Lectures on Psychological and Political Ethics: 1898

John Dewey

LECTURES ON PSYCHOLOGICAL AND POLITICAL ETHICS: 1898

*Edited and
with an Introduction by
Donald F. Koch*

HAFNER PRESS
A Division of Macmillan Publishing Co., Inc.
NEW YORK

Collier Macmillan Publishers
LONDON

The text of the Lectures on Psychological and Political Ethics: 1898
is © The Center for Dewey Studies, Southern Illinois University,
Carbondale, Illinois   62901

Copyright © 1976 by Hafner Press
A Division of Macmillan Publishing Co., Inc.

Hafner Press
A Division of Macmillan Publishing Co., Inc.
866 Third Avenue, New York, N.Y.   10022

Collier Macmillan Canada, Ltd.

Library of Congress Catalog Card Number: 76–14292

Printed in the United States of America

printing number
1 2 3 4 5 6 7 8 9 10

Library of Congress Cataloging in Publication Data

Dewey, John
    Lectures on psychological and political ethics, 1898.

    Includes index.
    1. Ethics--Addresses, essays, lectures. 2. Psy-
chology--Addresses, essays, lectures. 3. Political
ethics--Addresses, essays, lectures. 4. Social ethics--
Addresses, essays, lectures. I. Title.
BJ1008.D48 1976   170   76-14292
ISBN 0-02-847930-0

CONTENTS

PREFATORY NOTE

The lectures printed here for the first time were delivered by John Dewey at the University of Chicago during the winter and spring quarters of the 1898 academic year. No original manuscript is known to exist. The following text is based on notes taken by an unknown stenographer (or stenographers) which were then typed and duplicated—presumably for the use of Dewey's students. Despite the lack of information about the accuracy of the recorder of the lectures, readers familiar with Dewey's style will recognize that the stenographer did a very careful job in capturing it.

The original copy contained virtually no title headings, and in addition Dewey was indifferent about finishing up a given topic at the end of the lecture. Consequently, all chapter and section titles have been supplied by the editor, according to the actual sequence of topics Dewey followed. The analytical table of contents and the explanatory footnotes are also by the editor. Punctuation and paragraphing have been corrected. No attempt was made to change the text except in cases of obvious error. Most of the more serious errors were due to the defective hectograph copy, and in the case of the *Lectures on Psychological Ethics* there were three missing pages.

The *Lectures on Political Ethics* were transcribed from the copy at the the Duke University Library and checked against another copy in the possession of Grinnell College. The *Lectures on Psychological Ethics* were taken from the only known copy, now in the hands of The Center for Dewey Studies at Southern Illinois University.

I would like to thank the Duke University Library and Mary Gae Wyly of the Grinnell College Library for help in providing the original hectograph copies. Jo Ann Boydston, director of The Center for Dewey Studies, was very helpful in securing the best possible copy of the hectograph on *Psychological Ethics*. The St. Louis University Library supplied a microfilm of the latter at a time when the original was not available.

Special thanks go to Herbert W. Schneider for his helpful advice along the way, and particularly for aid in phrasing the chapter and section titles to reflect, on the basis of personal experience, the style Dewey actually followed. Elayne Magnan was responsible for typing the final copy. Alan McBeth, Gwendolyn Weaver, and Stephen Dickerson did work beyond the call of duty in proofreading the typescript. Katherine McCracken, as grammarian, did a heroic job of punctuating the manuscript, most notably at those points where Dewey's phrasing seemed to defy any clear interpretation. Finally, I would like to thank my wife, Kathleen, for many hours spent verifying the original copy and for unwavering support throughout.

Financial assistance during 1973, 1974, and 1975 was provided by Michigan State University "All University" research grants.

Donald F. Koch

EDITOR'S INTRODUCTION

I. BACKGROUND OF
THE 1898 LECTURES

In 1898 John Dewey was one of the most prominent young philosophers in America. After a successful early career at the University of Michigan, he had come to the University of Chicago in 1894 to head the departments of philosophy and pedagogy. Already written were a number of books and shorter works.[1] Yet to come were such now well-known works as *The School and Society* (1899), *Ethics* (1908), with James H. Tufts, *Democracy and Education* (1916), *Human Nature and Conduct* (1922), *Experience and Nature* (1925), and *The Quest for Certainty* (1929). An important bridge between the early and the later works is formed by a number of lectures given during the Chicago years (1894–1904), taken down by unknown stenographers and then mechanically duplicated for the use of students.[2] In them, Dewey tries out ideas that often turn up in later works; and, freed from the onus of public scrutiny which is the fate of the writer who submits his views to print, he reveals an extraordinarily systematic and comprehensive approach to his subject matter.

The present lectures are especially interesting because they attempt a unified presentation of Dewey's views on moral and social philosophy which is not found in any of his published works. The large scope of the enterprise can be seen through a description of the lectures in the University of Chicago catalog.

35. *The Psychology of Ethics*. This course will include particularly the psychology of volition, taking up such topics as impulse, intention, deliberation, effort, desire and pleasure, motive-choice, and overt action. Winter Quarter, '98.

36. *Political Ethics*. This course will approach the problems of ethics from the standpoint of social organization, as the preceding one does from the standpoint of the agent. The two courses are thus complementary. It will deal (1) with ethical statics, or the organized moral order, including a discussion of the ethical significance of social institutions and of rights and duties as related to institutions, and (2) with ethical dynamics, or the nature and conditions of moral progress in society as a whole. For graduate students. Spring Quarter, '98.[3]

The distinction between the "Psychology of Ethics," which studied the moral life from the standpoint of the agent, and "Political Ethics" or social ethics, which studied the moral life from the standpoint of the social organization, is fundamental in understanding Dewey's overall moral philosophy. It was first made in Dewey's 1894 book, *The Study of Ethics, A Syllabus,* where he maintained that "in analyzing conduct it is just as important to consider the situation as the agent";[4] yet a projected final section of the book that was to deal with "Social Ethics" was left unwritten. In 1897 the publisher Henry Holt contacted Dewey to ask him to write an ethics text for Holt's influential "American Science Series." [5] But when the book finally appeared in 1908, the bulk of the material on social ethics was not by Dewey but by his co-author, James H. Tufts. So, then, the present lectures are far more ambitious in scope than his other published works, insofar as they integrate his psychological and social theory in a single, systematic presentation.

This combination of these two enterprises in a single volume helps overcome a fundamental difficulty in our attempt to understand Dewey's overall moral theory. Near the end of the *Lectures on Psychological Ethics,* he points out that

> There is no way of telling what the capacities of the agent are, excepting as one takes for granted the environmental conditions with reference to which those powers are exercised. There is no telling, on the other hand, what the situation and its needs are, excepting as one takes for granted an agent free, with certain resources at his command.
> . . . the real self, psychologically, is always a synthesis of two distinct types and conditions, one of which we may call the agent or instrumental self, and the other of which we may call the conditions of the situation, or briefly, the environment.[6]

If, then, the real self is always a synthesis of agent and environment, and yet for purposes of study it is necessary to hold one of these factors constant while we study the other, any analysis that concentrates on one of them is going to take the factor that is held constant for granted without exploring its relation to the other. For example, readers of Dewey's contribution to the Dewey and Tufts *Ethics* can justly complain that his analysis of the moral life of the agent mentions the social factor in conduct while failing to give an account of it.[7] Or, to take another case, the social recommendations that Dewey makes in *The Public and Its Problems* [8] are not related to the individual psychology that he takes for granted. But in the present lectures Dewey begins his individual psychology with an analysis of the social aspects of individuality (*Psychological Ethics,* Chapter 1, Sections 1, 3). He treats his all important theory of the organic circuit *both* from the individual point of view (*Psychological Ethics,* Chapter 2, Section 2) and the environmental side (*Political Ethics,* Chapter 3, Section 1). His analysis of individual duty (*Psychological Ethics,* Chapter 5, Section 2) can be compared with the explanation of social rights and duties

(*Political Ethics,* Chapter 6, Section 5). In these and many other instances, the vast sweep and coherence of Dewey's undertaking provides
the reader with a unique opportunity to participate in the overall vision of
one of this country's great philosophers.

II. THE LECTURES ON
PSYCHOLOGICAL ETHICS

1. Dewey's Procedure in Ethical Theory

Those who busy themselves with ethical theorizing ordinarily expect an
author who is concerned with practical moral matters to give some general account of the nature of good and obligation, and then go on to give
reasons why the position he takes on some particular issue is consistent
with this account. How are we to react, then, when we are confronted with
the fact that the following lectures largely consist of an analysis of interests,
habits, the thinking process, and other psychological topics? How are we
to explain the absence of any sustained attempt by Dewey to formulate
general characterizations of key moral terms and his not going on to reach
specific conclusions? [9]

In other words, how can Dewey concern himself with "mere psychology" and still claim to offer us any conclusions of moral significance?
If, in the broadest sense, psychology deals with human conduct that has
been, is now, or will be occurring, what has this to do with good conduct
or conduct that ought to be? Granted that psychology can give some explanation of the origin of values and obligations in actual life, there is still
the open question whether the moral points of view which in fact happen
to arise are correct.

The answer to these questions, I believe, has to do with showing how
Dewey's procedure in ethics represents a radical break with tradition. To
see this, we need to consider more carefully the conventional methods of
moral theorizing and to see how Dewey's approach contrasts with them.
In the broadest sense, ethical theorists have utilized one of two alternative
methods of procedure. The first, originating with Jeremy Bentham, is to
ask the individual to take a reflective, unprejudiced point of view, and in
so doing get him to admit to agree to certain fundamental principles. Once
this is done, some attempt is made to show how the fundamental principles,
which are now agreed upon as acceptable to all "rational" men, are of
value in leading us to conclusions in particular matters.

But to many who grew up in "Darwin's Century," the fact of continuing human evolution precluded the possibility of men ever reaching such a
stable consensus. Dewey was one of these. For him the task of moral
theory was to find methods of coping with change, to find the means to
resolve the genuinely new moral problems created by new developments
within society, and to gain consensus by reconstructing the processes and

functions that produce problems. Actual censensus—sharing harmoniously in common social processes—was not something to be sought at the beginning of ethical theorizing; it was a goal to be pursued, the attainment of which would mark the end of theorizing.

A second common procedure in ethics is to hold that there is some rational basis for moral knowledge, no matter what anyone in particular happens to believe. This alleged knowledge may stem from some universal moral principle, from some perceived natural quality, or from some intuited right-making characteristic. But, whatever its source, adherents of the procedure maintain that moral knowledge is like scientific or mathematical knowledge in the sense that there can be true propositions apart from anyone's awareness of them.

How does Dewey respond to this approach in ethics? He does, as one might expect, try to show the inadequacy of particular knowledge claims. But, at best, this would only show the failure of particular instances of the method, while leaving the method itself unchallenged. So, in addition, what Dewey in effect does is to offer an alternative formulation of the task of ethical theory. His view, stripped to its bare bones, is as follows: moral theory is concerned with the analysis of actual practice. Its task is to observe the characteristics of human behavior in order to provide information helpful in the resolution of actual moral problems. Moral practice—actual moral behavior—is concerned with the successful experimental working out of solutions to these problems. Claims to moral knowledge, even if successful on their own terms, are unrelated to the practical question as to how those ideals were to be embodied and assimilated in practice. Hence, they are irrelevant to the concerns of moral theory.[10]

Three additional points about this method may serve to clarify it further:

1. It requires a procedure different from the first two methods that were mentioned. The procedure is different because its aim is not moral knowledge in the sense of some kind of cognition of moral principles but knowledge of how to go about resolving particular problems in act. This is not to say that theorists themselves resolve the problems, but they do provide us with a psychological and sociological standpoint that is instrumental in approaching their resolution.

2. Accordingly, the emphasis is on careful observation and analysis of the various aspects of human behavior. Theorizing is not primarily argumentative; rather, its aim is to provide useful information. For example, if one wants to say there is a role for reasoning in ethics, he is going to have to be aware of the actual reasoning process (see Chapter 3, Sections 3, 4, and 9). If he wants to take a position on the question whether badness is always ignorance, he must know something about the psychology of human failure (Chapter 3,

Section 7). If he wants to be aware of the value of pleasure, he needs to know something about its role in moral judgment (Chapter 4, Section 2).

3. If it is objected that information that is helpful in the resolution of actual moral conflicts is irrelevant to the true aim of moral theory (which is to discover just what an adequate "moral" resolution of the dispute would be), the proper reply is that Dewey has a different view of the aim of moral theory. For him, an actual resolution *is* an adequate moral resolution.

I am not trying to say here that Dewey's method in ethics is the correct method. I have only tried to show that it is not the usual method. How, then, are we to evaluate it? To see this we need to show how it functions in the resolution of a particular moral problem.

2. Dewey on the Problem of Egoism and Altruism

The egoism-altruism problem was one of the most vexing puzzles for moral philosophers of the last half of the nineteenth century. It has two aspects: psychological and logical. The psychological aspect occurred because many utilitarians defended psychological hedonism, or the view that personal pleasure is the sole object of desire. (Nonhedonists could hold to psychological egoism, or the view that all men desire personal good.) Most philosophers, Dewey included,[11] rejected both psychological hedonism and psychological egoism, and with it the implication that all benevolence is merely a disguised form of selfishness. But the logical aspect of the problem is more serious. For, even assuming that men have a choice whether to serve themselves or serve others, the question arises as to whom they *ought* to serve.

Broadly speaking, nineteenth-century ethical theorists approached the logical problem in two distinctly differently ways. Utilitarians and intuitionists tried to show that some form of benevolence was the rational course of action—an approach that most present-day thinkers would take for granted.[12] On this view it was not necessary to venture very far into the nature of the self, since men were presumed to be free to choose the more rational action. By contrast, the idealists—including Dewey himself prior to 1891—tried to show that self-realization was the moral ideal. Self-realization was not individual pleasure-seeking as the hedonists would have it but rather the development of the self in and through one's social station. And if, as the idealists tried to show, the self was basically social in nature, all that was necessary in order to get a man to act benevolently was to make him aware of his real self.

Now, Dewey does not reject the notion of self-realization as the moral ideal, but he does reject the idealist theory of the meaning of self-realization. The idealists had maintained that there was a transsocial order, other than the natural order, in which self and others were united. Dewey, by contrast, tried to work out a thoroughly naturalistic, concrete analysis of the development of self within society. In this section I will briefly trace the outlines of this concept of self as it relates to the problem of egoism. In the next I will begin to treat Dewey's analysis of society.

For Dewey, the psychology of egoism is very simple in principle and very complex in detail. He asks,

> Is the self a presupposed, given existence, or does the self exist only as it operates? Is the self a continual synthetic construction? If the latter, the question between egoism and altruism is solved by getting a different purchase on the whole thing. We would have to say that a man always does act as himself, but that that is a different thing from saying that he acts for himself as an end. The objectionable character of the conception that a man always acts for himself has the same origin as the objectionable character of the doctrine of [the idealist theory of] self-realization. It presupposes that a man is already there, and whatever he does, he does as the means to himself as an outside end.[18]

In other words, the contention that men can choose to serve themselves presupposes a fixed self which they are trying to serve. But if there is no fixed self, there can be no self-serving action. So the enterprise of trying to stop people from serving themselves is fundamentally mistaken.

Now, the purpose of this argument is not to inveigle the reader into believing that there are no moral problems in life and that men in fact live together in harmony. Rather, the aim is to suggest that we have the wrong psychological model for analyzing moral problems. We tend to think of the individual self as somehow posed between two alternatives, one of which it knows to be moral and the other to be self-serving and immoral. The moral task is, then, to overcome the latter tendencies and do what we know to be right. Dewey holds instead that the self is to be characterized in terms of what it does,[14] and that when actual doing is thwarted the competing values are not given at the start but have to be defined and controlled.

Dewey is willing to grant that at times in the development of the self it is outgoing toward the environment and that at other times it draws away from it.[15] But the latter is not altruistic nor the former egoistic. Both are phases in the process of self-adaptation. This process begins when specific interests come into conflict.[16] Its goal is to find new interests which reflect the whole self by finding an adequate division of labor.[17] The problem, then, is neither to suppress egoism nor to encourage altruism. On the psychological side, it is a matter of utilizing intelligence to resolve the problem. On the social side, the task is to stimulate interests that further the harmonious interaction of various selves.

Now, obviously, the enterprise outlined above will not be acceptable to those who hold to various forms of the doctrine that alternatives—both moral and immoral—are given to the self in advance of its acting. So, then, Dewey criticizes the hedonist's claim that it is the alternatives with respect to pleasure or pain that provide a criterion of action.[18] He criticizes the Kantian view that the principle of universalization is a guide to action.[19] He makes an important distinction between immediate stimulus and final object of desire, saying that the latter is often confused with the former. Hence, people often think that the alternative that is eventually chosen was there at the beginning of the deliberative process.[20] All these points of view are worked out in the process of Dewey's development, in the *Lectures on Psychological Ethics,* of an overall theory of the development of the self in act.

There is no space to go into the details of Dewey's psychology, nor has it been my purpose to show that he has given us a final answer to the problem of egoism. What I have tried to show is that, starting with a particular problem (the problem of egoism), we have been led to consider a number of philosophical issues and eventually to an entire theory of the nature of the self. We could have started with some other problems—say, the role of pleasure in the decision-making process or the function of moral principles—and we would have been led to take a similar course. In any event, it is Dewey's contention that most theoretical problems in ethics need to be reexamined in terms of an adequate theory of the active self. And it is the working out of the latter task that he regarded as one of his major contributions in ethics.

III. THE LECTURES ON POLITICAL ETHICS

1. Dewey's Early Political Theory

It will be helpful in trying to understand the task Dewey is undertaking in these lectures if we consider the situation he faced when he broke away from his early, idealist-oriented political philosophy. This early position is presented in an essay "The Ethics of Democracy" (1888)[21] and sections of his *Outlines of a Critical Theory of Ethics* (1891).[22]

"The Ethics of Democracy" was devoted to the thesis that

> society, as a real whole, is the normal order, and the mass as an aggregate of isolated unity is the fiction. If this be the case, and if democracy be a form of society, it not only does have, but must have, a common will; for it is this unity of will which makes it an organism. A state represents men so far as they have become organically related to one another, or are possessed of unity of purpose and interest.[23]

And in the *Outlines of a Critical Theory of Ethics* this same basic standpoint was expressed as the "ethical postulate."

> In the realization of the individual there is found also the needed realization of some community of persons of which the individual is a member; and, conversely, the agent who duly satisfies the community in which he shares, by that same conduct satisfies himself.[24]

The fundamental problem with this early formulation of the organic theory of society was that the proposed unity was at bottom an expression of a spiritual reality, something apart from actual life. In "The Ethics of Democracy" Dewey conceded this point.

> And if, as actually happens, society be not yet possessed of one will, but partially is one and partially has a number of fragmentary and warring wills, it yet follows that *so far* as society has a common purpose and spirit, *so far* each individual is not representative of a certain proportionate share of the sum total of will, but is its vital embodiment.[25]

The only plausible interpretations of this view is either that the individual is split into two parts, one will that is fragmentary and warring with the other, which is the embodiment of the common will, or that the common will is something apart from individual wills. Dewey at least implicitly rejected the former view when he held that those who think of life as having two parts, one animal and the other truly human, were wrong and accordingly the material and industrial sides of life were not just means to a higher life but were part of the ethical life.[26] Apparently, the only alternative was to admit that the unity was ideal (in the sense of something apart from the actual) and Dewey seemed to imply this in *Outlines of a Critical Theory of Ethics* when he said that where the ethical postulate was concerned "further inquiry belongs to metaphysics." [27]

But the situation was made even more complicated when, in the same paragraph that referred the ethical postulate to metaphysics, Dewey also said that it was analogous to the scientific postulate of the uniformity of nature. In short, "moral experience *makes for the world of practice* an assumption analogous in kind to that which intellectual experience makes for the world of knowledge." [28] This suggests that we turn away from metaphysical analysis and resort to action in order to make the ethical postulate come true, a view which was developed elsewhere in the *Outlines*.

> Consider again a person assuming a family relation. This seems, at first, to consist mainly in the satisfaction of certain common and obvious human wants. But this satisfaction, if moral, turns out rather to be the creation of new insight into life, of new relationships, and thus of new energies and ideals. We may generalize. . . . The secret of the moral life is not getting or having, it is doing and thus being. The getting and the possessing side of life has a moral value only when it is made the stimulus and nutriment of new and wider acting. To solve the equation between getting and doing is the moral problem of life. . . . It is essential to moral activity that it feed itself into larger life.[29]

This is basically the same viewpoint as was expressed in Dewey's post-idealist writings in social theory, but the problem at this time was that he simply did not have an adequate theoretical framework for developing it.

He did point to history and said that its development was marked by "new divisions of labor and corresponding freedom in functioning," on the one hand, and an "enlargement of the community of ends, . . . growth in 'comprehensiveness,' " on the other.[30] Yet he immediately went on to say that an ideal based on "physical facts . . . will have a somewhat external and physical manifestation," and he appealed again to a "truly spiritual" community.[31]

We can only assume, then, that four years later, when Dewey appealed again to the ethical postulate in *The Study of Ethics,* he had still not worked out an adequate solution of the difficulty. He did indicate the direction in which he was moving by dropping the appeal to metaphysics, and he reasserted the viewpoint that the postulate could only be proven experimentally, that is, by being acted on.[32] Yet the absence of a section on "Social Ethics" left the reader in the dark as to how this goal was to be accomplished.

In order to appreciate the task Dewey was up against, and which he undertakes to solve in these lectures, it is worth pointing out problems in an "experimental" social philosophy which were suggested by philosophers that Dewey was very familiar with. I mention them because I think they formulate, in an explicit way, the kind of intuitive apprehensions we have about the type of project Dewey is undertaking.

The first problem arises when we try to formulate a concept of moral progress along experimental lines. Before about 1892 Dewey had safely clung to T. H. Green's view that progress was a gradual realization of the eternal, spiritual element of the self. But in *The Study of Ethics* he was more and more sympathetic to Samuel Alexander's evolutionary naturalism and accordingly accepted his conception of progress as evolving. In fact, Alexander held that "progress" referred to any movement from one set of conditions to another that happens to be accepted by the whole of society.

> In changing from one form to another morality changes from what is right under one set of conditions to what is right under another set, and such change from good to good is what we mean by becoming better. To deny this is to find some other standard of advance than in the actual movement that has taken place. . . . Goodness and badness form a distinction within society itself. If there were only one society, whatever forward movement it made must be considered progress, for there would be no other standard of judgment. Goodness represents the solution of all the conflicting elements in the problem of social life, and hence whatever change the standard underwent would be considered as a change for the better.[33]

Dewey accepted a similar view: "One class of persons, as a class, is then, morally no better than any other; one period no more virtuous than another. Responsibilities not virtues, increase." [34] This view marked Dewey's final emancipation from Green, but it raised problems of its own.

For example, what happens if a society of cooks replaces a society of philosophers? Alexander did not equivocate.

> With that [new] society itself this ideal would be esteemed higher than that which it had replaced. It would be absurd to reply that the whole society had become degraded or had abused its trust, as we should certainly say of such a body of persons in our own larger society. For I am supposing that this is the only existent society, and the law under which the society lives is itself that which marks off good from bad. [35]

The point of these remarks is not that society is likely to kick out the philosophers in favor of the cooks. Alexander expressly denied that this was a real possibility. But the theoretical difficulty concerns the question of what is to be done when the cooks threaten the philosophers? Can the latter make any kind of appeal which would preserve the rationality and morality of their own stations, if not their necks? More generally, if our own society happens to be threatened by violence, facism, dictatorship, or any other force that could upset the established order, how can we say that these threats are irrational if we cannot appeal to some kind of abstract ideal?

These questions take on new significance when we realize that by 1897 Dewey explicitly denied that there was any dualism between the evolutionary process and the ethical process. In an article written during the summer previous to the *Lectures on Political Ethics*,[36] Dewey not only challenged T. H. Huxley's dualism between the evolutionary and the ethical but said in addition that the evolutionist's notion of "struggle" was an essential part of the ethical process.

> The ethical process . . . is one of constant struggle. . . . Oversight, vigilance, constant interference with conditions as they are, are necessary to maintain the ethical order. . . . The problem, however, is to locate this opposition and interference,—to interpret it, to say what it means in the light of our idea of the evolutionary process as a whole. [37]

> If the strugggle is still going on, selection is still occurring, and there is every reason to suppose that as heretofore, it is a distinct agent in social progress. [38]

At first glance, such contentions make us wonder whether what Dewey called the "loose popular argument," "that if the principle of the struggle for existence and survival of the fittest were rigorously carried out, it would result in the destruction of the weak, the sickly, the defective, and the insane," [39] did not apply against his own view. The question has two distinct aspects: (1) Isn't the process of "survival of the fittest" and the "struggle for existence" basically antithetical to moral progress? (2) Even if they are not, how can these evolutionary notions pertain to anything other than the means to a moral end which is given in advance of the struggle? In other words, isn't "struggle" merely a neutral tool which can be used either to enable one man to dominate another or to further harmony among men?

The first question is the easier one, and Dewey's reply to it in "Evolution and Ethics" prepares the groundwork for the answer to the latter question in the *Lectures on Political Ethics*. To begin with, Dewey noted that even Huxley did not hold that the ethical process was opposed to the entire cosmic process (since the moral life of man is part of the cosmic process) but that the part of the cosmic process that concerns the conduct of men is opposed to the part of the cosmic process exhibited in the stages of evolution before man's appearance on the scene.

Dewey then asked whether the notion of "survival of the fittest" was antithetical to the moral process. His basic contention was that we are used to interpreting the term "fit" with "reference to an [animal] environment which long ago ceased to be." [40] Our present environment is different, and so fitness takes on new meaning.

> The condition with respect to which the term "fit" must *now* be used to include the existing social structure with all the habits, demands, and ideals which are found in it.[41]
>
> The environment is now distinctly a social one, and the content of the term "fit" has to be made with reference to social adaptation. Moreover, the environment in which we now live is a changing and progressive one. Everyone must have his fitness judged by the whole, including the anticipated change; not merely by reference to the conditions of today, because these may be gone tomorrow.[42]

This argument is sufficient to convince us that "fitness" is relative to actual conditions and that current actual conditions do not require us to kill and eat our fellow human beings as a tiger would kill a deer.

But doesn't the "struggle for existence" imply, contrary to ethical practice, that one man serve himself at the expense of others? Dewey's answer, if I understand him correctly, is that struggle is not necessarily opposed to the ethical process and in fact is an aspect of it. When an act that was adapted to given conditions must now be adapted to new conditions, "struggle" simply refers to the necessity for this readaptation.

> Just because the acts of which the prompting and impulses are the survival, were the fittest for by-gone days they are not the fittest now. The struggle comes, not in suppressing them nor in substituting something else for them; but in reconstituting them, in adapting them, so that they will function with reference to the existing situation. . . . The tension is between an organ adjusted to a past state and the functioning required by present conditions. And this tension demands reconstruction.[43]

This is an appealing notion, especially when Dewey adds later that variation creates a new environment in which more species are adjusted without
interfering with others.[44]

The value of Dewey's remarks here is that we are warned against formulating ethical problems in terms of a narrow, either/or situation. If a
person loses his arms in an accident, the choice is not necessarily between
doing away with him entirely or putting up with an helpless cripple. You
can create an artificial limb which does away with both your problem and
his.

Turning to our second problem, the question whether evolutionary
struggle provides a moral ideal and not just the means to realize it, it
would seem that Dewey's rejection of the distinction between the natural
and the moral is a two-edged sword. It seems to be an open question
whether the material to be "reconstructed" is to be reconstructed for the
benefit of the other person or not. If we can build artificial limbs for the
person in need of them, we can equally well reconstruct him by turning
him into fertilizer. Dewey is not encouraging on this point when he says
that the "very meaning" of adjustment is that a life form "subjects conditions about it to its own needs." [45]

So he has a problem. The question, originally posed in our discussion
of Alexander, as to what ought to be done when the cooks threaten the
philosophers is still with us. It would appear that the only strategy open to
Dewey at this point would be to try to give an analysis of actually existing
society which would show that readjustment demands that we help others
rather than eliminate them, an analysis which would suggest that interests
are bound up with the positive rather than the negative reconstruction of
the existing situation. Such is the difficult task that Dewey tackles in these
lectures.[46]

Why say the strategy just outlined is the *only* strategy left to pursue?
The reason, I think, has to do with an 1891 essay by William James, "The
Moral Philosopher and the Moral Life." [47] Dewey read this article and said
in a letter to James that "the article rejoiced me greatly . . . two things
more than others . . . your statement that any desire, as such, constitutes a
claim and any claim an obligation, and your discussion of rules." [48] Later,
in *The Study of Ethics* Dewey maintained that the article was "a very
strong statement of the practical character of the moral judgment." [49]

When we turn to the actual development of these views in James's
article, we find a shocking rejection of the traditional viewpoint that one of
two actually conflicting (yet both claimed to be moral) demands must be
correct.

> We inveterately think that something which we call the "validity"
> of the claim is what gives to it its obligatory character, and that this
> validity is something outside the claim's mere existence as a matter of
> fact. It rains down upon the claim, we think, from some sublime di-
> mension of being, which the moral law inhabits, much as upon the

steel of the compass-needle the influence of the Pole rains down out of the starry heavens. But again, how can such an inorganic abstract character of imperativeness, additional to the imperativeness which is the concrete claim itself, *exist*? Take any demand, however slight, which any creature, however weak, may make. Ought it not, for its own sole sake, to be satisfied? If not, prove why not. The only possible kind of proof you could adduce would be the exhibition of another creature who should make a demand that ran the other way.[50]

No doubt, all this appealed to Dewey since his own recently published article "Moral Theory and Practice" (January, 1891)[51] was a polemic against those who regarded moral theory as "an attempt to find a philosophic 'basis' or foundation for moral activity in something beyond that activity itself." [52] But the plain fact of the matter which James's article so forceably brought home was that so long as two people made conflicting claims there was no way to say that one of them was correct as long as the other continued to oppose him.[53] The only way that moral philosophy could proceed was to formulate some kind of framework for the resolution of conflicts, of tension. But it could not do this by appealing to what James called the "validity" of one of the opinions. We can see now the difficulty of Dewey's task.

2. Reconstructing Social Psychology

Dewey's goal in these lectures is to provide us with an adequate theoretical framework for the examination and solution of the problems that arise when various groups within the overall social process come into conflict.

> . . . all I am going to give in this course is certain general principles and . . . their value is found simply in their value as method. What you get out of it will be the extent to which you will take the ideas and utilize them with reference to some specific social subject matter. I would like to . . . give you an instrument for thinking more deeply and criticizing more adequately the categories which you are using in your own thinking, whether historical, economic or socialistic.[54]

There has, Dewey thinks, been little advance in political philosophy because the psychology that controls its conclusions has never been seriously examined.[55]

Where do people go wrong? According to Dewey, they begin by assuming that men have relatively fixed wants which often come into conflict. Economists strengthen this image by picturing man as a creature with virtually unlimited material wants who is both willing and able to exploit nature and his fellow man in order to realize them. The next step in this mistaken analysis (according to Dewey) is to call upon ethics to point toward ideal ways of acting. It will tell us how we ought to determine our wills in contradistinction to our natural tendencies. The final step occurs when we take note of the fact that simply pointing out the ideal way to act will not be a force sufficient to insure that it will be practiced. After all, our natural tendencies are so contrary to the demands of morality. It seems, then, that politics on the theoretical side and actual governments on the practical side are necessary in order to discover and implement ways of controlling naturally unruly men for their own mutual benefit. Government may not succeed wholly in making men moral, but it can at least use force to restore some order to society.

This is admittedly a rough outline, not designed by Dewey as a criticism of any particular theory. But for those who are inclined to accept it, or something roughly like it, the consequences are no small matter. It creates dichotomies between man's natural wants (the subject matter of economics), his will (the subject matter of ethics), and external force (the subject matter of politics), which from the very start appear to preclude the achievement of the goals of any one of these disciplines unless we rule out the goal of the others. Instead of this inherently unstable state of affairs, Dewey proposes to eliminate the dualism between economic, moral, and political man and to call on government to exercise intelligence instead of force in the maintenance of social order.

But there is another serious consequence of accepting the dichotomies between economics, ethics, and politics. Moral disorder is assumed to be a function of individual wants in conflict with other individual wants. Men are everywhere scheming for power, for riches, for self-aggrandizement of any sort. Evolutionary theory, with its catch phrases like the "struggle for existence" and the "survival of the fittest," reinforces this image of man. Therefore, if *what is the case* in the affairs of men is so desperate, there is all the more need to point out *what ought to be*. Not to do so would be somehow to sanction individual evils; at least, it would be to concede that there are no rational sanctions against such acts. The philosopher's proper task is not to dwell on how things are but to tell us how they ought to be.

I have said enough to suggest that Dewey is trying to reconstruct our economic, moral, and political psychologies in order to convince us to change our metatheoretical approach to social philosophy. The lectures are not so much a commentary on current (1898) social problems as they are an attempt to provide us with a rationale for dealing with any social problem. We are to give up the metaethical requirement that social theory establish ideals, duties, and instead formulate a method for coming to grips with the actual conditions that produce trouble.

In setting forth Dewey's approach to this problem, his answer can be divided into two separate areas. The contention that man, especially economic man, is selfish has been dealt with in the previous section. By contrast, the problems centering about the regulation of man's conduct by society revolve around his functioning within the larger makeup of the social process. That is, they refer to Social Ethics, which deals with the "what" or "content" of conduct.

Let us turn to the actual development of the *Lectures in Political Ethics*. They begin with a criticism of various thinkers' views on the function of physical force in regulating individual conduct. And, accordingly, the reader would expect that in the following chapters Dewey would immediately begin to develop a social psychology which would pave the way for government functioning as intelligent resolver of social disputes instead of as an agent simply applying force to restore order. Instead, Chapter II begins with a discussion of the concept of the life process in general, proceeds to develop the theory that organism and environment are aspects within an already existing functioning whole, develops a theory of biological variation, and concludes with a definition of organism. Chapter III is mainly devoted to an explanation of the development of consciousness in terms of a continuous organic circuit of which stimulus and response are a part. It is only in Chapter IV that Dewey turns to the social process in general and asks whether society can be termed an organism.

What, then, is the function of Chapters II and III in view of Dewey's overall goal of giving an analysis of the social process which will be helpful in the resolution of disputes? I think the best hint is given by Dewey himself in an article about William James written years after the present lectures were given.

> One does not have to go very far below the surface in reading James to see that at his hands reference to biological considerations is a means of breaking down artificial barriers and compartmentalization from which philosophy was suffering. Previous empiricists had, for example, treated experience as something set over against nature, separated from it by a gulf. This fatal barrier to development of a genuinely empirical philosophy was broken down by James. The biological aspect of experience is far from being the whole of experience. But recognition of its existence cuts under, once for all, every theory of experience which rests, consciously or unconsciously, upon the postulate that experience is set over against the natural world and can be profitably studied in independence of our knowledge of that world.[56]

Substitute the phrase "social process" for "nature" or "natural world" in this quotation and you get a description of what Dewey is trying to do in the two chapters in question. In other words, just as James used a biological analysis to show that experience is not set against the natural world, so Dewey uses it here to show that society does not operate in opposition to individual interests. Accordingly, external force as used by a single sovereign body or government is neither necessary nor effective in securing the common good. This is not to say either that biological analysis is wholly sufficient to explain society or that we are to take it for granted that society is always a healthy organism; but it does provide a basis for the intelligent solution of social problems which arise when various functioning groups within society come into conflict.

Although Dewey's use of biological analysis is extensive, I think that three major points are made and later applied to the analysis of society:

1. *Rejection of the rigid dualism between organism and environment.* In Chapter II Dewey asserts that the notions of organism and environment are distinctions that we make within an already existing biological function whenever there is need for readjustment. The environment is that part of a function that resists the organism; it represents the demand for readjustment. The organism is the unity of function that persists, the point of initiation of a new function. The problem is to turn the environment into an adequate stimulus, one that restores the overall function to a new unity. In addition, Dewey points out that the environment is *all* the material the organism has to work with.[57] There can be no choice about this. Either the existing tension calls forth new modes of action, successful variation, or there is no evolution and the organism dies. But, if successful, variation lessens competition because the new variation no longer shares the same environment; it has created a new and favorable environment by turning the previous resistance into a sustaining factor.

The importance of this rejection of the dualism between organism and environment is that it suggests that we can study individuals (organs) as functional aspects of the larger process of society (or organism).[58] Individuals are not entities that sustain themselves either by themselves or in opposition to this larger process. This comes out in Dewey's discussion of the two aspects in our conception of an organism.

> First, there is a unity of process which is not merely an objective unity in the sense that a spectator can see that there is an underlying quondam of mass in energy which persists throughout, but a unity in which the later stages have reference to the earlier in such a way that they do not simply follow after them, but that they react into them so as to maintain them in their action; a unity which some writers term an ideal unity. . . . [But] if the term ideal or subjective may suggest to some that which is antithetical to real objectivity, the terminology perhaps might be objective to. . . .
>
> Second, this unity is maintained through some differentiations or distinctions of activities; if not of parts or structures, at least of the offices performed by the various parts. And of course the higher the organism, the more marked and specific this specialization or differentiation.[59]

It is clear from these remarks that Dewey is not using the conception of organism to argue that the state is an ideal unity but rather a series of interrelated processes. Elsewhere he says that the task of social psychology is to take specific social processes to "see whether there is any community of organs and of function or outcome."[60] The sciences, particularly those like biology "which deal with the points of contact, of application of life," will have to be developed in order to make clear functional interrelationships that create shared difficulties.[61] Eventually, "an organized science of sociology would . . . be practically identical with an organized newspaper, an organized system of the continuous statement and interpretation of the facts of social life which are relevant to the needs of the individual." [62]

2. *Development of the view that organism (the parts of society) and environment (society as a whole) are part of a continuous organic circuit.* In what way do the various organs in an organism interact? If, like Herbert Spencer, we regard the other parts of an animal as subordinate to the nervous system (since the nervous system alone is capable of suffering pleasure and pain), it would follow that if society is an organism it would have to have some "common sensorium" or whole to which all the other parts of the society are subordinate. But Dewey rejects this view, stating that just as the nervous system does not monopolize feeling but refers it to particular organs, so in society there is no whole apart from its parts.[63]

Now the biological basis of this criticism of Spencer's theory of the interaction of sense organs and the nervous system needs to be stated if we are to understand just how society is in part analogous to the functioning biological organism. Specifically, Dewey had by 1896 worked out the view that stimulus (from sense organs) and response (from the end organ, or brain) are not separate functions but part of a continuous organic circuit.[64] This view is restated in Chapter II, Section 2 of the *Lectures on Psychological Ethics,* and its importance cannot be overestimated in the development of the theory of the evolution of the social process as worked out in Chapter IV of the *Lectures on Political Ethics.* If sense organs and end organ are two aspects of a single function or activity, it follows according to Dewey that the control that the end organ exercises is not to subordinate the other organs (as Spencer would have it) but to adapt the various organs to each other. Accordingly, when we turn to the social process as a whole, the function of government is not to exercise power to control the various elements in society but to mediate or make adjustments between them.

Moreover, and more importantly, the focus of attention in studying the overall social process is directed toward the specific individuals in functional interaction with each other. Specifically, the process of their consciousness is social, that is, a function of adjustments resulting from stimulation from others and their capacity to call out activities from others.

> The agent A is at once excited to action and restricted in action by the doings of others, and reciprocally he is able both to call out their actions and to modify their activities.
> Now if we could get a statement of how these various actions interplay, how they act and react on each other, we would have a formulation for the content of consciousness at a given time. It is in that kind of consideration that we find the justification for the term social con-

sciousness. It does not mean that consciousness is possessed by society any more than the term individual consciousness means that consciousness is owned in fee simple by an individual. It means that the actual contents of one's consciousness, what one thinks, believes, hopes for, and strives for, are dependent on this continuous and complex interaction going on between these various individual activities.[65]

It should be clear from this quotation that the exploration of the organic interrelationships described here does not mean that we have to accept the view that society is exactly like an animal, but that we use the concept of consciousness being determined by action and reaction to others as a leading principle for further explanation of the actions of various individuals in their social setting.[66]

The technique of explaining consciousness in terms of reciprocal interaction is also used by Dewey to bridge the alleged gap between the moral and the natural. Early in the lectures, he had said that the question of the social or nonsocial character of the individual was not a question of the content or structure of the individual but of the process that he is a part of.

What kind of process does the individual stand for? What is the mechanism, the form of that consciousness which we call individual? What is it that initiates it? What stimulates it? In what direction, toward what ends does it function? No matter how individual it is in its form, if we find that in its genesis it is social and that in the part which it plays, in the service which it renders, in its outcome or function, it is social also, then we would call it social even if in its content you could not find a single element which was like an element found in any other personality. On that basis the criterion is the quality of the process that is going on, the value of the process that is going on, and not any particular thing that you can pick out here or there within them.[67]

Expanding on these remarks about "the value of the process that is going on," it turns out that rights and duties are a natural outcome of it.

We are both members and organs of society. As members of society we have duties, responsibilities, we have to respond to the stimuli which come to us as particular individualizations. As organs we are representatives of the whole, we are embodiments of the whole; we have rights; we have claims; we have specific modes of action. Or putting the whole thing into more distinctly political terms, all members were subjects, all organs were participants in sovereignty, were citizens.[68]

This quotation, in essence, summarizes the view of rights and obligations which Dewey develops in the final chapter of the lectures, and we will deal with it in more detail in the final section of this introduction.

3. *The vital role of competition in the specialization of social function.* We have already said in our discussion of Dewey's critique of T. H.

Huxley that he emphasized the positive value of the competitive struggle in the moral life. In 1894 Dewey had committed himself (without going into any detail) to the view that the "working out" of moral ideals was the heart of the moral life as distinguished from simply following a rule or ideal that was already given in advance.[69] The theory of competition, as borrowed from the theory of biological evolution and developed in these lectures, provides a kind of framework, or skeleton, for the interpretation of the moral role of actual social conflicts.

Dewey begins his discussion of competition in the biological sense with the assertion that in the higher organism each organ participates in a division of labor. The eye, the hand, the stomach—each have an individuality of their own in the sense of having a specific function. But, in a sense, the price the organism pays for this specialization is that it is both dependent on and in competition with other organs. Put another way, there are two extreme positions that mark the limit any organ can fall into. It can either try to "run on its own hook" and have merely "external and mechanical relations" to other organs, or, if it fails to resist other organs, it will "relapse into an over-labile, jelly-like condition . . . a relapse into a lower stage of organization." The more moderate alternative is for each organ in an organism to remain in dynamic interdependence with other organs while maintaining a relative independence for itself by competitively seeking out a specialized function for itself.[70]

Applying all this to the social process, Dewey utilizes the notion of the competitive process in society as the very basis for the possibility of locating a community of process. The notion of a common process is substituted for T. H. Green's "common good" in which all the members of society are supposed to share.

> It would be an interesting fact if we were to find a thousand different animals with the same kind of a stripe on the back, . . . but as long as we conceive an animal as a thing, as a pure object, and not as a process, that community of trait would simply be a peculiarity which would be interesting . . . [but] it would not introduce any real community. If [on the other hand] you were to find that they had that common trait simply because there is a common process of life involved in them all, that these thousand different animals are genetically all differentiations of one and the same process, . . . this common trait then would be a sign of some real intrinsic organic community. . . . Now the same way here [in the analysis of the social process]; if these resemblances between different individuals were used to reconstruct the whole theory, if they were used as proof that there is a single conscious process, . . . then the fact of resemblance and of community would have a positive social significance.[71]

But how are differentiations of function within this "single" process to be worked out? At this point, the strictly biological analysis of competition we have just referred to is supplemented by a more sophisticated analysis of the available tools for social action. Language, the "social sensorium," is a shared element in experience which, through the printing press, telegraph, and so on, makes knowledge available to those in need of it. Government, through legislators' discussion of the issues, can act to prevent tension becoming too great by finding out ways to resolve disputes.[72] The economic process is seen by Dewey as a procedure both for the allocation of resources and for the utilization of science in the production of goods. All of these devices provide for a constructive (yet competitive) working out of various conflicts which arise when there is a clash of social functions. Competition is utilized to work out a new social environment which can be shared by all of the parties to the previously existing conflict.

3. Pluralistic Sovereignty and the Identification of Will with Effort

Let us return to the two issues posed at the end of Section I, the question as to what ought to be done when the cooks threaten the philosophers and the problem of going about answering this question without making the presupposition that there is some "valid" point of view that states what ought to be done. In a broader prospective the first of these questions is reflected in the dispute as to whether sovereignty resides in a supreme coercive physical force or whether there is some sort of general will or social contract in which everyone, cooks and philosophers, share. And, in considering the moral and legal organization of society at large, the second question can be reformulated as the question whether might makes rights, whether rights extend only to the powerful and duties are forced on the oppressed; or whether there are valid rights, either natural or established by reason, and valid duties that state the ideal in contrast with the actual.

Now Dewey rejects Rousseau's version of the common will theory because his "general will" is too abstract,[73] and he thinks that a social contract theory like Hobbes's breaks down because there is no reason why an individual should yield up his unrestricted obedience to the sovereign if he wants to return to a state of nature.[74] Accordingly, he is faced with the prospect that sovereignty is nothing more than supreme coercive force, that it simply reflects the will of the stronger. Dewey had rejected this view in an important 1894 article entitled "Austin's Theory of Sovereignty," but he had concluded the article by posing the problem of discovering a new theory of sovereignty.

> The practical, as well as the theoretical problem of sovereignty, may fairly be said to be this: To unite the three elements . . . force, or effectiveness; universality, or reference to interests and activities of society as a whole; and determinate, or specific modes of operations—definite organs of expression.[75]

From one point of view the analysis of the social process that Dewey gives in the first five chapters of these lectures is a preparation for solving the problem posed here and formulating a theory of rights and duties based on a pluralistic theory of sovereignty.

Pluralistic sovereignty at least removes the threat of a single organ of sovereignty exercising coercive force over society at large. How does he work out this theory? To begin, the criticism of the rigid dualism between organism and environment can also be applied to relations between the individual and society. If so, a single individual could not be a sovereign, because any individual is already functioning within a larger social process. This is not to deny that there can be oppositions within society, but it does suggest, as Dewey tries to show in the case of the criminal, that the opposition of the individual to society is a function of his already being a member of some functioning social group *within* the social whole. That is, oppositions within society occur when some social function that was heretofore unquestioned is challenged by some other functioning group in society, as when labor strikes for better working conditions. Second, if the analogy between society and the continuous organic circuit is correct, society does not require an overall leader or leading group that exercises supreme coercive force to keep various factions or individuals in line. Instead, there is a vast and changing network of specific functional interrelationships that go to make up the modern society. Rights and duties are natural outgrowths of this process. Third, competition is not a struggle for power over others but a necessary condition of the various functional organs within society being able to sustain themselves and grow further.

All this is preparation. What is Dewey's theory of sovereignty? It is neither supreme coercive force nor does it have a single locus. Yet it is definite in the sense that it resides in specific functioning organs and pluralistic in the sense that every working functional relation within society is an aspect of it. Government is simply one mode of sovereignty, as are industrial life, family life, and the school.[76] Rights and obligations are "correlative phases" of the manifestation of sovereignty.

> Right represents the phases of organization which correspond to differentiation, or the movement toward individualization. Politically speaking it is the body of rights, the system of rights, which constitute the individual.
> We might almost say the rights are the individual and the individual is the rights which he possesses. The responsibilities, the obligations, are the organization on the side of association, on the side of interaction. I tried to show before that the organization necessarily, as well as matter of historical fact, did involve those two sides of the evolution of the particular organ: the aspect of individualization, the reciprocal relations of stimulus and response in which a given organ stands to others, summed up under the term association or interaction.[77]

From an institutional point of view the working action of sovereignty is found in the specific institutions themselves, while the "self-conscious" action of sovereignty is found in law.[78] And from an individual point of view, rights and obligations are the counterpart of structure and function, respectively. "Rights are the conditions which are requisite for complete action, and the obligations, the duties, are simply the abstraction of the various modes of operation involved in this complete function." [79]

The pluralistic theory of sovereignty does away with the possibility that sovereignty is supreme coercive force, but it still leaves open the possibility that the various functioning aspects of sovereignty are simply expressions of force. And, moreover, it would appear that on Dewey's theory these forces may very well represent the actual rights of the powerful over the weak. In dealing with this problem, I want to refer to two questions which we are inclined to think refer to separate issues. Yet, in Dewey's analysis of society, they refer to the same problem. The first question is whether force alone, in the sense of external force, is a factor in solving problems. That is, to take specific cases, does war solve the problems that prompt it? Does capital punishment eliminate crime? The second question is the one just raised, whether sovereignty and rightness as well are identified with force or external power alone.

Dewey's answer to the first question is to deny emphatically that force is a factor in the solution of problems. Early in the lectures he declares that "society is all the time discovering more and more that control of action from without by any external agency is superficial and ineffective."[80] Rather,

> the whole development of politics in the democratic direction has been simply moving in that direction to get a form of political control which shall not be external and coercive with regard to the individual, but which the individual would feel represented his own nature. . . . The feeling of patriotism, or in general loyalty and devotion to the state, seem entirely unaccountable for unless we assume that the state is regarded by the individual as some way or other an organic outgrowth of himself and as something which fulfills and develops himself.[81]

Psychologically, force alone cannot solve problems because thinking cannot occur when there is complete obstruction.[82] Dewey makes it clear, for example, that war is no solution to the problems that brought it about.[83]

Now, if it is a relatively uncontroversial point to say that force alone is merely an obstruction to the solution of problems, why are we inclined to say that this conclusion is irrelevant to the question whether sovereignty and rightness as well can be identified with power or force alone? The answer, I think, is that we conceive of any sovereign body as somehow ruling over its subjects as if they were somehow separate from the sovereign body yet we also hold that the sovereign body can exercise a club over the subjects. That is, the sovereign controls the subjects, but the subjects have no control over the sovereign. But if Dewey is correct in saying that the various organs of society are in constant dynamic inter-action, problems are common or shared evils. They arise when as a matter of fact old customs conflict with new demands, or (to use moral language) old taken-for-granted rights conflict with newly claimed ones.

In his unpublished 1895–96 lectures on *The Logic of Ethics* Dewey laid the foundations for a theory of common evils by developing the logic of resistance.

> The concept of resistance involves the idea of a system or totality within which that resistance occurs. If the resisting and resister were independent they could never get near enough, get the relations to each other, that resistance demands.

In short, there need be two sides if resistance is to occur; resistance indi-cates a shared problem.

In the present lectures Dewey points out that unless we can find some consensus of purpose and community of interest, the only test for a right is whether it can be exercised or not.[84] Let us suppose, then, that Dewey is correct in saying that resistance indicates a shared evil and that the task is to find some binding common end which resolves it. It follows that a negative answer to the question whether force alone is effective in resolving problems also requires a negative answer to the question whether sover-eignty can be identified with external power alone. For, if the so-called organ of sovereignty shares a problem with other organs in the organism of which it is a part, it has no choice except to exercise available intelli-gence in resolving the dispute. In my view, this conclusion is essential to an understanding of how Dewey proposes to utilize the existence of tension in order to resolve it.

But doesn't this analysis neglect the fact that the organ of sovereignty can simply eliminate the opposition if he could get away with it? Granted that such an elimination would not solve the common problem that existed when the opposition arose, it would at least eliminate it. In reply, it should be noted that although the spectator to the crime as well as the victim holds that murder is wrong, it is quite likely that the man who is about to commit it thinks that it is right. Both of these positions, if Dewey is correct, are social in the sense that they are approved and supported by some group within society. No philosophical analysis and subsequent demonstration can change these facts, yet the objection just posed seems to rest on the assumption that the failure of the philosopher *qua* spectator to demonstrate what he already believes in will somehow have adverse consequences. But now the question has become a matter-of-fact question as to the factors that actually influence men to give up their propensity to murder.

How, then, are we to judge which will is to prevail, that of the man against murder or the man who prefers to commit it? In answering this question, consider the concept of will that Dewey brings out in these lectures.

> Will cannot be defined . . . in terms merely of ends, or merely of ideals, abstract ends and ideals. Will implies that the end becomes to some extent a means and thus points toward operation or effectiveness.
>
> . . .
>
> Now applying that general psychological conception to society, the exercise of force, instead of being something external to and restrictive to aims, is the measure of the reality of the aim. . . . our test for the reality of the social conception is the amount of stir it can make in the world, the amount of positive effective application to life it can find in the sphere of space and time. Any other conception leaves us in this thorough-going dualism betweeen the moral and the physical, or the moral and the social. The moral becomes a mere ideal something—desirable to have realized, very nice if it could be realized—but it has no intrinsic force of its own.[85]

The effect of this doctrine is to suggest a choice for any ethical theory. On the one hand, if you separate the moral will and actual effort, you have an ideal with no means of implementation. Even if it is asserted that we can achieve the ideal provided we give up something we are now doing, there is still the problem of how to go about giving up this something. As long as actual effort is not put forth, then it is not yet clear in what sense the task prescribed by the ideal can be done.

On the other hand, if you say with Dewey that moral will and force are aspects of a single process, you are committed to a wholly naturalistic, evolutionary, and relativistic[86] theory of morals. This means that there is no way to judge one competing ideal against another as long as they are working wills in tension with each other. Only when there is a resolution can the moral dispute be settled.

Those who say that this theory sanctions murder neglect the fact that it is not the theory but specific people who commit murders. The theory simply says that the solution that solves the problem, that establishes a working conception of sovereignty with agreed-upon rights and duties based on mutually acceptable reciprocal interaction, is the solution that will prevail. Now sometimes murders will in fact occur, although they will seldom solve problems. And sometimes people will find "solutions" to problems which could be improved upon. Sometimes the strong will manipulate the weak. But the only way to change that is to affect the working wills of the strong. And the only way to do this is either for the social group that is strong to change the wills of its members through tension and subsequent reconstruction among themselves or for the weak to express their own working will against the strong. Dewey's lectures end in an all-too-brief discussion of the resolution of these competing wills through strife [87] and suggest a problem for future inquiry into the working out of actual moral conflicts.

Dewey gives no summary statement, no bringing together of his various observations into a "grand social design." Again and again in the lectures he reverts to the expression "if society is an organism" without seeming to answer it. What then are we to conclude?

It would be a mistake to think Dewey is using the notion of organism in order to give us an ideal picture of the perfect society. Rather, he uses the organic model, reinterpreted along evolutionary-biological lines, as a device or instrument for enabling us to come to grips with actual social problems. As was mentioned in the opening pages of this section, Dewey wants us to abandon the view that men are selfish by nature, that morality cannot be sustained, and that accordingly governmental force is needed to help keep people in line. The functional organic model of society is his device for doing this.

Well, then, is society an organism? Yes and no. It is an organism in the sense that in fact people are bound together in voluntary associations and accordingly share common ideals. Moreover, these voluntary associations are functionally interrelated, although at times they come into conflict and require the aid of government as a catalyst in working out new values which resolve the problem. All this is taken for granted by Dewey; it simply must be assumed if we are to account for the existence of society at all. On the other hand, it is clear that the organism is not perfect. As Dewey says, it "is a question of fact rather than principle as to how far the movement toward organization has actually gone." [88] Still, existing inadequacies do not justify rejecting the organic model. For when there is social stress, we must begin with the analysis of some heretofore successfully functioning relationship if we are to have any material at hand for resolving the problem.

NOTES

1. All of these writings are contained in John Dewey, *The Early Works*, ed. Jo Ann Boydston (5 vols.; Carbondale and Edwardsville, Ill.: Southern Illinois University Press, 1967–72). Hereafter referred to as *Early Works*.

2. For a list of Dewey's lectures during the Chicago period, see the bibliographical lists in *Guide to the Works of John Dewey*, ed. Jo Ann Boydston (Carbondale and Edwardsville, Ill.: Southern Illinois University Press, 1970).

3. *The University of Chicago Register, 1896–1897*, with announcements for 1897–1898 (Chicago: University of Chicago Press, 1898), p. 169. In addition, the catalog lists a course in "The Logic of Ethics" to precede the course in "The Psychology of Ethics." There is no known hectograph copy of the lectures, but the catalog description reads as follows:

34. *The Logic of Ethics.* This course will undertake a critical exam-

ination of the nature and conditions of a scientific treatment of ethics. It will involve a discussion of the relation of ethics to physical and social science, and of the methods appropriate to ethical inquiry and statement. The chief ethical categories will be analyzed, the following concepts being examined with reference to their content and scientific validity: Value, natural and moral; Standards of value and their application; the relation of Ideal to Fact in the ethical judgment; Law, physical and moral; Freedom, its relation to law, causality, and responsibility. For graduate students. Autumn Quarter, '97.

4. *Early Works,* IV, 229. See also the brief note, allegedly written by Dewey, on "Ethics and Politics" (1894), pp. 371–73 of this same volume.

5. Charles A. Madison, "An Editor's View of John Dewey," *The Dewey Newsletter* I (April 1967), 8.

6. *Infra,* p. 217.

7. Consider, for example, the second edition (New York: Henry Holt and Co., 1932) where Dewey points out that "the exercise of claims is as natural as anything else in a world in which persons are not isolated from one another but live in constant association and interaction" (p. 236). Yet he gives virtually no analysis of this world of associations and interactions.

8. Henry Holt and Co., 1927. Dewey's *Human Nature and Conduct* (New York: Modern Library, 1929) comes closest to the complete treatment in the 1898 lectures, but the analysis of the social aspect is not as systematic or detailed as it could have been.

9. Dewey does—almost offhandedly—characterize the good as "the attained synthesis of action as mediated through tension" (*infra,* p. 163) and the sense of duty as "the process of attention as expressed in the relation between the instrumental and the functioning self" (*ibid.,* p. 194). But these characterizations are virtually worthless without an adequate understanding of their psychological basis.

10. The viewpoint outlined here was first developed in an important 1891 article, "Moral Theory and Practice" (*Early Works,* III, 93–109). It is worked out further in the 1892 article "Green's Theory of the Moral Motive" (*ibid.,* III, 155–73) and the 1893 article "Self-Realization as the Moral Ideal" (*ibid.,* IV, 43–53). In the latter two articles, Dewey emphasizes again and again that the vague idealist concept of self-realization provides no guidance in action. For more on the historical development of Dewey's view that morality requires a resolution of the problem, see the next section of the Introduction, especially with respect to James's influence.

11. *Infra,* p. 208 ff.

12. And they also ignore Henry Sidgwick's skeptical conclusion in *The Methods of Ethics* (London: Macmillan and Co., 1874) that both egoism and benevolence are equally reasonable.

13. *Infra,* p. 209. The details of this view are worked out in the remainder of the section.

14. A view that Dewey took over from James (see *infra,* p. 178).

15. *Ibid.*, pp. 120, 212–13.

16. *Ibid.*, p. 37 ff.

17. *Ibid.*, pp. 45–47.

18. *Ibid.*, Chap. 4, Sec. 2.

19. *Ibid.*, Chap. 4, Sec. 1.

20. *Ibid.*, Chap. 4, Sec. 5.

21. *Early Works*, I, 227–49.

22. *Ibid.*, III, 239–388. The important sections are Part I, Sections XXXVIII–XLI (pp. 314–27), and the whole of Part II, entitled "The Ethical World" (pp. 345–52). The brevity of the latter section and the fact that Dewey ended it with the contention that "the consideration of specific institutions, as the family, industrial society, civil society, the nation, etc., with their respective rights and laws, belongs to political philosophy rather than to the general theory of ethics" (p. 352) shows the incomplete development of his political philosophy at this time.

23. *Ibid.*, I, 232.

24. *Ibid.*, III, 322.

25. *Ibid.*, I, 237.

26. *Ibid.*, I, 246–47.

27. *Ibid.*, III, 323.

28. *Ibid.*

29. *Ibid.*, p. 370.

30. *Ibid.*

31. *Ibid.*, p. 371.

32. *Ibid.*, IV, 234.

33. Samuel Alexander, *Moral Order and Progress* (London: Trübner and Co., 1889), p. 370. Alexander's influence on Dewey has not yet been examined, despite many favorable references to Alexander in both the *Outlines of a Critical Theory of Ethics* and *The Study of Ethics*. In Dewey's 1901 course on "Social Ethics" he refers in the April 11th lecture to *Moral Order and Progress* as "one of the most suggestive of all the modern statements of ethical theory, concrete ethical theory, not merely the analysis of the subjects, but the attempt to interpret them also in terms of life and social relationships."

34. *The Study of Ethics, Early Works*, IV, 261.

35. Alexander, p. 371.

36. "Evolution and Ethics" (1898), *Early Works*, V, 34–53.

37. *Ibid.*, p. 37.

38. *Ibid.*, p. 44. The importance of struggle in the ethical process was not a new idea for Dewey, but the idea that value could be attached to the "working out" of a moral conclusion could only be developed fully after Dewey had rejected T. H. Green's view that the moral ideal existed apart from any activity of the concrete, natural self. "Evolution and Ethics" was Dewey's first attempt to make an explicit analogy between the moral and the evolutionary struggle.

39. *Ibid.,* 39.

40. *Ibid.,* p. 41.

41. *Ibid.,* p. 39.

42. *Ibid.,* p. 41.

43. *Ibid.,* p. 46.

44. "So far as the progressive varieties are concerned, it is not in the least true that they simply adapt themselves to current conditions; evolution is a continued development of new conditions which are better suited to the needs of organisms than the old. The unwritten chapter in natural selection is that of the evolution of environments" (*ibid.,* p. 52). The point is developed further in Chapter II, Section 2 of these lectures.

45. *Early Works,* V, 51.

46. Dewey suggests an answer in "Evolution and Ethics." He imagines a case where the leader of an "early social group" is faced with the problem of whether to put the feeble, sickly, and aged to death (p. 40). He points out that to do so might be a short-run benefit but in the long run would not enable the tribe to develop habits of foresight and forethought which would be useful to it. "In a word, such conduct [aiding the sick man] would pay in the struggle for existence as well as be morally commendable" (p. 40). This case may be intended merely as an illustration, but such examples contribute to the feeling that Dewey is either overly optimistic about the ease with which progress is possible or is appealing to the *a priori* thesis that the conduct that pays and moral conduct are always compatible.

47. As reprinted in William James, *The Will to Believe and Other Essays in Popular Philosophy* (New York: Longmans Green and Co., 1898), pp. 184–215.

48. Letter of Dewey to James, June 3, 1891. As quoted in Ralph Barton Perry, *The Thought and Character of William James* (Boston: Little, Brown and Co., 1935), II, 517.

49. *Early Works,* IV, 227.

50. James, *The Will to Believe,* p. 195.

51. *Early Works,* III, 93–109.

52. *Ibid.,* p. 94.

53. There is no space here to give the reasons for James's scepticism. It basically was developed by Henry Sidgwick, but came down to James through A. J. Balfour's *A Defense of Philosophic Doubt* (London: Hodder and Stoughton, 1879), pp. 335–55, and Josiah Royce's *The Religious Aspect of Philosophy* (Boston: Houghton, Mifflin and Co., 1885), Bk. I, Chaps. II–V. James was very much influenced by the young Royce at the time he wrote "The Moral Philosopher and the Moral Life."

54. *Infra,* p. 245.

55. *Ibid.,* p. 244.

56. Dewey, "William James as Empiricist," in Horace M. Kallen, ed., *In Commemoration of William James, 1842–1942* (New York: Columbia University Press, 1942), pp. 52–53.

57. *Infra,* p. 279.

58. The contention that organism and environment are distinctions we make within an already existing whole is difficult to understand unless we realize that Dewey is making a functional rather than a substantive analysis. *Qua* substance my body (organism) is distinguished from the environment by the surface of my skin, the surface of my eyeballs, and so on. But as a functioning process the skin, for example, is not isolated from the atmosphere in which the body operates. Hence, there is no need to distinguish the surface of the skin from the environment which helps sustain it until such time as tension is produced, say, when the skin touches poison ivy. We could, of course, make the distinction, but it would have no functional import; there would be no need to make it.

59. *Infra,* p. 294.

60. *Ibid.,* p. 239.

61. *Ibid.,* p. 393.

62. *Ibid.,* p. 380.

63. For the details of Dewey's statement and criticism of Spencer's position, see Chapter 4, Sections 1 and 2.

64. Dewey, "The Reflex-Arc Concept in Psychology," *Early Works,* V, 96–109.

65. *Infra,* pp. 347–48.

66. Specifically, Dewey does this in his examination of interrelating social and individual factors in the production of the criminal and the genius. See Chapter 4, Section 4.

67. *Infra,* p. 238.

68. *Ibid.,* p. 298.

69. Dewey, *The Study of Ethics,* in *Early Works,* IV, 259.

70. This paragraph is largely based on the *Lectures, infra,* pp. 295–96.

71. *Ibid.,* 237–38.

72. Years later, Dewey considered this limited function of government to be a bit naive. "Our doctrine of plural forms . . . does not intimate that the function of the state is limited to settling conflicts among other groups, as if each one of them had a fixed scope of action of its own. . . . Our hypothesis is neutral as to any general, sweeping implications as to how far state activity may extend" (Dewey, *The Public and Its Problems* [New York: Henry Holt and Co., 1927], p. 73).

73. *Infra,* pp. 425–26.

74. *Ibid.,* pp. 434–35.

75. Dewey, "[John] Austin's Theory of Sovereignty" (1894), *Early Works,* IV, 90.

76. *Infra,* pp. 424–25.

77. *Ibid.,* p. 433.

78. *Ibid.,* p. 427.

79. *Ibid.,* p. 440.

80. *Ibid.,* p. 346.

81. *Ibid.,* pp. 249–50.

82. *Ibid.,* p. 364. This is not to say that force has no role in the solution of

problems. See Dewey's clever analysis of the liberating and restrictive role of force in Chapter 6, Section 2.

83. *Ibid.,* p. 335.

84. *Ibid.,* pp. 434–35.

85. *Ibid.,* p. 412.

86. The question how, for Dewey, morality can be both relative and objective is the proper subject of another inquiry.

87. *Infra,* Chap. 6, Sec. 9.

88. *Ibid.,* p. 331.

LECTURES ON
PSYCHOLOGICAL
ETHICS: 1898

SECTION 1. THE SOCIAL
BASIS OF INDIVIDUALITY

The point of which I was speaking yesterday, that the psychological individual represents the social individual freed from any fixed social relationship, may be illustrated by reference to a discussion in Aristotle's [*Nicomachean*] *Ethics,* Book I, Chapter VII, beginning with Section 10. I will take the liberty of reading about a page. The argument is that every man must have a function; every class has its special excellence and man must have his excellence too. His excellence must be in rational life in the exercise of his vital energies in obedience to and with reason. A good man's life consists in functioning well and nobly, in using his powers in accordance with their excellence.

This may seem commonplace, but it marks a great discovery and called Ethics into existence as a discipline; the discovery of man as man distinct from man as shoemaker, carpenter, or fruitseller; the distinction of man as a ruler on the one side and a citizen in obedience to the ruler on the other, from man as man who has functions and therefore has powers, energies, and faculties with relation to that end or function.

Now we have the two-fold historical and theoretical interpretation, one which regards man as man distinct from the ruler, the carpenter, as somehow if not outside of society, at least independent of society so that the social operation is regarded simply as a limitation or else as a mere outward mode of manifestation of the human function which inherently transcends society. The other interpretation is that which I gave yesterday, that this does not represent isolation, independence transcending the social functions and relationships, but simply represents the generic freeing of the individual or represents the conception of the individual in a free, flexible, progressive society instead of in any particular form of rigidly fixed society. The individual from that point of view considered psychologically is the individual who is abstracted from all special forms or social relationships in order that he may be a [fit?]* subject for any form. He is not taken as father or as ruler or as subject or as artist or as carpenter or in any other special social

* Word missing in original hectograph copy.

3

relationship, because it is necessary to view him with reference to all possible associations and relationships. As long as society was fixed in a caste system or, if not as rigidly as that, fixed in forms which lie definitely along racial ties or geographical relation of special communities, the Greek pitted against the barbarians, of classes within the community, as the free or working class distinguished from the leisure class; if any individual is taken as a member of a limited social group, we cannot have and historically did not have any psychology as psychology. Of course there was a good deal of implicit psychology, but as a science it could not come to birth because the individual as a possible universal had not come to existence. The object of any science as science must [?] be universal. The individual, then, must become universal, must become objective or generic.

That point is reached, the universalism of the individual, only when the individual is abstracted from particular, local, exclusive forms, so that he may be considered a possible subject of any and of every [form]. Now social life gets more fluent. The distinctions of classes become the simple functional distinctions. The points of view become simply limitations and barriers when they can view the individual from his possible position in society generally and thereby he is universalized and becomes the object of a science—psychology.

The emerging, then, of the individual as an object of psychology is at once a sign and a reflex of the growth of freedom in society; of the breakdown of all rigid, fixed separations within the social organization. It is a mark both of the growing community of society and of the fact that society is progressing instead of being fixed. Where we are liable to go astray, where so many writers have gone astray, is in interpreting this freedom—abstraction from any specific social relationship—in order that we may consider more general relationships, as if it was abstraction or isolation from all social relationships as such.

The two points, then, which may sum this discussion up as regards the psychological individual are that, first in connection with the matter of progress, the psychological individual stands for an element of variation and invention in social life. As long as society is of a fairly conservative type (as all primitive relationships are, social relationships being established by custom and all departure from custom being regarded abnormal, the fact being regarded as making one a criminal all along), there can be no question of any psychological individual. But when a society becomes progressive, then the initiation of variation is just as important as the conservation of the accessions or accomplishments of the past. When we get to a socially progressing society, then the two points have to be considered: the conservation of what has been worked out in the past—but equal importance is thrown upon the elements of discovery and invention, in general the element of variability. That element of variability can be found, of course, only through the individual; then the individual is taken psychologically. It is his departure from the customary, habitual, commands of social action which characterize him as this or that individual. On the basis of custom the only way to characterize him is by his status—that is, he has wife, children, is a working man, a slave; that is, he has a definite status. But in the progressive society the individual is defined by what he does that is different from what others have been doing. He is defined by reference to the new lines of activity that he sets going.

It is the tension then between the variable and the conservative factors in social life which throws the psychological individual into relief; which makes him conscious of his difference, of his own identity, and makes others conscious of their peculiar identities distinct from each other. As long as you define a man in terms of status he is still defined in thoroughly socialized terms. These distinctions of status are permanent. But when the individual breaks out for himself and contributes a [?] mode of action you did not have before, a variation, then you have, according to the terms of the psychology of sensation, the threshold difference which makes social difference.

The difference of the psychological individual from the social individual is the individual differentially defined, not defined by the social status that he fits into. You have the analogy, of course, here on the biological side between the generic and the individual in the theory of evolution; or between the hereditary element—which is the generic, and the element of variation—which tends towards the formation of new species. The very conception of evolution carries the distinction between the relative and the permanent distinguished as hereditary, and the progressive element which is called variation and which tends within the generic to the formation of new species: or if it goes far enough so that the variation becomes organized permanently, it finally becomes itself generic.

Psychologically this element of variation which constitutes the psychological individual shows itself in both what we term impulse and what we term reflection. Impulse and reflection are equally opposed to custom. The individual of a customary society is neither an impulsive being, a consciously impulsive being, nor a consciously reflective being; he is a creature of habits. He is a creature of routine.

Of course the romanticists of the last century, among them Rousseau, have pictured the wild, primitive man as peculiarly a creature of wild impulse, and he has been set up in that way against the habits of society; but recent research has turned this about. It is the primitive man whose life is prescribed to him practically along certain definite lines of social conformity. The breaking loose that he does is physical rather than psychological. As far as his consciousness is concerned he follows pretty narrowly along the curves of his society. Anthropological investigation justifies that view. Of course, too, he is not a reflective being.

We deliberate only when we are setting up new lines of action and the question is how to carry them out. As long as we are following customary lines there is no need of thinking. It takes care of itself. One step more or less automatically gives rise to the next. So the growth of the psychological individual in the introduction to conscious variation marks itself on the one hand in the freeing of impulses of new tendencies to action, and on the other side reflects itself in the rational deliberative proposal of new ends to the conscious seeking out of means by which to realize those ends.

Impulse, then—we must have some word to designate this; I take the word impulse—impulse is as distinct from instinct as thinking is from immediate response to suggestion. The impulse represents an instinct which has broken up. Of course the impulse is always based on an instinct, but it is that instinct which has got set free so the various tendencies to action now tend to run on their own account instead of simply with reference to a predetermined end of instinct. It might be illustrated best generically by the difference between the human language and the animal language; take the classical experiments of Spalding [1] on the clucking of the chicken and the ability of the young chicken to locate its food practically as soon as free from the shell or at most not making more than one or two false moves to locate the corn or an insect as well as its mother, without direct teaching. Now undoubtedly, if one accepts evolution at all, the reaching tendency we see in the child, its reactions of hand and arm are all of them based upon what have been recently fixed instincts or definite coordinations but now in the child are held together and limited each by the other so that they could work simply to one end; all that self-inclosed system, so to speak, has been broken down and the child simply has the impulse to move his hand, to move his eyes not from instinct but simply for the sake of doing—an impulse to act with his arm, impulse to close with his fingers. So his coordinations have to be got by putting together those tendencies which represent the unraveling or breaking loose of factors previously tied together in a distinctive coordination.

Both impulse and reflection are opposed to habit or customary element and these are embodied in the psychological individual, the growing individual in a progressive society who has been considered not as fitting into the particular conception or with reference to the movement of society as a whole but with the possibility of becoming the center of a new function.

Now it is just at these periods of disintegration, especially at their crises when the tension between the variable and the customary element is greatest, that the individual feels himself so consciously as differentiated, as a psychological individual, where the threshold of difference is so great between him and the customary action that he is led to think himself as being non-social, as being precedent to society, so that his social relationship should present various ways in which he as an individual chooses to act. He is precedent to future modes of action. He does represent new modes of action; so far as future society is concerned, the individual may be considered to be prophetic, to be symbolic. He is the basis of future society and wherever historically that particular conjunction of circumstances has been found, the individual has considered himself as the basis of the future element and therefore has considered himself as absolutely antecedent to society instead of being relatively antecedent, or being the point from which society reconstructs itself, changes from one point to another.

Perhaps a political example will make that clear. If we take the English political philosophy from the 15th or 16th century on to the beginning of this century, we will find that they begin by assuming the historic non-social individual. Then these individuals come together and make a contract and that contract is the beginning of society. They agree to give up the individual will to form a state in order to be more secure in their possession of a certain number of other things. The individual was becoming a social element in the sense he was not before society, because society was passing through the stage of custom into the stage of progress or variation. This individual was the outgrowth of a previous stage of society and was in opposition to the customary stages of society, which of course went on, for if it had not, society would have dissolved in anarchy.

What may be said, then, is that the psychological individual represents the social values getting subjectified, being translated over into subjective conscious form, while the conservative habitual element represents the objective phase of social action; and thus wherever there is progress in society, there is tension between subjective and objective in society, just as there is in knowledge between the subject (or the mind which knows) and the object (which it knows).

Now the point which we are coming to is that this tension or opposition is an opposition socially developed; it is between the progressive, variable factor, represented by the psychological individual, and the conservative, customary factor. At these periods of comparative social disintegration and reconstruction, once more, the moral life seems to retire into the keeping of individuals. It seems peculiarly a matter which goes on in the theater of the individual consciousness. Motivation and impulse as such and the social life without seem to be indifferent or even alien to morality.

Now just as I illustrated the other point with what went on in the 15th, 16th, and 17th centuries, this [new point] may be illustrated by what went on in the early years of our era, in Stoicism, Skepticism, a movement so generic that its causes must have been general, a movement putting the moral life in the individual consciousness. The real question is what the individual chooses to do . . .* himself. You find it in Stoicism, Christianity and, in modern times, in the Reformation. A socially organized institution is regarded as external and is indifferent if not alien to the interests of morality. The explanation, on the basis of what I have said, is that we have there a social disintegration going on and this indifference, this split between individual and the social constitution, merely means the inadequacy of the past customary social relationships longer to adequately motivate and control the actions of the individual. These institutions, in breaking down, are setting the individual free; that is to say, they are breaking down

* Word missing in original hectograph copy.

men's thought, they do not longer adequately stimulate and control him. Hence the individual gets a new social responsibility, the responsibility of reorganizing the social constitution. That is often felt or interpreted as if it were non-social because in this case it is interpreted with reference to what has gone before instead of what is coming after. That is, the individual is merely cut loose from institutions that have been, so the tendency is to throw the burden into his own consciousness instead of saying that these thoughts come on as the initiation of a new social condition. The individual has emerged out of the old institutions and new institutions must spring up through him.

Instead of interpreting the ferment in the individual consciousness as functional, let us isolate it and make it an end in itself and you will find that the key or explanation of all free, subjective, ethical theories, whether we take the excessive subjectivism of one-sided theories of Christianity or Stoicism or Puritanism or of the Protestant Reformation. There was this responsibility thrown on the individual, but it was made an end in itself in the individual's own consciousness, instead of all that was going on in the individual consciousness being seen to be a preparation of the instruments and tools of new social action. The introspective character of the Puritan morals, morals that went with the religion, give [an] example of what I mean. The moral split then is really within society, not between the individual and society.

And moreover the tendency is to identify the interests of morality too exclusively with the ideal side or with the side of the reformer. It is important at one of these periods to do justice to the full amount of the ethical content and value which is involved on the customary, habitual side. The tendency is, because there is reconstruction needed, to neglect the established institutions not only as indifferent but alien to morality. Now as a matter of fact there is always as much morality involved in the institution or customary habit as there is in the ideal of the reformer, and no ideal that fails to take into account the morality in the established institution will fail to bring revenge upon itself. A genuine reform is what the word implies—it is a re-forming. Now ignoring all the ethical value embodied in the institution leaves that without any substance to reform. There is nothing left to shape over. The whole thing has to be created *de novo* and the reform has become a revolution.

The psychological explanation is that things that are customary are valued so low as to fall below consciousness. The general law is that tension goes to the point of greatest weakness. So there is the law of defect in the institution as compared with the amount of substantial working truth there is in it. The consciousness, stress, or strain is located with reference to the failure. So naturally a sort of hysteria of consciousness comes and one point is greatly exaggerated at the expense of the other. Now I said the . . .* it avenged itself, the neglect on the ethical side, because the ideal of the

* Word or two words missing in original hectograph copy.

individual becomes empty and in becoming empty it becomes either senti-mental or arbitrary. There is nothing to control what content shall be given to the views of the individual. The individual is somehow to create his own motives in himself, as in the one-sided forms of Protestantism to which I refer, and the whole destiny of the thing somehow comes back to him. Now, in the very nature of the case when he is isolated from the institution in which he as a matter of fact, is bound up, there is nothing to give substance or meaning to the thing. If it becomes arbitrary, the result is revolution. Abstract idealism is found in the French revolution.

As a rule of course man's practical instincts will prevent them from taking such arbitrary revolutionary form as that, and then this neglect or contempt of customary institutions avenges itself in the ordinary customs of life. The habits, the customs which are displaced, avenge themselves by becoming the controlling motives of everyday life, while the spiritual or ideal ones are retained for special occasions; for instance the distinction between the weekdays as secular and the Sabbath as specially holy. These institutions of life must be put up with somehow and so they are endured or maintained but they are regarded as indifferent. But somehow they have got to be indulged in and kept up. That means that the spiritual side be-comes practically reserved for emotional stimulation. It becomes very largely a scheme of getting the feeling of doing a thing without actually doing it. Hence the distinction of the modern consciousness between the customary on the one side and the moral *par excellence* on the other with-out seeing how the moral sphere does get simply emotional sentimental value. The individual uses certain means for getting a certain frame of mind because that is regarded as the right thing, but the actual working habits of life go on very little changed right along with it.

The same general principle may be stated on the other side. The split is not only one in society, but also one in the individual. You may say it is in a society or in an individual. Morally you may say it is between the flesh and the spirit. In psychological terms you may say it is between [the] in-dividual's impulse to act and his reflections and thoughts which come in to check and control these impulses.

First and Second Chapters, *Data of Ethics*—Spencer.[2]

SECTION 2. PSYCHOLOGIC AND SOCIAL ETHICS IN THEIR HISTORICAL BACKGROUND

January 4, 1898

Psychologic Ethics discusses conduct with reference to the agent, with reference to the way in which forms of conduct originate and operate. So-cial Ethics discusses conduct with reference to the practical situation, the important function of the situation being the vital values summed up in it—

i.e., the values produced in past action and representing the raw material for the realization—effectuation—of future action. Psychologic Ethics discusses the "How" of conduct. Social Ethics discusses the "What" of conduct.

It is to be noted that both psychologic ethics and social ethics are but parts of social ethics in a larger sense of that term. The one is not the ethics of the individual and the other the ethics of society as if these were opposed to each other. The distinction may be said to be between two views of society—or (it might almost be said) between two views of the individual.

There is no society apart from individuals—no such thing as "society in the abstract." A theory of society which neglected the individual would be "*Hamlet* with Hamlet left out." But upon the other hand it must be said that the individual is a social being who acts in and with reference to the social situation. The individual must be recognized in social ethics and society in individual ethics. The individual may be treated as one in whom social values are incarnate, in whom they "live, move and have their being." But he may also be regarded as one who brings value into existence, one who varies it, who consciously assumes an attitude to it. The former is the social individual, the latter the psychologic individual.

In general we may distinguish the individual who is at one with his community, and the individual who marks himself off consciously from it. Both are social; and this very marking off of self from the group has a social origin and a social function. But in the former case, all the interest attaches to the *content,* the values focussed in the individual; in the latter, it centers in the *form* of a process—the way in which an individual consciously distinguishes himself from his community life and readjusts himself to it. And, as will be suggested later on, this latter discussion involves the question of social progress as distinct from that of social status.

In considering the family, for instance, the interest of social ethics is in parent or child as parent or child, i.e., in what special values are maintained by the parent, etc., in the family life; in the rights he possesses as representative of such values; in the duties devolving upon him as their bearers. So in political ethics the interest is in the individual as employee, employer, citizen or subject, etc.

In psychological ethics he is a certain member and organ of a practical situation. While we remember that the individual exercises his rights in social relations, these relations are of interest to us only as stimuli to the individual, only as they arouse and initiate a specific mode of action—specific in the sense of involving variation in the existing situation.

We may illustrate also from imitation. From the standpoint of social ethics the interest in the situation is in it as a conservator of values. From the standpoint of psychological ethics, the interest in it is in the mechanism of imitation, i.e., how it grows.

It is not possible actually to separate value from the process which maintains it, but this can be done in thought for the sake of clearness of treatment.

Psychological ethics takes action on the side of form. Social ethics takes action on the side of content.

Historically, conduct was at first group-conduct pure and simple; the individual had neither freedom nor responsibility, i.e., the individual as such. Everything was corporate—the individual was undifferentiated from his group. The individualization of conduct—the recognition of it as something coming from the individual—is a concomitant of democracy: the postulate that conduct springs from a free and responsible individual is the very basis and spirit of real democracy. For about two thousand years the tendency has been toward this individualization of conduct.

There were two sources of stimulus to this development:

1. The philosophic analysis of conduct in Greece—the Socratic movement.
2. The work attempted by Jesus and His followers.

The Socratic idea of the morality of the individual was that he could not be moral until he could define and comprehend his motives in action as these were embodied in universal principles. The individual was not truly moral save as actuated by recognition of the universal. Of course there were two assumptions underlying this idea:

1. That there is this eternal universal principle.
2. That the principle may be so comprehended by the individual as to become directive of his conduct.

These principles were calculated to work the downfall or the thorough reconstruction of Greek society as it then existed in Athens, for it was essentially an aristocracy. First, the Greek himself in relation to the barbarian was an aristocrat. Second, among the Greeks there were class divisions and distinctions which were aristocratic in the extreme—as those between the manual laboring classes and the higher classes. The Socratic idea, in theory, broke down these distinctions and reorganized the individual—looked at him from the standpoint of his relations to universal principles.

The actuating motive, the working principle of the Greek, was his local social environment. The Socratic idea proposed to enlarge this environment until it became cosmic—universal. Thus a great contradiction was introduced into Greek civilization: a contradiction between the scientific formulation of conduct and the circumstantial environment in which it was to be worked out and actualized—one which set the ideal individual over against the actual individual.

The individualism of Jesus and His followers was the polar opposite of Greek universalism. Jesus gave infinite value to the individual because of his possible present membership in the Kingdom of God. This participation of the individual in the Kingdom of God was so greatly emphasized that it outweighed and sometimes overshadowed participation in all other fields of activity.

The new view of the individual set to work to reconstruct the social unity. This effort manifested itself externally in the structures of Roman civilization—laws, general citizenship, etc.—various devices to make the Roman Empire outwardly and materially one. The inner reconstructive attempt was made in Christianity, in the spiritual unity of believers with each other and with Jesus and with the God of the universe.

It may be said that the political and industrial ididualism of more recent epochs is the direct continuation of the religious individualism of early Christianity as interpreted and formulated by the universalism of Greek thought. Greek thought claimed for the universal the right to control the individual and based the morality of the individual's action upon its motivation by the individual's recognition of this universal, but its universal and its individual were such that only in the cases of particularly favored individuals could the two be brought together, i.e., the philosophers and the leisured classes. Plato in his *Republic* sets forth a scheme for connecting the two, but this scheme was impossible because based upon a fundamental dualism.

Christianity upon the other hand, devoted its attention not to the universal, cosmic law and order, but to the individual—it had no worked-out scheme of the universe into which to fit its individual, i.e., it had no adequate view of the universal—just as [the] Greeks had no adequate view of the individual. The two, Greek universal and Christian individual, complemented each other. Very much that is known as Christianity is but the working out [?] of Christian individualism in forms of Greek intellectual universalism. The Greek individual was abstract—not concrete; the concrete individual, as individual, of the Greeks was of little worth, while the Semitic individual was concrete and was of infinite worth.

The problem has been: How can the space-and-time individual so bring it to pass that his action shall transcend all local considerations? Its solution has practically been a reconciliation of Greek universalism and Christian individualism. In other words, the salvation of the individual, at first intellectual and religious, is being worked out in other ways as well, as is illustrated in modern political and industrial individualism.

January 5, 1898

The weakness of Greek thought was in emphasizing for the individual the importance of the universal while providing for him no adequate means for coming into contact therewith. The only means, to the Greek thought, was the insight of intellect, and thus only those gifted with time and intellectual power could hope to come into contact with the universal in any saving moral sense. The Greek did not conceive of this objective order as so living in the individual as to express itself in his impulses and instincts. These last were indeed considered as things opposed to reason insofar that they must be controlled by it—they were not recognized as possessing value of themselves.

Christianity was strong in its conception of the individual as having in himself the divine principle which needed only to be freed through the act of faith and love in order to furnish him a motive and direction of activity. With the outward world—with its scheme and construction, the Semitic had but little to do. He thought that if the individual's motives were right, he would get a right view of the cosmic law and order. His position was that of those who consider science as of little import—religion will give man all he needs to know of the universe. He considered the inner impulses as both legislators and initiators of action. There was no conscious denial of the value of the Greek's cosmic law and order—only an ignoring of it.

Thus each conception demanded the other. The objective view of the Greek demanded a free individual who reproduced subjectively the outward order. This Christianity furnished, while the Christian individual needed just such a world idea as the Greek conception furnished.

While Christianity spoke of the Kingdom of God, it emphasized this much less than it did the individual. In working out the conception of the two, it gave attention to each; but the realization of the concept of the Kingdom of God is always approached from the side of the individual and his motive. In the New Testament very little is said about the ideal Kingdom of God. It remains an ideal without filling—save in certain lines, and these extend from the motive of the individual. This growing remoteness from the world of space and time, intellect and volition, increased after Jesus and his disciples' time; and eventually the Kingdom of God was reflected into the "other world." This came to a climax in the mediaeval period when the Kingdom of God—heaven—was simply the not-worldly. This was manifested in the dualism of church and state. The state got its only ethical content from being an instrument in the hands of the church used for the saving of souls. This purely ideal interpretation was the outcome of the lack of positive content in Christianity's conception of the outward world.

In the forms of Roman civilization, in law, citizenship, unity of government, etc., etc., of the Roman empire was furnished a field for the employment of the individual's ethical self, and also a rough outward structural type or symbol of the ideal unified law and order world of the Greek. It furnished an object lesson to the moral and ethical nature of the individual—an outward type of the inner and spiritual world of relations which should obtain among men. No institution can for a moment retain its grasp on men which does not furnish motives and materials for their moral life. Thus the Roman civilization in furnishing a place, orderly and under law, for the exercise of the powers of the individual, furnished a field for moral activity.

From the time of the Renaissance to the present, the individual has come to a definite realization of self in a social environment which the self may reconstruct. Our present social conditions embody to a degree the realization of the early Christian idea of the relation of the individual to the whole brotherhood of man. Science, commerce, etc., have conspired and culminated in freeing the individual; not by absolving him from society, but setting him in a flexible social whole which provides scope for his activities, demands them as individualized and at the same time gives to them its own acquired values—i.e., backs him up, as it were, by its sanctions and makes him its heir, giving to him funded capital. Thus the individual gets in a real way the infinite values conferred upon him (theoretically) by early Christianity, gets them here and now rather than in some far removed future world. His social environment makes him feel in any act the value of the whole system of which that act is a part: makes him feel it in two ways, as contributing to it and also as constituted by it.

The foregoing sketch is from a certain point of view the nature of the individual as that individual is regarded by psychology. We have seen that the growth of the self-conscious individual is the counterpart of a social growth. The growth of the conscious individual marks the growing recognition of an agent of social action in general, independent of any one particular form of social action or institution. The completeness and complexity of society and of the individual are parallel and independent growths.

This developing importance of the individual created and creates increasing demand for knowledge of this individual, because he comes now more and more to be considered as the mechanism through which social values are manifested. The more responsibility is placed upon the individual, the more ways in which he will work—in which he can be depended upon, or made to work—increase in importance as matters to be known.

SECTION 3. THE PSYCHOLOGIC INDIVIDUAL AND RECONSTRUCTION OF THE SOCIAL ORDER

January 6, 1898

As a matter of historical fact the theory of ethics was brought into existence by the discovery that man as man has a goal and a function which may be set over against the office and aim of any particular class of men. This is the significance of the Socratic movement. (See for example Aristotle's [*Nichomachean*] *Ethics,* Book I, Chapter VII, Section 10.) The discovery of man as man, distinct from man as ruler, parent, shoemaker, etc., marked both the possibility of psychology as a science and the possibility of ethics as a discipline of individual life.

The problem however is as to the interpretation of this discovery. Does it mean that there is any such entity as man apart from and outside of definite social relationships and offices; that his operations in society are simply mere outward modes of manifesting a capacity which inherently or inwardly transcends society? Can we ever find an individual who does not as matter of occupy some special social station and do some particular social work? And is this social definition a mere outward necessity or does it belong to man as man? (Out of this problem grew the metaphysical one of the relation of the universal to the particular; and out of the tendency to separate the two grew the divorce of knowledge and practice with the attaching of superior value to the former.) If the separation is real, we are forced to the conception of man in his inner nature as non-social. But if it is only an abstraction, the problem arises: why make this abstraction? Why not stick to the actual facts of the particular individuals, doing particular things?

Believing that the distinction is only an abstraction, the location of the abstraction will throw light on the problem of the nature of the psychologic individual. All abstractions arise for the sake of setting free some force which is not finding adequate expression; and they serve to set it free because they bring out some hitherto concealed unity, with reference to which it may function. In this particular case, the abstraction of the individual from any particular social status and work means that society is becoming conscious of its unity, of the necessity of defining the individual with reference to its unity, and is thus becoming consciously progressive. As long as society is fixed into mutually exclusive groups on the basis of local conditions, as long as within each of these groups there are castes or fixed classes of ruler and subject, of working class and leisure class, there can be no psychology: because there is no universal to serve as its subject matter—for every science must have a universal.

The emerging, therefore, of the individual as a self-conscious subject, is at once a sign and a reflex of the growth of the community spirit in society. It indicates the breaking down of rigid, fixed barriers within social organization. The individual is marked off from any fixed and local social group only that he may be seen as a member and organ of a wider and more flexible association—theoretically, he can now be defined only with reference to the most inclusive of all associations, humanity itself. Instead therefore of a self-conscious individual designating something separate from social relationships, he is the exact counterpart and correlate of the consciousness of intrinsic, inclusive social unity as such. He is free from a local social relationship only that he may be freed for a wider one.

But we said that this abstraction indicated progressive as well as a more unified society. The more inclusive society presents itself at the outset as an idea, as something which has still to be realized. Existing society in its positive institutions is still mainly a class society. These institutions present themselves as habitual, as customary; in other words, they are the organs of past social action. Now the individual who is getting free from absolute absorption in one of these groups or classes through his consciousness of wider association and of powers which can express themselves adequately only in a wider range of opportunities must serve as the organ of future social action. Through him escaping from the local institution and indeed turning against it to reconstruct it, must progress, the development of a free flexible comprehensive social interaction, be brought about.

Just at this point, as the individual turns against the attained institution, does he seem perhaps both to himself and to others, to be non-social. But we must remember that it is in the interests of progress, of effecting a social unity which can be maintained only in free interaction, not in the prescribed forms of past habits, that he can do this. The individual is no longer defined with reference to social status previously occupied, but with reference to the new modes of social construction which radiate from him: the demands that he can make, the stimuli that he can offer to others, and the problems which others can put upon him with some assurance that he, without further supervision, will undertake their solution. It is thus the tension between the varying element looking forward to a more functional social unity and the habitual or conservative factor which looks back to a more static unity, which throws the psychologic individual into relief.

Before showing just how this defines the psychologic individual as a universal or subject matter for science, we may illustrate historically the point just made. Just at the periods of historic reconstruction, when local communities are disintegrated through absorption into larger wholes, and special classes or institutions are breaking up through the demands made on them in the larger society in which they now operate, the individual is set free from the customary modes of action from which, since they are customary, he has not previously been differentiated. He thus becomes the prophet and the instrument of new social institutions. But there will be a period when he will be set off from the old and before he is set into the new. It is by making this historic epoch absolute, isolating it from its past conditions and future function, that there arises the conception of the individual as intrinsically non-social, and as inherently antecedent to social organization. For example, political philosophy from the 16th to the present century began by postulating non-social individuals who voluntarily come together and make a contract which is the basis of all associated life. Here the assumption is that pre-social individuals generate society. It is customary now to regard this doctrine as merely a crude aberration due to mere metaphysical speculation or else to an unbridled ethical individualism. But however false, it still has a great historical meaning. It shows society undergoing a tremendous democratic reconstruction in which as matter of fact the individual is being given more freedom and more responsibility, and thus is becoming the determiner of future social life.

Another historic illustration is found in the negative attitude assumed by the consciously moral individual or reformer to social institutions in the first centuries of our era, and also at the time of the Protestant Reformation. In the earlier period both Stoic, Epicurean, and Christian, as conscious moralists, regarded existing social institutions as external and as indifferent if not actually hostile to moral interests. But at the same time each set up the ideal of a new form of associated life to be reached through the individual himself: the Epicurean, the band of friends; the Stoic, the world Republic; the Christian, the Kingdom of Heaven. Now this moral indifference to the moral institution means simply the inadequacy of social customs and institutions taken as fixed or given adequately to stimulate and control the individual. This means that he has a new social responsibility, that of reorganizing the institution until it shall afford him an adequate theater of expression and an adequate principle of regulation.

The fallacy comes in when the historic reconstruction is conceived of as an essential split. The new social form is emphasized in its negative rather than in its positive relations to what preceded. Instead of being the old made over through the instrumentality of the individual, it is regarded as a creation *de novo* from the individual's efforts and aspirations as an individual. If we keep the historic connection, we see the individual as the nodal point of reconstruction, operating not as an isolated power but as the medium through which social forces are moving on. We see also the new society, not in abrupt opposition to what has preceded and therefore void of all definite content; we see it as previous society operating more adequately through the consciousness of its own unity which it has attained to in the individual.

We must therefore avoid the too frequent misinterpretation by which the whole stress of morality is conceived to be bound up with the ideals of the reformer, and the content and value embodied in the positive institutions ignored or denied. There is always as much morality involved in the positive institution as there is in the conscious ideal of the reformer. If the reformer overlooks this fact, he becomes isolated, turns into either a sentimental dreamer, a harmful fanatic, or a self-conscious Pharisee. His ideal, being severed from institutions, has nothing to give it positive content. It is left to the arbitrary caprice of his own images and emotions. The psychological explanation of the tendency to this abstract idealism is the fact that conscious attention always goes to the point of greatest strain, while that which is habitual is taken for granted and thus falls below consciousness. Thus there arises a sort of hysteria of consciousness on one side, and a corresponding blank on the other. It is interesting to note the practical split which this abstract idealism results in. Just because the ideal of morality is set over against the existing institution, it has no leverage upon the latter. They cannot be displaced, they cannot be made over. As a result the customary side persists and furnishes the controlling motive for everyday life, while the so-called spiritual or ideal values are placed in another distinct region and reserved for special occasions and emotions. There arises a systematic compromise and adjustment between the two sides.

More important for our purposes is to see how this marking off of the individual as the organ of social progress in its movement from a more dynamic to a more static unity of values shows itself in the definition of the individual himself. If we can thus define the individual we have fixed for us in outline the main factors and problems with which psychological ethics has to deal. It will not be simply a question of hunting around empirically and finding certain phenomena, but of discovering what the individual is, considered as this intermediary.

In general terms the psychological individual is defined in impulse and reflection. These processes mutually implicate each other while they are both opposed to custom. Primitive man, instead of being the creature of impulse, is in reality the creature of habit. The wildness, the breaking loose which romanticists have ascribed to him are simply from our standpoint. So far as his own consciousness is concerned he sticks closely to the grooves of his own social group. But the break up of a habit or an instinct means the setting free of impulses, of initiatives in action. Of course all action is impulsive, but *an* impulse means a mode of action which has its value defined in marking on one side a departure from established values, and on the other side in marking an introduction of new values. Conscious thinking or reflection, moreover, is equally relative to reconstruction. As long as we follow habit there is no stimulus to nor sense in deliberation. We deliberate simply with reference to new aims and their execution. The impulse would carry us into action, but action is a matter of the object as well as of the subject. It involves a setting, a lodgement of the impulse in the actual world of conditions. What does the impulse thus projected and set mean? This anticipation is the function of deliberation.

Not only are both impulses and reflection marked off from habit, but they are strictly correlative to each other. The nature of their mutual dependence and interaction shows the psychical process as intermediary to the social. The impulses represent the disintegration of the former coordination. The fixity of the coordination has broken down and as a result the various factors previously organized into it are set free and operate for a time, each on its own hook—each strives to become a controlling or impelling center. Compare for example the difference between the striking and locating instinct of the newly hatched chicken in getting an insect [or] a grain of corn with the slow and toilsome process with which the child acquires the ability to coordinate eye and arm. If one accepts the doctrine of evolution, the reaching tendency of the child must have its origin in what was once a similarly definite coordination. But in the child that coordination has broken down, the self-enclosed system no longer exists; what we have is the various elements in it working more or less independently with the necessity of building up the new activity through consciously bringing them into mutual adaptation with each other. The impulses, in thus representing the break up of an old coordination, furnish the multiple, analytic or discrete phase of the volitional process as individualized. Reflection stands for the new coordination which is to be built up in the mutual stimulation and control of these various impulses. In thus standing for the new—the future—it presents the synthetic factor, it indicates the unifying phase, just as impulse does the diversified. When the solution is reached—that is, when the various impulses are harmonized in a new mode of activity, we have the new plane of social conduct established out of which, in turn, new impulses and new deliberations may arise.

January 10, 1898

The psychologic individual marks a phase of *social* development in which the variant factor is set over against the social customs factor. It marks a phase in the *individual* development wherein habit is set over against imitation.*

According to Weber's law,[3] a "stimulus" does not give rise to a conscious reaction until its power reaches a certain ratio to the level of that which is already in consciousness of the effected adjustment; so the conscious individual represents a certain variant in social custom—coming consciousness, because it departs to a certain extent from the existing plane of social adjustments.

From the social standpoint, one may say that society requires that all variations be accounted for. That this, that, or the other is customary means that it has come to be expected of the individual under given circumstances. Anything else is immediately noted and must be accounted for by the individual to society. This comes out prominently in those stages of society wherein all variations are felt as criminal—all anthropology is full of illustrations. Amends must be made to custom, sometimes in one form, sometimes in another. Very frequently the customary in the form of religion demands reparation—or possibly the customary in several forms (religion, politics, tribal customs, etc.) demands apology and restitution. Note for instance that in Rome long after bronze had been supplanted by iron in all other uses, it was still retained as the only metal proper for the religious casts.

As civilization progresses, men come to discriminate between disadvantageous and advantageous variations, punishing the one, tolerating or rewarding the other. But for a long time the presumption is against the variant, and it is always against the man who varies too much. But the limits within which variation may go without meeting formal social disapproval are constantly widened. The more complex society, the less variation threatens it.

The psychologic individual is defined as a reconstruction of social order. He is defined between two termini:

1. The previous mode of social action in which the individual was implicated and of which he formed a part.
2. The future mode of social action which is now in process of becoming established and of implicating individuals, and which will, when it is

* This probably should read "initiation," not "imitation."

once established, for a new level from which new variations will diverge.

The Psychology of Ethics has to do with the intermediating process of social transition or reconstruction which is referred to the conscious individual both by himself and by others.

NOTES

1. For an account of D. A. Spalding's experiments, see William James, *The Principles of Psychology* (New York: Henry Holt and Co., 1890), II, 396–400, 406.
2. Herbert Spencer, *The Data of Ethics* (New York: D. Appleton and Co., 1879).
3. Ernst Heinrich Weber (1795–1878), professor of anatomy and physiology at Leipzig. A more detailed account of Dewey's interpretation of Weber's Law is contained in his *Psychology,* in *Early Works,* II, 49–51.

CHAPTER 1

THE PSYCHOLOGY OF
THE MORAL SITUATION

SECTION 1. THE MORAL
SITUATION AND MORAL
DECISION

This reference to conduct as individual gives us the standpoint from which to distinguish the moral from the practical. In one sense the practical is a more generic conception. The larger part of our conduct is considered as the subject of non-moral judgments—as something to be governed by pure matter of fact or expediency. But wherever any portion of conduct is identified with the self, it is then thrown into moral perspective. Very much of conduct we regard as non-moral. All such falls within the sphere of a taken-for-granted self. The only thing questioned in such cases is how the thing is to be done. Very often this moral indifference may seem to attach itself to ends, but whenever this is true, close examination will reveal the fact that this end is taken as the means to a larger end. This distinction between the practical and the moral is a shifting one—an action may be now in one category, now in another.

Of course it is true that every act of the individual does affect the self, but it is not needful in all of them to consider the bearing of this reference to the self; however, it may come about that under some new conditions, it is necessary to examine the bearing. At such times the action gets into the moral sphere. Any item of conduct gets moral value insofar as it embodies the conscious self as conscious self, the agent as agent, the person as person.

In order to clear the ground by a broad illustration let us take the case of a captain of a fishing smack on the New England coast. He is a man of family—has his home—is in the habit of going annually at stated times to "the Banks" for his catch. At length, a year comes which brings illness to his family—wife and baby sick, let us say, as the time approaches at which he is wont to set out on his annual trip.

He finds himself in a quandary as to what to do. Previous to this time his conduct has been a unity, a positive one. The needs of his home, those of his calling, the interests of himself, his employers and his employees have supplemented each other; each activity has stimulated and played into the hands of the others. But now the ethical situation has a new element in it—it has become disorganized. His family's sickness must be recognized and must be dealt with as a factor of the situation which must be harmonized with the other factors. What was before a conscious unity is now a discord—that which was taken as homogeneous is found to be heterogeneous. A new mode of unification must be discovered. Unity becomes for the time being an ideal to be put into the new situation. Something must be done, this man knows; but what?—this he knows not. With reference to previous entity [unity?] the present situation becomes unreconciled diversity. He desires to go to sea—he desires to stay at home—the elements of the situation are immediately in conflict with each other.

The man's sense of diversity, of conflict, in the situation is due to his sense of the existence of the ideal unity—as when a man anticipates satisfaction in the future it is proof that he is not satisfied with the present. Two statements of one fact—"I will be satisfied"—"I am dissatisfied." The sense of conflict represents difficulties in the way of attaining the integration—the difficulties calling for a new unity. It follows that it is the thought of the new unity which breaks up the previous line of action and brings out different factors in it which have never before come into consciousness as different.

But all the different and conflicting factors finally gather in two parties —in two "polar bodies," opposed to each other.

January 11, 1898

It may be thought that these two poles are there from the first, i.e., it may be said that our captain has two courses of action open to him from that start—he may go fishing, he may stay at home, both he cannot do—they are objectively, diametrically opposed to each other—are so from the first, and our captain recognized them as such. In a certain sense of "recognize" this is true. They may be present in his consciousness—though they are not often so—as two objective poles. But even so, this mere presence in consciousness as two incompatibles is a very different thing from feeling the pull and struggle between them. Our captain may have recognized before that he could not both go fishing and stay at home at the same time—he may have seen the two polar opposites there, but this was very different from being called upon to go both ways at once, as he is in the instance under consideration. Again one may be so placed that he is conscious of the struggle, he may feel the conflict, but unless he is under the necessity of deciding in favor of one or the other, he gets not the fullest realization of the meaning of the struggle—it does not become subjective, in other words. The importance for the self must come into consciousness before the external incompatibility becomes the internal conflict.

It is a matter of experience that there always are two poles—two alone. But why? Why does the situation always thus dichotomize itself? One set of factors—those gathering about one pole, are those having most to do with the past; the other polar cluster will be found composed of those having to do with the future. This dualization means that the agent must choose between defining self in terms of what he has been or in terms of what he may be.

Two types of satisfaction consciously present themselves to him: first, those springing out of following habitual, customary lines of conduct; second, those springing out of possible lines of action different from those which are habitual and customary. The first refers to the past, the second to the future. The former is related to the psychology of desire, the latter with the psychology of effort.

Habit comes always to be in the end a satisfaction, a means of pleasurable activity. Almost any activity continued until it becomes a habit becomes pleasurable, and when discontinued becomes a source of pain and dissatisfaction. So with the sea captain and his occupation. The habit of going to sea calls him to go. He is, as it were, arrested in his progress. The arrest, the not going, robs him of a means of pleasurable activity, and thus gives him pain, or at least discomfort. Again, his family represents certain activities which are represented in staying at home. These two sets of tendencies, two habits which have previously been unified in one activity, are now pulling against each other and some new method of unification must be found. In this case the tendency to stay at home may be called the ideal self, the tendency to go to sea the customary self. Note that the ideal self is more than a mere ideal—it is based upon habit; while the habitual self is idealized, i.e., as what he can do.

But we may ask: if the habitual self is idealized, and if the ideal self is embedded in habit, what sense is there in this distinction? Just this— that in one case the end is emphasized from the standpoint of powers which have realized it, while on the other hand the individual feels he must evaluate these acquired powers in terms of their function; hence the push and pull—the conflict. Habit says: "I am the definition of the ideal," and this is true. End says: "I am what controls and values the habit," and this is also true. On one side the means—as have been in the past—attempt to define the end as it is to be in the future; while on the other, the end as in future—the ideal—attempts to define and decide how the means as they have been in the past shall work. There is the feeling that customs (means) must be reconstructed in terms of the new situation—the new end.

We observe that the distinction between the ideal self and the habitual self is not one of existence. There are present psychical existences which stand for habits; there are other present psychical existences which stand for ends. The ideal has a motor force—the tendency of the individual to go in a certain direction, and which, but for obstruction, would be carried out. The distinction is one of kind of work done. The habitual self represents powers and capacities as defined and organized in the past, and as ready now to go to work; those which make up the ideal self stand for tendencies to modify the acquired tendencies and thus control future operations. This is the point upon which the categories of psychical activities depend. (See Chapter II, *Dewey's Psychology*.)[1] Upon the one hand we have habits which demand satisfaction; upon the other we have the ideal element which demands exercise in the future, but which cannot get it without a reorganization of the other elements.

The real problem is that of adjustment of means and ends; the conflict occurs because there are two points of view. We may put it in either of two ways; we may say the agent puts before himself two courses of action, or we may say that only one course of action is possible from the beginning, while the agent is divided; i.e., we may say either the agent is one and the courses of action are two, or vice versa we may say there is but one course of action while the agent is divided. This distinction between ideal self and habitual self arises within the whole working self.

But our captain decides to stay at home. This means that the ideal unity which was the cause of the whole difficulty has at last realized itself— means and ends are unified with reference to each other and to themselves. The habits, acquired powers and capacities have finally been adapted to each other, and a single line of action is the result.

Note here that while, externally speaking, the agent has simply chosen one of two incompatibles, psychically and morally he has reattained a unity, within which, morally, the value of both the competing ends is contained. Psychically our captain is doing one thing only, i.e., staying at home, but morally he is doing both. The value of that decided on is derived from that [with] which it competed. The staying at home is now, now that it is the followed course of action, what it was in ideal—it is more—it has gained by just the value of that which it conquered.

This does not mean that the staying-at-home's added value is that given it by being made a fiat of the will—that its value as a process is its value as ideal plus this fiat value, but rather has it undergone a qualitative change with reference to its value as an expression of his selfhood, for his whole self is now expressed in the act of staying at home. This is the meaning of choice, i.e., that if one really decides, there are in the decided-upon action all the powers otherwise engaged in both competing tendencies. One must get his whole self into the action decided upon. If our sea captain does not do this, only part of him remains at home—the other part has gone to sea. If a man, after having nominally decided upon a certain course of action, keeps thinking of what joy he might have gotten had he taken the other course of action, he is, just insofar as he does this—not decided. He is doing wrong in thus looking back—he is doing what is the essence of hypocrisy. The hypocrite who says one thing intending to do and to feel another is almost a psychologic impossibility; but the hypocrite who says, who thinks, that he wants to pursue a certain course of action but who at the same time indulges in daydreams of another course of action, and who takes delight in picturing himself in the midst of such a course of action—he is the real hypocrite of everyday life, who [?] is comparatively plentiful. He is fooling himself as well as others; his footsteps take hold upon the way which, if pursued, will inevitably lead him at last to some moral breakdown which will surprise and astound both himself and his friends. It is a man's duty to decide and, having decided, to throw no backward glances—to resolutely recall his thoughts from dwelling upon the opposite course—to avoid reconstructing again the duality, the polarity, the conflict, and the moral split within himself.

This state of mind is very often really illustrated in the one who says: "Well, I did not choose to do so and so; circumstances forced me into this course and I had no alternative." This shows his real choice was not gained, else it would have included all the values of both contemplated lines of action. His mind was not really "made up," else his whole self would have found expression in the line of action chosen.

See [The] Study of Ethics (Dewey's Syllabus), pp. 127–30, in particular the reference to Martineau.[2]

SECTION 2. THE PSYCHOLOGIST'S FALLACY; CHOICE; DELIBERATION AND DESIRE IN THE DYNAMIC SELF

January 12, 1898

[Last quarter we ?] began by attending to what Professor James calls "the psychologist's fallacy"[3] as the root of false interpretation in this matter. The psychologist's fallacy might almost be called the historical fallacy, i.e., the reading into the early stages of a development which can only be true of the later stages, and can only be true of them just because it was not true of the earlier stages. Our tendency to do this arises from the fact that common sense is always interested only in products, in proceeds; not in the process but only in the outcome. This means common sense is interested only in the value of the process, i.e., in the outcome. This focusing of interest at this spot leaves us no motive for considering the process—the *modus operandi*.

Now this habit of being interested only in products is so strong that when we turn back to investigate the process it is almost impossible not to read into it the thing so all important to us; i.e., we take the function of a process and read it into the whole process in its course of development; i.e., we see the function somehow as if it were there at first and the process grew up about it while it remained unchanged. Thus the function of attention is to establish unity—to focus. Many psychologists speak as though that focus had been there from the start; but if this were so, then attention would simply have been already developed. The end of the volitional process is to constitute the person in a certain desire, effort, attitude. The outcome on the intellectual side is to define for him the two modes of action which are psychically competing with each other. But we falsely assume that the individual began with these two distinctly recognized, competing lines of conduct—ends of conduct, clearly in consciousness, and then in some way the final decision is given between them.

There are two ways in which this choice—this decision—is supposed to be given: first, a power of will comes in between those two ends and chooses one of them. Second, these two competitors fight it out on the arena of consciousness and when one has the other down so that it stays down, this victor then is the will.

Each of these theories assumes that the competing ends and desires have been there all the time—this is the psychologist's fallacy of reading into the process at first what is only there at last. Only when the decision is reached do the competing ends present themselves with clearness, and the whole process up to that time has been the evolution of this distinction as consciously valued (into consciousness?).* We have the competing ends because we have got to choose—not vice versa.

Thus the process of desire is the process of finding out what we desire. The ideas of desire and effort do not represent forces, psychic existences, operating at the time and leading up to the choice. They are attitudes assumed by the self in the process of choosing. The whole process is one of choice. The poles are not there at first. They are not there to provoke choice but they are there as a product of the choice. The psychological fallacy in this case consists in assuming that the two incompatible springs of action are there, definitely, from the outset; but it is only in the necessity of coming to a unified mode of action that the incompatibilities are defined.

The conflict is within the individual—between the incompatible expressions of himself. Each checks immediate action on the part of the other. The more he starts to follow one line of action, the more closely the other's value stands out. Action in one direction brings out the value of action in the other direction. The self of the past is not a fixed-form self. It is a self which urges us forward. Ordinarily we do not think of the self; only when the self is blocked in its expression in some way [do] we become conscious of it and then scrutinize it. To bring self to consciousness means to arrest the tendency to action, while the natural tendency is to go ahead —not to think of self. The particular value which the individual gives the motive on one side, and the habits on the other, will be brought out in the movement toward unification. In starting to do, we act impulsively, but only when another impulse starts up and conflicts with the first is impulse by and through this very conflict thrown into the intellectual arena and we are set thinking of them and thus making them into motives. In and

* The material in parenthesis probably represents the hesitation of the original stenographer.

through the conflict itself are these impulses made into motives. The individual's motive is his consciousness of himself in a given mode of action. The conflict occurs because he can't reconcile those two expressions of himself. At the outset he was in it; now he sees and feels himself in it. The competing motives are within the self, the growing analytic defining of the self.

We may sum up by saying that the root of the matter consists in seeing the self as dynamic and in seeing the moral process as one of conscious discovery, revelation, and definition of self in act. If self were there at the outset, a moral conflict would be meaningless. The self is constructive—built up and organized in and through the process—it is all a process of self evolution. Choice marks the point where the self finally sees itself in a unified way. Desire, effort, deliberation are aspects of the process of self definition. The self is a dynamic synthesis, not a fixed entity. The self is a synthesis of function, of operation. It must continually be reconstructed.

See *Syllabus of Ethics,* Dewey, "Will." [4]

See James's *Psychology,* II, "Will." [5]

January 13, 1898

The self is a dynamic continuum, a dynamic synthesis. The selfhood represents an active coordination of coordinations. The factors in selfhood are a series of coordinations acting upon each other in such a way as to call for a continual recoordination. Each coordination struggles to represent the whole self—to be the supreme coordination. In this process is a continual interplay between them which demands the rebuilding of coordinations on a basis more comprehensive and more stable. The self is not the mere act of coordinating—nor is it the mere materials which are coordinated. The self is seen in the entire coordination. The materials and the putting of them together are divisions of labor within the entire process of active coordination. The whole process of moral decision is a volitional process in that general sense which makes volition have to do with conscious determination of action. The process rises out of action, represents conflict in action, a readjustment in action, of these conflicting elements, and finally terminates in action. The process is action all through.*

[Let,] A–K. Course of action in which self is expressed, or represents self in action.

A–B, M–N. The unified self (unified course of action) before and after the choice and the preceding split or conflict.

B–M. The split self, the self in conflict and coming to a decision—or the split action in which self is expressed.

B. The split, the unraveling of the past, the point where habitual self,

* Apparently the following is a reference to a diagram not reproduced in the original hectograph copy.

unified self, or course of action encounters a "snag," and conflicting elements come into consciousness.

XXX. Conflicting elements or points of view, at first wholly divergent —but gradually grouping themselves about two points—poles, represented at QQ.

QQ. The two poles about which the many conflicting elements gradually arrange themselves in two conflicting parties.

M. The point where the two poles of QQ have become one and where unity of action, of selfhood—of ideal and habit—is once more attained and the action again proceeds free from conflict.

The whole process A–N is intrinsically active and volitional—not merely internal and mental.

It is valuable to note at this point the tendency in psychology to regard movement as merely external—as a mere by-product. The process A–N is one of action—movement. The internal and emotional phases so often set over against action really represent action in its divided phases. The real opposition is between action when it is in process of unification, and action when it has attained a certain degree of coherent unification. The tendency of modern psychology is to make the intellectual and volitional process more and more motile.

Deliberation must be stated and interpreted in volitional terms. This intellectual process is one of defining particular impulse to action in terms of the coordinations to which it has belonged, and to which it may belong. The intellectual process is looking at the impulse until it comes to consciousness—until we see what it really is. This intellectual process moves in two directions, as mentioned above. The psychologic process of deliberation is a process of working back and forth between suggestion and retrospection. The presentation of suggestions to the mind is the intuitive factor. Nobody tells when suggestion comes. One is moving forward— suggestion simply represents the sense of moving forward—of forward movement. It is probable that one sex trusts more to the suggestion factor, the other rather to the deliberation factor.

But feeling is also a bringing of the impulse to consciousness. The difference in this regard, between feeling and intellect, is in the way in which the impulse is brought to consciousness. The intellectual process is the process of defining the impulse in terms of other processes. We say: "What will happen now if this impulse is allowed to go on? What other courses of action will be entrained by the course of action in which it will eventuate—realize itself?" Feeling, emotion, is the immediate sense of value in the impulse. All other impulses of self are retracted into this particular one—it becomes loaded down with the self and this feeling of its value. We say: "I feel a certain worth, value, in carrying out this impulse." We are unable to analyze it because of its very immediateness.

Knowledge—objective.

Feeling—subjective sicle [*sic*]* of experience.

Emotion has two aspects. 1. The projective. 2. The retractive. The first is desire, the impulse felt in its forward movement. It is related to suggestion on the intellectual side; it represents the felt congruence between impulse and end, i.e., when image of the conditions strengthens impulse, we have desire. Again when image of end checks the impulse (suggests opposition, difficulty) readjustment by the outcome can be gotten. This is effort. The second [is] the retractive aspect. The sense of effort equals the sense of discrepancy between the present self and the future self (the self in ideals).

We never have merely desire or merely effort, but always the two together. The thought of the end never only stimulates the impulse, but arouses opposition also. We never have effort *sine* desire, or desire *sine* effort—if there is any conflict—i.e., if any volitional process is present at all. Desire and effort each represent tension—when the tension ceases we no longer want the thing. (We may have it or may have forgotten it.) Desire and effort, pleasure and pain, are logically opposed, but not so psychologically. Psychically both can be felt at once—indeed this is our normal state—a sort of balance or equilibrium—a tension between the members of those two pairs—desire-effort, pleasure-pain.

There are certain points of view, certain tendencies in modern psychology, in harmony with this point of view:

1. The conception of every idea as having a certain motor tendency— no idea is merely intellectual—it is action—it is movement so far as it goes.
2. The James-Lange theory of emotion,[6] i.e., emotion is the consequence, the reflection of action; what we feel is the reverberation of what we are starting to do.

See *Psychological Review,* November 1794 and January 1795.[7]

SECTION 3. THE REALIZATION OF AIMS IN THE DYNAMIC SELF

January 17, 1898

At the last time I attempted to give a somewhat generic analysis of the volitional process, with a view to showing the relation borne by the intellectual process of deliberation, and the emotional, desire effort process, to the development of self in and toward final choice—the attempt having been made to show that that relation was an organic and intrinsic one, that the intellectual and emotional processes present to us aspects of the volitional process rather than anything which is external to it.

There is one controversy to which I may refer in connection with this

* Side? or cycle?

general analysis. The question is often asked: Is attention a cause or a result? You remember James discusses it from that point of view.[8] The same question is asked regarding desire, regarding effort, regarding choice: Are they to be conceived of as original causal activities, or to be conceived of as products?

The outcome of the previous statement is that they are neither, and that the disjunction is a misleading one. These terms express attitudes, relations, and not simple causes on one side, or simple products on the other. Now that term attitude may seem somewhat vague, but surely there is some meaning in stating, for example, that attention represents an attitude of the self, considered as intellectual. It is a posture, if that word be used in an active and not a merely passive sense, of the self. Concretely we say: I think, I desire, I strive, I attempt. There is in this expression the idea of the organic unity between the self and the want, the self and the striving. But in our scientific reflections we say that the I, the self, is somehow common to all these different attitudes, and expresses itself in a great variety of thoughts, and desires, and struggles, and so we get into the habit of thinking of an I, or self, somehow outside of all these states; and so on the other hand we think of a desire as if it were an objective psychical existence instead of simply being that I in a certain stage of its progress, or aspect of its realization—instead of being I in an attitude, in other words.

The psychological standpoint I have been trying to present is that of the common man when he says: I think, I want, I am trying to do so and so, and if there is no self or I outside of this particular experience causing it, neither on the other side is this condition of the I a result of some desire or thought, which is somehow acting on the self. What is the relation of a flower or a leaf to the plant? It would be about as absurd scientifically to set up a similar disjunction there and ask whether the flower is caused by the leaf and bud and stem, or if on the other hand the leaf and stem and bud were caused by the plant. They *are* the plant; and that is what I mean when I say that the thought, desire, etc., are attitudes. They *are* the self in a certain outcome, or in a movement toward a certain outcome.

From this general statement I pass on to a more detailed analysis. The psychical beginning is always with some activity or doing, taken as a whole. In biological terms we cannot get behind a function, and all further, all later developments are developments out of the function. Or, in physiological language, we start with some coordination, and later stages of growth are in and from that coordination. Now this original activity, however crude, is still a whole and not a composite. It is not a putting together of existences, states, which somehow lie behind it. Our psychological distinctions emerge as the original activity, or doing, is brought to consciousness.

The primitive acts, those of the infant, so far as we are concerned with them psychologically at all, are acts—concrete wholes. They are not impulses in the conscious or psychological sense of that term. We are apt to regard them as impulses, because we, as spectators, see what their later history and final destiny is. We see what that act is going to lead up to, and then think of it in relation to the final upshot and term it an impulse. Thus we take the kickings and graspings of a child, his first babblings of more or less articulate sounds, and his first acts in balancing himself or in creeping, and we call them all impulses because we are thinking of them with reference to some later outcome. We call the babblings impulse, because we see in them the potency of speech. But to the child they are not impulses, because he is not conscious of the end; and not being conscious of the end, he is not conscious of them as reachings toward an end.

Considered from the standpoint of the one who experiences them, these early acts, so far as they have conscious value at all, are ends in themselves. To the child who is cooing, kicking, grasping, these activities are just as final as anything the adult can do is to the adult. When we say they are simply blind impulses on the part of the child, it is simply because we know that if they keep on they will sooner or later result in something, and that their practical importance consists in just this fact.

Now the significance of this statement is that conscious impulse and conscious idea are correlative and contemporaneous. No one can have conscious impulse on one side, until he [has] conscious aim before him on the other. The activities will become conscious impulses to the child when he begins to feel and see for himself the outcome to which they may lead, and begins to look at them—to value them as possible or probable outreachings toward that end. So every birth or consciousness of purpose or aim of possibility on the part of an agent brings to birth also a consciousness of impulses, demands, powers, on the other side.

This might be illustrated historically in what goes on in the consciousness of the slave as he begins to demand, or think of, his freedom. At the same time that freedom becomes an ideal to him on one side, he becomes aware, on the other, of powers and capacities which hitherto have lain dormant, but which now demand expression. It is an historical fallacy to suppose that the slave had been conscious of the powers and capacities on his part and yet has remained a slave. If he had been conscious of them he would not have remained a slave. If he had been conscious of them he would not have remained in slavery. We can generalize from the person whom we technically call a slave, to the individual in any class or condition who has a feeling of opportunities hitherto not taken advantage of. When any man sees an opening before him as a possible ideal, it awakens on the other side a feeling on his part that he now has certain capacities which can operate in such an ideal situation and which hitherto have been unexpressed.

Another illustration is that waves of moral idealism and of moral sensualism occur in conjunction. One is called the reaction from the other and is sometimes spoken of as the swinging of the pendulum back and forth. That is of course a mere phrase and does not explain the problem. We want to know how it is that the two extremes accompany each other. It is simply the consciousness of the ideal on one side accompanied by the present demand, or impulses, on the other hand. And the more comprehensive and far-reaching the ideal asserted, the more numerous are the impulses awakened. On the other side, the more clearly the ideal is conceived as something to be sought for in action, the more urgently the impulses demand their satisfaction on the other side. Take Greece at the time of the Sophists and Aristotle. You have exactly the same phenomena. On the one side the assertion of the ideal, and of a unified ideal, a single principle of virtue in a sense far beyond anything before in consciousness and on the other side a medley of appetites and a constant demand for enjoying them. So in the early Christian centuries the extreme asceticism seen among the Christians and also among some of the Stoics was the other side of that excessive and willful search for a new and hitherto unheard-of sensual satisfaction and enjoyment. Similarly phenomena present themselves in the individual in the psychology of adolescence, where the consciousness of a new ideal or relation in life is manifested on the other side by the arousing of a consciousness of desires, appetites, capacities hitherto dormant. The same thing is seen through all the period of choosing a vocation. A vocation represents on one side the purpose, the idea which is going to dominate and unify a great variety of otherwise diverse acts; and also reflects itself in the knowledge that one has capacities and powers now within him which could find an outlet in that calling. The consciousness, in other words, of an activity or demand, and the consciousness of a purpose which would function that power—that is, which would give it a sphere and scope of operation—are necessarily correlative.

I would suggest in passing that the contemporaneous character in consciousness of ideal and impulse defines the difference between the animal and the moral consciousness. The animal consciousness is one of mere impulse and appetite, upon which afterwards an ideal or rational judgment supervenes. The animal consciousness is simply the consciousness of a direct start towards doing. It is again a case of an historical fallacy when we look at the animal consciousness and interpret it as being one of conscious appetite to the animal itself. It is not present in consciousness at all. But let this activity, doing, come to reflective consciousness and then we get it interpreted as impulse or active demand on one side, and as conscious purpose, or end, on the other. We have two typical periods or epochs in the conscious development of the relation between impulse and idea. The first is where the impulse and the idea, or ideal conscious end, are not separated from each other. They are practically simply the two sides of one and the same thing. It is all one to me, for example, as I decide to assume a certain vocation, whether I say, I now have an ideal, a purpose, which will control the activity of different acts, or whether I say that I have certain powers and capacities which are going to find expression and satisfaction. But in the other epoch the impulse and the end and aim stand in conflict with each other, and a unity has to be constructed.

First, then, what is the process by which the original, naive, unreflective doing comes to consciousness in the way of a unity of impulse and purpose? Now the general answer I give is that some decisive attainment which is accidental, so far as the individual is concerned, marks the level to which future actions must consciously come up, unless there is going to be dissatisfaction. Activities which at first have no conscious aim, deeds which the child does without their having any conscious reason at all, accomplish something—they culminate in a period of success, and that success, which so far as intention or purpose is concerned is accidental, fixes the plane from which future life proceeds. It then becomes a conscious end or aim, to which one must live up, and at the same time it makes the person conscious of impulses or powers in his own nature. Because I have done it, I can and must do it in the future. That is the side of the coming to consciousness of the aim or ideal. Because I have done it I have powers in me which enable me to do it, and that is the side of coming to consciousness of impulse.

For example, once more, in the case of the child. The child does certain things with no conscious reason or motive, which finally culminate in the act of locomotion. The various kickings, crawlings, throwings, and reachings which he has performed finally sum themselves up in this performance of the act of walking. There is an achievement in the way of their coordination. Now, the child has a new standard, a new level. That becomes now the conscious end or ideal, something which he must live up to in the future, while it arouses him to the sense of powers and capacities leading him to assert himself in a new direction of which he was not aware before. The same thing could be said about his learning to talk. He learns to talk through babblings which had no conscious motive at all at first. Speech is finally reached through accidental means, and the achievement is of such importance, has so much significance in his development, that it becomes the conscious plane from which further action proceeds, awakening impulses and other powers. We have then a lucky success; and it is out of the success that consciousness of powers grows, and the consciousness of aim, and purposes for future achievement. I think you will find that this is the same principle as that laid down in James's *Psychology,* Volume II, pages 487–88, as the first principle of volition, that an act must first be done without any purposes or motive; that this leaves* . . . [im]age of what it is like to do that. If one can accidently move one ear and be left with a sense or image of what [it is?], he can make it a conscious object of the future. So he lays it down as a principle that the accidental must precede the intentional.

* A line is obliterated in the original hectograph copy.

In the case as thus discussed there is a unity of action. The sense of aim on one side and the sense of power on the other are not separated from each other. We can say there is an idealized impulse or a realized idea. That is, the impulse, the power, is interpreted through the idea of what it will do for us; of what it will accomplish. That is what I mean by saying that it is idealized. On the other hand the idea is not a mere object of contemplation, it is a motor idea, it is a thought which carries with it a demand for its own fulfillment, and carries with it the power for such fulfillment.

NOTES

1. Also in *Early Works,* II, 18–27.
2. Also in *Early Works,* IV, 345–48.
3. James, *Psychology,* I, 196–97.
4. Also in *Early Works,* IV, 237.
5. James, *Psychology,* II, XXVI, 486–592.
6. James, *Psychology,* II, 449–67.
7. The reference is to Dewey's two articles under the general title "The Theory of Emotion." They are "Emotional Attitudes" and "The Significance of Emotions." Reprinted in *Early Works,* IV, 150–88.
8. James, *Psychology,* I ,447–54.

CHAPTER 2

INTERESTS AND HABITS
IN THE ORGANIC CIRCUIT

SECTION 1. INTERESTS, HABITS,
AND THE PROCESS OF
READJUSTMENT

In going on with the discussion of the cases where the impulse and idea get separated from each other and opposed to each other in consciousness, it is necessary to note that the end of which we have been speaking is embodied in a diversity of acts which follow each other in a series, and that at different points in the series different acts and different organs are predominant. Take speech, for example. There is a very great variety and diversity of acts performed in speech. There are acts of hearing and of seeing. Of course these take very little part in the development of adult consciousness but in its earlier stages acts of hearing are more important than are visual acts in seeing the things that we are talking about, and so on. All these acts are harmonized and make up a single line of action. At different periods different ones will be predominant. Now it is focused in the ear, hearing; now in the eye, seeing; now in the motor reproduction of sounds. That would be the case with a child. Take locomotion again. At one period consciousness may be focused on the image of some distant thing, which is the reason why I want to take a walk. On uneven ground it may be the mere act of walking. Again it is centered in the eye as I look around to see what path I will take, or try to find some signboard. It is all the same act but expressed in different overt acts, and each of these temporarily comes to be predominant and then subsides to a subsidiary position and contributes to the next. You remember that James uses the curve as an illustration of a sentence.[1] That would apply to any organized action. The words come up and then go down and we have to think of each word as successively coming up to the sphere of consciousness and then passing by. We do not keep all words in consciousness simultaneously. It is realized in a series of successive centers of foci.

With the growing comprehensiveness of the complexity of these modes of action there is increasing likelihood of conflict. In an adult these organized modes of action are what we call callings or vocations. They are pursuits. It is difficult to get a word which expresses one of these conscious modes of action in all its phases, but I shall employ the term interest, used in an objective sense. I have an interest, or such and such a man is following a certain interest. That seems to me to convey the idea of a somewhat systematized series of acts which have a conscious, felt, value, and are not merely biologically systematized. As an interest becomes more complex in its scope, there is great likelihood of the various minor or specific acts in which it finds expression coming into conflict with each other. In any interest or pursuit organized by action, there is a certain amount of resistance between each successive pair of acts. This is true so far as the interest remains conscious and is not reduced to mechanical habit. Each act being conscious has a certain value of its own. In biological terms it has a certain inertia. It tends to persist, therefore. Personifying it for the moment, we may say that it dislikes to give way to the next act. It wants to hang on as long as possible and there is a certain amount of resistance—or what in a more developed stage will be called effort—to displace that particular act and make room for the next. This resistance calls out adaptation or adjustment at each step in the series, and it is this necessity of adaptation which keeps the act in consciousness and makes it an interest.

As soon as the whole line of action gets so thoroughly . . .* we call habit, and the whole process then falls below consciousness. It no longer represents an interest at all. But here the process is intelligent and not merely one of mechanical habit, it supposes that there are periodic nodal points at which each act has to be adapted to the next to bring it to consciousness.

I should like to call attention to the point which Mr. James has made concerning the stream of consciousness, and the alternation, according to him, of the substantive portion and the transitive portion, or he calls them in other places points of rest and points of movement.[2] I think the general theory just given explains that particular alternation in consciousness of substantive content and what he calls fringe. Supposing you have that organized portion of conduct which I call an interest. That will be expressed in a series of acts which may occupy five minutes, or an hour, or a week. Now in the carrying out of that interest in a series of overt acts, it is almost certain that there will be things that are easy, that are already mastered, which have taken the form of habits, and which can readily be performed. That represents the straight line where we are simply going ahead. It is not purely mechanical because we know why we are doing that particular thing. We have an image of the end in view and recognize that it tends from dissatisfaction to satisfaction. The movement to it will be what James calls the fringe. When that particular act is reached, completed, we have to stop and think what we are going to do next and what the relation of that act is to the one just performed. Some adaptation has to take place, some deflection. We must arrest the act we have been doing and modulate

* Part of a line missing in original hectograph copy.

it over into another act, and that will be the point where we stop and reflect. That is the substantive portion in the stream of thought.

Take a man who has started out to go from a certain place to another
place to do a certain thing. He thinks where he is going and outlines the
first stage of his journey. That may carry him to the end if the journey he
is taking is familiar; but if not, when he gets to that particular point he will
stop, see where he is, and conclude that he has to turn in this direction.
Then he follows that clue for a time and then again stops to lay out the
further plan for his journey. That will give a mechanical illustration of the
fringe and the substantive portion. They are related as points of relatively
easy and of impeded execution.

January 18, 1898

I pointed out yesterday that every general line of action or interest is embodied in a series of particular overt acts, each of which not simply passes
on the stimulus to the next, but enters as a contributing factor into the
conscious value of all the others. Thus each step in the act is not isolated
consciously, but we somehow feel in it the meaning of what has gone before and foresee in it the significance of what comes after. As I also
pointed out, this necessitates a series of adaptations of greater or lesser
importance at each point as we go on from one overt act to another.

Today I wish to discuss more specifically the reason for, and the
nature of, that adaptation. Each organ enters into a great variety of conscious functions. Think of the multitude of different lines of action, for
example, into which the hand, or the eye, or the ear enters. Now the eye
has to act somewhat differently, has to receive its stimulus in a somewhat
different way and respond to that stimulus in a different way for each of
the many interests in which it shares, in which it cooperates. It may be
called upon to cooperate in something which the hand is doing. It may
be writing, it may be drawing, it may be some kind of constructive work,
it may be scientific investigation. The eye will not act in quite the same
way as it operates in reference to this variety of ends. There will be certain
features of the eye activity which will practically remain the same, untouched by the variety in the context. But there will be other features
which will have to vary with the context. What is true of that organ is true
of every other.

It is this fact that each organ participates in a great variety of different
interests which presents occasions for conflict and which necessitates a
period of delay and reflection in which adaptation and adjustment take
place. We may imagine, in our example of the last hour, that the eye is
stimulated into action in the interests of speech. We hear someone say
something and we watch his face in order that we may better get the exact

shade of meaning. In the normal course of events that stimulus will simply react to the vocal organs. We are about to say something and what we want to say will depend upon the exact thought caught from the other person. That would give us a circuit of this sort. From hearing what the man is saying, A, to the eye, B, and then in turn to the organs of vocalization, the throat and mouth, C. But supposing as the eye is called into activity in that interest, it happens to notice something else—which it might very well do. Then there will be a tendency to a diversion of the activity along the channel D. We might see some sign of emotion on the man's face which we had not suspected, and that might switch off our interest in another channel. In certain cases after the eye is called into activity there will be a tendency to start out on any one of four, or five, different channels. Then comes the question: Which of these channels is it going to follow? In what interest is it going to operate? It is the possibility of a number of alternative directions which implies a readaptation and makes the nodal points in consciousness of which we were speaking yesterday—what James call the substantive portion or the place of rest.

If these interests are not stable and well organized, no such conflict and readaptation will take place. Take a little child. Any one of these interests is relatively so slender, has such a slight hold on him, that as his eye catches this thing he is as apt to follow that tract as any other because of the facility with which the child's attention is diverted. This is one limit to conflict calling for adaptation: the lack of a sufficiently definite organization in the habits, so that activity may, at any junction, branch off. There is a limit in the direction of organization which we term habit or routine. As against the chance of being switched off or diverted at any point, is the chance of having one activity so thoroughly worked out that it practically takes control and there is very slight temptation to follow any other line. If we take a child before he has learned to walk, the act of pressing the sole of his foot to the ground may stimulate a great variety of possible reactions. It would be a matter of chance which one the child follows. But to us who have established the habit of walking it is probable that no diversion would take place. This would simply stimulate another act along the same general interest. We may say that this particular groove is so deeply worn that all the other channels are relatively at a great discount.

These are the two limits, then, within which this process of readjustment and readaptation goes on. They find their typical illustration in the scatterbrained person on one hand; in such cases of extreme association by contiguity as novelists and dramatists present us in the nurse in *Romeo and Juliet,* for instance, and Mrs. Nickleby in Dickens' *Nicholas Nickleby,* possessed of an overflexible, loose-jointed temperament. The other extreme is the martinet, the one whose lines of action are definitely made out in advance, or the person of fixed routine who rarely swerves. These are simply the objectification of these two limits; but the limits themselves are present in every person's conduct, and the actual course of conduct is an interplay between them.

This suggests then two topics for further analysis: One, the consideration of the more permanent, stable aspects of conduct; the other, of the more flexible and variable ones. These two cannot be rigidly set off against each other. They are simply the two limits within which action goes on. Or put somewhat differently, in all cases there is always something which remains identical, which remains stable, and within which and from which the variation branches off. It makes no difference whether action takes one or another course. There will still be some elements in the coordination which will remain the same. Shove the variation back as far as you please, you will still find some identical organic elements. For the fact is, however great the diversity of acts, there is behind them all the life interest and the life process. When that is broken in, you will get actual double consciousness, an alternation of subjective personalities in one and the same being. On the other hand, except in extreme cases which may be considered pathological, this element of fixity or stability does not become so predominant that it is not accompanied by slight variation. We are apt to take extreme cases like walking. I mean the cases which have become most automatic and most mechanical.

But we must bear in mind that even in extreme cases there is a normal recurrence to the end to which that habit is subservient. There is no habit of walking at large. We are going here or there, or we are walking for exercise, or we are going to business, and the act is colored by the particular end so that it must be adapted, adjusted. If we take the case of a man walking in a treadmill as a punishment, we would find a practical division of the permanent stable element from the variable one. There is no end which controls the action. He walks because he has to, and his thoughts may go on independently. But in the normal state of things there will be recurrent points at which the two have to be brought together, where we have to think what we are about, so that the thought adapts and varies the habit, and the habit embodies that particular thought.

If we do not take the extreme cases which have become so thoroughly organized, the same fact is more obvious. In the multitude of daily habits which make up our lives there is a continual need of adapting these more permanent elements to some special end. I mention this point because I am going to discuss the two factors separately, but I do not want the fact that I am discussing them separately to leave the impression in your minds that they are actually separate.

I begin with habit. Habit then represents in any given case the mode of action which is so generic that it continues or persists in spite of minor changes. I think that defines habit for us so we can use the word intelligently. It is that mode of action which persists in operation in a variety of different directions of interest.

From this standpoint we may discuss the usual accounts given of habit. It is generally said that habit is formed by repetition, sheer repetition. This statement is defective so far as it pretends to give an accurate account, for two reasons. First because it is partial, and secondly because it actually perverts, or inverts, the true state of the case. It is partial because it fails to note that habits when forming are normally related to ends. Biologically, nothing could be selected and organized into a habit until it contributed something positively to the welfare of the organism. Even if we gave the most mechanical explanation possible, it would be true that those lines of action which were selected had a teleological result in helping maintain the animal in its struggle for existence; while the other variations which were not organized into habits failed to have any such purposive value. The dice are loaded in the formation of habit.

It [the theory that habits are formed by repetition] inverts the true place of habit because it ignores this fact of end. To say that we have a habit by repetition implies more break than there really is. It is rather persistency than repetition. The habit is lying in wait there trying to break out whenever it gets a chance. All that it needs is the removal of the obstruction; all that it needs is an open channel and it at once shows itself in action. We have to conceive of the habit as latent and somehow compressed, inhibited by the activity of some other habit. Now let the other habit begin to subside and let there be a channel open, and the energy which is organized proceeds to manifest itself. It is putting the cart before the horse to say that habit is formed by repetition, because when a man can easily repeat a line of action it shows that he has a habit formed. If he could repeat it, there would be [no?] reason for forming the habit. It is a variation, rather than a repetition, which forms a habit. Now because of that variation there must be another habit. You cannot form a habit except where there is another persistent habit in existence, and every habit is formed as a variation of some other habit.

A lot of examples might be found, but I will take one used by Lloyd Morgan when he lectured here on "Habit and Instinct." [3] He told about a dog which, as a puppy, kept poking about a gate, trying to get through. Finally one day his nose struck the latch and the gate came open, purely accidentally. The next day the dog floundered less than he had previously done and got through after a comparatively small number of trials. And in a few days he went to the latch the first time. That is given as an example of the formation of habit through repetition! If he had kept on repeating the first day's acts he would not have opened the gate at all. His first acts were wrong and repetition would have hardened and settled him in them. It was a variation which set up the habit. When there was success the tendency was strengthened. There was a deeper habit of the animal expressing itself; but it was a variation which caused the new habit. It is success or achievement which constitutes the basis of habit, rather than repetition.

I could expatiate at length on the pedagogical bearings of that subject. It is thought in our schools that if you can only get a child to do a thing enough times, he will finally learn to do it instinctively. That is wrong psychology, but it is the root of all so-called drill. The normal method is in getting the child to feel that he is accomplishing something: in having him do a thing once and seeing the value which it has. If any one does a thing once and realizes that it has a positive value we need not worry about his doing the act over again; the tendency to the habit, the stimulus to persistence, is secured. So one marked success is worth a thousand futile drills. It marks a level or standard for future activity.

From this standpoint I am going to criticize the account given by James in the first volume of his *Psychology*.[4] On the whole I think that it is the best statement of the prevalent view that we have. James reduces habit practically to a mechanical result of which there are two factors: On one side the plasticity of the nervous structure, on the other the outward agent. The outward stimuli pour in through the sense organs. The excitations are conducted to the brain, the central organ, and that agitation must find some way out. It pours out along a certain channel and then through the influence of nutrition there is a modification left behind. The tendency is the next time an excitation comes to the centers, to take the same channels as before; and so finally these paths or grooves are worn. The lines of easiest discharge are the lines of least resistance. The interesting point is to account for the path which is traversed the first time. For, granting what Mr. James says about the plasticity of the organs, it may be admitted that the path chosen tends to be followed the next time.

You know how marked this is in children. It makes not so much difference what is done. If it is done once under a certain context the child wants the same context the next time. A child in a family where a lame doctor was employed supposed that all doctors were lame, and whenever he played doctor he always got a cane and limped. A little boy whose mother was sick in bed was given reins and told to hitch them over the bed as his horse. The next day he said to his mother: "Mother, you go to bed and I will play horse." The tendency to play horse could not reinstate itself without all the original factors. It is a principle that any coordination once set up tends to persist, no matter whether the elements which enter into the coordination are intrinsically related to each other or not.

The whole point of interest in the discussion comes to this: Why does the discharge take such and such a channel at the outset? Mr. James assumes that that is merely a mechanical matter. I do not doubt that the process as a process is mechanical, but I want to point out that reference to an end comes in there. It is all very well to say that action will always follow the lines of least resistance. But how does this particular line happen to be the line of least resistance? This particular line is the line of least resistance because in the past that line has conduced to the end of the organism.

SECTION 2. SENSORY STIMULUS
AND MOTOR DISCHARGE IN
THE ORGANIC CIRCUIT

Mr. James himself makes the suggestion on which we may base the further discussion. He says the nervous system is a mass whose parts are in states of different tension tending towards equilibrium.[5] That is, you have in the nervous system a point of high tension and a point of low tension. The tendency will be to redistribute the energy until you attain an equilibrium. Of course when the excitation has come to the brain, there is your point of highest tension. Some part of the brain will be thrown into a state of highest tension and some part of the periphery will be in lowest tension. Your path will be from the highest tension to the lowest.

Now following James's line of suggestion, and using his own terminology largely, I would say that that is normally a reason for a particular point being in highest tension and another in lowest tension; and that reason is teleological. It is related to the whole system of the organism's actions. There is no sense in regarding the incoming current as something foreign and external to what is going on in the brain. We get that idea only when we isolate the thing in an abrupt way and forget to inquire what was going on before. When we ask the relation of this point of activity to the preceding, we see that the excitation from the periphery and the central changes have some positive relation to each other. We have no right to begin with this abrupt isolation and speak as if the incoming current might be everywhere in relation to the existing state of brain action. The beginning of the activity, as well as the end, is a matter of different tensions pointing toward an equilibrium.

Changing from James's language to my own, we have all the time a coordination of minor points in the larger act. The incoming current is there for the sake of the outgoing. It is not as if it were a mere matter of accident that you have an incoming current, and the brain, and an outgoing current. You might as well try to account for the telephone exchange in that way and say: There are a lot of wires meeting at a certain point, and because they meet a third activity is set up. The whole thing is a system. The incoming wires, and central switchboard, and the outgoing wires are all there playing definite parts in this system. It is exactly the same with the brain. The sensory stimuli, the central activity, and the outgoing motor currents all occupy certain places in the coordination.

Now the fallacy of this supposition of an abrupt incoming current is seen in the fact that the current which does come in will as a matter of fact depend more or less upon the outgoing current, and the higher the organization of life the more relevant this incoming current will be to the preceding motor act. This is seen in the discussion of attention. We give one false account of sensation and then usually attempt to correct it at another time by a false account of attention, instead of bringing the two together and seeing that the stimulus which prevails is always to some extent relevant, and is selected on the basis of relevancy.

There is no one in this room who is instantly open to all external stimuli. It is not true as a physical or mathematical fact that every set stimulus has an equal chance of influencing your next act. The stimuli that are going to act upon another intellectually or practically will be the stimuli that are relevant to what we are engaged upon. Of course we ignore a vast multitude of stimuli: the pressure of the clothing, the particular objects in the room which physiologically affect the eye. They do not enter into the next act at all, because the activity is already persistent in a certain direction, and the incoming currents get their value fixed by that fact. The usual procedure is to have the incoming stimulus not a mere matter of accident, dependent upon external considerations, but to have it largely controlled, or at least influenced by the existing type of activity as expressed in the last motor reaction.

Let the dotted lines represent the preceding activity.[6] The reaction, when it takes place, will tend to return to the point of origin and thus in turn affect the subsequent sensory current which I will represent by the heavier lines. In James's language this point will be the point of lowest tension, and consequently the outgoing current will return to that stimulus. Wherever there is any continuity in action at all, we do not have what is termed a reflex arc as if one activity came in on one channel and went out haphazard along any other. The reaction is a response. Take the ordinary instance of a child putting his finger in the candle flame. Here is the incoming stimulus—the heat, the burning—and there is supposed to be the outgoing current. The child draws his hand back. As a matter of fact there are no disconnections. There is a circle, not a mere arc. The child in drawing his hand back modifies the stimulus, and that is the reason for the occurrence of the reaction—namely, to change the preceding stimulus. It is this fact, that every change exists for the sake of modifying the stimulus, that constitutes the nature of the response.

I will refer you to my article in the *Psychological Review,* July, 1896, on the reflex-arc concept.[7]

January 19, 1898

I pointed out yesterday that while the motor discharge might be regarded as the important thing in setting up a habit, yet that motor discharge cannot be isolated or treated as if it had nothing to do, except in a purely external way, with what has preceded it; that the sensory stimulus which persists is for the sake of securing the motor responses; that it reacts in, and modifies that sensory stimulus; and that, moreover, that sensory stimulus itself has to be considered as related to some previous response. Or put positively, we have to regard the motor discharge as a factor in the coordination.

Now my further point is that just insofar as it is actually a member of such a coordination does it succeed in forming a habit. We will say that there are three or four lines of motor discharge going on at once—that one of these discharges which sets up most adequately a coordination will be the one which will tend most to the formation of a habit. The functional discharges with relation to this coordination may be regarded as simply byplays or offshoots, and will not groove so deep a path, and therefore not fix the subsequent paths of discharge. There are habits which are pure motor tricks, which have no such teleological significance at all—habits of biting one's nails or twiddling with a button—mere tricks which get fastened upon one. But it inverts the whole psychology of the matter to make these typical at the expense of the trunk lines, so to speak, of action, which are all of them teleological, and do really subserve ends. One may fairly say that these motor tricks are subsidiary to and offshoots from the main coordination.

Somebody, I cannot now remember who, has suggested that the maintenance of thinking requires the continual recurrence of sensory stimuli, but of such a nature as not to distract the thought; and that, moreover, the energy which is accumulating in thinking must drain itself off somewhere, and that consequently these bypaths, so to speak, are taken. One gets rid of the excitations, the arousing of energy which accompanies the thinking, by having it drawn off into these irrelevant channels; and again the return of the stimuli from the conditions thus set up provides new store of excitation in order to keep the process of thinking going, so that it is teleological, so that these mere tricks which have no positive value of their own are yet to be interpreted on the teleological basis.

A man is engaged in thinking on a hard problem. This means a certain amount of excitation, of brain energy that must go somewhere. If it goes off an important channel, it will produce effects which will interrupt his thinking. If it is drawn off in channels which do not amount to anything, like playing with a pencil, it will not interfere with the continuance of thinking, and may supply energy to help maintain it.

This is a minor point. The important point, that the motor discharge will be likely to form a habit becoming the determining path for future discharges which serve most adequately in maintaining a coordination, may be illustrated in this way. Suppose some discharge does not unify the organism. Suppose it does not accomplish any definite results. It is simply a chance, random overflow. The result will increase the confusion. For every motor discharge there will be a new sensory stimulus. Suppose one discharge goes to the eye, another to the hand, another to the foot. That changes the conditions and that change is reported in so many different sensory stimuli which do not coordinate. These stimuli come into the brain and a series more of chance stimulations is set up. Under these conditions these discharges all tend to negate each other, cancel each other, just because they do not cooperate, do not unify. There is no probability that the second discharge is to follow the path of the first, no reason why one dis-charge should groove a deeper path than another; and the outcome is fatal and nugatory.

Now suppose, on the other side, that a discharge (which we will admit for the sake of the argument to be purely random) does succeed in effect-ing a unity, in establishing a coordination. What does that mean? Precisely now, it unifies all the different stimuli so that they reinforce each other. A twofold result follows. First a continuous activity is set up, underlying variety. As long as your stimuli do not reinforce each other in the re-sponse, and as long as the different responses set up a lot of different stimuli unrelated to each other, you simply have a shifting, diverse series of acts more or less spasmodic. If the stimuli do reinforce each other in a single response, that tends to set up a single stimulus which maintains the existing condition of action. Secondly, in the future this special path will stand much more chance of being selected, simply because there are a number of the stimuli which find their outlet in this particular path. Sup-pose a half dozen elements in that particular discharge. Then let any one of the half dozen stimuli come in and this same path will be repeated; but if not, they will be likely to take different paths at different times. So we can see on purely physiological grounds how it is that that path of motor dis-charge is most likely to be more deeply grooved and thus maintain a basis for future discharges which succeeds in effecting a unity, because all stimuli reinforce each other; while otherwise they are working at cross purposes and therefore serve largely to annul each other.

The formation, the origin, of any habit, is a variation of existing habits in such a way as to make the end involved in those previous habits more definite. It does not separate from the previous end by any means, but it brings out that end in a more coherent and specific manner. Now it is on this account, once more, that this other phase which I am now going to discuss, of the adaptation, or bringing in of the novel element, is not some-thing really distinct from habit itself. We talk about habit and its adapta-tion and adjustment as if there were really two things there. But of course there are not. The habit is there for the sake of adaptation, for the sake of adjustment, for the sake of accomplishing some end which it cannot ac-complish without cooperating with other modes of action. Now wherever there is a necessity for cooperation, there is a chance for competition. Wherever you have a variety of means necessary to reach a given end, you have the possibility of conflict among these means; and if each one of those means is a means for a variety of ends, they are almost certain to have conflict under certain circumstances.

I go on now to speak of this conflict among different modes of activity as necessitating conscious adaptation.

I. This conflict arises within the system of the self, or system of con-duct, and not from without. To refer to the illustration given before, sup-pose I raise my eyes to watch somebody's countenance as he speaks and

I see a fire. My eye will probably function in quite a different direction from that which I had intended to have it do. We may say, then, that there has been distraction from without, and think of this as a purely external interference.

My point is that it is not external to the whole system of conduct. It is external only if we identify the self with the existing form or mode of conduct. Just because that has been the thing of predominant interest, from its standpoint this new activity is external; it is a stimulus from the external world; it is pure distraction. In moral terms we would regard it as a temptation, as something hostile to the integrity of the self, a solicitation from without. But it is external only with reference to this previous line of action; and just because that is not a supreme, perfectly adequate representative of the interest of the self—because it is, after all, a representative in a particular direction—this new mode of action is just as internal, intrinsic to the whole system of conduct, to the whole interest of the self, as it is to the particular mode of activity with reference to which it is a distraction.

There is the fallacy here, then, of supposing that what is true with reference to a certain particular mode of self or interest is true with reference to the whole self. It is just as important that the eye should recognize fire as it is that it should follow the gestures or expression of a person speaking. That interest is just as legitimate an interest under given circumstances as is the other.

Now it perhaps may add meaning to that if I say it is equally true of a moral temptation. The temptation just as much reflects the man's self as did the virtuous line of action in which he was engaged and from which this tends to distract him. It would not tempt him unless it was an interest. I do not say the interest is psychologically justifiable, but simply that except as it mirrors himself it is not a temptation at all.

What we have in reality is a number of various interests which are practically equivalent to division of labor. Each interest has a certain part to play in the whole self, but no one is supreme; and while we may call one external with reference to another, we cannot say that any one is external to the whole self, because they are all representatives of that self.

[II.] Secondly, this so called diversion is not only intrinsic, not only legitimate from the standpoint of the whole self, but it is absolutely necessary. To put it in biological terms, there must be in a healthy organism not only that stability which is reflected in division of labor, differentiation of organs, but there must be that flexibility which is seen in their mutual interaction and stimulus of each other. In an organism, in a machine, in anything which is to accomplish an end, you must have both stability and flexibility, and a certain balance between the two. Given only flexibility and you have a scatterbrained, futile activity which will wander around at random as it happens, passing from one center to another; but if you have any success on the side of stability, organization becomes mere mechanical routine. That excess is just as futile as is excess on the side of the easy passing on of stimulation. Habit, considered as a division of labor, has been evolved on the basis of past conditions. Now simply to repeat what was appropriated in the past, without any readjustment, it is just as certain to result in failure in the long run as is the mere random striking out into new paths. The situation of course changes, as well as has certain permanent features, and the healthy organism must take account of both sides. The organism that does not take account of both sides dies out. It is important then, it is essential, that the eye when aroused to activity should start to function in a possible variety of ways incompatible with the line of activity already entered upon. If it does not do that, there will be mere routine. Any line of action once entered upon must be seen through to the bitter end.

This tendency on the part of the organs to distract the line of activity, to make a shifting of interest from one center to another, simply means that the agent is thereby kept alert to notice any changes in the situation which would call for a change in his line of action.

Attention has two features, concentration and alertness. Of course concentration stands for the side of persistence along given lines. But that will become rigid if not accompanied by continual alertness, being on the watch for changes of stimuli. Now this starting up of new modes of activity which are incompatible with the one already entered upon is not only not mere distraction, from the standpoint of the organism as a whole, but it is absolutely essential in the needs and interests of that organism. It represents the possibility of shifting from one habit to another as occasion makes that desirable; and more than that, even if the same general line of action, the same interest is finally continued, as quite likely it will be, that one continues in a more intelligent way after a survey of the whole situation and the observation of other features in the situation, instead of going on blindly. I should say it was that start-up of competitive interest which keeps action intelligent instead of making it merely mechanical. Of course it is difficult to get a psychological statement of the difference between animal and human action, but. . . .*

January 20, 1898

As I pointed out yesterday, the conflict of habits involved in different interests serves to throw into definite relief, or objectify, in intellectual form, elements of quality or meaning hitherto bound up in these interests, so that we become conscious of specific qualities in an objective form. But it also serves to bring out the importance or value, in a conscious way, of these interests. It is hardly necessary to call attention to the fact that we have here come upon, once more, the intellectual and emotional aspects of con-

---

* Final line of the original hectograph copy is unintelligible.

duct. This throwing of the qualities into definite form represented to consciousness is the intellectual aspect. This awareness of the value or importance of the habit is the feeling or emotional side. The difference between interest and emotion, and the relation between them, will occupy us later on, but I think it ought to be clear in a preliminary way what we mean by saying that emotion always represents a disturbed interest. The interest is relatively calm and quiet and objective; that is to say in the sense that while there is a feeling value, it is completely bound up with, or lost in, the object. Take the artist who is interested in painting a picture. So far as that interest functions freely, there will be no emotional disturbance in his consciousness. There will be feeling, of course, but it is all interfused with the work which he is doing. Or take anyone in a normal relation of friendship or in the normal relation of love. As long as it functions freely, there is no subjective disturbance of the feeling. The feeling is attached to the objective concern. Let any of these interests be interrupted; let something threaten the friendship; or let removal or death come in in the relation of the interest of love and then the interest is thrown back upon itself in a more subjective form. There is all that stress and excitation which we associate with the term emotion as distinct from the term interest.

Now having come around again to this matter of the breakup of the interest, organized habit in distinct impulses, and to the fact that these impulses carry with them both emotional tone and intellectual quality, we have the further topics for analysis outlined before us. I shall go on to take up the intellectual side and then the emotional.

NOTES

1. James, *Psychology,* I, 278–83.
2. James, *Psychology,* I, 243–48.
3. C. Lloyd Morgan (1852–1936), English biologist and philosopher. See his *Habit and Instinct* (London and New York: Edward Arnold, 1896), p. 153ff., for a more detailed analysis of the example Dewey refers to here.
4. James, *Psychology,* I, Chap. IV, "Habit."
5. *Ibid.,* p. 109.
6. Apparently a reference to a diagram not reproduced in the original hectograph copy. Compare Dewey's view in the following with James's account in his *Psychology,* I, 24–27.
7. Dewey, "The Reflex-Arc Concept in Psychology," *Early Works,* V, 96–109.

CHAPTER 3

THE INTELLECTUAL PROCESS

SECTION 1. ITS GENESIS
AND LIMITS

The intellectual process has its genesis in the breakup of the interest or organized activity in conflicting impulses. It has its outcome, its limit on the further side, in the reattainment of unity in conduct, or in the setting up of a new interest. That, of course, would include within itself the idea of the unified modification of the old. It comes in between one interest, then, and another, finding its start in the breakup. Its material is the impulses which are left in this disintegration of previous habits; and its working is the piecing together, knitting together of these *disjecta membra,* in the organization of action. This intellectual operation is conditioned genetically on the breakdown of the previous coordination, the previous system of action, and its function is to build up a new coordination. The intellectual process continually looks both backward and forward. Baldwin continually used the categories of retrospective and prospective without explaining why the intellectual products have this retrospective and prospective outlook.[1]

On the basis of what has been said, the intellectual process on the side of its genesis will be retrospective. On the side of its function its looks will always be prospective. The actual intellectual process itself is the working back and forward between one point of view and the other; between the intuitive element which represents the anticipation of the new mode of action, and the empirical element which represents the reflection on past experience with reference to the assistance which it may give in building up the new experience. You cannot help looking at every intellectual product from these two points of view and you cannot help organically connecting them. If you separate function from genesis it loses, and if you separate genesis from function it loses. The retrospective view is always for the sake of getting material to go ahead with. On the other hand your demand for the prospective view is due to the breakdown which is just behind you. The motive for the conscious looking ahead is simply because what you have had failed you, and also that must furnish you the material, the stuff, for building up and realizing your prospective glance. In more psychological terms it would be the strict correlativity of anticipation and recollection.

We recollect for the sake of anticipation, and we anticipate because we cannot recollect, because we cannot unify.

The same general idea may be put in another way. The intellectual process has for its purport to discover and construct an adequate stimulus to action. Or what is the same thing on the other side, to discover or construct a coherent response to the varying existing stimuli. I say the two statements are the same thing. You cannot have a current response unless you have an adequate stimulus. Consequently we must discriminate mentally between the meaning of the terms stimulus and response in their objective sense and in the conscious sense. It is an error which has very serious consequences to confound that act which is generally termed sensory stimulus with the conscious sensation as stimulus. The stimulus becomes conscious in the form of sensation only because the objective stimulus is failing us. The same is equally true on the side of response. It is the easiest thing in the world to use sensation in this double sense, meaning by it sometimes the active objective stimulus, and meaning by it at other times the condition and value in consciousness. And yet we cannot say that what is true of one is true of the other, because the sensation in the sense of a sensory stimulus is found only in the organized action. The sensation as the conscious state or value is found only in the breakup and readaptation of such habits. For instance, in the act of walking we say that the contact of the foot with the ground is the sensory stimulus to lifting it up and putting the other one down as the motor response. Or we say that the hearing of a certain sentence in a conversation is the sensory stimulus to our reply as a motor reaction, and so on indefinitely. Now in those cases, all that is meant is that there is an adequate stimulus to action; that you have a series of organized acts, of which each one initiates the next of the series. A initiates B, and as soon as B is set up it initiates C, and that in turn initiates D. As that goes on there is no sensation in the sense of a presentation in consciousness. By stimulus we simply mean that particular act which excites another and introduces it into this organized coordination. It is really no more sensory than motor. The act of putting the foot on the ground has its motor side as much as its sensory side, and the putting of the other foot down again has its sensory side as much as its motor, but we name it from that particular interest which is predominant at the time.

The sensory stimulus in the objective sense is simply what we mean by the relation which one act bears to another in any orderly habit. Each act is stimulus to the next and that is response to the preceding. It is only when that habit comes into conflict with some other habit that the sensation is thrown into conscious relief or presented as a state or value in consciousness. That is what I mean by saying that the intellectual process is a process of discovery or the constructing of an adequate stimulus. It is because the objective stimulus has failed that we must work out another one intellectually. So the outcome of the intellectual process may be stated just as much to find the sensation that we want as it is to find the idea that we want. There is a continual tendency in psychology to suppose that you have all the sensations on hand at the outset and that your further intellectual process is simply manipulating the collection of sensations that you already have. So it is in a sense. But that manipulation consists not simply in associating: it consists in selecting some of them and rejecting others, and that act of selection is a constructive act. We do not merely take the sensations that we have originally; we search for sensations, and the intellectual process is just as much a searching for certain sensations or sensory qualities as it is a building up of concepts or ideas. I do not suppose that will be perfectly clear at this stage of the discussion. Subsequent discussion will bring the point out more clearly.

Take the scientific man who is working out some problem; take the biologist with the microscope or the astronomer with the telescope. He is looking after new sensations. He is neglecting many that he might have, because they do not help him. He is after sensations that have a certain relevancy determined by the problem in view. The error, then, which is apt to creep in at the outset of the discussion is supposing that we have the sensations already given and that the only problem is to find some response, or to form some idea which somehow corresponds to the sensation. What is really the whole reflection works in both directions. It not only builds up ideas as the basis of the response, but it is also building up sensations as a stimulus to further action.

Now the material of course that is on hand is the impulses. It is out of these impulses and their interaction, their reciprocal stimulus on each other, that the new coordination must be built up. Psychologically that is absolutely all that there is there.

Now in saying that, you remember that that interaction between the impulses is just as intrinsic as are the impulses themselves as distinct impulses. These impulses have emerged out of a unity, and therefore they normally [do not] go beyond the limits of that totality or system. When they do, the state is pathological. The person is insane when any impulse has entirely escaped the bounds of the system to which it belongs. So while I shall go on to speak as if these impulses were relatively independent of each other, that is simply a convenient mode of speech. It is the very nature of the impulse to stimulate another impulse and to respond to other impulses. These relationships are not external to it. That is where the fallacy of the empirical school is apt to come in, as in the theory of association—regarding them as in themselves independent, and therefore as associations, as being an external thing, because it is not seen that these impulses are not originally given as separate and distinct, but that their distinction is due to the breakup of the preceding interest. We must think of them with reference to a unity out of which they have emerged and of a unity to which they are converging.

Now the quality of the impulse—that is, its discriminating quality—constitutes the intellectual side. That intellectual *latus** has itself its own double look. It looks backwards, and forwards. I mean by that that it has a value which has to be stated with reference to the past, and it has another value which has to be stated with reference to the future. Its value is indicative. It is a value pointing out something else. It is the very nature of any state of consciousness, as knowledge, to refer to something beyond itself. The moment you have a state of consciousness absorbed in itself, you no longer have an intellectual condition. That reference, that indicative power, may be in either of two directions. Putting that in concrete terms, sensation and idea are not names for two distinct physical existences. I mean by sensation, conscious sensation. They are one and the same intellectual content named from the direction in which it points. If it is defined with reference to what preceded, we call it sensation; if it is defined with reference to what we expect to follow, it is image. The distinction between sensation and image is thus one of direction, of movement, depending simply on the way we take the mental state. If we would isolate the psychical existence from its place in the movement we could not tell whether it was sensation or image, and we would have no ground for calling it one more than the other. This point determines ethically the significance of what we call the sense appetites on one side and of moral ideals on the other; and because it does that, it is an exceedingly important point to get straight.

I think the point is that animal activity simply goes on from one center to another. If it shifts off, then the old line of activity becomes at once quiescent, and one is simply substituted for the other. But in the human being this tension occurs. The previous interest does not subside at once but continues to assert itself, and other modes of action called into activity by it assert themselves, and there is not the possibility of merely following the original line of action or merely shifting from one to another—there must be selection and adaptation.

Just as the formation of habit, then, means the definition of the end, translating it over into more precise and accurate terms, this interaction of habits and their mutual adaptation makes that end wider, more comprehensive, and more flexible in consciousness. It stands for the interdependence of the various habits on each other, or the various interests on each other, and stands for the unity of the self as a whole, as distinct from the particular interest of the self which has found expression in any one habit.

Thirdly, it is not, strictly speaking, true to say that habit is adapted to new conditions or circumstances, but rather that one habit is adapted to another habit. It is [through] that mutual adaptation, and the conflict that goes on because each one tends to persist as it was and thus resists modi-

---

* Side or aspect.

fication by the others, that the new conditions emerge in consciousness, while on the other side the habit is thrown into relief.

Suppose we take the case of a child forming the habit of writing. He has certain habits already formed. He has the habit of seeing. He has the habit of language, both hearing it and speaking it. He has the habit of using his arms and hands, the muscles, to hold things, to move things, to accomplish ends. Now his formation of the habit of writing must mean that those three habits are to be adapted to each other in such a way that each loses a certain supremacy that it had before and is reduced to a subordinate character. When he begins to write, he no longer sees for the sake of seeing as before, or uses language for the sake of using it. He does not follow these interests as primary and ultimate, but he uses them as subordinate with reference to the others. He looks at the copy with reference to the use of his hands, and the use of language will be controlled by that use of his hands. He will think of a word in order that his hand may be guided. He must no longer use his hand as supreme, but use it as suggested by the eye. The difficulty of forming this habit, then, or any other, is simply due to the fact that the previous work has been so well done. These other interests have been so well worked out that there is a persistence of each on its own account. It resists surrender to the others, and yet a new habit cannot be made except as they are subordinated so that a new coordination can be built up. With the attempt at mutual adaptation a lot of new sensations arise in consciousness. They may be sensations of confusion, and probably will be at first. A boy from the country, put into the city, must adapt certain habits to each other. The first effect of that adaptation will be a sense of bewilderment. But to go back to the previous case—the child will see the words more distinctly than he ever has before. This power of seeing will be broken up into distinct qualities, simply because, now, instead of being used for its own sake it must be subordinated to something else. He will be conscious of the movement of his hand and arm when he is using them as subordinate to another end as he was not when using it for itself.

Take another example, that of drawing, where necessarily the eye habit and the hand habit must be adapted to each other, where a person must learn to see over again. There must be not simply new muscular sensation but the object must be seen in a different way. The old habit of interpreting objects by touch must be broken up and they must be interpreted in their various lights and shades. The great difficulty is to learn to see over again, to learn to see in terms of the eye qualities themselves which are thrown into relief and distinctness when that power of seeing is made simply a subordinate stimulus to the powers of reproduction in drawing.

If you will go over this principle in your mind, you will see that the adaptation of one line of action to another compels certain things to stand out as sensations and that it is this mutual adaptation of habits that persist to the new conditions in consciousness, instead of the habit being adapted to those conditions, as if they were already there. On the other hand, the resistance which each habit or interest offers to its adaptation to another habit, being made subordinate, makes that habit stand out more clearly. The child who must learn to write values the independence of action of his hand, and eye, and speech organ as he did not before. This brings out the longing to continue what he did before—to see simply for the sake of seeing, and to use his hands simply for the sake of using his hands. This accompanies all readjustment and makes the departing thing seem more valuable than it ever had done before. It is when we are going to lose a thing that it means the most to us. Put in moral terms, a man may have been following a certain line of action without thinking very much about it or being aware that he attaches much importance to it, but let him be convinced that he ought to surrender that mode of action and he at once sees what it means to him in a way that he did not as long as he took it for granted without questioning it at all. Suppose he uses a stimulant or narcotic and has had no occasion to put that act into the moral sphere at all. What it meant to him he never has defined, but let him begin to feel moral reasons for giving it up, and as a rule there will not be much doubt left in his mind as to how much importance he has attached to it in the past without knowing it. The habit as a habit is thrown into relief when various habits have to be subordinated to each other and thus form a new coordination.

SECTION 2. THE ROLE OF
SENSATION AND IMAGE

January 25, 1898

The point under discussion was the relation of sensation and image. The principle stated was that they are not differences of psychical existence but rather distinctions of value with reference to one and the same existence— that distinction of value depending on the place which the state occupies with reference to the direction of activity; or, more accurately, we interpret the state as sensation or as image, according to the direction of interest. It is the movement of interest that makes one and the same state, now sensation, now image, according to what is wanted of it, and what can be done with it.

Before attempting to establish the later point, I will make some remarks and criticisms on the assumption that there are differences in the psychical existence itself, between the sensation and the image.

In the first place every image is really sensational in character, taken as an existence. A good many psychologists, following Lotze,[2] have said that the image of red is not color, that the image of a tone does not resound, and so on. Those who can visualize colors tell us that colors *are* colors, and in the image are illuminated, just as they are in the sense perception; that tones do possess pitch and other direct sensational qualities. There are probably some of us who cannot image red or blue, but those who can visualize red or green or any other color, always find that the color is projected in space and that it is definitely illuminated, and is an actual shade of color. All the investigations of image tend absolutely in this direction, that the images, as directly in consciousness, are purely sensory in quality. There are touch images; if I can image a touch on my shoulder, then it is, so far as it goes, as sensational in quality as if someone had actually laid hold of me.

If we take the images of language we find that on analysis they reflect themselves in certain auditory sensational qualities on one side, and on the other side in various sensations of the movements of articulation. Sensations come to us from tongue, and lips, and the. . . .*

. . . to inversion, thinking that as an image becomes intense, it is a sensation, and as the sensation becomes faint, it is an image. All sensations decrease in intensity, as sound grows less and less as the distance increases, but we do not think of it as changing into image, but simply as a decrease in quality. I may be more conscious of it as sensation when it gets faint than when it is more intense. I think we can read into his statement without much difficulty that it is rather the direction of movement that is concerned. Anything which stimulates to the reconstruction of the existing level of consciousness will be regarded as sensation, whether faint or intense. Anything which, on the whole, goes on within that level and tends to build it up further, rather than giving it another switch off, will be interpreted as image. (Of course the English psychologists have worked out this difference simply as one of intensity, much further than James has. It has been the characteristic distinction since the time of Hume, that the image is simply decaying sensation, and in Herbert Spencer you will find this built up in a most elaborate way.[3] Külpe in his *Psychology* has criticized this point of view and suggested another differentia as regards sensation and image.[4] It is rather complex and I shall not state it except in a general way, which is: that is regarded as sensation which is novel. That is the peripheral excitation. That which is familiar is image, and that is the central excitation. The central excitation arouses a feeling of familiarity. That of course is particularly true in what he calls the memory image. Külpe himself states that this is a distinction which has to be learned. As we learn to interpret photographs in relation to their originals, so we learn to interpret our images. Thus he approaches the doctrine I have stated: that it is really a difference of interpretation rather than any inherent property of the sensational states. In bringing attention to this idea of familiarity and novelty, he gives half the truth, as James has the other half. I

* A page (approximately 800 words) of the original hectograph copy is missing.

should say it was a distinction with reference to action. We feel anything as familiar which arouses the sense of power and control. Something comes before us. We are doubtful about it, but in a moment a sense of familiarity comes to us. It is simply the feeling of our reaction to it, and the feeling that these reactions are harmonious, that there is no particular difficulty in the way. The sense of novelty in the sense of having to determine a new reaction. It is not so much that the quality is new, but that we must deal in a new way, and the sense of newness is in reality the sense of change in the direction of our action—James's change of level.

Now to apply the result of this critical excursion to the original proposition. The sensational state will have the value of image to us insofar as it affords a basis of control. It is because it does relate to the more familiar, that it puts at our disposal the element of control secured in the past. That which is given the value of sensation is, on the other hand, that which needs control. It is that which arouses or stimulates interference in some way. It marks the point of deflection *to* which attention has to be given, just as the image marks the organ or instrument *through* which attention may be given. Now I said that was only half the truth. The other half would be this: While the image represents what is familiar, taken as the basis of control in the present emergency, it also represents what is wanted. It represents the direction in which activity is moving, while the sensation represents a consciousness of what *has* been reached. It tells us the direction from which activity is moving. So far as we refer a value backward, so far as we are thinking of it with reference to its origin, it is sensation. It is image as we are thinking of it with reference to what we are going to do—not the object that we have had, but the object that we want to get. Any conscious state will always have these two values. Take one example, a familiar psychological illustration, the walking on a plank at a high altitude. If that same plank were on the ground, we would go ahead and there would be no conscious sensation, or image. That plank being put in an unaccustomed place the eye habit contradicts the equilibrium and locomotion habits, and most people have very curious sensations of an action which . . . . *

. . . as opposed to what will be ignored and thrust back out of consciousness. Wherever there is any condition which is intellectual, as distinct from mere feeling, there will be both of these elements; there will be a feeling of tension between the past and the future. If in that tension the conditions are more important for us, then we call it sensation. If on the other hand, we are engaged in formulating what we want and how we are to utilize it, it becomes image. This whole process is a tentative one, an experimental one. We move a little while in one direction and then in the other. First we think of what it is we want to do, so as to get a clear image of what we are about. Now if we keep on thinking of what we want to do,

* A page of the original hectograph copy is missing.

we will go wool-gathering or to building castles in the air. When we have a clear image, we must turn around and apply it. Then we must begin thinking of our data for action, what the present situation is. We must get sensations, and in getting them we test our image, because we use that image as a basis of selection. If we find we are making headway on the side of sensation, we are satisfied with the image—if we find that we are getting hold of the stimuli to action in such a way that we can react easily. But if after reaction, we find ourselves making no headway, we have to return to our image and think that out a little further. Then we come back again to our sensations, to the present immediate data. The normal, unified outcome, the sensation, is built up more and more on the basis of the image, and the image gets saturated with the sensations. Apperception is the image on one side, and sensation on the other.

To take a scientific illustration, suppose a botanist sees a flower with which he is not familiar. He does not know how to classify it. The intellectual process is set up. Will he not first go over his stock of images to see what he has to control that experience with? He will think over the kinds of flowers that most resemble this one, and when he finds one which he thinks is a good one to work on, he will go back to the particular flower, and search for sensations. Will this flower give the sensations I ought to have if it is a flower of this kind? He does not succeed, and he goes back to the image side and modifies it, perhaps only a little, perhaps a great deal. On the basis of that image he comes back, and again searches for sensations. It takes the shape of working backward and forward until he can identify the image with the sensations, until he can find the image embodied. He can select the sensations required, while on the other hand his sensations become unified on the basis of the image which he has.

SECTION 3. THE MORAL SIGNIFICANCE OF THE INTELLECTUAL PROCESS

January 26, 1898

The outcome of the discussion yesterday was that image represents immediately the new formal activity and that it has the function of thus controlling and directing the present activity; that the sensory aspect stands for the activity as interrupted and thus has the function of locating the problem and of giving the starting points from which further activity must proceed. Having now attempted to suggest the strictly correlative character of sensation and idea or image, I will go on to discuss the habit process more concretely with a view to leading up to the discussion of its ethical significance.

We begin then with a confused sense of interruption and of striving onward, forward. We have to use the two terms here, interruption referring to the past and the striving or urging with reference to the future, but of course there is only one actual experience which we are naming in two different ways. There would be no feeling or interruption unless there was a feeling of trying to get ahead. We would not feel that we were restive if we did not feel some urgency onward. One thing would be as good as another and hence would not give rise to any sense of obstacle if it were not for the feeling of activity as somehow going on, nor would the ongoing of activity come to consciousness as a striving unless it were somehow arrested. As long as we can go ahead freely, easily, we are not conscious of that as onward striving or urgency. We are simply taken up with what we are doing, and that is the end of it. But when that doing runs up against something, we feel the urgency to get ahead. Now it is the feeling of the ongoing activity which needs to be cleared up into a definite idea of an end. At first it is simply the feeling, the impression, the presentiment, and the problem for us is to translate this correlated vague presentiment into a clear-cut thought which may really serve to guide action. Now the clearing up of that impression, transforming it into a definite thought of an end—that is, an ideal—means that we can interpret it on the basis of our past experience, and so fast as we can do that it becomes an image, and thus gets the intellectual quality of an ideal or basis of control.

The feeling of interruption needs of course to be translated into objective intellectual terms. We want to get rid of the mere sense that we have come up against an obstacle, and be able to locate that obstacle, and in locating it to show just what place it occupies in the situation which confronts us. We have to see just what that obstacle means with reference to what we are trying to do, or the future direction of action, and that translation out of the mere feeling comes about on the side of sensation. That is, our vague sense of interruption, or confused sense of interruption and of obstacle in the present situation, is made coherent when we look at it with reference to its adaptation to our future movements.

I will give one illustration, not so much psychological as ethical on the points involved here. Suppose men smarting under a sense of injustice. That will mean that they feel their legitimate lines of activity interrupted. Suppose that we imagine working men who feel that they are being unjustly treated and go on a strike where they feel they ought to win and find themselves gradually getting beaten. Now so far as that situation can be translated into intellectual terms, it will remain in this vague sense of feeling in both directions. There will be a vague feeling of right, of justice, something not met by the present situation. But if we ask just what that is there will be no answer. Or in a vague way they will say: "We only know that we ought to be doing or having something that we are not getting or doing." And this will resolve itself into the inability to locate exactly what the source of the disorder is, or to tell exactly what the point is to which they have a right to object and what they want reconstituted. The result is blind resentment, simply an indefinite striking out, a kicking back against anything and everything in their immediate surroundings. It is a matter of ordinary experience, as well as of social psychology, that discussion on the intellectual side is almost always accompanied by appeals to blind force on the practical side. The more freedom is allowed people to meet and discuss, the less likely there is to be any such appeal made to immediate physical force.

I take that illustration because there is an explanation of the psychology of it. The whole process of deliberation which reflects itself on the social side in the talking, and writing, and communicating of ideas to each other, serves to clear up the original confused sense of the difficulty and translates it over into a definite plane of action on one side, and [it results in] the ability to tell what things are disliked, so that the objects are located and there is a definite point fixed where energy can be directed. But where the intellectual discussion does not take place, there is no such mediation of the impulses into intellectual channels. They are simply damned up and when they find expression it is in a meaningless, unrelated way.

The practical moral would be that no society needs to fear anarchy, in its destructive sense, where there are adequate facilities for the discussion of the situation and where there is a feeling of the capacity to intellectually clear up the situation so as to give a definite plane of action and a definite point of attack in the existing situation. If there is a fear of anarchy, you would have to show that there were not adequate facilities for the discussion of the situation, or else that it was felt that that would not be effective, that it would be smothered somewhere. If there was the feeling that the discussion would be extensive enough, there would be the trust that that would itself clear up the situation and lay out the lines of future action. In individual psychology, when a person feels that he is in a box, that he is penned or trapped in, it is practically sure to result in this mere physical reaction against the existing situation. The whole impulses and feelings remain in this confused state because there is no means of transforming them on the basis of an intellectual statement of the situation in terms of the plane of action on one side and the specific obstacle on the other side.

That would mean that the function of deliberation is rationalizing, is to clear up, to illuminate the active situation, and that it does so by translating the impulses over into the language of an end or aim which will operate as a plane of action on one side and state just what the obstacles are on the other. It marks the difference between "that" and "what," in other words. It is one thing to know "that" we want to go on, or "that" we are interrupted; it is another thing to know "what" we want to do and just "what" the obstacles are. And the intellectual process puts the "what" in the mere fact of the "that."

I will now apply this first to the nature of deliberation as a process, secondly to the nature of the ends or ideals, and thirdly to the nature of the sensory states.

Deliberation is a rehearsal of action. While it is intellectual it is not a mere indifferent consideration of objective things. It is not thinking about certain possibilities and results; it is imaging these as actually operative and at work. It is imaginative experimentation. We set up the end just as the scientific man in the laboratory sets up the working hypothesis; and we try it on exactly as he tries it on, excepting that when he tries it to see how it will work he makes an actual manipulation of certain external facts, while in this moral-practical deliberation we try it on simply in our imagination. We say virtually, suppose we do this or that. We try to see the scenes which would happen if we did thus and so, and on the other hand what the scene would be if we did the other thing. I think introspectively there is no difficulty in carrying that out.

In the accounts that are given of deliberation in the Psychologies and Ethics there is a neglect of that dramatic, dynamic experimental character of deliberation. They talk of weighing things as deliberation. I take it that we put ourselves into those data which we are weighing. We do not simply set them before us, we project ourselves into them and imagine ourselves doing this or that, or we pull them into ourselves and look at ourselves in the light of them. This dramatic character then, of deliberation, is the first thing I would insist upon. That dramatic quality, that rehearsing of action means that we are anticipating. We do not get quite to the point of overt action in this rehearsal; we do not quite go and do the things of which we are thinking. We simply do it in our minds, in our images—though at times I think the dramatic rehearsal will become so intense that we will be carried into decision almost without knowing it, and the picture gets so motor that it carries us over by one swish, so to speak. But normally it does not take us at once into that overt statement. To say that it is rehearsal means that it is mental. We anticipate future action and future experiences then, in order to see what they are like, and to see whether we like them or not and whether they would like us, to see as we bring them before us whether they coalesce with the image of ourselves in such an harmonious way as to bring satisfaction. This deliberation is not the mere putting of certain data before us. We project ourselves into this imaginary result. If we can do that, we get a feeling of satisfaction and will be certain to go ahead on that line unless some other obstacle intervenes.

The value of this anticipation is to preclude one-sidedness of action. An interest which is dominant at the time is the particular mode of operation. Now it need not be partial simply because it is particular. If our whole needs, if the needs of the whole being are met by that particular line of action, there is nothing partial in it. That it is particular means that the whole self is defined in a particular way. That is, if the organism can be best served by using the eye, the fact that the dominance of action in the eye does not permit the ear or hand to be dominant does not mean any one-sidedness. There is an equation between the organism and the organ, that particular organ. But when conflict arises, to act in a particular direction would be at once one-sidedness, because the other interest is there and is asserting its claims; and unless both sides are allowed to have a fair hearing and to present their own claims, action would be one-sided.

Deliberation, then, consists in looking at the conflicting interests in the light of each other. It consists in bringing up into the imagination the whole of action formed on the basis of imagining one impulse acted upon and executed and then of the other impulse acted upon and executed, until there is a whole scene imagined in which the claims of these two impulses are met so that they coalesce and it is possible for the self to project itself consistently into the imagined scene. Now if the conflict is one of any depth or scope, more and more considerations are brought into play. The area of imagination widens. If I am simply debating in my mind whether to go downtown, it is not likely that any very large scope of interests will come before my consciousness. If I am deciding upon the choice of a profession, it is likely that many more considerations will present themselves before me, and if we take the typical moral conflicts of life which touch our interests, I suppose we may say that one after another all the interests of the self come into active operation, are put upon the scene, and play their parts in the rehearsing of the final action.

Now this anticipation then, which brings more and more interests into active play all the time, keeping the self from going off at once on any partial line, means the following things:

1. The existing impulses are temporarily inhibited. We say: "Stop and think." That is tautology. The thinking is stopping and stopping is thinking. That is, the inhibition of an impulse will throw it into the region of idea.

2. This deliberation will mean the revaluation of the various competing interests. We look at their value, not simply as it has been, but as it may be in the light of possibilities in future experience. We consciously compare one interest with another and value one according as it reinforces another, or as it tends to degrade or tear down another.

3. It means possibly, though not certainly, its overt modification. The thing will be different when it is finally done than it would be if there had been no previous reflection and deliberation. Even if we finally do one of the things that we thought . . .* will be quite different.

* Several words are unintelligible in the original hectograph copy at this point.

But . . . of its being somewhat different externally, . . .* as well as being different in meaning. This deliberative process, then, anticipates future action by bringing it over into the region of imagination, and may be said to have for its function to objectify the impulse. I do not mean anything new by that, but simply a word to name the process I have been describing. This objectifying the impulse is translating the impulse into terms of the experiences which it may render possible. Suppose a man is angry and starts to shoot another man. As he starts, that impulse is checked by the thought, perhaps I will kill him and maybe this, that, or the other thing will happen. That means simply that the original thought is translated into an intellectual content which is the experience which might follow if that impulse were acted upon. I also used the term mediation of impulse to express exactly the same idea; that the impulse is no longer taken as it is, merely by itself, or isolated, but is looked at in the light of other impulses and in the light of future experiences.

One thing more in general about deliberation. This anticipation is virtually the consideration of possible consequences. This point will occupy us at greater length further on. I want to point out here simply that there is no reason for regarding those circumstances as external. The consideration of consequences has a bad name with many theorists. They say as soon as you consider consequences you are lost morally. You must simply decide what is right and go ahead, and if you begin to weigh consequences you will be deflected into selfishness. That makes the consequences to be something external. The consideration of consequences is nothing but the thought of the impulse. It is nothing outside of the impulse. It is the impulse turned over into terms of relationship. It is the impulse seen as an index to other experiences.

So far I have been discussing anticipation in relation to its value in defining our end for us, in defining our ideal—anticipation in the sense of making us see what sort of thing each impulse really is when we look at it in its relations instead of taking it in a one-sided way.

Anticipation has a value in the other direction also. It helps determine not only what we should do, our end, but it also helps decide how we shall do it. This dramatic rehearsal in advance of action helps us because it puts at our disposal in advance instruments of action which would escape us in the heat and stress of the activity itself. Put ethically, we are more apt to have presence of mind, to be cool-headed, and to have command of all the available resources of the situation according to the degree of clearness with which we have thought the thing out in advance; and that is the value of planning—not simply to decide what we are going to aim at, but to decide in advance in what direction we are going to turn to get help in carrying out our decision. Our habits, which are our powers, are, so to speak, tied up with specific ends and interests. Now by deliberation we

* Several words are unintelligible in the original hectograph copy at this point.

loosen them. We think of them as being used for different ends, and by thinking of them in relation to new ends we are enabled, when the stress of action comes, to devote them to those new ends in much quicker time, and in a much more effective way than we would if we had to make the adaptation at the moment.

That is not always true. Sometimes the heat of action will enable one to do things which he would not have anticipated doing at all; but when a person does have so much clearness of judgment under the stress of action even when there has been no anticipation, it is because he has a habit of deliberating action in general, and he reaps in this particular case in an unexpected way the benefits of the habit which he has formed. The general would be most apt to know what to do quickly at an unexpected crisis of battle, who had the habit of anticipating the turning points of battle and thinking what he would be likely to do under the circumstances. The whole process can be put as follows: The value of deliberation is to transfer conflict from the overt sphere to the mental. Conflict, then, must be wherever there is any necessity for choice, and necessity of deciding. The question is: Where is that conflict going to be located? Are we going to be pulled and hauled here and there in action itself? Are we going to have action divided because one part is drawing one way and another another, or are we going to carry on the conflict in idea so that when we come to action the conflict will be unified and coherent? That means that deliberation assumes a possible unity of conduct, of action, and the conflict is reduced to being mental or imaginative simply because it is all carried on with reference to finally reaching and maintaining a unity of conduct.

Let me give one example on the social side. What measures the value of intellectual discussion? Certainly on one side there must be diversity of points of view, there must be a certain amount of opposition. If two persons look at things exactly alike there is nothing gained particularly by discussion. It is more likely to be fruitful if there is an intellectual opposition. A conversation will be fruitful to the degree that the unity of result is postulated by the two participants. They do not need consciously to say there is a whole truth of which we have only fragments, and by bringing the fragments together each will get the value of the other's thought; but if the results are to be fruitful, that is what it means, or else the discussion is simply argument and the end is not to attain a unity of view which will include the ideas of both but simply to down the opponent. In that fruitful discussion the conflict is transferred simply into the region of ideas, the assumption being that there is a whole which will organize and unify the diverse parts. And so with moral deliberation, the assumption is that there is a unity of conduct which will organize the values respectively presented in the various competing impulses and desires. The perception of moral deliberation is that conduct is organic, that it is a system, and the value of it is to introduce that system into thought.

SECTION 4. HOW WE
BECOME CONSCIOUS
OF AIMS

February 1, 1898

The last time I spoke of the moral significance of the intellectual process in general. Today I propose to continue the same discussion by specializing it with reference to the consciousness of aim on one side, and the consciousness of the existing status on the other.

The consciousness of aim is primarily the consciousness of the tendency or direction of action. The aim neither represents a mere mechanical manipulation and juxtaposition of previous experiences, nor something formal to the action supervening from without. We sense the activity, so to speak, in the direction in which it is moving. I think that is what Mr. James, in his analysis of the stream of consciousness, calls the fringe.[5] I am speaking, not so much about the content of the aim, but rather the consciousness of it as aim; the consciousness that there is such a thing; and that represents the reflection in consciousness of the way in which activity is going, or in which it is tending to go.

Activity cannot be absolutely arrested. It is never a question of stimulating activity as if what existed were simply a non-active condition and the aim were required to come in and stir us out of a condition of pure torpor. The stimulation which takes place represents the deflection of activity from one line or type of interest to another. That we are conscious of the direction or tendency of our activity is due to conflict and obstacle. As long as action is thoroughly harmonized there is an end, in the objective sense, that is reached; but there is no end in the subjective sense, as being something definitely marked off as ahead of us and distinguished from what we now have. It is the negative element in our activity, the resistance met, which makes us differentiate our sense of the direction of our action from the existing make-up of that action. But it is not enough to know that there is an end generated through this conflict. At first there will be a mere presentiment, a vague feeling. We feel the ongoing direction of action in a formless confused way as set over against the present accomplishments and the present obstacles, but that formless feeling of the persistence of action must be given definite content; or, in our previous language, this feeling must be transformed into an image. Now this image of the end, the feeling given content, represents experience adapted to defining the direction of movement. Instead of being the mere sense of where we are going, or that we are going on, it is the definite statement of that direction through bringing to bear one's past experiences or habits.

Psychologically that means that no image is ever a mere copy. Every image is a reconstruction. We talk about calling up images out of the past or out of our storehouse of images, as if they were all there and all we had to do was to pull a string and pull out one above consciousness where we could look at it. But this process of recollection is a process of reconstruction. Our experience as we experienced it was an image in no sense. It was a total reality, a totality, an integral whole, and the problem is how that totality in the process of reproduction becomes reduced to being an image. We are apt to think, and our Psychologies are apt to speak, as if the image were a mere copy of an original experience taken as a model. That term copy or reproduction, if we take reproduction in a literal static sense, simply slurs over all the difficulties in the case. In reality the previous experience becomes an image in the process of being adapted to give us assistance in the present emergency with reference to the future direction of action. I am speaking of course, now, of the primitive conditions of things, not of certain later complexities; but in its origin and development, to have an image means that we need assistance with reference to what we are going to do, with reference to defining the direction of action, and that we bring our past experience to bear in order to get that experience, and that in so doing we reduce that experience from its complete totality of value, and make it simply a means or an instrument. If it were not for anticipation, I do not believe there would be any recollection; or if it were not for the necessity of anticipation, I do not believe there would be recollection. It is metaphor to speak as if these things were stored away in the mind and emerged, or popped out, or were pulled out with no real motivation in the process of action for it. The image is a reflection of experience with a view to adapting it to our needs.

Now the extent, quality, and character of this reconstructive modification will depend of course on the importance attaching to this further direction of action. If what we are going to do does not strike us as anything of very great consequence, then the modification which takes place in our adaptation of previous experience is very slight, because the amount of reconstruction that is going to take place is not very great. It is not necessary to make over experience much to accomplish that deflection, but if the branch off of activity is great, and if much significance is attached to it, then not only a great deal of our past experience may be before us but it will get an entirely new setting. The empirical justification of that statement is the fact that in crises of life one sees himself and his past in such different ways than he had seen those things when they happened, or had originally viewed them. We look very different to ourselves; our experiences that we have been accustomed to have look different to us at such periods of reconstruction. It is a common situation in the drama and in the novel where this looking different is so great that one hardly recognizes himself and his own past at all because it is seen in the light of its adaptation to a large and important modification in the direction of action. Ethically that would mean, of course, that a project of reform as to the future reflects itself in condemnation as to the past. The consciousness of the necessity of a future direction of action places our previous experiences in a wholly different setting. We look at them from a new standpoint of view so that what was pleasant is abhorrent and what was abhorrent becomes positively attractive to us. It is usually considered that a person first disapproves his habits and then sets about to reform them. On the contrary it is the dawning of reform, the dawning consciousness of the possibility of a new mode of direction, which makes one change in his attitude toward his past and his customary habits.

Now we have here again that apparent paradox with reference to the image which has met us before—that in form the idea, the end, represents the new, while in content it is filled up with the old and familiar, and this gives the basis of control. The end represents the new in that it represents the ongoing direction of action; but when we come to tell what that direction is, when we come to fill up that formal sense of ongoing action with a definite content, the only way in which we can do it is by freeing our past habits and restating them from the standpoint of this direction of action.

We have the intuitive and empirical elements in the formation of the end. That there is an end is purely projective, but the what of it will be gathered, re-collected, out of our previous experiences. The function of the aim, then, of the purpose, is to bridge precisely this gap between the past and the future. It is the bridging of that gap. On the side of its form it is the direction, a change in the direction of action. But on the side of the content, and what fills it up, it is simply our own habits, our own accomplishments adapted to effect this change. The purpose, then, will subserve its reason for existence just in the degree in which it effects that mediation or redirection of action with the maximum effectiveness and the minimum friction. Later on I shall have more to say about the direct ethical significance of this in forming the moral value of ideals and getting the criterion for the value of our ideals; to distinguish the empty ideals from those which are effective and which, therefore, ought to be cultivated.

We now turn briefly to the other aspect of the intellectual process, the sense factor. This stands for that which presents the obstacle, which makes the resistance to the ongoing of action, and which therefore calls for the ideal, the image. It is our feeling of the present facts, not as something final, but as something which is to be left behind or made over. We would not have, then, any consciousness of the sense factor if it were not for the felt obstacles and resistances in action. It is this split in action which throws that element into relief over against the consciousness of purpose on the other side. These obstacles must be interpreted with reference to the needs [?] and possibilities of the future and thus are changed from obstacles into means, into instrumentalities. There is the paradox, both intellectually and morally, of our sense life, that the very thing which presents itself at first sight, at the outset, as a factor of resistance, as an obstacle, is the only means we have for going on, and if our mere presentiment of change, progress, ever succeeds in it realizing itself, it must be because we can realize the very obstacles and make them into positive initiations, positive stimuli, for the maintenance of action. Of course this is exactly what happens in any scientific investigation. A scientific man has a theory all formulated about the sun, for instance, a theory which interprets all the facts that are known. Now suddenly, all by accident, or as the result of special research, he sees a lot of new phenomena, say peculiarities in the sun spots. Now these sense observations are obstacles. They represent the breakdown of his theory, of his coordinated system of ideas about the sun; and yet it is these very things with which he must deal to find positive clues for further advancement. That is the very meaning of the question. How shall these apparent obstacles be transformed into the positive stimulus? He would not inquire if there were not an obstacle, but the function of that inquiry is to take the obstacle and translate it into a classification of some sort.

Now ethically this means that our sense nature cannot be an obstacle, per se, to moral ends; and that there can be no ultimate moral dualism. That would be a psychological impossibility. You cannot have an ultimate dualism because our sense nature, which offers the obstacle to moral purpose, is the only medium of realization for those very aims or ends. It is the soil in which the moral seed must be planted. More than that, it is the only source of nutrition for that moral gain. The sense nature, then, does not represent a positive obstacle to moral action, it simply represents the necessity for a change in the direction of action. It is obstacle, not with reference to the ideal generically, but with reference to this or that end.

One point more, still in general. The very consciousness of it as an obstacle has a positive function to fulfill. If it were not for this resistance, our mere feelings of ends would [not?] be made over into definite and comprehensive form. It is the sense of the obstacle that keeps us at work in elaborating our ends. It would be sheer waste of time to build up elaborate ends if they were not required in order to function these apparent obstacles as stimuli. The consciousness of moral ends would have remained in the most chaotic condition if it had not been for the resistance which these ends meet in their execution. It is as it is with a scientific hypothesis. The scientific man forms an hypothesis which seems very nice and complete. He tries it on and it does not fit. Then he has to go back and put more meaning into the hypothesis. He has to make it more specific and accurate. It is the resistance which he meets which makes him conscious of its undeveloped condition and which sets him about working it out. It is just the same with our moral ends. If our moral ends are more definite; if they are more specifically presented to us than were those of two thousand years ago, it is simply because of the fact that those ends of two thousand years ago met this resistance, that they ran up against this sense obstacle, so that this sense element is a positively important factor, not merely because it furnishes the instruments of realization, but also furnishes the motive to the development of the ends themselves.

This includes* a discussion of the psychology of the intellectual process in this outline way. Two things remain concerning it, one of which I shall postpone till later on; the other of which I shall take up right away. The aspect which I shall postpone is the discussion of the fact that the habit of engaging in this intellectual process is the virtue which is known as conscientiousness: what the Greeks call wisdom, but we call it con-scientiousness. The discussion of the . . .† in this process and the habit of doing it, I shall postpone.†† . . . compared with certain other views. It involves the same principle already discussed, but it happens that there are historical views which run counter to this one and it may serve both to clear up this view and to give an organ of criticism if I go over this discussion of theories which seems to be inadequate. You will understand that if these theories did not happen to be current there would be no need for their discussion.

The point thus far made is that this process of deliberation has an intrinsic moral value because it is part of the evolution of selfhood. Now that point of view is challenged at once by the theories which maintain, either explicitly or implicitly, that this intellectual process is a mere antecedent of, or a mere concomitant of, the strictly ethical process. Those who take this view in general are subdivided into two schools, a division which we find running through ethical theory, the intuitive rigidistic school on the one side, and the empirical and hedonistic or utilitarian school on the other. The distinction between the Cynics and the Cyrenaics in the Greek thought, between the Epicureans and the Stoics of the Roman thought, and between intuitionalists and utilitarians in modern thought. Both [schools] agree in making an external relation between the delibera-tive process and the moral locus. Both virtually agree that this intellectual process, as a reflective one, has simply to do with the calculation of con-sequences. The intuitional school places the gist of the matter morally in an act of choice which lies outside of the deliberative process; and the other school finds it in the emotional values, in feeling, to which this deliberative process is merely antecedent and external. It is a mere means, not a necessary means. The intuitive school holds that morality is found in the motive which determines choice, and that that motive has no essential connection with the intellectual process.

The empirical school holds that morality depends upon consequences of acts, and that that is a matter which bears only an external relation to the intellectual process. They split motive from intention—motive being

---

* Probably "concludes."
† Unintelligible word in original hectograph copy.
†† First part of the sentence is unintelligible in the original hectograph copy.

that which impels to action, being found in the agent himself: therefore an intention which represents the foreseen consequences and has to do with the act as an overt act, not with anything in the agent himself. They distinguish between character and conduct, between agency and action. The intuitive school says that morality is measured by the motive impelling the act. The utilitarian school says it is measured by the results in conduct, by the act which the agent happens to put forth. Now they agree in spite of this opposition in that they make this split between character and conduct, between agency and action, and they make that split because they fail to see that the intellectual process is the mediator from one to the other—that the intellectual process is the real bridge over which the character passes into conduct, and the agent realizes himself in action.

The problem then, which meets us, is the discussion of the difference between motive and intention. Up to a certain point both schools agree in their definitions of motive and intention. We ask a child: Did you mean to do it? And the child says: I did not mean to do it. Now that is intention; having an idea of the thing before it was done and having that idea somehow operate in effecting action. Intention is what a man aims to do, and everybody is agreed that an act has no quality at all unless one meant to do it, or meant to do something like it. No one is held legally responsible if it can be shown that he did not mean to do the thing, unless he was culpably careless. The motive is why a man means to do this or that particular thing. Why did you mean to do this rather than something else? What gave this intention a hold on you and made it an impelling force? A man means to kill someone; that is his intention. But his motive may be patriotic, as a soldier in battle. His motive may be self-defense, or obedience to law (as when a sheriff hangs a man), or it may be avarice. The intention would be the same, simply the deliberate aim to kill the person. The motive would vary according to the actuating reason which made him intend to do this particular thing. There is something important in the distinction. The question is: What is the significance, what is the real distinction between what a man aims to do and why he aims to do it? Is the distinction really a separation? Can we draw any marked lines between motive and intention, or do motive and intention represent typical stages in our intellectual analysis of an act so that there is no real objective difference between the two at all, but simply one of convenience in representing to ourselves certain phases of the concrete whole? Of course which [sic] I shall try to make is the latter; that intention represents a more or less superficial analysis of the aim which has its own reason for being, and the motive stands for a more or less fundamental analysis, carrying the act back to a deeper level.

I would like to say that you will find in the *Syllabus of Ethics* quite a number of references which give pretty much all the discussion that there is on this question in English since the time of James Mill.[6]

SECTION 5. MOTIVE
AND INTENTION IN
MORAL JUDGMENT

I shall take up the discussion from both ends and show first that what the intuitionalist calls the motive has nothing to do at all if you separate it from intention—that is, taking him on his own basis; and then try to show that, taking the utilitarian on his own statement, the intention has no meaning when it is separated from motive.

February 2, 1898

I begin with the school which attaches moral value to character, or to motive, in the sense in which it is distinguished from the act on the side of intention. The first proposition is that the impelling motive, used in a sense in which it is distinguished from the anticipation of consequences, has no specific psychological meaning and has no moral content attached to it. [By contrast I hold] that the impelling motive, in any sense in which it can be said to have moral bearing and quality, instead of being exclusive of the anticipation of consequences, always includes the latter, and is determined by the latter. If we leave out intention or anticipation of consequences, there is nothing left excepting the bare feeling—in the popular sense of the word feeling—a bare impulse; and that feeling or impulse is simply one factor which emerges in the process of defining self, of defining conduct. It is in no sense coextensive with the whole of the operation, or it is in no sense by itself an adequate representative of the self. It simply expresses the self taken in one particular phase or attitude, just as the anticipation of consequences presents us with the self in another, and the whole of the moral valuation of the self can be found only in the inter-action of these two.

I take the illustration from Bentham's *Principles of Morals and Legislation,* page 107.

> To the pleasures of curiosity corresponds the motive known by the same name: and which may be otherwise called the love of novelty, or the love of experiment; and, on particular occasions, sport, and sometimes play.
>
> 1. A boy, in order to divert himself, reads an improving book: the motive is accounted, perhaps a good one: at any rate not a bad one. 2. He sets his top a spinning: the motive is deemed, at any rate, not a bad one. 3. He sets loose a mad ox among a crowd; his motive is now, perhaps, termed an abominable one. Yet in all three cases the motive may be the very same: it may be neither more nor less than curiosity.[7]

Consequently, Bentham, who of course is an anti-intuitionalist, says that there is no such thing as any sort of motive that is in itself a bad one, or that no motives are constantly good or bad. If they are good or bad it is from the effect. And as to their effects it appears that they are sometimes bad and at other times either indifferent or good. In the remainder of the chapter he gives a whole lot of instances, of which I have simply quoted one.

Now if we admit that there are any such impulses or motives as that expressed here by the term curiosity, Bentham's statement that no moral quality attaches to them in themselves—they may be good, bad or indifferent, according to circumstances—seems to me entirely unanswerable. It is the object or end to which that feeling or impulse attaches that gives it its moral value. If it is directed in one way, we call it good; if it is used in another way, we call it bad; or if it functions in still another way, we say it is morally indifferent. It may be said that that is not true in the case of all feelings. Take feelings like compassion or sympathy or generosity: that they would be intrinsically right or possessed of moral quality, and that others like indolence, maliciousness, and avarice would be intrinsically possessed of bad quality, and that the illustration which I have chosen seems to prove the contrary [is] only because it belongs to the class that are indifferent. Regarding that latter proposition I would say two things. In the first place, in all such terms as benevolence, malice, avarice, we tend to shove in something besides the mere feeling or impulse in itself. We tend to conceive it as already attached to an end. In other words we are not dealing with pure impulses or feelings at all, but with impulses or feelings that are operative with relation to the results that are anticipated. We are speaking of interests, not mere feelings. That would be the case with reference to avarice. There is no such feeling as avarice. If we go back to the instinctive psychology of childhood we may find a passion for collecting, but that passion would not be evil per se. It is evil only when it takes a particular bent which interferes with the rights of others or the person's own development. The same may be said of malice. It represents, not a bare feeling, but a feeling interpreted by being attached to a certain type of end. We may find, in going back to childhood again, an instinctive pleasure in teasing, but an adequate interpretation of that would show that the real animating motive is to show one's own power, to feel one's self reflected in a social act. That is mischievousness, and while that may lend itself to bad interests, so also it may be treated so as to function in a right direction. So the force of the statement [that some motives are intrinsically bad] depends largely upon our failure to analyze it, and upon our using the term feeling or impulse in two quite different senses—one the legitimate psychological sense, and the other putting into it the whole content of the problem under discussion, namely the reference to anticipated consequences or to ends.

The other point is that when we do take such a thing as benevolence, or pity, or vanity, as mere feeling, it is absolutely without moral quality. There is hardly any supposition which is the root of more mischief practically, than just that sort of supposition. That leads to the sort of cases where a man excuses himself for acting in an unregulated way by saying that he meant well; and that means that he had certain feelings that he wanted to gratify, and there is no more morality in gratifying the feeling of benevolence than in gratifying the feeling of hunger. Simply to act for the mere indulgence of feeling apart from its objective interpretation with reference to the kind of act that it is going to result in, is bad. It is just as necessary for a man to control his benevolent impulses as it is to control his instinctive feelings of aversion to a certain person; or his instinctive impulses to protect himself.

The other moral question refers simply to the way in which the individual makes those impulses operate in action. Towards what sort of an end does one make them function? It is safe to say that what the intuitionalist has in mind when he says that the moral quality attaches to motive is that he is conceiving of motive as equivalent to interest. Now interest, objective interest, involves what the other school terms the intention. It is the active attitude toward a certain end. It is an active attitude. That is, not a mere attitude of passive contemplation but an attitude which is directed toward the realization of that end, toward transforming it from mere idea into actual fact. It is an attitude because it manifests the whole self, or the whole character defined in a specific way with reference to this particular and instead of some other possible end. Now these ends, then, to which the impulses are attached with reference to which they are made to function and so are transformed into this active attitude; these ends are the presentation of consequences which are anticipated to result from the operation of the impulse. I shall not go over that again. That is simply the whole import of the deliberative process to present the impulse in objective terms, to anticipate the kind of situation it will give rise to if acted upon, and therefore to direct this impulse in its expression. The motive is thus the original impulse or feeling determined, illuminated, through its intellectual interpretation, and the latter is the intention. It is what a man means to do.

One of the chief reasons, I think, which has militated against the recognition of this fact that the motive is a meaningless thing excepting as it comprehends the anticipation of results is that such a narrow content has been given to the term consequences. The consequences have been thought of as necessarily meaning simple pleasure or pain, or they have been thought of somehow as merely external results which happen to occur if one acts upon a certain motive. Now the first point I do not propose to discuss here, as to whether or not the consequences are to be reduced to mere pains or pleasures. That is another and further problem. Of course the whole tendency of what I have been saying is that they could not be reduced to pleasure or pain. But on the second point it must be realized that the consequences are in no sense something extrinsic. We do not have the motive *and* its anticipated results. The anticipated results are the impulse presented to one's self in intellectual terms. What anger is, what benevolence is, what pity is, we do not know except as we conceive of them in terms of the outcome. The outcome is the impulse manifested, and how should we get hold of a thing excepting in its own realization? If we sever it from its manifestation, of course, there is nothing left to us; we are simply playing with abstractions. The consequences of the act are the consequence of the act—that is to say, its importance and meaning. We get into the habit of considering certain consequences as more or less intrinsic, and of others as more or less extrinsic. The intrinsic consequences are those we are most accustomed to have happen, and the extrinsic are those we are not looking for. It may turn out that the consequences that we had thought to be extrinsic are really part of the normal outcome of the working of the impulse itself, and then we must change our whole view of the matter. In any case it is the business of the individual every time to anticipate the consequences which a reasonable being would regard as relevant if he took an impartial view of the situation. That of course is tautology. The reasonable being is one who does take an impartial view of the situation. A man under certain circumstances would not hesitate about eating fruits because he had never found them to be attended by consequences that were evil; but if he were sick he would be obliged to take into account, he would be obliged to anticipate, the possibility of consequences and to control the satisfaction of his appetite correspondingly. So no hard and rigid line can be drawn between the intrinsic and extrinsic consequences.

Now I will turn to the utilitarian side of the matter. I might say in passing that there is one phase of the separation of motive and intention, the Kantian, of which I have not spoken here. It is a peculiar development of the theory and I will not complicate matters by going into it now.

The utilitarian says that morality is measured by consequences: that the motive may have something to do with the worth of the agent, in Mill's language, but it has nothing to do with the morality of the action. The morality of the action is dependent upon the intention, and the intention is the consequence foreseen. Now the point I shall try to make here is, that just as the other side's use of the term motive is ambiguous, shifting about from the mere psychical impulse to that impulse as operative for a certain end, so the utilitarian's use of the term content is ambiguous. He is shifting about from *de facto* consequences to conceived consequences. When we confine him to the first standpoint his statement ceases to have any meaning, and when we take him from the latter standpoint it is impossible any longer to separate intention from motive.

I am going to begin the discussion with the footnote on pages 26–27 of Mill's *Utilitarianism*.[8]

      There is no point which utilitarian thinkers . . . have taken more pains to illustrate than this. The morality of the action depends entirely upon the intention—that is, upon what the agent *wills to do*. But the motive, that is, the feeling which makes him will so to do, if it makes no difference in the act, makes none in the morality: though it makes a great difference in our moral estimation of the agent especially if it indicates a good or bad habitual *disposition*—a bent of character from which useful, or from which fruitful actions are likely to arise.

The point there to which I wish to call your attention is: "The motive, that is, the feeling which makes him will so to do, when [*sic*] it makes no difference in the act." It is conceivable that there should be a motive that makes no difference in the act. If we admit that little clause, I think Mill's position cannot be controverted. If it can be controverted, it will be that as a matter of fact the feeling which impels him to action not only makes a difference in our estimation of his character but that it also makes a difference in our estimation of the particular act.

Mill quotes from Mr. Davies:

> Surely the rightness or wrongness of saving a man from drowning does depend very much upon the motive with which it is done. Suppose that a tyrant, when his enemy jumped into the sea to escape from him, saved him from drowning simply in order that he might inflict upon him more exquisite tortures, would it tend to clearness to speak of that rescue as a "morally right action"?

Now Mr. Mill answers:

> I submit that he who saves another from drowning in order to kill him by torture afterwards, does not differ only in motive from him who does the same thing from duty or benevolence; the act itself is different. The rescue of the man is, in the case supposed, only the necessary first step of an act far more atrocious than leaving him to drown would have been.

Now of course the point I want to make is that what Mill says there has to be said regarding every instance: that these two cases do differ, not only in motive, but that the act itself is different. The act externally is the same in both cases: one man pulls another man out of the water. The whole question is: What kind of an act is that? And Mill himself has to admit that *what* kind of an act it is depends upon the whole context of the act, the sort of a system of which that act is a part. It depends upon the reason for which that act was done, and if you isolate that act from the system to which it belongs you have no basis left upon which to pass upon it morally. Or in other words, what Mill says here is that the "rescue of the man is only the necessary first step of an act far more atrocious than leaving him to drown would have been." Generalizing that, I would say that the intention which we distinguish from motive is only that first step, and the only reason for distinguishing the intention from the motive is because we have occasion to distinguish between the first overt act and the whole act of which that is a part.

If you simply take intention in the narrowest sense how can Mill say that the act is different? In either case the man means to save the life of this other person. If he does make a difference it is simply because he has to take into account a larger intention of which that act is simply a partial expression, and my point is that the larger intention will always be identical with the motive. What we have is a distinction between means and end where they are not external but the means represent the realized content of the end. The motive and the end are always identical. The intention represents the analysis of the end into its approximate means.

To go back to Bentham's case on the other side. No one intends merely to set a wild ox loose, or intends merely to read a useful book; or so far as he does intend merely to do so, there is no moral quality in the act. It gets moral quality only when we regard it as approximate execution of a motive. In the illustration of yesterday, no one intends merely to kill another man. He intends to do his duty as a soldier, and that comes in as the means—not external means but as a part of the end. He means to defend himself, and the killing of another man is incidental to that; or he intends to conform to the law as a sheriff and so he kills another man. He intends to kill that other man, but that is only a part of the larger intention; and you have his interest, you have his impulses attached to certain anticipated results, and they function for the sake of bringing about the realization of those results as anticipated.

I shall take two cases which I have discussed in the *Syllabus of Ethics* of those who deny the identity of the ultimate intention and the motive.[9] One is the case by Bentham. On pages 85–87 [of *The Principles of Morals and Legislation*] he gives nine different alternatives of the case of the shooting of the English king William II by Tyrral. He shot at a deer, and the arrow swerved and killed the king. Now Bentham's second case was this:

> He saw a stag running that way, and he saw the king riding that way at the same time: what he aimed at was to kill the stag: he did not wish to kill the king: at the same time he saw, that if he shot, it was as likely he should kill the king as the stag: yet for all that he shot, and killed the king accordingly. In this case the incident of his killing the king was intentional, but obliquely so.[10]

It might not at first sight seem that he really meant to kill the king, but insofar as he anticipated that as a possible consequence at all, it must seem that it entered his intention and indicated his interest. He was a man who had not sufficient regard for human life to refrain from the pleasure that he would get in killing the deer. It therefore was a part of his intention and can be used in indicating both what kind of an act it was, and also it indicates what sort of a man he was in doing it. On the other hand, if he did not foresee that consequence at all, then of course it had no bearing on the question of intention, or the question of motive.

The other case is that given by MacKenzie, who says that the killing of Caesar was no part of the motive of Brutus; that Brutus did intend to kill Caesar but that it was no part of his motive.[11] That is a perfectly unintelligible statement. We may say his motive was patriotism or that it was ambition. Of course a man is not actuated by patriotism at large, nor is he actuated by ambition at large. Whether his motive was patriotism or ambition, it includes within itself the killing of Caesar. He was moved to act by the thought of Caesar as dead. That thought actually impelled him to action. Not that thought in its isolation, but neither is the murdered impelled in that way. It is the relationship that attaches to that anticipation: that he will have revenge or get money, etc.

We cannot tell what the intention really is until we know the motive. We cannot judge the act really until we know the motive. A great variety of authors make this difference between judgment of the agent and the judgment of the act. Kant and Green differ from Mill and say we cannot judge the agent. All we have to go by is the overt act. Now I would say that if that is all we have, we have no right to judge the act either from any moral point of view. We never can say an act is right or wrong until we know what the real intention reflected in that act was, and if we know the ultimate intention we know the motive and are in a position to pass judgment on the character.

February 3, 1898

As I suggested yesterday, the utilitarian's use of the concept of consequences is ambiguous. At different times he means different things when he says that the morality of an act depends upon its consequences. And it is that ambiguity which prevents him from realizing the organic connection between intention and motive. Sometimes he says we must judge the act on the basis of its actual results or consequences. At other times he says we must judge the act on the basis of intention or foreseen consequences. Now when he says the latter, the gap between his statement and that which says that morality depends upon motive is very slight, because it is the foreseen consequences as moving to action, as interest, as having a hold on the attention and getting motor force, that make up the intention; and of course when we take them in that way it is practically the same thing as the motive itself. Otherwise there will be no difference between this intention and any purely objective scientific contemplation, if we leave out the interesting features of the consequences as foreseen.

The connecting link between his two ambiguous senses of consequences is, without doubt, the following: intention is foresight of probable consequences, but in framing that foresight one has to have recourse to past consequences. One has no way of telling what the probable results of a certain course of action are, excepting by reference to similar cases in his own past experience, or in other men's experience. So what the utilitarian really means is that the rightness of any act will depend upon its foreseen, anticipated, consequences as they are worked out on the basis of past experience. It is not the mere consequences of some past act which makes us say that that act was right or wrong. It is those consequences as used in helping us determine what we shall do next. It is those consequences as set before one's self in imagination in the process of evaluating the next line of action. For example, take the stock instance: a surgeon performs an operation which results in a man's death. If the utilitarian meant what he seems to mean in saying that the act is judged simply by its consequences, he would call that a wrong act; he could not distinguish between that and willful murder. But what he has in mind really is that when that surgeon, or other surgeons who know of the case, come in the future to judge of the rightness of a further act of a somewhat similar character, they must take into account the past consequences of acts of the same general sort; and that excepting as they do thus reflect on the proposed act in the light of similar acts already performed, they have no basis for deciding whether it is right or wrong.

I hope you see the difference, then, between judging of an act simply by its consequences as they have already occurred, and utilizing that particular experience with its results to determine the wrongness or rightness of a proposed act which exists only in anticipation. What the utilitarian has in mind in all his constructive work is the latter use of the consequences. It is on that basis that he criticizes the intuitionalist who says that morality simply attaches to motive, in that sense in which motive means an original impulse in a given direction. And from that point of view there can be no doubt that the utilitarian is right.

As I said yesterday, the mere impulse, the mere motive in a given direction, is without moral quality unless it is weighed with the sort of results it is likely to lead up to, and of course in figuring on what sort of results it is likely to lead up to, we must realize past experience. The man who says: "My motive is right and I must therefore act upon it without reference to probable consequences, or without reference to how similar motives when acted on have turned out in the past," is a monomaniac. He is under the influence of a compulsory idea. His whole moral consciousness is rigid.

What the utilitarian stands for is keeping the character fertile by bringing judgment to bear upon impulses as they present themselves. As soon as we realize that that is really what the utilitarian means by the morality of an act depending upon consequences, namely, that we must utilize past consequences in determining the value of any proposed direction of action, the supposed gulf between intention and motive has disappeared.

We start from the impulse to act in a given direction. We want to see what its probable outcome would be if it were acted upon. We want to measure its real worth in some sort of objective terms, and to do that we have recourse to our recollection of other actions along the same general line. So that what we get when we are through with that process is simply the original impulse mediated and interpreted, put over into objective content, through material supplied in the medium of the imagination. Intention, what one means to do, is simply the judgment passed upon the impulse—that is, the recognition of its quality on the objective side and the concrete union of the impulse and its meaning. That is to say, the impulse worked out in terms of its meaning is a motive.

We may get at the same result by insisting upon the utilitarian's raising the question: "Why does the individual form a certain intention, foresee certain consequences? How does it happen that he sets up a certain intention? Where does that come from? Where is his point of contact with his consciousness and with his present experience?" The question suggests its own answer. He formulates this intention because he has a certain tendency in a certain direction. He is somewhat doubtful about carrying that impulse into effect and he asks himself: "What will this impulse signify? What will be its consequences if I act upon it?" And the answer is: it is the intention. The formation of the intention thus presupposes a motive, and the motive is worked up, elaborated, cleared up, in the intention. There is always a motive, not merely to the act: there is a motive to forming the intention, there is a reason why we mean so and so—that motive of course being found in the underlying tendency to act. The formation of intention is necessary that we may know what we are about, that we may act sensibly. All that intention means is that we may know what we are doing, that we may put a certain estimate or value in consciousness upon the thing that we are about to do. Intention thus states the whole of action, and the motive is not merely why we do a thing, it is also the final statement of what we do.

It is false psychology to put the motive as something antecedent strictly to the action and then impelling the self on toward that action. The motive simply expresses the hold of the proposed line of action upon the working self. It simply measures the presence of the self in the projected scheme of action. I set and think of twenty things, all possibilities. Some go through my mind as daydreams. They do not move me, because they only reflect myself to a very superficial degree. Some other proposed suggestions stir me deeply. The very fact that I am so stirred shows that it is not something outside me. The stirring is the index of the extent to which I find myself already present in that proposed mode of action. The intention therefore establishes the identity of the agent with the act in the intellectual sense. If a man injures another by an absolute accident, we do not consider it his act at all. It is a mere event of nature. As legal phraseology has it in extreme cases, it is the "act of God" which relieves the person of responsibility. But we do not in any case consider it the person's act unless we find that he was willing to have it happen. That is what I mean by saying that the intention establishes the identity between the act and the agent, and the motive takes that same relationship at a deeper level. It establishes the identity of the practical and emotional sides as well as upon the intellectual.

It is simply the completed consciousness of the organic identity of agent and act, of character and conduct.

There is one more point I should like to make here. This transformation from intention into motive is going on all the time in the process of deliberation. It is not merely a terminal point. It is often presented as if there were a conflict of intentions, possible purposes for a while, and that finally one of those was settled upon and became the motive. But as a matter of fact all the shading and emphasis of attention all through the process of deliberation is a process of changing intention into motive. A suggestion comes before the mind. Does it awaken interest? Does it arouse and hold the attention at all? Insofar as it does, it is just insofar a motive, and it becomes *the* motive when it gets the exclusive hold of attention. There is no difference in principle in the hold which an idea has upon the mind in the process of reflection, and the hold which it finally has in overt action. It is a distinction of degree, not of kind.

I will take one more example. A man falls on the ice and breaks his arm and suffers pain. If the utilitarian really means what he seems to mean, he would call it a vicious act because it interferes with other lines of action. What the utilitarian does mean to say is that if it came to a question of doing that thing a second time, that that person or other persons who knew of that result are morally bound to take that into account in forming their intention, and allow it to have some weight, some influence. Therefore an individual who did that a second time without due consideration would be morally culpable. We really have no way of estimating the value of projects of action, suggestions, impulses, excepting as we look at them in the light of their probable consequences; and that of course is the point of view to which our whole psychological discussion brought us.

What the utilitarian finally stands for is opposition to an abstract view of character. Ordinarily he opposes conduct to character from the standpoint of the moral judgment. But what he is really protesting against is that partial view of character which identifies it with mere feelings and impulses, a view of character which shuts it up in a self-embodied entity cut off from its manifestation in overt action. What he means positively is that character can be judged only as seen in action, and that when we pass judgment on our own character we do it either as it actually shows itself in conduct or as we imagine it in action. We consider it as if we were acting by anticipation and thus get a basis for estimating character; but excepting as we take it actually in action, or view it dramatically as if in action, we have no criterion for deciding whether this or that trait of character is worthy or unworthy.

On the other side, what the intuitionalist stands for is the necessity of judging conduct in its relation to the self. What he really means, as distinct from what he nominally means, is that to get any standpoint for valuing conduct we must view it as the expression of the self, as embodying the interests and motives of the self.

Character and conduct are thus strictly reciprocal. In fact they are so reciprocal that the real problem is: Why do we distinguish them? Since there is no character excepting as manifested in conduct, and there is no conduct excepting that which expresses character, why should we have the two concepts? The reply is that it is convenient and valuable to regard the self from two points of view: the point of view of initiating action, and the point of view of the outcome of action—just the distinction between the organism and the environment which some of you had last term.[12] We wan to know what we have to start with, what our resources are. That standpoint of initiation, of the start out, is that which defines the concept of character. Now we also want to know how these tendencies are going to come out, what their upshot is going to be. We want to know, if we start from here, where we are likely to go to. (It is only so that we value the initial side.) We must get its bearings before we have a standard for measuring its worth, and that standpoint defines the concept of conduct.

Put in slightly other language, character means capacity, means equipment, but the only way to determine the value of that equipment is to see what we can do with it, to see what we can accomplish or secure with it. And when we get to the standpoint of attainment we are on the side of conduct. Character, then, is not a fixed thing—that is, all made up. It is simply the available resources, or the equipment, and like any statement of resources it becomes utterly meaningless the moment we make it a finality in itself. When we are talking about resources, we are talking about something which we can do, not about something that has been done.

Of course ethically, the question involved here is the possibility of reform. If character were a finality, something fixed and accomplished, then a good man would always stay good and a bad man would stay bad. But since character means simply resources or instruments for further action, since it has to be defined, not on the side of what has been done, but on the side of what is going to be done, there is always in character the possibility of change, of development.

SECTION 6. INTUITIVE AND DISCURSIVE FACTORS IN MORAL JUDGMENT

The question we have been discussing thus far is: What is known or thought of as having moral value attached to it? We come now to another aspect of the intellectual process: How do we know it? Presumably we have settled the question of the what, that which we judge. We have not discussed another side of the controversy between the intuitionalists and utilitarians: of how it is that we judge.

In fact this controversy is so mixed up by the participants in it with the previous one that it adds to the confusion which hangs around the whole matter. The intuitionalist not only holds that what we judge is the motive in a sense apart from consequences, but he holds that we know the rightness or wrongness of that motive immediately, without any reference to experience or any reflection. That is why he is called an intuitionalist. The utilitarian is an empiricist and holds that there is no immediate knowledge of right and wrong, that we must use our judgment and memory in this question as we would in any business or scientific question. The proposition advanced on this point is first, as already suggested, that both an intuitional and an empirical factor, in the psychological sense, enter into the way in which we decide moral questions; but that neither of them separately, nor both of them taken together, decide the morality of the act in any final sense. Psychologically both factors are concerned, but morally neither of them nor both together decide the matter. On the other hand it is the intellectual process in its intuitive and discursive aspect that shows the kind of morality already existing; they manifest and they test the kind of a person one is. They have to be tested by reference to something behind them instead of their having an ultimate criterion of morality in themselves. So we have two points of discussion.

I begin with the first. Every project, every purpose as project or purpose is intuitive. The very fact it is thrown ahead shows that there is something new in it and it is an impossibility to get the new out of the old by any amount of jugglery of the past. We may say that everything remains the same but differently arranged. This different arrangement however is a novelty; so we attempt to get rid of the new element by reducing all quality back to identity of quantity with change of form. But the change of form still has to be accounted for. We might as well recognize the problem of novelty frankly as to try to jugglery it out of sight. You cannot account for its being there by mere manipulation of past data as past; you must recognize an element of movement, a process of ongoing action in those past elements before you will get anything more out of them. Psychologically the novel element represents a consciousness of the ongoing movement—this being brought to consciousness through a conflict which throws this tendency into relief by bringing it in contrast with the obstacles which have hemmed it in and which are relatively stationary. With a project, a proposition, there is no focus to the reflective empirical side of our intellectual process, and there is no limit set up.

There would be no point to our reflective process, and there would be no control of it, any holding it within bounds, if it were not for the intuitive element. And that reference to past experience as the discursive side of our intellectual activity is held down to a certain limit beyond which it does not go. It has a certain pivot about which it all revolves, and that pivot is set for us by the intuitive factor. If we were left merely at the mercy of the discursive process, logically the thing would go on forever; there is no end to consequences that we could imagine, and the past experiences that we might call up. Where would we stop? How far would we go in reflection on our past experience and in imagining new combinations and possibilities, in anticipating future action, if there were not all the time the project of some fundamental interest of our own to determine what is relevant and what irrelevant, and keep us within a certain scope or field?

February 7, 1898

At the last hour I was speaking of the intuitive element in the deliberative process. I tried to show that there always would be such an intuitive projection because it marks really the means of activity as ongoing. It is that which is projected. We throw it on ahead of us some way. And I showed that the value of that must be to supply a focus for the discursive process and to furnish the limits within which it should go on.

So far as this intuitive element fails in any given character, you would find that character irresolute and subject to the paralysis of doubt and scepticism. You would certainly have a wavering, unstable person, and in morbid cases we get the insanity of doubt where every suggestion is questioned. They do not get as far as reflecting on the means for doing a thing, because no project comes up before them that is not immediately replaced with another. It occurs to a man that he will wash his hands and he at once thinks maybe the water is poisoned, infected with disease. No matter what occurs to him, the skeptical attitude arises and it may be hours before the person can bring himself to do anything.

In terms of our discussion it marks the failure of this projective power of the activity which manifests itself in the positivity of the intuition. It is this intuitional element which supplies the factor of self reliance, of independence; the element of directness, of freshness and originality as distinct from the type of character which is conventional and second handed, a type where one is always dependent upon thinking what someone else will think about the thing before he can come to a positive conclusion about the matter. Furthermore, this intuitive projection will be prominent just in the degree in which interests are well organized or systematized. You will find this intuitive element in the play of a child insofar as the play has a unity of value and meaning which tends to continually evoke new suggestions and carry out those suggestions. But we find it most prominent in the expert of any kind, in the man of professional or technical skill, in the artist, and in the social life in what is known as tact. It is the immediate response to any presented situation, the response which takes the form of at once striking out, blazing out a possible mode of dealing with the situation. The painter, the sculptor, the architect, the landscape gardener, the carpenter, the host or hostess of large social experience, all these would suggest cases where this intuitive projective response is prominent.

I think one reason why this element has tended to be minimized by psychologists and ethical writers is because they are engaged in professions where the intuitive element is at a discount and the reflective factor is at a maximum, and consequently the accounts which may be true of their own individual experience become much less applicable when we transfer them to people whose lines of action lie in constructive immediate directions, as engineers, generals, men of affairs upon the whole.

As we go toward that type which is distinct from the investigator and reflector, we find the intuitive element relatively assuming a more important place. If that is the real meaning of the intuitional element, it is hardly necessary to say that it possesses no final moral value. It possesses value for conduct, but there is no decisive criterion for value here. The worth of the intuition will depend upon what kind of a character you have there; it will depend upon the sort of a man one is. The intuitions of a good man will be good and the intuitions of a bad man will be bad, and that is the proof of the badness of a bad man that even his suggestions have become perverse and deflected. If you could get hold of a man's intuitions, you would have a sure index of his moral character. They reveal his balance or one-sidedness, and they reveal his predominating interest and his amount of organized activity in any given direction. But the forger and the burglar have their intuitions which serve to regulate their conduct just as the philanthropist or moral hero has his intuitions which serve to regulate his action.

So we cannot say that the fact that intuition exists throws any light upon the content of that intuition. Hence the necessity of the empirical factor. This intuitive suggestion must be tested. One must examine into its worth. We must see what it is like in detail, what it will mean when it is carried out. It is counting the cost and making the plans when the idea occurs of building a house. That may be intuitive, but before one knows how valuable that suggestion is, one has to go through a certain amount of putting it, placing it, intellectually. That involves the recourse to past experience, of which I spoke before.

The exact character and relationship of the empirical and intuitive factors is thus always an individual matter. Consequently no general rule can be laid down as to the amount of one as compared with the other which is morally necessary. Some individuals, some classes, some vocations, probably one or other of the sexes have a distinctly different ratio in this matter. In one the intuitive element may predominate and in the other the empirical element may be most prominent. And about all that can be said is that anybody and everybody should get the benefit of his strong point, while checking that by being aware that it involves a certain danger.

Suppose a man of an intuitive type should systematically distrust his ways of arriving at conclusions. He would succeed in depriving his action of all effectiveness. If he lost that criterion, he could not get anything in its place. So of the person who has to arrive at conclusions by a more logical and analytic process. But on the other hand the intuitive type may be sufficiently aware of the danger of unreflective, impulsive action to strengthen the weak spots and to guard against going off at a tangent; while the empirical type must remember that that tendency carries with it a danger in the direction of over-prudence, over-caution, of secretiveness and reserve which tends toward selfishness. That is, in terms of types of character, the failure of balance on the side of intuitive form would give us persons expansive, generous, and outgoing in their conduct, but tending to be unreasonable and capricious, and capable of doing a good deal of mischief with the very best intentions. The over-reflective type would lend itself to this endeavor, to guarantee all possible results in advance, and would dislike to act until one could become certain that it was going to turn out just right for one's self—an endeavor to eliminate all the risks, which leads to selfishness.

For it must be remembered that the value of the consideration of past experience is not to set up from the beginning the end of action. It is simply as a measure, as a test, the ultimate ongoing in action. It is a stating of one's self. While the object of reflection is to reduce the element of venture and of risk to reasonable limits by illuminating the proposed course of action, it is not to eliminate absolutely that factor of risk and of uncertainty. That experimental element must remain in order that character may be tested. That is the lasting truth I think in the religious formula which has played so large a part in Puritan development: that life is a probation, that man is on trial all the time, and that the kind of intuitions he sets up and the kinds of responses are not only manifestations of character but are tests of character bringing out the weak points and bracing up the strong.

The ultimate test, then, of both the intuitive and discursive factors is found in action. They in themselves are tentative and experimental. They are both hypothetical. They are instrumental. That is, they exist for the sake of unifying the course of action, and their success can only be measured in that test of action. They are working hypotheses whose ultimate value can only be found by acting upon them and seeing what happens.

In terms of character this means that the conscientious man deliberates with reference to the needs of action. He does not indulge in self-scrutiny at large or in general, but with reference to the actual needs of the situation. Then, when he has reached the conclusion, instead of holding that rigidly, he submits it to the test of action and is therefore open and anxious to learn from the results of his own test. The conscientious man is the exact counterpart of the experimentor in science; a man that frames an hypothesis in the light of the data at command, then submits that to experimentation, and then revises his hypothesis, measuring it by the light of the actual outcome.

I shall come again to conscientiousness as a virtue, but I will here note the fact that the conception of conscientiousness is apt to be one-sided, emphasizing simply the necessity of acting upon the idea after it has been once formed, but neglecting the equal necessity of revising the idea by the fuller content which is given it in action. The man that merely says, "I had to follow my conscience," and who does not equally say, "I have to keep my conscience open and flexible to learn from the results that I get when I act conscientiously," is a dangerous man. We may not call him vicious, but the fact that we do not is probably due to the limited progress of our moral standards. Of course this decides in principle the whole question of criterion. I do not mean that it gives us a ready-made answer as to just what things are right and wrong, but it shows us the nature of criterion which is used normally in the decision of matters of right and wrong.

SECTION 7. THE RECIPROCITY
OF THOUGHT AND ACTION
IN MORALS

Before I come to that point more specifically I want to speak again of this question of the relation between knowledge and action. I have said that this whole intellectual process, the whole knowledge process, both on its intuitive and discursive sides, takes place because of the need of action and is itself tested and valued by passing over into action.

Now we are all familiar with the so-called Socratic paradox that knowledge is virtue, that the man who knows the good will of necessity do it, and that wrongdoing is always involuntary and due to ignorance; that the fact that the man does the bad is proof positive that he does not know the good, that he takes the bad to be the good, so that the only virtue comes to be wisdom, and the only vice ignorance. Is the result we have identical with that, or if not, what is the distinction?

The modern attitude, the popular attitude on the whole is very averse to this Socratic-Platonic theory. We call it a paradox. It seems strained, forced, unreal to us; and moralists of all schools are fond of calling attention to the fact that it is a matter of commonest experience that we know the better and then follow the worse; that everybody knows really much more than he does and that the real need is not for more knowledge but for more active motivation to act upon the good that we already know.

And yet it is possible that there is more truth in the Socratic statement than in this modern reaction from it. Or at least, it is possible that there is a truth in the Socratic statement which is entirely untouched by this criticism that we continually know the better and then do the worse. The real question is: What is the nature of moral knowledge? And the Socratic statement at least lends itself to this interpretation. I do not mean that that is just what Socrates and Plato meant by it, but it lends itself to this interpretation: that that only is knowledge which issues in action. If it is put that way, then of course the statement is identical with the point we have reached, that the deliberative process itself is not the final criterion of moral value; but it has to be tested by passing into action, and it is that action which reveals its worth.

With the invention of printing and the multiplication of means of communication, knowledge has come to have two meanings. The early Greeks, at least before Plato, had only one. With Aristotle we begin to have the two. It is direct knowledge which is realized, and if a man does not realize a thing he does not know it. And so the Socratic paradox in its modern interpretation would be: if a man realizes a thing, unless he is crazy he will act on it. The knowledge that is not acted upon is simply symbolical.

February 8, 1898

The two significances of knowledge spoken of yesterday are those of knowledge of and knowledge about. Of course it is true that knowledge about moral truths gives no more guarantee for right action than would knowledge about mathematics or hydraulics. Of course what Socrates had in mind was not this knowledge about. It was direct and immediate knowledge of. The image of knowledge which was in the Greek mind was that of participation in reality. The earlier philosophers bring that out in clear, even if crude ways: that the act of knowing is one in which the reality is somehow absorbed in the knowing self, or in which the knowing self somehow actually takes a share of participation in the object. Now with that highly direct and immediate conception of knowledge in view the Socratic statement loses practically all its paradoxical character.

I spoke yesterday of the multiplication of books and of means of communication as having introduced the second sense in which the term knowledge is used. Another great means was that of formulative education. Schools in which anything approaching our methods of professional teaching began with the Sophists who were almost Socrates' contemporaries. Now, that making learning a professional thing which may be communicated, taught, by one to another, presupposes that there is a certain body of knowledge which is external and objective, which does lie outside of the immediate personality, and which therefore may be handed around from one to another. As that conception of formulated education grew, it tended to reinforce this idea of knowledge which did not directly affect the individual and his conduct because it could be transferred from one person, the teacher, to another person, the pupil. Much of the virulence of the attack on the Sophists, that they bought and sold knowledge, wisdom, or tried to, is a reflex reaction of the personal coloring and therefore the moral coloring which had attached to knowledge before this time. If knowledge is a personal and moral thing, to make it a matter of barter is to make it like any other act of prostituting spiritual matter to material ends.

In its essence then, the Socratic position is a theory about what moral knowledge really is. Nothing can be called genuine moral consciousness excepting insofar as it does show itself in action. There is no doubt, however, that Plato at least and possibly Socrates went further than this and conceived of this identity of wisdom and virtue, not simply as an adequate account of wisdom, but also as a complete account of virtue; or that, as Aristotle accuses him of doing, he overestimated the factor of knowledge and underestimated that of habit and impulse. That is, Plato realized that moral ideas determined action, but he failed to see that they grow out of action as well as determine it. He tended to make the ideas absolutely fundamental and the action a mere reflex of the ideas without seeing that the reason that the intellectual process has such significance is because it arises out of the necessities of action, so that there is a dynamic motivation behind it as well as an ethical function ahead of it.

It is interesting to note that Aristotle himself, while criticizing Plato, suggests—if we read between the lines, though he did not say so in so many words—that if all men were only intellectually adequate Plato's statement would be really true, but that taking human beings as they are with their limited intelligence, you have to conceive of virtue as a union of the practical factors of habit and impulse and the intellectual factor of reflective deliberation. Because of the Platonic failure to see that ideas grow out of action as well as determine it, we have the demand made that all conduct is to be examined into and rationalized. There must be a complete and comprehensive survey of the whole scope and relationship of conduct, and action must depend upon that.

Now the theory that has been previously advanced sets the limits of course, as well as the value of this deliberative process. It is out of the question, it is not only impossible but it is harmful to attempt to rationalize conduct as such, absolutely, to bring it all within the scope of reflective analysis. The demand for reflective analysis arises only at the crises where the conflict is taking place and where readjustment is required. That is its value, but that is also its limit. Just as psychologically it interferes to give attention to that which is thoroughly under the control of habit and we cannot do as well as when we go ahead automatically, so it is paralyzing to action, it is a dissipating of energy, of freshness and directness, to be eternally subjecting conduct, as such, to scrutiny. There is a motive for scrutiny in the necessity of adjustment; and these demands for adjustment occur frequently enough so that one need not be afraid that the moral consciousness on the intellectual side will not be kept active if he only attends to these as they arise. There is no need to seek for such opportunities; no special gymnastic is required.

Just because Plato did not recognize the genesis of the intellectual process out of action, he could not set any limit at all to it. Among other consequences of this is his practical separation of the common man and the philosopher. He recognizes the impossibility of the ordinary man having either the time or the ability for any such exhaustive analysis. Therefore it is necessary to have a particular class set apart for it; and Plato's statement that the philosophers must be the rulers is only one way of stating this principle that we have been discussing. If you admit the necessity of this absolute rationalization of conduct, Plato's conclusion of a particular class which shall set the moral norms for all other classes and which shall direct, in general principles and even in details, the activities of the other classes is inevitable.

Another corollary is the rigidity with which Plato conceives the moral life, not only in the *Republic* but even more in the *Laws*. When you have the whole thing once rationalized, then you have only to hang on to it. Any change then is corruption and Plato lays down that principle in so many words, that given once the ideal situation and all change is deterioration. We must screw ourselves up to the highest level and then after that conservatism must be the law. There is no provision made for moral progress in the Platonic scheme after this process has once taken place. I say Plato because he is the typical representative here, and because he was conscious of the implication of his views.

Not that he was the only sinner in these respects. The tendency among almost all moralists has been to assume the superiority of the rational element [to] the practical and to subordinate the latter to the former, and hence to make the objective element as made known by the intellect the final criterion of action instead of saying that that intellectual process comes in to mediate action. So there has been a tendency toward class morality. And this particular class who are the representatives par excellence of virtue and morality are conceived of as having some particular hold on moral ideals and interests, and as being the saving salt of the rest of society, the spring from which moral influence must radiate.

There has been equally the tendency not to deny moral progress but to conceive of it as negative, as marking merely an approximation to this state of perfect rationalization of conduct due to the degree in which we are removed from it, so that if we could get there, progress would cease; only we are sceptical of our ever getting there, but to Plato it seemed possible, at least when he wrote the *Republic*. We are not so consistent as Plato was in insisting that all change must cease insofar as we do rationalize conduct. It is felt that action, instead of carrying with it its own criteria, instead of carrying the principle for its own evaluation, has to be submitted to rational considerations which proceed from an extrinsic source, and that action, per se, would be disorderly and chaotic.

I will briefly apply this principle on the practical side. Here we have the limits as well as the positive value of moral introspection, moral self examination. Here we have the principle of how far we shall carry our conscious investigation of our character and our conduct.

First, this process of self examination is normally an objective one. It is an examination of the self, to be sure, but not of the self in or by itself as if any final moral value either of goodness or badness could attach to the self in itself. It is an examination of the self in the attitude which it takes toward conduct. Now that is just as objective a question intellectually as can be. There is nothing morbid about it. In one sense there is nothing introspective about it. It is dramatic rather than introspective. It is putting the whole situation before one's self and putting the self in as a part of the situation, to see how it looks; to see how it fits in; to see how it operates; what its action and reactions are. The question: "Was I bad, for instance, in doing so and so?" is not a question which can be resolved on the emotional side nor on the subjective side. It is simply the calling of an entire situation before the self and seeing if the right relationships and adjustments were made between the agent and the needs of the situation.

Second, it is just as harmful to introduce it where it does not belong as to forget it when it is needed. Just as at certain periods there is a neglect of the examining process and too much reliance is placed on mere custom and the mere expectations and demands of the community, on the whole since the Reformation there has been an excess in the matter of moral scrutinizing and introspection simply because an attitude has been set up (which we must assume in general and more or less all the time) instead of there being a recurrent demand at the nodal points of reconstruction in the direction of our activity. It has to be admitted practically that life carries its own moving spring within itself; and reason does not originate that, and reason in one sense never gives it its final measure or evaluation. Life must carry itself on and measure and work out its own value, and the process comes in—while the chief factor, still as one factor—in carrying on that self movement of the life process as a whole.

On the theoretical side (under the Teutonic influence) there has been an exaggeration of reflection. The Teutonic assumption is that you can get your clues absolutely in reason and that you must reason out the whole thing somehow in advance. Reason is a very respectable thing, but it has no such place in life, either individually or socially, as that. You must go back to the formed interests of men and their formed habits, to get the main springs of conduct; and it is when they temporarily fail by coming in conflict with each other that the conscious reflective process comes in and opposes those habits and interests by penetrating to a deeper level and thus allowing the more fundamental interests and habits to get under way and effect a unity. The real value of the rational process is that it sets free some fundamental interest which would otherwise have been clogged up.

This general point of view may be further brought out by what is known among ethical writers by the "inner life." What is to be said morally of the inner life? You will find an interesting chapter in MacKenzie on this subject.[13] It is the sphere of ideals and emotions, the sphere of personal cultivation. We all know that at certain periods the cultivation of the inner life has been made the important thing in conduct, generally under the influence of religion, although of course the Stoics tended to do the same thing without the religious sanction which we find in Christianity.

Regarding this inner life, it may be said that in one sense it is no more inner than is any form of experience. The individual is complex; he finds himself in a great variety of situations and relationships in life. Sometimes he is thrown with other people and his action is what we call overt because it comes directly in contact with their action. But a good deal of the time the individual is alone, he is left to himself, and then what is termed the inner life becomes prominent. But personally I cannot see that there is the slightest difference. That this life is inner and the other outward is simply because the situation, the direction of forces, becomes somewhat different than it does at other times. It is no more a time for merely cultivating the self than is that of ordinary social intercourse; a man simply carries on his life with a certain emphasis here and with another emphasis there, but so far as principle is concerned, one is as external as the other. The element of recreation, the aesthetic and artistic elements, come in largely in the period when one is relatively left to himself, and recuperation is going on. We may say that the individual is a whole community in himself and when there is no one else with whom to carry on conversation, he carries it on with himself. He has a variety of interests and points of view and it is not a mere matter of accident that so much of our inner life is a conversation between the inner selves. I imagine that most people carry on this inner life largely in terms of at least quasi-dramatic personification.

The second point of which I wish to speak is meditation. It may be said that meditation does have a positive moral value and yet it is not an intellectual process which goes on with reference to immediate needs. It is not for the sake of making a plan for any particular adjustment which must be made. If we emphasize the word immediate there is truth in that. The pressure of immediate action tends to throw us into routine and that tends to narrow the range of consciousness. We get caught in the machinery of our daily conduct and we get no perspective of it. We are swallowed up with immediate details and lose the sense of its relationship. We do not get the whole value of the particular thing we are doing because we cannot get off far enough to get a view of it.

The value of meditation is to counteract this tendency to get caught in the wheels of our daily routine. It is getting out of the immediacy of our actions and viewing them in their larger bearings and relationships. Meditation, then, so far as it is morally valuable, does not escape from the limitation of the general principle that I have set forth. It is for the sake of reconstructions and readjustments of action; it is in order that when we come to the details of action we may see them in a freer and more flexible way. Any other principle makes a division in life, a disintegration. The details remain as before and this period of meditation becomes an indulgence, a contemplation of ideals which has no modifying influence on the habit side. Meditation is for the sake of getting a better view of the ordinary routine interests. It is for the sake of reconsidering and reviewing and giving them more content or else it becomes simply daydreaming, an emotional indulgence which tends to the division of character.

The third phase of the inner life may be termed emotional excitation which goes along with the imagination, with the fanciful rehearsing of possibilities. The same is to be said in principle of this as of meditation. This arousing of emotional excitation, this imagery is valuable insofar as it enables one to get away from certain immediate bonds that hold him in and restrain his thinking and his action, and thus help him use his existing habits in a freer and more vigorous way. It is harmful insofar as it becomes an end in itself. If the strong use of the emotions creates in any sense a reservoir which will carry the man further than he would have been carried if he had not through his imagination created this excitement, there is some value to the thing. In general principles it is simply a case of the use of stimulants. The use of stimulants is justified if it has this outcome, but when separated, when the emotional pleasure or excitation aroused becomes an end in itself, it becomes harmful.

There is no great difficulty about the theory, but there is difficulty about the practice. It is a matter of decided delicacy to tell how to give this factor sufficient play so that we may imaginatively get beyond the limitations of our routine conduct and get a new point of view, and yet not allow the thing to get out of focus and become an end in itself. The difficulty is to be sure that this will react in the form and content of the daily life. The tendency is to go from one extreme to another. It is a fine test of character for a person to give the right amount of play to this, and yet not too much. The practical type of character prides itself on its common sense, considering imagination and the accompanying excitation as a waste of time interfering with the affairs of life. The sentimental person represents the opposite type of character, and somewhere between these types—the practical and hardheaded man of the world and the sentimental character—there lies the type which might be characterized as mellow, juicy, whose experience is rich and fertile both to himself and to others.

These three phases cover in general what is meant by the inner life and give the theoretic criterion for its treatment. Historically it may be said that the excess of the meditative and emotional sides shows itself at periods of general social reorganization when important ideals are looming up into view which however are confronted with tremendous obstructions in the immediate situation. Now excepting with persons of very unusual force of balance, the tendency at such a time must be to make the cultivation of the ideal an end in itself, or the getting of the emotional excitation which goes along with the imaging of the ideal as an ultimate end. The illustration of this is in the early centuries of Christianity when the most comprehensive of all ideals in form came into view—that of the absolute unity of humanity, the necessity of controlling the conduct of the individual with reference to the unity of humanity, the possibility of the unlimited access of the individual to the truth required for the conduct of the person. All the ideals were there, but if he looked at the immediate political situation he saw hardly anything but contradiction. It was necessary that there should be a reaction, and the attempt would be made to keep the ideal alive and postpone the attempt to act upon the ideal or to make it a controlling force in the details of life until a more auspicious time.

SECTION 8. THE RECIPROCITY OF INTUITION AND CONSEQUENCES

February 9, 1898

I propose to take up today a problem connected with the same general considerations that we have been discussing, but dealing with it in a different application. The controversy between the intuitionalist and the empiricist has two phases which are frequently confused with each other, and are confused because they are necessarily connected together. One of these phases, the mode of knowledge of moral distinction, we have already discussed. The other phase, that which we are now to take up, is whether the moral quality is intrinsic to an act or whether it is secondary and due to some sort of association. The intuitionalist as to mode of knowledge has always insisted on the intrinsic character of the moral quality. The empiricist has insisted on some sort of genetic theory, something which made the moral quality depend upon reference to previous and indeed extraneous experiences. So what we shall discuss now is the intrinsic versus the genetic theory.

The principle involved has already been discussed in pointing out the ambiguous way in which the empiricist uses the term consequences. If the moral quality were dependent upon the purely objective consequences of an act (the *de facto* consequences, independent of the use made of these consequences in the deliberative process), then any reference to consequences would make the moral quality an extraneous matter and one of association and transfer. So they say there is no moral quality in any act itself, or in any motive itself—it depends merely and purely upon its consequences. We may come to associate certain consequences with certain lines of action and hence we judge these lines of action as good or bad. But it is merely by this associated transference—not on account of anything in the experience itself.

The intuitionalist, holding that the moral quality is known directly and immediately, holds on the other side that the moral quality belongs to the impulse or the motive itself; that is, one is intrinsically good and the other intrinsically bad.

The disjunction is due to a wrong conception of the whole process. The putting of the genetic interpretation over against the intrinsic interpretation is due to this original faulty grasping of the point at issue. Moral quality is both intrinsic and genetic. That is the proposition which I wish to put forth as distinct from the two under consideration. We cannot put the *either/or* just where these two schools put them. We cannot say *either* the moral quality belongs to the action entirely independent of previous experience *or* else it is transferred wholly into association with reference to present experiences.

The moral quality belongs to the act, but it is certainly not independent of previous experience. When the motive is isolated in that way, it possesses no moral quality at all; it is neither bad nor good; it has simply psychological quality, natural quality, not moral quality. But when we say that, it is not the same thing as saying that its moral quality is due to simple association with past experience, the consequences of past action. Use is made of the consequences of past action to determine the meaning of the present suggestion, the present project, the present impulse. Insofar as the past experiences and their consequences come in simply to interpret the present, then surely the quality is intrinsic to the present experience. We see what the present experience means, we work out its bearing only by taking advantage of our other experiences. By the fact that we throw light on the present in that, we certainly do not deprive the present experience of that value, that significance. But insofar as we do have to refer [to] that previous experience in order to work out this interpretation, in order to get any adequate valuation of its significance we may say the consciousness is genetic.

Here is an impulse, an aim. Now we want to know before we act what the import, what the content of that impulse is. The only way in which we can find out is by viewing that impulse as if it were acted on, thinking of it in terms of overt action. And the only way we can translate it over into terms of overt action is by going over our experiences along identical and analogous lines, so that the genetic element of the reference to other experiences coming in as the instrument by which the intrinsic significance of that impulse, or project, is brought out and realized.

The impulse or motive of the intuitionalist is [an] abstraction. We know what it is concretely only in terms of its relationship. The empirical process brings out those relationships, but in doing so it answers the question: What is the real impulse? What is the real motive? For example, someone under a supposed motive of benevolence gives money to a child, a beggar, and finds out afterwards, either accidently or because he has interest enough in the matter to follow it up, that in so doing he is supporting certain adults in idleness through their making use of the child. And he finds that he is really depriving that child of the necessity and opportunity of getting an education ,and of following out some line of action that would afterward be useful.

Now of course my point is that in finding out those consequences he has not simply certain external results which he can associate with that benevolent impulse and thereby measure its moral value; he has light on that impulse itself. He began with a narrow, imperfect consciousness of that impulse. Now through this experience the consciousness of its real nature widens and can be more adequately determined, and hence he has a new criterion for determining the value of such impulses as they arise in his future consciousness. That does not mean that that absolutely settles the value of that impulse. The next time he must judge how far this case is identical with the previous one, how far he can carry over the previous range of considerations and apply them; that is part of the balancing, weighing and measuring that he must go through in the deliberative process. But insofar as he has reason to conclude any identity between the two cases, insofar he will use the previous case as an instrument of interpretation for the next case.

If you stop to think, it is a queer position anyway, because we learn from experience that what we learn is not organically connected with the things to which we apply it; it is a mere matter of external association. Insofar as it is a matter of external association, it shows that we have not learned much about it. In the degree in which we have really learned, we take the results of past experience and somehow incarnate them into the present experience, carry them over into the present experience. It is well enough to say that a child who has burned his finger in the fire associates that pain with the fire, but psychologically the connection made is a good deal closer than one of association. There are not two things for him after that: there is one thing. There is not the fire plus pain: there is a burning fire. And the weakness of the associational school in all cases is the failure to see that just in the degree that the experience is thoroughgoing, we do not associate it with other experiences, but we transfer it bodily into the next experience. What we have is a chemical union rather than any sort of association in time and space.

There is an interesting case given by Professor James in one of the earlier numbers of the *Philosophical Review,* the record of the case of a deaf mute in California who had been accustomed to petty thefts and had no compunctions of conscience in consequence. This individual stole once a sum of money.[14] I do not recall the amount, but we will say—on the supposition that it was a dime—that it turned out to be a gold eagle. Now without any instruction at all he felt that he had done something wrong. He became uneasy, he had remorse so that he went and confessed to somebody.

Mr. James gives that as an argument on the intuitional side. There were no associations of an extraneous type; he was not punished, had not been detected. That illustrates this principle. A person acts on a certain impulse. Now in case that impulse has certain momentous consequences, he must reconstruct his view of that impulse. If the results are not srtikingly marked there is no new evaluation of it. But the interesting thing in this case cited by Professor James is that the very bulk of the consequences, the fact that he had so much money to spend, threw him into a state of great uneasiness and he felt that he had done something wrong. The mere quantity of the experience that he had threw a new quality into this tendency or impulse of his.

We do not in our ordinary experience get cases as pure or typical as that. We are subject to more or less moral reproof and made to suffer from previous action, but in principle that is what is occurring in everybody. One starts out to do something either with the assumption that it is all right, or else that while other people say it is wrong, on the whole he thinks it is right for him and he is willing to take the risks of it. The results, the consequences, may not be such as to change his attitude, but if they pass the customary limit he has to reconstruct his attitude toward that whole line of conduct. It now becomes a moral problem and he must take some definite personal moral attitude towards it.

Of course the strict intuitionalist ought to say, in the case which James cited, that while he [the deaf mute] had the thieving impulse at the time he ought to have known that it was bad. So the case would tell against the strict intuitionalist as much as against the strict empiricist. But it seems in line with the interpretation that I have been giving.

The acting upon any impulse, then, any interest, always has the possibility of bringing to light relationships and values not previously taken into account. There is no end to that process. Consequently there can be no limit to moral evolution. We may say that everybody has always known that it was right to regard human life, that it was right to guard property and to tell the truth and so on. But when we come to any specific statement, we find that the whole process is an evolutionary and a genetic one. The things that one puts under the head of regard for life, property, and truth are in process of development. The primitive social man will include under the head of regard for life his own family. But everybody outside his kin is on that account an enemy and it is a virtue to kill him and not a vice. So what is conceived of as property is changing with the actual situation. The same is true of truth telling. In other words, the acting on impulse reveals and constructs a new situation and the value of the impulse is transformed and reconstituted. It is difficult to see but there could be any limit to that process of rhythmic readjustment.

This general principle may be carried a little further and applied to the evolutional statement of morality (I mean evolution in the biological sense). Does the evolutionary statement of morality destroy the intrinsically ethical quality of conduct? Of course it has seemed to many persons that it does, that the only way of justifying the moral content of action is to make an exception in its favor with reference to the process of evolution, to show that that is not evolved in any way. What difference should it make with its intrinsic morality whether it came in *ex abrupto* or whether it came with genetic continuity? What peculiar authority attaches to this introduction from without? The answer is that what we had before was merely providential. If we say that out of that the moral consciousness was evolved, we are reducing it to an animal plane.

Now just the same principle which attaches to the genetic element in everyday experience applies also in this larger problem. Particular lines of action which were formerly on a nonmoral plane come out on the moral plane in the history of every individual. If we take it from the baby up to the adult, we can say that all lines of action are gradually passing over from the nonmoral plane into some sort of moral plane. But if we confine it to the adult, we know that our attitude changes. What we thought was nonmoral we now conclude to be innocent and right. Other things that we conceived as having no moral quality at all we now conceive as wrong, the principle being that through experience we come to perceive relationships that we did not know before, and interpret the experience from the standpoint of the relationships thus brought out.

If we take Darwin's statement, in his *Descent of Man,* that moral consciousness arises out of the social instincts appertaining to animal family life, the relations of parents and offspring, and to the general gregariousness of some forms of animal life; that the first rudimentary moral distinctions were the direct outcome of the social instincts on this family side and on the side of gregariousness, herding, and flock living; and of course that the origin of herd living found in natural selection, the value given, the value of the family life, would have to be found in the same way.[15] And that takes the moral content out of moral consciousness.

But does it? Why should we hesitate to admit that the content, the substance of the moral consciousness, is found in such social instincts and habits as these which previously were merely biological? The moral element would come in at just this point when it was necessary to take a definite attitude toward these instincts on the basis of their reference to determining future action. As long as the animal acts on these instincts as instincts, they simply have certain *de facto* results; they have no moral consequences. But let there be a question for the animal to tell what he is going to do and let it be a question of his making use of these instincts and their past experiences for deciding upon any particular line of action, and you have a moral consciousness. The animal is no longer a mere animal. In other words we have all the differentia needed between the animal and the moral. The moral comes in with the consciousness of what was biologically not merely reflex consciousness, but a consciousness which looks toward the future, which utilizes or adapts these habits to the selection of some particular line of conduct.

To make up a particular case which is slightly grotesque: let the animal get food for its young even at the risk of personal danger to itself simply because it is impelled forward by instinct, and we may say that its action is altruistic in the objective sense. But we cannot say that there is any morally altruistic content. Now let the animal consciously conceive of this danger to itself and then have its social instincts demanding of it that it get food for the offspring, and then, on the basis of that conscious reflection and of its instinct, determine its future conduct; and I do not see but what its act has such moral quality as the act of a philanthropist would have.

To sum it up: it is the objective consciousness of the biological with reference to the determination of action (which of course throws the emphasis into the future) that makes at once the transition from the animal to the ethical, and the distinction between the animal and the ethical. That is, as far as the principle is concerned. As far as the actual historical details are concerned, I think we do not know enough to say much about it.

February 10, 1898

Herbert Spencer has attempted the reconciliation of the empirical and the genetic views both in metaphysics and in ethics. The general principle is the same in both: that certain principles are *a posteriori* for the race and *a priori* for the individual.[16] Certain feelings and ideas have been so thoroughly worked out in the experience of the race that they have been organized in the constitution of the individual: thus in metaphysics ideas like causation and space and time. And so also he would account for moral intuitions. They are the transmitted outcomes of centuries and centuries of registered consolidated experiences.

Regarding this it may be said that Spencer seems to admit a great deal more for the intuitionalist than it is possible or advisable to conceive, and also that his statement is a confused one. I shall not attempt to discriminate these two lines of criticism. They run together. If we attempt to get any clear conception of the way in which experiences of this sort are registered and transmissible, we must recognize that the consolidation is primarily on the motor side, not in any sense on the intellectual side. There is no conceivable apparatus by which an idea, a thought, a feeling would be organized and handed down from one person to another. It is conceivable that certain habits, certain coordinations should become so generic by natural selection, and (from Spencer's point of view [regarding] the transmission of acquired characters) that they should influence their offspring.

In other words the idea of habit becoming instinctive, and in the form of instincts being transmissible, is not only a possible thing but it is an undisputed thing. There is a dispute as to whether it comes from natural selection or acquired characteristics, but of the fact there is no dispute. When Spencer is talking about the inheritance of moral intuitions, we have to translate that over into the inheritance of certain habits of action and reaction. There is no intellectual conception of an idea of that sort which is transmissible. You no more could transfer by heredity an idea of truth telling than the idea of the telephone. The same is true of the idea of space. Animals get certain habits of reacting in space to space conditions. And so it may be conceived for the sake of argument that they may get certain habits in connection with preserving or destroying life, and these ways of reacting may be transmitted. It is only fair to suppose that that is what Spencer really means, but his statements are so vague that it is difficult to put any very clear meaning into them.

If we grant this formation of generic habits, their reduction to instincts, and their transmission, we may say that any of those lines of activity will, under certain conditions, give rise to certain feelings. There will be a feeling of pain, of uneasiness, when the instinct is thwarted just in the degree of the fundamental character of the instinct. And the most rational interpretation that can be put upon Spencer is that he means by the moral intuitions the feelings which accompany either the pleasurable or painful workings of these instincts. Taking the theory in that form which seems to me the only intelligible one, it must be said that there is no moral value which attaches to those feelings at all, no direct moral value. They possess value as data for morality, but neither the habits nor the feelings which accompany them give us a decisive value. The habit has been worked out under prior conditions. The feeling which attaches to it, therefore, may be a sign or index of its worth under those conditions, but it has no ultimate character with reference to present conditions. The whole moral problem is the adaptation of the habit (which was adjusted to prior conditions) to existing conditions. The habit and the feeling which accompanies it may be an obstruction to right action as well as a facilitation of it.

Pathological cases seem to leave no doubt that there is in some persons, in certain degrees of excitation, positive pleasure in the sight of the shedding of blood, even of the infliction of physical pain. With the average individual [this] never arise[s], but the abnormal cases show that it is really there. It is possible to see how that should be when we consider the struggle for existence, the necessity for shedding of blood in the defense of life and in the procuring of food. There is no moral quality attached to that. It makes the moral problem more difficult. In principle we would say the same thing even about the habit of truth telling and the feelings accompanying that. If it is more valuable it is because that habit is of value in the present situation. The whole question is in all cases one of its present utilization, and the mere fact that the habit has been formed in the past has no final value, although it may have instrumental value.

Without going into the disputed question of the transmissibility of traits acquired through use, it may at least be said that the most important transmission of moral principles has been, not through direct biological continuity, but through the continuity of the social tradition. In other words, that education, conscious education and unconscious intuition, has been tremendously more efficacious in maintaining the body of ethical precepts and points of view which are common than any amount of this biological registration. Of course on the biological side the relation which human life bears to prehuman life is very slight. Although so far as there has been a fixed heredity on that side, it would be harmful instead of helpful because it would express an adaptation to prehuman conditions if it has become fixed and rigid on that basis. But every social type, every community, formulates its own habits in the demands and expectations which it makes on all new individuals brought into that group. Of course at later periods it formulated its habits in religious ideals and aspirations, but in any form it formulates its demands, its habits.

In the way of practical instances, there are certain things which it is required that a man should do and certain other things that he should not do. And it is those typical expectations and demands on the individual in order to make him form for himself what the group as a whole has formed which without a question form the great trunk of what we may call the moral intuitions. They are intuitive with reference to the individual in the sense that they are expectations which meet him, confront him, from the first, before he begins to recollect at all, and which influence and mold his conduct both consciously and unconsciously. It seems to me that is the positive sense which may be given to the concept of general moral intuitions. They are the customary social expectations or demands which are built into the individual by the whole way in which he is treated, by stimuli brought to bear upon him, and the responses that are required of him. They reflect, they embody the habits of the social group, be it narrow or be it wide, conceived of as necessary to its own maintenance, to its own integrity.

Now that gives a certain positive significance and positive value to those intuitions, but of course in no rigid or final sense. This particular social environment will have certain expectations in common with others and it will have certain [expectations] which are more or less peculiar. In a larger whole, say the United States, there will be certain expectations that are common with the rest of humanity and some that are peculiar. Then there will be certain families, say in the central western portion of the United States, having their expectations. With reference to the individual those intuitions will vary depending upon the particular type of social group with which the individual comes in most direct and immediate contact. That means of course that these intuitions, while they are useful and important, while they facilitate the acquisition of moral experience by the individual, they economize his time, they direct his experience so that he learns more in less time than if he had to work out the whole thing de novo, [yet] they are always subject to revision. The individual is called on more or less to decide how much value he will attach to them. They control his ways of thinking or acting before he knows it and would seem intuitions to him. But they themselves need to grow, to be adjusted. Insofar as the individual feels himself called upon to be a reformer, to take a conscious active part in social progress, he will be called upon to defy more or less the moral intuitions in which he has been brought up. If reform were simply a matter of getting rid of evils, it would be a simple matter; but it always consists in eliminating something which probably the majority of the people consider good. It consists of modifying and reconstituting this trend of the social expectations and demands.

Of course we are subject all the time to the historical fallacy here. We take it for granted that we would have been on the side of the reformer because it is a perfectly clear question and it seems as if there must have been a stubborn resistance on the part of the many. This means that it has been worked out for us. But when the question was up it was still working out and the most intense opposition usually comes from the good portion of the community. It is apt to be from the most highly moralized and conscientious part of the community, insofar as they have brought themselves into line with the demands and social expectations. The moral intuitions become more or less conventions and the moral reformer must shock the conventional. There is always more or less convention to work against. They have been worked out on the basis of the more or less local environment having its own particular peculiarities. Now when you try to extend the conditions, what was appropriate to some particular condition would have the essence of convention. What I mean is by the nature of the case they must have a phase of conventional coloring attached to them, and insofar have to be made over.

One word in conclusion about the intuitionalist's position. The intuitionalist has been forced more and more from the conception of an immediate moral sense to the conception of a peculiar faculty which makes known merely general principles, the application of these principles being left for experience to determine. The earlier writers, the moral sense school, held that we had a certain immediate reaction to actions which told us they were right or they were wrong. If there was any such equipment as that, and life were fixed and not progressive, it would undoubtedly be a very useful thing. There would be no opportunity left for ethical development, there would be this ready-made inventory and every new phase would be referred to that at once. There would be no process of finding out and testing what is right and what is wrong (such a process as now develops moral character) but simply a rigid application of principles already fixed.

It has been shown, however, that there is no such thing as this immediate sense, and so the intuitionalist has been forced to generalize his conception. When we get to Kant we find this principle more generalized and left with only one moral intuition: the fact that it is our duty to do our duty, that obligation is absolutely obligatory, and the particular content of that ultimate generalization of morality has to be supplied.

Now regarding these intuitions of a more and more general form, it may be said first that even if they existed they would possess a metaphysical interest rather than an ethical one. The actual moral problems of life, and the actual strains on character, do not come with reference to finding out whether honesty in general is right or wrong, but in reference to doing this or that particular thing. The whole moral stress is in just the factor which the intuitionalist in the modern generalized form leaves out—the adaptation of the principle to the individual case at hand. When we act it is some particular thing in some particular time and place, and the question is to adapt the general principle to that case. And even more than that, these fixed general principles would be obstructions rather than helps. There is always a gap between a merely general principle of that kind and a particular case to which it must be adapted.

I have a number of fixed, uniform principles—honesty, truth telling, regard for property and life, chastity, and so on. Here is a particular case. What particular principle shall I adapt to that particular case? Suppose there are two or three principles which might apply. How shall I tell which one to apply? A burglar comes to my house at night and starts to take away my property. What is the intuition which applies to that case? Is it regard for property or life? Shall I let him steal out of regard for life, or try to shoot him out of regard for my property rights? That is a coarse case of the sort of instances that are always coming up in more delicate ways, and these fixed intuitions, if there were such things, would really tremendously complicate the situation. It would make it much easier for a careless person. But [you] increase the difficulty for a conscientious person: the more conscientious, the more in doubt he would be.

The second point I have already made. I simply repeat it. The generalized principles are simply the formulation for educational purposes ultimately—purposes of controlling, by the mature, the conduct of the immature. They thus represent the dominant habits of the social life. And just because those habits have no ultimate value, because they are instrumental, these intuitions must be held open to revision and readjustment. They cannot be applied rigidly, even educationally, to the immature individual. You must interpret the principle by the individual as much as to control the individual by the principle. These rationalized moral principles, then, are convenient devices (I do not mean to underrate them by calling them devices) for educating both ourselves and others, and for shortening the deliberative process by setting before us in advance certain of its more salient features and for increasing the likelihood of a rational conclusion. They are, so to speak, weapons for attacking and analyzing the particular situation. They suggest a number of questions which are to be asked. They do not give a number of heads or pigeonholes in which acts are to be sorted out, but they do suggest the questions that it is important to ask about the given case or situation. Thus instead of our having to feel around indefinitely and for a good while in deliberating on the particular case, they reduce the number of points of view to a number of heads that are fairly typical, and in our process of surveying it, they put at our disposal the experiences of others. They are ultimately educational devices in which we use the experiences of others, or we give others the benefit of our experience. So we may apply the same principle that we apply to the intellectual process. It is a scheme for bridging over the present conflict of impulses into a unified and valuable mode of activity as quickly as possible.

SECTION 9. REASON AND
PASSION: KANT VERSUS
HUME

The next problem which I shall take up is the statement of the relation between the rational and sensory factors in general. We have discussed all the principles involved, but historically we have on one side an author like Hume who says that reason is and must be the slave of passion. On the other side we have an author like Kant who says the moral motive must be direct from reason and that any motive from the feeling side of life is, and must be, bad. When you get an opposition as extreme as that there are some fundamental questions involved. I shall discuss this entirely on the basis of Kant: his statement regarding the universal legislative reason as capable of supplying motivation.

February 14, 1898

The general tenor of the criticisms to be passed on authors like Hume on one side and Kant on the other has of course been anticipated in the previous line of discussion. It is that in their respective conceptions of sense and passion or of reason they erect into independent entities and give an independent value to what are really only functioning factors in the whole process of determining action. The reason that we happen to have these two schools coming up so persistently is precisely because each abstracts one of these functioning factors in action and attempts to make of it something that is supreme over action.

The course of Kant's argument is about as follows: all man's natural inclinations are for getting pleasure. These natural inclinations in themselves—that is, as they are in an animal—have no immoral quality; but whenever the motive, the determining principle of action, is found in one of the natural inclinations, then the will of man is made subservient to an animal or sensible aim and immorality results. If the man is to be thoroughly free, if there is to be genuine morality, then the determining principle of the will must be found outside of any inclination; that is as regards the formation of the motive, all the natural inclinations must be ruled out. The only thing which you have left from which to seek your motive when you have ruled out all your natural appetites is the bare form of will itself in its generality. The will must find its motive in the will. Now this form of will, separated from all particular empirical content, is just what is meant by reason, and so the reason is to determine the will. What is this bare form, however, of volition which has excluded all content because that content is particular and self-seeking? Simply the conception of generality in general. The motive must be such that it can become a law for action, that it must be capable of absolute generalization.

All reason means is this formal universalization. The universal which is formal means uniformity and that gives the point of view for the criticism of Kant, namely, that this formal universal which includes [excludes?] the particular impulses and inclinations utterly fails to subserve the true purposes of a universal. It is the universal only in name. The real value of any universal is in its capacity to organize the particulars, and such organizing power is lacking in Kant's formal universal. Undoubtedly Kant contributed a very positive factor to moral theory in this conception that right conduct is the conduct which can be universalized. The right motive is precisely that which is, or may become, a law for action. It is not a mere principle that we happen to act upon in an isolated way in this particular case.

But the difficulty is that if the universal were what Kant says it is, it is something exclusive of motivation, of inclination and impulse. We never could use this criterion which he sets up in order to make good his own principles. In order to utilize it we have to anticipate the meaning of reason, of the universal, in quite a different way. Any motive can theoretically be made uniform, can be made self-consistent, or noncontradictory, if you isolate it from the whole body to which it belongs. Now when Kant rules out all the impulses, he gives us just exactly this isolation. The false way of putting the question of the universal is this: Can I at all times and in all places without contradicting it act upon the identical motive upon which I am now acting? To a question put in that way you can answer: Yes, you can at all times and in all places act upon the identical motive on which you are now acting, or that you never can act upon it under any circumstances. As Kant's critics have pointed out, you can act upon the motive of destroying life or property universally without contradicting that particular motive. What you do contradict is a certain system of action, or a certain organized situation, but to get that criterion of the organized unity of conduct, you have to go outside of the mere formal law of identity and consider what Kant rules out as being empirical content.

For instance, Kant says, a man has been given a deposit. The question comes whether he now shall return that deposit, the circumstances being such that he will not be detected if he does not. Kant say yes, because if he were to keep it, it would be self-contradictory. No one would ever make deposits if universally they were not to be returned; so, to act in that way would be bad, because it contradicts itself. Well, what of it? Supposing no one ever did make deposits. There would be nothing particularly immoral about that. Or put from the other side, what the act contradicts is not itself; it contradicts a form of social organization in which people have the habit of confiding money or property to each other. That is a purely empirical matter. According to Kant it is people's inclination which leads them to make these deposits and their is no particular reason why that should not be.

Some critics take these cases and show that it is not the more formal motive that is contradicted by the wrong action. It is really some organized interest in action which is contradicted by the failure to do so and so, so that Kant's real criterion of the universal is not found in the formal self-identity, but is really found in this thought of the organized relations involved. As Mill points out, you might claim Kant as a utilitarian.[17] It is the inconsistency between the present motive and its consequences that he really judges by. From that point of view any and every motive might be made universal without contradicting itself. It might contradict a situation of which it is a part, a unity of which it is a member, but the actual detailed consequences Kant has no right to take into account.

But he [Kant] says that no mode of action could ever be made universal. The same circumstances never do repeat themselves. It is because no moral act is merely a duplicate of some act which preceded it. There are some different factors, some different circumstances; and from that point of view, a universal, in the sense of the uniform, is impossible. When is the man going to give the deposit back? The next minute, or the next day, or the next year? It is not simply a matter of giving it back in general, but of giving it back at a particular time and in a particular way. And the next case that involves a trust would involve a certain variation of those factors, so if you attempt to prescribe absolute uniformity of action, the law which would hold good in the first case would not hold good in the second, and so on indefinitely. Kant's scheme of the universal in the sense of the merely uniform would lead to continual conflict.

As I said the other day, supposing a man is attacked in his own house by a burglar. What uniformity is the one that covers that particular case? In more complex circumstances a man might have a line of conduct to which any one of a half dozen principles would apply. On Kant's basis if he were to take one, he must rule out all the others. But what the agent really needs is not arbitrary selection, but a comprehensive unification. If each principle is kept in its rigidly formal universality per se, that comprehensive reconciliation is not possible. The law of reason, then, instead of being something which is set over against consequences, and set over against inclinations, means simply a concrete unification. The universal is not a thing by itself. It is simply the way in which one factor in conduct cooperates with another factor in conduct. If you rule out those factors on the ground that they are empirical, you have nothing left but the bare thought of adaptation, the bare thought of adjustment, with nothing to adapt or adjust. You have the merest, emptiest, schematic form which will fit anywhere and nowhere, as I have already said.

Conduct is presumably [as] organic as a piece of music. Supposing a musical critic were to develop a theory of the unity of a given symphony on the ground that you must rule out all the particular sounds and notes because they are simply sensations; that the value of music is in the ideal element and that would be simply in the form or relationship which these tones bear to each other, but that in thinking of these relationships, in order to get a pure universal, you must rule out all the actual tones themselves. It is pretty evident that there would be nothing left to think about, because the universal is simply the relationship, it is simply the way in which one tone bears upon another tone which leads up to it, and is in turn interpreted by it.

And so with the rational element in conduct. Instead of being something which can be set over against consequences and inclinations, it stands for simply the adaptation of one of these elements to the other in the construction of the unified whole of conduct. The reasonability of truth telling is nothing which you can find in truth telling if you isolate it from the rest of conduct. The reasonableness of truth telling is in the fact that that particular mode of action maintains the organized character of conduct as a whole. The unreasonable character of untruth is that it disintegrates, making the unity of conduct as a whole impossible.

In other words, it is a very important thing to duly recognize the function of the universalization of conduct, and Kant was the first to do this. But you might say that he fixed his mind on it with such rigidity that it lost its place, it lost its function; so that he transformed the useful and necessary idea of the universal in conduct into the conception of a universal outside of conduct, thereby making it meaningless and futile.

We can imagine a man putting this question to himself, "I propose to do thus and so. Now can I generalize my motives so as to make it a universal law?" What he will really do will be to call before him the probable consequences which he anticipates from that mode of action, and see whether they fit into each other or not, and as he extends his range and thinks of different results, he will continually ask himself. "Do all these reinforce each other? Will they maintain a unified situation, or do they work at cross purposes with each other? Will acting upon these impulses thwart the action upon another impulse which is important?" Now if he finds that he can create a unified situation out of acting upon this impulse, that he can act upon it in such a way as to reinforce the due claims of all others, he would say that that line of conduct was generalized. But if he found that it would perpetuate conflict, he would conclude that he had not generalized it. Generalization means organization, and organization not merely in general, but of the concrete factors which make conduct what it is.

The same line of criticism may be briefly repeated from a different point of view. Kant makes a divorce which is practically complete between the moral motive and the natural springs to action. This question continually presents itself in his system. Supposing we waive all the objections just made, supposing a man could decide by his criterion just what it is right to do. That represents rational intuition on his part. How is that going to become a working motive? How is it going to get any leverage so that it will become a dynamic spring to action? All a man's springs to action lie on the other side. They are all inclinations which are particular and self-seeking. Where are you going to get any connection between this natural self-seeking motive, and this recognition of the proper course to pursue? Before a man can act, the universal must be particularized. It must become somehow an impulse which will operate well.

Kant attempts to meet that by saying that there is one feeling which is rationally produced and which therefore does not seem to be simply after pleasure, that all our feeling nature comes into collision with the law of reason, with the universal, and it feels its own subordinate, subject position. It feels the majesty, the authority of the rational principle, and that feeling we may term either humility or reverence. Humility marks the inferiority of the natural inclinations. It is the recognition of the superior moral law, the rational principle, and in that way the moral law, in this form of reverence or of humility, becomes an actual working spring.

The criticism that is continually passed there is that if Kant has the machinery by which one feeling can become moralized and rationalized, he is bound in logical theory to admit the possibility of other inclinations being rationalized also, not being merely self-seeking. Why should the feeling of reverence have any such superior place over the feelings of family affection, or over the feeling of patriotism? Why should not the mother's passion for her child be just as rationalized as this feeling of reverence for moral law in general? The gist of that criticism is that Kant must not do two things at once. He must not in one and the same breath proclaim an absolute separation between the natural and rational, and also provide a bridge across. If his separation is ultimate, then why should the natural feelings feel the majesty of this moral law? If the feelings were what Kant claims they were, purely selfish and particularistic, certainly the recognition of the universal would have no moral meaning for them.

That is a criticism of Kant along the line of his own self-consistency; but there is a deeper meaning than that of personal consistency. It means that our natural inclinations and impulses cannot be interpreted as essentially hostile to reason, to the universal. A given impulse or inclination may become such, of course, historically. It may get out of focus; it may get out of balance and need to be wheeled back into line, it may need to be rationalized after being nonrational. But that is a different thing from saying that the inclinations as inclinations are nonmoral. We must find the moving spring to action in something which has impulsive power. Now its rationalization means what I tried to show that it does mean, that it is the interpretation of one impulse in the light of the whole system of conduct, that while there may a great deal of conflict in detail, while there may be a great deal of reconstruction necessary, there is no essential dualism. But if rationalization means something which lies outside the sphere of inclination as such, then the moral life involves hopeless conflict. Any connection that can be set up is arbitrary. It is one thing to say, for example, that even a person's impulses in the way of benevolence, compassion and family affection should be subordinate to reason; should be isolated by no means, but be treated as members of a larger system; and that when so treated there will be a certain amount of opposition to the immediate form in which the impulses present themselves; that the acting on them right will necessarily have to be suppressed and they will have to be interpreted before they are acted on. But to say that these inclinations can never become a motive to action, that we must refer them over to another source to get them rationalized and moralized, means that only a wholly self-conscious pedant could ever act morally at all. It would involve a sort of operation which the average human being is utterly incapacitated for going through, and for which he would be the worse if he did go through.

To take a sort of stock illustration, this case of the mother's affection for her child. It has to be rationalized in the sense that it has to be brought into relation with other impulses so that it becomes a factor in the whole system, but to say that she could not act until she had referred to the principle of duty and lay aside all her impulses until she could say, "I will act upon this impulse because I see that it is my duty, and my only reason for acting upon it is because it is a duty," would be to make the moral life wholly pedantic and destroy the ordinary wellsprings of conduct.

This general principle may be given a much wider extension than its application to Kant. Reason on this basis does not mean any special faculty, it means rather a certain value. There is no particular entity or faculty called reason which comes in and operates in any way. We have simply the interaction of our impulses which are translated into images. Now when this interaction and interpretation goes on in such a way that we get organization, then we can say that there is reason, or that the conduct is rational. Reason is a name for this worked-out organic unity of conduct, not anything which comes in and operates upon action from without. It is simply a name for the degree of system attained.

At the other extreme we have the school which says with Hume that reason is and must be the slave of passion; which says, not only is action measured by consequences, but the consequences are always consequences in the way of mere feeling, pure pleasures and pains. I have criticized this utilitarian conception in its general form without taking up what kind of consequences they are, but this hedonistic school limits the consequences which should be considered to this matter of mere feelings. All reason has to do is to collect the probabilities as to whether a given line of action will give us a maximum of pleasure or pain. That is what Hume means by being its slave. It is an instrument which we utilize to see whether if we do a certain thing the result will be pleasure or pain. But apart from its coming in that way to figure out a balance on one side or the other, it has no meaning at all.

I shall simply now pass two criticisms very briefly on this point of view.

First, it overlooks the fact that we have recourse to reason just because the passions, the impulses, have broken down as affording us any immediate guidance to conduct. It is because the passions, so called, the inclinations, have got into conflict with each other, because if we act upon them we will simply make confusion worse confounded, that we go through the intellectual process at all. Otherwise we would simply act on habit, on our prevailing interest.

The second criticism is that no amount of consideration of results in the form of mere feelings would ever give any guidance to conduct. Such consequences are extrinsic to our impulses. On the score of mere feeling there is no reason for saying that any line of conduct will ever have any particular set of results. If I do this, will I get more pleasures or pains? That is absolutely an undeterminate problem. There are so many factors entering into the simplest case that nobody would ever have any data for answering it at all. That is the basis of Spencer's criticism on the older utilitarians, that it was purely empirical. He says we must be able to deduce from the laws of life and existence that certain lines of conduct will necessarily result in certain pleasures and pains.[18] The moment you do that, you are not judging conduct from the standpoint of pleasures and pains: you are judging pleasures and pains from the standpoint of conduct. You may still call yourself a hedonist, but you have virtually reversed your position.

NOTES

1. Probably a reference to Baldwin's discussion of the imitative and inventive aspects of mental development. See James Mark Baldwin, *Social and Ethical Interpretations in Mental Development* (New York: The Macmillan Co., 1897), Chap. III.

2. For Lotze's view, See James, *Psychology*, I, 522, note.

3. Probably a reference to Herbert Spencer's *The Principles of Psychology,* I (New York: D. Appleton and Co., 1897), Part II, Chaps. I and II on "The Substance of Mind" and "The Composition of Mind."

4. For Külpe's analysis, see Oswald Külpe, *Outlines of Psychology,* trans. E. B. Titchner (London: Swan Sonnenschein and Co., 1895), pp. 29–44.

5. James, *Psychology*, I, 258 ff.

6. *Early Works,* IV, 276.

7. Jeremy Bentham, *The Principles of Morals and Legislation* (New York: Hafner Publishing Co., 1948), p. 107. This is an exact reprint of the 1823 edition.

8. John Stuart Mill, *Utilitarianism,* 2nd ed. (London: Longmans, Green, Longmans, Roberts and Green, 1864).

9. *Early Works,* IV, 273–74.

10. Bentham, p. 86.

11. John Stuart MacKenzie, *A Manual of Ethics,* 2nd ed. (London: University Correspondence College Press, 1894), p. 40.
12. Dewey discusses the organism-environment distinction again in Chapter II, Section 1 of the *Political Ethics.*
13. John S. MacKenzie, *Manual of Ethics,* 4th ed. (New York: Noble and Noble, 1925), Bk. III, Chap. V, "The Individual Life."
14. William James, "Thought Before Language: A Deaf-Mute's Recollections," *Philosophical Review,* I (1892), 613–24.
15. Charles Darwin, *The Descent of Man,* new ed. (New York: D. Appleton and Co., 1890), esp. Chaps. IV and V, "Comparison of the Mental Powers of Man and the Lower Animals" and "On the Development of the Intellectual and Moral Faculties During Primevil and Civilized Times."
16. For the basis of this view, see Herbert Spencer, *First Principles* (New York: D. Appleton and Co., 1888), note p. 179, and *The Principles of Psychology* (New York: D. Appleton and Co., 1880), II, Part VII, Chap. XI, "The Universal Postulate," esp. Sec. 433.
17. Mill, p. 78.
18. Herbert Spencer, *Social Statics* (New York: D. Appleton and Co., 1873), pp. 11–27, on "The Doctrine of Expediency."

CHAPTER 4

THE EMOTIONAL ASPECT
OF VOLITION

SECTION 1. THE ROLE OF
EMOTIONS WITHIN THE
LIFE PROCESS

February 15, 1898

The intellectual process just discussed represents the valuation of action on the objective side. By objective, we mean simply that one experience is determined or measured in terms of another experience which it makes possible. It is the very nature of any intellectual condition to refer beyond itself, and it is that extra self-reference which constitutes its activity. As we said, in deliberation we valued an impulse by rehearsing the consequences which would probably result if that impulse were acted upon. We turn over the impulse in terms of its outcome, and by seeing it in its outcome we objectify it. The end of that intellectual process is found, of course, when the process of valuing reaches an equilibrium, when some unified, self-consistent value is mentally presented. We call that, in ordinary language, making up one's mind. The deliberative process has been one of inquiry conditioned upon doubt; we were undetermined about the real value or worth of the competing impulses. When we make up our mind it means that we have come to some conclusion, we have figured out a certain worth. In other terms, this is the process of decision, of determination, signifying that the limit of this intellectual process has been reached, and that consequently the point of overt action has been reached.

Now the emotional process parallels the intellectual one. More strictly speaking, the discussion and analysis of it parallels the other one. In reality there is only one process. We have previously isolated the objective side of that process, that single process, and now we turn to its subjective, or feeling side. Its commencement is conflict of habits; its course is one of valuation, but of immediate subjective valuation; and its terminus is preference—preference being just the same thing on the emotional side that decision, or resolution, determination, is on the intellectual.

What is meant then by subjective or immediate valuation is that instead of measuring worth in terms of something else, we take it just as it is. Any worth which is immediately appreciated is feeling. In one sense there is no definition of a process, there is simply an identification of it. That is what we mean when we say "feeling." The impulse A not only has a worth which may be stated in terms of other experiences, B and C, which it leads up to; but being an experience, it has a certain value of its own, direct, and on its own account. So too, B and C, as they are called before the mind, not only have a value in reference to A, but they themselves, as experiences, as mental rehearsals, possess a certain attractiveness or a certain repulsiveness, immediately, on their own account.

The word feeling, then, in its broadest sense, is a name for this purely immediate, face-to-face consciousness of worth. Now just because it is so immediate, it is not finally trustworthy. That is, the intellectual process is in a way necessary in order to make up for the deficiencies of this too direct valuation. Things which seem to possess a negative value immediately may possess a very positive one measured in terms of final outcomes, and vice versa. But on the other hand, the intellectual process would all be in the air if it did not terminate in feelings, in direct appreciation. We value A in terms of B and C. What value have B and C unless they have some immediate value? We must determine them in terms of something else, and so on indefinitely. There would be no limit to a merely intellectual process, and they would always lead on to something else by association, by suggestion.

As a matter of fact the intellectual and the feeling sides are always checking each other. What we term pleasure and pain are the most striking instances, of course, of this immediate value. A man may resolve to carry out a certain line of action against great obstacles and at great hazard because he has determined that it is right, because he can anticipate certain further experiences which seem to him of the proper sort; and yet his immediate consciousness may be a natural dread of doing this thing, a natural shrinking from it, so that immediately the thing would be given valuation.

Feeling has a narrower sense as well as this wider sense. In the narrower sense emotion has to be distinguished from feeling. In the narrower sense feeling is directly stimulated and aroused, while emotion is conditioned upon the presence of an image. A man has heart disease and he gets certain organic feelings corresponding to that, feelings of choking, suffocation, palpitation, which are painful. Or a man hears some bad news and is what we call "sick at heart." The actual sensations in the two cases may be very much alike, but the second case only would be an emotional condition, because it would have been stimulated by some image— hearing of the loss of a friend, or of the failure of some cherished plan, something of that sort. Feeling in the narrower sense is what we sometimes qualify by the adjective "physical." These feelings are so immediately aroused, so directly stimulated, that so far as their genesis is concerned, there is no ideal element present. But wherever we have an emotion, we have an ideal excitation for it; that is, there is an image which arouses it.

Observation of infant life will show that there is no emotion as distinct from feeling until the child is capable of expectation. To be capable of expectation means that one hold an image distinct from the sensations which refer to the present situation. Before this time the child would have feelings of comfort and discomfort due to matters of food, temperature, physical ease and dis-ease; but now the child has an image of himself engaged upon something, and that image arouses a feeling, or that image is interfered with, and the emotion of disappointment is felt. In physiological terms the distinction is that feeling in the narrower sense is peripheral excitation and emotion is central excitation.

Both feeling and emotion would be distinguished from interest. Interest is like emotion in that it is always ideally conditioned. It differs from emotion in that the feeling attaches directly to the idea or image. In that respect it is like feeling in the immediacy of its excitation, save that it is an ideal that arouses it; while emotion is found when there is a certain tension or conflict between the image and the feeling reaction. Emotion involves disturbance and agitation. Whenever there is emotion, there is a divergence between the sense situation and the image situation. For instance, hope is an emotion rather than an interest because in it there is a continual oscillation, a continual alternation between the image situation and the existing situation. There is tension between the two. Of course it is just the same in fear, surprise, curiosity, anger, dread. You cannot find a completely unified situation. Where you have such an emotion you must speak of it in terms of tension and vibration back and forth between the sense and image sides. Now let anger become settled hatred and that disturbance and agitation due to tension disappear. The person simply settles back into a continuous present disposition or attitude toward the thing which is hated. It may spring up, flash up, in emotion, at particular junctures.

So too, hope would cease to be emotional and become an interest when it was transformed into a persistent endeavor in a given direction, when it became a definite interest in realizing the thing which before had been simply hoped for. So when curiosity is transformed into investigation, it ceases to be an emotion and becomes an interest. The feeling is now attached directly to the idea in its execution. The excitation, then, the disturbance which is characteristic of all emotion being stirred up, is due precisely to the fact that the given situation is thrown into relief over against an ideal situation; the image situation is accelerated by its contrast with the given situation. Anger is about as sheer an emotion as there is. It comes as near being a pure feeling before it becomes indignation; but even then there must be the image element, there must be the thought of the object against which the feeling reaction is directed. There must be the thought of that as being changed, being hurt, or something of the sort, by the outgoing reaction. Let that image disappear, or let that image become identified with the feeling of the immediate situation, and the emotion of anger will disappear.

We get then, on the descriptive side, the feeling factors in the analysis of an emotion: two habits, at least two habits, conflicting with each other and inhibiting each other, each lacking the complete and overt manifestation of the other. In this mutual lacking we get an alternation of stress and of partial discharge. The point of highest tension is found now on one side, now on the other. This action and reaction seem to be very characteristic of the emotional condition. Emotions proverbially go in waves. We have our ups and our downs on the emotional side. It shifts around from the ideal side to the given side, or vice versa. Now this alternating of partial discharge, or stress, goes on until one dies off from sheer exhaustion, or until the energy aroused on both sides is deflected along some single channel: when we either get a relapse back into a state of mere feeling, or an advance into the stage of interest.

In this alternation of stress from the given to the ideal side, positive value may seem to attach to one side or the other. As one becomes positive, the other becomes negative. If the positive value is attached to the feeling of the existing situation, then the feeling that goes with the image side will be felt as an intruder, as something which is to be got rid of, expelled. In other words, we shall have the emotional motive of aversion. If positive value is attached to the image side, if it is welcomed, found attractive, then the reaction is against the feeling of the existing situation, and we have desire. Now since there always are both elements present, simply with the shifting of stress from one pole to the other, there is no such thing as an unmixed condition of desire or aversion. When there is aversion against the image state, there is desire for the maintenance of the present, there is desire for it to become unimpeded; and when there is desire on one side, there is dislike or aversion of whatever interferes with the unimpeded engrossment of that which is felt to be desirable. In other words, emotion always involves a mixed condition of satisfaction and dissatisfaction, of pleasure and pain as ideally conditioned.

We may say in passing, although it has more psychological value than ethical, that this distinction between the painful and pleasurable, the disagreeable and agreeable, has only been made very recently. The agreeable and disagreeable [are?] the pleasurable and painful that are ideally conditioned. It is the painful and pleasurable on the level of emotion instead of being on the level of feeling in the narrower sense. When we talk of anything as disagreeable or agreeable, it shows that there is an image there which provokes the feeling reaction.

On the stage of interest, this feeling of pleasure and pain becomes, say, joy and sorrow, happiness and misery. Happiness, like the agreeable, is ideally conditioned. It is aroused by an image but it marks a more settled disposition and attitude. It marks a disposition of character and conduct in general instead of an excitation which waxes and wanes with the rise and fall of any particular image.

Restating this in terms which make it a better basis for the ethical discussion, emotion is the immediate appreciation of the conflict between impulse and idea, conflict in which the impulse at once tends to arouse and excite the impulse to realization, and tends to check and inhibit it by bringing into play some other impulse. Now if we say that the impulses represent the executive capacity, then they represent powers of execution, while the idea stands for aims to be realized.

The significance of the emotion is the conflict and the need of adjustment between the formed element in action and the ideal element. It represents the lack of equilibrium between active power and tendency and aim. Of course the movement is toward an equilibrium, toward an equalization. Hence the importance of the emotions. Action without force behind it, without power, is meaningless. Action which represents simply force is disorderly and ineffectual for quite another reason. It has no ideal regulating it, controlling it. It represents then the strain of adjustment between excitation and control, the impulses urging forward all appetites, inclination to action; the image, the idea, springing up to check these impulses, throwing them back on themselves in these waves of disturbed agitation.

That general principle may be made more significant by referring to Darwin's theory of the expression of emotion. In this connection I would refer you to two articles in the November 1894 and the January 1895 numbers of the *Psychological Review,* in which I have discussed at greater length the psychology of the emotions from this point of view.[1]

Darwin's theory, in its most important aspect, is that so-called emotional attitudes represent the reduced survivals of acts that were once directly serviceable to the agent. All the characteristic attitudes of anger, for instance, the throwing up of the head, the pushing out of the chest, the tightening of the muscles of the arms, the doubling of the fists, the peculiar expression of the face, the retraction of the upper lip, possibly the gnashing of the teeth: they are simply survivals of the original overt act of attack, when our semihuman ancestors actually threw themselves on the prey and these movements were needed to carry out the act. If we take the emotion which is antithetical to anger, fear, the characteristic expressions of the emotion of fear are survivals of an original act of evasion or retreat. The bashful child puts his hand before his face, or gets behind his mother's apron. It is simply a miniature act of retreat, of getting out of sight.

Darwin was deeply interesting in discussing the expression of emotions, but I think you can at once see that if the principle is correct, it has a wider scope. It throws great light on the psychology of the emotions themselves, giving us the point of view from which the emotions have to be typically considered. We begin with certain fundamental, or racial, life habits, habits which pertain to the most fundamental necessities—the procuring of food, the avoiding or the attacking of enemies, and the association with others, either in the form of mating with one of the other sex, or associating with those of the same herd or flock. There would be, then, those race habits which would lie at the basis of all our fundamental emotions. Now as long as these modes of action are not inhibited, there is no emotion, in our sense. As long as they are not brought into contact with images which tend to check their immediate expression, there is no emotion. We talk, travelers talk, about the rage of the lion about to attack his prey, as if it were the same thing that we call the emotion of anger. But there is no reason to suppose that the growling and the lashing of the tail are anything more than parts of the action, preparations for the action. Undoubtedly there are accompanying feelings, just as there are feelings accompanying getting satisfactory food; but supposing that there is an emotion—it is reading more into that than there is any call for.

But let one of those fundamental modes of action become intention, with an idea, or with an image, and then it will be turned back on itself and come to consciousness in an emotional form. Now as we all know, these animal types of activity are in the human being met at once by ideal suggestions. They have to function in certain social situations that are very different from the conditions under which they were evolved and they are at once contradicted by images which correspond to the existing situation, and which attempt to control in the interests of the existing social situation. When I say animal, I mean animal in the sense that their continuance in some form is necessary to the maintenance of life. However refined their expression becomes, we are dependent upon the presence of these fundamental modes of action as ever was any animal. There must be this instinctual reaction with reference to the things which are absolutely necessary to the maintenance of the race of the individual: food, sex, and the more immediate relations of association, either in a friendly or a hostile way. Now the fundamental emotional excitations such as anger and fear would represent original, complete activities reduced to partial tendencies through being inhibited by ideal suggestions, these ideal suggestions being the counterpart of the existing social status.

February 16, 1898

The point of view suggested yesterday, being an interpretation really of Darwin's work on emotions, is that certain race habits which mark the most fundamental adjustments of the environment, along the line of food and sex particularly, become organized into the individual structure; that, however, these activities have to be readapted to the changed situation, the changed environment; and especially in the human agent, to the fact that the environment has become consciously socialized and that the adjustment of these two factors to each other is what brings about the disturbance and the agitation. That [is the] general theory, which I think accounts for the so-called mysterious, deep, unanalyzable character of our emotions. They well up from sources which are back of the individual's consciousness; they are the emergence in the individual of these racial habits. It is as much a source of surprise to the individual, therefore, as it would be to anyone else, when these great emotional waves roll in on him. He seems to be at first, rather, a theater, at which they display themselves; or as a passive spectator, he seems to come from behind his individuality and to be intellectually unanalyzable.

We know how a school of writers has emphasized tremendously this refractoriness of the emotions to any conscious intellectual treatment. It is in general the standpoint that puts the heart in a superior position to the head, and which proclaims that a man must live in and through his feelings, get his moral inspiration through his feelings, and that the intellect is simply a machine for cold analysis and should occupy a very subordinate place. That is an exaggeration, but it has some justification in the fact that the typical emotions do arise in the adaptation of the race factors in the individual to the variable factor which is connected with the existing social situation.

The urgency of the fundamental emotions is connected with this same principle. The fact that at first in child life they lie so utterly beyond control, the fact that so many of the moral problems of life have to do with the regulation of these emotions, that to some the emotions seem the great disturbance of equilibrium, has led some ethical schools to go to the extreme of saying, as the Stoics have done, that the emotions must be gradually crushed out, starved to death, that reason may become supreme. But they misinterpret the place occupied by the emotions in life.

Physiologically the race habits would be found in motor and vasomotor coordinations centering in taste and smell, and immediate contact, especially with reference to sex. The images to which they have to be adapted represent lines of activity which are mediated particularly through the eye and the ear, which stand for more indirect and remote value in experience; so that the emotional disturbance would be largely found, on the physiological side, in the adjustments of the motor and vasomotor habits which originally center in these immediate activities relating to food and sex. The suggestions coming through the eye and ear represent in a way a sort of dislocation, the severing of their attachment to the immediate sense life as found in the tasting and smelling and contact, and transfer the values over to the eye and ear. The motor and the vasomotor activities would here present the stimulation, while the eye and the ear activities would represent the control of the stimulus. The eye and the ear of course represent the remoter stimuli, the remoter considerations which influence conduct, the eye the remoter in space, and the ear the remoter, of course, in space: but more particularly on the side of time through language and ideas communicated by both in order to influence the conduct of the individual.

The intensity of the emotion measures both the difficulties of effecting this adjustment of the immediate and the mediate factors, and also the importance and necessity of effecting that adjustment. What we term the feelings, as feelings, insist on immediate expression and gratification. These feelings become emotionalized in tone by being attached to the images of the remoter consequences which we get hold of especially through the eye and ear. When these fundamental habits conflict with each other, an inhibition takes place through the conflict with each other, an inhibition takes place through the conflict so that the acts are reduced to active attitudes, and to dispositions. Not all overt motor discharge and vasomotor discharge are suppressed of course; some immediate overt expression still occurs. It would be a physiological impossibility that all this energy should be damned up, that none of it should find any outlet along the outgoing nerves. This outgoing discharge results in the change of sensation, and it is through that change of sensation that the active part of the emotional conditions comes into consciousness. That statement I give as an interpretation in the light of the general principle laid down by James's theory regarding the emotions.

James's theory, as you all know, is that there first takes place an instinctive reaction. Then that reaction causes certain changes in the muscles and in the viscera, in the whole circulatory system, thus making itself known in changes in contact sensations, in organic visceral circulatory sensations, and in what we may term for convenience a muscular sensation; and that those sensations, the resonance of these instinctive responses, are what constitute the emotion as a conscious quality. Or, as he puts it epigrammatically, we do not run because we feel afraid; we feel afraid because we run.[2] There is an instinctive withdrawal from the threatening object which throws the organism into a certain condition: and that condition has its own sensational report, and that constitutes the emotion on its conscious side.

It seems to me there can be no doubt of the correctness of Mr. James's statement. The chief thing against its general acceptance, aside from failure to understand it, seems to be the fact that he leaves the active side (what he calls the instinctive response) and this conscious, sensorial side into too external relations to each other. There does not seem to be any intrinsic, organic connection between the dynamic reaction and the sensations. The theory under development I think explains and interprets what James presents as the purely empirical nature of introspective observation. Instead of these instinctive responses being arbitrary or disconnected or incoherent in any way, they represent the necessary fundamental adjustments to the environment. They are simply the race habits expressed under certain conditions. That expression, like the activity, reflects, repeats itself in certain sensations. These sensations, therefore, do not constitute the whole of the emotion, as James seems to make them; they constitute simply the immediate feeling side of the emotion. The ordinary man includes in his conception of anger, not the mere feeling of anger, but he thinks first of all of this active tendency or disposition, his tendency to hit somebody or to crush out something. On the basis of what has been said, that is a normal element; it is the primary element in the emotion, but that as finding partial expression, partial because of inhibition, gives rise, like all conflicting activities, to sensation; and that constitutes the feeling side of the emotion, while the growing consciousness of qualities to which the activities are directed constitutes the objective or intellectual factor in the emotion.

In other words James's theory is perfectly true if we confine it to the one element of the emotion which we may term the feel[ing] of anger or hatred or whatsoever—the immediate particular coloring that it has in consciousness. But the emotion includes besides that the dynamic tendency to act in a certain way, and also the image qualities or values which the active attitude tends to produce or to destroy. In other words, out of the general confused consciousness which follows directly upon the conflict of these habits with each other gradually emerge two types of conscious value. The particular sensations which are objectively definite sensations, which are mediated through the eye and ear, become the intellectual con tent, become the image, in other words, which represents the future direction of action. The other qualities thus mediated through the organic conditions in general, the vasomotor and the muscular, become the sensational or the direct feel[ing] side of the emotion as an attitude.

James puts the matter as if we first had a perfectly clear perception or image, as if that brought about an active instinctive reaction; and that then came the emotion, the feeling, which is the reverberation of action. In an illustration on which he uses more or less, a man first sees a bear. Then he has an instinctive adjustment or reaction as an intellectual content. And then finally he feels the physiological reverberation or resonance of this reaction.[3] First, the idea; secondly, the action; thirdly, the emotional feeling.

Now without questioning at all his statements so far as relates to this one element of the feel[ing], I think I cannot accept what he says of the relationship which these three elements bear to each other. There is a certain activity going on, say, the activity of seeing, of looking. It is not a definite intellectual content but it is primarily an activity. As an element of the content of that activity there comes the sight of a bear. Now there follows the reaction to this action. And in that action both the intellectual factor and the feeling factor emerge and are set over against each other. At first he does not see the bear as an enemy, but he reacts; and not only in the reaction does the feeling side emerge. The intellectual side also emerges, what the bear means as an objective fact.

If you take the case of an immediate fright I think the point will come out. You hear a sudden noise as you walk on a dark night on some Chicago street, and you feel suddenly a scare. You get a sensation of fright. I think if you will notice such cases, you will find that the relation presents both the emotion and a distinct intellectual idea. We jump, or get ready to jump, or our flesh creeps. That is reaction. Then we feel that and it constitutes the emotional tone. And as the excitation subsides there arises some definite intellectual consciousness of the probable object which, as we say, caused the fright. We think of a burglar or of a dog running along through dead leaves, or the creaking of a tree. But that definite intellectual location comes after the reaction, and in and through the reaction, just as much as does the feeling side. It is psychologically false to suppose it was there before. We say: "Oh, it was only a dog which frightened me," and we speak as if we had known it all the time. But we read our causal explanation back and make of it as something which presented itself at the time, when as a matter of fact it did not do that.

You will recognize that this is simply an application of the same general principle regarding sensation and image that we had in the discussion of deliberation. You have the activities conflicting with each other, then the period of confusion, and then the gradual defining of that in two directions: one the sensory one, and the other the image one.

We could not on this basis adopt the hypothesis which James leaves open to us to adopt, that simply the coarser, more physical emotions are cases of direct reverberation, while the more ideal ones are without this sensational quality. The only difference, of course, between the two would be in the degree of mediation. That is, in the so-called higher emotions, relatively speaking, the image value is the important one; say, in the case of art receptions, or the religious emotion, or the intellectual emotions, curiosity, or the discovery of new truth where all the importance is attached to the image side. But it would still be true that the feeling tone, which keeps it in the region of warm passions at all, would be the feeling of the direct active attitude assumed. Those things do not stand out in consciousness by themselves as they do in cases of fear or ordinary anger, but they are there and constitute a sort of bath of feeling in which the intellectual content is sunk or absorbed.

I will go on to speak briefly of the principle on which the emotions may be classified. I shall not attempt a classification in detail. You will remember what James says about the tediousness of a descriptive classification of the emotions and how little it amounts to. That is perfectly true, I think, if we can get nothing but descriptive classification; but if we can get a genetic classification which differentiates the emotions with reference to their different modes of origin, the classification would have some significance. It is just the difference between the old classification of plants and animals, first the collecting of a lot of them and then looking them over to see the common attributes, and the modern classification on the evolutionary hypothesis of the community of origin. The basis for the classification of the emotions of course would be the particular type of the adjustment of the organism to the environment and of the environment to the organism. In general, the organism accomplishes its purposes either by movement toward or by movement away from the stimulus. Each of these typical modes of activity would be subdivided according as the activity was directed either towards getting rid of the object, subordinating it to the organism, or as the movement was directed towards cherishing and building up the object and, relatively speaking, subordinating the organism to the development of the object.

For instance, anger would evidently be a case of movement towards the object of a destructive sort, of a sort which tended to make of the object a mere means to the organism. The angry animal or the angry man denies the value of the thing against which the movement is directed—he wants to get it out of the way or reduce it to a mere factor; while love in sex form or more highly idealized forms would be a positive movement towards the object of a cherishing sort, where the relationship is reversed and the organism is subordinated to the care of the object in question. Of course the parental relations, especially of the mother in the care of the young among the animals, would be an example of the same sort.

On the withdrawal side, we would have either withdrawal to get rid of a threatening element—flight, fear, caution, and so on—or else withdrawal into self for the sake of nourishing, cherishing, and building up something. There is the isolation, the withdrawal always in the care of the young, the hunting out of a safe place. And there is isolation and withdrawal in the saving up of food. Now at the outset that is possibly conditioned simply by fear, but it soon comes to function in the positive direction, in the interest of cherishing a certain form of life. All cases of protection, pity, compassion would be cases of this type; so also would ordinary prudential activities, self-protection, not simply against some immediate danger, but where a man becomes prudent, looking out to save things with reference to possible emergencies, and lays up a store of things greater than there is any immediate demand for, for the sake of future possibilities. There the cherishing function is exhibited in the direction of withdrawal rather than in the direction of movement onwards, movement towards a thing. We have in the activities themselves a continual rhythm. They could be traced back, if one had accurate knowledge of details, to a chemical and physiological statement: expansion leading to the appropriation of food, or sex attachment, and contraction, either for the sake of avoiding an obstacle or enjoying and protecting something which has been secured. In higher forms it is the rhythm between consciousness in selecting, defining particular elements, and the utilization of the material thus secured in building up further capacities.

If we were to work out a scheme for the classification of the emotions we would find that they would be reduced to these four types or of course to a combination and interaction of the four types. The more complex, the emotion the more difficult it would be to classify it. It might be found possibly to have more or less of all the elements within it. I shall not go into any such inventory, however, but will simply make two suggestions.

First, we will find later on that this rhythm between the movements of contraction and expansion is for two purposes, both equally necessary to the realization of life. It throws a good deal of light on the moral question of so-called egoism and altruism, or of self-love and benevolence. Psychologically egoism and altruism are just the typical expressions of the conduct in the movement of the self away from the environment for the time being, on the one hand, and the outgoing active movement toward the environment, on the other.

The other suggestion is that if we take the emotions that we call sentiments in the good sense of sentiments, the emotions in which the image element has become predominant, we would be able, in theory at least, to get a genetic development out of the more primitive and therefore cruder adjustments. It has, moreover, a positive ethical bearing as indicating the economical importance of the emotions, that they have to do somehow with the adjustment of the organism to the environment; and that the more complex and spiritualized emotions like reverence and compassion simply mean that the agent and the environment between which the action has taken place are more conscious, or more socialized, and are definable in more mediate terms, while the coarser emotions simply represent the adjustment between the organism and the environment of a more immediate sort.

Take reverence, for example. On one side that must represent a form of fear, of socialized fear; the dread of doing anything which will awaken the disapprobation of others; the fact of being ashamed before others at doing certain things. Of course reverence is not simply this socialized fear and dread. It has on the other hand the element of the active going out of the individual in becoming instrumental to the maintenance of certain positive values, the subordination of the individual to the ends maintained by the community as a whole—a subordination which, instead of lowering the worth of the individual, dignifies him because he can fight for and help maintain the social group. If you take reverence as a highly complex emotion at present and trace it back, you will find it growing out of the interaction of these two elements: on the negative side fear in the form of shame, and on the positive side the defense and maintenance of the public good.

The value, then, of this psychological theory of emotions growing out of a sort of combination of Darwin's and James's theory is that it gives us the point of view from which we may interpret the significance of the emotions in general. Where we are not able to trace the definite relationship and content in detail, we still, because of our general theory, have a right to assume that the emotions mark certain great constructive attitudes which are turned by the habits of the individual to the needs of the environment in which the individual finds himself, and which he presents to himself in terms of images.

SECTION 2. THE PSYCHOLOGY OF PLEASURE AND PAIN

February 17, 1898

In discussing pleasure and pain we have to distinguish between that which is in physiological language peripherally aroused and that centrally excited: that is, between the pleasure or pain which gives tone to the sensation, and that which depends upon the intervention of an image. Directly, conduct has only to do with the latter. The immediate pleasures and pains in themselves are accidental, and with reference to them the agent is not an agent. He is a patient. That is, he simply accepts or receives what fortune or environment throws his way. He does not actively enter into the determination or possession of the feeling. When a man eats a good meal there is a certain immediate feeling of pleasurable satiety. If his finger is cut there is an immediate feeling of pain. Now no direct moral quality can be said to attach to feelings of that sort. I mean immediately there cannot. They are sheer gifts of fortune or of nature on the face of them.

Here is one criticism of the hedonist's point of view. He puts on the same level the pleasures and pains which are dependent upon the given structure of the agent, upon his direct reactions to stimuli, and into whose happenings he does not therefore actively enter; and the pleasures and pains which are attendant upon the images which the agent presents to himself and over which therefore he possesses active control. While the pleasures and pains are feelings in both cases, in the first instance they are relatively passive depending upon the contacts of the individual, while in the second they are relatively constructive because they rise and fall with the images which occur inside the deliberative process of the individual. The immediate pleasures and pains feelings enter into the moral life insofar as the individual has to assume a certain general attitude toward getting them or going without them; but that is always dependent upon the intervention of the image. In the sense in which the term physical was used the other day, pleasures and pains are purely physical, not moral. But as the image of these pleasures and pains recurs to the individual, he practically adopts a certain attitude toward them, either seeking them out or avoiding them, or of just going about his business and allowing them to come as they naturally would come. Now because of that necessity of assuming some kind of an attitude toward these pleasures and pains, they become tremendously important factors in the direction of the moral life.

A certain type of virtues and vices is defined mainly on the basis of exactly this attitude. The vices of the glutton, of the voluptuary, for example, simply mean that certain attitudes, through the intervention of the image, have been taken toward these pleasures and pains, that the individual has formed the habit of seeking the situations which produce certain pleasures. He cannot produce them at will, but he can select the situations in which they do arise. On the other hand, the value of temperance—in the Greek sense of temperance: self-control, right-mindedness—means that another attitude as taken toward the pleasures. The individual no longer seeks them out as an end in themselves but pursues another course of action based on other considerations and allows them to take their natural course. If they present themselves he gets the pleasure; and if not, he does not. Anyone familiar with Greek ethics knows how much store the Greeks set by that capacity of being influenced by pleasures and pains in the sense of not being an ascetic, but having the ability to enjoy the pleasures when they came, and enjoying them to the full; and yet having the habit of determining the ends of life on other principles and not allowing the pleasures and pains themselves to become ruling ends, but simply present themselves as they would normally while in the pursuit of other ends.

Both Plato and Aristotle define courage on the same basis: the disposition to assume a certain attitude toward fear.[4] It is neither hardening one's self against fear nor seeking to expel it from life. Plato in the *Laws* criticizes the Spartan idea of the elimination of this feeling while the Athenians recognize that it belongs legitimately in life.[5] It is simply taking such an attitude toward the feelings as will utilize it in a given direction. To the man who determines his end through other considerations, if the pleasure feelings present themselves—well and good; he simply takes them as incidental to that course of action, but he does not allow them to become the determining motive and end.

That is practically the analysis which Plato and Aristotle give of courage and temperance. It contains a very positive contribution to all ethics, but it serves as an illustration of the way in which pleasure and pain elements, possessed originally of no moral quality at all, become influential factors in the direction of the moral life. We must resist the allurements of certain pleasures as imaged, so far as allowing them to become the determining factor in conduct, but not resist them insofar as attempting to expel them absolutely from life. The Greek ideal attempts to get a balance between asceticism and self-indulgence; and certainly as an ideal, whether the Greeks really lived up to it or not, it did maintain that balance much more thoroughly than any later type of ethical theory has done. You will remember that Plato in the *Laws* defends a certain amount of the orgies accompanying the Bacchic festivals on the ground that a man was not really temperate unless he could indulge himself in a certain amount of pleasure without allowing it to become a determining motive in his conduct.

February 21, 1898

The other day I was speaking about the pleasures and pains which are immediate, or which in physiological language are peripherally stimulated. Such pleasures and pains represent the accomplishment of certain fundamental adjustments. In their more immediate form they gather about the satisfaction of the appetite for food, the general physical well being, the adaption to the larger features of the environment (like temperature), and the general balance of the internal organs that maintain life, so-called organic sensations, and the sex appetite. Whenever we have any one of these fundamental adjustments which are necessary to the maintenance of life effected, we have a certain pleasure. Whenever we have one of these adjustments interrupted, or failing to accomplish itself, we have corresponding pain.

We are of course very far from the possibility of any adequate biological statement of the origin and development of pleasures and pains, but we can state two factors that enter into the problem. One is that a reservoir of energy which is in excess of the normal demands of the environment would be a useful thing. We can imagine an animal developed in such a way as to have just enough energy to meet the stimuli which it usually encounters. As long as that environment remains uniform that animal would be at no disadvantage. But if there were any shifting, any unusual element encountered, there would be an element of strain to which that animal could no adopt itself; while the other animal which was no better fitted to cope with the ordinary circumstances that it was meant for, having an excess of stored energy, was able to effect an adjustment and bridge over the gap. The principle then of excess of energy, the storing of excess of energy, is in the long run economical, although in a shorter view it might not be useful, or even might be hurtful, as of course it takes the expenditure of energy to store up energy. Now some way or other it is reasonable to suppose a connection between this principle of excess of energy and that of pleasure-pain. I think the particular scheme suggested by Grant Allen in his *Physiological Aesthetics*[6] is both vague and imaginative, but the general purport of his theory may be justified by assuming that there is some connection between the two. Pleasure does not mark the mere effecting of an adjustment, as if the organism just responded to the stimulus with the exact amount of energy required and none to spare, but marks the response with a welling forth of energy, a pouring out of energy which is in excess of the exact amount required to effect this particular combination.

The other factor is that, on the theory of natural selection, pleasures must associate themselves with the activities which upon the whole are useful, and pains with those which are upon the whole hurtful. An animal that found pleasure in lines of action that were mischievous either to it as an individual or to the species to which it belonged would eventually get wiped out in the struggle for existence.

These two statements put in ethical terms would mean about the following: pleasure is valuable and is to be sought for insofar as it is a mark of vitality. Pain is to be avoided, morally as well as prudentially, insofar as it is an index of depression. Just because the pleasure has, upon the whole, accompanied and grown out of this reservoir of available energy, this superfluity, so to speak, of life, it is itself a stimulus to expansive, generous activity. Just so far as pain has grown up under contrary circumstances, the suffering of it and the inflicting of it tend to paralyze and to restrict action, to give it a mean and stingy quality which it would not otherwise possess. The faculty for enjoying pleasures is a morally desirable end. It is an end to be cultivated.

The other point concerns them, not as ends, but as clues, as signs. Because pleasure represents upon the whole action that has proved advantageous, it has a certain indicative quality. But that is only presumptive, not in any sense final. It is just as important morally to note the limitation of the sign quality, as it is its existence. There are at least two limitations. In the first place it represents favorable adjustments on the basis of past situations rather than of the present. Pleasure accompanying a certain action does mean that that mode of action has been useful, but that of course does not settle the question that it will be useful now. There is [still] a further problem to be raised: How far does the pleasure situation agree with the conditions under which this line of action was evolved and in which it proved advantageous? Of course this means that there is an element which has to be dealt with morally there. The situation has changed in some respects, so much that modes of action which were once directly advantageous, and which still are pleasures, must be inhibited and deflected into quite different channels of activity. There is no doubt that there is a pleasure accompanying the rush of ongoing activity in anger. There is no doubt that that measures, biologically, a past utility in maintaining the species and the individual. But of course it is equally true that the factors must now be reckoned with. It is not merely a sign or clue to be unhesitatingly followed.

It is interesting to note how Mr. Spencer, who has attempted to combine an evolutionary statement with a thoroughly hedonistic statement, who has endeavored to show that pleasures and pains not merely have a certain indicative value but have an infallible indicative value morally, has attempted to escape the import of the principle just laid down. He has to recognize that as things are at present, pleasures and pains are not necessarily satisfactory guides and he gives a number of points in which they fall. But he says that is due to the imperfection of the stage of development reached, and he sets up an ideal condition of completed development, as he calls it (arrested development, I should term it), in which because the whole process has been worked out and a final adjustment effected between the organism and the environment, the pleasures and pains will be absolutely safe guides.[7] So he makes their failure now to be incidental to the imperfect stage of evolution reached. With respect to that, we can say that we are living in this imperfect stage of development. The concession means that for our purposes they are not trustworthy guides. We can afford to let the people who live in the other condition reckon with the pleasures and pains consequence on such a condition. They have no working significance for us, even granting his argument.

The other point would have to do with his whole conception of completed evolution and the absolute equilibrium between the adaptation of the organism and the environment.[8] I shall not go into a criticism of that general principle excepting to make one suggestion. Unless we imagine some revolution in the organism, such complete adaptation, while it would not be painful, [it] would neither be pleasurable. It would mean a reign of habit. There would be no more adjustments or readjustments to be made, and in consequence the feeling element would drop down below consciousness. If such conditions were conceivable, I do not see that human beings would be different from a machine which has avoided friction and is running smoothly. Objectively it would be very nice to look at, but subjectively there would be no pleasure any more than there would be pain. In such an ideal condition pleasure would not be the guide more than it is now, because there would be no pleasure.

The second limitation to the indicative value of the feeling is that since it has been made with reference to the past, it represents certain average features of the environment, rather than exceptional ones, and represents present, rather than varying ones. That is, we can say that they are signs upon the whole, but we cannot say that they are signs every time. Perhaps the simplest illustration of this would be the pleasure accompanying the sensation of sweet. The sugar of lead is as pleasant as cane sugar. Obviously the indicative value in the two cases is very different. That means to me that upon the whole, with reference to the great majority of stimuli from the environment, the substances which give us the sensation of taste have been foods, have been positively advantageous to the organism. But there could be no guarantee in that fact that every substance which stimulates the nerves in this particular way should also be a food. If poisons which afford a sweet taste had been just as frequent factors in the environment as foods which possess it, we should probably find the sweet taste painful, or sometimes painful and sometimes pleasurable. But since upon the whole foods are frequent and poisons rare, we simply have this uniform reaction, and consequently it cannot be trusted absolutely. There may be value as a presumptive sign, but how far we can presume upon it must be determined by the interpretation of the signs, by the use of one's intelligence and judgment.

That a thing is pleasant means, in other words, that it favors the activity of some particular organ. It is probable that even in the case of sugar of lead the immediate nerve endings are stimulated to advantageous activity and we get a pleasant taste, but other parts of the organism are differently affected, of course. On the whole there is this presumption that what favors the development of one set of organs would be favorable to the organism as a whole, but that is far from being an absolute assurance in every particular case.

Now it seems to me that the results of such a psychological analysis agree with what we might call the unsophisticated judgment of the common man. Not that we can appeal to the latter as a final criterion in this matter, but it is a thing which has a certain amount of weight. Now this average moral common sense (seems to me) takes the ground precisely that pleasure is not something to be avoided for fear it shall lead them astray. It is rather a positively valuable factor in life and, under the limitation which common sense puts on the term, innocent occasions for pleasure are to be multiplied and sought for. There is always a reasonable presumption that the course of action which a healthy person finds pleasant is likely to turn out moral also, but no one must allow himself to make this principle absolute and say that simply pleasure, and only pleasure, and pleasure at all hazards is to be sought for; nor yet that in this particular situation, while the course of action is pleasant, it is at the same time immoral. That is, the moral common sense, it seems to me, is neither ascetic nor hedonistic. It neither considers pleasure as a worthy element, or regards it as something dangerous, nor as a thing in itself to be sought for. And that would agree precisely with the outcome of this psychological analysis.

Pleasure and pain have not only this sign value, but they have a stimulating value. Because they have a sign value, certain nascent activities tend to start. They are accompanied by feelings of pleasure or pain. Now under normal circumstances that accompaniment will tend to reinforce or to check the action. If we start to do something and as we start we find it pleasurable, we will go ahead with additional interest. If it is painful we will stop and think, and wonder if it is worthwhile to do it or not; and the tendency is to check and divert the action. This principle must have been the dominant one in animal life. It must have been the governing system of stimuli and checks to action. Not that the pleasures and pains originally stimulated the action; that is physiologically impossible. It started instinctively, but as it got to going it had a reflex in pleasure or pain, and the animal instinctively trusted to this, either to reinforce or check the starting action.

This holds, I think, to a very considerable extent in human life as a psychological fact. But the principle is complicated by the fact that we can do what the animals probably cannot, that is, re-present. We can image these pleasures and pains and then make them ends in themselves. The hungry animal gets hold of food. That reports itself to him as pleasurable, and that pleasure reinforces, continues the activity. But when the activity ceases, the pleasure dies too. Now the human being can re-present that feeling of pleasure and thereby become an epicure or consciously self-indulgent person with reference to food, while the animal cannot. Consequently the sign value which the direct pleasures and pains have does not hold true to any such extent of the imaged pleasures and pains. The direct pleasure grows out in action which the organism has already entered upon and which presumably has been stimulated by the whole needs of the organism. But the activity which follows an imaged pleasure has no such guarantee of connection with the needs of the organism as a whole. It is the difference, in the ordinary phrase, between eating to live and living to eat. In the former case the pleasure of eating is a positive, and within certain limits, a reliable guide. In the second place the imaged pleasure becomes the stimulus. The particular activity of taste, the pleasure of taste, is isolated; it is made an end by itself, and in being thus isolated it loses its normal stimulus—that is, the stimulus of the organism as a whole. So far then as image, pleasures and pains become the ends of action, our cues become miscues, we are misled, and pathological conditions ensue.

The difference may be otherwise stated. Our appetites are not originally aroused with reference to pleasure and pain at all. Pleasure and pain, however, as soon as the appetites begin to work, come in to influence their quantity and also their direction. But the appetites themselves exist simply as instruments for the satisfaction of the needs of the organism as a whole. Now reason supervenes; more strictly the imaging power comes in. That imaging power may be used in two different ways: in one case to clear up and broaden the consciousness of the condition of the activity, and to interpret the sign value of the pleasure by placing the particular act in a larger situation—what we ordinarily mean by reason controlling the appetite. Or the image may come in and attach itself simply to the pleasure and pain, may hold them up and endeavor to stimulate and direct action by it. In the latter case we get what we know as sensuality or voluptuousness in some of its forms.

February 23, 1898

Not only the immediate pleasures and pains, but the images of such, must be distinguished from the feelings aroused by images. There is a difference between a reproduced or re-presented feeling of pleasure, and the pleasure which is evoked by the reproduction or the construction of a certain situation. Of course the distinction is one of degree and each type shades into the other. We cannot reproduce even a so-called physical feeling directly; that is, if we want to call up the feeling of pleasure got by eating, we will have to image the food and ourselves as eating it; we will have to bring up as much of the objective combination as possible in order to get the feeling reproduced.

But nonetheless there are feelings of pleasure and of pain which are concomitants of an ideally constructed situation which is very far from being a mere reduplicate of anything which has been experienced before. Perhaps some of the greatest joys of life attend in this way the anticipation of lines of action which never have been entered upon before. Consequently the feeling of pleasure cannot be explained as a mere revival through association of a like pleasure previously experienced. Take the pleasure, for example, attendant upon just starting out on a tour of travel which has been anticipated for a time, but yet to which there is no immediate analogue at all in past experience. The image there represents a nascent activity, starting out along certain lines, and it aroused directly its unique response in feeling according to the kind and amount of energy which is represented in this image. Undoubtedly the new line of action will gather into itself and embody, coordinate, a large number of previous modes of action, habits, and elements in habits, but the significant thing is that it does not merely combine to associate them mechanically; they are recoordinated, and each of the old lines of activity is modified by the new mode of action whose starting up is represented by the image.

In other words, we must say of the feelings what is said of the image. It is never a mere reduplicate of any previous experience; it always represents the adaptation of that experience to a new situation or aim. So these ideally evoked pleasures are not copies nor combinations of copies of pleasures and pains previously experienced. There would not be the image if there had not been the previous experience. Neither would there be this pleasure attendant upon the forming image unless there had been experiences along somewhat similar lines before, and unless pleasures had resulted from those experiences. But that does not change the fact that the image is a unique construction when it comes, and not a mere revival or association of previous sensations. Nor does it change the fact that the feeling thus evoked is original and not the mere combination of previous experiences.

The significance of this fact is that it shows the sense in which we can legitimately speak of moral pleasures and pains as distinct from physical pleasures and pains. Of course in one sense they are all physical, they are all physiologically conditioned. But in another sense they are all psychical. Insofar as one feeling is immediately aroused through the contacts which result from a certain line of action, and insofar as the other is aroused by the construction in imagination of a given course of action, we can distinguish between the two as physical and moral, or as sense feelings and as ideal feelings. It means that we have to recognize distinction of quality in pleasures and pains, and not a mere distinction of quantity.

According to hedonistic and associational psychology there would be only degrees of intensity. Even the most highly moralized pleasures, those which are aroused by anticipation of the right course of action, and aroused by it as right, would be nothing but survivals and associations of pleasures that originally had a purely sense origin. That result follows because the associational school regards the image as a mere combination of previous experiences through association, instead of seeing it as a unified and novel experience not in any sense caused by the previous experience, but having its origin in the failure of these previous experiences adequately to function.

Concerning the value of the ideally evoked pleasure, we may say that it serves as a clue or index. It bears the relation of a register to the activity that is going on and like any registration serves to guide future action. That is, just as we look at a thermometer first to tell us how hot it is, and then utilize that registration as an index as to what had better be done next, so the pleasure and pain here is like a thermometric or barometric reading which reveals to us the status of the existing action. We are unconsciously steering ourselves by these signs. We conceive a certain course of action, but pain feelings start up at once. That serves as an unfavorable index to attention; that image tends, other things being equal, to fade out. We conceive another mode of action. A pleasurable reaction follows and that image tends to be selected. The attention goes in that direction and that sort of an end is built up. We are continually steering ourselves by just such reactions. Regarding that as a logical fact it seems to me there can be no doubt.

The question that further comes up then is: What is the moral import of this guiding, steering function attaching to these pleasures and pains? I note three limitations.

1. They are clues, not ends in themselves. At most these pleasures and pains tell us how good or how bad a line of action is. They do not constitute that goodness or badness any more than the thermometric reading constitutes the heat. Consequently, when they are made ends, as of course relatively they may be by dwelling on them and isolating them, the conduct becomes pathological. We said, in speaking of the direct pleasures and pains, that making them ends of action was what constituted psychologically a sensualist—the one who instead of utilizing these pleasures to function normally makes them a controlling end of action. The person who makes this particular type of pleasures (the mediated pleasures) the end of action is a sentimentalist. So far as principle is concerned there is no difference between him and the sensualist. He has made a feeling the controlling end of action. The difference is a psychological one, not a moral one.

One class of persons takes a kind of pleasure which is evoked in one way and the other class of persons takes the kind of pleasure which is evoked in another way, but the man who makes the pleasure of benevolent doing the end of action is morally on the same plane as the man who makes the pleasure of eating the end of action. Through the growing comprehensiveness of images, and their growing complications, there come to be pleasures which are clues to moral action as such. That is, we have distinctly moral pleasures which accompany, and in a sense reward, right action. A man may make those pleasures his object. He may do a right action simply for the sake of getting the feeling of a satisfied conscience, moral complacency, the glow of having done a right thing. But of course morally, just the same contradiction results as results in the case of the sensualist, which has come to be known as the hedonistic paradox. Pleasures are normally the accompaniment of certain ends of action, and the way to get these pleasures is through normal conduct; it is by making the action the end, and letting the feeling be stimulated by that. When the feeling is made the end, it never is got satisfactorily. The energy is in the wrong place and there is always dissatisfaction and irritation. The same thing is true of the man who seeks the pleasure of a satisfied conscience as of the man who seeks the pleasure of satisfied appetites. He can only get a pumped up and more or less factitious mimicry of the genuine article.

Historically there has been a tendency to put these two types of pleasure seekers on different planes. That is, a sensualist is practically universally regarded as insofar forth a bad man. The sentimentalist is regarded as good, or at least as one who means to be good, but who has a somewhat mistaken idea about it. The fact that the pleasure which he seeks is ideally isolated, that it accompanies the thought or right modes of action, has seemed to put it on a higher plane than that of the man who aims at the satisfaction of his physical appetites. I see no justification for making that distinction, unless it be that the man who seeks the ideal pleasure, or the idealized pleasure, is more easily turned into the right course of action than the other man. I must confess personally, while I can see that there might be some arguments in that direction, I do not see that they are very conclusive. It seems that such a person is about as likely to be hopeless as the sensualist is. In fact, insofar as he is apt to pride himself upon the cultivation of these emotions, he is in some respects harder to reach than the other man. It would be in line with the fact that great moral teachers, Jesus particularly, denounced the Pharisees more severely than he did the publicans and sinners, in that their evil seemed to be of a more sophisticated character. And because their consciousness was more highly idealized, they represented less a failure to get on the right track and more an actual deviation and deflection of it.

2. These feelings and clues measure and test the character, or agent concerned, more than they do the value of the particular act concerned. That is, so far as one is already a good man, his feelings of pleasure in the contemplation of certain lines of action will be pretty safe clues. Insofar as he is a bad man, just the opposite would be true. The pleasures taken by him would be rather a symptom that the action was in the wrong direction. If you could tell just what images a man takes pleasure in, you would not have any measure of the real worth of the images, but you would have a mighty certain index to what sort of a man he was. The

pleasures and pains he images would exhibit the nature and tendencies of his interests.

That gives a basis for dealing with a certain class of facts which are continually quoted by the hedonist in support of his position. He says the martyr must find a satisfaction in suffering for his cause or else he would not do it, that in a certain sense he is animated just as much by pleasure as the sensualist is. The story has become current in ethics, regarding Abraham Lincoln. He saw an animal lying in a ditch as he was riding by one day. After he had gone by he turned back and helped the animal out of the ditch. A fellow traveler remarked that he must be a very good man to take so much pains. Lincoln said, no, not in the least, that it was because he felt so uncomfortable that he went back to get rid of his feelings of discomfort. What we have is really the measure of the character involved. It is true that the martyr gets more satisfaction out of being true to his convictions than he could out of being false to those convictions and saving his life. It is simply a question where his interest lies—not interest in the sense of getting a certain advantage—but interest in the sense of the active projection of himself.

It does not follow, however, that he does the act for the sake of the satisfaction, but that he cannot get satisfaction in any other way. It simply reveals the kind of character which is behind. So with Abraham Lincoln, the feeling of the discomfort shows the benevolent element present already in his character. Another man might feel equal discomfort for having passed a saloon without getting a drink. The feeling would not tell whether the particular act was good or bad, but insofar as we decided on other grounds that the act was good, the feeling of pleasure would reveal a good man. Insofar as we decided on other grounds that the act was bad, the feeling of pleasure would reveal a bad man. I think Lincoln rather modestly misstated the true facts of the case. He did not go back merely to get rid of a certain feeling of discomfort. Undoubtedly that was an impelling motive in his going back, but I doubt if we are called upon to say that he isolated that feeling from the objective and active content concerned.

3. This point simply follows out of the two preceding. These signs have to [be] brought out of the merely psychical sphere into the moral. I mean by that, that instead of accepting them at their face value as signs, one must consciously get outside of them and ask how far they are trustworthy signs. I do not believe it would be possible to exaggerate the extent to which we do, under average circumstances, follow the clues of these feelings; not that we make them our ideals, or our motives, but that we instinctively adjust ourselves to them. On the other hand it is not possible to overstate the principle that the good type of character, the conscientious type, is the one who has the capacity, the tendency, whenever any reason presents itself, of getting out of these instinctive adjustments

and impartially surveying the whole thing and judging of the value of these signs, instead of simply following them.

Take a case where a certain person seems himself to be doing right. He does not think much about it; he is doing what seems to be good; he thinks he is doing the natural and inevitable thing under the circumstances. To other people it seems that he is doing wrong. That is not an uncommon case because the distinctions are not cut and dried. It is not simply a question of [not] killing people and not stealing, etc. The problem often involves a great range of complicated elements where it is a very delicate matter to get hold of the differences and distinctions. What makes that difference to the man himself and to other people? Or suppose the same man comes to the conclusion later on that he was acting selfishly then, though all the time he seemed to be doing the natural and inevitable thing. What makes the difference? In one case he is following the clues without stopping to judge of their real value. The other person, or himself at a later time, is taking the clues as tests of the man's character. If he says to himself: "What I am doing now is running smoothly and it affords satisfaction. Why should I not keep on with it?" The other person says that the fact that he did take satisfaction in it, that it did run smoothly, was evidence of some carelessness in his makeup or character, of some positive interest in another direction which ought to have been supreme and dominant.

I may speak later of the psychology of remorse, but just here I will say that it seems to me that the essence of remorse is that he now feels that the satisfaction he previously got out of a line of conduct exhibits its worthlessness. He says: "What a bad sort of person I must have been to have got satisfaction out of what I now see to be so wrong." What I am indicating is, that while under certain circumstances it is all right to follow the clue of these feelings, it is not necessary always to be deliberately reasoning out everything. Yet one must have a formed habit of being ready when it is necessary, to deliberate, to consider the worth and significance of signs which under other circumstances he follows habitually. That is what I mean by getting them into the moral sphere. They get into the moral sphere when they are judged, when they are reflectively estimated so that they enter into the constitution of action through the value which is put on them in this process of reflective consideration.

SECTION 3. EMOTIONS AS PART OF THE DECISION PROCESS

February 24, 1898

I return to the discussion of the emotions in general, particularly with reference to the stirring up of energy in the aspects of excitation, agitation.

It will be noted that we have in emotion precisely the same conditions that we have in attention—namely, the habit or power more or less organized on one side, and an idea or image on the other, with the necessity of mutual adaptation. That is, we have these two in a state of tension and not in one of an achieved coordination. The image stands for the interrupted activity which has projected itself and is endeavoring to find a new coordinated line of discharge; and the habit stands for the accumulated energy of the discharge which is temporarily damned up, or held in check, because of the uncertainty as to its final direction. In attention, this shifting about of the habit and the image serves, on the one hand, to develop and construct an image which will stand for the unified mode of action and thus focus the energy which is otherwise scattered and conflicting, while it also serves to reshape the habit, to readapt the habit, until it will serve as an instrument in the one desired and selected end. That of course is simply a review of the points made in the discussion of deliberation.

Now the emotion is simply this same process on its subjective side; it is this tension as immediately reflected in consciousness. As psychologists we may afterward isolate it and speak of the emotion as if it were a psychosis by itself. Of course in reality it is nothing but the immediate or subjective side of the whole attention movement. In addition, this immediate phase of the conflict tends to be referred to the habit when we are discussing emotion, since the habit becomes in the tension the subjective factor. It is the factor which marks the agent as distinct. It is the agent which stands for the subject of action as an attained result, and as a basis from which further action may proceed; while in attention, which we ordinarily think of in its intellectual aspects, our emphasis is turned on the side of image, of the object, the outcome which is in process of construction. Just as the habit is that factor in the tension which represents the subject, so the image, since it symbolizes the aim, stands for the objective side. So while both the intellectual and the emotional processes are phases of the tension between image and habit, yet on the emotional side our interest centers in what is going on in the habit, while on the intellectual side it is that reconstruction which is taking place in the image that is of moment to us.

There are two reasons why we tend to overlook the necessary connection between the emotion and the attention movement. One of these is simply a case of the psychological fallacy. In attention as an intellectual process, all that is of import to us is the outcome, the objective unification and distinctions that we arrive at through the attention. All the adjustments and readjustments and trials, struggles and conflicts, that are precedent to this objective result, are intellectually not useful. In fact they are hindrances rather than of any use, and so when we review the process from the intellectual standpoint, the thing that stands out in our mind is simply the result, the solution which we have finally reached, and we ignore all that went before as being merely subjective, or of no account. We either forget, or we purposely overlook all the preparatory strains and stresses which we call intellectual. All we have any demand for is the unified states of consciousness that have emerged out of these conflicts. But when we avoid this psychological fallacy and go over the whole process as it actually took place, we become conscious of the fact that there were risings and fallings in the subject, in the agent itself; and that was brought into tension with the aim because of the lack of any adequate definition in the aim, in the object, and that consequently the whole process had its emotional side. This fallacy is increased by the very nature of the case. The people who discuss these matters are the persons in whom the speculative and strictly scientific interest is uppermost, and naturally they write from the standpoint of their own predominant habits of mind in which that element of emotional stress has been reduced to a minimum as compared with the average man. But the average man who would be most adequately conscious of the emotional side is the one who by the nature of the case does not write psychological discussions.

The other reason for failing to see the close connection between the emotional process and the attention is that it becomes a distinct object in attention as an intellectual function to reduce the emotional element to its minimum; not simply to ignore it in retrospect but at the time of having the attention to get just as little of the stress of emotional disturbance as possible. It is economical, in other words, to get rid of that factor when attention has a distinctly intellectual purpose.

The reason is obvious. With reference to overt action the stirring up of the emotion is a good thing because it stirs up the energy which is necessary to carry out that action. When a man is going to do something directly, it is good policy for him to allow his emotions to get a certain headway and momentum. He will have so much less to do when the moment for action arises. But when one is aiming at simply an intellectual result, all the energy he needs is just enough to maintain the process of thinking. He does not want any surplus with reference to what is going to come after. If he does get up more steam than is necessary to maintain the process of reflection and investigation, that energy comes between him and a clear view of the intellectual results he is getting, and thus serves to defeat his end and aim. That accounts for the statement that used to be made in psychologies regarding the inverse ratio between sensation and perception. As the sensation element increases, the perceptive is at a minimum, and vice versa. The sensation excitation that accompanies looking at the sun is in inverse ratio with the clearness with which we apprehend the object, and so in other cases. So far as the result wanted is a merely intellectual one that of course is true, while it is not true insofar as a more practical and overt result is aimed at. The result is that along with the growth of science, partly as a necessary condition of that growth and partly as a result of it, in the intellectual class at least, the emotional concomitants of the emotional process have become very much reduced.

We have no right, however, to take our typical illustrations from that sphere because this marks a highly specialized development of attention; this is not a normal or average case of attention by any means; it is a technical case. What we call the sphere of prejudices and opinions is the normal and average case; and one only has to think of these prejudices and the part which they play—not simply for bad, but for good as well— in the life of the ordinary man, to realize how truly the emotional element is bound up with the intellectual. I do not remember who said that if men's interests and passions were as much concerned with the outcome of reasoning in geometry as they are with the outcome of the reasonings in religion and politics, the former would be a matter of just as much dispute as the latter. If you choose between such a statement as that and the part the emotional aspect plays in the intellectual process, the former is certainly nearer the truth. The emotional agitation is harmful, disadvantageous, in a strictly scientific process because it tends to attach too much interest to the outcome while the scientific man must be relatively indifferent as to what sort of a product he is to get. He must be equally open to have his thoughts move in any line where there seems to be a fair prospect of reaching any conclusions. He must not load down the process with reference to any one result. That is a different attitude from that of the ordinary man where the emphasis must be on getting a certain kind of result.

This lack of emotion in the formal attention which is most usually brought up in psychological works is really an indirect testimony to the very point in question. It marks really an achievement. It marks the power of inhibiting this emotional stress and therefore testifies to its presence in the usual case. However, even in this highly specialized form of attention— while we have succeeded in suppressing to a considerable extent the excitation, and have reduced it simply to an interest, curiosity, wonder, an interest which attaches to the form of the process, not to the result to be reached—in these cases we must not overlook the excitation following the thought process itself.

The story of Sir Isaac Newton will illustrate this point. When his calculation regarding the moon upon which depended the verification of his theory of universal gravitation was approaching completion, he was obliged to give the calculation to somebody else to continue because he was in such an excited state he could not carry it on. That simply illustrates the disturbance when any tension is approaching its climax. There is a reverberation, the resonance of which James speaks,[9] all through the physical frame. More usual cases would be the excitation that accompanies all intellectual processes that assume an artistic form, the direct creative form, or in such a thing as oratory where the person's main interest may be in a train of thought that gets warmed up and reflects itself in the heat and passion of his delivery.

Such facts as these are unaccountable when we say that attention is on the objective side an emotional process. I may seem to have dwelt at unnecessary length on this point, but it has a positive intellectual significance. In the first place it allows us to admit about all the facts that the hedonist has regarding the influence of feeling on action, but yet enables us to get those facts in their proper perspective and to give them their proper interpretation, namely, that this emotional feeling side comes in as a concomitant of the whole movement of action as found in attention, and as thus indirectly influencing the more intellectual and rational side. But apart from its bearing on any particular theory, it helps us to see the whole intellectual process in a more real and less schematic way. It obviates that tendency to think of pure reason as if it were an absolutely logical, cold, impartial process, which is a state in only a few individuals, and probably in those few comparatively rarely; it enables us to see in the ordinary man that the emotional and intellectual sides are bound up with each other and consciously acting and reacting upon each other so that speaking in the rough, we are as much influenced by our feelings as by our cooler judgments in reaching results. It thus not only enables us to recognize the facts of hedonism but also enables us to avoid the errors of one-sided rationalism and intellectualism.

I speak of that mutual relation between the emotional and intellectual side of the attention process, as preparatory to speaking of the stirring up of energy, which is the chief mark on the dynamic side of emotion. As was previously said, the tension produced by conflict, preventing any immediate outgo of energy, throws the subject back upon himself; that is, the energy accumulates within, the organism becomes a reservoir of clogged energy. Now the further this emotional excitation extends, the more all portions of the organism are brought into play and stirred at deeper levels.

It is from this fact that the moral significance of the emotions, as distinct from pleasures and pains, emerges. Psychologically, the emotion represents at least a temporary contradiction. It is the lack of any clear end or aim, any unified direction of action which brings about the emotional disturbance. Up to a certain point this is a good thing because it stirs up energy that would otherwise be dormant. The arousing of power that accompanies an emotion need hardly be dwelt upon. It is a commonplace. Even in what you might call the more negative emotion of fear, provided the fear does not become pathological, the statement is still true. One gets an acuteness in avoiding danger and in planning a retreat which he would not have in the ordinary unmoved condition. But on the other hand, this very accumulation of energy tends to throw the agent out of balance and lead him to purely arbitrary and meaningless discharge of force.

In other words, one tends under the influence of emotion, to be carried away by the very momentum of the energy aroused prematurely, before the channel along which it may be most advantageously directed—that is, before the image—has been cleared up. Anger affords a most striking instance of that fact. There is no doubt about the energy aroused and about the tendency to strike out blindly, to let it go off absolutely arbitrarily. In savage tribes they often kill the man who brings bad news. That is one instance of the irrational, arbitrary character of the emotional discharge— simply being carried away with the excitation of the moment. Such discharge is of course wasteful and destructive. We must condemn anger because of the uneconomical character of action which follows. It gets in its own way. Insofar as one under the excitement takes anything and everything as the obstacle and reacts against whatever lies nearest, he wastes his own energy. What is true there is true of any emotional action. Insofar as we would regard it as bad, its badness consists in the fact that instead of the energy being directed by the objective end so as to accomplish something, it goes off more or less at random.

Hence, the moral problem might be stated as that of finding the mean between two extremes, or better to establish the balance between two opposite forces.

On the one hand we have the tendency to regard the emotion as per se bad and immoral, and therefore to be suppressed, to be crushed out: what used to be known in treatises of moral education as breaking the will in order that the child might be prepared to submit himself rationally to law.

The other extreme is that just spoken of, to allow the energy excited to discharge just as it happens, to allow it to take care of itself. What is wanted then is the stirring up of this disturbance, the arousing of the energy insofar as this can be utilized, can be made serviceable, first in defining the end, that is, in making the thought of the end so interesting that one will dwell upon it till it is worked out; and then in realizing that end. The transformation of anger into what is called moral indignation would of course be a typical instance of the happy solution of the problem.

Say a man who often helps in cases of distress, a philanthropist, sees some person suffering a great injury. His blood boils and tends to make an immediate reaction, but whether he does or not, his blood continues to boil so that he thinks about the problem. What has made this abuse possible? There the energy functions in holding the man's mind on the image until he has elaborated the thing intellectually. The average person might be just as angry for the moment, but that would be the end of it; the excitation would not stay by him to compel him to keep his mind on it. After the philanthropist has made out the thing intellectually, then the emotion serves him in gathering all his powers together in attacking the evil.

First, then, I shall speak briefly of the part played by the emotion in shaping the image, in defining it. Much that is said in a general way about the relation between interest and attention belongs here. Of course all that was said in general about the emotion as the subjective accompaniment of the attention process belongs here. What is said in the psychologies about the part played by emotional congruity in shaping the association of ideas belongs here also. If a man is in a certain mood, then the ideas which suggest themselves to him are those which are congruent to that mood, those which might be serviceable as means in producing it as an end, or to which it as a means might be conducive. We all know it is practically impossible in certain emotional conditions for ideas of a certain class to get any lodgement, while everything which runs along with that mood is dwelt upon and cherished. We have extreme pathological cases where these moods become so fixed that a man cannot get outside of them. In cases of melancholia a man gets to dwelling on everything dark and gloomy and dwells on them so long that they come to possess his consciousness, and something like travel or a new occupation is required to get him out of it. A person who has a continuous depressed mood will unconsciously invent causes for it and thus lead to hallucinations. A man who feels bad all the time will come to imagine that he has lost his property or that he has some powerful enemy who is seeking to kill him.

We have then the general principle that the energy which is stirred up in an emotion will go to shape the image of the end with reference to which the energy stirred up is to be expended. The stirring up of energy does not provide merely a direct practical stimulus, it also provides the indirect practical stimulus, that is, the intellectual one.

What was said about following the clues of pleasure and pain would also be in place here. We all of us come to realize the possibility of playing upon our emotions in certain ways in order to build up, or to elaborate certain images which we want to get, working ourselves up to a certain pitch as the two sides act and react on each other. The emotion aroused tends to bring up the image and then by dwelling on the image we keep whipping up the emotion and so we develop the image and the hold it has on us, and so on. We find under certain circumstances that the best way to get at a certain mode of action is not to do it directly but to try to get ourselves into an emotional state, and that emotional state will automatically go on to develop the images that are relevant to it and which are the ones we are after.

February 28, 1898

I was speaking the last time of the utilization of the energy aroused in the emotion with reference to forming the image. I shall speak today of its use in the final discharge in overt action. In thus speaking of it under two heads, we must of course be careful to keep in mind the fact that we have here simply two stages in the development of one and the same process. The forming of the image is simply the earlier stage of the discharge, and this final overt outlet is the completion of the forming of the image. Physiologically we can say that the energy is mainly expended in effecting the central restimulations and combinations in the case of the image. Then when the central rearrangement has been made, the energy goes out in some more or less unified mode of discharge. It is this intimate connection between these two modes of using the energy which of course gives the basis, on the moral side, for discussing the final reaction. The problem is to effect just the right balance as to time and circumstance as to the amount of energy which is expended in effecting the central rearrangement and that which is expended in the overt peripheral direction.

As was said the other day, too speedy emotional reaction is not good because the energy in that case is undirected; it finds its outlet according to any path which happens to be open, whether that is the most useful path under the circumstances or not. In other words, it would tend to follow the lines that would correspond to previous habits, without taking into account the relevancy of the use of these habits in this emergency. This formation of the image on the energy side represents the inhibition until the central energy is put in shape to discharge along the line of—not merely least momentary resistance—but along the line of greatest probable effectiveness. When I have spoken before of the mediation of the emotional discharge by the image, it is not to be thought that the image formation lies outside of the emotional process; it rather lies inside of it and marks the certain direction of the energy.

But it is possible to fail in securing proper balance at the other end, as well as in that of the too speedy reaction. This is what we know popularly as the suppression of an emotion. The angry person may only seek and find an immediate outlet for his excitation, but he may also, by the presentation to himself of certain considerations, suppress all direct, overt manifestation of it whatsoever; that is, all apparent overt expression of it. Now such a person, according to the kind of considerations which he utilized to repress this expression, will become sullen or else highly malicious and revengeful. The sullen child will represent one in whom the excitation has been checked in this immediate way. It does not find an outlet in any particular action. It does find outlet then in setting up a certain disposition of action. It tends to effect a more or less permanent readjustment of the central connections.

The person who acts on the anger at just the moment will by that action drain out the energy so that there will be no permanently hostile attitude set up. The combination is effective, but it is effective in this particular action. If the particular act does not occur, it becomes much more set. We simply know that it is so, not how it is so. The failure to find an outlet simply drives the person back into himself so that he brooks on his injury, shuns others and becomes more or less morbid; or in the case of a person who lays a plot to revenge himself, that will take some time and shows ingenuity in preparing for the active use of the energy in building up the image. He carries the elaboration of the image further than is necessary with reference to this function in giving that energy an outlet, so that that over-matured treatment of the excitation is morally just as pernicious as the premature treatment of it. Now of course, just where the balance lies, just the exact point of time and circum . . .* two limitations here is one that is perfectly sound.

All attempts in education to suppress the expression of emotion may suppress it outwardly for the time being, but they do so at the expense of complicating the moral problem by making the elements involved more subtle and refined, and making them more difficult to get at by driving them back further into the person's subjective consciousness. The smoldering fires of passion are proverbially dangerous because we do not know when they are going to suddenly explode, or we do not know what ingenuity will be displayed by the person who feels injured in order to get a more marked, and for him perhaps a safer, expression of the feeling which he is still cherishing.

What is necessary then is a transformation of the motion through utilizing it to express itself up to a certain point in imagery. When this transformation fails, we have one form which, when it becomes habitual, is regarded as immoral. When the transformation is deflected too far, so that it is carried over into a line of action which is not relevant to the original stimulus, we get another type which, when habitual, is also immoral. When the transformation succeeds and becomes habitual we get a moral interest. Then we get, not unregulated exhibition, nor suppression, but simply expression, so that the whole self manages to express itself, to move out and onward through this particular channel. This must always be so when the emotion is expressed adequately—that is, when all the energy involved is economically employed.

Now the criterion of marking out suppression from expression is simply whether the controlling force is one which is relevant to the emotion, or irrelevant. That is, supposing an angry child has his exhibition suppressed simply because he is sure that he will get punished if he expresses it. Now his dislike to physical pain or humiliation begins to operate and check any overt expression of the anger. That is a motive that is external to the anger. It does not make the anger any different; so far as his own volition is concerned he is as angry as before. It is simply that he sees that it would not pay to express that state. If the imagery, however, is controlled, the overt exhibition of anger is one which does have some intrinsic relationship to the anger itself, to the whole coloring of the emotion itself. It is transformed and gets a different moral and internal meaning attached to it. That is, if the person realizes that he has failed to accomplish what he wanted to by giving way to his anger, because the very nature of the circumstance was such that it defeated his own end, then there would be not simply suppression, but somehow mediated and transferred expression. It is simply a case of controlling the emotion through anticipation of its own legitimate consequences, that is, transforming it through the power of objectively presenting itself to one, of

---

* Apparently a line is missing in the original hectograph copy.

seeing what it means. In that case it cannot be said there is any suppression whatsoever. The emotion finds more organic expression of itself, instead of less complete expression, than it would if the person had at once an immediate reaction upon it; but if the consequences which come into play are of a kind which are simply external, then we get suppression.

What I said incidentally the other day about the social responsibility is applicable to this case. The business of society in moralizing the emotions is to set up the conditions which will make the agent realize the failure involved in the expenditure of energy excepting when it is directed into certain channels. The child who is spoiled is one who is allowed to let his excitation overflow without being made to feel their return weight, without having the conditions supplied by others to make him appreciate and realize in his own consciousness the failure involved in thus acting. He is continually humored and artificially protected from realizing the nature of his action through its consequences.

On the other hand we have a constant checking and thwarting by bringing motives to bear which are not strictly relevant to the act itself, but which lie outside of it—in appeals to fear, or in appeals to hopes of bribery, or expectation of a reward. In that case also the emotion is not controlled by the image of itself. It is not controlled through any self consciousness. It is controlled simply by reference to what we ordinarily term considerations of expediency.

SECTION 4. THE TENSION BETWEEN DESIRE AND EFFORT IN THE MORAL ACT

I go on to the question of desire and effort. First I will discuss them together and then in their relation to each other. These terms really sum up and review the whole discussion up to this point. They are processes that have intrinsically both an emotional and an intellectual aspect. There is no desire or effort where there is not some process of deliberation or emotion. The whole psychology we have been working out thus far is the tension that arises in the conflict of active powers with each other, a tension which finally arranges and crystallizes itself about the tension between habit and idea, between the subject as represented by habit and the object, the end or aim, as represented by idea. Now desire and effort are simply the names for this tension. It is desire, or it is effort. I think more or less confusion arises through using these words ambiguously. Sometimes we mean by them what the practical man means by them—namely, the whole active attitude. When in common language we say: I want something, I desire something, I am going to try to get something, we do not mean a mere state of consciousness; we mean the whole bent and direction, the attitude of the agent.

In psychology desire and effort are sometimes discussed, not as such entire personal attitudes, but simply as the states of consciousness which accompany them. There is no object to using the terms in the latter sense if the psychologist warns us that he has not the whole attitude in mind, but simply this abstraction which he is making for purposes of psychological examination; but it is important that we should not confuse the feeling which we have in desire and effort with effort and desire in the practical popular sense of these terms. When I say that desire and effort are the tension, I am speaking of them in the practical and popular sense, as the whole condition that the person is in when he desires or when he is putting forth an effort. I do not mean the mere sense of desire or effort that he has.

I may remark that there is a good deal of difficulty in the mind of some regarding James's theory of the emotions. It is because Mr. James himself is not explicit on this point (because he does not state that he is speaking simply of the consciousness side and not of the practical side) that the common man feels that something is manipulated away when he is told that effort is certain organic visceral sensations, together with certain feelings of muscular stress and strain, when he is told that is all there is to effort.[10] It does not correspond with his experience, for he does not mean merely the consciousness of effort, he means the whole attitude that he is in, the whole thing that he trying to do, and the reason that he is trying to do it. Desire and effort then, being both names for the tension, cannot be discriminated from each other unless we mark off different points of interest in the tension. If they both name one and the same process, they must simply name it from different standpoints.

I have used the illustration of the commercial exchange, but it is applicable here. There is only one process, but you call it buying or selling according to the standpoint in which your interest finds its origin. It will depend upon the end from which you name it. With desire and effort the tension is effort if our interest centers in the hither side, in what is going on in the habits, but we call it desire if our interest is in the thither end. Both name the activity as divided and as striving toward recoordination. That is what I mean by the tension. The activity is broken up but has not become divided. The activities are striving toward a unity of expression and that still holds them together. Now desire is this movement towards unity. That is, it names the process as moving on towards that unity. Effort denotes the fact that this unity can be attained only through such transformation as will get rid of the division. Desire is thus the recognition of the synthetic; effort of the analytic. Desire is the movement towards the end in spite of the obstacle, effort the concentration of energy in order to reach the end. In desire our whole attention is on the end, the aim, the final good; the obstacle comes in as coloring our end; but in effort we are thinking about the obstacle, and the end comes in simply to give value and location to the obstacle.

These are general statements, but they are necessary to get the right psychology, either of effort or desire. Desire presupposes opposition but emphasizes unity; effort presupposes unity, but designates the opposition, the obstacle. The tendency is to think of effort as if it were merely a state of opposition, as if we were merely struggling against something instead of realizing that the struggle against something is simply part of the positive attainment of something.

Almost the commonest theory about effort is that the self is struggling to overcome something outside of self. That ignores the unity involved and it compromises . . . .*

. . . with which to illuminate the topic by which to solve the problem. In nonvoluntary attention there is no conscious distinction between means and end at all. The child at play has no end outside of what he is doing immediately. Take the child at play as a typical example of the so-called nonvoluntary attention. It is quite a different thing subjectively in experience from the voluntary attention. Indeed it might almost be questioned whether having the same word for those two very distinct mental attitudes is not misleading. The same way here with the distinction between this naive distinction of desire and effort and the case in which each is reflected because of its conscious connection with the other. A dog will sit by the hour watching a hole in which an animal has gone, or watching an animal in a tree. In one sense he is very persevering; in one sense he is putting forth effort to maintain one activity for so long a time. But it is probably a purely immediate thing—it is renewed from moment to moment by an ever present stimulus. There is not a definite consciousness in the dog's mind that if he watches long enough the animal will appear, and he is not directing all his activities in the meantime in connection with that end; so there will be no effort in any conscious sense.

Watch a young child and see him put forth much energy in a very concentrated and persistent way. He will keep at a thing which interests him until he is exhausted and seems to show great persistency in meeting and overcoming obstacles; but certainly in some cases, probably in most cases, he is simply not conscious of them as obstacles at all. The child of two or three may appear externally to have more persistence than a child of five or six. People often wonder what makes the child become so lazy after there has been so much activity before. It simply marks the fact that he sees the obstacles as obstacles; he relates them consciously to an end which is more remote, and in doing so concludes that the "candle is not worth the game." It does not pay. While the persistent child at the earlier stage is not moved by the consciousness of the end at all. He is simply taking the energy that is there and directing it continuously with reference to the last thing that he runs up against. The same thing may be said of desire. There is a difference between the natural, unmediated want, the active going out for and insistence upon a certain thing, and that peculiar state of consciousness which we call desire; because in the latter case we are aware of the difference between the present and the future. We are

* A page of the original hectograph copy is missing.

aware that this end is only an anticipated end: that is, ideal; in other words, not actual.

I think the parallelism could be worked out to some advantage in political economy. There is a natural want or demand which has not met resistance and which does not, therefore, have to measure itself against the resistance, against what has to be overcome. Then there is the consciousness of cost which is precisely the mental attitude of valuing this original demand or want in terms of the energy which has to be expended in satisfying it. Then there is the distinct economic want, the want that is aware of itself and which will pay a certain price. The consciousness of value in the form of price is the counterpart of the estimate value in terms of the cost. This original want expresses the unmediated psychological desire. It is objectively a desire, but not subjectively. The cost *is* that getting mediated through effort, and then after being mediated coming out and setting a certain value on the thing, called exchange value.

In the naive condition then, the obstacles are not realized as obstacles, but they simply stimulate, arouse. The end is taken for granted and it fascinates, hypnotizes, just as the child keeps pegging away at the thing until he is thoroughly exhausted. He is under the domination of his end and cannot get outside of it to see whether it is worth all the energy which is being expended in its behalf. Now when the consciousness of disparity comes in, when one feels the overt incompatibility between his means and his end, he reflects upon each in terms of the other. This opposition between the two, this disparity between the two, is what makes him try to value each and tell what each is worth. It is the act of sitting down and counting the cost. Now when this state arises, effort no longer attaches merely to the means, the chief effort comes to be in hiding the end. The effort is no longer to do something, it is rather not to do it until the idea has been worked out; or the effort is to keep one's mind upon the idea so steadfastly and firmly that the idea will become motor, not merely in general, but become the dominating motor tendency. In what we call moral courage, the difficulty is not so much in doing a certain thing as in facing an idea frankly and fully.

Now when one has found that there are great obstacles in carrying out an end (in other words, that it takes much effort with references to the means), then he must revalue his end, he sees that end in a new light. At first he has taken it superficially. He starts to act on it and finds it takes longer than he expected; that it involves sacrifices of which he had not thought, or the general concentration of his energy. Then he must go back to his end, see it in a new light, and either give it up, or drop some of it out so as to make execution easier, or else brace himself up again through the renewed consciousness of the end. On the other hand, in this same process the desire must come to attach consciously to the means. That is to say, the interest which originally attached to the end must be consciously transferred or made over to the means. The individual must so identify what he is immediately doing with the outcome that he hopes to arrive at, that what he is now doing will possess for him the worth of the end to be reached, and therefore will keep his desire alive. That is only to apply to this particular case the general principle laid down by emotion that in its moral development it must come to function as interest. The effort that attaches to the means shifts over to the end and the desirability that attaches to the end shifts over to the means.

Now in that process of working consciously from one to the other, in realizing to one's self the value of each as brought into tension with the other, the desire and effort get their moral coloring. They get it because now the nature of the self is seen to be involved there. The question of desire is: What kind of a self does one really want? The question of effort is: How much does the self want it? How much is it willing to pay for it? And that question of how much it is willing to pay, exhibits the value which is attached to that particular kind of a self. That may be illustrated from the case of good intentions. A person says he meant to do a certain thing, he really wanted to to do it, and we are asked to take his intention, his want, for the deed. When do we agree to that, and when do we refuse? Suppose he says he really wanted to but forgot. The retort is that he did not want it very badly or he would not have forgotten. The fact that he forgot shows that he was not so very anxious. He meant to, but some obstacle came in between. The fact that he made an obstacle of it so as to give it up shows that he did not want it as much as he wanted something else. The only cases in which we accept the intention or want, for the deed, is when the individual can show that so far as he was concerned, he did act on the want, but some unforeseen circumstance, some power which relatively to him was external, came in and interfered with the consummation of the deed. Morally, then, effort is the content of desire. Effort is the desire in its motorization, while desire is the animating spirit and motive of the effort. The whole question of the moralization of an individual is in securing just this organic connection between desire and effort. That is, to have the individual mediated over from one to the other in just this way, instead of having a conscious separation between the two.

That may perhaps be illustrated negatively: that is, from failures to secure this intimate interdependence; from the tendency to action which gives effort without desire, or the form of desire without effort. On a higher scale the desire that is effort is exhibited in much that is said about duty for duty's sake. The effortless desire finds its expression in the mere pleasure secured. But without taking illustrations on so highly developed a plane I will suggest one from the current antinomy in educational theory and practice. There is a current opposition between the idea of discipline and the idea of interest. You hear it said, and find it still oftener assumed without being said in so many words, that discipline implies that the student must do something which he does not like to do, and in spite of the fact that it is disagreeable, put forth his effort to do it. That discipline cannot be got in any other way. That is, the measure of the discipline attained is the natural repulsiveness of the task to be done. There you have the conception set up of effort distinct from desire.

The implied reasons for this point of view are two. One on the objective side is that the person will have to meet a good many disagreeable things in life anyway, and he must be disciplined to meeting and facing them; and on the subjective side, that one puts forth more energy in those cases, and hence gets a strength of fiber and backbone which he does not get in other cases. Now an examination of that statement will reveal the psychological futility of effort which is not organically enough related to desire. What is the stimulating motive in this case of the effort, which is supposed to give discipline? One cannot get stimulus out of the thought of the thing to be done because that is disagreeable. The more he thinks of that, the less he will do; the more likely he is to run away from it. Where then will the point of connection be found? It must be found in some other image or suggestion which holds the mind of the pupil. In other words, he will have to think of the disgrace of failure, or of the adult as displeased with him, or failure to make his mark high enough, or failure of promotion, or the possibility of being punished, or he will have to think of some other disagreeable result, or agreeable result, which will happen to him if he does this thing. If that is a true statement psychologically, then this means simply that he does not get stimulus out of the thought of the thing itself because it is disagreeable, but must get it from something else.

What becomes of the statement then that a person gets discipline out of doing disagreeable things which he dislikes doing? Is he likely to be able to meet disagreeable situations better in after life? Not at all. He simply acquires the habit of seeking for some extraneous motive such as hope of reward to brace himself up with. How is the person who has that habit any better off as regards facing the disagreeable tasks which everybody must face in life? Is he not just as likely to dodge them as anybody would be who had not this so-called discipline? Is he not in a more or less servile position, always waiting until he is prodded up by somebody else and not ready to go at them himself? The most intrinsic motive that a person can get in such cases is when he becomes conscious that doing these things does give him a sense of power. Undoubtedly power is thus gained. A man says: "The harder the thing is, the more energy it will take and the better I will feel after it is done." That means simply that there is in the act itself, in spite of its disagreeable factors, an element of intrinsic interest. It is difficult to see how a person can be got to take that attitude excepting as he has, through interest, been led to do things which were at first disagreeable, and thus got the sense of accomplishment.

Take it on the subjective side. Is the person building up fiber and backbone there? The statement that he is confuses effort with the consciousness of effort, particularly with the feeling of strain. The feeling of strain is very far from being any accurate thermometer of the actual amount of effort put forth. When we do not feel like doing a thing, the putting forth of a little energy will seem like putting forth more effort than a hundred times the actual expenditure of energy will in other cases. It is almost a commonplace that a man puts forth the most energy when he is not conscious of it as strain. When he is conscious of it as strain, his activities are more or less divided. The soldier in battle who does the best fighting is the one who forgets himself, not the one who nerves himself up to fight. The latter will use more energy in thinking how hard it is not to run away than in the actual fighting. So where it is a conscious sense of effort it is the same, and there is no position psychologically more absurd than this idea that we are getting some moral result by creating a position which gives a sense of strain, of conscious difficulty in the work to be done.

This sense of strain has its value, but that simply means that this sense of strain ought to have a functional value and we ought to treat it as a clue or sign, as we do any other feeling; we ought to use it to control and direct our energy with. That sense of strain locates the difficulty for us, and insofar it has a positive value if it directs energy. But if not, then it simply gets in our own way. It is what often happens with students in trying to study subject matter with which they are not familiar and feeling the strain of giving their attention until it gets between the subject and the object and they have only the feeling of giving attention left. In other words, the subject will put forth most effort in an active way when he can find the point, the value or interest in the work which he has to do and can utilize that so as to interpret and direct the elements and activities which otherwise are disagreeable and repulsive. Discipline is not concerned with the mere disagreeableness of the thing to be done; it is simply the forming of habits which lend themselves to the service of worthy ends. Discipline is nothing but organized power, and the sense that discipline involves some opposition to interest, involves something which is done because it is disagreeable, or done simply through subjection to some external authority, is a psychological monstrosity which it is hoped will die in due season.

Now if we take the other side, the separation of desire from effort, we find it is in the abuse, the misuse of the theory of interest in education. That is, I mean by misuse the attempted justification for the continual exciting and amusing of the pupils, sugar coating everything in such a way that it arouses an immediate sense of pleasure and then relying as a motive on the immediate sense of pleasure aroused rather than on the mediated consciousness of the value of the thing to be done.

The interest means the consciousness of value in relation to the active powers. That is, it is the consciousness of finding the activities of the self realized in some anticipated course of action. Now the abuse of that idea is simply in saying that anything and everything, the object, the end, must be presented so as to awaken a feeling of pleasure, and then that feeling of pleasure is to become the motive for attaining to the object. That involves the deflection of energy into wrong channels just as much as this misconception of the theory of effort does. There are certain powers there. Those powers must be appealed to, they must be interested, they must be engaged; but legitimately they are engaged by furnishing them the object with respect to which they may function, which serves to stimulate them, to call them out and release them. But when the pleasure excited is made the motive, then this power is simply excited or stimulated just as it is, and what the child gets is simply the feeling of the formal exercise of that power. That which is a means is made into an end; there is a stimulus just as much as in the case of appetite. It is possible to make a child as eager for bright colors or for pleasant sounds as it is to arouse his taste to demand certain pungent stimulants or certain pleasures. One is just as disintegrating as the other, simply because in either case the momentary formal exercise of the organ there, power is made an end in itself instead of the exercising of it with reference to the accomplishing of a certain result. Hence there is no development of power, there is no objective result of that sort got; there is rather disintegration and loss of capacity. The only development that comes is purely by accident. It may happen that somehow the more intrinsic interest may develop itself to which the child will respond. Moreover the inevitable result is to create a demand for more stimulus, just as in the case of the drunkard. The more he drinks, the more desirous he becomes of the feeling of the satisfaction of that appetite. Or as the tongue comes to demand stronger and stronger stimuli when it is isolated and made an end in itself, so a person instead of getting the interest really gets blasé and is thrown into a condition of boredom from which he can only be aroused by some new form of stimulus, or some more intense stimulus than he has had before. He does not get interest or the power of interest any more than the other person gets discipline. What I mean to indicate by this example is the futility of the conception of effort which is not the organic outworking of desire, and the futility of purely immediate desire that does not express itself mediately through effort.

In order to avoid misapprehension I will add that this sort of desire and effort are different from the naive desire and effort. There was no conscious separation, no consciousness of desire as desire, or of effort as effort; but in the typical cases the desire becomes conscious; and my whole point is that effort and desire should not become conscious excepting in their relation to each other, that then they come into the moral sphere because they represent the valuation of the self, the valuation of the self appreciating and measuring itself, which is the process of moralization.

March 2, 1898

It was implied in what was said yesterday that when desire and effort are consciously referred to each other, they come into the moral sphere because they bring to light, or effect a conscious valuation of the self in terms of an act, or of an act in terms of the self; and it is that conscious construction of one in terms of the other that has been suggested from the start as giving differentia of the moral. That particular indication may be developed by reference to the ordinary distinction between physical effort, intellectual, and moral effort. According to some writers these terms mark either two or three distinct sorts of action of the self. They are qualitatively different. Different writers disagree as to just how they would classify them. Those who hold to different activities of the self involved here mark off physical effort from the other two; but some classify intellectual with physical, and others classify the intellectual with the moral. It is possible that some writers make three distinct sorts of action here, though no illustration comes to my mind of such an author at the moment.

Against such a separation, of course, what is involved in the previous treatment is that there is only one activity designated, but these different terms which it names differ according to the direction which it takes. Moral effort is not a different kind of energy of the self than is found in physical effort, but the activity of the self accomplishes one sort of results, effects one sort of value in one case, and another in another, and we name it from its objective reference.

More specifically in connection with what was said yesterday, when the energy is directed in a unified way towards the means, we would call it physical effort. When it is directed towards the end, we call it intellectual. When it is attempting to maintain either one in terms of the other, when it is trying to mediate one, keep it in its balance with the other, we term it moral effort. The term physical, or the term animal, as used in psychology, will almost always, if not uniformly, be found to refer to the direction of energy towards the immediate obstacle to action so as to transform it into an instrument or means. The distinction that is familiar to us is the distinction between the peripheral and the central. It is not located in the place where it is ordinarily put, but needs to be defined with reference to the place where it starts. The distinction is to where it is directed, where it ends, where the interest lies. This distinction between the peripheral and central is equivalent to that between the physical and the intellectual. The senses do not have a peripheral significance simply because they lie on the outside of the body and are open to external stimuli. The meaning is rather that they have to be on the alert, they have to be on the look-out with reference to these external stimuli. It is not their receptivity that is designated, it is the teleological direction of their energy.

If we take as a case of physical effort that involved in lifting a stone, it is the energy, whether psycho-physical or strictly psychical, it is the same self and the same activity that is involved there as is involved in attempting to maintain one's integrity in telling the truth when the temptation is to lie. But in the physical effort, when it is called merely physical, there is no division of the activity of the self, it is simply all directed towards the act which has to be done, as the means of accomplishing something else. We may say the energy is directed towards the stone, but it is at most an elliptical expression. The energy is towards the act of lifting the stone because of that as instrument in some other activity. If the person found that he could not lift the stone, that might become, for the time being, an end. The problem is: How shall I lift that stone? He ignores for the time being the larger activity and concentrates all his powers on this as an end. He begins to reflect, to seek for devices by which the stone can be lifted. So far as it is toward that as an end, it is intellectual in character. The whole thing is to tell what kind of an act the act is. Taken as a means, one must go right ahead and do it as an overt thing; but when we cannot do it, when that activity which we call physical in inhibited, then the problem is to define the act to ourselves, and there we have it as an end and also the intellectual process.

Now I said that the moral meant bringing one of these consciously into relation to the other, means to end; or in terms of the present discussion, physical to intellectual. Supposing the person is tempted to quit lifting the stone because of the obstacles which he meets, because he finds he cannot do it as easily as he expected to. Then the question arises: Why do it at all? Why not give it up? What is the reason, the real motive for engaging in that activity at all? So far as the agent's consciousness is in that attitude we cannot say that he is either dealing with the act as a means or end. He is dealing with the relating of means to end. If one should not highly value the end, should feel that it did not amount to much, and that as means it might easily be given up, one would be deciding in effect that there was no moral significance attached to the act, while if one should reflect that the lifting of that stone meant the relieving of another person's suffering in some way, or if one should conclude that his own power of perseverance, of not getting discouraged at obstacles, was at stake, then in that process of moving back and forward he would have brought that act into the moral sphere, because he would see that it was a necessary organic part in an end which he felt somehow to be necessary to the integrity of himself as an agent. I have emphasized, defined the means in terms of the end. The other side is there. It is the obstacle that one meets in the act as a means which makes him turn around and consider how much importance he really attaches to the end.

If we work from the other sort of illustration, one that is obviously moral on the surface of it, as the effort involved in truth telling, we see that both physical factors and intellectual factors are involved. It would not be difficult to be truthful if we did not have to tell the truth, if it did not have to take the peripheral direction, if it did not have to take the outward direction, just as much as the act of lifting the stone does. What gives the thing its difficulty is precisely the fact that we are facing a point where this act is going to strike the environment, and the difficulty is in effecting that lodgment of the act in the environment. There is an apparent opposition between the two which repels us just as much as in the case of trying to lift the stone when it is too heavy. Then there is the intellectual element involved. There is a tendency to shy from the thought of the end which involves all these difficulties in its realization. The easiest way to lie is simply to forget to tell the truth—to just let the image of the end as desirable go. Just to let ourselves drift. It is the easiest, and commonest, most natural way of doing wrong. We do not have to positively decide upon this wrong end, all we have to do is to shove it aside out of consciousness and decline to make it the active and controlling factor.

That means on the other side, that the moral effort must be directed towards maintaining the end clearly in consciousness, and that is what we mean by intellectual effort when taken by itself. It is moral simply because we are reflecting upon it; we are defining it in relation to the other factor which by itself we would call, under other circumstances, simply physical.

I would say here what might have been said as well at any other point in the discussion, that you may find it helpful not only to work out these illustrations from occurrences which present themselves in your own experience but also from problems as presented in novels. Take any novel of importance that has a distinct ethical problem in the development of character involved and see how the author has unconsciously brought out the psychical forces involved. Tolstoi in his *Anna Karenina* gives us as good an illustration of the fact that evil is not so much a course decided upon as a mere shying from a certain kind of an end and letting things drift. There are other novels but none in which this is brought out more clearly than in the life of the heroine of that story.

Moral quality then arises in consciousness just whenever it becomes necessary to construct, that is, to value an act in its relation to the agent, and that of course on the other side means that the agent is being reflected upon, is having his value expressed in the act.

Before going on to speak of desire and effort separately, I will briefly mention the general problem as it now stands. This general problem is to give each its right placing in the whole volitional process. The false psychology and the false ethical inferences arise from isolating them from the place which they really occupy in the whole active process. When these are isolated, then the active unity of the self—that is, the will—is disintegrated and the results is that we have to conceive it as either a separate and independent factor operating from without the process upon the process, or else we conceive of it as a mere effect of the play of other psychical forces; a sort of epi-phenomenon, as Huxley said consciousness was.[11] The usual procedure is to regard desire as something acting upon will, when the divorce is made an effort, as being the expression par excellence, of the will, resisting and dominating—trying to dominate—from without the desires which are acting upon it. Or one goes to the other extreme and holds that this mere play of the desires as psychical forces is the whole thing, and that effort then is in one sense an illusion, that it is simply the reflex or the reverberation of the results produced in the interaction of desires as so many mechanical forces.

The points that I shall try to develop are that desire is the active out-reaching of the self in the form of acquired powers as these powers are re-inforced and brought to consciousness by an image of an end; while effort is the same outgoing of the active powers of the self controlled by the conception of an end in such a way that the conception of the end involves the reconstruction of the powers. Positively, then, what will have to be shown regarding desire is the organic connection of the image of the end, the conceived satisfaction, or the ideal, and of the feeling with the activity.

There are two distinct points of view from which this organic connection is ignored. One regards the desire as aroused by the feeling of pleasure which accompanies a certain image. That is, it puts the feeling and the thought which the feeling accompanies before the activity of the desire. That of course is the hedonistic psychology.

The other point of view may or may not hold that desire is sometimes our end, naturally produced in this way, but holds that moral desire ought to be aroused by an ideal furnished from reason. These two theories are of course at the poles from each other. One seems to identify the morally desirable with the most intense desire. It seems impossible to get any distinction between the natural and the moral. In ethical terms it seems impossible to get any particular meaning for "ought." We seem forced to say as Bentham did say that "ought" is a meaningless and mischievous word.[12] It is simply a question of what we desire and what the most intense desire is.

The problem for the other school is how you are going to get any connection between the moral and the natural; that is, it seems to have made them so very distinct that the question is whether there is any leverage of one on the other at all. It seems radically to separate the desirable from the desire, just as the naturalistic point of view seems absolutely to identify them.

SECTION 5. THE CONFUSION BETWEEN IMMEDIATE STIMULUS AND FINAL OBJECT IN THE THEORY OF DESIRE

Our problem then, as it breaks up, takes such forms as these: What is the relation of the idea of the end, the idea of satisfaction—that is, the ideal—to activity, to the arousing of desire? And again, what is the relation of the feeling element, the pleasure, to the idea, and also to the function of desire? Is our consciousness of the ideal a simple formulation of the way of getting pleasure, the easiest way in which to get pleasure? Or is it something which supervenes from reason outside the desire process and has for its function to subordinate and control the latter? Or do both idea and feeling and the relations between them emerge within the process of doing and serve simply to bring out the value of the doing? Of course in the general survey already given, the question has been answered in the latter sense. The point will be, then, to work out that answer in more detail.

In discussing desire it is quite common to confuse two senses in which we speak of the object of desire. We sometimes mean by this term that which stimulates, which awakens desire; and at other times we mean the object towards which desire tends as affording it satisfaction. Now I shall try and show later on that there is such a close connection between these two that it is not difficult to see why the confusion arises;[13] but for the present I will try to point out the fallacy in this immediate identification.

Precisely the same sort of ambiguity with the same misleading results occurs in discussions regarding knowledge as in those regarding object. It is sometimes used as that which sets up and arouses the knowing activity, and sometimes as that which is known. Certain sections of the Scotch school of psychology used to hold that the object of knowledge was the last change that took place in the brain antecedent to the sensation, and it has been by no means uncommon to find the sensory stimulus, the vibrations of ether or the sound wave, or the excitation of the nerve organs, spoken of as if they were the object of knowledge. You will find the implication in the statement that our knowledge of red and green is subjective, that the real knowledge is the vibrations concerned. What is meant in such cases is that which stimulated or set up the knowing process. In common life we talk about the object of knowledge as being the values which are got hold of through the knowing process.

Exactly the same confusion takes place in discussing attention. By the object of attention we sometimes mean that which is immediately present to attention, that which stimulates it, which keeps attention alert; and we sometimes mean the outcome which is reached when the movement of attention has completed itself. For instance, here is a case of a man who is climbing a mountain where there is no distinct trail. His object is to get to the peak of the mountain. Now what is the object of his attention, what is the focus of his attention? I think you will find in discussion of such cases as that a continual unconscious vacillation between the two points of view, sometimes speaking of the end to be reached as if it were the focus and, at other times, the last stimulus—the blaze on a tree or the sight of a stream of water—as if that were the object of attention. As I said before, we have a tendency toward the psychological fallacy, speaking as if the focus were all the time there, when, as a matter of fact, when we get the focus attention disappears because it is no longer needed. In each of these cases the term object in one sense means stimulus, and in the other sense it means the factor which exercises control. When we talk about the object of desire we must define whether we mean that which excites and arouses desire, or the final cause for the sake of which desire exists—that which will mark the satisfaction of desire, that which will mark its fruition.

I will try and show in the next lecture that both the hedonist and the rationalist confuse these two senses of the object.

March 7, 1898

At the last hour I was speaking of the current confusion in the use of the term object of desire, having the meaning sometimes of the excitation of desire, and sometimes the meaning of that in which desire will find its fruition or satisfaction. The importance for our purposes for being aware of that confusion and avoiding it is the fact that as soon as desire has a conscious object it ceases to be desire, the condition becomes transformed into effort or interest or an organized mode of action. This consciousness of a definite object of desire represents the outcome of desire as desire, and when therefore we put that back into the earlier stages and treat it as the exciting, or as the excitement of desire, the whole treatment becomes vague to the greatest degree.

If you will read, or if you have read, either Ladd's account of desire or Sully's account of desire,[14] which are fairly representative of the current discussions, I think you cannot avoid the impression (which will be more marked as you realize their statements) that they are going around in some kind of a hopeless circle between various factors in desire; that they discuss desire by pointing out that there are three factors involved in it: the intellectual image or object, the feeling element, and the active element. When they are discussing the object, they point out that that arouses feeling, an accompaniment of feeling, and that either directly or through this feeling accompaniment it excites action; that when they get to the discussion of the feeling, they point out that feeling excites action and that it at least reacts upon the intellectual element, or that that feeling must be there, in order to give a differentia between the intellectual object in desire and that in contemplation; and when they get to action, they point out that action is necessary to feeling and is necessary to the intellectual object. That is, at each point of the discussion you are really referred to the other points for the explanation of the thing you are dealing with, and it keeps chasing itself around in that circular way. You never get a clear single view of what the desire process is and just why and how it involves the feeling element, the intellectual element, and the active element. Now this circular mode of explanation has its root, I think, in this confusion of the two senses of the term object of desire.

Without discussing that point further just here, I will now attempt to make good my statement that so fast as the excitement of desire becomes transformed into a definite object or aim of desire, insofar forth the desire state as such is transformed into something else. What then is the excitant of desire? The perception or image of some object stimulates to action. That is the first coefficient of the excitation. Now if we ask why it excites action, the answer in general is a reference to the principle of suggestion, or the principle of ideomotor action. There is nothing in that fact which is in itself peculiar to desire, or characteristic of desire. It is simply a case of the principle of ideomotor action. Psychologically the object is nothing but a possible series of coordinated stimuli and responses. The miracle, or the thing to be explained, is rather the cases when the object does not arouse action, rather than the cases when it does. There is no sensation which is not a stimulus to movement and there is no movement which does not react into and modify, differentiate the stimulus, and the object psychically is simply the grouping of these customary excitations and reactions, a sort of equilibrium of stimuli and inhibitions.

If we take the stock case of a child who sees some candy, the problem is not to tell why the sight of candy arouses him to action. It is simply a question of explaining what candy as an object is to the child. What is candy to him? It is primarily something to be eaten and which when eaten affords an agreeable satisfaction. Of course incidentally to that, it is white, or red, or striped, and has a certain touch to the hand and a certain quality of touch also to the mouth, and so on; but all of those are simply various other actions of seeing and touching which the child can perform, and in this case are subordinated to the tasting action on the part of the child. Then the fact that the child when he sees the candy is stimulated to reach for it means nothing except that the idea of candy tends to complete or fulfill itself. Merely seeing candy is only partly candy. The real noumenal candy is the tasted candy, and the seen candy is simply the phenomenal candy, simply the sign of the noumenal. I said it is simply a suggestion. There is no problem at all as to how an object becomes the suggestor of activity. That is what it is and that suggestion goes on to fulfill itself, and that is the normal state of things. It is the failure and withdrawals that really have to be accounted for.

Perhaps the principle would be plainer if stated in physiological language. The candy as seen means an activity of the visual optical apparatus. The activity of that apparatus is nothing isolated. The child's eye and the visual centers in the brain are not a little nervous region by themselves. It is nothing but the specialization or differentiation of the whole organization, and, as such, is connected with other centers and with other organs, both sense organs, glands, and motor organs. So far as that connection is defined, we have of course a habit; that is what the habit is. Hence this visual activity tends to communicate itself to the other organs of action with which it is associated habitually. It tends to discharge in the arm, to reach, and tends to discharge in the organs of taste—the child's mouth waters, in other words.

As the reaching activity and the tasting activity are stimulated, they of course tend to in turn stimulate the eye. It is a coordination of circular reaction. As they are excited the energy set free propagates itself along connected lines and goes back to the eye, and so the eye has a reason or, in psychological terms, has a motive for looking at the candy which it did not have before. At first it might be that the child's eye was simply roaming around and lighted on the candy, but after the motor reaction takes place the child looks at the candy because he is thinking of it in terms of his arm movement and in terms of his tasting activity. So far we have only excitation of action, not excitation of desire. But it is perfectly futile to my mind to attempt to discuss the excitation of desire by itself, apart from the general psychology of the excitation of action, apart from the principle of suggestibility. The question is to get the particular differentia which mark off action taking the form of desire. From this general type of case which we have discussed so far then, it is found in the presence of an obstacle, or of a competing activity which inhibits the fruition, the immediate realization of this particular form. If the child can reach right out and get the candy, desire is at most an exceedingly transitory state. Even if it is present as desire in consciousness at all, at most it simply comes in because of the friction that there is between the seeing and the reaching and the getting it to his mouth. If he had to walk a few steps or change the position of his body, that slight amount of resistance might serve to throw this activity into the desire form, but that would be only very transitory, and so far as the principle is concerned, if there is no obstacle there will be no desire— simply a suggestion which proceeds at once to execute itself.

If we take the other part of the stock illustration, namely, that the child had been forbidden to eat it, or that he is sufficiently mature to remember that he was sick the last time he ate it, or if he gets any suggestion which sets up any competing object, we have the conditions necessary for desire. There is then the perception of another object which also has its suggestive form which is more or less antithetical to the motor suggestion furnished by the sight of the sugar. Each one of these possible modes of action is thrown into relief over against the other and that competition of two suggested activities with each other is the excitant of desire, or the two-fold perception of the excitant of desire. When we are discussing that which excites desire, it is just as necessary to note one of these factors as it is the other. It is not the mere sight of the sugar which arouses desire any more than it is the mere thought of punishment for disobedience, or possible sickness, or possible discomfort, or displeasing someone to whom one is attached, that arouses the desire. The latter considerations do not represent mere negations which come in to check the expression of desire. They come in as integral factors to excite and arouse the desire. We must have a differentiation between the immediate, direct outgoing activity, appropriation of desire, just as on the other hand we must have a differentiation to mark off absolute sheer rejection. Direct appropriation is not the desire any more than direct rejection is aversion. It is the tension between the appropriating movement and the rejecting movement which excites desire.

Psychologists in discussing desire always note the conflict of desire as an empirical fact. That is, it is a fact that hardly escapes observation that when there is desire there is conflict; and they also recognize with varying degrees of clearness that that conflict is somehow involved in desire; but so far as I know they overlook the full significance of this fact, that when there is desire there is conflict. There is the tendency for them to speak as if the two desires were there ready-made and somehow came into conflict.

Of course I am making the point that this conflict is the excitant of desire itself, it is that which generates it. Up to this point there has been no special object of desire. Here it is that the conflict comes in of which I have spoken. The piece of sugar as a seen thing is confused with the piece of sugar which will satisfy desire. Now it is not the same piece of sugar psychologically. Of course it is physically, but it is not psychologically. The piece of sugar which excites desire is the visual activity as in tension, inhibited, by some other. The piece of sugar which is the object of desire is the activity of appropriation, value measured through this conflict.

If we take a case on a somewhat higher or more complicated plane, the child's father is a lawyer. Through his general admiration for his father, through the talk that he hears about that profession at home, its successes, its rewards and so on, he is led to the idea that he would like to be a lawyer. Now insofar as those facts are set over in his mind against the obstacles—that is, against the length of time and expenditure of energy in study, etc., that he must go through before he can be a lawyer—so far this must be a rudimentary desire to be a lawyer. But now to be a lawyer as the object of desire consists in some kind of clear appreciation of what that means: what it means objectively in its relation to other things, and what it means subjectively in terms of experiences that he must go through in order to become a lawyer. I think it is easy enough to see that that represents a more mature state of mind, that it represents the completion of a certain relative swing or rhythm just at the first, which serves to set up the desire or excite it. It is the relative and initial stage of the movement; the object is the excitant worked out, objectified. It is the excitant value presented to oneself in terms of its meaning and significance, and insofar as one does that, the mere state of desire as such passes out of existence, it is transformed into endeavor, into some kind of consciously [?] directed expenditure of energy. It is in the valuing of the stimulus, then, that the object of desire, both as regards its content and as regards its feeling accompaniments, emerges.

Green points out that the hedonists make the mistake of supposing that the desire can be excited by the anticipation of its own satisfaction.[15] Of course you see the self-contradiction involved in that, the reasoning in a circle in saying that the desire can be aroused by the anticipation of its own satisfaction. The point is simply this. They say the object of desire is pleasure and then pleasure excites the desire. Well, how does this thought of pleasure, or of pleasurable satisfaction, arise? Only because there is a desire already present and then the anticipation of its satisfaction is of course pleasurable. They regard that pleasure as in turn somehow awakening the desire. I think that criticism is justified, and when its full meaning is realized it is conclusive, it seems to me. It is simply a particular case of this confusion to which I have called attention.

Because it is only a particular case the same type of criticism will apply equally to Green's own position. He holds that moral desire must be awakened by the consideration of the moral good. You think of the desirable and think of it as desirable and then that thought either awakens the moral desire or it makes the natural desire already existing a moral one. What is that but simply saying over again that the contemplation of the fruition, of the realization of the desire, will excite the desire? What does the desire mean except the fulfillment of desire? What sense is there in the term "that which should be desired" if you eliminate all pressing desire? The ethically right is desirable and altogether lovely only on condition that one already has certain movements of self in that direction, and then this desirable thing presents itself as the completed fulfillment in ethical terms of that movement. That serves to reinforce the desire, but it serves to control it, to reveal the desire to itself. As I said yesterday these two senses of object do lie very close to each other and it is not difficult to see why they are confused; it is the fact that that which reveals desire does in turn react in the desire and restimulates it, or at least reinforces it, and serves to give it control and direction. That transformation is precisely the function which ethically we are after. It marks the attainment of the purpose for which the desire operates.

March 9, 1898

The outcome of the discussion of desire the other day was in substance that desire is the consciousness of divided tendencies to action, or divided activity, and that it was from that as a basis that we had to fix the relation of the so-called object of desire to desire itself, and also have to fix the relation of the feeling side to the pleasure-pain side, the first stage of desire. I should say that, concretely taken, it is a condition of uneasiness, of restlessness. Locke, in his discussion of the will, as you remember, made a great deal of the factor of uneasiness as furnishing the motive.[16] I do not suppose that we could accept all that Locke says about the relation of uneasiness to the will, but he has located there a factor which much of the discussion since his time has tended unduly to ignore.

This tendency to uneasiness is the reflection on the immediate consciousness of the condition of divided activity in which one is. This uneasiness is really simply the awareness of the alternation of these partial and obstructed motor discharges. The moment we desire we really begin to act, we stretch out in the reaction to the excitant cause of the desire; and then reaction, even if it does not go so far as gross action which would be visible to others, still exhibits itself in muscular contractions, in glandular excitations, and in visceral and other organic disturbances. Now as one of these partial discharges is set going and then is checked in its complete discharge by the starting up of another phase of the activity, the person is in this condition of restlessness. He feels himself starting to do one thing and then starting to do another incompatible thing. It involves then the sense of discharge of the activity and also the sense of obstructed activity. The sense of merely obstructed activity would not give rise to restlessness, neither of course would the completely operative suggestions give rise to it; but the mixture, the confusion of the two, throws one precisely into this condition. I should say that this was the initial stage of desire and, in perhaps the average case, represents almost the whole of desire, until finally the division is put a stop to through the selection of some single path of response. But whether this is simply the first part of it, or whether it is the larger part of it chronologically, there is here no very definite consciousness of any object of desire. I should say that it was a characteristic of desire just as desire—I mean taking it in its most intense and typical forms—that we really do not know what we want, or that the object of desire is not clearly presented to one. Our consciousness is rather filled up and clogged with these alternating partial discharges and these obstructed returns in the self.

I am aware that that goes quite contrary to the general current discussions of desire, but it is what my own observation has lead me to and I am confirmed in it by the fact that it would not be economical upon the whole to have attention fixed upon the object as the realization of desire. When desire discharges itself it finds out what its object is. After we get something which there has been this striving for, then we know what that desire was after all the time, and then in a retrospective discussion of it we attribute this awareness of the object as revealed in the final outcome to the desire in its earlier stages.

Now of course that is an introspective question and I hope you will take occasion to do some observation on that special point. Notice the cases of your own desires, especially the more intense ones, the ones that arise most unexpectedly, and see if it is not true to a very large extent that your objective consciousness is directed rather to the stimulant of desire than to the object of desire. My experience is that we keep recurring, either in fact or in imagination, to the conditions which excite the desire; we think of those or we look at those, and that keeps up this perpetual partial discharge; just as the child will keep his eye going back to the sugar and thus maintain the discharge. His thought, the intellectual part, is not really fixed on what is going to happen when that desire is satisfied; he directs his attention to the stimulus and in that way keeps his activity going; keeps it primed. To a very considerable extent that is an economical procedure; that is, insofar as instincts and habits have fixed for us a certain kind of ends, nothing is to be gained by consciously dwelling upon those ends. The problem rather is to get up steam enough to move on toward their realization. It is a question, in other words, of keeping up the stimulus rather than of discovering the proper mode of control, for the proper mode of control will be to a considerable extent organized into our system. Take such cases as eating and drinking, all the ordinary physical desires as we might term them. It would be comparatively futile—worse than futile, it would be waste—to keep the mind fixed upon the end, upon the object. If we can only get the activity going it will take care of the end in its own due course; but what we do have to attend to is getting the energy going which will carry itself forward to the reaching of these ends.

Now in emphasizing this point I do not mean to go to the extreme of saying that the object, the what is wanted, is not presented to consciousness at all. If it were not, there would be no desire, there would be mere direct want and appetite. I am simply trying to bring out the point of view that it is in a decidedly subordinate position with reference to the rising tension. Just because the desire is a partial discharge, so far as it does discharge it does fulfill itself, it does call up its own object or realization. We may say figuratively that the desire is pressing forward to an end but, like an instinct, without knowing what the end is; but the nearer it gets to it, the more it succeeds in getting, the more it becomes aware of itself, and in that sense the object of desire is continually present. But it is present in and through the activity itself, not outside of it to start it up or make it go.

Just the same thing which has been said about the object in the sense of the content must be said about the feeling side. Our activity is pressing onward, urging itself onward. Insofar as it finds a unified channel which represents the onward movement of the agent, insofar pleasure is felt. Insofar as it is obstructed, and there is the activity simply turned back on itself without effecting anything, there is the pain of dissatisfaction. But both the intellectual content of the object of desire and the feeling tone or accompaniment of this are registrations of the self-movement, of the desire process. They are it in its coming to consciousness of itself, in its own evolution. They are to be discussed and defined with reference to this active tensional discharge, rather than it with reference to them.

To put it back in the case of the child with the sugar, it is not by thinking of the satisfaction of desire that the child arouses desire or keeps it alive, but there is a stimulus on the principle of instinct or of habit, a suggestion that awakens its own immediate response; it is an activity and calls out an activity. That activity is inhibited as that activity unifies the checking element involved in it and expresses itself. Then the child comes to consciousness of what he wants. He knows it on the intellectual side and also on the subjective side, or what it means for him in terms of his own feelings. Now insofar as that comes out and plays a part, we get the desire in its more mature and developed form as distinct from this condition of restlessness, which represents the more primitive and undeveloped type. That consciousness of the object, or that self-consciousness on the part of desire of an object, serves to control the desire—not to stimulate it, but to control it, to direct it, to illuminate it. It is of course simply the deliberative process. The whole thing could be brought in here as representing the growth on the part of desire, of the nature of its own objective end; and that consciousness serving to instruct the desire, to show it what to do and how to operate. Now so fast as that control takes place, desire as desire ceases, and we get effort, or we get endeavor, or we get active interest, an insistent demand for the realization of this end. Now that is interest rather than the condition of desire. The way a man keeps himself continually in a condition of desire is by not putting before himself exactly what is involved in the satisfaction of that desire. Insofar as he does face that question and see what the fruition of it will be, he has something with which he can turn around on the desire and regulate it and eliminate the factor of restlessness, the factor of emotional stress which gives the coloring to desire as a psychical state. The man who has found out just what he wants is not in the state of conscious wanting as before; he is ready to act, his mind is made up, he has reached the point of resolution and the question for him now is to gather all his energies together and make them function along particular lines symbolized by that end.

Take a case where it is not physically impossible but where it is morally absolutely out of the question. Morally the satisfaction of the desire is impossible. A man's moral duty is then to turn his activity pretty energetically in some other direction so that that desire will cease to possess him. If he does not do that, he keeps toying with the morally forbidden end, he keeps imagining the satisfaction that he would get if he were to act in that way. He says: "I am not going to; but if I should, I should get such and such satisfaction." And he images it to himself and gets a certain amount of pleasurable satisfaction. That represents a partial attainment of the object. His desire as desire is a partial attainment of the object because it is this partial discharge. Of course it is not the complete attainment and so is not the overt attainment, for the overt act comes in at the point of the completed unification, or the synthesis of the activity.

The condition of desire then, so far as it is regulated by the anticipation of its own fruition, becomes transformed, it modulates over into interest, into passion, into affection, into devotion—that is, into an organization of all the means of action with reference to accomplishing this end. If we say it is desire, we must at least recognize its very great psychical distinction from desire in this other form. It is desire now, not as the conscious psychosis, but desire simply objectively, it is having one's heart set, one's energies bent upon the realization of the object. Just as the intellectual process of deliberation finds its own limit in determination or in decision, so the more emotional form of desire finds its limit in preference, in active preference, which is just this functioning interest or demand for the realization of an ideal. Preference is the name on the emotional side for the same thing that on the intellectual side we call determination, or on the concrete side what we call choice.

Before I go on to speak briefly of the moral bearing of this, I would like to read something which I found in a newspaper, from Goethe. It seems to contain more good psychology than is found in most of the psychological books. He said: "Our desires are the presentiments of the faculties which lie within us—the precursors of those things which we are capable of performing." It is simply the precursor because it is running against something which is running in another way. "That which we would be and that which we desire, present themselves to our imagination, about us, and in the future we prove our aspiration to an object which we already secretly possess." That is, this object is, so to speak, implicitly given, it is teleologically given; but as the desire keeps working itself out, then this thing which we secretly possessed all the time becomes an overt possession.

> It is thus that an intense anticipation transforms a real possibility into an imaginary reality. When such a tendency is decided in us, at each stage of our development a portion of our primitive desire accomplishes itself under favorable circumstances by direct means, and in unfavorable circumstances by some more circuitous route, from which, however, we never fail to reach the straight road again.

That conception of desire as "the presentiments of the faculties which lie within us—the precursors of those things which we are capable of performing" is practically giving the whole thing in a nutshell.

The importance of the distinction I have been making for purposes of theory is this: it makes the consciousness of value arise in the process of becoming conscious of action. Both the hedonist and the rationalist assume that we present to ourselves in consciousness certain goods, certain values, certain satisfactions, and that the presentation of that good or that value excites and keeps up the desire. One school takes one sort of value which he calls the rational good, the reasonable good; the other takes the subjective good which it calls feeling, pleasure. But just as in the other cases, although these two schools are strongly opposed to each other, they are alike in assuming that somehow the mind presents to itself a satisfaction, a good, and it is that which is responsible for the desire. Now just the reverse is true. The desire as active is the primary thing, and our consciousness of goods, of values, of satisfaction, represents simply the self-consciousness of these active forces. Instead of defining the desire in terms of good, either rational good or hedonistic good, we must define the good in terms of our desires—not the desires merely as phenomena, but desires in their relations, as indices of the active strivings of our own nature. On the basis of this psychology of desire the good is the attained synthesis of action as mediated through tension. Now it is because the discussion was going to lead up to this point that I have brought out this distinction between the excitant of desire and the object of desire, but if you find that the excitant is in the condition of divided action itself, or is an activity which is divided, which is disintegrating and falling apart, then you will find the object of desire in that activity becoming self-conscious or aware of itself, and then using that self-awareness as the instrument of direct organization. But if you take the other, you must find your excitant of desire as well as your object in something which lies outside the active process itself, and then you are forced to become either the ethical hedonist on one side, or the ethical rationalist on the other.

I hope you will work this round in your minds back with the discussion of deliberation. Here is really where the deliberation comes in play. It is in this process of self-consciousness, of the desire process serving to direct and control the active process, representing its passage over into active, operative interest or conscious endeavor, the expression of realization of the valuable idea.

I will call your attention to the article on the "Psychology of Effort" in the *Philosophical Review* of January 1897.[17]

March 14, 1898

I shall pass over any further discussion of effort in making the transition to the next topic, which is a consideration of the relation of conduct and character. For the sake of review of what has gone before I will make the transition from the point which was involved in the last discussion, that of desire. The distinction there made between the excitant of desire and the object of desire is a sort of distinction which holds all the way through this whole process. The entire intuitional procedure—just like attention, which is the intellectual aspect of this intuitional procedure—may be described as a process defining the relation of stimulus and control. It is a process of defining the stimulus so as to bring it under control; or it is the process of transforming the stimulus as an excitant into an organized instrument of control.

It should be obvious from the previous discussion that there is no sense in inquiring after the stimulus to action in general. There is no such thing, and the very conception of it is absurd. If you had a condition of quiescence, or real inertness, nothing ever would arouse to action. We talk about the stimulus of an act or of a particular mode of activity; that means the inquiry after the conditions which lead activity in general to assume this particular mode of manifestation, or after the conditions which deflected the previous mode of action into this particular channel. Any discussion is bound then to go astray which does not recognize that the problem of stimulus is really one of the deflection or diversion or mediation of action from one form into another. To discuss the question at large, apart from some particular transition or reconstruction, is therefore futile.

As has been already seen, the excitant always represents the loose ends of a previous coordination; these in their felt pressure and pull on each other, the influence which they are exerting on each other in the building up of a new coordination, constitute the process of stimulation. The conscious stimulus therefore represents the loss of the practical dynamic stimulus. As long as stimulation is practically effected there is no consciousness of stimulus. As long as each step in an activity is adequately motived, is adequately set going, and not only set going but set by the activity which precedes it, there is no consciousness of stimulus, or response to stimulus at all. We have simply an ordered series of acts. But let that adequate practical stimulus be wanting and then we get the conscious feeling of excitation. The failure in an adequate practical stimulus becomes the stimulus to finding and determining another adequate stimulus.

A man is shooting at a mark, hitting it regularly, and about as regularly he begins to miss it. That failure, that obstruction as regards reaching his end becomes at once a stimulus to think, to examine the various factors in that end, to search for something which may in turn become an adequate stimulus to successful shooting in the future. He examines his gun and ammunition, or looks for possible changes in the direction or the velocity of the wind. In that process previous stimuli in the objective sense, in the sense that they were there and were motivating his activity, are brought into consciousness; they are brought into consciousness in order that he may hit upon that which will give him the adequate clue or signal or organ for his subsequent activity.

We must, therefore, keep clearly in mind the distinction between the stimulus in the sense of the excitant which is found while the reflective process and the emotional process are going on, and found while the evolution is still occurring, and the attained or adequate stimulus which marks of necessity the termination of the intermediate process. The stimulus in the sense of the excitant is simply the divided state of activity as reflected in consciousness. But that division has grown out of a unity which moves through interaction, inter-stimulation, on toward a further unity. The stimulant then can never be merely subjective—that is, a feeling, nor merely objective—that is, a thought. And as we have· seen before, the line of cleavage between the two ethical schools which have been repeatedly criticized is the tendency on their part to forget that action is the germ of action, is the stimulus to action, one school isolating the feeling factor to get its initiative, the other abstracting the rational factor to get it. In either case the factor thus selected is made inexplicable because it is taken away from the action of which it is a sign. That is, the feelings of uneasiness, the feelings of pressure, of being pushed on, are simply the accompaniment of the divided activity; so the thought whether the recognition of an object or the formation of an image is some aspect of the divided activity projected into another form, projected as a rule [on?] to some special sense organ.

Now the control side represents simply the growing consciousness of the unity which underlies this division, it represents the thought of the unity utilized to effect itself, to control itself by—and thus terminate—the division. Now that unity cannot be anything of course outside of or beyond the divided activities themselves. We cannot talk as if we had divided activity and somehow decide there a consciousness of unity. The consciousness of unity is nothing but the sense of the interaction of these particular elements; it is the carrying out of the stimulating influence which each of them has upon the other. We think of A in terms of B which it incites, and we think of B in terms of its arousing of A, or the reaction which it has upon the A, and so on. The control, in other words, represents simply the developed consciousness of the stimulus. It is the same distinction we have had so many times before; it represents the consciousness of what the stimulus is, instead of simply that it is an excitant. It is finding out what sort of a thing it is after all.

As was suggested in the discussion of desire, there are two types of this relation between stimulus and control, the distinction being found in the matter of complexity, or the relative emphasis due to complexity. In probably the vast majority of acts, certainly in the vast majority of the acts of a person who has not subjected himself definitely to intellectual discipline, the stimulus side plays a much larger part in consciousness. There is simply just enough sense of the unity of the attendant outcome or end to hold the process together, to center it and to steady it. There must be some consciousness of the object, that is, of the fulfilled outcome; but the chief interest of the agent is on the other side, it is on what is immediately before him, it is on what is pushing him ahead, and on the next step that he is going to take to go ahead. He has no special interest in determining to himself what sort of a result he will get to finally, or in using that conception of the result to direct his activities, but he finds his guides simply in the push and pull of the stimuli themselves. He allows them to work themselves out.

This is relatively the more instinctive form, the more immediate, impulsive, intuitive type of action. The other type is where the circumstances are so complex, or where the individual by his habits of thought makes them so complex, that the end must be pretty definitely anticipated, all the impulses must be evaluated and therefore directed with a good deal of definiteness on the basis of that anticipated end. Here the person's interest becomes more in the process of deliberation, in the imaginative elaboration of the outcome, and consciously thinking of the intervening stages in terms of the outcome. Different social classes would present instances of these two types, but every individual under different circumstances finds himself at different poles. It is in effect the same distinction we find in discussing the relation between the initiative and the discursive phases. But the general principle remains the same in both of these types of relation of stimulus and control. In any case the control factor is the excitant clarified, it is the excitant interpreted with reference to what it is going to do if it is allowed to operate, the distinction being that in one case a comparatively slight though of this outcome is enough, while in the other it has to be gone over thoroughly and comprehensively. So far as the excitant is turned into an instrument of control through being related to its outcome, it ceases to be a mere exciter and becomes a director, or what in ordinary terms we call the motive—the motive being simply this excitant conceived in terms of outcome.

Now as fast as this transformation takes place, the immediate stimulus becomes modified in consciousness of the point of application of energy. Take a person conscious of a growing uneasiness and restlessness until it reaches a point of irritation. One feels that he must do something, but the interest having been on something else, there has been no attempt to think what it is one ought to do or why one ought to do it. Now there is the excitant there, but there is no clear or coherent consciousness of its nature, simply the pressure to do something, and in certain cases the man may allow himself to be guided by habit and do something he is accustomed to do simply because he is irritated. What he does may be relevant to his feeling or it may not. If one, however, begins to reflect at all, what he virtually does is to define and locate that excitant, to say to himself, it comes from just this point, it proceeds from just such and such a source, and therefore my energy must be directed, to be efficient, to that particular point.

That is then really the function of the restlessness. It is to stimulate us, not directly to action, but to incite us to find out where the point is which needs attention, the point which needs to be looked after; and as we do that, then of course we become conscious of the point to which our energy may be most economically and most fruitfully applied. I take a very trivial instance. Suppose a person engaged in some activity becomes suddenly aware of physical discomfort and also of a tendency, which is annoying, to have his activities diverted; and yet he is very much engaged in what he is doing and he hates to be diverted, but still the discomfort keeps up and finally gets attention, and then he locates it and sees it is a draft from a window, or one's shoe pinches at a particular point. There that immediate indefinite excitant marks the division of activity and has succeeded in inciting him to locate it, and the value of locating it is that when it is located we know the focus or the center at which to aim our next action. Thus the excitant, when thus reflected upon, represents the aim in terms of the spot to be aimed at. It is obvious that a sufficiently important consideration in realizing an aim is to know just at what point to discharge the energy; that is the function of the sense side. In the first place it is to show the point of weakness or strain, the thing which needs to be looked after, and then, when more positively defined, to serve to focus the expenditure of effort that we are going to put forth.

Now I think exactly the same process is gone through within any completed volitional development. Imagine yourself plunged into any complicated moral or social situation in an unexpected way. As long as the feeling side of confusion, uneasiness and pressure dominates one, a large element in the confusion is that you cannot tell the point at which to react. First you cannot define the difficulty. The situation presents itself in such a way as to almost suffocate one or it is seen in a kaleidoscopic view, one phase rapidly changing, the whole thing shifting all the time. The moment we can pick out the point of greatest obtrusiveness, that moment we can also select the point against which to direct our first attack; and when we do that, we have the stimulus under control.

The psychological fallacy coming in here is well seen in the discussion of attention. Attention is treated as if it were directed toward certain sensations, but the great problem of sensation is to find out what sensations we must attend to—the sensations that are really the keys to the situation; and the attention process is a process of tentative selection and reaction to values, possible clues, until one gets hold of just the sensation which he does want so that the process may go on in an unimpeded, successful way. With reference to the excitant then, control means the definition of the path of discharge or, in practical terms, the getting hold of the next thing to be done. Just as fast as on the immediate side, the peripheral side, we become conscious of the point of attack, on the mediating side, or the central side, we become conscious of the organization of all our powers or habits with reference to effective application and expenditure at this point. Thus we have a period of organization of action succeeding this period of estimation, valuation, and emotional stress. Instead of having an image of an end simply set over against the immediate situation as sensed, we have that consciousness of the end transformed into terms of sense, into terms of operating habits or attitudes.

Nothing is more futile pedagogically and morally than the consciousness of the mere end, that is, the end which is not transformed into a working hypothesis. That is the basis of the inefficiency educationally of developing attempts for mere words of command, or the direct immediate presentation of certain ends. You can tell a person to stand up straight physically, but the primary thing is for him to know what standing up straight means. In other words, how it is to be effected; what particular action or adjustment on his part is necessary. Insofar as he does not comprehend what adjustment is called for, insofar he will do nothing[?] or throw himself into some other distorted attitude. Not knowing what application of energy to make, he does not know the direction in which to apply his powers and capacities to that point. In other words, so far as the volitional process is successful, so far as unification is effected, the distinction between the immediate and the mediate loses its meaning; tension ceases and we get, instead of it, organization. Now we as observers may draw a distinction between the objective point to which the energy is directed and the subjective gathering together of the energy for discharge on that point. But there is no such distinction in the consciousness of the agent himself. As soon as you have one you have the other. It is a perfect equation or balance.

Just so far as this coordination [?] is attained, the state of consciousness is also changed. The emotional stress, the uneasiness, gives way to a feeling of relief, to a feeling of calm; or if it is a very important matter, to a feeling of great peace. The feeling of relief amount[ing] to peace is found in religious experience, for example, and marks exactly such a termination of a period of suspense in divided activities. It is the feeling of attainment of a satisfactory level from which one can thereafter proceed. So the feeling of uncertainty changes to a feeling of being settled, to a feeling of going ahead and knowing what we are about—a slightly different feeling from that of simple relief.

On the intellectual side, instead of having this duplex consciousness of an immediate situation on one side and an ideal imaged situation on the other, with incompatibilities between them, we have the image of a complex integral situation, into which what one is doing at the particular moment fits. Take a man who has his mind made up, his plan of action settled on. He has an image—it may be vague, but still an image—in his mind which covers the whole procedure, covering perhaps days or months, and each particular act has its place in that whole situation. It is that whole situation taking shape, taking form. The immediate overt act is placed in its bearings in other words. This is the factor of additional value which has been brought about through the conflict. Previous to the conflict what the person was doing fitted into an organized scheme or situation in the same way, but just insofar as that situation has never fallen to pieces and one is not aware of the incompatibilities between various parts of it, one has not a sense of this value, of that and how each act is an expression of the whole complex situation, so that the value of that whole is in every one of its particular modes.

The termination then of the period of tension, of suspense and of positive unification, does not mark a simple relapse into the original condition of unity. We get the benefit of the conflict that we have been through, in this deepened and extended sense of the relation of the particular act to the whole system which it embodies. In practical terms what we now have is a status of choice, preference, or decision.

SECTION 6. DETERMINISM VERSUS INDETERMINISM

March 15, 1898

I shall attempt to dispose of the question of choice rather summarily, as in a way the whole analysis up to this time has really been an analysis of the process of choosing; that is, the process of movement of action toward definite outcome.

The two fallacious views of choice isolate the two factors of coordination which were under discussion yesterday—namely, stimulus and control. They arise from a difference of interest leading to a difference in emphasis, that difference of emphasis resulting in a fallacy because it leads to an isolated abstraction of the factor in which the particular school is interested, and this leads to the ignoring of the whole direct coordination in which that factor really has its placing.

The indeterminist school is interested in the initiation side of action. It is interested in the way in which a new mode of action gets under way, gets started, and as a result it emphasizes the agent and his supposed faculty—to the presence in him of a faculty termed will—of arbitrarily initiating a certain mode of action. The determinist school is interested in the direction that the activity thus set going is likely to take; it is interested in seeing to it that the activity results in a certain outcome which is regarded as valuable or desirable. Its interest, in other words, is in the question of the control.

James is quite right in saying that the ordinary criterion for deciding between these two views is the ethical one.[18] I do not mean by that that the real thing is to be decided on ethical considerations because the psychological analysis enables us to see the whole circle of coordination in which both intuition [or initiation?] and control have their place; but as between these two schools, the side on which one ranges himself depends upon the direction of his ethical interest. James speaks as if the distinct ethical interest were on the side of indeterminism, and as if scientific interest were on the side of determinism: that as a scientist one would believe in determinism, and as one interested in human conduct he would want to see the scales tip on the side of indeterminism.

But that overlooks, I think, the ethical motive that is really operating on the scientific side. The desire to find order, to find law, is just as much an ethical desire at bottom as is the desire to get intuition and spontaneity. That comes out very clearly in John Stuart Mill, as representative of his whole school. They were all determinists. I think that it is in his *Autobiography* that Mill states that he was anxious to believe that the action of everybody else was determined, while his own was not.[19] How his desire to bring the activity of others under the principle of determination was simply that he might have some assurance of the possibility of reform. If action is determined, then you have some guarantee that people are going to grow, provided they are presented with that which induces it. The whole question of moral reform comes to be one of forces, conditions. If you can set up conditions which will make it worthwhile for the agent to shape his actions in a moral direction, he will do so if he is a determinist, but if not he will not do so. Do the best you can with institutions, there is a factor that is utterly unaccountable. The individual may pay no attention to this elaborate structure that you have built up, or he may tip the whole thing over because he feels like it. Now that feeling that on an indeterminist basis you have no certainty of a continuation of social growth on the moral side has been the disposition that has animated the determinists. It is not simply that they feel their scientific sense satisfied in bringing everything under necessity. Why should they have this interest in reducing everything to the determinist's point? It is simply because that is the way in which they get action under control.

Paradoxical as it may seem then, the interest of both schools is in the question of reform, but they tackle the question from different sides. The determinist wants to be sure of getting pressure to bear on the individual with some certainty that if that is brought to bear, he will respond and modify his conduct accordingly. The indeterminist sees that all this is bootless unless the individual does respond. It is this possibility or capacity of response to the conditions which are presented which they emphasize. Each school always assumes implicitly the standpoint of the other. The determinist assumes the capacity for response which the libertarian school emphasizes, and the libertarian school always assumes the motive operating from without the individual's will but presented to him and at last influencing him, inciting him, soliciting and possibly tempting him.

This mutual assumption by each of the standpoint of the other is perhaps best seen in the standing quarrel between the individualist and the socialist. The socialist says all the evil is the outcome of institutions. Change the institutions and you take away from the individual all the egoism and aggressive disregard of the interests of others; take away the competitive constitution of industrial society and reorganize it on a collective and cooperative basis, and nobody but an insane man would willfully do anything which would injure another—it would be too obviously injuring himself. So if you want to change the individual, change the institution. As long as you do not change the institution and preach at the individual, you are wasting words; it is nothing but an exhibition of words. The practical motives that animate him are all the other way, so they say reform is from without and not from within. That is all right in a way, but how are you going to change the institution? If you change the institution, you change the individual. They assume that the institution is a fixed thing operating on the individual. If that is so, how are you going to get your leverage to modify the institution? They are practically doing the same thing that they criticize. They want the institution changed but they must start with the change of the individual or else they have a cast-iron wall of an institution which must persist just as it is.

On the other hand, the person who says we must always reform from within is trying to bring arguments to show the individual why he must reform from within. If you simply preach to a man, you are bringing external considerations to bear, you are presenting to him motives in terms of operating conditions and institutions. The moment anyone goes a bit further and says: do right because it is right; the moment you go as far as that and attempt any explanation of what is meant in its being right, you get outside the mere limits of the individual's consciousness and attempt to influence his conscience in terms of an objective situation— of an institution in other words, in some form or other. The individualist has to assume some institution as there as affording the scene or theater of operation, and also as furnishing the stimuli, the incitations to action. All it does for the individual is to reserve for him in a rather nominal way the capacity to choose arbitrarily between these different excitations that are presented to him.

Introspectively, the libertarian appeals to the individual's consciousness that he can move either way, that he can choose in either direction. The necessitarian for the most part relies upon indirect arguments rather than any direct appeal to consciousness; he appeals to the supremacy of law and order and to the scientific meaninglessness of introducing the factor which is not a factor, introducing a power which you cannot treat in the same way with the other powers with which you deal. This is really an appeal to the miraculous and the supernatural and thus violates the whole tendency, the whole spirit, of philosophy—which is to explain facts in terms of their relations to other facts. But the necessitarian does to a certain extent appeal to introspective consciousness. It says to the agent: Did you not really have some reason for deciding as you did decide? You say you decided from sheer power of your own will, that you chose the weaker of two motives or of two desires as against the stronger, but why did you do this? Was there not some other reason why you chose this weaker one? Did you do it because you felt that it was right, and that duty had a supreme hold upon you? If you did thus decide in view of any further considerations, that consideration was the motive that was operating and was adequate to determine your conduct.

What is the merit, respectively, of these two appeals to consciousness? A man feels that he can choose either way. So he does in the earlier stages of his action, because as a matter of fact he is choosing both ways. It is not simply that he can, but he does. In other words his self is divided; there is a tendency in two directions which, objectively considered, are opposed to each other. A man stops at a signboard, hesitating whether he will take the right or the left road. For the moment he is taking both, though he may not move his body an inch in either direction; but psychologically he is now going in one direction and now in the other. Of course he feels that he can go in either direction, but I do not see that this appeal of the determinist means anything more than that the agent is in the state of divided action, and he is conscious of that division. His consciousness of alternative forces in tension with each other is a necessary feature of the process of bringing the agent to consciousness with reference to an act. Those two divided courses of action are both himself. It is he that is divided.

The libertarian appeals also to the consciousness of a man. I did decide that; it was not decided for me. As Martineau says, he is not like a log tossed about by psychical waves, but he takes a hand himself in telling how the thing is going to come out.[20] Of course he does simply because he is the waves instead of being either the log or an umpire between them. The choice represents precisely the agent unifying himself in and through this process of division.

Now what the necessitarian appeals to on the other side is the consciousness of the agent that the deed is absolutely his own deed, that that deed is himself. Being what he was, you have that deed; you must have that deed. You must have it because the deed is simply the exhibition or the realization of the agent himself. At the very last moment the libertarian shifts his ground. Up to a certain point the thing which he is emphasizing is that the deed proceeds from the agent and not from any outside consideration, but at the last moment, so to speak, just at the moment of choice, the libertarian thrusts in this purely indefinite thing in the agent, this capacity to choose in either direction. Well then the deed proceeds from that capacity; it is that capacity which is responsible. It would be perfectly legitimate for a man to argue with the libertarian: Here you are blaming me because I have done a certain deed. Now I have a capacity in me of choosing either way, and at this particular juncture that capacity chose for reasons known entirely to himself, with which I have nothing to do. Now if you can catch and isolate that capacity, you may punish it and hold it responsible, but why should you blame me for doing it? In other words, how are you going to identify such a capacity with any concrete historical agent? The determinist now comes in and says: No, the person that did the deed was this particular person, this person with certain habits and interests. He did it because he was just that kind of a person. Now of course where the determinist makes his mistake in interpretation is that he then shifts his ground and introduces exactly the same break between the deed and the agent that the libertarian has done. He begins to regard the deed as a merely external affair, as a mere result, and the agent simply as certain causes which somehow operated to produce the result.

Now from the point of view which we have been discussing so long, the particular deed, the product, is not an external result or effect, it is the process come to a head, come to a definite, identified outcome. You might as well regard the point of a moving cone as somehow the product of the base of the cone and the mere result of the base of the cone, as to conceive of the deed as an external result of certain forces which have preceded it. It is those forces come to the point of exhibition, come to the point of explicit clear recognition.

We are free because the whole process is one of coming to self-consciousness. The whole process is one of discovery and self-revelation on the part of the agent; it is a process of liberation by its very nature. But that freedom is a determinate matter; that is, the action in its onward movement has its own law, its own order, and in reflection, theoretically if not practically, the conditions can be stated. Theoretically that action will be put in terms of concrete facts and their relationships, just as much as any physical activity can be.

The popular view in this matter is eclectic, I should say. It takes both views by turns. It takes both up to a certain point, just as regards the quarrel between the individualist and the socialist. The ordinary man is eclectic and says: It is quite true that the institution modifies the individual, but the individual has the power of changing his own motives in such a way as to change the institution. That has a certain practical truth at the bottom of it, but that truth is got at and stated in a very confused and ambiguous way. There is no clear consciousness on the part of the common consciousness as to how both these opposed views can be true at the same time. That confusion arises because of lack of insight into where the two factors come from, how they arise, and how they enter into relationship with each other. That want is met by recognizing that the distinction between the agent and his capacity on one side, and the environment or the conditions and their controlling force on the other, arises within the process of coming to self-consciousness; it arises as an assistance, an economical device within the process of valuing action. In other words, there are not two such things as the agent and his capacity on one side and the environment and its influences on the other; but the self in action, in attempting to get an adequate view of the whole thing, finds it convenient to make that distinction.

If I am ignoring the logical aspects of the thing, it is because they were discussed last quarter—the whole question of the relation between subject and object, or between organization and environment.

SECTION 7. NO POLARITY
BETWEEN CHARACTER
AND ENVIRONMENT

This latter point, this statement just made, brings us then to the discussion of the positive meaning to be put into the term agent or character on one side, and the term environment or conditions of action on the other.

The complete agent, the full self, is found in a unified way in an organized and valued mode of action—what we term practically an interest or a pursuit or a calling. Of course, if we use the word calling or function, we must take it in a wide and flexible sense which will include under the term calling a child playing with a ball or building a block house. That is, we cannot limit it to what in the adult sphere would be called a pursuit. These adult callings are not different in principle, but simply in the range and comprehensiveness of the organization attained. Perhaps an interest is as good a term as any. In the interest there is no conscious distinction between subject and object, between agent and act, between motive and consequences. In an interest, in the function, so far as it operates integrally, the person is engaged, as absorbed, is found in the act. It is the condition which psychologists have termed nonvoluntary attention. On the other hand that object is not a mere object; the agent has not lost himself in a bare external thing. It is equally on the other side that the object has been taken into the individual's self, has been centered with his purposes, feelings and aims. It is nothing as an external thing; it is everything in the part that it plays in carrying on and maintaining the activity. In other words, you have an activity which has its subjective side because it has meaning and value and its objective side because it has content, because it is action which is realized through things as its instruments and organs; and those things as its instruments are combined in perfectly regular ways.

Now we come once more to the principle of some break, or some interference. That is, the interest, the activity has to be revalued before it can continue to operate successfully, and at this point the distinction between the agent and his powers on one side and the environment and its influence on the other will prove serviceable—a distinction in reflection, in analysis, in power. The agent, so to speak, draws himself up and off, he looks at himself, searches himself to see how much of an agent he is, he takes stock of himself precisely as a bank would see what its assets and liabilities are or a merchant would take an inventory of what he has. The agent, in other words, views himself not as in action, because he does not know what to do in action. As long as he can view himself in action, he does so normally. But now there is obstruction of the immediate identification of the agent and his act; so he looks at himself in the light of his capacity for action. That is advisable, is necessary as an adequate preparation for the action. As long as you can walk ahead successfully and easily, you do not need to examine your instrument; but if it becomes a question of what you are going to do, it is good policy to see what you have as an instrument for doing things with.

On the other side one will set over against this power or capacity the scene or situation in which the agent is to operate. That is, just as a bank would not only strike a balance in a static way of its assets and liabilities but would also inquire whether business was extending or contracting, whether there was a general feeling of trust or of distrust, it would not only examine itself but it would also draw out, abstract, the scene of its operations. It does both of these, it does them correlatively in order to find out what the next line of action should be, or to value and bring to consciousness the action. Now this abstraction on both sides is one which occurs within the problem for the sake of solving the problem. It is just as much a device for purposes of solution as putting all your knowns and unknowns together in algebra or as bringing your pluses and minuses together are. There is a question to be solved: What is the valuable mode of action? What is the interest? Now you can get at that from either of two ends. Sometimes you may use one, sometimes the other, sometimes you may find it desirable to look at it from both sides. You can either say: What am I as an agent with reference to the scene of action? Or: What is the scene, what are the conditions, with reference to me as an agent? The instrument cannot be defined excepting in terms of what it can do. The moment you attempt to define an agency in terms of itself, it becomes contradictory. But on the other hand conditions and their influences can be defined only in terms of what can be done with them. What are they good for? How can they be manipulated to advantage? This distinction then is for the sake of realizing the problem more distinctly. It is not that there is a thing called the agent on one side and something else called the environment on the other. The only reality is the whole activity, but it is problematic and in order to bring that to consciousness it is advisable to split up the thing and look at it on one side of the instrument of action from which the activity will immediately proceed, and to consider it also from the side of the conditions, since what that instrument will succeed in doing will depend upon these conditions. To study the conditions represents the action defined in terms of probable outcome, just as the agent represents the activity defined in terms of probable starting points.

March 16, 1898

Yesterday I attempted to state the economical reasons for drawing a distinction between the agent and the conditions of action; to suggest that that represents an intellectual survey of the field and the marking off of the problems requiring solution in order to facilitate the adequate mental realization of the process. If that be true, then the so-called interaction of agent and condition, the influence which one exerts upon the other, will represent the solution of the problem thus put; it represents the solution of the equation. It is not a process in any sense which one as a fact is exerting on the other as a fact, but it is translating our somewhat abstract view of the process or situation into a more adequate one. The interaction is an intellectual process and not a factual one; it represents the building up again of the whole situation from the standpoint of the abstracted parts. Through stating the situation in its dualistic form, we bring it to consciousness more adequately than in any other way.

Now if we feel reasonably sure of our conditions and our main problem, our main deficiency lies on the side of the agent; that is, if we are obstructed in bringing the whole process to consciousness because of our imperfect realization of the nature of the agent, then all our attention goes to the agent. We regard him as the all important thing, not because he is really any more important than the conditions are, but simply because to us, in bringing the process to consciousness, he is more important because we have the other already fairly at command. If the whole type of interest is of that sort, the person would tend to become an indeterminist. While if one felt the varying and uncertain thing was the conditions, if one felt that the subject was pretty well understood, if one located the difficulty in telling what was to be done on the side of the conditions, just the opposite tendency would set in; all the attention would go to the conditions as the important thing, and the agent would be there simply for those conditions to operate upon.

In practical terms then, the issuing of character in conduct means the solution of the problem. It represents action in its intellectual form, its form valuation passing over into activity, in its overt or practical form. The character which is set up prior to issuance in determinate conduct is an abstract, but it serves the purpose of a working hypothesis. It is a tentative definition of conduct. The overt activity represents simply the limit of the whole movement. It is not, strictly speaking, something that supervenes after the deliberative process and after the emotional stress; it is not the mere state that follows upon the process of valuation. It is the process of valuation itself arrived at its limit. Every step in the mediating process involves character passing into conduct. It is all overt, but in this preliminary stage the various overt activities check each other because they are discrepant and the net result on the overt side is inhibited for the time being. Here what we call the overt act is simply a unification of the discrepant overt acts which have been going on simultaneously up to that time. Their unification involves that they become visibly objective both to the agent himself and to others. Or to change the language, there is motor discharge all the time in the deliberative process and in the emotional stress, but the motor discharges do not reinforce each other along a single definite line until the process of mediation reaches the point of decision or choice. When that mutual reinforcement is reached, the activity becomes obvious.

Starting from the other end, the overt activity is simply a nodal point in the process of self-revelation. It is not something that takes place after one has arrived at an adequate valuation. That point may be got at by asking what our criterion is for deciding when the unified overt act ought to set in. How long should the process of deliberation and emotional stress go on? If the whole process is one of self-evaluation in practical form, in the form of action, in the form of doing, that must give the criterion for the answer to the question. There comes a time when the only way to carry the evaluation further is to do some deed. The agent has virtually exhausted the conception of the situation along that line of procedure. If he is going to get anything further, he must do it by setting in active motion the conditions which he already feels sure of.

Put it in an extreme case on the other hypothesis. A man says he will not act until the knows all the conditions. Such a position is psychologically contradictory for two reasons. First, he is acting all the time he is knowing. He cannot say: "I will not act until I know," because his very knowing is an active directed movement as far as it goes.

On the other hand there is a point at which he cannot know any more conditions until he does act. Suppose a person should say that he would not apply for a certain position until he was sure he would get it, or until he knew all the conditions. It is obvious that the act of applying may be one of the conditions and the chief condition in finding out what the situation itself is. This point is precisely analogous to the stage where actual experimentation becomes necessary in science. The experimentation serves not merely to test the hypothesis, it serves to elaborate the hypothesis, to clear it up, to define it simply as an intellectual concept. There comes a time when a man ceases to become a scientific investigator and becomes a word mumbler. If he goes on to elaborate his hypothesis further, he must bring this ideal, temporarily abstracted, up into contact with particular conditions in order to see what it is. The same is true on the moral side. A man puts a certain value on a situation. The only way in which he can test that and also the only way in which he can build it up and carry it on further will be by bringing it into immediate connection again instead of mediate connection with particular facts, through acting upon it. The overt action then—from this point of view, that is, where it is marked off from what has gone before—indicates the particular point in the process of valuation where one must assume unity in order to discover unity. That of course is only another way of saying that the moral process is an experimental process just like the scientific process.

Through the distinction between the agent as capacity and the conditions of the agent's action becoming generic, there arises a distinction which may be conveniently termed that between the instrumental self and functioning self. Every adult has in a general way a certain conception of his own habit and powers and interests, lines of action. He has also in an equally general way a conception of the probable sphere of exercise of those powers; not simply the sphere in the geographical sense, but also in the question of the people and the things with reference to which he is probably going to be called upon to act. Now we carry around with us then all the time in advance those general conceptions, which of course are both abstracts, but like all legitimate abstracts they have value in facilitating and freeing action when the stress of it comes. In other words, these distinctions shorten very much the period of tension, the amount of deliberation and anticipation required, and make it more likely to have a successful issue. We have worked out in advance certain features of the situation and therefore are freed from the necessity of directing our attention to them, and can locate it upon the peculiar features of this particular situation. Now the conception of the agent which we thus have built, that form of self-consciousness, represents the instrumental self. We know in a general way what we are good for, what lies within the scope of our powers, what it is reasonable for us to attempt to do, and if we are called upon to do something what resources we can bring with us.

It would be interesting if there were time to trace the development of this self-consciousness from infancy up in terms of modern psychology, but if you will simply look over what James says about the growth of the empirical ego consciousness,[21] you will see that all the time self is being defined in terms of what it can do, what it can probably effect. That is the legitimate, as distinct from the morbid, consciousness of self. The little child is defining himself in terms of his bodily sensations. He is doing that from the standpoint of motor reaction. He will draw a line between what he is and what he has, on precisely that basis. He does not take all the bodily sensations and work them into his self-consciousness; but insofar as these sensations influence or direct his mode of action, they will become bound up with his sense of self. He bruises his finger. He may at first put it in terms of I have so and so, rather than I am so and so. It is an objective fact which he recognizes. But if that bruise upon his finger influences what he can do and what other people do to him, if it becomes a center of action and reaction of a social sort, that bruised finger becomes a part of his own ego consciousness. If you take the child's concept of his empirical ego from his crude consciousness up to the developed adult, the principle is always the same. The range of the actions, the importance attaching to them, is of course changing continually, and in that change the growth of the concept of the self consists. But the principle that remains active everywhere is that I am to myself, I am in my own consciousness whatever I feel I can predicate future action upon, that which I can use to initiate and effect action and reaction. That is what I mean by the instrumental self.

The empirical self is the instrumental self and is not then merely empirical; it is not merely a chance grouping of sensations which without rhyme and reason become identified with our own being. If you will make an empirical study along the line suggested by James in his *Psychology* [22] of your own peculiar sensations of self, you will find them in certain muscular strains and characteristic bodily reactions. There is a reason for that which lies deeper than anything James gives. Some people have located them in their cheeks, others in their eyes, others bring in wrists or hands, or vocal chords also; but whichever you take, I think you will find upon further examination that they relate to the organs from which you habitually initiate your lines of action, or which you have come to associate with the initiation of action. Of course there are many subtle associations which come in here to complicate the matter.

Now as distinct from that what the philosophers call the transcendental self, the spiritual ego, the moral personality is the function itself; that is, the self that is not abstracted as capacity for action, but which is actually in action. That represents unity and it represents universality, but it represents it in a dynamic way, in a practical way and not in a static or intellectual way. That functioning self is the organized motor synthesis of the habits and interests. Character is of course identical with the instrumental self, the historical ego; it can never be identified with the whole personality.

NOTES

1. *Supra*, p. 34, note 7.
2. James, *Psychology*, II, Chap. XXV, "The Emotions," esp. pp. 499–67.
3. *Ibid.*, p. 449.
4. Plato, *Republic*, 429a–432b; Aristotle, *Nichomachean Ethics*, 1115b–1116b.
5. Plato, *Laws*, 632d–650b.

6. (London: Henry S. King and Co., 1877).

7. Herbert Spencer, *The Data of Ethics* (New York: D. Appleton and Co., 1881), Chap. X, "Relativity of Pains and Pleasures."

8. *Ibid.*, Chap. XIV, "Conciliation."

9. James, *Psychology*, II, 457.

10. Apparently, Dewey is not attributing this view to James. Rather, the latter's theory is ambiguous enough to permit this interpretation. For another view of James's theory of emotions, see Dewey, "The Psychology of Effort" (1897), in *Early Works*, IV, 152, note.

11. "On the Hypothesis That Animals Are Automata," in Thomas Henry Huxley, *Method and Results* (New York: D. Appleton and Co., 1898).

12. For a statement and analysis of this view, see C. K. Ogden, *Bentham's Theory of Fictions* (London: Routledge and Kegan Paul, Ltd., 1951), p. cxxix *et passim*.

13. *Infra*, Chap. IV, Sec. 5.

14. George Trumball Ladd, *Psychology, Descriptive and Explanatory*, 4th ed. (New York: Charles Scribner's Sons, 1903), pp. 601–08, and James Sully, *The Human Mind, A Text-Book of Psychology* (New York: D. Appleton and Co., 1881), II, 169–209.

15. Thomas Hill Green, *Prolegomena to Ethics*, 2nd ed. (Oxford: The Clarendon Press, 1884), Secs. 158–62. Dewey discusses this issue in *Outlines of a Critical Theory of Ethics* (*Early Works*, III, 254) and in *The Study of Ethics, A Syllabus* (*Early Works*, IV, 266).

16. John Locke, *An Essay Concerning Human Understanding*, Bk. II, Chap. XX, "Of Modes of Pleasure and Pain."

17. John Dewey, "The Psychology of Effort," *Early Works*, V, 151–63.

18. William James, "The Dilemma of Determinism," in *The Will to Believe and Other Essays in Popular Philosophy* (New York: Longmans Green and Co., 1897).

19. John Stuart Mill, *Autobiography* (London: Longmans, Green, Reader, and Dyer, 1873), pp. 168–69.

20. James Martineau, *A Study of Religion*, II (Oxford: Clarendon Press, 1889), 213–15. Dewey discusses this illustration at greater length in *The Study of Ethics, A Syllabus* (*Early Works*, IV, 345–50).

21. James, *Psychology*, I, 291–329.

22. *Ibid.*, 299–302.

CHAPTER 5

PSYCHOLOGY OF THE VIRTUES

SECTION 1. THE PROBLEM OF CLASSIFICATION

I have said these things, not only because they seem to have a certain importance in themselves in relation to the problems that are always presenting themselves, but as a preparation for a discussion of the nature of virtue and the classification of virtues. If the moral process represents, in the language of our last discussion, the continual valuing of the instrumental self, the agent for action in the process of action, the continual passing over of the instrumental into the functioning self, then the virtues must find their interpretation with reference to this process. Stated intellectually—that is, on the intellectual side—the virtues would represent the various attitudes assumed by the agent with reference to the action that he is to perform. Stated on the emotional side, they would represent the types of interest which appear as the agent manifests himself in action. Or stated in active terms, they represent the chief modes of organized action which arise, these modes or types being distinguished from each other simply upon the basis of the part of the process of mediation which is emphasized.

But those very general statements perhaps had better be put in a more concrete form. The general problem is whether there is any basis for the classification of virtues and for the definition of each particular virtue. Can we do anything more than simply catalogue the various virtues in an empirical way? Can we say, as a matter of fact, such actions have been regarded as virtues, or are not regarded as such? Or do they represent an organized system? It is interesting historically to note that the attempt to make a science of it arose in the belief that virtues were an organized system and that the primary ethical interest was the discovery of the right basis of classification and definition of the virtues. The question was asked continually in the ethical dialogues of Plato: Is it one or many? If one, how does it become divided into many; and if many, how do we call them all by the common name? That question soon got pushed to the background historically. I think it is easy enough to see why. Certain intermediate psychological and metaphysical questions came up which had to be answered antecedently. A satisfactory answer to that question could not be got until a whole lot more were answered. Putting that question stirred up a lot of other questions that gradually pushed it out of sight, and so at present the theory of virtues is regarded as more or less an arbitrary annex to ethics proper. The value of it is being seen to lie in its getting an opportunity for the presentation of pedagogical maxims.

I think the original Greek instinct was the correct one. The whole question comes in the nature and relationships of the virtues. That is, the only object of all the rest of the inquiry is to find out what the forms of the chief types of valuable life are—so that all the preceding discussion in a way ought to be regarded as preliminary, its value consisting in the hold, the insight which it will give us upon virtue as a psychological system. I think Greek instinct was right not only in classing this problem as fundamental but also in the answer which it brought out.

I think we have to come back to the four original Greek virtues, but we can do so on the basis of a deeper insight into their psychology and have a better hold on their organic* . . . four types of virtue would be conscientiousness, self-assertion, self-control, and the fourth, which I should term justice-love. It is not designated adequately by either term: there must be a complex term for it.

Conscientiousness is the interest of the agent in the process of mediation. The moral process is the process of bringing the self to consciousness in an act; it is the process of valuation. Now the habit of attaching proper value to the process of valuing is conscientiousness. That may seem a little summary, but you will see in a general way what is meant by the habit of attaching the proper value to the process of valuation: seeing if it is properly performed without overdoing it or without slighting it.

Self-assertion is the process of mediation from the standpoint of the initiating of impulses. That of course is the Greek courage, just as what I call conscientiousness is the Greek wisdom.

Self-control is interest in the process of mediation from the standpoint of the outcome. Of course self-control and self-assertion are strictly correlative; they take the process of mediation from the two ends.

The fourth type of virtue is the interest in the organization of conduct in overt action. That is, it is the interest in the issuing of the mediation into the overt sphere. It is the interest in interests—not in process of mediating interests—that is conscientiousness, but the interest in the content of our interests, not their form. Therefore it is what we call love, affection, simply interest itself in its full development and realization. If we take it with reference to its distributive rather than its integral aspect, that is, as applying itself to the proper adjustment of this act to the other act, we call it justice. My point is that if we take the process of mediation as a whole it is affec-

---

* Part of a sentence is obscured in the original hectograph copy.

tion or love. It we take that as getting the proper distribution of attention so that each shall have its due weight, it is justice.

SECTION 2. CONSCIENTIOUSNESS

March 21, 1898

Going on with the discussion of the system of virtues, I begin today with conscientiousness. Conscientiousness is habitual interest in conduct from the standpoint of its organic relation to the agent; it is the interest in seeing to it that conduct is an adequate manifestation of agency; or from the other end it is seeing to it that agency is valued with reference to its outcome in conduct. It is the interest in the process of valuing action; or it is attention to attention. To say that a man is conscientious does not mean simply that he attends to matters in a proper way; it means that he is that because he is attentive to the whole process of distributing his attention. A man may do right in this, that, or the other thing; that is, the valuing process is carried on in a right way, but we would not call him conscientious unless we can get a habit of attention lying back of this particular case, unless he is interested in general in securing that distribution of his attention that would insure the proper evaluation. That interest in the proper control of attention is substantially what the Greeks term wisdom; it is the attention as thus directed to conduct; it is what in modern times has come to be called conscience.

But we have to recognize that in its popular connotation conscience has a rigid meaning attached to it. Instead of being simply attention as directed in the evaluation of conduct, it is by many supposed to be a peculiar organ or faculty which reveals a peculiar kind of knowledge. In other words, in the popular conception it has lost its flexibility and has become identified with the social traditions and fixed social demands which the individual feels to be made upon him. In fact we often see it held up as the supreme merit of the conscience that it is something different from mere attention to this specific question of valuing conduct, that it is something entirely distinct from any ordinary working of intelligence and is more reliable, sacred, holy, and mysterious, because it is irresponsible from the standpoint of attention in general. Conscience has thus been changed from organ or method of interpretation into a fixed revealer and fountainhead of finely constituted moral truths. Conscience has been interpreted as the method of valuing proposed lines of conduct and is simply intelligence in general taken in its particular working; it is as broad as one's working interest in moral problems and moral issues.

There are three characteristic attitudes in which conscientiousness manifests itself. The first of these is practical and relatively unreflective. Perhaps some would deny to it the name of conscientiousness at all simply because it is so lacking in the reflective phase. But in any case it is necessary to note the facts there in order to understand conscientiousness in its more reflective aspects. The whole process of setting up an end, of desiring and choosing a good, is the process of approbation. What a man selects, what a man decides upon, shows what he really holds to be good. He may say that he approves something else, that he really values something else more. But he is either trying to deceive you or himself when he says that, if he does something else. Because that process of building up the end in attention is the process of valuation. That means that the agent is proving himself in his process of approving. He is testing or exhibiting himself in the ends which he elaborates, or which he presents as his goods, as his values.

Now the essence of this whole matter is to get a clear conception at the outset that approbation is primarily a practical process. We do not have a lot of goods presented ready-made and then say we approve this or that and it is good, or that we disapprove the other and that is bad. But the person all the time is engaged in finding out what he really takes to be good, and choice simply marks the fact that now for the first time he has a settled, clear notion of what good is. On the other side he is simply showing himself out in that process. The kind of a good he builds up shows what kind of thing he wants and, in showing that, shows what sort of a person he is.

The bearing may be brought out in discussing two questions that are often discussed. First, the question of good intentions. A man justifies himself for a certain line of conduct on the ground that his intentions were good. He meant right, and his conscience having prescribed a certain course of action to him, it was his moral duty to obey his conscience come what may. He must act on his good intentions even if he turns everything upside down in doing so. Now this justification as already given simply ignores the fact that this state of things may be the man's condemnation instead of his justification. The fact that he thought these intentions were right may be just the basis from which we would condemn him. Just turn the thing around on the man. If you thought that sort of thing was good, it shows how immature or disturbed your character is. No well-balanced character would ever arrive at such a result as that, would ever dream of this thing as being good. In other words, to offer good intentions as a final excuse for an act which turns out badly shows an inadequacy of the man's own character. He excuses his particular act, if you please, but only by carrying the the blame further back in his own character.

More particularly, this offering of good intentions as an excuse shows a static conception of the nature of approbation instead of the dynamic character which was just attributed to it. It shows that the agent has some fixed conception of good, instead of seeing that all action is a process of discovering and determining good. That is in one sense what action is for, so as to bring character to self-revelation. A man has certain fixed categories of good from which he will not swerve, and he does not develop and build up any further but tries to put all particular cases under his preconceived ideas, that is, under his prejudices. He might as well think that he was making valid a scientific error by saying: "I had a prejudice that way," as to suppose that he is excusing himself morally by saying that he had a good intention. A man may argue, for instance, that the sun really does go round the earth because he had a prejudice that way. The whole question is as to what a man scientifically conceives to be valid and, ethically, what he conceives to be good. And simply to say that I did conceive that to be good is to beg the whole question; it is to destroy all responsibility.

In other words, conscientiousness is seen here in its first form. It is the degree of openness and flexibility with which one arrives at his conception of the proper end of a good, not whether a man acts on his intentions or not. (Everybody does that.) The question is whether he was sufficiently interested in mediating his action, in valuing his conduct. Now if a man does not hold that question open and let himself learn every time over again by whatever characteristic features the particular situation possesses, it means that he is falling back on some past habit or on some past acquisition as final. And thus there comes in a form of morality under the guise of devotion to morality. A man says: "I felt so certain this was good that I had to stick to my convictions." What he means as shown by what he does is: I was so satisfied with my past attainments in goodness that I insisted upon making them the standard for the whole scope and range of goodness.

In other words, all abstract devotion to morality, apart from interest, is seeing what morality really means and requires in this particular case, and shows that the individual is taking himself as an end instead of redefining himself as an agent. Now this taking one's self as an end instead of as an agent is the essence of any form of immorality, and I think it may fairly be said that the setting up of abstract goods, abstract moral ends, and then insisting that one is good because he is attached to these moral ends, is the most subtle form of vice and the most pervasive form of vice of the so-called good class. It is the particular vice of good people just as sensuality would be the vice of recognized bad people. It is the essence of Phariseeism in the great variety of forms which it is capable of assuming. Instead of finding out what is good and then proving goodness of character through the assiduity and openness with which one attempts to determine the good both in knowledge and in action, one simply takes for granted a certain end as good and then says: "See how good I am because I am devoted to this good."

Now all that arises from a practical misconception of the nature of the process of approbation. The reason I took up that particular case is that it shows what happens when we fail to note that approbation is the process of presenting and defining to one's self what the good really is. It was because the Greeks felt all this they laid so much stress on wisdom, this necessity of getting some objective statement of the self and of its goodness, stating it in terms of a situation, as knowing in reason, rather than in stating it in terms of the individual's prejudices, misconceptions, and ignorances.

Here we find the ultimate moral significance of science not directly, but indirectly, just because science does reveal to us the situation. It is nothing but the process of mentally constructing the situation, and it is only through this mental construction of the situation that the good can be determined. With the development of chemistry, bacteriology, and physiology, the content which we attach to any virtue must modify itself because we have at once a more enlarged view of the situation with reference to which action must take place, and therefore better organs for determining what the good really is. The static conception of the process of approbation would rule out the scientific process; it makes it irrelevant to moral progress.

Before passing on to the next topic I would like to say that this gives us the basis for defining aspiration as a virtue. It does not mean a sort of tense attachment to an ideal in general; it means simply the absolute openness to growth. As aspiration is often conceived, it seems to mean that the individual sets up an ideal of the ideal, the ideal of the good in a very fixed way, and then hangs on to it by main stress for fear it will get away from him. It is practically a static virtue. Now if valuation is a dynamic process it means this continued openness in revising one's past conception of what goods are, and this positive willingness to learn from every situation what the real ideal of the good is. Everybody feels his to be good after a fashion. The real question is: What is this thing that you conceive as good? And that leads up to the other problem of which I was going to speak.

The scholastics used to say that every person's desires were *sub specioni,** under the species of the good. Whatever he desires, he desires as good. There is no such thing as the desire for the intrinsically evil; if he desires it, it is because he subsumes it under the good. That doctrine, although it has the sanction of the most orthodox scholastics, is objected to on the ground that it puts all on the same level. The criminal as well as the saint does what he deems to be good and it is argued that it is then simply a question of ignorance, as Socrates would have put it, or that it makes the whole thing simply arbitrarily subjective. I want this or that and it is good for me. You call something else good and that is good for you, and there is no common standard at all.

That is hardly a legitimate statement. It is true that Socrates resolved all vice into ignorance.[1] But even if he were certain that that was the root of all vice, it would be nonetheless something to be struggled against, both in ourselves and in others. Instead of having eliminated it we have located it, have shown where the stress comes, have found out where the fight must be made. That is ignorance, an ignorance of a particular kind, growing out of lack of interest in and attention to the discovery of the value of self in action. But such an ignorance as that is certainly as important a matter as one could well come across. Or, in other words, the criminal as well as the saint does what he takes to be good; but what one takes to be good is the measure of the worth of the agent. The doctrine is the furthest from elimi-

* Probably *sub specie boni.*

nating responsibility or moral goodness as an essential thing, but it does have great pedagogical significance both in the individual's treatment of himself and in his treatment of others. It shows him where to look for the fundamental defect and shows him how to overcome it. This thing is good, the other thing is good—therefore do these things. But the whole moral development has been that on the whole it is more economical to get the individual in the right attitude as regards his habits of using his attention, and that leads to specific overt results.

I do not mean to say that we have practically arrived at this outcome in a consistent way. Theoretically we appeal to a person's conscience and leave it to him to decide in specific cases the right or wrong. Practically we are afraid of that amount of flexibility and we insist upon it as a *sine qua non* that the individual shall regard certain specific things as goods, whether he sees any value in them or not. The first point is, then, that conscientiousness is exhibited in the process of approval, that process of approval consisting in the presentation and elaboration of certain ends as good and therefore to be acted upon.

I now turn from the prospective to the retrospective aspect of conscientiousness. As we saw in the process of deliberation, we can set up an ideal only through images which are reconstructions of previous experiences. During, therefore, this process of setting up goods, one takes an attitude toward his past.

At this point I think the distinction between good and right comes in. Good refers to one's conception of what he is going to do. It marks the proposed end as unified and therefore satisfying the active self. But when one says right, he is thinking not of an act or an end as the synthesis of a situation, or the synthesis of his own powers; he is rather placing the particular act, which once was an entire end or aim, as a factor in a larger situation. That is, action that has already taken place is revalued with reference to the position it occupies in further development. As long as we are looking ahead, we think in terms of good and bad. When in looking ahead it becomes necessary to look back and decide whether the given good really is good with reference to its being itself a factor in a larger, moving whole, we use the categories of right and wrong. If the act done fits into progress, if it becomes itself a constituent factor in future development, we call it right. If it hinders the attainment or the progression of the new good, if it presents itself as an obstacle which must be done away [with] before the new good can be realized, we term it wrong. Right represents the good with reference to the place which it occupies in progressive action.

Some would consign the term conscientiousness to this judgment of right and wrong as distinct from good and bad. I do not care to bring that out, but we will simply see the relation between the two, the good as exhibited in one's process of deliberation and choice on one side, and [right as the] judgment one afterward passes on that as one views it with reference to the function it has in the further determination of action. The whole thing begins with some doubt, some uncertainty. One asks himself, "What shall I do?" In the course of finding out what he shall do, the concept (both intellectually and emotionally) of the good comes out. The good is that which will maintain the integrity of the self. Now in discovering that, one will pay more or less attention to past ends or results aimed at. He views it not as projected ahead, but he sees it in the light of the future movement of the self. If he goes back, and sees that that does fit in, that it is an instrument that reinforces his further good, he calls it not only good but right. Or if it does not fit in, if it obstructs, if he must turn back on that end and overcome it before he can get ahead to what is good, he calls it wrong.

I wanted to work out the application to what is meant by self-approbation and self-condemnation. I have discussed approval and choice in the practical building up of aims. We have self-approval or self-condemnation, complacency on one side and remorse on the other; or moral approbation and moral condemnation. Now of course the whole point is contained in what has already been said. Judgment has no business to arise in reference to ourselves or anybody else except in the construction of the future action. Judgment of morality, right or wrong, of moral self-approval or [self]-condemnation, has no legitimate function excepting when it is a question of estimating what has been done with reference to what is going to be done. Nobody has a right to say: "I am bad or I am good," or "Somebody else is good or is bad," as a final fixed fact. Judgment is passed when it comes to relating, in an organic action, what has been done with what needs to be done.

March 23, 1898

I was speaking of the judgment of right and wrong and was to go on to apply that to the nature of moral satisfaction or dissatisfaction with one's own conduct or that of another. Normally moral self-satisfaction has no reflex existence at all. As it is stated in my *Syllabus,* the good man is satisfied *in* what he is doing, not *with* what he is doing.[2] That is, it is the very nature of the rightness or of the goodness to set up a complete identification of the agent in his act. The agent is the act, taken of course not in merely an overt sense but in its full value content. Now if he, over and above the satisfaction which he gets in the action, thinks of himself as good because he is doing the action, it shows that there is not this organic identity; it shows that there is something in him which is held over against the act, outside of the act; and insofar the act lacks the very criterion of goodness— that of organic unification. A man may judge reflectively that his act is right, but as was said at the last time, that means simply a way of assuring himself that he is on the right track as regards what he is going to do. It is not that he congratulates himself that he is good enough to do such an act; he is not thinking about himself but about the relation of the act done to the value of the subsequent act.

Now on the contrary, moral dissatisfaction is always with the self and not merely with the act. Self-reprobation or condemnation does not attach to the act as such. When it is simply the act that is condemned we say to ourselves: "It is a mistake, that was not the best thing to do; it was not the wise thing to do." We make a distinction in that case between the act and the agent. That is to say, we admit that the act was not a wise one, that it did not fulfill the actual requirements of the situation, but we do not on that account condemn the agent. That is a state of things which must be accounted for. It may seem contradictory to the theory. The distinction, however, is this: when the man simply says that the act was mistaken, it is because he has found no reason to attribute its inadequate character to anything in himself. He attributes it to causes which lay outside of his own control, or to ignorance, in a sense in which he conceives that he is justified in attributing ignorance to the normal agent under similar circumstances.

That is, we make two cases of ignorance: one in which we say that the fact that the man was ignorant shows that there was something lacking, that the normal agent would not have been ignorant under those circumstances; and then we have the other case where we think we are justified in saying that any agent, as such, would have been equally ignorant or liable to misconception. Now that does not really mean that that act was wrong; it simply means that we know more now than we did before. It is not that act which is judged even as inadequate; it is that act as reconstructed in the imagination with reference to its possible happening again. In other words, the conditions have changed so that the same act could not be repeated, but the moral condemnation is always of the self. That is, in that case the act is regarded as having its quality through the agent which it manifests and realizes; so if there is anything the matter with the act, it is the agent with whom the blame lies.

But once more, the moral conditions for blaming the self are not present excepting when it is a question of the reconstruction or reform of the self. Swedenborg is reported to have said that remorse or self-condemnation is simply one form of self-conceit. It simply means that the agent still has an excessive interest in himself that he should think it worthwhile to focus all his attention on himself and to go through with spasms of agony and remorse and blame, and so on. It shows that his interest is still subjective instead of being objective. That is perfectly true if we mean by self-condemnation the condemnation of the self in a fixed sense, in a static sense, as something apart from a phase in the future development of action itself. It is possible for a man to feel so much remorse, and feel remorse in such a way, that he is secretly priding himself on the fact that he is capable of having such remorse. He feels as if his capacity for suffering remorse were an atonement for the wrong action which he has committed. Some people become virtuosos in remorse, in self-condemnation, and of course such remorse as that remains futile;

it does not show itself in any positive reconstructive course of action. It is simply an emotion which gathers about a certain objectified content of the self; and when treated in that way, that emotion becomes a form of self-indulgence just as much as any other isolated emotion is self-indulgence.

The real self-condemnation and the real emotion of remorse are simply the accompaniment of the process of reconstruction. When Green says that conscientious consists in examining ourselves to see if we were as good as we ought to have been in certain cases,[3] it makes just exactly that isolation of the past acts from the needs of the present situation which leads to overconscientiousness. Real overconscientiousness is impossible. You might as well talk about a truth as being overtrue. If the examination is directed to the consideration of the future self, the valuation of the future act, if it is directed to that, there is no question of overconscientiousness. It is an active question; it is a question of distributing one's attention correctly. If you conceive of conscientiousness as thinking, reflecting on whether one is as good as he ought to be, apart from the reference to the immediate or the coming situation or action, the instrumental self is isolated, it is made an end in itself; and we get only the phenomena of the subjective, morbid consciousness.

To say then that the self was bad is simply one way of saying that the self must be made over—not made over at large, merely. (I mean by "at large" not made over in the abstract but made over with reference to action.) It means that the interest, of which the particular act that is now regarded as bad is considered as an expression, must be modified and revalued. In other words, this judgment of badness locates the point of greatest need of reconstruction. To say that a thing is bad does not mean necessarily that it always was bad. It may mean that it was once good, but that the maintenance of future good—that is, of dynamic good—is dependent upon turning against it. The bad thing is the thing that must not be done any more. It is not only that. That would mean simply that we might ignore it. It means also that we cannot do the things we should do excepting as we mediate the habit of which that act is the expression.

That point may perhaps come out better with reference to the approval or condemnation of others. Legitimately, the moral approval of others means simply encouragement to continue a given line of action. When another person is approved independent of this stimulation to a certain course of action, it means that his little ego is being set out in an isolated way and simply that self-conceit is being fostered in him. Everybody knows that in the case of a child there are two ways to approve of him. One way is to fix his attention on himself. The other is to fix his attention on the act, on the quality of the act and on the need of measuring himself with reference to this quality of the act. So with condemnation, fixed condemnation, that is, condemnation of a man as he has been or as he is, apart from the stimulation of him to a different course of action. It is not only paralyzing as regards that other person, but it is favorable to the growth of moral self-conceit of the person who passes this judgment of moral condemnation. To condemn another is in place when that condemnation is a factor, not in the abstract but in the concrete, with reference to his reconstruction.

In other words, there is always a responsibility attaching to this question of condemning others. We have a criterion for telling when it is in place and when it is not in place. It is not in place when it is not part and parcel, an organic element in the cooperative process of reform. It means that we are called upon, when it is in place, to do something, as well as the other man who is condemned. It means mutuality of responsibility and participation in agency. Otherwise we get simply class morality, one class of people standing out by themselves and condemning the acts of another class of people as bad; and that means that they are congratulating themselves that they are not as these other people are. In the other case it is recognized that there is an evil situation for which there is general responsibility. The other man is not condemned as bad in himself, as distinct from one's own self, but there is a felt need for bringing him to recognize the real significance of the situation.

Of course that same principle can be applied to the whole question of punishment. What is the moral criterion for punishment? It is ethically effective insofar as that negative reaction brings the individual to appreciate, to value the situation more adequately. It is a way of bringing him to self-consciousness. That, insofar, is justifiable. But insofar as it does not do that, it is ethically paralyzing to the person punished and its reflex influence on the person who does it is bad, in that it leads him to set himself off from the whole scene of action.

That does not mean that punishment is always not justifiable in society where its only obvious effect is repressive. We have to stop some things from being done simply as things, and it is all right to restrain the individual at such times whether we feel that there is any reaction in his own appreciation of the situation or not. But there is no moral significance attaching to it. It is all right to consider that a moral necessity, but there is no ethical value attaching to it one way or another. It is on par morally with shutting up an insane man so that he will not hurt himself or other people. Or it is on a par with seeing a man about to fall off somewhere and you scare him to prevent his doing it. There is nothing moral about it. You are simply preventing a thing which is harmful.

As I said, that aspiration was a name given to conscientiousness with reference to the future, so we may say that humility is the counterpart for conscientiousness as it looks toward the past—not that it is self-depreciation as such, any more than aspiration is mere attachment to the ideal in general. Humility is simply willingness to reconstruct, to transform all attainment into instrumental terms, or it is not virtue at all, but simply a name for weakness. There is no value in anybody's depreciating himself as a self. There is value in a man's being always open to revalue what he has done and what he has accomplished, so that instead of treating it as possession, as acquisition, he treats it as an instrument for accomplishing something further.

I now come to the third aspect of conscientiousness which is again directed toward the future as was the first form. But it is a more generalized form because mediated by the judgment of right as passed with reference to past habits and acts. This is the conscientiousness of duty. Out of this reflective estimation of the self of which we have been speaking, or along with it, arises the consciousness of the need of reform. We might say that this is the same mental attitude that we have been discussing, only it looks toward the future instead of to the instrument through which that outcome is to be effected. The more naive and unreflective building up of the good is the process of approbation, but under certain circumstances we find that we cannot approve the self excepting as it is made over. The self, therefore, with which there is satisfaction is the self of the reform, of the making over. Now the sense of that in contrast with the self as it is if it were left unmodified is the consciousness of obligation in its psychological aspect. That is, I can approve of myself, I can conceive myself as good, present myself to myself as good, only in case I make over the habit or interest which it is now apparent that I have. If we look at that from the side of what must be made over, it is condemnation; if we look at it from the side of this projected self which would receive approbation as mediated through his reconstruction, it is the sense of duty. Hence as all moralists recognize, conscientiousness culminates in the habit of being conscious of duty and of being moved to action by duty. Only we ought now to see that that sense of duty is not a supervention from outside, that it is not an extraneous factor in the process. It is the sense of the process in its integrity as reached through the turning against, or the turning over, of an existing habit.

We begin with the consciousness of good in the projective sense. Then we criticize that: we measure it with the concept of the right, and then we reconstruct again our good in terms of the right. We conceive of it, not as good simply, but the right good, and then we have the sense of duty. Now if we take that in its more naive form (that is, the consciousness of the good that always looks ahead to the unification that we are going to attain in action, of factors more or less discrepant), then we come to see that some of these are successful and some are not, and that the success or nonsuccess depends on the way the agent conceives of himself. Hence the projected self gets a modified meaning. We see in the law, the standard, with reference to which particular actions have to be determined. So the sense of duty is nothing but the sense of the active process, taken not merely as a fact but in the function which it performs.

Good, the consciousness of good, mental good, is the consciousness of an integrated self, a synthesized self reached only through action. That is not a special characteristic of the moral consciousness; it is characteristic of any practical consciousness. But when we get to the point of seeing that that integrated self constitutes the basis of all evaluation, that is not only good, but morally good, and insofar realization as a unity requires the transformation of existing habits, the sense of obligation. Hence certain characteristics of this sense of duty. One is imperiousness, the authority, the majesty of duty—what Kant calls the imperative quality of it. This simply means that since it represents the active functioning self, it represents the self as complete. The attained self is partial and if set up as an end, as law, it is isolated and hence disintegrated. It explains the fact recognized by all moralists that conscientiousness is summed up in the attitude taken toward duty.

Conscious reconstruction is the essence of the whole moral process, and the sense of duty is nothing but the generalized sense of this reconstruction. The sense of duty is the consciousness of the import, the value of the moral process.

Once more, we get the criterion for deciding when the sense of duty is called for and when it is not called for. There are two extreme views regarding the function of the sense of duty. One class of moralists, like Kant, says that no act is right excepting when done from the consciousness of duty as its motive. Another schools says that the sense of duty is always evidence of partial morality, that the ideal agent would not have any sense of obligation at all, ever, that he would do everything from direct interest in the good, or direct love of the right. It would not be necessary for him to brace himself up by any recourse to the sense of duty. He would do right as the stars move in their courses, because that was the inherent, organized law of his nature, and until he gets to that point he is only partially moralized. So Spencer says that with increasing moralization sense of duty will disappear.[4]

I think that the theory that the sense of duty is the consciousness of the self as a reconstructed self does away with the apparent meaning of these two extreme views. It is certainly unnecessary that every right act should be done with a sense of duty as its motive. There are large planes of action which fall within the scope of an organized habit or of an organized interest. The rightness of all those particular acts is found in the general interest of which they are the specifications. For a man to reconstruct consciously at every point would be to fritter away his strength, it would throw him into a continual attitude of questioning, doubting, and bewilderment, and he would never get any straight momentum of action. Think of a man who would always ask himself not only if he was right but if he was doing it simply and purely because it was right! A principle that would destroy action practically cannot be a right principle of action. On the other hand, excepting on a purely static conception of morality, he never would come to know when a sense of duty would be entirely out of place, since a progressive life means reconstruction; since what was only an end must be made over into a means, and that can be done only with effort, only as one thinks of a reconstructed self alone as receiving approval.

There will always be rhythmic periods when the sense of duty will necessarily emerge; hence once more, in a certain way, the vagueness and formal character of the sense of duty. There come times when the only reason that a man can give for doing a certain thing is that it is right to do it. He can define his past self, his past attainments; they are all there. He can state them in terms of actual content. But the real self, the moving self, has no such realized content. There is a sense in which the moving self is there and that it is in a general way of a certain kind, and that it involves this overturning of attained habits. But one simply cannot translate that sense over into any specified content. I do not mean that one always cannot, but simply that there are certain cases where one cannot. So the sense of duty is simply the sense of the on-moving self. Just because that on-moving self has not realized itself, we cannot tell just what it means, and so cannot put it in very definite terms just why we must do a certain thing. So we get the explanation of how a man would be justified in falling back and saying: "I cannot tell why I should do it, excepting that it is right and I must do it." The cases in which that legitimately arises must be distinguished from the other cases where such statements represent simply abstract attachment to some moral preconception.

To sum up then: the sense of duty is the process of attention as expressed in the relation between the instrumental and the functioning self— the instrumental self standing for attained habits as constituting the capacity for future action, the functioning self representing simply that action as effected through the habits. That is the real significance of the doctrine of the higher and the lower self. Not that there are two fixed selves, one eternally higher and the other eternally lower, and the higher sending down orders to the lower; but the distinction arises within action itself. The lower means that however much it may once have been the function, it has now a position simply of means [or] instrument; and the higher self, being simply that motor projective self which would unify and realize—that is, utilize—all the agencies constituted by the habits. Such a theory as Kant's fails because it does not see that this is a distinction in action, and that therefore it is a constantly changing distinction. That which is the higher self at one time is the lower self at another, and must be so as long as action is progressive, as long as the only way to get ahead is in the realizing of ends, making the last end realized the subordinate factor in a larger coordination.

The other school represented by Bain and Spencer finds no place for the sense of duty within the self.[5] If you leave the self to itself it would have desires and inclinations, but according to them it would never have any consciousness of obligation. That must arise from without. Social pressure must be brought to bear on the individual, demands must be made upon him for obedience, conformity to the demands set up by society, before he will have any sense of duty. According to that the consciousness of duty is extraneous to the whole self-process.

That view originates from the failure to see that the self is essentially active, or in psychological terms that it is essentially a motor synthesis. And because it is, there is always opportunity for contrast to come into consciousness between the needs of the motor-projected self and the attained-sense self. However, the particular fact[s] which writers like Bain and Spencer bring up, showing as a matter of fact how this sense of duty arises in the child, seem to me very relevant and important. I doubt if this sense would arise very much if the individual were left to himself. But the question is as to the interpretation of those facts. Does it mean that we have something outside the individual introducing the factor into his consciousness which does not belong there, which does not belong to his normal psychical process at all, or does it mean simply that the social stimuli are necessary to get an awareness of that process? It is one thing to say that the individual will be brought to recognize his functioning self largely through the demands that are made upon him by others. It is another thing to say that the consciousness of duty is the consciousness of something outside the self and imposed on the self. The first simply makes social stimuli a mediating factor in bringing the individual to self-consciousness. That that state of things should exist is not a matter for scorn. Isolate a person from his environment and he would not come to consciousness of anything, because the individual is social. Put him in the social environment and you have the stimuli which will bring him to awareness of himself as such. But this theory is strong just where the Kantian theory is weak. It is inexplicable on the Kantian theory why social stimuli should play any part at all in bringing the individual to social consciousness. He has shut up within his own consciousness the two selves—the sensuous, appetitive self and the higher self which ought to make its commands and ideals known. As a matter of fact, consciousness does not arise excepting through the social stimuli and social inhibitions to which the individual is subjected.

SECTION 3. COURAGE AND TEMPERANCE

April 4, 1898

At the close of the last lecture I said that I would continue the discussion of the virtues for three or four lectures in order to complete the dicussion of the last quarter, and also in part because the latter part of the discussion will make a connecting link between the psychological and the social.

The virtues were defined and classified with relation to the process of bringing the self to consciousness, to conscious value in an act. The generic virtue of conscientiousness was discussed as consisting in an interest in that process, the habit of paying attention to the relationship existing between the agent and his deed.

The second type of virtue which I will take up is that designated by the Greeks as courage, or which may be termed more generically self-assertion. The process consisting psychologically in the mediation of impulses, it is necessary that the impulsive side shall mediate itself; that is, in emphasizing the mediation of the impulses, we must also remember that it is impulses that are mediated, that they are not suppressed or eliminated, but are simply controlled through recognition of what they mean when carried out in terms of experience. Now the process of reflection, of bringing to light the content of any impulsive tendency, may reveal the consequences as distinctly unpleasant or disagreeable, or indeed to involve so much misery that "unpleasantness" and "disagreeable" are very mild terms, and yet the situation may be such that the facing of these unpleasant consequences is necessary to the adequate self-expression of the agent. Under those circumstances the maintenance of the impulses in their integrity becomes a matter of distinct determination; it becomes a matter of mental attitude, and that attitude taken toward the expression of impulses in spite of uncertainty of consequences, or of the disagreeable reaction of the consequences, constitutes this virtue which the Greeks call courage. Whatever name we give to that, it must be recollected that it is a type of mental attitude, and not any particular external operation. Thoroughness in work, patience, endurance, perseverance, calmness, cheerfulness, everything which has to do with the tenacity with which an ideal is clung to and carried out in the face of difficulties, would come in there.

There are three particular features of this group of virtues of which it is worthwhile to speak more specifically. So far as this attitude represents attachment to an impulse in spite of obstacle and objection, it represents the tendency to initiate. The habitual, the customary, is always to a certain extent the conventional. It is that which has become acquiesced in, not only by one's self but to a certain extent, at least, by others. That anyone has a habit means that there has been a certain amount of active as well as passive cooperation by others. No one can form a habit without receiving either passive sympathy or active encouragement. The impulse, as representing a break in the habit, represents an emerging, a springing forth of native original power in ways which have not yet received the sanction of society; it represents the element of valuation and of initiation. There is therefore in this virtue the only guarantee we have of securing the introduction of variations into the existing order. Certainly under modern social conditions, the greatest test to which the virtue is ever put is to stand up and assert a new tendency or a new conception in the face, both of passive discouragement of conservatism and the more active obstacles of all sorts thrown in the way by those opposed to the change.

Secondly, because self-assertion means interest in maintaining personal variation or initiation, it represents faith in self, and faith in self in the most thoroughgoing way; that is, faith as an adequate organ of the universal order. If the individual felt that his impulse was a mere variation, a chance accident, it would be impossible for him to attach himself to it with any very great degree of sincerity; or we take his attachment in such cases to be evidence of his lack of balance, of his—perhaps not insanity—but at all events, crankiness. The only distinction that we draw between the persistent attempt to vary the order of things that is worthy of a fair field of competition in the struggle for existence, and that which we would consider as simply an individual whim, must be in the former case these intuitions, while expressed in the individual, express forces deeper than those which lie in the individual as an isolated being. The impulses thus represent the outgoing, the active self. Courage represents faith in them as ideals. To give the impulses then due weight, to insist that they do have a chance to assert themselves and work themselves out to see what they will come to, means that one realizes that one is an organ of universal forces, that one is an organ of the absolute. It is the same virtue which in another aspect we term faith, not in the sense of an intellectual adherence to certain objective formulae, but faith in the sense of trusting to an impulse or to an ideal so thoroughly that one is willing to stake his whole agency upon it. It is this virtue, in other words, which has at once brought about and resulted from the development of the individual, and the sense of the meaning of individuality. That is, that it stands for something, that it is a real integral factor in the makeup of things and not a mere capricious accident.

In the third place the attachment to the impulses must exhibit itself in the effort to carry them out; otherwise there would be a mere nominal assent to the ideal as determined by the impulse, and not a real one. The reality of the thing can show itself only in actual effort put forth to overcome the obstacles in the way, and from that point of view it is what we call sincerity: it is the test and pledge of theoretical conviction as manifested in action. Now if we call to mind all that intuition means, all that self-confidence (which is a poor term to express this) means, and all that executive force as manifesting sincerity or depth of conviction, means in life, we get a rough sense of the scope of this particular virtue.

What more may be involved in the conception of self-assertion will perhaps best come out by considering the apparent counterpart, self-sacrifice. The conception of self-sacrifice made absolute has certain very obvious difficulties on the basis of the psychology which has been presented. In the very nature of morality it is the bringing the self to consciousness in an act, or discovering the act which gives the value to the self. Self-sacrifice in the absolute sense will be the very negation of the moral process; it would be more than incompatible, it would be its absolute antagonist. Yet the facts that we commonly term self-sacrifice certainly have a legitimate and necessary place in any moral scheme. It is the question then of interpreting the sense in which the term self is used. It cannot be the self as the self, because that would mean annihilation of the very root, and removal of the very meaning of the whole moral process; and when it is not as complete as that, sacrifice as an end means weakness. The self being the agent of all action, voluntarily to sacrifice that self would mean to throw away the power which is necessary, which is essential to moralization. Moreover, self-sacrifice as an end means the narrowing of the whole moral horizon; it means limiting the content and substance of ideals. If you find anybody who habitually looks at anything from the standpoint of how much he can give up, you will find somebody who habitually has a narrow sense of the worth and claims of personality anywhere. The man who is contented with a narrow scheme of existence and the partial play of powers for himself cannot possibly conceive, by the very nature of things, of an existence very much different for anybody else.

That self-sacrifice as an end means a certain amount of weakening of force is generally recognized; but this other aspect of it, that it means the hemming in of the whole moral power, that it means the limiting of the content which is attached to individuality, is not so often recognized. But it comes out clearly historically. You see it in the Puritans; the willingness to give up, making a virtue of giving up certain values of life for themselves, changed itself into the positive assertion that those things were wrong for other people. It was not simply that it was wrong for them, but anybody who tried to get them was perforce vicious, and the whole scope of life was closed in so as to shut out the play of those things. The concept of self-sacrifice then, as an end, as a virtue in itself, means that the conception of the possibilities of life is restricted. It is a habit of putting up with the absence of certain things. Thus, even when it is assumed to be a virtue, it really marks a lack of courage in the broad sense in which that term has been used. It really means that there is not sufficient energy, sincerity, and sufficient faith to face the possibility of the introduction of new ideals and new values in life.

On the positive side the sense in which there is a practical meaning to this is significant, I take it: the subordination of the attained self to the active, what I call the functioning self. It is not foregoing, or going without. It is the will to put to use, to positive use, everything that one has. Sacrifice really is devotion to these powers to the end in view. It is the willingness to use them instead of simply holding on to them. Now that is conceived as sacrifice simply because there is a certain amount of effort which is unpleasant involved in that transformation or reconstruction. That is, it is difficult to deflect a habit into a new channel. It is hard work to take the acquired powers and ideals and switch them around so as to make them work for another end, and when we look at it from the standpoint of pain in reconstruction, we conceive of it as sacrifice. But this is conceived of as sacrifice in the sense of giving up only insofar as choice is still incomplete. When a person finally conceives of any particular act as an act of sacrifice, it always shows itself in a demand for some kind of compensation or return. If anyone feels that he has made a sacrifice in the sense of positively giving up something to which he was entitled, he cannot help feeling that it must be made up to him somewhere if there is any justice in the universe. The thing contradicts itself. It is not sacrifice, it is simply credit to be made up to him at some future day. It shows therefore that the interest is still in the self as an end in itself; that the interest is really on what the self is going to get by performing the act of sacrifice, instead of being in the discovery of the self in reference to the needs of the situation. Emerson says somewhere that any honest person will admit that he has never made a sacrifice. That is an extreme statement, but it suggests the fact that whatever the act one has done, he has done for some reason, or some motive; there has been some value attaching to the act, and that value seemed at the time to be the adequate motive for the act. Now of course everybody is at times in situations where he does forego certain things in the interest of certain other things and where he would prefer to have the circumstances such that he would not need to do it. That is what we mean practically by sacrifice. We do not simply give up what we think is good, but we give it up for something which we conceive to be of more adequate value.

It may be said that as long as those situations occur, sacrifice does come in as a positive element in life; that the individual has to sacrifice his own individual interests and powers for the sake of social demands made upon him which he feels to have more moral weight than the expression of his own powers, and yet which involve a certain limiting, and really a sacrifice of his own capacities. Well now I do not wish to minimize the occurrence of those situations in life, but there are two things to be said. In the first place one's own powers and capacities do have a certain claim. Nobody, in other words, has a right, to say nothing of the duty, of making the sacrifice, to yield to the situation until he has exhausted all ways of throwing the burden on the other side. One must be certain that the demand is a moral and not a conventional one, and he must be certain that he is not giving in to it simply because it is easier on the whole to conform to the conventional demand instead of making a fuss which would call down the displeasure of others. Nobody has a right to make a sacrifice of himself to the demands of the situation before he has insisted that the social situation shall assume a certain amount of responsibility also.

Take the case of a young man who feels that he is called upon to follow a certain profession to which his own immediate surroundings are very much adverse, but where he feels that he can make his mark. How far is he called upon to sacrifice, not only his own inclinations, but his own powers in the interests of the social situation about him? He evidently has no right to until he has thrown all the burden that he can on the other side, and made them prove their side of the case instead of simply accepting it. This self-assertion of impulses means faith in individuality, provided one is, after due consideration, certain that he has those powers which can find expression only in that way, and which will be sacrificed if he gives up a certain mode of action. He must recognize that he is just as absolute as anyone else is, and it is simply a question whether he thinks it is of sufficient importance for him to stake himself upon and see himself through in spite of the fact that it is against the recognized moralities of the situation. It is only in that way that any progress has ever been made. If moral progress were simply a question of fighting against the recognized evil in social environment, it would be a comparatively easy matter. The chief obstacle of reform is that the reformer has to set up a new standard of good which involves the condemnation of that which is regarded as righteous. Now in a lesser way that same question comes up every time when the individual is called upon to do what he conceives to be a real sacrifice of his own capacities to the needs of his social environment. I do not mean that there is any ready-made scheme for settling the question, but one must be very certain that he has gone over the whole thing and has compelled other people to go over the whole thing; and if they then decide that their individuality is of preeminent importance, I do not see that there is anybody who at the time can say them nay. The only thing is to try it, and insofar as the person has been sincere, so far the presumption is on his side.

The other point is that whenever a person does decide, it is his business to throw all his powers into the course of action for which the decision calls. In other words, it is his business to minimize the element of sacrifice so far as he possibly can (in the sense of going without). I do not say that it is possible to absolutely shut it out, but it is necessary to reduce it as far as possible, that he may get the benefit of the particular line of action into which he finally goes.

I now come to the next type of virtue which the Greeks called temperance, as set over against courage. The Greek conception as developed in Plato and Aristotle is whole-mindedness, it is sincerity, not the mere curbing of the appetites, or abstinence from excess of indulgence, which our English word temperance so often signifies. It is self-control in the positive sense of that term. There is no particular object in controlling the self by itself. The self is controlled because it is an instrument or organ for realizing certain ends; and the dominance of the end, of the purpose in the appetite or impulse, is the true meaning of this expression. Just as in the idea of courage we discuss the mediation of impulses from the standpoint of the impulse, so in self-control it is the same process from the other end, from the standpoint of the reason, which interprets and therefore directs the impulse. Self-control is a name for the direction of power with reference to an end or aim. Hence self-control is called for in the region of the emotional impulses and the appetites, to see to it that they function with reference to accomplishing something objective, instead of simply leading up to their own indulgence.

I suppose self-sacrifice might have been discussed as well under this head as the other. The negative aspect of self-control must be subordinated to the positive. Temperance is not abstemiousness, it is not even simply setting definite limits to one's impulses or appetites and saying that they may go just so far and no further. You cannot get self-control in eating by figuring on how many ounces you ought to take and saying I will take just so much food and go no further. A man who would go at it in that way would not be likely to be a man of positive self-control. It is his capacity to use his appetite as a positive tool to control his eating and drinking from the standpoint of being himself efficient which would be likely to result in anything very valuable. The more emphasis is put on the positive side and the less upon the negative side, the more likely the virtue is to be a healthy vigorous thing.

SECTION 4. THE CONTINUITY
BETWEEN JUSTICE AND LOVE

April 5, 1898

The fourth of the cardinal virtues of the Greeks was termed justice. The psychology of that virtue is that it represents the active cooperation or organization of habits on the basis of a unifying end; that is, justice is the cooperation itself with the two aspects of the contributing habits, impulses, on one side, and the objective unification on the other side. All cooperation involves the minor activties which are coordinated, the various elementary activities which are organized with reference to each other, and the function or active end which is mediated and effected through the cooperation of the minor activities. Insofar as this organization is attained, we have this virtue of justice. It is the equivalent on the ethical side of the concept of organism itself on the biological side.

That is, the virtue of justice is not a peculiar thing which is superimposed on the psychological makeup; it is simply the name given to the psychic structure to designate its thoroughly organized character. The very idea of an organism involves that each contributing organ, each constitutive member, shall have its due place; that it shall have a certain specified sphere of action within which its claims are undisputed—within which, moreover, they are guaranteed by the activity of the other organs. But of course a mere multiplicity of organs operating side by side with each other would not interfere with each other; each must act in such a way through reinforcing the activities of the others so as to maintain the functioning of the whole. That is, we must have the functioning of the whole (not a mere aggregate) to which all the constitutive members actively contribute.

Now that gives the skeleton, the framework of the nature of justice as a virtue so far as that can be expressed in psychological terms, leaving out the social content side. A man is just to himself, or just in himself, when all the impulses and habits which enter into his active makeup are allowed proper play, are given due position and their due weight. If you ask what the criterion is for telling what "proper" and what "due" means, the answer is found in its relation to the unity of the whole self. The due position and the due influence of any particular impulse or habit is the functional contribution it makes to the unity of the self. If it is suppressed—that is, if it does not have sufficient play to maintain, to further the fullness of the whole self—there is no justice done it. If any particular impulse or habit gets exaggerated at the expense of the others, and therefore at the expense of the welfare of the whole self as an active unity, there is no justice. So in this principle we have the limits on both sides. That is the reason that, as Plato remarks, justice is not so much a name for a particular virtue as it is a name for the equilibrium of all virtues, of all the powers of the self.[6]

As I maintained before, the antique conception, the classic conception of justice has been supplemented historically through the introduction of Christian ideas. The virtue of love is not really an additional virtue; it is simply a reinterpretation or deepened conception of the facts of this organization of conduct which the Greeks termed justice. If we realize the absolutely organic character of the relation existing between the part and the whole, between the particular habit or impulse and the entire self; if we realize that the connection is not an external one of means and ends but that the welfare of the self is such that it must reflect itself, it must show itself in the care and attention given to the parts; if we realize on the other side that it is impossible that any particular habit or organ should have its end defined in terms of itself, that what it is is its devotion to the interests of the whole, we realize that this process of the organization of the self in action may be designated by the term love. If our emphasis is on the relation of the parts to each other, if we are thinking of the whole in terms of the constitutive parts and the necessity that each part shall be in equilibrium, then we would throw the emphasis on what we might term the justice side. If our attention is on the relation between any part and the whole as the definition of the meaning and worth of the part, then we would term it love.

The dualism between justice and love (that is, the assumption that they mark two distinct mental and moral attitudes) has its root in a fixed conception of the self. The idea of justice turns about the relation existing between the particular act and the whole self. Now if the self be regarded in a rigid way as something which is metaphysically there, already made, instead of something which is always in process of construction, the act, as we saw before, must be conceived as more or less external to the self; it is a product of the self; or a possession or attainment, or accomplishment of the self. On that basis the notion of justice, or maintaining the equation between the self and the act, will have to be interpreted in an equally external way. The term equivalency, justice, would simply consist in making the self enjoy or suffer an equivalent amount for the particular deed which it had produced. A man steals. He has a certain fixed self, ego, that chooses to manifest itself in this particular deed of stealing. Justice then will consist in making up to him an amount of suffering which will equal the amount of enjoyment which he has got, or tried to get, through this wrong deed which he has performed. Here is your self already made and that issues in an act, and justice would consist in the return back upon that self of an objective equivalent for the deed which it has performed. Now if the self is active, and if it is a continued motor construction, then the self is itself only in the act. The act is not an effect, or product, or result of the self and somehow lies outside of it and causes it. The act is itself focused, brought to a head. The equation between the act and the self would not consist in any external return to the self; it would consist in bringing one into consciousness of the organic presence of the self in the deed. Justice, in other words, would consist in making that supposed thief realize what he had done in stealing; it would consist simply in bringing him to see that particular act as an expression of himself; it would consist simply in making him come to self-consciousness in that deed. What is called then frequently the return of the deed upon the doer is partial and inadequate, save as that return is in the individual's consciousness, excepting as it is a return in his valuation of himself and of his acts. Simply making him suffer a certain amount as an equivalent for the wrong that he has done is a mechanical conception of equivalency. It simply tries to establish an equivalency between two external acts; it does not bring out the equal value of the doer and the deed.

Now in many cases this process of realizing one's self in an act, of bringing to consciousness that that act does characterize or manifest the self, would be a painful process and involve self-condemnation and remorse; and one may, if he please, say that that is simply justice, or simply punitive justice. But that should not blind us to the fact that if the self is an active process and not a mere given existence, this suffering of pain and of penalty is a factor in the process of self-valuation—that is, a factor in the process of bringing the self to an adequate conception of itself. Now when we say that, the process ceases to be one of mere justice in the external sense of that term, and we get the standpoint of love. What has happened then in this dualism of the virtues of justice and love is that a higher, more comprehensive ethical point of view has been laid on top of an older psychological and metaphysical conception, without the latter having undergone the necessary modifications, and this is what happens in general in the relation of the Christian conception of life—what we might call the Christian psychology in relation to the Greek and Roman conception. In the Middle Ages the Christian conceptions were simply superimposed on those of the Greeks and Romans. The Greek and Roman standpoint was practically adopted wholesale—as you will find in the Christian Fathers—as an adequate account, as far as it went. It was supposed to explain the natural virtues, and then on top of these were put other virtues as Christian or supernatural, which the older standpoint could not account for. That is, instead of realizing that Christianity gave a new meaning to the self and therefore require[d] the reconstruction of all the virtues as habits of the self, attitudes of the self, the old conception was left up to a certain point as a natural foundation, and then the Christian conception was superimposed on top of that. While our position is not now as thoroughly dualistic as the Middle Ages', the average moral consciousness was still in an inconsistent attitude as regards this matter; there is still the view which would make of the self an object as the Greeks did and which therefore conceives of the act as product and effect. There is also the Christian conception of the self as an active realization of the universal principle, and therefore of action as simply a continual manifestation of that self.

I have given only a very general and schematic account. I have done so because I wish to be brief so as to get on to the next point. Certain considerations which have been involved in this discussion will, when brought out more explicitly, mark the transition to the standpoint of social ethics.

NOTES

1. For example, *Protagorus,* 351b–358d.
2. Dewey, *Early Works,* IV, 293.
3. Green, *Prolegomena to Ethics,* Secs. 297–309.
4. Dewey elaborates on this aspect of Spencer's theory in his *Outlines of a Critical Theory of Ethics* (*Early Works,* III, 330–31).
5. There is a more detailed discussion of Bain's and Spencer's views on this matter in Dewey's *Outlines of a Critical Theory of Ethics* (*Early Works,* III, 328–33).
6. Plato, *Republic,* 441c–445b.

THE PSYCHOLOGY OF SELF-REALIZATION AND ITS APPLICATION TO THE EGOISM-ALTRUISM CONTROVERSY

SECTION 1. THE MEANING OF SELF-REALIZATION

The principle of morality, or the virtues, has now been stated to be the realization of the organic unity existing between the self and the act, between the doer and the deed. That would apparently give us the principle of self-realization as the most general category of moral life, the most general point of view from which to consider the particular facts of morality. That phrase, however, "self-realization," is not self-explanatory. Everything depends upon what one conceives to be the relation existing between self and realization. There are very serious objections to making self-realization the unifying moral principle until one has an adequate psychology of the self. As perhaps the doctrine has been most often stated, it breaks down just at that point because the self is regarded as something fixed, something given; it is regarded as after the manner of an object to which action may be ascribed as its forth-puts, as its products.

Now the realization of such a self as that would be a very different matter, have a very different meaning, from the realization of the self which is an active synthesis—that is, which exists only in action and which is an abstraction excepting as we find it operating in deeds. If you take the former conception of self-realization, it would always have to consist in getting something for the self that was already there. It is not getting pleasure, to be sure—that would give us the hedonistic idea. But it is getting happiness, or culture, or experience, enriched life, or more morality, or perfection for the being which is already in existence; it throws the emphasis on the side of acquisition and of possession. I do not see that it makes much difference what a man gets as long as you define moral life from the standpoint of getting. Moral perfection as something to be got has more content than getting pleasure or riches or intellectual culture, but morally it seems to be tainted with the same radical defect of selfishness. A man is after a thing because it is a good thing for himself. If he is wise he will perceive that there is more in it for him to get moral perfection than to get intellectual culture, more in intellectual culture than in simple pursuit of the pleasures of the senses. But in principle one does not differ from the other. It is the idea of the self which is somehow there and which sets out to get something for itself, to make certain acquisitions. It interprets perfection from the standpoint of acquisition.

You will find an interesting article in the last number of the *International Journal of Ethics,* April 1898,[1] on the discussion of self-realization as a practical working principle, in which the writer tries to point out that there are certain times or periods when self-realization is an adequate ideal, and there are other times when it is not. For example, the period of youth, at least for those who are getting an education, is a time when distinctly the principle of self-realization comes into play. There is a duty to get all the self that is possible. But when the person comes to maturity, to adult life, and adopts a certain vocation, then the point of view must shift: service, the rendering of social equivalents, becomes the main principle rather than self-development or than self-realization. I am far from saying that there is not a certain amount of practical truth in those statements. But the essence consists in supposing that the self is something that is given as an individual fact, so that there is a distinct difference between self-realization in the sense of getting learning and getting additional experience, getting culture, and social service as displayed in the form of a business pursuit or a vocation.

On the other side of the self the question would be all the time: What is the self as defined in terms of the act which expresses the situation? It would not be that the youth was engaged in college in self-realization, and that when he has taken a pursuit it must be service of others. It is simply that he is called upon to define himself in different ways, being in different conditions. The self has no existence excepting in terms of what it has to do, and what it has to do is a function of the whole situation. It is perfectly natural then, that one sort of act should be called for at one time as an expression of the self, and another sort of act should be called for at another time as an expression of self-realization.

In other words, on what I may class the motor or dynamic theory of the self, the self *is* the realization and the realization *is* the self. You do not know what the self is. You have no self until you find what we may call the realization. It is absolutely impossible to define the self either metaphysically or psychologically if you take it apart from the situation in which the agent operates. The concrete self, the psychological self, the ethical self, is specifically different with every act because it *is* only in the act. That is what I mean by saying that the realization *is* the self. It simply means that the act alone is the adequate definition of selfhood.

Now on that basis self-realization must be a social process. If you take the self as given, as simply a bare existence having certain powers, self-realization may or may not be a social process. Intrinsically, essentially, it is not possible to see why it should be a social process at all. As a mere matter of abstract theory it ought to be possible for the self to expand, to realize itself. Simply as a matter of fact we find that this given self exists along with a lot of other selves, and they act and interact upon each other so that the realization of one is conditioned upon the attainments reached by the others. But that logically is an external accident of the situation. The fact that a lot of selves do happen to operate in the same world and do run across each other is not due to anything in the self as such.

That comes out clearly in Green's *Prolegomena to Ethics* where he points out that as matter of fact the self cannot be realized excepting through the medium of institutions. At certain points he emphasizes the doctrine very strongly that self-realization is a social process; but at other times he points out that institutions are limited, that they are contracted, and therefore no institution can by any possibility be an adequate medium or channel of self-realization. Self-realization would be reaching perfection; it would be infinite development, complete exhaustive development of all powers.[2] It is obvious that when a man lives in institutions, he does not live at large in that way. He lives in some particular family and some particular town, and all this from the standpoint of a fixed conception of the self is pure limitation. The individual then is in this hard case: he must realize himself in social institutions and yet this holds him down so that he cannot get complete self-realization. If that were merely a logical contradiction on Green's part, it might not be a matter of special significance; but it shows what is intrinsic in any theory which conceives the self as existing apart from the act and treats the act as simply product or result. From that point of view the act must always be limited. The capacities of the self are so large, so infinite, that you never can squeeze them into the act. The act as an act is fixed by the environment. That is, no matter what a man's aspirations are, when he comes to act he must act in the world of space and time, in the now and here. He must act in a finite situation and so the sphere, the theater of his expression and realization as long as he stays in this world, prevents his adequate self-realization.

Now from the other point of view, this supposed limited situation and institution, instead of being a restriction of the activity of the self already there, is simply a means for defining the self. It simply marks the emerging of the self out of something abstract into something concrete. It is the specification or particularization of the self. Or put more concretely, the only way I can tell what I am, what my capacities are, the only way I can determine or value them at all, is by looking at some specific situation into which I as agent enter and then define myself in terms of the part to be played in that situation. So that situation, instead of being a restriction, is an absolute necessity to my realization. Now that situation is a social situation, which would mean that the man can define himself, he can tell what he is, he can be what he is, only in terms of the practical social situation which involves others as well as himself. There is no self until you ask what the self is called to do in relation to other people. The metaphysical self—that is, out of space and time relations,—that is, out of a specific situation which requires the doing of some particular deed—is simply a nonentity. It is simply a pure abstraction.

From the standpoint of the psychology of the self as an active synthetic process, you must define realization in terms of a social character because the situation affords the elements which are to be synthesized. The individual as simply psychological will afford you the machinery of synthesis. But it will not give you the content, the stuff which requires synthesis, nor will it tell you what particular form the synthesis must take at any particular time. The more you define the self as a synthetic activity in general, the less clue you have as to what you are going to get at any particular time. What is the synthesis that is required at this particular point of time and space? If the considerations which answer that question are a different sort of considerations entirely from those which determine the form of the synthesis, the moral life must be a hopeless dualism. But if the materials to be synthesized also show what particular form the synthesis must take at any particular time, then realization of self can be stated and worked out only in social terms.

SECTION 2. EGOISM
AND ALTRUISM

April 7, 1898

I will take up today the topic of egoism and altruism from the standpoint of the psychology of the self already set forth. The question which has recently taken form under the terminology of egoism and altruism, mainly under the influence—that is, so far as the terminology is concerned—of French positivism [3] and largely through George Eliot in English under the title of the relation of self-love and benevolence,[4] is the question whether all action is for the self, or whether such a thing as strictly disinterested action is possible. Or put in its extreme form as some writers would have it, whether any action is moral at all that occurs for the self, the assumption being often made, perhaps more often in popular discussion than in scientific, that morality and altruism are identical. Some moralists have laid down the principle that benevolence is the supreme ethical principle. The assertion has been made that the theory of self-realization denies the strictly altruistic or benevolent action—at least it always makes it a subordinate form of action for the self; the real end is to realize the self; it simply happens under certain circumstances that the best way to realize the self is through attention to the needs and interests of others. Hence the relevancy of this topic at this time.

At the last discussion it was shown that there is an ambiguity in the concept of self-realization, an ambiguity which is solved by a more adequate definition of the self. That same point of view can be applied to the analysis of the present question. Certainly from the standpoint of one conception of the self there is no alternative excepting either to say that all action is for the self and that altruism is simply a form of disguised selfishness in the sense that the self would not attain its own full development unless it did this particular kind of act that we call unselfish, or else to say that self-realization holds up to a certain point and then beyond that it must be supplemented by another theory of action for the welfare of others.

When Kant attempts to give a more concrete statement of morality than is found in his metaphysical writings, he gives that dualism. A man is to act for his own perfection and the happiness of others. He must not act for his own happiness. He must not act for the moral perfection of others, because he cannot. Every individual must moralize himself. It is a question of his own internal motive which nobody else can determine for him. If anybody else attempts it, it is simply an impertinence or interference. So we are in this strange plight that morally a man is bound to seek for something in others which in himself would be immoral. To get happiness for himself is immoral, but to get it for others is benevolent. Why happiness should be good for somebody else and bad for one's self is not clearly explained, and that is the basis of any theory which attempts to have two criteria of action, which says that action is a combination of rational self-love and rational benevolence, so that the truly virtuous man combines both a reasonable interest in his own well-being and a reasonable interest in the well-being of others. The difficulty is to find a unifying principle, to find a principle which tells where the limits of one cease and where the other begins.

Now in terms of the discussion of the other day, the discussion is futile excepting as one has some conception in advance of what is meant by the self. Is the self a presupposed, given existence, or does the self exist only as it operates? Is the self a continual synthetic construction? If the latter, the question between egoism and altruism is solved by getting a different purchase on the whole thing. We would have to say that a man always does act as himself, but that that is a different thing from saying that he acts for himself as an end. The objectionable character of the conception that a man always acts for himself has the same origin as the objectionable character of the doctrine of self-realization. It presupposes that a man is already there, and whatever he does, he does as the means to himself as an outside end. On that basis the relation between the act and the self is external. The self is the real end or aim whatever the pretended one may be, and the act that is done is a mere means to the welfare or the building up of that presupposed self. But if the self is identical organically with the act, then we can say that the act is [not] simply means to the welfare of the self. The act *is* the self. The man must do the act because it is himself and do it as himself—that is, throw himself thoroughly into it, put his whole being into the act. That is quite a different thing from saying that he acts for himself.

Or to state it [the objection] in terms of interest, one school says that a man's conduct is always motivated by his interest; that his interest will always control his action, and hence benevolence is really an enlightened selfishness. Once more, the objection to that is the false psychology that is back of it, making a difference between the man's interest and his act. The interest is set up as something ultimate and fixed, and the act is regarded as a mere subordinate means for subserving this presupposed interest. It is simply a tool. The same thing would apply to the utilitarian theories in their wider aspects as regards happiness, where the happiness is regarded as a fixed thing which is already known and the act is to be merely tributary to keeping up that totality of happiness.

On the basis of the other psychology of the self, the act is the man's interest. His interest is not something aside from it and beyond it so that the act comes in as an intervening state toward his interest, but you know his interest by seeing him act. He does what he does as his interest, not for his interest.

Now the defect on the side of the altruistic theory is precisely the same psychologically. They have exactly the same conception of the self that the egoistic or utilitarian schools have, but they see the practical moral objection to making that ultimate, and so they try to correct the deficiency by putting in another self. You must not act simply—or sometimes they put it as strongly as to say not at all—for your own interest, but always for the interest of some other self.

Now the difficulty in that point of view has already been suggested. Why should anybody else's self be better than your own? If the self is a thing of a presupposed rigid kind, why should another self-end have any more claim than my self-end? Why should the self in anybody else have superiority over the self as found in you? Consistently you must either say that the self is a nonmoral principle or else that it is a moral principle. If it is a nonmoral end, then it is so wherever it is found. It is just as bad to further it in somebody else as in yourself. If it is everywhere a moral end, then the ego and the alter both stand exactly on the same plane, the same level. Whatever a man takes to be his interest, he does. A sane man could not possibly do anything excepting as his interest, but that does not mean that he sets up his own welfare, his own good as a thing to be attained at all hazards, and then makes everything else tributary means for getting this thing for himself. It means on the contrary that the moral problems arise because a man does not know what his interest is; and the whole moral process of deliberation and of effort and desire is a process of the discovery of interest, of finding out what one's value, what one's worth or meaning is.

We get two radically different conceptions of interest from the standpoint of the two psychological definitions of the self. It was said the other day that while the self is in a continual process of construction, it cannot be adequately made up excepting in terms of the content which it supplies for the situation in which the agent has to act. That would mean in terms of the egoism and altruism question, that the self cannot define itself excepting in terms of a larger whole, a larger situation in which others, as well as one's self as an agent of action, are involved. All action would be altruistic in the sense not that others are its end or aim but in the sense that in finding out what the self is, of valuing it in terms of the individual act that needs to be performed, one must have recourse to others who are involved as necessary conditions.

What is the criterion for an act of charity which is presented as a claim? Upon what basis does one decide whether he shall or shall not do something for a needy person who offers himself? There would be, on the basis of what has been said, two false and two right ways of getting at that. One of the false ways would be to take the past interest, the established interests and habits of the self as final and simply say: What would myself from the first up to the present time get out of it for me (meaning by me the acquired, presupposed self)? The other false way would be to say: Of course my moral duty is to do always what I can for somebody else and here is an opportunity for me to be benevolent, to be self-sacrificing, and if it is really such an opportunity it ought to be embraced. The fallacy is that although seemingly altruism and egoism are so opposed to each other, they both have the same fundamental psychology: that of supposing it possible to define the self either in the ego or the alter without reference to a comprehensive situation.

If we take the two right ways of getting at it, the question is either what am I myself with reference to this particular case, or what is the other man with reference to the particular case. What am I as identified in the act, or what is the other man, similarly identified? The real criterion is found in the ego or alter with reference to the whole situation. It is only as you get beyond the fixed self, the given self in either case, that you can get any criterion at all for dealing with the problem. Otherwise you must settle it on capricious, or arbitrary or sentimental grounds; arbitrarily, if you suppose there is some outside canon which fixes the question whether you are to give or not, or sentimental if you allow the feelings of the moment to determine what is to be done. The probem then between egoism and altruism is solved by recognizing that there is no such problem, the supposed distinction simply grows out of a false psychology of the self. All action is egoistic in the sense that the act is the self defined; it is all altruistic in the sense that one must, in defining one's self as end, take account of others, must define one's self in terms of relationship to others.

That solution, however, may seem so general as to be rather unsatisfactory. It may be said that there must be some distinction between generous action and selfish action, between self-regarding action and other-regarding action, and that the theory laid down would merge those distinctions in one swamp. That leads to two further points, the one in which egoism and altruism may be distinguished from each other and from which both are morally legitimate, and the other, the case in which egoism and altruism do become conscious and reflective.

There is no doubt that there is a certain psychological distinction which has validity between egoism and altruism. That simply means, however, that there is a certain rhythm, a certain alternation in the attitudes which the self is called upon to assume. It is expressed crudely by Mr. Spencer in his discussion in *The Data of Ethics* when he says that a man must live before he acts. I will ask you to read his chapters on egoism and altruism to test the theory that I am giving. He has covered all the ground first on one side, then on the other, and then both together. The statement is given by him that a justification for a certain priority of egoism over altruism is that self-preservation is the first law of nature. After a man has secured himself in existence, he will have leisure for being altruistic, but if he does not look out for himself enough to keep himself alive, he obviously cannot do anything for anybody else. So the primary principle would be egoism. I say it is expressed crudely because it has no real existence. A man cannot live except in action; so to talk about living before he acts is absurd, but the truth involved there, I take it, is that there is a rhythm of attitudes. I would say that one is prior to the others; it is simply rhythmic alternation. It is a question whether the interest is in means or end at a given time.

There are circumstances under which the means is the end. That is, you must fashion the tool, you must perfect the instrument before you can use it. Now under those circumstances the principle of egoism would be the dominant principle. There are other times when the situation is such that it calls for the full functioning and operation of the instrument or organ even at the cost of loss to the organ as an organ, and under those circumstances the principle which might be termed altruism would be the dominant one. Now that, however, is simply a psychological distinction of the two phases which the self assumes: the self as agent and the self as function; the self as instrument for use and the self in use, in realization; the self as means and the self as ends. It does not mean that there is any fundamental dualism between self and others, but simply that the whole situation is such that at one time the development of the organ for future possible use is the chief thing, while at other times it is the actual use of it. It is the rhythm between preparation and realization, between income and outgo, between possession and use, between tool and operation. Physiologically one might say it is the rhythm of the anabolic and katabolic processes: at one time the building up of the self is the chief thing, and at other times the kinetic expenditure of that energy is the chief thing. A man saves money that he may invest it; a man learns a profession that he may practice it. When the emphasis is on the learning of the profession or the saving of money, the interest is egoistic; while in practicing the vocation or in using the money it is altruistic.

That is a distinctly different use of that term from the one which prevails in the ordinary discussions where the ego is set in antithesis against the alter. In this latter distinction the whole situation or function is taken for granted. It is assumed all the time that there is some function, some active operation; but we see that before that can take place, the instrument for it must be got ready, it must be sufficiently built up. On the other side, after that has been built up, then the emphasis is thrown on its outward direction, on its active use. But the ultimate end and justification are not that it is for others; it is simply that there is an organ which must function, and in functioning service for others results. But the activity is its own reward and its own justification; we do not refer it to the fact that it will benefit someone else in order to get its justification.

Here we have the two stages which we have seen in the process of attention. On the scientific side, the stages of building up an hypothesis and then putting it into use and experimenting on the hypothesis. Up to a certain point attention must be given to defining the theory. That would be the egoistic attitude. But after the concept has been built up to a certain point, then, in order to verify it, experiment based upon it must occur.

The other aspect of the discussion is what we may term reflective egoism and reflective altruism. Both of these are equally virtuous or both are equally vicious. That reflective egoism is vicious we need not argue. That is what we mean by selfishness in the bad sense, when a man puts up his own welfare as a fixed given thing and then reduces other things to means for realizing it. The whole difficulty there is simply that one does not recognize the impossibility of what he is trying to do. There is no such self fixed there beforehand as an end. What the self is, what the end is, has to be found out experimentally through deliberation and through desire and effort. The self is always being discovered and valued, brought to consciousness. For that reason reflective selfishness in this sense is a comparatively rare thing. There are few people who have consciously and deliberatively set up their own welfare as a supreme end.

The form in which selfishness ordinarily presents itself is simply that of undue absorption in one's immediate interests. It is simply failure to mediate sufficiently the direction of attention and of interest. It is comparatively rarely that a man says: "I am going to have my own good at all hazards and I do not care how much I sacrifice other people." It comes in a much more subtle way than that. One is engaged on something which has a positive value; it is a good so far as it goes. Then the person becomes so absorbed in that immediate occupation which has defined himself in the past that he is not observant of new stimuli which would compel a broadening of the scope of activity, and which would involve that he subordinate this particular line of interest to something more comprehensive. The judgment that a man is selfish means that he ought to be defining himself on the basis of a wider situation, that he ought to be taking into account factors which as a matter of fact he is neglecting. It means inadequacy almost always. It generally means lack of adequate self-consciousness. It means a narrow vision of the situation which should be used to tell the self what it is.

On the other side, reflective altruism is vicious too. That is, to consciously make the welfare of others (whether their happiness or their moral good) the end, the supreme criterion, will always result in conduct which would be inadequate and defective as much as if one consciously or thoughtlessly made one's self the supreme end. That point, probably, that altruism is defined in that sense as being as vicious as egoism, may not be quite so obvious. I will therefore suggest three or four reasons for considering it so. As an illustration: For what motive should business be carried on? How shall one define the end and the ultimate criterion? Is the only moral justification for a pursuit of a certain business or profession conscious desire as the supreme thing to do good to other people? If one says yes, aside from the fact that that would condemn about everybody that is doing business and following professions, there are two theoretical reasons why such a view is to be rejected. On one side you say the business is a simple means where the welfare of others, either as happiness or moral perfection, is the real end. That externality between the means and the end is a fatal objection to that point of view. That means that there is no adequate moral criterion within the business itself. It means that it does not carry its own moral standard and justification on with it. At every point you must get away from your business and think about the welfare of other people; and in that outside consideration, which is more or less remote and external to the thing you are doing, you must seek for justification and for guidance. That of course means that you cannot give your full interest to what you are doing. Nobody can do thoroughly well what does not command his full interest and attention. If a man cannot find his motive for action in what he is doing, he cannot do it with his whole being, and therefore he will do it imperfectly. There is the contradiction. Any moral means, to be moral, must be one which is identified with end; it must be the end. In its immediate aspect it must be the end as it presents itself at this particular point in time and under these particular circumstances. If you say that the justification for business is the contribution to the welfare of others, then organic identification of means as end is lacking. You must get at it from the other standpoint: a man must be made to believe that this particular line of action is called for by the whole situation, and then believe that because it is called for it does involve the welfare of others. There is an altruistic paradox as well as a hedonistic one. The hedonistic paradox is that a man cannot secure happiness as the end unless he forgets it. He must forget it and devote himself to the thing in hand in order to be really happy. So here on the altruistic side, before he can really do good to others, he must stop thinking about the welfare of others; he must see what the situation really calls for and go ahead with that, and the reason is the same in both cases. Whenever one makes his own good or the good of others the end, it becomes and extraneous end.

On the other side, what criterion have you by which to tell what the good of others really is? You are going to work for the good of others, making business a simple means to the welfare of others. What is the content for the well-being of others or the good of others? How are you going to tell what that really is? Because your means is external to your end; you cannot give your whole attention to the means, and equally when the end is external to the means. That means that it is inadequate, it is empty, it has no definite content. Persons who persist on that theory are always thrown back on a sort of emotional utilitarianism in order to define what the welfare of others is. There is no rational way of telling what the welfare of others is. The man who looks at the situation and goes on to see what he can do has a standard, a basis on which to put content into welfare; it enables him to realize what the good of others is in the abstract. But if you turn in the other direction and set up the good of others in the abstract and reduce professional and industrial activity as mere means for that end, you are at the mercy of any sentimentalist or any dogmatist to tell you what the real good of people is.

April 8, 1898

The insufficiency of altruism in the sense of making the welfare of others the supreme end of action may be further illustrated in two ways. Because of the lack of any criterion as to what the good or welfare of others is on that basis, the natural, practical tendency of altruism as a principle would be to induce selfishness in others. It puts the other person, the alter, in the attitude of having something done for him. It puts everybody in a passive or recipient attitude as regards others. It is true that there is an active side (that is, everybody is to promote the welfare of everybody else), but on the other side he is to be an object whose welfare is to be cultivated. I say the practical tendency would be to cultivate in the individual a sense of his own happiness or good as something which he has a right to demand to receive from others. The thing not infrequently occurs in some families where the members of the family make self-sacrifice the supreme end. The result is that those upon whom the self-sacrifice is lavished tend to take it as a matter of course and to expect such treatment as their normal due. It has a tendency to exaggerate the sense of the ego and what is due to it: its rights, privileges, possessions. Moreover, if this principle were universalized—which it never has been (it has always been a class principle—that is, a principle of superiors in some form to inferiors, the conferring of benefits by one class upon another)—but if it were universalized, morality would be reduced to a competitive contest regarding self-sacrifice.

It comes out very neatly in Mr. Spencer's final ideal state where he states that the highest form of altruism consists in the waiving of the right to make other people happy.[5] The chief form which self-sacrifice can take is allowing somebody else to make you happy instead of your trying to make them happy. The greatest self-denial a man can exercise under those circumstances would be the denial of the pleasure he found in making other people happy and in waiving his rights and allowing others to do these things for him. The theoretical difficulty that underlies that absurd practical outcome is that there is no basis for the unification or organization of a system of complete altruism any more than of a system of complete egoism. You have so many distinct selves, you have no system, no organization which as a unity defines and measures each one of these egos. The result is that the moral claims of one individual would be apt to cut across, to a certain extent, those of others, and you must have some sort of compromise. That is where Spencer comes out with a sort of working compromise of the claims of these individuals in relation to each other.

With relation to the agent himself there are certain practical tendencies also likely to result which would not be at all desirable. It is very difficult practically to keep the desire to do good to others entirely without any flavor of the desire to regulate their conduct. The thoroughgoing and systematic altruist is quite likely, under the guise of doing good to others, unconsciously perhaps to set up a good and insist that others must have it whether or no, all the more so because the agent is really sacrificing himself in giving the other person that good. Virtually he says: What greater criterion of my sincerity can you demand than the fact that I am willing to sacrifice so much to give it to you? The fact that one is sacrificing for another is taken as evidence that that is the good. Of course puritanic morality is a very common thing on this side. What was a perfectly sincere desire for absolute freedom of thought became the standard to regulate the lives of others just at the point where one demands freedom for himself; that is, in the definition of what the good really is and in the selection of means for realizing it.

Moreover, another reaction upon the self which is not at all desirable is to build up what some author has called the "egoism of renunciation." It is quite possible to make this pleasure the end, in which case you have a refined form of hedonism. The feeling that one is sacrificing something, and the satisfaction that one gets out of that, is quite capable of becoming a person's working measure for the rightness of what he is doing, and the securing of that doing becomes the end, the ideal. One measures one's goodness by the amount that he does to promote the happiness of others, and from that point of view his goodness can be maintained only on the condition that he do as much of this as possible, and that works into the previous point of view. The conferring of pleasure upon others, since it is the measure of one's own moral attainments, lends itself really to subordinating other people as instruments to securing the proper plane of goodness on the part of one's self.

The previous criticisms may be summed up by saying that in this reflective altruism, or the promotion of the welfare of others as the supreme end and test of morality, there is no organizing principle and there is therefore no objective principle. We come back, in order to get a unified principle, to the conception of the self as the active synthesis of all the conditions, all the elements; and to the further fact that under different circumstances one arrives at and discovers that active synthetic self by throwing the emphasis upon either of the two poles involved in it. One can discover the act which will define and identify the self by going at it from either of two sides: either from the side of the capacities of the agent, or from the side of the needs of the situation. We get back to the conception of function as the working unity of organism and environment to the possibility and desirability under different circumstances of defining function in terms of organism at one time, or in terms of environment at another; but whichever we consciously emphasize, we select because we presuppose the relation to the other.

There is no way of telling what the capacities of the agent are, excepting as one takes for granted the environmental conditions with reference to which those powers are exercised. There is no telling, on the other hand, what the situation and its needs are, excepting as one takes for granted an agent free, with certain resources at his command.

Take the illustration given the other day of the relief of suffering. The self there, the right self, the psychological self has to be discovered in the act which will unify all the factors. One may arrive at a solution by saying: Here am I and I have certain powers and limitations. What I do here I cannot do somewhere else, it is a question of utilizing my power to the utmost—and decide the question by throwing the emphasis on that side. But it is obvious that he cannot tell what his powers are or how much he can do with them until he virtually assumes certain conditions with which they are to operate. He will take into account the claims of this particular person as compared with other claims which will be made upon him, and the fact that the time and energy that are spent here could be spent somewhere else. Or he can throw the burden of the problem on the other side and say: What are the real needs here? Just what are the claims of this man as compared with the claims of the other? If he puts it from that side, it is because he is assuming that he is there as the agent. The only reason that he asks about the needs of the situation is to get light upon the direction of himself as an agent, just as on the other side the only reason that he asks about himself as an agent, inquires into his own powers, is in order that he may determine what the active need of the whole situation is.

That might be summed up briefly by stating that the real self psychologically is always a synthesis of two distinct types and conditions, one of which we may call the agent or instrumental self, and the other of which we may call the conditions of the situation, or, briefly, the environment. Thus we arrive once more at the point I have spoken of two or three times, that the moment you give up the conception of the self as a fixed entity, the moment you give up the conception of the self as an ontological being already in existence and having certain powers already made with which it can produce certain acts or results, you get to the conception of the self as an active synthesis—that is, a unification—realized only in action of a variety of factors; and if you call part of those factors internal then you must call the others external, if you call part of them individual you must call the others social. An act as an act always transcends mere individuality—that is, mere absolute individuality. An act occurs in space and time and embodies these space and time factors which lie beyond the individual.

We have at least then, so to speak, as a presumption, this point of view for the consideration of the social ethics. The self, psychologically examined, turns out to be an active synthesis; therefore the self is a social self in the sense that it involves intrinsically within itself a content which lies beyond its own formed habits and its own achievements, and with reference to which all its attainments and accomplishments must be considered as purely instrumental, as so much capital with which to do business, as so much resources for laying hold of, appropriating and working up into personal form the conditions and materials supplied by the environment. Thus, while the psychological examination throws itself into an investigation of the form, of the machinery of the self, this very examination finally compels us to go over to the social side. It is not simply that after we have completed the psychological investigation we can take up the social investigation, but that the process, the machinery revealed at the psychological examination, is seen to depend upon a content which is social; that that content is what constitutes the peculiar character which the form has and that the varieties in the content are what differentiate one form or mode from another. From this point I shall go on to consider the social and political ethics proper.

NOTES

1. Henry Sturt, "Self-Realization as a Working Moral Principle," *International Journal of Ethics,* VIII (April 1898), 328–44.

2. Green, *Prolegomena to Ethics,* Secs. 183–91.

3. See Auguste Comte, *System of Positive Polity* (London, 1875), I, 73–75, and *The Positive Philosophy of Auguste Comte* (London: Jay Chapman, 1853), II, 554–55.

4. For an analysis of this aspect of Eliot, see Josiah Royce, "George Eliot as a Religious Teacher," in *Fugitive Essays* (Cambridge, Mass.: Harvard University Press, 1920), pp. 260–89.

5. Spencer, *The Data of Ethics,* Sec. 98.

LECTURES ON
POLITICAL
ETHICS: 1898

CHAPTER 1

HOW DOES SOCIETY
REGULATE THE INDIVIDUAL? [1]

SECTION 1. THE RELATION OF
POLITICAL ORGANIZATION TO
MORALS

The social sciences are commonly and conveniently classed under three heads, Ethics, Politics, and Economics. The classification is so convenient that I shall take it is as the point of departure.

First, and for the present very briefly, about the ethics. There are at least three types of views regarding the part played by social forces in moralizing the individual. One of these is the typical English theory represented in the present generation by Bain and Spencer, in which the individual naturally, the individual as a psychical being, follows after his own pleasures, aims at his own private satisfaction. Social forces come in, however, and inhibit certain desires of the individual; they facilitate the satisfaction of others and, in general set up certain standards, certain laws present to the individual, certain duties or obligations. The origin of duty, of obligation, is always extraneous to the natural self according to all orthodox English psychologists. You cannot say that it is a man's duty to secure pleasure: he simply does so by the makeup of his being. If there is any duty to follow moral law, it comes in because others attach to certain actions of the individual rewards and to others punishments; and then as he gradually learns to look at his conduct on the side of how others are to treat it, he gets moral consciousness. Spencer mentions three types of social forces which act on the individual—the priest, the policeman, and public opinion: the social forces organized in the church with supernatural sanction, those summed up in government with definite penalties attaching to certain kinds of actions, and the approval or disapproval of public opinion. It is because he associates with his conduct what others think of it that the moral comes in. There is a dualism between the psychical and the social as the originator and impressor on the natural individual of the moral relationship—the dualism between the natural psychical individual and the playing upon him of social forces. Note that that theory does not say that the social stimuli bring the individual to consciousness of what he really is, that the social pressure and influences mediate and interpret the activity of the individual.

That is the theory that has been advanced. It is a matter, on Spencer's theory, not of interpretation and mediation; it is a matter of combination.

Another type of theory is that of the universal self as a metaphysical principle. There is in the ego a distinction—Kant is perhaps the best type here—between the historical sensuous self, which agrees practically with the English utilitarian school. It does not differ essentially so far as that goes. But there is another aspect of the self, which is the noumenal or transcendental in Kant's terminology, the self which is universal, which being universal does not aim at particular pleasures but is controlled by the end of law, of reason; and on the basis of that universal self there is found a bond of connection and identity between the various particular egos. Just because it is necessary to constitute selfhood as such you have a common element, an individual element on the basis of which the social superstructure may be reared.

I am not going to criticize that view at this point, but simply say that the great problem historically is to get these two aspects of the self in any kind of working relation to each other. It has had a good deal of difficulty in combining the actual historical particular self of John Smith with this universal, metaphysical, rational self which was present in him. In concrete social terms, even admitting that there is an identical self, an absolute universal self present in all the variety of different selves, that is a connecting link, a common element, a bond of synthesis. When you come to social organization you must get some grip on the part of that principle on the empirical selves; the concrete problem, say, in the family organization, or in the school organization of a city ward. The problem does not lie with this metaphysical self, but in getting this great variety of empirical egos to recognize mutuality, community of interest, and to control their own particular tendencies on the basis of that community of end and purpose and value. This theory, then, while it seems to have a factor that the other does not, has found historically great difficulty in making that available for working social purposes.

The third type of theory is of course substantially that there is no self ego as an entity ready-made once for all, that the self is a continuous construction, a continuous organization; that that organization involves continually a reconstruction of habit, of agency, with reference to the performance of functioning, and that the social considerations come in to determine both the quality and the quantity of that immediate reconstruction; that the social considerations come in at the time to enable the individual to define himself in terms of the acts required. A good substitute for this distinction between the empirical self and the metaphysical self is this other distinction between the self as agent and the self as operative function. And that latter is not the bare identity of content, or bare metaphysical community—it is always a concrete unity, organization, or function, which is what it is through the uniting, putting together of the practical elements which enter into the statement of the situation.

This is all I shall have to say at present regarding the strictly ethical side. I think the problems involved will come out better if we shift the point of view, and so I shall state these same problems as they appear from the side of politics and the general theory of economics. The general point I am trying to get at is the same, that is, the underlying psychology of the self which is involved in the different statements of political views and of economic views.

April 11, 1898

I will go on with the discussion of the general question of the relation of ethical conduct to social life, but instead of taking it up further from the standpoint of morality itself, we will reverse the point of view and consider the various groups of theories regarding the relation of political organization to morals—the theories regarding the relation of politics to ethics. In considering these theories I shall not follow any historical or chronological order, but rather take them up as illustrations of the typical ways in which this relationship has been interpreted, with a view to bringing out the main factors which enter into the problem.

The underlying point which I wish to bring out is the extent to which political theory has been controlled by psychological assumptions. There are disputes as to how far social science should be psychological. It always has been psychological in the sense that the current idea regarding the nature of consciousness, the relation of consciousness to the world, subject to object, and the relation existing between the acts with their consequences and motives have been at least unconsciously assumed, and have fixed the underlying political categories. So far as any change is taking place, or is to take place, it would simply mean that as psychology itself gets its methods better developed, as it becomes more conscious of its own procedure and gets results in ways which are more controllable, political philosophy can criticize and utilize in a critical way the psychological assumptions which hitherto have been taken for granted in a more or less dogmatic manner.

The common assumption of all the theories which I am going to present is that of the self as somehow an independent ego or soul which is a given entity in itself that is apart from the process of consciousness. Such selves internally and ethically must be independent of each other. They are ethically independent because they are psychically independent. Each is what it is in itself. Of course it might not develop itself in the same way if there were no other selves, but its existence as a self as not dependent upon other selves. The acts of these selves, however, because they are not matters of mere internal consciousness, but because they take place in the sphere of nature, bring these independent selves into contact with each other and, because in contact, into possible conflict. The area of politics, then, of society as governmentally organized, is to institute the proper adjustments and relations with reference to these external acts. Each self in its inner being is unapproachable as respects every other self; that is the nature of the ego, and taken in its own sphere—that of motive, or will, or personality—it is sacred, inalienable to itself. Each of these independent selves manifests itself in a certain sphere, motives expand into acts, and then these spheres of action coincide with each other, or collide with each other—and hence the necessity of some principle of adjustment with reference to this sphere of outer action, the political organization of society. That is precisely that which has to do with this matter of delimitation, and the preventing of friction, the restoration of harmony in this external sphere. All the theories agree in that general assumption. They differ in subinterpretations of which I shall speak.

I have divided these theories into five groups.

A. That represented first by Hobbes, according to which each of these independent selves aims at the maximum of possession and enjoyment on its own behalf. Each ego is absolutely egoistic, self-centered, and the nature of the external expression of this desire for self-assertion is such as to bring all these selves into necessary conflict with each other. Now these two assumptions do not necessarily go together, as we shall see later. The liberalistic school has agreed with Hobbes as to the first assumption but holds that on the whole there is a harmony of the various selves in getting individual satisfaction, so that one's efforts tend rather to assist others in their efforts also. But according to Hobbes the ego of one is so thoroughly negative in relation to the others that its efforts to realize itself of necessity bring it into hostility and opposition to the others. Each for himself and the war of all against all. This natural man is not only nonpolitical, but nonsocial and nonmoral. You cannot say it is immoral, simply because there is no consciousness of duty at all for the only law is the law of the strongest, and the only obligation for anybody is to get all he can get and to keep all he can keep.

Morality then, according to Hobbes, is originated by the state. It is the state as formed by a compact of these individuals which for the first time imposes obligation. The sphere of moral obligation and the sphere of political obligation are synonymous. All law and order proceeds from the commands of the sovereign. The sense of obligation is simply the recognition of the necessity of subjecting the individual self to the will of the state. There you have a thoroughgoing view of the identity of the ethical relationship and the political relationship founded, however, upon the conception that the ethical relationship is arbitrary in that it rests simply upon the authoritative declaration of the political sovereign. The political sovereign can do no wrong, simply because it alone is the standard and criterion of what right and wrong are. It cannot do wrong any more than God can do wrong in His sphere, and for the same reason, because the arbitrary will of God makes right and makes wrong.

That theory seems thoroughly arbitrary and perhaps rather unreal. At the time it awakened very bitter reaction among the English moralists. (Hobbes was born in 1588). It awakened reaction in two general directions. One school held that man is not naturally egoistic but has sympathetic tendencies; and the other tried to show that morality was intrinsic and not the enactment of a political superior. Hobbes's theory, however, is of extreme significance, more important than the contributions of most of his opponents, because it represents the feeling for some sort of necessary connection between social organization and morality. Of course the lack comes in in supposing that this social organization was simply a matter of arbitrary agreement, an authoritative enactment; but below all that, what gave Hobbes's thought an element of vitality and truthfulness was the feeling on his part that the isolated individual was not only nonsocial but nonmoral, and that moral relations must somehow arise and be bound up with social relationships.

If you come down to Austin in this century, you get in his theory of jurisprudence an interesting variation of Hobbes's point of view. According to Austin there is a definite distinction between the sphere of legality, or of politics, and of morality; but the distinction is simply this: when the command or injunction comes through a definite social organ and has attached to it a definite fixed penalty, we are in the sphere of law in the legal sense; when the command comes in a vaguer way, not through a specific organ but in a more intangible way, through pressure of public opinion, and the penalty its not attached by some person, we have the moral sphere, or the sphere of morality. Both political responsibilities, then, and moral duties have exactly the same origin in kind; that is, both come through social demands. But the distinction is in the much more definitely organized command on the political side, and the relatively loose and vague way in which the moral claim is exercised and in which its sanction follows.

B. Following up the line of thought started by John Locke (born in 1632) we have the conception which in the last century and in this developed into what may be termed liberalism. According to this point of view there is a tendency toward a natural harmony in the expression of the various subjective egos. Metaphysically and psychologically, each is an independent entity, but they are turned out more or less on a common plan. They have, therefore, many interests in common and the tendency to agree is just as natural as the tendency to disagree and oppose. The state, then, comes in mainly in a negative way to remove barriers and restrictions and to prevent, so far as possible, collisions between these various individuals, and at all events to rectify them after they have occurred. According to Locke the real need of the state is to get an umpire. It is not that there is an absolute war of all against all. The state of nature is a social state up to a certain point, but there is a certain amount of disagreement as well as agreement, and there is no final court of decision as to what is right in these cases of conflict. There is no recognized person who shall carry out the common interest; so the state comes in as the representative of man's natural common interests, as the judge to show where the interest really lies; and it also comes in as the executive force to carry it into effect after the judgment has once been passed.

Now such a theory is naturally somewhat ambiguous as regards the relation of the political to the ethical. You see it must differ fundamentally from Hobbes's. The ethical is there already in the natural social tendencies of man. It is the category which is current in the metaphysics of the time, of similarity, and the ethical is based in that element of likeness and the acts which spring from it. The sphere of the state, then, of politics, is distinctly subordinating on the ethical side.

There is a divergence in two directions. According to one school the state is without ethical significance entirely. It simply comes in as a practical agent to prevent clashing and to get back to an equilibrium as easily as possible when the clash has occurred, simply for practical reasons, not for ethical reasons. It is better in a practical sense to get along without friction. The other point of view tends to give the state a sort of negative ethical function. That state comes in to reinforce and to execute the natural moral tendencies of man. It thus has a derivative if not primary moral function. The political economy school, known as the Manchester school, gave the first point of view its most interesting development.* Their assumption is that this natural harmony between the interests of various individuals, this natural agreement, is very great and very important; that if you can only get rid of artificial restrictions which have been built up into class interests and factitiously maintained by government, the perception every time will be that the intelligent self-interest of one individual will agree with that of another; that you get the maximum social order when you get every individual seeking his own happiness under free conditions, where the government has not come in and by various kinds of laws restricted the action of the individual.

That school has lost its vogue, but it is very interesting to see how thoroughly that scheme was believed in, and how influential and prevalent it was in the early part of the century. The doctrine is more or less misrepresented. One side only is presented, that of universal self-seeking, but in the mind of those who held this view, the other side was as important— that is, that if you can get complete freedom, harmony will naturally result. There was the virtual, if unjustified, assumption that there is a universalism implicit in the individual, that there is an intrinsic social factor in him which, if it can be free, would bring about the most active unity of

* Presumably a reference to Richard Cobden (1804–1865) and his followers who favored free trade and the repeal of the English corn laws.

itself. Of course there went along with that the idea that the function of government must be reduced to a minimum, the laissez-faire conception. The essence of government is the seeing that something is the matter. Government is the doctor that comes in after something has gone wrong, and its function is simply to get rid of the obstructed elements there, to give the system itself natural free healthy play. As the function of the physician is to make himself unnecessary, so with government. There you see the government has no ethical function, in one sense, at all. It is rather a sign that something has gone wrong; the natural harmony of interests has been disturbed.

Herbert Spencer's theory represents, in a way, a union of factors derived from Hobbes and from the liberalistic school. His point of contact with Hobbes and with Austin is in this theory of obligation; that the sense of duty as distinct from the sense of self-interest arises only through social pressure. His point of contact with the liberal school is that he too believes, not indeed in any absolute identity of the interests of these various individuals, but in the progressive tendency towards harmony in their various expressions, and he attempts to explain this by reference to the theory of evolution, trying to show that by the very conditions under which life is developed, there is a continual tendency towards the reconciliation of egoism and altruism, that on the evolutionary hypothesis life could not maintain itself and could not develop, excepting as there is a trend in the direction of the individual interests harmonizing with those of others.

C. We have the transition of liberalism into modern radicalism with John Stuart Mill as the most influential factor—that is, in English thought. According to liberalism the only function of the government is to get rid of the artificial barriers which the individual meets in his attempt to get individual satisfaction. Here is A. He is after the greatest possible happiness, or the greatest amount of wealth with the least possible effort, or after freedom. Now all that government has a right to do for him is simply to get certain obstacles out of his way, and those are only the artificial ones. If it attempts to get rid of his natural obstacles (that is, what man has not put there, but nature) it will defeat his own effort and the final outcome will be worse than if he were left to work the thing out for himself.

Mill represents the growing recognition that that conception would be all right if the ideal state of things had already been reached. That is, if such a theory were not necessary it would be true. But as matter of fact, no such line can be drawn between natural and artificial restriction. Or put in another way, the conception of the individual who already knows what he wants and knows how to get it, the individual who has an intelligent broad survey of the situation and knows what he wants and asks nothing of anybody excepting to take the stones out of his path which somebody else has put there, is the kind of an individual that you get only with the completed development and organization of society. It is simply a nominal thing, a verbal thing, to talk about giving the individual a free external sphere of action unless you have some guarantee for supposing that his internal powers, his intelligence, is capable of recognizing the sphere of action and taking advantage of it. If a typical individual is developed to the point where he clearly recognizes his own welfare, knows what it is and how to get at it, and other individuals are on the same plane, it would hardly be worthwhile to have government even to remove the obstacles.

But the real difficulty is farther back. The individual's consciousness is so dulled, he is so unresponsive, that he does not realize the obstacles, much less that he is on the aggressive to attack and get them out of the way. Mill recognized that the defect of early liberalism was that it did not see how external conditions react in and influence individual perceptions and motives. They supposed that the whole difficulty was in the external sphere and that if the deck was clear for action the individual would go ahead and operate freely. Mill saw that that presupposed a mythical individual, that the real defect was further back, that the individual consciousness was so blunt that he did not see the situation or that his sympathies were so untrained that they did not respond. Hence the state must come in, not only to provide an external sphere for the research for happiness, but it must also attempt to awaken and develop the individual's sense of himself and of his happiness.

Moreover, Mill also saw that the earlier liberalism, and economics, of the Manchester school were defective in that it had after all only an external guarantee for harmony of interests. Suppose my only reason for aiming at the welfare of others is that I believe that by so doing I best subserve my own interests. The earlier liberalists had supposed that was sufficient. Of course that is after all external. There is no absolute guarantee in any particular case that the interests of the individual are going to coincide. They may ninety-nine times out of a hundred, but if the individual should think he saw an exception in the hundredth case, he might go ahead on the egoistic basis. Mill said that the individual must be trained, educated to believe in an intrinsic identity of interest; that is, his sympathies must be so worked up that he will not have to see intellectually in particular cases that his own interests do coincide with those of others. All the institutions of society must be modified, externally modified, so as to tend in this direction.

Here now then we have two spheres of influence for state action which liberalism does not recognize at all, and both of which are ethical, or at least quasi-ethical; namely, that all the institutions of society must be shaped, not merely to give the individual an external sphere of action, but so as to react into his consciousness, making him feel what he is and what his good is. The other point is that they must be so shaped as to culminate in fixing in the individual the sense of his social nature as an adequate motivation of action. Mill continued to conceive of himself as a utilitarian and as a member of the liberal school, but there is here a very profound movement away from its psychological process as well as its ethical conclusions. Here is a marked tendency toward the recognition of a continual action and reaction of one on the other, and [the development of the view] that in shaping the external you must take into account the way in which it reacts in the individual's recognition of the valuation of life and in his emotional appreciation and sympathies. Now that view of Mill's brought about the modern radicalism which is at least semi-socialistic in character. It believes that government has a tremendous active work to do, not only in the direct sense of the term, but that all institutions are effective in the way in which they unconsciously react on and modify the individual's views of things and his motives. Spencer does not believe in public education of the school type. Schooling ought to be left entirely to the individual. He either wants it or he does not want it, and it ought to be left to private initiative. The radical school has transformed the conception of public agency, not only with reference to education but in other respects. Everywhere where it is worthwhile government should take a hand to free the individual; to see to it that he has intelligence to see things and that he has practical powers to take advantage of them.

Thus we have the paradox of English politics in the last half century, that right out of laissez-faire liberalism there has grown up a powerful party which believes in strong and continual strenuous action. They both have the same fundamental premise, but the radical school says that before you can get the individual as an end of himself, you must do more than simply take away certain negative restrictions: you must enlarge the sense of himself and his sense of his environment. Practically it seems to me we have an approach to the true view there; there is practically a recognition of the relationship between individuals and the institution, but the defect is that the school has theoretically kept the old psychology, the psychology of an isolated consciousness which is simply acted upon by stimuli which in turn act upon them, but which is in the nature of a thing, in the nature of an entity, or object.

April 12, 1898

D. I will take up today under D the conception of the Kantian school regarding the relation of political authority and obligation to moral conduct. The interest in the views of this school arises from the fact that it attempts to establish a peculiar equilibrium or adjustment of spheres between the ethical and legal. Kant is strenuous in the assertion that morality of conduct is due entirely to the motive which actuates it, that the only moral motive is recognition of the dutiful character of the act. Now it would follow from that naturally that he would be very solicitous to avoid even the appearance of any external interference with our consistent use of this inner freedom of the will as expressed in motive. It is obvious that he must in a way regard the political and legal sphere as morally insufficient; but at the same time he is anxious to give a moral basis to political authority, so that while legal regulations themselves shall not be ethical because they are external, yet they shall have an ethical reason for being.

His connecting links there are about as follows. The moral motive is always universal: that is, the moral maxim is: so [act] that the principle upon which you act might be made a law universal—so that all agents under similar circumstances would follow the same principle. You must act as if by the fact of your acting your motive were going to be legislated into effect. Would you be willing that the principle on which you are acting should become a law of nature as certain and unchangeable as the law of gravitation? That is really the criterion. An act which does flow from the recognition of universal law flows from reason as practical, or it flows from the will, in Kant's sense of the will, and thus it and it alone is really free. An end which is dictated by appetite simply, or personal convenience, is controlled by a more or less external consideration, and hence is not really free.

Now it follows according to Kant, that the external act of any agent ought to be such as not to interfere with the possibility of free acts on the part of others. That is the supreme principle of the legal sphere. The external acts of A must be such as to coincide with similar free acts on the part of everybody else. That which is externally wrong—that is, legally or politically wrong, not simply morally wrong—is that which hinders the exercise of freedom on the part of others. Now that hindrance of the free act of another implies constraint put through the action of one upon the free expression of the will of another. The authority of the state comes in to use constraint against this constraint; or as Kant puts it, it comes in to hinder the hindrance of freedom.

The principle in form is not unlike that of the liberal school in England. In fact Spencer's formula is almost identical with that of Kant, that every man ought to be free to act as long as he gives the like freedom to others, but if he uses his freedom to interfere with the freedom of others, he misuses it, and it is right to put constraint upon him to prevent that interference on his part. The state, then, or civil and political authority in general, comes in precisely in that negative way to secure the conditions of the free exercise of will. The state has its justification negatively, exactly as it had in the liberal school. The only difference is that in the liberal school the state comes in to give every individual the proper sphere for the satisfaction of his wants. Its motivation is economic rather than ethical. It is to see to it that A can have a fair chance to make known his wants and satisfy them, provided he does not infringe upon the equal right of somebody else to satisfy his wants.

With Kant the ultimate justification is ethical rather than economic. The thing which must be secured to each individual is not so much the opportunity to satisfy his natural wants but to enable him to act freely in the sense of following the principles of reason or the laws of morality.

These motives may be perfectly universal; that is, he may be acting from the sense of law and recognition of duty. Can he carry that motive into effect? Can he carry it out in action? Not until certain conditions are present, not until certain regulations are observed: and so the state comes in to see to it that the individual that wants to be moral, that wants to carry his moral motives into operation, shall have a free and unhindered chance to do so. So the state in that indirect and somewhat negative way comes to possess an ethical function. In the translation of Kant's *Philosophy of Law* by Hastie,[2] you will find the gist of the discussion in the Introduction, between pages 43 and 58, and then on pages 155 to 165.

Thomas Hill Green represents in his *Principles of Political Obligation*[3] the attempt to carry out Kant's idea in a less formal way. The underlying philosophical principle is pretty much the same, but he attempts to work it out in a less abstract way and in a way which is more consonant with the modern social and political conditions. Green too takes the ground that it is the very essence of morality to be spontaneous—that is, to arise from free choice and interest of the agent concerned. Consequently he says, page 34, that moral duties cannot possibly be enforced because moral duties are duties to act from certain dispositions and with certain motives, and nobody can force a man to have a certain disposition and a certain motive.

It is not a question, then, whether the state shall try to enforce moral duties or not; the very conception itself is unmeaning[ful], because, he goes on to say, the only motives which the state through the use of force can appeal to are fear of punishment and hope of reward, and these are non-moral motives and under certain circumstances are immoral rather than moral. So then, the kind or quality of motives which is open to the state to appeal to is such as to make it desirable for the state to restrict rather than expand its action. The only means at its command, pages 35–37, are pleasure-pain, offers of reward, and employment of physical force. Now to utilize those motives too freely would tend upon the whole to weaken morality rather than to strengthen it. Now there we have the negative aspect of Green's teaching, that is, the dualism that he sets up between the moral as strictly internal, and the political and external. However, Green is not contented to leave us with that sheer dualism between the ethical and political. He wishes to get more positive import into the sphere of organized institutional life; so he too gives that state an indirect ethical function just as Kant does, only one of greater importance. Here is his general statement: the value of institutions, of civil life, lies in their operation as giving reality to capacities of will and reason, and enables them to be exercised. That is, the individual in himself may have a moral capacity or moral disposition. Now comes the question: Can that be operative? Can it become active? Can it be exercised in a relaized form? Does it enable this individual motive and disposition to translate itself over into objective form, to become realized? If we are asking not after the possibility of a purely external capacity of morality but about the moral conduct objectively considered, the possibility of moral action on the outward side—that is, on the side of the action—the state has a very important ethical function to perform.

Put more briefly, institutions give reality to the capacity called will. Thus the sphere of political obligations, so far as they are what they should be legally, is distinguished from the sphere of moral duty. It is essentially distinct and yet relative to it. It is distinct because political obligations are capable of enforcement while the moral are not. You can insist on a man acting in a certain way. You can tell him that he must not do certain things, or that he must do certain things, but you cannot insist that he shall do them from certain motives. The motives that he does them from politically are indifferent. It is enough that he does the act. That is, if I am habitually honest and pay my debts, it is not of the slightest importance legally and politically from what motive I do it: whether I do it because it is right, or because it is good policy, or to get a good reputation that I may later on be able to steal more. As long as I do, or refrain from doing the acts, that is enough for the state.

On the other side the sphere of the legal and political is relative to moral duty because only through this legal organization, only through the possession of rights and the obligation on the part of others to observe these rights, can the power of the individual freely to make the common good his own have reality to it. Rights are what may be called the "negative realization" of his power to make the common good his own (p. 45). The habit of acting for the common good is the essence of morality. It is that common good that is substituted by Green for Kant's universal law, and on that account Green is less abstract than Kant. He has the conception of a good which, when realized by one, furthers, helps on the interests of all; that is, a good so common that when the individual acts to bring it into effect, he by that fact enables others to participate in it also. Without these institutions, then, and the rights and obligations that go along with them, the individual cannot, or at least is not certain to, make his interest in the common good effective.

So then, rights are the negative realization of this power to bring about a common good. They realize it in the sense of providing for its free exercise; but they do not realize it positively, because their possession does not imply that in any active way the individual makes a common good his own. If the individual wants to act out of regard for the common good, the legal and political sphere will enable him to do so; but if he does not want to do it, there is no assurance or guarantee that he will do it.

I was going to raise the question later on, but perhaps it will be well here, as to whether this equilibrium is a stable or unstable equilibrium. Can you go as far as Green does in ascribing a moral function to the state without going further? Now Green states in so many words that of course it is not merely the external act to which the legal procedure has reference.

The mere fact that one man kills another does not make him a criminal, does not subject him to the action of a political superior. You must establish intention; that is, intention is necessary to an act. He says that expressly on page 36: "An act necessarily includes intention." If the act does include the intention, and if the law takes account of intention, how can you say that it deals simply with the external? Green says it is not a determination of the will as arising from certain motives and certain dispositions, and he goes on to say that a certain motive, say fear of punishment . . . but here, while it does affect action on its inner side, it does this simply for the sake of the external act. "Its business is to maintain certain conditions of life, to see that certain actions are done which are necessary to the maintenance of these conditions, others omitted which would interfere with them. It has nothing to do with the motive of the actions or omissions, on which, however, the moral value of them depends." These two questions come up: Can you draw this line between intention and motive; between aim and disposition?

In the second place Green himself admits that the law does appeal to one motive; that is, when it threatens punishment, it at least tries to influence a man by appealing to his motive of fear of pain. Thus it does affect action on the inner side, but he says it does so simply for the sake of the external act. Supposing it does. We now have the political in the sphere of motive. Now having admitted it there through that back door, are we justified in saying that the state can appeal only to that motive? How does it happen that the only motive which the state, or society, can get at should be simply this low one of the hedonistic kind? To put the two questions together in a more empirical manner: Can you make any division between motive on one side and external act on the other? Are motive and external act anything more than correlative abstractions that arise in the process of realizing conduct? That point was discussed last quarter. The answer being in the negative, I shall not go over that whole matter again. But supposing that the state does influence motives simply for the sake of influencing the external act. Is there any object of controlling the motives of anybody excepting that it is the way in which you do [?] control his activity? Or putting it practically: Can you really be sure of controlling the action of a man as long as you appeal merely to his fear of consequences, or to his hope of consequences? If it is admitted that the state for the sake of controlling acts does influence motive, why should it not be permitted to make a thoroughgoing job of it, that is, to do it in the most effective possible way? Supposing you were trying to influence the conduct of an individual and you felt that you had appealed to him only so far as his fear of consequences was concerned. Would you not feel that you only had a partial hold upon him? As long as the pressure of fear is on him you will have some hold on him, but when that becomes uncertain you will not have any real hold on his action.

Is not the action which Green allows wholly inadequate to the end?

The end is to secure a condition which will make the common good realizable, which will put it into operation. Is there not a tremendous gulf between simply personal fear of consequences and the maintenance of conditions for the realization of the common good? Will a man who has not some positive interest in the common good be interested in maintaining the conditions necessary to the common good? Can you get him to do that simply by appealing to his sense of bad consequences to himself?

If we had time to go over the specific questions which Green discussed in a very interesting way—the sovereignty of the state, the right of the state to punish, the right of the state over the individual in war, the right of the individual to life and liberty—you would find that Green is continually vacillating between the two sides, the dualistic and the organic side of his conception of the relation. When he is going ahead, following the swing of the concrete subject matter, his tendency is to emphasize the rights and obligations affording the material for the realization of the common good, making the individual see the common good, making him take an active interest in it, and securing him in his interest against interference and interruption from others so that he can devote himself in a full and efficient manner to it. When he comes back to his preconceived theories, he begins to hedge and point out that we can only do that in an external and negative way. On page 131, where he is talking about force as not the basis of the state, he says: "The state is an institution for the promotion of a common good." And on page 133 he says that the state, because it does exist for the sake of a common good, is a moral institution and not a physical institution. In a number of places he says that the only reason the individual is given rights at all is on the presumption that he is a moral being and it is assumed that he is interested in the common good and that he will exercise his right in such a way as to contribute to it, and that it is only in cases where this principle is violated that the state comes in as a coercive agent instead of a reinforcing instrumentality.

I will have to leave you to carry that out further. Green is the oldest of the English writers on this subject of political obligation. I hope you will find an opportunity to read his statements for yourselves. The point I want to suggest is that here is an attempt to distinguish the legal and political from the moral and yet to give the political a definitely moral basis and a moral function.

The question, as I stated before, is whether there is an unstable adjustment set up there, whether if you get so far you must not go further or else make the dualism still more complete and go back to the position of liberalism and hold that the function of the state is simply economical, to assist or prevent interference in the satisfaction of moral aims. Can you ascribe any ethical function to the state unless you are willing to admit that the regulations of society intrinsically affect the consciousness of the individual? The peculiarity of Green and Kant is that they limit the state to the external act, not letting it in to operate, to affect intrinsically the conscious process itself, and yet attempt to give it a moral import. Is not that a contradiction in terms? If the state is confined simply to the external you must draw one of two conclusions: either that it is confined simply to the external and therefore has no moral significance, or it does have moral significance and therefore the whole dualism between external and internal breaks down. You cannot shut up the individual motives in the individual's breast apart from action in any such way.

E. Another view I will call E [is] that of modern socialism. If we regard the older liberalism as economic and the view of Kant and Green as quasi-ethical, modern socialism is the culmination of the two—that is, of the economical and at least the quasi-ethical.

April 13, 1898

In discussing this socialistic conception of the relation of social organization to moral conduct in the individual, I do not find it possible to refer explicitly to any one author, as the point of view is rather involved in the discussion; but the continual assumption that you will find in at least a certain number of the socialistic writers, so far as they discuss the ethical aspects at all, is that all selfishness is the result of a premium put upon egoistic conduct by existing economic arrangements, that the present competitive system is one which positively requires of the individual, whether he would naturally wish to or not, to make his own private gain, his own individual end, the supreme object of his endeavors; otherwise he cannot live at all. The capitalistic and competitive regime is by its very nature one which stimulates the individual in an egoistic direction; and the legal institutions which make supreme the present economic system are all of a kind simply to protect and guarantee the individual in his selfishness, being build finally upon the institution of private property.

That conception is as old as Plato. If you read in his *Republic* his arguments for communism, you will see that they are primarily ethical. The ideal is the unity of the state and that every individual should feel the interest of the whole as his own interest and act upon it, but the institution of private property, and according to Plato that of private family, makes it a practical necessity that the individual should conceive certain ends in a narrow way, that he should attempt to appropriate certain things for himself and exclude others from him, and so it is a contradiction to try to get thorough organization of effort for the common welfare when any man can appropriate a thing to himself and base his ends upon it. The modern socialist rarely goes to the extreme of Plato, but you will see it continually assumed that if you have common ownership and state control of industries and economic operations put on a common basis, all the motives that exist now for objective egoistic conduct will be done away with. The individual will have equal regard for the welfare of others simply because he will have no reason for not doing so. Beyond this point there does not

seem to be any very consistent theory as to whether this resulting benevolence of conduct will simply have this negative guarantee or whether there
is some posiitve guarantee back of it in the very constitution of human
nature. Various writers are not very clear, nor do they agree with each
other. Some go no further than simply to say that the motive for selfish
conduct will be removed; others go so far as to say with Rousseau that man
is by nature good and that institutions have made him bad, so that if you
can only change the external conditions, the natural social instincts and
benevolence in the individual's nature will have an opportunity to assert
itself. In the latter case there is a virtual assumption of some universal
factor in the individual's nature which needs only a fair chance in order
to show itself and make itself valid.

All the five shades of opinion presented have a common theoretical
principle as their basis: that is, the assumption of a dualism between what
is termed the inner and the outer, the assumption of a dualism between the
conscious self of the individual and the world, both of society and of
nature, in which that self exists. It is very frequently assumed that the
question of the relation of consciousness to the external world, the objective world, is simply a metaphysical speculation at most with no practical
interest attaching to it. But as matter of fact all these concrete political
and economic views that we have been discussing are so many workings
out of that metaphysical assumption that consciousness is one thing which
somehow inheres in the given subject, and that the world, nature, is another, and that the relation between these two is at most external.

If we were to go at the problem historically it could be shown that
this metaphysical dualism is simply the formulation of the practical dualism
of the social and the economic. That is where the inability of the Greeks
is seen, particularly of Plato who formulated the thing, to find any way
to unite the supposed higher spiritual and moral nature of man with his
lower appetites and wants, which were regarded as physical and simply
economic. This finally worked itself out in a rigid metaphysical dualism of
the world of self-enclosed spirit of mind on one side, and of the equally
self-included and self-comprehended world of physical nature on the other.
However, the point of interest here is simply the limitation of the conception of selfhood, of consciousness to the particular ego or individual
regarded as an entity, as a being, a thing, which exists somehow, and then
has around it and outside of it certain external conditions.

As I think was brought out incidentally at least in discussing the [five]
views, it is assumed in all cases that the moral has a purely internal origin
and aspect lying entirely in the conscious motivation and disposition of the
individual; that the social sphere, the institutional sphere, has no way
directly and intrinsically, organically, of getting at and developing that
internal consciousness, but is limited to the sphere of external acts and
conditions, and reacts, indeed, to a certain extent, vary[ing] in the views of
different schools, in this internal consciousness. The most you can say is

that the external conditions indirectly modify consciousness, but they are not supposed to be involved in and necessary to the process of consciousness in the formation of motive and in the building up of the individual. That is what I meant by saying that there is a certain psychological theory of the self involved in the whole discussion.

Comparing the various views with each other, it must be said that from one point of view Hobbes's theory is the most consistent. If the self is an independent, given existence, then an atomic egoism—that is, the war of each against all—would be the legitimate outcome. All the other theories, therefore, represent departures, to a certain extent, from the assumption of the individual as an absolutely given entity. The factor of likeness, or similarity, or, in Kant's case, of absolute identity between the different selves, is introduced. Or as in the case of liberalism and of socialism, even if there is no explicit theory as to how there comes to be this like element in the different selves, it is practically asserted that there is such.

Now these departures from the logical rigor of individualism as found in Hobbes make it possible to square the theories much more with the existing state of things. But after all there are contradictions, there are compromises. They consist in smuggling in factors which have no business there and which simply contaminate the purity of the doctrine. If you start with the assumption that the self is a fixed existence, what would it mean even if you were to find out that a number of these different selves did have something resembling each other in them, or that they had something common, identical?—there would be still the peculiarity of the individual. If a person is cut off, isolated, the fact that there is something in his makeup like other people would be an interesting scientific fact, but it would not change the intrinsic quality or makeup of his being. It would be an interesting fact if we were to find a thousand different animals with the same kind of a stripe on the back, or with the same coloring or markings; but as long as we conceive an animal as a thing, as a pure object, and not as a process, that community of trait would simply be a peculiarity which would be interesting but would not militate against the fact that each one of these was just itself and nothing else; it would not introduce any real community. If you were to find that they had that common trait simply because there is a common process of life involved in them all, that these thousand different animals are genetically all differentiations of one and the same process, then of course the thing would be different: this common trait then would be a sign of some real intrinsic organic community, not because it is a common trait, but because as a common trait it has been shown to witness to a common ancestry which under varying circumstances has branched out in all this variety of forms. From that point of view the animals cease to be given things—they are differentiations within a unified process. Now the same way here; if these resemblances between different individuals were used to reconstruct the whole theory, if they were used as proofs that there is a single conscious process, and that the different selves, the different individuals, represent a variety of organs and agents with reference to that single social process, then the fact of resemblance and of community would have a positive social significance. As long as you conceive consciousness as something shut up within a given individual as his possession, and upon which other things and other people simply operate in a more or less external and mechanical way, the basis for interpreting this common element or this like element as intrinsic ethical community of purpose is entirely lacking.

Summing up that criticism, what I want to suggest is that the question of the social or nonsocial character of the individual is not a question of the content or of the structure of the individual. It is a question of what kind of a process the individual represents just as an individual. I alluded to that point the other day indirectly in speaking of Mr. Baldwin.* It seems to me that the point where he, in common with that whole school, goes astray is in the more or less conscious assumption that you cannot establish the social character of the individual until you can find in the content of his consciousness something like somebody else's.

A composite is not a universal, and an individual who was a mosaic, made up out of pieces of individuals, would no more be social than when he started out. It would be an interesting fact if he was constituted in that more or less composite way, taking by imitation and putting together the elements taken out of other people; but if that were all there were to it, you might as well call the mosaic social because it is made up out of a lot of bits of rock, or as to call the composite photograph a universal. It is inevitable, when you try to find sociality on the side of content, that you will make your criterion purely quantitative, and then you have no further criterion for telling how much or how little of this agreement or identity of content you must have between different individuals to constitute that sociality.

Now the other point—which seems to me the only point of view of any psychological portent—would put the question: What kind of a process does the individual stand for? What is the mechanism, the form of that consciousness which we call individual? What is it that initiates it? What stimulates it? In what direction, toward what ends does it function? No matter how individual it is in its form, if we find that in its genesis it is social and that in the part which it plays, in the service which it renders, in its outcome or function, it is social also, then we would call it social even if in its content you could not find a single element which was like an element found in any other personality. On that basis the criterion is the quality of the process that is going on, the value of the process that is going on, and not any particular thing that you can pick out here or there within them. The whole process of development is recognized to be the process of differentiation.

* Apparently an incorrect reference.

That is, if you compare biologically the higher type of organism with the lower, the ground on which one is classed higher than the other is precisely that there is greater variety of structural organs within it than in the lower organism where the same tissue will perform many functions while in the higher the tendency is to specialize, set apart one particular structure for the performance of one function. Now we have on the biological side passed through the same transformation of the criterion of judgment that we must pass through on the social side. If you take the preevolutionary biology, its theory of classification is simply the finding of objective identification. Plants were put together, or animals, belonging to the same family or same genus because you could find features which were regarded as characteristic, alike, or common in them all; and thus there grew up the theory of organic structural types which were somehow embodied in the great variety of species and of individuals.

The theory was carried out by Agassiz [4] most consistently and logically. There you have the same assumption that the principle of organization is simply identity of content and the problem on that theory is the same as that of Aristotle and Plato, the relation between this generic structural element and the purely individual. What is the relation between the genus and the individual? How far does the individual go and where does he merge into the generic and how do you hitch these together in one and the same being? You get the whole metaphysical problem of the relation of the universal and individual because you are conceiving your universal as simply an affair of objective content instead of a dynamic process in the continuity of development. From the modern biological standpoint the very differentiation may become your proof, your evidence of organic connection or organic unity. If you go into a factor and find different people doing very different things, you do not say: What chaos there is here, what lack of system and organization. You would take that very specialization as an evidence of system, of a controlling and comprehensive unity, provided you could find that all these specialized activities contributed dynamically to each other, that there was a common end to which each was relative, and with reference to which each one somehow reinforced each of the others. It is precisely that same point of view which must be carried out in the social psychology, to stop conceiving of the individual as an objective entity, the sole criterion for whose sociality is the finding of certain identical elements of content, and conceive of the individual as a process and then ask: What is the relation of this process, no matter how different in form from every other, to the processes of others?—to see whether there is any community of organs and of function or outcome.

To apply that briefly to the topic which will occupy considerable time later on—the phrase social consciousness: many of those who hold there is such a thing and many of those who deny it take as their standard of interpretation and criticism, either consciously or unconsciously, the idea that social consciousness would be a particular kind of consciousness, that is, would be a consciousness of certain things, or a consciousness inherent here, there, or somewhere else. Now from the standpoint of what I have been saying, the meaning of the phrase would be simply asking after what any consciousness really is. It is not a question as to whether there is a consciousness over and above the individual consciousness, or whether the individual has another kind which is somehow social. It is an inquiry after the nature of consciousness wherever you find it. What sort of thing is consciousness as a process? Is it anything which can be predicated in any intelligent sense of an individual, or is the very nature of consciousness as a process such that we must call it social?

The whole case is prejudged because of the almost universal assumption that consciousness is already owned by some individual, and then you have a peculiar problem on hand of how it is that the consciousness which is purely individual can also be, or become under certain conditions, social. The very theorists who will assume that consciousness is purely individual and who ridicule the conception of social consciousness as a piece of meaningless metaphysics will be equally ready to ridicule the problem of individual consciousness when it is not labeled that way, but has all the implications of it. For instance, you perceive this table. Does that table belong to you? Is that table a mere state in your consciousness? The same man would ridicule the idea of there being anything in the term social consciousness, who would waive it aside as a piece of transcendental metaphysics, would actually laugh at the idea of that table as a state in his own mind. If consciousness is simply individual, why is not that table a state of your own consciousness? Or if that table which you perceive is something more than a state of your own consciousness, how can you avoid the conclusion that consciousness is at least universal, is something which the individual does not own and appropriate but—if we are going to use that metaphor—is something which does control the individual? That universal that is involved there in seeing that this table is objectively a table is really a social factor. That is, the fact that we can know anything as a thing is itself a proof of the social character of consciousness.

All this is simply anticipating, but I want to bring out the root of the problem. It lies in this, whether we are to conceive of self and consciousness as a fixed existence, the criterion for whose sociality is to be found in certain elements of content; or whether we are to conceive of it as a process, the criterion for its sociality being what kind of a process it is considered on one side as to its genesis, and on the other side as to how it operates or the functions it fulfills.

I do not think it would be worthwhile to criticize other views. I would simply point out that socialism states the problem as its own solution. That is, socialism as an end insists upon existing actual diversity and opposition of interests. It paints the picture of existing society according to which existing society is practically what Hobbes said the state of nature was when the hand of every man is turned against every other man, every individual trying to get the greatest quantity of economic good for himself, and because of that egoistic exploitation treading everybody else down or trying to make them subservient to his own interests. The ideal of socialism sets up an absolute community of ends and a thoroughgoing cooperative system where the activities of everybody reinforce those of everybody else. Of course that is the formulation of the problem in the most extreme form. There is the whole thing taken for granted, the actual opposition and conflict, the ideal unity and community of organization. It states the factors of any social problem and makes a demand for the solution, while on the other hand it states this problem in such an extreme form, without any connecting links, without any process of mediation, so that logically it seems to leave us with the very contradiction itself. It states the problem in such a way that there can be no solution. The very completeness with which they state community cooperation as the ideal state of things, and the abrupt way in which each is set over against the other, makes it practically impossible to find any solution, any transition from one set of terms over to the other. If man is naturally so social, if that is his normal condition of things, then how did things ever get as bad as they are? Why should the actual be so entirely opposed to this natural state of things? Or from the other end, if the existing economic system is so thoroughly egoistic, and if that is the natural expression of man's tendencies, how are you going to get any guarantee for any other state of things?

Now the reason that I mention that is because logically socialism seems to me to present, reduced to its lowest terms, the elements of the problem—of the relation of the individual to the universal. The real question is to discover the universal in the individual or the individual as universal, to discover a much more organic connection between the actual and the ideal than socialism finds, or else give up the whole job as a bad business and say that human nature is so bad that it naturally expressed itself in the evils of society, and there is no hope, unless we get a millennium or find a Utopia, of having anything more than incidental improvements in detail here and there.

SECTION 2. THE ROLE OF PHYSICAL STIMULI IN CONTROLLING CONSCIOUSNESS AND ITS RELEVANCE TO THE RELATIONSHIP BETWEEN ECONOMICS, POLITICS, AND ETHICS

April 14, 1898

The point I was making yesterday was that the problem of the psychology of the self is involved in all the political theories advanced and that the chief point there was the principle of interpretation for determining whether or not the self is social or what the universal quality of the self really means. That carries with it a subordinate question, still on the psychological side, the relation existing between the self and acts, as to whether the act [has] involved in it an element which is external to the self as self, and also the question of the relation between motive and intention—between the reason for doing an act and what one aims at in doing it. That point was touched on in the discussion of Green.

Leaving that point there, then, the second main problem involved on the psychological side is the question of the relation between consciousness and the stimuli which are used to affect or modify or control action which proceeds from that consciousness. The point that I was discussing yesterday was the relation between the self and the manifestations of the self, the relation between the ego and the output from the ego. The question I just suggested involves the same principle, but from the other end—not the relation between what the self does and the self, but what is the relation between the influences which are used to direct self and the self. It is obvious that one consciously acts on another only through the medium of the physical world. Even in such apparently direct transmission of thought as we have in language, it is true that we have at first the translation of the thought of one in terms of physical agent, and then those physical agents in turn being interpreted by the consciousness of the other. Now in political organization it is clear that in every case it is certain regulations, requirements, commands, expectations which are manifested in terms of physical agencies which modify the conduct of the individual. The political regulations which remain merely in the region of subjective consciousness would certainly never be political, never would be legal. It always calls for a certain kind of overt acts and it always utilizes something existing in the nature of overt action, some sort of physical condition or stimulus of some sort to control the action of the individual. Take the case on the political side of punishment. Shutting a man up or taking his life, or fining him a certain amount of money is evidently the utilization of certain physical conditions to induce a state of consciousness. Now the underlying question involved there is: What is the relation which exists between the stimulus to consciousness and the consciousness itself?

We may have there three types of theories.

First, that the physical stimulus influences action through the medium of consciousness only because it arouses certain feelings of pleasure and pain, or arouses the expectation of such feelings; as when you tell a man that if he does a certain thing you will thrash him, and the fear of the pain of the thrashing enters into his consciousness so that it controls his future action. Or a man is led to believe that if he labors so many hours a day he will get so much wage and that he can secure a certain amount of pleasurable feeling with that wage, and that anticipation leads him to act in a certain way. That is virtually the theory that is found in Hobbes, which is found in the liberal school and which is found in Green, on the negative side of Green of which I have spoken, where he denies any direct moral function to the state on the ground that the only way in which the state can get at motives is in the region of fear, the expectation of pain or of pleasure.

Another view would be that the individual brings into the world with him ready-made a number of faculties, of innate powers and capacities, and that the physical stimulus is necessary simply to set these off. Physical stimulus represents the turning on of steam, or the pressing of the electric button that will set the conscious machinery going. It is all there in a latent, dormant condition, whatever those adjectives may mean; but it will not operate, it cannot find actual exercise until contact with the external world sets it off. This sort of relationship between the stimulus and the psychical power is assumed, but after all it is of the most external kind. You have two things, just as much as hydrogen and oxygen are separate from each other, and you will not get reaction until these two distinct things are brought into contact with each other.

The third theory would be that what we term the stimulus is in reality an integral part of the process of consciousness, that the distinction between the psychical power on one side and the physical stimulus on the other is simply a distinction which is made in the analysis of the whole process of conscious experience.

Now according of course as we adopt one or another of these theories psychologically, we will get a very different conception of the relation between political authority and moral conduct. The positive physical element involved in the institution which serves to stimulate and arouse the individual could not be regarded as anything external; it would have to be regarded as entering into the process of his coming to consciousness so that the dualism between the political and ethical would break down. On the basis of the other theories, we still maintain the dualism between them.

The whole question comes to its head in this problem which is essentially involved in the discussion of the nature of the political authority or in the nature of sovereignty. That is, what is the relation between will and force? Will is evidently the generalization of the ethical, the ideal, the psychical factor. Force is evidently the statement of the physical stimulus in its most general terms. Now you will find that the dualism between the political and the ethical always reduces itself on the psychological and physical sides to this assertion of some radical distinction between will and force. The ethical is conceived to be the sphere of will and the political is conceived to be the exercise of force. One theory only, that of Hobbes, attempts to carry this distinction out rigidly; but the rest of these theories are trying to make some kind of bridge over to connect these radically unlike factors.

I am trying simply, here, to bring out the problem. At the same time I am anticipating in a general way the solution that I shall try to advance, but mainly I want to bring out that there are psychological assumptions involved in this problem, and the kind of psychology that we work out will control the conclusions we arrive at on the side of political philosophy. One reason that there is so much argument in this sphere with relatively so little advance is precisely because there is no thoroughgoing analysis of the underlying psychological concepts. The analysis is on the surface until we get back to the fundamental question of the relation between the agent's disposition and his act, and the relation existing between the stimuli which direct his action on one hand and his acts on the other.

In noticing this latter point, namely, that all political agency must be exercised through the medium of the physical world and involves the exercise of force, we have prepared the way for discussing the next question: the relation between economics and politics and ethics. The part which the world of nature plays in politics, while perfectly real, is subordinate. Our interest is in the way these physical agencies are used; but when we come to the discussion of economics, the interest then is precisely in this question of the physical world and its relation to the individual and to consciousness. The economic relationship is the relationship between the wants of the individual on one side and nature, which is supposed to provide the material for the satisfaction of those wants, or the means for the functioning of the activities, on the other side.

I wish to point out that the underlying psychological and philosophical dualism set up between individual consciousness and the external world will also be reflected in the underlying assumptions of economics. If we compare for a moment the relation which is assumed to exist between the individual and nature on the economic and political side, the popular assumption is this, that the economic relation is the natural one between the individual and the physical world, while the political one is relatively an artificial one. Naturally the world of nature is there just to give the satisfaction to our wants or appetites, to supply material for fulfilling our demands. We have certain wants and here are things which are adapted to the meeting of these wants. That is a purely direct and natural relationship, so natural that it is often treated as if it were practically simply an animal relationship, excepting that man has an intelligence which the animal has not and therefore is capable of manipulating the adjustment of the materials of nature for the satisfaction of his wants in a way that the animal has not, but that, apart from the superior intelligence of man with the greater control of nature which it gives, the economic process is practically identical with the animal on the biological side. But it is supposed that on the political side these natural means are used through the intervention of the government as more or less artificial instrumentalities for producing certain results in the individual. That a man should take cotton fiber and attempt to make it into cloth to satisfy his demand for physical comfort, decoration, etc., would be regarded as perfectly natural. That somebody should attempt to control the way in which he did that so as to produce a certain state of mind in him, or so as to set up a certain other end for his action, would be regarded as involving a certain amount of legal or political interference and control, and in that sense as artificial.

This conception of the economic process is expressing the natural relationship between the individual and the physical world, while the political expresses a relatively artificial attempt on the part of somebody or other to adjust one of these to the other in such a way as to bring about some moral motive, is, I think, what underlies the popular definitions of ethics, economics and politics in their relations to each other. Economics is supposed to have to do with natural values, that is, values in the way of the satisfaction of the natural wants and appetites of the human being.

The ethical is distinguished from that by being concerned with the moral good, that moral good being somehow marked off from the natural goods which satisfy man's economic wants and desires; and politics comes in either to adjust the ethical to the economic, to establish some sort of equilibrium or external adjustment between them, or else it comes in to adjust one phase of the economic process to another phase. That is, according to Kant and Green, it would come in to get some kind of equilibrium between the individual natural tendencies, which would find their expression in the economic side of his activity, and his higher and spiritual or moral nature, finding its expression in ethical conduct. Or according to the liberal school and Spencer, it would come in simply that the economic activities of one [man] to find satisfaction for his appetites might not unduly interfere with similar efforts on the part of other people.

In the more popular conception, while the economic region is conceived as that of egoism, the economic process is the one in which the individual as individual seeks for his own private personal desires. The ethical process is the altruistic one in which the individual either conquers his natural selfishness or egoism, or lets another part of his nature have play; and the political comes in again to keep some kind of equilibrium and adjustment, to keep these things from interfering with another, to keep one's ego from encroaching on another ego, to restrict these natural tendencies of the ego to certain limits, or to make a balance between the egoistic tendencies of men and their altruistic tendencies.

I would like to make a brief digression here. I do not know how many of you are engaged in studying some line of social study—either economic, sociological, or political science—but I would like to say that all I am going to give in this course is certain general principles and that their value is found simply in their value as method. What you get out of it will be the extent to which you will take the ideas and utilize them with reference to some specific social subject matter. I would like to give it from that point of view as far as possible, to give you an instrument for thinking more deeply and criticizing more adequately the categories which you are using in your own thinking, whether historical, economic, or socialistic. I would like to ask you to keep this point particularly in mind, to ask yourselves all the time, what is the underlying psychological assumption there, what sort of a self is presupposed, and how is that self supposed to operate, to be stimulated to activity with relation to other people and with relation to nature?

This question has not been examined very thoroughly in literature. The only book is Bonar's discussion of the relations of economics to philosophy,[5] and that is valuable as a statement of facts rather than from any great depth of interpretation. On the side of facts you will find a good deal of material there that would be of use to you. If you read the account of James Mill and John Stuart Mill, you will see how definitely and how consciously that whole school of economic theory was built up on the basis of psychological assumptions; or if you will read John Stuart Mill's section on the logic of the social sciences in his *Logic* or the early essay [6] which he wrote on the method of political economy, you will see that his psychological assumptions are those of the English sensational and associational school.

That psychology is practically discredited today among psychologists. The economic theories have not made use of the new psychological categories to restate its own matter. What I have said is also true of the general theories in political science. So far as the English theories are concerned, they are based on the psychology of Locke, Hobbes, and Hume. And even in sociology, where not having the traditions behind it it might have been expected to utilize the modern psychological methods, you will find in many authors that the psychological assumptions are of (I will not say a prehistoric character) the psychology of the eighteenth century rather than of the last half of the nineteenth.

I would like to suggest some of the influences which have tended to modify the rigid separation theoretically set up between the economic and political and ethical spheres, the historical influences, I mean, which have arisen from practical or scientific motives, not from any conscious formulation of the problem on the philosophic side.

The so-called historical school working independently in jurisprudence and in economics has discovered continual interdependence and interaction of the economic and political factors. The general theory of jurisprudence up to the present century was always entirely *a priori* and abstract, but particularly, beginning with the influence of the followers of Hegel in Germany and of Savigny* in his investigations of Roman Law, the theory has been worked out legally in the present century. That historical school has shown as matter of fact that the system of political organization and of political rights and duties which obtains at any given time is always a reflex, to a considerable degree, of the industrial habits or the industrial type of social organization found; that a simple agricultural

---

* Friedrich Karl Von Savigny (1779–1861), founder of historical jurisprudence. He found the origin of law in custom and the actual will of the people, rather than pure reason.

community may be said to have a different form of organization of government from a commercial community, or from a manufacturing community, or that when one industrial class is uppermost, say the landed interest or the banking interest, you will have at once modifications in a purely political system and so far as any organization has been discovered for the evaluation of political form it has been the economic and industrial ones; that the political side tends to follow and to guarantee, to reinforce the prevailing types of industrial life.

Now the historical school in economics, as distinct from the older abstract school, has reached an analogous conclusion from the other end. The criticism of the German economists upon the English school amounts to saying that there is no such thing as the isolated man with his industrial habits as was presented by the followers of Adam Smith, but that the leading status of society always has to be taken into account in determining what men will do economically.

April 19, 1898

This relativity, mutual dependence between the industrial organization and the political, which I mentioned at the last time as having been brought to light through the investigations of the historical school, has been one of the influences, on the scientific side at least, which has furthered the development of the socialistic theory. The German school of socialism take this mutual dependence as discovered by historical investigations as part of its fundamental data and goes on from that to assert the necessity of a new and different political organization in order that different economic processes may be carried on or that different ideals may come to control the industrial processes.

From a more theoretical standpoint than the consideration advanced at the last time, the liberal school has tended to do away with the distinction between the political and the economic by holding up the economic as the most adequate mode of control. I think it can be said without exaggeration that the underlying assumption of James Mill and his followers in Great Britain was that political organization in governmental form is a rude and clumsy way of getting results which can be got much more economically and expeditiously through the natural play of supply and demand of economic tendencies. The government at best, from this point of view, is rather a bungling apparatus for trying to do in an external way what can be done automatically in an internal way through the development of commercial relations themselves, provided you have sufficient intelligence to regulate that economic play.

As I mentioned the other day, the attack of the liberal school on the extension of governmental functions, its plea for the reduction of them to a minimum, and its adoption of the laissez-faire doctrine is based on the assumption that the interests of men may be most effectively served when left to the natural, free play of individual attempts to satisfy their respective wants and in the growth of mutual dependence that accompanies this. Government, according to this school, is really necessary only when there is ignorance on the part of individuals as to what their real interests are, or when barriers to the satisfaction of these wants have been set up by previous governments and some overt stop has to be taken to get rid of them.

Spencer in his *Sociology* [7] has presented the theoretical justification of this position better than anyone else and I will refer you to Volume I, Part II, Chapters IX and X on The Regulating System and on Social Types and Constitutions. The whole point of the chapter on the regulating system is that government, in the ordinary sense of government, arises on an external basis through the necessity of defense and attack when you have different societies isolated from each other without any common basis; but that as social interaction grows more complicated, as the walls of division between various societies are broken down, an internal system of regulations based on the needs of various individuals and classes within the society arises, and it suggests that on the whole the greater part of social regulation today is exercised not by the formal medium of government but by the various agencies by which the individual makes his wants known and secures satisfaction for them. The great railroad corporations, the banking interests, if we look at the thing really and not only as far as names are concerned, are exercising political control; they are positive regulating functions. They set the great limits for human activity, and a large part of the legislation is really nothing but ratifying, or else formulating, the modes of social control which have been independently worked out in the industrial organization itself.

In the next chapter he classes the industrial type over against and higher than the militant type, the military type being that in which formal government exercises control in directing one state in its hostilities against another, but as the hostility grows less, the internal regulating system based on the actual organization of agriculture, manufacture, and commercial exchange grows up. The progress of society, then, according to this view, means that political control is located more and more in, and is exercised more and more by, the economic processes themselves, and that government is continually regulated more and more to the background simply as a sort of last resort when the more natural economic mode of control breaks down. One school of modern anarchy simply carries this position to its logical extreme, holding that governmental control is in all cases ineffective and unjustifiable, and that the whole control of society must be found in the mechanism of the play of the industrial forces.

As regards the relation of the political process and the economic process to the ethical, the same point may be made, that the investigation of these subject matters from the historical standpoint has shown that as matter of fact ethical practices have grown up along with and out of both the industrial organization of society and its political organization, and that in turn political organization, at least, has been effective only insofar as it did grow out of and express the general moral sentiment and ethical beliefs of the community; that as matter of fact as revealed by all ethico-logical and anthropological study, primitive forms of government were conceived of as not only moral but as under religious sanction; that the very conception of the separation of moral from the political is, compara-tively speaking, a very modern idea (what is known as separation of church from state is a very late outgrowth); that for centuries and cen-turies through the earlier and formative periods of development the politi-cal organization was the great ethical organization, not only in theory but even more so in practice. That which was morally right was that which was expected and insisted upon by the customs of the community, and the political organization was nothing but the social customs crystallized into definite form and expressed in regular modes of procedure. So here, once more, however it is meant theoretically, it must be confessed that as matter of fact for centuries and centuries the ethical and political were more than closely connected together, they were practically identified [with each other].

On the more theoretical side we have the attack on the economic theory and practice when that is set over against the ethical. What is meant perhaps may be best got at by referring to writers like Carlyle and Ruskin who have drawn up an indictment of what they take to be the typical industrial procedures of modern society on the ground that they are thoroughly selfish and insisted that it is perfectly absurd to proclaim the supremacy in life of moral principles and then set up a sphere which is the largest part of man's activity and say that in that sphere moral principles are superseded by a set of principles which would be regarded not only as nonmoral but as positively immoral.

If we take a survey of these various considerations, we can, I think, formulate a statement which will be wholly moderate in its terms regarding this supposed tripartite division. It certainly seems natural to say that a political organization which is simply limited to the use of force, which grows out of the necessity of bringing pressure to bear on individuals, and which is restricted in its function to bringing force externally to bear upon individuals, would be a much less stable type of organization than that which grew out of the individual's own needs and nature and which suc-ceeded upon the whole in satisfying and expressing that nature. It certainly seems wholly within the bonds of reason to say that the whole develop-ment of politics in the democratic direction has been simply moving in that direction to get a form of political control which shall not be external and coercive with regard to the individual, but which the individual would feel represented his own nature, both economically and morally, so that he would identify himself with it because he does associate it with the protec-tion and the continuing realization of himself. The feeling of patriotism, or in general loyalty and devotion to the state, seem entirely unaccountable for unless we assume that the state is regarded by the individual as some way or other an organic outgrowth of himself and as something which fulfills and develops himself.

Whether we go to the extent of the liberal school and of Spencer, or not, it certainly seems within moderate limits to say that as matter of fact very much of what is consciously governmental at one time is intrusted to the automatic play of commercial forces at another. When we look at the facts of the case, how can anyone deny that the controlling agencies, that the influences which really control man's actions at present more than any others are the great commercial and industrial enterprises, and that the formal government is largely reduced to simply registering automatic industrial play or in harmonizing various phases of it so that the industrial process will run more smoothly and with less friction. The great railroad corporations in the United States certainly exercise more social regulation than multitudes of historical states and provinces ever dreamed of exercising. If you take any of the petty states into which Germany was divided, or in which all Europe was divided at one time, none of them exercised one tithe of the influence that the Vanderbilt railroad does today.

The fact is that the tendency in that direction is so strong that it becomes a political problem to prevent the government machinery from falling too much into the class that is industrially dominant. When the agricultural class is dominant you have landed aristocracy on the governmental side, and now that it has passed to the banking classes there is a tendency for laws to be made and administered on the political side in a somewhat one-sided way in the interests of this class. It is impossible to prevent political supremacy from going along with industrial domination; and whatever may be the theories of the relation of the ethical process to these others, it would seem to be true that men's working ideas as distinct from their professed moral creed are attached in the closest way to their economic practices and to their political organization. If it is true that the industrial process is simply a purely egoistic one, it is inevitable that the law of brotherly love should be reduced to a pious wish. Men must first get their living, they must establish themselves as agents, and whatever they may profess as ideals, their working ethical principles may be nearly allied to what they are actually doing for the greater part of the time in the great bulk of their endeavors.

Now I mention these points to indicate the desirability of the reconstruction on the theoretical side of the premises which underlie the assumption of three distinct processes or three distinct ends. If we are led, both on the basis of historical study and on the basis of the facts as they obviously present themselves, to question the rigidity of the separation and the division, it certainly is advisable to turn more closely to the fundamental assumptions which have made this division current, which have led people to accept it and to see if it is possible to find a theory of the relations between them which will introduce some kind of organic unity. What is the assumption then which has led to considering ethics, politics and economics as dealing with three distinct spheres, three distinct subject matters? I stated that matter briefly from the political side; now I will state it from the economic side.

SECTION 3. THE UNEXAMINED PSYCHOLOGY OF THE ECONOMIC THEORISTS

Economic theory, like political, has taken for granted the ready-made self existing in an external world which is equally ready-made. Here is nature. It is all there, the things, the objects, the forces are all there. Now into that nature is introduced practically, from without, as far as anything in nature itself is concerned, a human being who has a consciousness of his own and has wants of his own. It happens fortunately that these objects and forces of nature will satisfy the wants of the individual. But the fact that practically the two do work together, that they do show some kind of working relations to each other does not affect the underlying theoretical dualism of the world and what it is on one side, and the consciousness and its wants on the other. On the side of the individual we assume that he as an agent has certain desires already fixed in his makeup. We assume also that there is a certain scale of importance in these wants and in their satisfaction; and on the other side, we assume that all this stuff, this world, is present, simply to be seized upon by the wants and transmuted into material for satisfying them. Intelligence and action are on this theory simply intermediary, simply go-betweens. You have the fixed agent on one side and the fixed world on the other. Now that world [which] is to furnish satisfaction to the wants and intelligence somehow comes in as a convenient instrument in subordinating material to these wants; so the man's activities come in simply as intervening steps in the process of transmuting objects into the satisfaction of the wants.

The so-called ethical school in modern political economy has objected to the current statement of the economic man. The doctrine of the economic man is that the individual is so constituted that he aims at the greatest possible amount of satisfaction with the least possible expenditure of effort on his part. That is, he wants to satisfy as many desires as possible through the intervention of his intelligence and action but with the least possible use of his intelligence and of his action. He wants to save up as much of his activity as he can in order to satisfy other wants with. The ethical school objects that that is not a fair statement of the case. Besides the wants of the individual of this kind, man has also sympathetic, social desires, and some people are so constituted that they actually like to work, actually like the activity for its own sake.

But this ethical school I should say upon the whole has not brought about any large measure of reconstruction of the psychological and philosophical premises. It has simply insisted that besides these wants and tendencies as formulated in the so-called orthodox school, there are other wants and tendencies that come in to modify, direct, and that they ought to be taken account of in the formation of an economic doctrine. While on the ethical side it is important that relatively they should become more and more supreme, controlling. But it has not effected any great measure of theoretical reconstruction because it has about the same psychological basis. It does not try to show that the want itself and the process of trying to satisfy the want is of such a nature or quality that the economic process is ethical. It admits a given individual, and his appetites already given. It simply says that that is not the whole—he has some more desires which are higher than these egoistic appetites, and that the natural self ought morally to be subordinated to the higher, ethical self.

Now if we take this philosophical assumption of the dualism between the individual and the external world as the basis of current economic theory, we find that this underlying philosophic assumption is one that has been very seriously questioned on the philosophical side. There can be no question that since the formulation of philosophical dualism in the six- teenth century, growing out of the practical dualism of the Middle Ages, the movement of philosophy has been in the other direction, towards some form or other of what, comparatively speaking, is monistic. Or to make the statement as modern as possible—that the older dualism has been modified and reconstructed in the direction of recognizing some kind of fundamental relationship between subject on one side and object on the other. Now it is a serious matter intellectually when one holds at large or as matter of philosophy certain principles, but holds as matter of science, as matter of concrete detail and of working investigation, quite a different set of principles; and yet that is practically the condition that we are in intellectually, so far as the general principles themselves are concerned. The whole movement is away from this fixed dualism and towards some kind of recognition between consciousness and the world of nature, and yet we have this important branch of social inquiry practically based upon assumptions of quite a different kind. Now that kind of divorce cannot be healthy. We ought either to reconsider the thing and modify from one standpoint or the other: either bring general assumptions into line with the concrete specific inquiries, or else modify the latter so as to bring them into harmony with our underlying philosophical principles.

I do not mean that economists start out by asserting definitely this dualism. I only mean that they actually proceed as if there were a purely external relation existing between consciousness and nature, between the subject and the object; that their method is controlled by an unconscious assumption which is a relic of the time when spirit, when consciousness, was regarded practically as something injected externally and miraculously into the world. Whether it was said in so many words that consciousness was supernatural, that it was miraculously thrust into the world, is a matter of little importance. The substance of the thing was, practically, that nature would be exactly as it is if consciousness did not exist; and on the other hand, that consciousness itself in its main structure and processes would be just what it is if there were no world, or in any other world; the details of it would be modified as it went from one kind of a world to another, or it would not have been admitted that the content of consciousness, what is known, what is felt, would have been the same without the world or in some other world; but it is assumed that consciousness in the sense of capacity would be just the same in any other world or with no world at all, excepting that it would not have the chance to exercise itself, would not have the material to call it out unless there were some sort of a world for it to do it in. Now if we are in earnest with the philosophical assumption of some kind of organic connection between subject and object, if we believe that consciousness as a process involves and requires objects—and objects of the kind which we actually have—we certainly ought not to be contented with that as a pious isolated faith but ought to see that that principle takes effect, that it gets is validity by becoming an organ of specific inquiry.

Put more definitely, the economic process, on the assumption of this positive connection between subject and object, has to be conceived of as the process of the evolution of wants instead of having a being which is ready-made, either a lot of particular wants in detail or a big want that seeks to get everything that it can. You must recognize that the essential meaning of the industrial process is that it is one by which the agent is brought to consciousness of his own activity in the form of wants, and that instead of these wants having at the outset a fixed scale of value, this economic process is the process by which he learns to value his wants; he comes to consciousness of what the meaning, the worth, the significance of any want is as compared with any other want.

Or put on the side of the object, the economic process is the history of the evolution of objects. Not that we have objects already there which can be utilized and the economic process is simply how you are going to get hold of the objects and subordinate them, but it is through the tension of subject and object that the objects have come to be what they are as objects.

Putting that same idea more generically on the side of the object, the economic process is the same as the biological process. It is the evolution of the environment as an environment. On the other side the economic process is the same as the psychological process considered simply as a mechanism, taking the psychological process simply as a piece of machinery.

From the evolutionary standpoint I do not see how we can avoid regarding the machinery of mind as economic development. The getting of the sense organs, the getting of a central brain organ and the development of that brain organ would biologically have to be put on the same basis as getting claws or getting teeth or getting an erect posture. It would be simply a question of an advantage gained in the struggle for existence—and that struggle for existence is the economic process, it is the continual development of an environment through the organs to the functioning of the life process.

On the other side that would mean that the differences between the *grassa** as it is to be the various orders of life from the simplest up to man, or the difference between rock as an object, is primarily and fundamentally an economic difference. I do not mean by that that there are not other differences which may become more important, but the immediate difference is that the thing seems something different in the process of life. If we are to get at and understand the other differences, we must start from this primary and immediate difference—the fact that it has a different relation to the maintenance of the life of the individual and of the species.

Now I have simply indicated the point of view which I wish to carry out in the reconstruction, that is, the necessity of reinterpreting the economic process as equivalent to the process by which the relation between organism and environment, or, in terms of consciousness, between subject and object, have developed; and then having worked that out, to consider the bearing of that upon the relations of the economic process to the political and to the ethical.

Tomorrow I will go over the ground a little historically, particularly with reference to Plato, to suggest how, as matter of fact, the dualism formulated by Plato between spirit and matter grew out of his psychological dualism between the economic nature of man on one side, which he made material, and his ethical nature on the other, which he made spiritual.

April 20, 1898

Three ideas are inseparably bound together in Plato's statement. The industrial or economic activities in society arise out of appetites and wants, these wants arise out of the physical side, the animal side of man's nature, and are directed at or upon the material aspects of the world, their final cause or aim being simply the appropriation of these objects in order to satisfy wants in the form of giving pleasure. The appetites are in themselves essentially disorderly, essentially individualistic using the term individualistic to mean that which opposes man to man, that which is exclusive and private, and therefore anarchistic, on the side of action.

Hence it follows on the political side, as well as on the individual moral side, that the process of satisfying wants, since it is so exclusive and so materialistic in character, needs to be regulated by a higher power, by a spiritual power which is extrinsic to anything in the wants themselves—the function, as Plato termed it. In the individual the appetites and desires need to be strictly subordinated by the ends which reason sets up. Reason

* Things that move about.

must indeed permit these appetites and desires to get a certain amount of satisfaction; otherwise the individual would not live at all, but left to themselves the appetites would always go beyond the subordinate function of maintaining the individual in existence: they would attempt to overrun and appropriate his whole being. Reason comes in, therefore, to limit them in their exercise, to hold them down to their proper place. In society the industrial class is simply aiming at the accumulation of wealth as an instrument of luxury; and, hence, when it becomes the ruling class of the state, it always tends to social disintegration, hence the need in the organization of the state of a higher ruling class which shall control the working and the commercial classes, to see to it that they do not work for wealth or luxury or display, but that they be restrained, to give society its moral basis that the higher powers may have a chance to express themselves.

The whole dualism is practically summed up by Aristotle when he said that man must live before he can live nobly, before he can live ethically, spiritually. The bodily appetites and the economic process which is relative to them are necessary to give the individual and society their substrata, simply that there may be that physical existence which is the substructure of a higher ethical life. But this process in itself is mechanical, it is base; consequently it is to be turned over to slaves, and when this subclass on which society rests has done its work in providing society with its material base of supply, then there is a possibility of a higher, free, cultivated life on the part of the higher classes.

Now those three conceptions are inseparably bound up together—the economic process as connected with physical appetites (physical appetite as having its root in the animal side of man's nature, springing from the fact that he is not pure spirit or pure soul, but that his soul is lodged in a body which upon the whole is a prison to the soul); and that the aim of the wants is simply their own individual satisfaction in the form of pleasure; and that that striving for pleasure, if left to itself, is absolutely unlimited, and becomes, without any principle of limit in it, a principle of disorder and of disorganization. The beauty of Plato's and to a certain extent of Aristotle's politics and ethics is the consistency and thoroughness with which that fundamental psychological conception is carried out. Plato, to be sure, puts in a mediating element between the positive animal desires which are so disorganizing and the higher unifying organizing reason, on the other the conception of the *thumos* which it is difficult to translate into English equivalent, sometimes called spirited nature, but which is equivalent to men's generous outgoing impulses. The characteristic of the appetites is that they are all trying to draw something in to the self to get possession of it. Now these emotions, while they are feelings in a way, while they are not in themselves rational and orderly, at least have the quality of being outgoing. They do not coincide in modern phrase so much with benevolent impulses as they do with the idea of loyalty, loyalty to one's country. There is the same conception then here. It is an impulse which reaches out beyond the individual. Instead of regarding the individual as an insatiable maw into which the whole universe is to be received, these outgoing instincts will at least lend themselves to the ends of reason, to law and order.

Now the thoroughness and consistency with which this dualism was formulated by Plato (he carried it out in his cosmology and metaphysics as well), and still more the agreement of the formulation with the actual facts of society at the time, have given this view, this theory, a tremendous hold on thought ever since Plato's time. It is a category which a great many thinkers have used who professedly would have only contempt for Plato as a dreamer; but their own fundamental conception of the relation between the animal and the physical on one side, and the ideal on the other, is practically an inheritance of this formulation by Plato.

There is nothing more instructive than a careful reading of Plato and Aristotle with this point in mind, to note the way in which they refer to industry, especially to the process of manufacture and of commerce. They both give a certain amount of ethical content to agriculture, not so very positive, but that it is at least necessary to the maintenance of society, and they do not contend that the reaction in the individual is so very bad. The fact that he is simply working to satisfy his own needs is not very elevating, but it at least saves the individual from corruption. But when you come to commerce the process is wholly evil. Man is working simply for money and all he wants money for is luxury or ostentatious display, or else simply to give him power over other people. Moreover the assumption is that the man who is engaged in these pursuits must be a person who on the artistic side has a narrow horizon, a person without any liberal outlook on life, without any culture, a man who will have no sense of literature or art or social life as ends in themselves, but who looks at everything as means, for what he personally can get out of it.

Now that dualism between the industrial aspect of society and its ethical ideals has got pretty well consolidated into our habits of thinking, in spite of the fact that the industrial development of society has been so great since the time of the Greeks, in spite of the fact that it has got to the point of revolutionizing, not only the earth, but forms of political organization, in spite of the fact that modern manufacturers are carried on rather from the standpoint of the exchange, the interdependence of different peoples and classes representing different local environments, than simply for luxury, the practical conception still is that the industrial processes grow out of something which is more material, more animal, and that its end and purpose is relatively private, selfish and narrow, and that the higher spiritual and ethical aspects of civilization are somehow grafted on these, or that they are to be maintained by more or less perpetual warfare against the lower interests to prevent them from becoming predominant.

Now if we take the school which has given to the wants and desires of the individual, and to the attempts to satisfy them, the most important place—I mean the modern liberal economic school—we find that as matter of fact the assumption is now that the wants do have a principle, or organization, of generalization within them. That is, the practical assumption all the time is this belief that with free competition and a fair opportunity for every individual to get at nature, the harmonious structure of mutual interdependence and of the highest possible individual development will come about. It is now assumed that instead of intelligence, reason, having to control these lower appetitive processes from within, intelligence itself is subordinate to the feelings, to the wants, just as Hume said, on the psychological side, it must be the slave of passion. It is simply an instrument to advise the individual how best to satisfy his wants and to make him shrewd and successful in satisfying them.

But in spite of those differences there is no fundamental psychological reconstruction of the premises. The want as a ready-made possession of an isolated individual having its end and aim in feeling, that is, in getting pleasure and activity simply as an intermediary between two extremes, still remains. Students of political science who have read much in the German writers on political science will find that they all, even when professing to write from a strictly scientific standpoint, assume that there is a great distinction between society and the state. Bluntschli* lays down the doctrine that society has no unifying principle in itself, that the animating principle of society is in the cross play of private activities. Hence, society is amorphous and more or less disorganized, and only the organization of a definite authority which lays down universals will check this chaotic disorganizing play of private interests and introduce the element of regularity and of organization. Regarding the state as a sort of entity by itself, either in the socialist school or in the school in general which favors strong centralized authority, the defection of the state will be found to go back to this assumption that the individual as an individual is a purely private affair and is expressed as an individual in his wants and desires in which he is trying to secure the maximum of pleasure for himself: so the necessity of some central authority that will come in to check the purely egoistic nature of man. According to some, simply check it; according to others, gradually modify it and make it more socialized in character.

Now if we compare all this with the tendencies of modern psychology, we certainly must be conscious of a pretty wide gap. It would be pretty difficult on the basis of modern psychology to maintain the conception of any fixed distinction between higher and lower wants, between wants on one side which are purely material and impulses on the other which are ideal and spiritual. Apparently we must materialize all of them or spiritualize all of them. It certainly cannot keep Plato's naive conception any longer, that appetites which are connected with man's stomach are animal, and the tendencies which grow out of his brains are spiritual. I do

* Johann Kaspar Bluntschli (1801–1881), Swiss professor and writer on international law.

not mean that Plato literally said that, only he did assume that man's appetites were connected with his body while his reason apparently acted without any intermediary. Now we are satisfied that they are all on the same plane, that the highest thought, no matter how spiritual, has its physical concomitant, its physical instrument, as much as the supposed lowest physical appetite of food or sex.

Moreover the biological way of looking at the matter would make us conceive of a continuous relationship as existing between the so-called higher and lower, that the higher is the lower transmuted, mediated. Now if the lower is capable of such transmutation, if it lends itself to such transmutation, then it must be something more than merely lower. If in the process of development the struggle of man to get food, say, has expanded into disinterested interest in science and art, all the higher values of civilization, then we must recognize that tendency in the lower and we must interpret it from the standpoint of that capacity. It ceases to be a rigid fixed thing, set off by itself, and comes to be the most immediate instrument in which the whole value of activity has presented itself.

Put somewhat differently, we must interpret all wants from the standpoint of realization or development of the self. We must recognize that because that self, which is in process of development, is one, the wants are all organically connected with each other, the so-called lower is just as necessary, just as ethical in its place as the so-called higher, and that the higher, the nominally more ideal, is just as disintegrating in its tendencies as is the desire for food or sex if it gets out of place.

Modern psychology also tends to a changed view of the position and relations of intelligence. Of the older views we have our choice between two. From the Platonic standpoint it is an outside governing and regulating force; from the hedonistic and utilitarian point of view it is a subordinate instrument. In either case it is something extrinsic, outside of the want and the normal expansion or expression of the want. I think the statement is within the bounds of moderation when we say that the whole tendency of modern psychology is to conceive of intelligence as necessary to a conscious want, as consisting, indeed, simply in the objectification of the want. It is impossible to maintain the conception now of one power which wants, and of some other faculty which recognizes an object which would satisfy this want. The feeling of want and the intelligent consciousness of the object which will satisfy that want are seen to be two correlative aspects of one and the same process. We can no longer set feeling on one side and intelligence on the other. Feeling and intelligence are at least more organically related to each other than that.

Once more, the location of action is changing. We again have our choice of two views according to which of the older schools we adhere. Either action comes in to carry out the behests of reasons—that is, instrumental to intelligence; or that it comes in to satisfy the wants, to give us pleasure. Of course the more common view was that activity per se was indifferent. Activity is an external thing, it is muscular, not spiritual or ideal in character. It is like a crowbar, a thing which can be used for different ends according to one's own choice, so one can direct his activities so as to carry out behests or satisfy his wants, or sometimes do one and sometimes the other, but in itself it is an indifferent capacity which is ready to be turned to any use. Once more speaking about tendencies. Rather than saying that psychology has arrived at this as a conclusive result, psychology is now trying to interpret both feeling and intelligence in terms of action, to make action the chief psychological category and to define and explain the facts of feeling and the facts of thought with reference to the part which they play in the development of activity.

Now all these changes that are going on in psychology must demand a reconsideration of the underlying concepts of the social sciences, or else the psychology must be modified to meet the conditions of these concepts of the social sciences, but we cannot permanently have one set of ideas for psychological consumption and another set for use in the social sciences.

SECTION 4. CRITICISM OF
SOME CURRENT THEORIES

I am now going to give a random discussion of four or five different authors for the purpose of giving illustrations of what I have been saying, to show that I have not been setting up a man of straw. I have simply attempted to generalize the statements and have not made them applicable to any particular writer, and I will take four or five writers from different standpoints to serve as an exhibit of the theoretical statement.

Beginning I think two years ago in the *American Journal of Sociology,* there was a series of articles by Professor Ross on Social Control.[8] If you will turn to the first of these you will see that the primary assumption is that the individual left to himself is merely individual. The problem of control then is: How are you going to deflect the individual from his natural egoism into some positive regard for social welfare? It assumes there that the individual possesses wants at the outset as an individual, and that the social control has been the process of trying to bring pressure to bear on these wants so as to modify their quality and the kind of satisfaction which they demand. Not that the social process has been a process of generating wants, of leading them out, but that it has been a process of gradually modifying this original set which the individual has, so as to give them a more social coloring and evaluation. You will also find it assumed in that article that man's will is something different from his feeling and from his judgment.

Another article that I turn to is one by Dr. [Sidney] Sherwood, "The Philosophical Basis of Economics: A Word to the Sociologists," published in the *Annals of the American Academy of Political and Social Science,* 1897.[9] As the title suggests, this paper professes to give to various individuals engaged in sociological study an authoritative statement of the proper philosophic basis. I refer to this because it is the best single statement of the point of view of the ready-made individual on one side, and ready-made nature on the other, that I know of. Dr. Sherwood's primary contention is the necessity of recognizing psychical factors, postulates, in all the social sciences, and particularly that economics is essentially a science built upon psychical data which must follow the psychical method. That was rather effective to me, I thought that was good doctrine for psychologists, but when we come to see how he interprets the psychical, we get this result.

> The beginning of all knowledge is the recognition of the reality of the individual mind. The *Ego,* or the individual mind, thinks, dreams, sings, builds houses and temples and systems of theology. It works in association with other minds, like itself, and produces laws and a political organization and various social institutions . . . they are psychical phenomena (pp. 60–61).

In other words psychical is interpreted as equivalent to an operation in an individual consciousness, or as a product of that individual consciousness. You start with so many individual minds and they produce laws and a political organization and social institutions. This individual mind thinks, sings, builds houses and temples and systems of theology. I do not think it does; but that is not the point so much as is the character of that assumption. I do not think anyone ever saw an individual mind build houses and temples and systems of theology. Certainly all the minds we have ever known to do these things have been minds working under social conditions.

> Besides the reality of the psychical world which is thus proved, another fundamental primary judgment must be emphasized—namely, the separateness between this psychical world and the physical (p. 62).
> Psychical processes are thus directed by mind toward chosen ends while physical processes go on, independently of any discoverable teleology (p. 63).

Psychical processes are teleological while physical processes are purely contingent, mechanical, nonteleological. I will not stop there, but there you see is the virtual assumption that into the psychical there is introduced the element of end which is absolutely lacking in the natural. In the natural sphere we have the purely mechanical display of force. In the human another element supervenes, which so far as Dr. Sherwood says anything is absolutely externally superinduced. He does not even use the biological as a connecting link between the physical as mechanical and the psychical as teleological: ". . . psychical forces proceed from the acts of individual minds . . . and upon this individual basis the structure of society is built up and social activities are carried on" (p. 65). Or again: "The individual with his wants, his choices, and his self-directed activities, is the starting point in the scientific investigation of social phenomena and the end of all social science as well" (p. 65). You take an individual; you give him wants, choices and self-directed activities; and then you build up your knowledge of the structure of society from that—and in turn the whole structure of society comes back to the individual. Why it should come back to him I confess I do not know.

> Economics, like all the psychical sciences, rests upon this funda-
> mental antithesis between the subjective and the objective view of the
> world. It studies the relations of the individual regarding the satisfaction
> of his wants, utilizing himself, society, and nature (p. 66).

> Economic forces, . . . in their last analysis, find their beginning in
> the minds of individuals. Individuals feel wants, recognize their environ-
> ment, judge of the means necessary to attain satisfaction of these
> wants, value the relative importance of various satisfactions and the
> disagreeableness of various efforts involved, make choices accordingly,
> and pursue those ends (p. 67).

There you have the whole business. You feel wants, recognize the environment and judge of the means necessary to attain satisfaction of these
wants; that is, make the adjustments of the objects to the wants, put value
upon the satisfaction of these various wants. Now just think about the
actual facts. Take the individual who has not been brought up subject to
social control, whose sense of valuation has not been acted upon at any
point by social forces, and what wants would he feel, and what environment would he recognize, and what sense would he have of the relative
importance existing between these wants?

Then he goes on to say a good deal about choice: "All social action
is a resultant of the forces set in motion by individual wills, and science
can only explain these activities by tracing them to their starting points in
the choices of individuals" (p. 68). The very structure of society itself is
built up out of the choice of the individual and "The family . . . is the
result of the choices of individuals" (p. 68). "Always and everywhere the
individual stands alone. The kernel of his life is in himself" (p. 69).

Going on to the relation of psychology to the social sciences:

> The essential form of thought is the antithetic proposition of indivi-
> dual subject (*Ego*) to object. . . . The recognition, then, of the funda-
> mental difference between the psychical sciences and the physical is the
> first step in the classification of the sciences (p 73).

Having got the first step, the next is to ultimately coordinate them. "These
two radically opposed points of view may be harmonized by the assumption of an ultimate and essential unity in both orders of phenomena"
(p. 75).

The next thing is the relation of economics to psychology. He says:
"Psychology is . . . the science of knowing" (p. 76). Consciousness
knows. It knows itself and its environment. The next of these general
psychical sciences studies mind utilizing its environment: "Psychology may

be relied upon to do this for consciousness itself, for man as a *knowing* thing. A new general science is needed to do this for man as a *practical* thing, for consciousness in action" (p. 76). The assumption is that consciousness as consciousness is shut up, not within itself exactly, because it knows objects, but it does not act because when you get action you have a positive relation between mind and the world, and when you come to consciousness in action, man as a practical being, you must have another science, and that he says is economics. That deals with all motives which find expression in choice and in action. You have in economics a broad fundamental science, psychology being simply a side issue. You must trace back all the phenomena of social action and organization to individual consciousness.

> They [aesthetics and economics] . . . all trace, or attempt to trace, the way in which these individual mental processes become general social laws, in accordance with which masses or groups of men have the same feelings, thoughts, and judgments (p. 80).

Then the conclusion gives all the points over again.

Here is his summary of Adam Smith: "Man's wants, man's labor to satisfy these wants, man's happiness as the end to be attained, these are the things studied in the 'Wealth of Nations'" (p. 86). The underlying conception here is the individual with his wants. Growing out of these wants and the necessity of satisfying them are effort and intelligence, and the end is individual happiness. That is the psychological scheme upon which the whole is built up. Want is the beginning, man's action coming in as intermediary leading to the satisfaction of the want as an end.

As an example of how far he goes:

> If there were only one man in the world all the fundamental things of economics would still remain. Goods, utility, value, labor, capital, wealth, wants, consumption, production, dynamics. These are facts in the economic life of every man, not only as a member of society, but as a solitary individual (p. 90).

The problem which always arises where mind confronts matter is the problem of the utilization by the conscious subject of the external object.

He ends up by saying: "The term 'society' is a convenient methodological symbol which we employ for certain purposes of reasoning and which must again be translated into terms of the individual before the matter is intelligible" (p. 91).

April 21, 1898

I do not intend by any means to go over the whole ground of Ward's *Psychic Factors of Civilization*,[10] but simply to pick out one point, the distinction which Mr. Ward makes between the end for the individual, the end of nature or physical process, and the end for evolution, the latter being identified with the social end. As Mr. Ward sums it up in chapter XIII, page 80, the statement is:

1. The object of Nature is Function.
2. The object of Man is Happiness.
3. The object of Society is Action.

The latter point is also taken up more at length in Chapter XVI entitled "Social Friction."

I reviewed this book I may say, in the *Psychological Review,* Volume I, Number 4,[11] and a more extended statement of what I am going to say now will be found there.

The individual is impelled by feeling. The motive, the stimulus for all action is desire, and desire is feeling. The nature of desire is simply a memory image of a previous pleasure accompanied with the feeling of pain because of the absence of this feeling which is represented in memory. That stimulus to action, and the sole function of the activity from the standpoint of the individual, is to do away with this pain, and the doing away [with] of the pain gives a feeling of pleasure. That in rough outline is his theory of the dynamics of individual action.

The individual, while he is stimulated simply by pain, and is moving simply to get pleasure, incidentally however brings about results which he does not aim at, and which are nothing to him as an individual. For instance, the pain of hunger in itself aims simply at the pleasure of food, but it calls into operation the structures or the organs that are connected with the various processes of nutrition, and those structures, being called into activity, are modified so that a functional development of them takes place. So while the individual is not aiming at all at this development of function, while it is nothing to him (all he is after is a certain amount of pleasure), yet because he cannot get that pleasure excepting through the use of the organs and structures which develops them structurally, we get this incidental aim, and that, as Mr. Ward says, is the end or aim of nature.

> . . . the satisfaction of a desire leaves the subject in the same condition psychologically as before the desire arose. . . . In many cases it does not leave the subject in the same condition *physiologically.* This is because it results in function (p. 77).

You get the law of improvement through use, and this structural perfection renders higher organization possible.

> Too great stress cannot be laid on the fact that *function is the object of nature,* in order to bring it into sharp contrast with another new and startling fact, yet not less a fact, that *feeling is the object of the sentient being* (p. 783).

Nature cares no more about feeling than the individual does about function, but as the individual in trying to get pleasurable feeling has to build up structure, so it happens that nature through the medium of feeling can further function. Nature in itself, however, is utterly indifferent to both pleasure and pain.

Now there is a

> third something involved in the satisfaction of desire, which, for want of a better term, has been called *action*. Totally distinct in its nature from both feeling and function, it nevertheless invariably accompanies these and mediates between them as the direct consequences of the former, and the necessary condition to the latter. In itself, and except as such consequence and condition, it is utterly useless both to Nature and to the organism. To the former it is simply a mechanical means, to the latter it is a costly burden (p. 79).

To the individual it means effort and effort is costly, it is expenditure. The doctrine is that all action as such is effort and therefore is not necessary in itself, but is simply a necessary evil because it is a means which lies between the organism and the more remote satisfaction which occurs in the form of feeling. "Of what use then is it?" he asks and adds: "The only beneficiary that can be conceived of is organic progress or evolution" (p. 79). That is, action ultimately furthers the whole movement of the thing. The beneficiary, "without any forced interpretation and in a true and literal sense, [may] be called Society" (pp. 79–80). That is to say, the individual through his efforts, through his labors, is instituting changes in the environment, making material transformations which will result in benefit to other individuals. That is, it so happens that the effort that he puts forth not only involves the exercise of function and thereby builds up structure, but it also happens that it modifies the external world. The individual sows a crop of grain, his object is simply pleasurable feeling, but in doing that he will have to exercise his muscles and you can imagine some industrial pursuit of that kind carried on long enough to modify the muscular system. That goes to the credit of nature; nature is so much ahead. But in doing that he may also manure the soil, he may improve the kind of ground or seed with which he started out, he may invent plows and harrows and so on, and while to him they are simply nothing but means in order that he may get more pleasurable satisfaction, yet being modifications of the environment they persist, and thus result in the advance of society. The individual does not do it for the sake of society; man never made civilization an end of his efforts but his efforts do result in material civilization and society is the indirect beneficiary of that gain.

There are many other points of interest in Mr. Ward's attempt to change sociology from a biological science to a psychological one, as he has consciously attempted to do, but it is his attempt in his psychology to divide off these three spheres—of nature, the individual, and social progress—that I want to call your attention to, because it seems to me to be a beautiful illustration of the very natural tendency to take a single process, split it up by abstractions into different phases, and having done that, regard these different aspects as if each were a complete and independent affair in itself. Simply to suggest the reconstruction there which would bring out the unity of which we have here three abstracted phases, it might be stated as follows: Action is the primary thing. That action has to be presupposed in nature before you can get function. Function is simply that activity considered from the natural standpoint—that is, the biological standpoint. You must presuppose, before you can get pleasurable feeling, the idea of a mere feeling, a mere image of pleasure, and of course he takes an image to be simply a static intellectual copy having the power to move an organ to action. It is of course incredible. In the first place we do not get any rationalization on that basis for the existence of pain at all, and he says from the standpoint of nature, feeling is absolutely irrelevant, is absolutely unaccountable. If you mark off nature in that way, when you do run across pain you must treat it is a phenomenon of a different order, something which is absolutely inexplicable and mysterious. The other reason that it is incredible is that feeling, which is by its very nature a state of passivity, could not give rise to action. The supposition that it can shows how much less advanced the psychological science is than the physical. To conceive of feeling as feeling somehow starting off action, and not merely psychical action but physical, is exactly on the same level as trying to account for moving bodies by some other body that did not move at all but by some mysterious power started other bodies in motion!

The same thing of course is to be said in general for the wall which he sets up between structure as the object of nature and the natural goods that come about from action as being connected with progress, and particularly with social progress. It is a perfectly arbitrary thing to make a cleavage there between the two kinds of results that action has. It is true that action on one side modifies the organism and, on the other side, that action modifies the environment, but those are simply the two phases of one and the same process. Mr. Ward, however, marks them off and regards one as a purely natural and physical thing, and the other as a purely social and evolutionary thing.

Take it in terms of evolution. What is the sense of setting up one end for nature and the other for evolution? If you set up evolution it is the statement of the working of nature. Whatever is the end of evolution would *ipso facto* be the end or object of nature. Why cannot Mr. Ward recognize that? Simply because he has to conceive of action as a simple go-between, as a simple intermediary between feeling on one side and satisfaction on another. Nature, therefore, simply as nature has to be conceived in a static way as exemplified in structure; and when we find that that structure leads to action and the exercise of that structure in action leads to permanent changes, which because they are permanent are participated in by others, these facts have to be regarded as something separate, to be accounted for by reference to distinct principles.

The distinction made by Mr. Ward serves to bring out some of the factors which enter into any thoroughgoing consideration of the problem.

What is the relation of the cosmic process as exhibited particularly in biological terms, in terms of the life process, to the end and aim of the individual, which we may call the psychic end? What is the relation between this psychic process and aim and that of society? And again, what is the relation between the social progress and the life process taken simply as cosmic, as biological? Is there any way of getting all those three into line with each other? Is there anything in an adequate statement of the biological which leads us on to the psychical and to the sociological? Is there a fundamental unity of operation and of aim, or have we, as Mr. Ward would hold, three distinct spheres of operation, each with its own law? It is particularly as bringing out that problem so clearly as to the relation of the biological, the psychical and the sociological, that I refer to it.

I take Mr. Seth's *Study of Ethical Principles*,[12] only on one point, as to the ethical relation existing between the individual and society. I take that also simply for one reason, to indicate what is by no means uncommon in ethical theory, the attempt to carry water on both shoulders, to state two things which are contradictory and assert that both of them are true.

> . . . these two spheres of life are inseparable. The interests and claims of the social and of the individual life overlap, and are reciprocally inclusive. These are not two lives, but two sides or aspects of one undivided life. You cannot isolate the moral individual; to do so would be to demoralize him, to annihilate his moral nature. His very life as a moral being consists in a network of relations which link his individual life with the wider life of his fellows (p. 19).

Verbally the contradiction begins to come out in that last sentence. That is, first he has a life, and then that life consists in a network of relations that link his individual life to something else. There is a verbal contradiction, but that is not the point.

> Man is a social or political being. On the other hand, the individual is more than a member of society; he is not the mere organ of the body politic. He too is an organism and has a life and ends of his own (p. 19).

Having stated first that he has no life of his own, that he is a social being, he then says that he is more than a social being, that he does have a purely individual life of his own.

> The Good is, for every individual, a social or common Good, a Good in which he cannot claim such private property as to exclude his fellows; their good is his, and his theirs. Yet the Good—the only Good we know as absolute—is always a personal, not an impersonal good, a good of moral persons. The person, not society, is the ultimate ethical unit and reality (pp. 19–20).

I think it is not too much say "Pay your money and take your choice" as to which of those views you will have.

On the social side:

> I have not . . . discovered my own true End, or my own true Self, until I find it to be not exclusive but inclusive of the Ends of other Selves. The centre of the moral life must be found within the individual life, not outside it. The claim of society upon the individual is not to be explained even by such a figure as that of the social organism. The moral Ego refuses to merge its proper personal life in that of society (p. 144).

"Personality is essentially universal" (p. 265) and therefore, as he goes on to say, is social.

> In a deep sense we are separate from one another, and each man must bear his own burden (p. 281).

> The walls of personality shut us in, each within the chamber of his own being and his own destiny (p. 283).

"By nature . . . he is a social being" (p. 283) and similarly on page 285 he asserts again the correlativity of the individual and society. You will find there an excellent statement of the organic connection between the two. On page 288 however, we find that individuals can only come into external relations with each other; morally, we cannot even strictly cooperate with another individual. "Such is the solitariness of the moral life."

Now from page 309 to page 323 in the discussion regarding the function of the state and the relation of the state [to the individual] you will find the same contradiction again.

> . . . the State must be regarded as a means, not as in itself an end. The State exists for the sake of the person, not the person for the sake of the State. The ethical unit is the person (p. 304).

> . . . a closer analysis reveals the fundamental identity of the State, in its idea at least, with the ethical Person (p. 311)

and no longer related as means and end, but as the correlative expression of one and the same principle. "The right of the State is, therefore, supreme, being the right of personality itself" (p. 312). First the person is the end; now the state, representing the right of personality, is therefore supreme because as against it the individual self represents a local and more or less arbitrary self.

I do not mention this simply to convict Mr. Seth of a personal contradiction, but simply because that view is fairly common now. You will find it in a good many writers—a wavering back and forth, stating one thing and then saying that the opposite view is true also. On one hand the individual is the ultimate reality and society is subsidiary and instrumental; and on the other hand, the individual is nothing excepting in and for society and therefore there is some identity between the two. Now for so able a writer as Mr. Seth to be wavering back and forth between the two views shows that there is some more fundamental conception that has not yet been analyzed, that there is some controlling conception that has not been worked out, and therefore there is no definite criterion for the position one should take. The conception left unanalyzed is as to what the nature of the self is after all, or on the other side what the nature of society is after all. It seems to me that such writers as Mr. Seth have in mind what is in reality two different situations. Now on one hand it is perfectly obvious that there is no society excepting in individuals, there is no society over and above individuals. That is what Mr. Seth means, I take it, by saying that the end must after all be finally personal. But that simply means that society is expressed in persons. [Standing] over persons are the organs, the barriers, the consummations of society. Now to the man who will say that and not carry out the analysis, it will occur to him to say that individuals are the ultimate thing, that the whole thing ultimately is just individuals. True, but those individuals are all *social* individuals. It is practically tautology: society is society, society is considered in individuals, individuals are the organs of society, they are society. We are going around in a circle, but it is worthwhile to go around in a circle in order to bring out all the points in its circumference.

Then at another time we think of a particular individual coming into a society already there, and requiring to be socialized; that is, every baby that is born into society comes at first as a natural being and it has to be socialized through the play of social forces. One who is thinking not of individuals as individuals but of a particular individual will be apt to emphasize the other side and speak of society as the controlling thing, and the necessity of subordinating that individual by the larger social relationship until he himself becomes socialized. From that standpoint it is perfectly true—only that is just as much a process of subordinating the individual as a natural being to the society that is already there. If we are studying simply the process of his growth in individual capacity, we would still have to take account of these same factors, the play of the social stimuli upon him and the responses which he makes to these.

I was going to call attention in Mr. Kidd's works [13] to the dualism which he sets up on the psychological side between reason and feeling. He gives us just the opposite side of the shield from Mr. Ward. It is feeling which is altruistic to Mr. Kidd, it is feeling alone which generates social action; reason as reason is wholly subservient to individual well being; it is purely an instrument for figuring out a comfortable, satisfactory state of existence for the individual. So if our reason controlled us, we would put a stop to all progress because it involves tension and that is painful and troublesome; and if we allowed our reason to come in, we would say: We will quit this struggle, this conflict, this high strain of action, and simply make things comfortable for ourselves even if we let down the plane of existence to a much lower level. There is the conflict between the individual and society. The individual would, if left to himself, simply aim through his reason at securing the maximum of personal comfort; but the larger force, nature or God, working through the individual, sacrifices the individual to the process of evaluation,* to the process of growth; it renders the individual, against his own reason, an instrument in advance of what Mr. Ward would call function in bringing higher types of life into existence, in raising the plane of being. Well, until man comes in, nature seems perfectly adequate to this task of keeping things going, but when man gets reason he begins to question the value of any such sacrifice and says: Go to now, let us make ourselves comfortable and let the future take care of itself. And so there must be some check to this action of reason, and that is found in the fund of altruistic feeling. It is impossible to exaggerate the extremely antithetical way in which Mr. Kidd sets one up against the other.

We have this contradiction. Mr. Kidd uses as proof of altruism exactly what other writers have used to prove the entirely nonmoral character of nature—that is, the continual conflict and sacrifice of the individual—which some writers have used to draw an indictment against the whole natural process, that it is simply bent on the further evaluation † of life irrespective of the satisfaction of any individual. Mr. Kidd makes the basis of altruism and morality simply having something which will keep the individual sacrificing himself to the conditions of future progress, and that sacrifice consists in the struggle for existence. As Mr. Kidd states over and over again, it is simply keeping up competition. The kind of altruism which shows itself in the most extreme forms of competition has something strange about it, and the contradiction comes out here: We are sacrificing ourselves for progress, that means the welfare of society that is going to be in the future. That society must sacrifice itself for the benefit of that which is to come next, and so on. What is the value of this progress that never gets there? The more you progress, the greater is the demand for the sacrifice of the individual to the future. So the logical conclusion of Mr. Kidd is that there is an antagonism between the ethical process and the biological or cosmic process, and the conditions of life are absolutely antagonistic to individual devleopment as development.

NOTES

1. Continuation of lecture for April 8, 1898.
2. Immanuel Kant, *The Philosophy of Law, An Exposition of the Fundamental Principles of Jurisprudence as the Science of Right,* trans. William Hastie (Edinburgh: T. and T. Clark, 1887).
3. Thomas Hill Green, *Lectures on the Principles of Political Obligation,* reprinted from Green's *Philosophical Works,* Vol. II (London and New York: Longmans, Green, 1941, 1950).

* Probably "evolution."

† Probably "evolution."

4. Louis Agassiz (1807–1873), Swiss born naturalist, professor of zoology at Harvard. See his article "Evolution and Permanence of Type," *Atlantic Monthly* XXXIII (1874), 92–101.

5. James Bonar, *Philosophy and Political Economy in Some of their Historical Relations* (London: Swan Sonnenschein and Co.; New York: The Macmillan Co., 1893). See also Dewey's 1894 review in *Early Works*, IV, 214–17.

6. John Stuart Mill, *A System of Logic*, 10th ed. (2 vols.; London: Longmans, Green, and Co., 1879); *Essays on Some Unsettled Questions of Political Economy* (London: Longmans, Green, Reader, and Dyer, 1871).

7. Herbert Spencer, *The Principles of Sociology* (3 vols.; New York: D. Appleton and Co., 1898).

8. Edward Alsworth Ross, "Social Control," *American Journal of Sociology* I (March, 1896), 513–35. This was the first in a series of fifteen articles which were later rewritten into Ross's best-known book, *Social Control, A Survey of the Foundations of Order* (New York: The Macmillan Co., 1901).

9. *Annals of the American Academy of Political and Social Science* X (September, 1897), 58–92.

10. Lester F. Ward, *The Psychic Factors of Civilization* (Boston: Ginn and Co., 1893).

11. *Early Works*, IV, 200–10.

12. James Seth, *A Study of Ethical Principles* (Edinburgh: W. Blackwood and Sons, 1894).

13. Benjamin Kidd, *Social Evolution* (New York and London: The Macmillan Co., 1894). See also Dewey's review in *Early Works*, IV, 210–14.

CHAPTER 2

THE BIOLOGICAL PROCESS

SECTION 1. ORGANISM AND ENVIRONMENT IN THE BIOLOGICAL PROCESS

April 27, 1898

I am going to divide what I have to say into six heads, of which the first three are in a way introductory, or at least preparatory. I am going to discuss first the biological process with special reference to the concepts of the organism and the environment, because that seems to give us one way at least of attacking the general problem of the relationship of individuality to the universal. Not that individuality there is consciously taken simply as biological, but at least we get external, objective individuality defined for us in the organism. Secondly, I will discuss the psychological in relation to the biological. That is, following up the biological process, what does consciousness appear to stand for from this question of the relationship and adjustment of organism and environment to each other? And then thirdly, as growing out of these two questions, in what sense may society be termed an organism, and what is the relation of society as an organism to the biological process and to the psychological? From that as a basis I will go on to discuss the positive subject matter, subdividing that as I have already done by way of anticipation, in the fourth, economic process of society. Fifth, the political process. And sixth, the ethical. The first three heads are to help us fix our method, and the last three are the application of the method to the more particular problems in hand.

I begin then, with the life process, the biological side. I want to discuss that as intermediary between the cosmic process, the universe in general, and the psychological process as revealed in the study of consciousness. And the point of view which I hope to bear in mind and to have developed in your minds is the necessity of interpreting the distinction and the adjustment of organism and environment, which of course we at once run across in an examination of the biological from the standpoint of the larger and more fundamental unity of the cosmic process. No matter how much one school may insist on the organism, no matter how much another school may insist on the environment, it is certainly true that both are parts of a common world. We have no right to assume anything in the nature of either matter or motion, either of man or energy, which is peculiar to environment as environment or is the direct possession of organism as an organism. From the larger standpoint we must have one thing, one reality, the world at large, and the distinction between the organism and environment and their adjustments to each other must be capable of definition and interpretation from the standpoint of this larger whole.

In the first place, what is the distinction between the organic and the inorganic? I do not mean the distinctions in detail between the living and the nonliving, but what is the standard which we implicitly use when we mark off one thing as organic and another thing as inorganic? It seems to me that the distinction may be stated virtually as this: In the inorganic the series of changes which occur may be treated without any significant loss as a mere sequence in which the various earlier members of the series disappear and are replaced by subsequent forms or appearances. Of course the scientific man assumes that there is something unchanging, that there is something permanent in this sequence of mechanical changes, but it is possible without appreciable loss to regard that permanent element as purely quantitative: it is simply the element of mass which remains the same in quantity in spite of the great variety of forms which it assumes in the sequence of change. There is no qualitative identity which persists through the series of changes. (A) and (B) go and their place is taken by (C), and (C) is another fact, another event. It is true that there is a certain quantitative identity which might be represented by (M) which was present first in the interaction (A-B) and which is now present in (C), but there is no qualitative unity or identity of any sort which it is necessary for us to recognize when we are dealing with the inorganic.

Now if we take anything that we regard as organic, as living or vital, we do not find that such is the case. I will admit, both for the sake of argument and because I personally believe it, that all the changes which take place in the organic must be stated in purely mechanical terms; that is, a detailed physiological statement in ideal has no use for anything but physics and chemistry—namely, has no right over and above the forces which are known to physics and chemistry to assume another force, call it life, and attempt to ascribe causal force to it. When I say there is a distinction between organic and inorganic, it is not because I think we have a right to bring in any other kind of force into the organic than we have in the inorganic, but when we take a series of changes as a whole, we find the outcome, we find the resulting values different in what we call the organic from what we call the inorganic.

For instance, take a log of wood lying on the ground undergoing slow combustion by rotting, or by fire, and take the tree growing. As I just said, if we take the inorganic aspect, the rotting log, we will have (A) a certain chemical constitution of the log; we will have (B) certain atmospheric conditions, the soil, etc., and then through the reaction of (A) and (B) we have that (A) and that (B) disappearing in the new fact which we may call (C), the phenomena which represent themselves in and through the rotting of the log. Quantitatively the (M) is exactly the same as the (m), but it can all be stated simply as a series, a sequence, and from the inorganic point of view. I do not see that anything would be lost in thus stating it as a series of phenomena simply connected by their valuation of quantitative identity.

Now in the tree that is growing we find we get what has to be conceived of as a circuit rather than a row or series. (a) represents the changes going on in the living tree. We find that those changes in (a) are calculated to produce changes in (b) in the surrounding circumstance and that those changes in (b), while they may lead on to (c), lead on to (c) simply as a by-product, an incidental product of so much waste, that so far as the process is organic, the changes in (b), to a considerable extent, tend to react and maintain (a), and maintain in (a) the structure and capacity which will again produce changes in (b). It seems to me that purely from a descriptive standpoint we are justified in drawing that distinction in the organic process. We find that there is a qualitative identity which maintains itself, not merely against change (of course the rock to a certain extent maintains itself against change), but it maintains itself through change. The changes which occur in it are of such a nature as to lead to changes in the surroundings which in turn perpetuate (a) in existence.

The food process is the most typical example of what I mean. In ideal we ought to be able to state the movement of the plant or of the animal to get food as a purely physical and chemical thing, simply as due to its varying pressures in plants, and due to its disintegrating as a chemical compound. We ought to be able to state the getting and digesting of food in terms which would be as mechanical as those in which we would state the explosion of gunpowder or the action of an acid on metal, but there is the difference that, in the former case, these changes which take place, instead of leading to the disappearance of (a) and the substitution of a new fact, (c), react and return in such a way as to perpetuate this (a) in existence. These changes which are going on in it are of such a nature that they make good the waste involved, the running down of energy involved, and restore to the structure the capacity of bringing about similar changes again. If we ask when the plant or animal dies, it is at the point where this return or reaction ceases. Of course the living being does not maintain itself immediately and directly through its own changes, but the changes in it carry along with them such changes in the environment as in turn bring about other changes in the organism through which its loss is repaired.

It may be said that as matter of strict fact the new animal or the new plant is as much different from the old one (I mean the animal of tomorrow compared with the animal of today) as the products which occur in the rotting of the tree are different from their antecedents. Strictly from an external standpoint that statement of course is true, but nonetheless we do ascribe a qualitative individuality in spite of the change of material in one case, while we do not do anything of that kind in the other; so that the conception of the living process is bound up with the conception of a qualitative individual which maintains itself in and through change. Since we cannot find that qualitative identity maintained in the material, in the content of science, in the life process, the stuff that there is always in continual flux just as much in the growing tree (probably more in the growing tree) than in the rotting one.

That qualitative identity must be interpreted in a functional sense—that is, in the teleological sense. It is because we have a center of interest, a center of reference, and a center of outcome of product which are all the same, that we ascribe this qualitative identity.

When the scientific man investigates the action of acid on metal, he does not care for the particular individual piece of metal, he does not care what becomes of that, he is simply interested in the statement of the relations, the conditions involved in the certain sequence of changes. Now when we get to anything organic, the interest is historic interest. It is not in a simple formulation for the changes which occur. It is historic in the sense that we assume a certain individuality of being there which focuses our interest, which we start out with and which we follow through the series of changes; and we are interested in those changes not simply as changes, nor in their relation to each other, but we are interested in those changes as they bear upon the destiny of this individual, this qualitative identity which we have assumed. The sequence of changes which occur is interpreted by us not as a mere series external to each other and yet connected together by certain quantitative identities, but they are interpreted by us as being the realization, the development, or the growth of some single being.

Next time I will go on to speak of the distinction between the organism and environment, between structure and surroundings: man with reference to this functional process of which I have been speaking today.

April 28, 1898

In bringing out the conception of the organic yesterday, I virtually implied a distinction between the organism and the circumstances or environment within which and upon which that organism operates, and—even in speaking of the inorganic—that it was necessary to mark off two factors or two existences, two things which operated upon each other and led up to the third thing—the effect in the series. But even in this latter case the distinction is really a distinction due to our interest; it is an intellectual distinction. Of course in the process of nature itself, there is nothing which marks off the log of wood from the temperature, the moisture in the air—there is simply a redistribution of matter and motion. Now when we come to the organic proceses there is no ground in the process itself for making that distinction as long as there is immediate unity, or as long as there is complete harmony in the process. All we could strictly say is that there is a functional unity, a unity of the life process which maintains itself in and by means of a continuous series of diverse changes. If we take the process of breathing or the process of digestion, or of circulation, or any other organic process, so long as it is going on uninterruptedly, as long as all the conditions of the process are adequately met, there is nothing which would make us draw a line between organism on the [one] side and environment on the other. There is simply a process of continual integration and dedistribution going on.

The distinction of organism and environment is a distinction which arises because this functional activity is maintained only through readjustment, readaptation. We commonly talk of the organism and the environment and of the adaptation of one to the other. For practical purposes there is no harm in speaking in this way, as if there were first an organism and an environment and then some adjustment of one to the other; but when we come to an analysis of the factors involved, it is quite necessary to start from the unity of function and see that the distinction of organism and environment arises because of adaptation in that process, not vice versa.

It is not true in the ultimate sense that adaptation occurs between organism and environment; what is true is that readaptation, readjustment, has to take place within the function, or the functional activity, or the organic process, and that at the time of that readaptation it is at least a teleological necessity to make a distinction between phases or factors concerned in that readjustment. What we mean by organism is something which exercises one function, has one office in the readjustment of function; and what we mean by environment is something which has another purpose to serve in that readjustment of function. So then, I repeat, ultimately we must define organism and environment from the analysis of adaptation, and not adaptation from the synthesis or composition of organism and environment. So much for the point of view.

If, now, we see that the function ceases to operate adequately, that some of the conditions for its adequate performance are wanting, or that the various elements or minor activities which enter into it conflict with each other, do not harmonize or unify, we find at once that that part or that factor in the function which is regarded as offering the obstruction or producing the disturbance will be regarded as environment, while that aspect of the function which endeavors to persist unchanged, which for the time being represents the whole functional unity, will be regarded as the organism. Now if we define the environment in that way, not as something given, but as simply this factor which emerges out of the whole function when friction or lack of unity is introduced into it, we find that a double function is ascribed to the environment. On the one side it resists the organism; on the other side in that resistance it excites or arouses the organism—that is, the positive and negative aspects of one and the same thing. On the negative side it resists the organism, on the positive side its very resistance excites the organism to continued activity. If the function of seeing, say, were always exercised without difficulty, if there were never any effort or readjustment required in the process of seeing, there would be no necessity for making a distinction between eye as organ and the light conditions as the environment; but now let some difficulty arise in the process of seeing, and at once in considering that process, we locate on one side the obstacle, and on the other that which is still striving in spite of and against the obstacle, to perform the office of seeing. Whatever it is that presents itself as in any way hindering or interfering, that which intervenes to prevent the full exercise of the function, whatever it may be, will be regarded as the external, while that element in the function which still persists to perform it will be regarded as relatively internal.

I think it is not making an over-subtle refinement to say that that factor which we call environment has been before this time to some extent a factor in the function. As long as the function was performed freely and successfully, it was there to some extent, if we say only implicitly; it was there as a contributing factor, just as all actual seeing is the cooperation of the light conditions on one side and the eye on the other. And, implicitly, whatever goes along with those light conditions, whatever is necessary to maintain that light, which is involved as a factor in seeing, is indirectly itself a contributing element in the process. Now if this element which we regard as external, set over against the eye, were merely external, that would be the end of the matter. But etymologically I think the term object is significant: it is something which is thrown over against. But after all its primary function is this of offering resistance, it is that which objects, which offers opposition, makes an obstacle in the free performing of the function; and the subject I think is also that which subjugates, that which functions in order to overcome or remove the obstacle. That distinction of subject and object is a psychological distinction, but in dealing with the psychological relation, it is in general outline the same as the organism and environment distinction, except that it is in consciousness instead of in reflective analysis. As I was saying, if this external were merely external, that would be the end of it, it would not be environment. Environment is something more than that which merely offers immediate resistance to the performance of function. That resistance also tends to excite, as I said, or stir up the continued activity of the organism. It serves, in our ordinary phrase, as stimulus.

Now if we turn to the organism, we find a precisely correlative distinction corresponding to the environment as obstacle or resistance. It is the organism as end to be attained; it is that to which the environment is an obstacle; it is an end to be opposed. Simply because this obstacle has come in, the function is no longer adequately performed, and it depends upon the organism to see that it is. The organism is therefore immediately identified with the function, it is the representative of the function, but because that identification is not attained, it presents itself as end, as something to be attained.

Relative to the environment as excitant is the organism as response, as putting forth energy in order to overcome the obstacle and to utilize the obstacle. At the outset, as long as the environment presents itself mainly as obstacle, it is only an indefinite stimulus. That was what I had in mind in calling it at first an excitant instead of stimulus. But if we call it stimulus instead of excitant the point to be kept in mind is that if it were a perfectly determinate stimulus it would cease to be an obstacle. To say that it is an obstacle and an indeterminate stimulus is one and the same thing; or going over to the side of the organism, the stimulus being indeterminate, the response is diffuse and indeterminate also. The problem for the response is of course to become adequate, to become an effective response, a response which hits the nail on the head, or which deals with the obstacle with the maximum of efficiency; but that means that the indefinite stimulus be transformed into a definite stimulus.

We are liable in analyzing this process to fall into the psychological or historical fallacy and confuse the concept of adequate stimulus and response with this stage. When there is adequate stimulus and response, there is perfect unity of function. There is no essential reason for making a distinction between stimulus and response. We have a series of adjusted acts in which every act is perfectly organized with reference to every other, but the peculiarity of this state of development is that the stimulus is indefinite and the response is therefore inadequate, it is not properly directed, and the problem for that response is to control the stimulus, to modify the stimulus.

If we express it in the form of a circle, here would be the environment, which simply as indefinite arouses the organism to some kind of correspondingly indefinite activity; it is tentative, experimental. Insofar as any portion of that tentative response succeeds, it will modify the stimulus and bring that stimulus under control, so that the next stimulus of the environment will be more defined and therefore will call out a more precise and concentrated activity; and so on, until that modifies the excitant again so as to make it more the kind of stimulus that is wanted, and so on, until for all practical purposes the excitant has become really an adequate stimulus to action. Then the response will be in turn effective, it will be really a response.

To go back to the instance of the seeing, the moment that function ceases to accomplish itself successfully, there will be a consciousness of something to be seen; some particular object or mass of color, of moving color, of light and shade will present itself, and it presents itself as an excitant, it irritates us; we want to know what it is. Is it a horse and buggy, or is it a cloud of dust or a crowd of men, and so on, and as that calls out the various organic reactions, we fix the eye upon it instead of perhaps allowing the eye to roam around and the muscular adjustments are held there to solve that question, and one draws upon his other resources to find any distinguishing characteristic to show that it was a crowd of men or that it was a cloud of dust. One uses at once all one's available organs to solve the problem, to define the obstacle so that it will cease to be an obstruction and fit into the system of action. That activity is experimental. The excitant is the problem. What is it? What can be done with it? How shall one react? The only way to find out how to react is to try a lot of reactions, some of which are off the track. Maybe all of them are more or less off the track, but the putting forth of the energies serves at least to define the excitant; they bring out the conditions of the problematic thing more particularly so that the next reactions are less wild and are more in the nature of a response, and so it goes on until one disposes of the objects somehow, the limit being purely practical—that is, what we want of the object. What would serve to dispose of it satisfactorily at one time will not at another. Sometimes the lack of equilibrium would still keep up, but the limits would always be found somewhere there—we would get what we want of the object or fit it into the existing trend of action. I have taken a case where consciousness is involved, but I think there is nothing in the analysis which depends on the presence of consciousness, I think the same thing would hold equally in the search for food.

There is one objection which I will speak of here—perhaps it has occurred to you: in a case like food, the stimulus often seems to proceed from within the organism while according to the theory advanced the resistance is the environment, or the environment is the resistance and the stimulus. In the case of hunger, the animal does not wait until it sees something which might be food, the hunger arises from within and excites the activity of hunting for the food. But in that case some other part of the organism, some other organ or structure is environment to the particular organ with which we are most immediately concerned. Or to bring out the real point involved better, the environment may always be stated as the friction or resistance between various organs in the same organism; it is the friction or tension and also the mutual stimulus of one organ and another, projected.

In the case that I gave of seeing, if it were not for some other organ implicitly involved, there would be no friction, the eye would be as well pleased with that patch of color as with a cloud of dust or a group of horsemen. It is because some other organ comes in which is related to the object and which wants to determine it that the factor presents itself as resistance. If one were to relapse into a purely aesthetic consciousness, there would be satisfaction in tracing the varying lights and shades of color as they present themselves—there would be no problem; but because one wants to do something else in which the center of action would be somewhere else than in the eye, this tension or resistance presents itself. What we call an adequate adjustment of the organism to the environment is always just the same thing as an adequate adaptation of all the organs to each other. You can state it either way. I want to thread a needle. I can state that as the adjustment of the eye organ to the needle as environment, but I can equally state it as the adjustment of my eye activity to my hand activity. A certain kind of eye activity and hand activity adjusted will give you the threading of the needle. The advantage of stating it in terms of the relation of the organism to environment instead of the relation of one organ to another organ is that the environment is precisely that which serves as means, as intermediary, go-between, between the two organs in effecting their unified, functional cooperation.

We may state that on the side of variation, of difference, the environment represents the demand for variation in the organism. The environment is first the indeterminate demand for variation, for readjustment in the organism. The organism is relatively the initiation of variations which lie in the direction of the end. We regard the environment as indifferent to the end, as hostile to the end, as opposed to the immediate end. Of course, while the organism initiates variations which lie along in the direction of the end, we regard that as putting forth effort in the direction of realizing the variation [?]. On the side of the identity involved, the end, so fast as it is transformed from excitant into stimulus—that is, from an indefinite into a definite cause of activity in the organism—is means. It is means or material. The environment cannot be merely obstacle in any case, because as environment it presents all the material the organism has to work with. It is exactly this same thing which at first is the problem, or the obstacle, in seeing, which later on will be developed into the recognized object, into the adequate basis for the next activity. It is just the same environment which produces hunger in the animal that must satisfy that hunger, and the satisfaction of the hunger will consist simply in the transformation of that environment. It is obvious that all the supplies, the material, to deal with, must come from the environment. That is what I mean by saying that the environment as transformed from excitant into stimulus is the means for the functioning. On the identity side, the organism then is the end which is subserved through the environment as means.

Now if our emphasis is on the earlier stages, then we would conceive the relation of organism and environment as one of excitation and initiation; we would put all the exciting-cause side into the environment. We would ascribe the initiation to the organism—initiation in the teleological sense, the successful activities, the activities that contribute toward the successful realization of the end. That is what we call the organism. Wherever we find that which calls out the activity, we call it environment.

At a later stage, when it has passed beyond the more merely tentative stages to one of approximation to adjustment, then the relation of environment and organism presents itself as that of means and end. It is obvious from this that we cannot identify offhand the organism or environment with anything in particular, we have to first find out what stage of progress has been effected in the transition from one function to another. For instance, which shall we say is stimulus, and which shall we say is control? We will say that we will call the environment stimulus and the organism exercises the power of control over that. That would be true if the process is at a certain stage of development, but at another stage it would be truer to say that the environment exercises the control. In the more tentative stage the organism is looking about blindly, seeing what it can do and the environment is regarded as affording the more permanent factors which ratify or reject the various tentative excitations which the organism puts forth. That is the way in which I would account for the fact that various writers make exactly opposite statements in regard to this matter: some writers speak as if the environment were the permanent thing and new species had to be accounted for as variations in the organism, others say that the organism as organism is always the same, it is just this protoplasmic structure, but the environment changes and the play of the environment on the organism changes, and it is that which produces new species and develops new organs, and so on.

Of course in reality you cannot possibly have one changing without the other changing, but the problem is quite different at different times, the stress of the problem is located at different points, and hence one school of writers interested in a particular problem will regard the organism as fixed and the environment as introducing variation into the organism while another will reverse the process. Darwin practically does both. At one time he emphasizes the variation in the organism as giving the environment something to work upon in order to produce new organs and new species; at other times he throws all the emphasis on the changes in the surroundings. Practically he is justified in doing that, and that is the advantage that he has over the later biologists, that he takes the problem at the time, instead of trying to carry his generalities so far as to be one-sided, as it seems to me the later writers growing out of that school have done.

May 2, 1898

As I mentioned the other day, in the various discussions that I have carried on regarding the relative importance attached to organism and environment in the process of evolution, there is an element of uncertainty and of indeterminateness, which makes the discussion practically futile. That element of vagueness arises because the terms environment and organism are taken as something at large, something having a fixed meaning once for all. The argument that then goes on is practically without any limitation at all, just as it would be in mathematics where the terms used had no assignable limitations at all. The term organism and the term environment, taken simply at large, without any statement of the function that is under consideration, and the historical development of that function, is a term to which there is no basis for ascribing any particular meaning. Whatever meaning is given to it will be more or less arbitrary, it will depend on what the person using the terms has in mind. Somebody else, having another problem in mind, may use the terms in another sense, and so you get practically opposite views, but no basis of deciding between them.

Thus you have a school like that of Lamarck* and of Herbert Spencer, who lay all the influence of evolution on environment, who conceived of the organism as something which some way or another is there, waiting to be played upon and moulded and worked into shape somehow by the environment; so in Herbert Spencer's full theory of the development of life and of mind, you will find that the organism is continuallly conceived of as fixed and all the determining force is located in the environment, which finally, through its repeated and persistent operations, succeeds in moulding the organism into a certain amount of conformity to itself or, in Spencer's terms, a certain amount of parallelism to itself.[1] The question is not asked, how, if the environment is so all determining, there came to be any opposition between the environment and organism, or how, if the organism is so merely passive and pliable, it does not remain unorganized and mere responsive material the way other things do under such circumstances. It is not explained how you can get this high degree of complexity of structure and of chemical composition through the action of this all-important environment on the organism, which for all practical purposes has no more to it than a lump of putty.

To those interested in another problem, we find the spontaneous variations of the organism assumed to be the determining thing, and you get the standpoint of Weismann,† who reduces the positive influence of the environment to a minimum but conceives the organism as somehow breaking up into arbitrary variations from within from time to time. Or if it is conceived in a more teleological way, you get the school represented by the American naturalist Cope,†† where the organism is conceived as somehow having a type latent within and responding to external stimuli in such a way as to evolve this involved type, which is explicit within it, so that variations come along determinate directions which would serve to carry out this preestablished harmony.

I will go over the discussion of the last time very briefly again, to show how importance shifts from one side to another according to the stage of realization reached in the transformation of one form of functioning into another. If we fail to notice the unity of function, we can begin at either end. We can think of the environment as acting on the organism in new ways and therefore calling out new reactions, or we can think of the organism as varying from within. In any case those variations in the activity, in the structure of the organism, must occur if there is to be any evolution. There we have initiation. So when we are discussing the standpoint from

* Jean Baptiste Lamarck (1744–1829), French naturalist best known for his theory of the inheritance of acquired characteristics.

† August Weismann (1834–1914), German biologist who rejected the theory of the inheritance of acquired characteristics.

†† Edward Drinker Cope (1849–1897), American zoologist and paleontologist.

the initiation of a successful specific variation, we cannot help falling back on the organism. But these variations are competitive with relation to each other; they are tentative, experimental. Or because there is a great variety of variations and only some of them lie along the line or direction of success in responding to new excitants, these variations have to be conceived of as competitive with reference to each other. So while at the start we find initiation in the organism and the environment presents itself simply as that which has to be adapted and all initiation rests with the organism, it is simply a question whether these variations are going to succeed in adapting themselves to the environment or not; but when we think of this initiation as consisting simply in variations which compete with each other, then the importance shifts to the environment. It depends upon the environment which of the variations is going to be successful. If initiation belongs to the organism, fulfillment, execution, the working test of all these things, can be found only in the environment. So when we are thinking, not of the commencement of a new series, but of the attainment of it, the whole weight of thought goes over to the other side, and we think of the environment as determination, adaptation. In biological terms the struggle for existence is located in the organism while the environment exercises the office of natural selection.

Now if we take the new function as it is developed, that is the variation which has succeeded, which has got developed and selected, that is fixed, we find that the new organ or new form of structure has been transformed which gives us another new species, or a new variety. We have, in other words, the survival of the fit, which is simply a name for this same process as it reaches its completion.

Stated in other terms which are those used by Mr. Baldwin in his book on mental development,[2] we have the process treated as that of habit and its accommodation. You remember in Mr. Baldwin's earlier book the two categories which he works chiefly to unify the biological and psychological statements are habit and accommodation.[3] I have never been able to see that there was any finally thought-out view of the exact relation which exists between habit and its accommodation, they are treated as two factors which are correlative and indispensable in all growth, but just how they are correlative and indispensable does not seem to me to be explained.

I should say habit and accommodation are simply the correlative distinctions which arise within the analysis of the reconstruction of function. There are not two things, habit and accommodation. Where does the accommodation come from if they are two different things? We have only habits to form accommodation with. The habit that is not accommodating itself is a mere abstraction. That is all it is for, for purposes of use, and all use involves a certain amount, however small it may be, of so-called accommodation or adaptation. The habit represents the abstraction of the structural or organism side of function—that is to say, those factors in function which remain not fixed, not fixed enough to be utilized in maintaining the continuity of life. It is not that there is anything once for all which can be marked off as habit, but that teleologically whatever can be depended upon to assist us without further attention, without further change, in reaching an end, is good enough, that is permanent and fixed enough, and whatever you can count on in that way will be regarded as habit; while on the other side, as function breaks up, or as friction arises in various parts of it, it ceases to be unified. The environmental side, that which makes the demand for the use of the habit in order to maintain the function, will be regarded as the conditions of adaptation. Environment is that to which the organism must adapt itself; the organism is that which can be utilized for purposes of adaptation. You cannot define either one or the other really, excepting in terms of adaptation, excepting in terms of inter-action.

Put in logical terminology, we have here simply the abstraction of the two elements of identity and difference, which are involved in all processes either organic or inorganic. We abstract the phase of identity and baptize it by the name of habit. We abstract the phase of difference or distinction, and name that conditions of adaptation, and then we think of the process, the only real thing, the transforming identity, as adaptation of habit to environment. Perhaps that may be made clearer by calling to mind that all important biological adaptations are dynamic in character.

Mr. Spencer, in his *Psychology*,[4] treats the development of mind as a process of adaptation to a wider space environment, a larger time environment, with more and more complexity and variety in both space and time. He contrasts the mental action of a North American Indian who lived in this country three hundred years ago with that of a white man today. The special environment to which the Indian adapted himself was comparatively limited in range, a local habitat; and not so very many features in that local environment were responded to by him. He lived mostly from year to year and during that stretch of time there were comparatively few events which were responded to. Take a business man here today and his special environment might include things all over the globe. To a dealer in wheat, changes in Russia or India might be of as much importance to him as those in his local environment, and infinitely larger details in space and time would be responded to. That conception as developed by Mr. Spencer seems to imply that that space and time environment was there for the Indian as much as for the American of today, but the former only adapted himself to a little of it, and the hypothetical merchant of today responds to a great deal more. From the psychological standpoint that is a case of the historical fallacy. What has taken place has been the development of the environment, the creation of the environment, the evolution of the environment, not a mere increased adaptation of the environment already there. The mental development has shown itself on one side in bringing that environment into existence. Or if we take it more as a biological matter, the increasing control over the environment is not as if the environment were something there fixed and the organism responded at this point and that, adapting itself by fitting itself in, in a plaster-like way. The organism reacts so as to bring the environment into use. That is what I mean by saying that the important adaptation is dynamic in character. It modifies the environment so as to subordinate it to the needs of the organism. It would be just as true to speak of the adaptation of the environment to the organism, to the needs of the organism, making it more and more subservient to the life process all the time.

The psychological or historical fallacy is likely to come in here and we conceive the environment, which is really the outcome of the process of development, which has gone on developing along with the organism, as if it was something which had been there from the start, and the whole problem has been for the organism to accommodate itself to that set of given surroundings.

I illustrated this in the other class with an illustration which I will use again. Take the desert region of the great West. The people that lived in precarious existence there a few hundred years ago with no advanced social or industrial life, moving about from place to place in small groups, were adapted to that environment. The great agriculturist that goes out there now introduces irrigation, saves up the water supply and grows large crops, is equally adapted to the environment. The first is a static adaptation which marks simply the arrest of the given evolution. Wherever you have growth continued, you always have dynamic adaptation or the transformation of the environment, to render it serviceable, to bring it under control. This taking of habits and accommodation as if they were two separate processes somehow is simply an aspect of the historical fallacy which makes us conceive of that which is the result of evolution as if it had been there all the time as something to accommodate to.

In terms of the discussion of the other day, it is only at the end of the process that we have the stimulus—that is, that we have the adequate working stimulus—so it is only after the adaptation in the function has been worked out that there is this environment here, which we look at retrospectively and consider as something all the time conditioning the process of determination.

SECTION 2. EVOLUTION:
VARIATIONS AND COMPETITION

We now go on to consider the process of evolution in a little more positive way, though it involves no new ideas. Begin with the effect of the environment on the organism, taking those terms in the functional meaning which has now been given to them. There is no sure thing as the absolutely direct influence of environment on organism, excepting to wipe it out of existence. Of course if a stone rolls on an animal and kills it, you say it is the direct influence of environment on the organism: that is, not an evolutionary modification of any sort. Now excepting in that way of destruction I do not see how we can talk about any absolutely direct influence of environment on organism. There is, however, a relatively direct influence. Insofar as environment furnishes the material of the function, the food supply of the function, the environment enters into function; it is a constitutive part of function, and as entering into function as supply or material, it may influence in a relatively direct way the organism. It is only relatively direct; it is always mediated through the performance that is going on.

To give a simple example of what I mean by that: an abundant food supply might easily lead to increase in the size of organs and of an organism. We know that in the human organism an abundant food supply increases the birth rate, thus increasing the number of organisms in existence, if not the structure of any one organ. Apparently the colors of flowers of plants can be changed by changing the food supply. If they assimilate different material there is a reaction which takes place in the structure. All such changes may, I think, be said to be comparatively superficial and unimportant. They might lead to new varieties, but it is difficult to see how they could lead to any new species without going further than anything that has been said. It seems also that such changes would be relatively unstable. I do not see that they would be likely to become so ingrained into the habits of life as to constitute a species.

Theoretically speaking it is hard to distinguish between the species and a variety, but it seems to me that the difficulty is not so great because the distinction is a practical one, a teleological one; it is simply a difference in the habit of getting a living and in the organs which are subordinate to that, and so while theoretically you will have all grades of changes and you cannot say that varieties leave off here and a species begins there, yet we do find that when certain variations lead to a change in the mode of living, we call it a species. This is the point I was getting at: when the change of material, the change of the environment, reacts so as to affect the nutrition of the process, the influence ceases to be a relatively direct one and becomes relatively indirect, and then the changes which take place in the structure are much more important with reference to growth. Supposing for instance that the flower changes color at first simply because something in its soil surroundings has changed. Suppose that the roots tap some different-colored food material that dyes the flower temporarily. For a while that would be temporary I think, but if that change of coloring should have an influence on the insects which visited that plant, it is conceivable that that might affect the nutritive side of the plant, might affect not simply the reaction which the food supply it gets has upon its externals, but might influence its ways of getting food and its ways of propagating itself. That change would cease to be simply a change adapted to the environment and would become an adaptive change; that is, a change which leads to a more dynamic adaptation, a change of structure which has a positive function to perform and which would then be selected because of the part which it played in the struggle for existence. It would be a specific variation.

It seems to me that the line to be drawn between these two sorts of changes would be right here: the amount of tension that is set up between the organs of nutrition and the other organs. If the change in the color of the plant's flower does not influence its nutrition, I do not see that it is a change which would lend itself in any appreciable degree to the evolutionary process; but if for any reason it calls for a different mode of action on the part of the organs which supply the animal with food, or if it leads to different results in the action which those organs put forth, then an adaptation has to be made within the plant between the structures which subserve nutrition, or the way in which they subserve nutrition, and the other organs.

If we ask then what the influences of climate, physical surroundings, etc., are on organisms, and how they have an influence, we have here the standard for the answer. A merely direct influence is out of the question, but insofar as the environment reacts and thus stimulates in new directions the organs which get the food and the organs of reproduction, they do influence the organism. Now that tension which I spoke of may—under certain circumstances will—show itself as variation in the structure. It seems to me that we have to account for variations simply as the signs of breaking up of a previous function or coordination. That function has been going on in an organized, unified way, but the materials which enter into that function vary so as to call out new modes of action in the organism, and those are what the biologist calls variations. It is simply the loose ends, so to speak, of the previous function. The energy which has been utilized along a certain line is now set free in quite a number of different channels. These variations, then, will naturally occur in times of great change in the environment, because great changes in the environment will mean change in the material which, through the exercise of function, is entering into the structure of the organism, and some of those changes of structure may affect the food-getting and food-assimilating structures themselves.

Now of course only a biologist could give any statement of the nature of these variations or how they occur, but since such biologists as Romanes* and Weismann allow themselves to use the term variation without explaining what they mean more than that changes do take place, a layman might be allowed to say something, and it seems to me that the essential thing in the variations must be tension between the nutritive structure and the other structures of the organism. A mere superabundance of food does not seem to me would be likely to produce evolutionary variations. The mere shortage of food would not do it. Mere superabundance would lead simply to fat, or perhaps to increased size. Mere shortage would lead simply to weakening and enfeebling. But if you can get a tension set up

* George John Romanes (1848–1894), British biologist best known for his popular writings on evolution.

there—on the one hand certain conditions which supply food in excess in certain directions and thus give a superabundance of material for energy, and on the other side the tendency toward a shortage of nutrition in some of the organs of the organism and the necessity for an unusual amount of effort, or expenditure of energy—it seems to me that you would have the conditions for variation.

I suppose in biological terms this would be a tension between the anabolic process, with reference to certain organs, and the katabolic, with reference to certain others. That is, while more food is got easily, or what is got is utilized so that there is excess in certain directions, that is not merely stored up in fat or in the increase of size but is expended in some katabolic way in another direction, and through the medium of a high tension the equilibrium is preserved.

There is much discussion among speculative biologists as to whether the variations are determinate or indeterminate. If we realize that the variation is a variation, it is indeterminate; that is, insofar as the variation is tentative, insofar as it is experimental. If we look at it the moment it occurs with relation to its future development, it would be indeterminate; but if we remember that every variation must be a mediation of function already in existence, that that variation cannot break in arbitrarily from the outside, nor break loose arbitrarily from the inside, but that it represents simply a reflection of the activities, of the life habits previously exercised, we would think of the variation as determinate. It is mere mythology to say that there is nothing at all which controls it. Of course it is controlled all the time by the function of which it is after all simply a modification, simply a mediation.

From that point of view it seems to me there is no mystery about variations always being determinate—that is, changed on the whole along certain lines—rather than as Darwin by his language often seems to assume that they occur indefinitely and impartially in a whole multitude of directions. If we treat the variation simply as a variation, it would be irrational to suppose that that variation is likely to occur in an infinity of possible variations that happen to be useful. If the habits of an animal's life tend in a certain direction upon the whole, then the variations must be relative to that mean habit of life; they cannot diverge very far from it without the result being the immediate death of the organism. To go back to the statement regarding habits and accommodation, the changes to which the habit has to accommodate itself must be relative to the habits already there, and so those habits must fix the limits of variation and fix the channels along which variations will go on.

May 3, 1898

According to what I said yesterday, variations are to be interpreted as the accompaniment of tension in the operations of the organism, that tension itself being due to a disturbance of functional unity. The main point was that it was necessary to conceive of these variations in the relation which they bear to previous functional activity. If we take living matter in its very lowest forms, we cannot get it so low that there is not some functional activity there. There must always be, in however small a form, the operation of appropriating the material of the environment and transforming it in such a way as to make good the waste involved in the expenditure of energy; and if we please to get beyond living matter, we never get any matter, however inorganic we may take it to be, which does not still have energy of its own. It seems to me futile to attempt to find anything which lies behind that activity, and if we start from that, then the variations and the subsequent process of development must be interpreted as outgrowths, developments, in some form or another, of that existing activity. That functional activity does something, accomplishes something; it produces certain results. It modifies in a certain way the existing food conditions, and thus it is through that modification [that] its own activities react into itself. The question then seems to me to be whether this existing function can stand, so to speak, the results of its own activity. Can it meet and adapt itself to the changes which [it] itself has brought about? Of course if it cannot do that, death must ensue. The nature of that change required in the function, in order that it may meet the results of its own doing, constitute the essence of that adaptation which we find in growth.

Now if we take the kind of instance that would seem most to contradict the statement just made, it will serve to test it; that is, put the change as much as possible in the environment. Suppose that a plant growing on the mountainside is slipped down the slope in a landslide, and is moved to a much lower level. The climatic conditions are quite different. Now of course it will be said at once that that change is nothing which the plant has done. It is not a question of its adapting itself to itself, the function being able to meet the change of conditions which it itself produces; but it is simply the question of the adaptation of the plant as a whole to a change in environment beyond itself. But the only way in which this change of environment can influence or modify the plant in any biological way is still through the medium of the function of the plant itself. Of course we could say that it is so much warmer below that the plant is at once killed, but if that does not happen there will be no direct influence of the environment on the plant structure. That plant has already certain habits of living and unless it is killed it goes on exercising those habits. Now, however, the conditions having changed, the net results of its activity are different from what they were before, and the question is whether the habits that were formed with reference to the previous environment can adapt themselves to the change of work which those habits do.

Let H represent the habits which are relative to the existing structure of the plant. We will see that exercise of them results in the conditions which we will term V, V signifying the getting of the conditions necessary to the vigorous growth of the plant, and thus to the maintenance of H. The environment is suddenly and arbitrarily changed. Let E express the environment as the mediation between the habits and the results of their activity. That would be changed suddenly to E'. Now the effects of H acting in E' are X, and the problem from the standpoint of that plant will be whether H can adapt itself to X or not, whether the conditions which are expressed in H will harmonize with the conditions which are expressed in X. That is not saying that the environment does not play an exceedingly important part there. It does, but the part which it plays is that of the mediation of the function. It comes in as a means, as a middle term, not as something which there is to be direct adaptation to on the part of the organism.

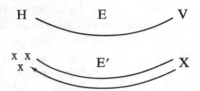

You could work out the same thing if you took the case of persons who had worked out certain industrial and political habits as giving them control over a certain environment, and then regard them as colonizing themselves in quite a different environment. Now that environment will call for a different kind of an activity than the former one, but you cannot tell what different kind of an activity will be called for, you cannot describe it, or value it, excepting as you call before yourself the activities, the habits which these people had previously. On the principle of habit those activities are going to maintain themselves with the least amount of modification possible and the question of just what change, what adaptation will take place, will have to be decided on just that basis. Given the old activities operating under changed conditions, what modifications will have to be made in those activities in order to make them effective, in order to maintain them in this consistency and coherency? You cannot tell what the nature of this new environment is, this E', excepting as you define it with reference to the part which it plays in this activity H. If you have a half dozen different kinds of plants that come down in the landslide, the problem will be different with each insofar as they are typically different from each other. You will have a half dozen different environments there because you have a half dozen different sorts of activity going on.

Now if we take these variations as set up expressing this tension (variations are the tension, not the result of tension), we have conflict and competition. They are in logical terms rival hypotheses; they are rival propositions regarding the nature of the function; they are so many attempted solutions of the problem, and which is the better solution, or approximate solution, can be told only through the process of experimentation. Each variation attempts to maintain itself. That is not something different—that is, simply, the variation is a mode of action as such; it operates. Now if it succeeds in subordinating the environment to itself, or controlling the environment, in reducing it to nutritive material, that variation is encouraged and all other minor variations that break out in it are encouraged also, until we get a specific variation established.

Now the point which I think is most essential to be noted there is that this competition occurs primarily within one and the same organism. Primarily this conflict is not to be interpreted as between different organisms. I do not mean to say that there is no competition between different organisms. There is; but so far as development is concerned, the important thing is, as it seems to me, the experiment testing of the variety of variations which occur within one and the same organism. As between two different organisms the variation means rather a lessening of competition than an increase in it. If we have two organisms of the same species, A and B, they do compete with each other, if there is a limited food supply, because they both have the same environment. Now let A develop a certain variation and that means the opening up of a new environment. Just insofar as it is a variation which affects its nutritive habits, it has a new food environment and therefore the pressure between it and B is removed.

Instead therefore of the process of evolution being interpreted as one which is affected by rivalry between different organisms, it seems to me that the reverse is true. Every advance step, every specific variation, must mean the constitution of a new enviroment which relieves the conflict previously going on between organisms that are homogeneous in their life habits. If we have a given plot of ground, say, a square yard, it is perfectly obvious that a greater number of individuals of different species live there than if they were all of exactly the same species. Of course I do not mean to say that would always be so, but under certain circumstances such would be the case, because a certain number of those individuals will draw different food elements, or will have new resources for utilizing the same food elements, and moreover, insofar as they are different, they may in some way cooperate with each other in growth. As far as they are all the same kind, they are all making drafts upon the same food elements in just the same way. The conflict between organisms of the same type, the same species, may be conceived of as perfecting the species already in existence, but I do not see any conceivable way in which, simply as conflict between the different ones, it would originate any new species, any new specific variations. If you have a lot of embryonic horses started, I mean variations along the horse line, there their competition would tend to weed out the less efficient ones of this type, and perpetuate and fix the more favorable specimens of that particular variation. It seems to me almost a truism to say that to get a new variation started, you must have something which leaves the main line of competition and starts out in a new line in such a way as to discover or constitute a new food environment.

If the competition then, so far as it relates particularly to specific variations, is within the organism itself, the process of natural selection is virtually the process of testing and confirmation. In logical terms it is the verification of one hypothesis and the rejection of another. It is the generalization of the variation, that which, as we say, fixes it so that it is no longer conceived of as a variation. We think of it no longer from the standpoint of the old species A; it is now a part of the definition of the new species B, and we say that the new species is established when the variation is constituted as a transformation of the previous life function. There you have, then, a unified or organized mode of activity; you have a coordination set up which in turn would be the plane or level to which future variations would be referred.

It occurs to me that on the more strictly biological side that point of view accounts for the absence of transitional forms. They are absent just because they are transitional; they represent simply experimentation. If we could find them, they would not be transitional; they would be just as individualized in some direction or another as the forms which we now find. It is the very nature of a connecting link not to attain to objectivity; it is a mere mediation over from one organized form into another. The supposition that we could get an absolutely continuous graded series is not only unnecessary as matter of fact, but it is absurd logically. As Mr. Stirling said, "You never can call nature half in and half out."* Any form that you could get would have to be different from other forms. It makes no difference, excepting in a practical way, whether it is so big, or so big. It is a jump and if you conceive of evolution as requiring an absolute series of graded degrees, it is a violation of it just as much to have a comparatively small variety of forms as if that variety were larger. It would be simply a matter of detail. The process is continuous, but you never see the process anyway. What we get is only the forms, the products, the various stages of objectified attainment, and those cannot be purely serial and continuous in any case, they must be discrete. In mathematics, the maximum and minimum within which a certain function increases or decreases, as the limits, are comparable to the forms, the species. The species are always the attained limit, the definition of the process of growth that is going on and it would be therefore unnatural to suppose that we could find in objective form in the geologic record anything but these limits which represent at least temporary solutions of the tension. The tension itself we cannot find, so we cannot find the so-called connecting links, because they were never there as settled existences.

If the distinction between organism and environment is a distinction with reference to the process of growth simply, the process of readjust-

* Probably a reference to James Hutchison Stirling (1820–1909), Scotch philosopher and commentator on Hegel.

ment of function, we ought to be able to state the process in terms which should ignore the distinction. We can treat it as either a cosmological process or as a biological one, and not simply as if it were about half and half, or a compromise between something which is biological on one side because there is life, and something cosmological on the other side because there is no life there. Before I go on to the psychological process, I will endeavor to show what we get when we describe this process first in cosmological terms and then in biological.

Stated in cosmological terms the process is, I think, simply one of redistribution of energy. The quantity of energy, according to the law of the conservation of force, would have to remain the same. But the amount of that energy that is available for the standpoint of certain ends is indefinitely increased. This redistribution of energy, in other words, cannot actually give any increments to the amount of energy that is externally there, but this redistribution, this change of position and relationship can increase the amount very much with reference to certain interests or aims with which we identify ourselves. It is worthwhile to note in passing that the definition of energy itself has a teleological implication. It is the power of doing work, it is the power of effecting certain results. You cannot even define energy at large excepting as you have in mind the accomplishment of a certain result. If one asks what the absolute quantity of energy is in the universe, the problem is a meaningless one. No physicist ever measures any form of energy except that which is limited and set off against another. Speaking from the standpoint of a particular kind of work in which we are most interested, there is then a great increase in the available energy of the universe through this redistribution.

If we take a little wider view of the evolutionary process and suppose, as is usually done, that the start is made with some kind of comparatively uniform distribution of nebulous gas, we find that the evolutionary process is, as Mr. Spencer says, the continual concentration of mass, and that with that continual concentration of mass, that segregation and consolidation, there goes along a continual increase in energy of position.[5] The energy that at first existed in an indifferent radiating form, going along with the comparatively diffused state of mass, is gathered up into centers of high potentiality. That means that the paths of motion are correspondingly limited. In your uniformly diffused condition the paths of motion theoretically are indifferent, also radiating out in comparatively even rays in all directions. In the concentration of mass you get more or less definite paths of motion limited. Now the living matter, especially as we find it organized in the animal organism, represents a very high stage of such concentration of mass, the organic molecule being infinitely complex in structure compared with the inorganic, and represents also a great amount of energy of position, together with the possibility of discharging that energy along certain specific limited paths.

From the strictly cosmological standpoint these seem to me the most important characteristics of the living being which have occurred to me. Of course at first the concentration of mass is instrumental, it is subordinate, it is simply necessary to getting this reservoir of energy, this energy of position, and getting it in such tensional relations to other similar reservoirs that its path of movement will be limited instead of being indeterminate. From that standpoint then, the process is an economic process, as more of the energy is available for ends in which we are interested, and through the limitation of the paths of motion it is available in a much more effective way. There is more stored up to use and it is possible to use what there is stored up with less incidental waste, to make it all go more directly to its mark.

If we take the distinction between plants and animals, or between the various orders of animals from the so-called lower to the higher, those seem to me the important distinguishing characteristics.

Stated in biological terms we get the familiar idea of division of labor or specialization of organs, and mutual interaction between these specialized organs, so that they all reinforce each other and cooperate toward a common end. The specialization of structure, differentiation of organs, is of course comparable to the concentration of mass and the accompanying getting of energy in the form of energy of position; while the interdependent side, the interaction of various organs upon each other so as to give harmony of result instead of waste, is, I think, comparable to the limitation of the paths of motion from one mass to another. In either form what we get is continual definition, continual specification, movement toward individuality, using that term individuality now to mean simply this differentiation so as to increase the centers from which energy may proceed, and interaction or interdependence to express the fact that these various centers have these modes of action and reaction upon each other more and more limited to certain definite forms.

SECTION 3. DEFINITION OF ORGANISM

May 4, 1898

We may sum up the previous discussion in such a way as to arrive at a definition of organism. I mean by definition here a statement of the factors which are necessarily involved in the concept of organism. Very much of the discussion as to whether society is an organism, for instance, seems to be wasted because there is either no definition of organism at the outset, or a merely nominal one. Some writers have defended the conception of society as an organism on the ground that you can find something comparable to various organs of the body in it, something comparable to stomach, head, etc. I think it is Bluntschli who argues that monarchy is the highest type of organism because it has a head, and the vertebrates which possess heads are higher types of organism than the acephalic type. Others have denied that such is true, calling it purely allegorical. It is obvious that there is no standard behind such a discussion as that; it is all arbitrary argumentation.

The point that MacKenzie has grasped clearly in his *Introduction to Philosophy*[6] is, first, the statement of just what it is that we conceive of as necessary to constitute anything an organism.

First, there is a unity of process which is not merely an objective unity in the sense that a spectator can see that there is an underlying quodam of mass in energy which persist throughout, but a unity in which the later stages have reference to the earlier in such a way that they do not simply follow after them, but that they react into them so as to maintain them in their action; a unity which some writers term an ideal unity to show that it is a unity in and for the thing itself and not merely a unity which can be more or less arbitrarily traced by an observer. If the term ideal or subjective may suggest to some that which is antithetical to real objectivity, the terminology perhaps might be objected to. For that reason I generally use the term functional unity; but the point is that it is an individuality in and of the action itself through this return of the later phases of it into the activity which manifested itself in the earlier.

Second, this unity is maintained through some differentiations or distinctions of activities; if not of parts or structures, at least of the offices performed by the various parts. And of course the higher the organism, the more marked and specific this specialization or differentiation.

Attempting to reduce these distinctions to their typical form we naturally state it in terms of the interaction of organism and environment. The first typical specialization would be that which has reference to the active appropriation of the environment by the organism, that which in the higher organisms we call muscular and motor operations; but before we have muscles we have certain operations whose function is to get hold of food stuff. That activity must be on the whole katabolic, it must change energy of position into kinetic energy. A corresponding activity on the other side would be the transformation, the assimilation, of this seized material over into living structure, making it really food, digesting it, changing it over into part of the life structure. That activity is anabolic, it results in the giving up more energy of position for future use.

Now as this is of course a purely schematic or typical treatment, the third set would be that which serves to mediate these two, or to maintain the balance. The animal gets food only by using itself up. As far as it is concerned, there is the out-go. The assimilation of this food, since it results in making good the waste of the organism, might be called the in-come, and then we have the mechanism which equates the in-come and the out-go. Of course in the lower organisms that will not be structurally marked off. About all the distinction at the outset will be that between the outside and the inside, but since it is the outside which naturally leads toward the appropriation, and the inside which has to do the assimilating, that difference of function develops itself into further differences of structure. The nervous system is the great scheme or piece of mechanism which is finally specialized as having the office of putting the outreaching appropriative function into cooperative relations with the internal assimilative changes.

So far then, we have as the concept of the organism a unity of end, of teleological process, which is kept up through diversity of operation, and to a minimum at least of structure. That is all that is essentially involved. A machine of course closely simulates this idea of an organism, in that there is there also a unity of end which is maintained through diversification of parts, which in this diversification interact in such a way as to maintain a general unity of process, but of course there is no provision in any machine which has yet been constructed for making good its own waste. That is, the products of the machine's activity do not return into the structure of the machine in such a way as to maintain its own workings, while in the organism they do.

The third head, which is simply a further analysis of the two already given, is with regard to the way in which the different organs or structures cooperate with each other so as to maintain the unity of the organism as a whole. The problem of an active organism is the same as an active machine. It is to secure the balance of stability or resistance, and flexibility or transfer of action; the bearing of one part on another. If we compare a higher form of organism with the lower, what makes us call one higher is not the fact that there are more organs there simply, but rather that each structure has a greater inertia or momentum, a greater independence of its own. It is more fixed as a specific organism. In the lower organism of course, one part of the organism may exercise the function at one moment and another part at another; there is no special fixity in the structure. It has no special individuality of its own. Now the division of labor that we speak of as characterizing the development or organic life means that certain structures are more and more set apart as having a certain sphere of action as their own—therefore a relative independence or isolation. The eye, the hand, the stomach, each is like a little organism, a little world in itself having its own specific modes of action which no other organ can adequately perform for it, but which it strives to perform on its own account as if it were a complete organism of itself. Of course we have to set right over by the side of that the statement that the higher organism has not only this greater resistance of one part over against another in attempting to maintain its own particular line of action, but there is also much greater flexibility of interaction in the way in which one of these organs acts upon another.

Those are the two limiting principles. If the principle of stability or resistance goes too far, of course the organism is likely to disintegrate into a number of separate centers which have simply external and mechanical relations to each other. The best organ would be one that has got to running entirely on its own hook while the free paths of interaction, inter-connection with other organs had got clogged up or in some way broken so that you would have either congestion or starvation. But if you do not have an adequate amount of stability and resistance, you have a relapse into an over-labile, jelly-like condition; you have a relapse into a lower stage of organization. Psychologically we might say that hallucination or absent-mindedness represents the extreme of too great stability or particu-larization on the part of some given structure. A man thinks he hears voices, he has auditory hallucinations. His ear apparatus is running on its own hook; it is not in such organic interaction of stimulus with other organs of the body that it is controlled. If you take a case of dreams or of loss of presence of mind where the whole consciousness is diffused, you would have a case of too complete reduction of the stimuli, too complete inter-communication without resistance at any given point enough to bring the thing to a definite head or focus. If we take the aspect then of specializa-tion, of individualization, we find a tendency on the part of each organ to become the representative of the end. In other words, to become the center of action. We may say that there is all the time going on a competition in the various organs of the body for domination for each to be the end so that the others may be put into a subordinate position to it. Of course in any healthy organism this tendency is so arranged that we get a rhythm, a succession of dominating centers, but in order to illustrate the point we will say that the tendency of each to become the controlling center remains. It may be illustrated on the side of consciousness. We may say there is a conscious competition of the eye or hand to become the controlling center of consciousness, to be that in terms of which the world will be reported, the factors from the other senses simply coming in to help out and rein-force the account of this dominant sense. But if this tendency becomes more than a tendency; if the tendency of any one organ becomes so marked that that has a preference, a fixed preference, over the other organ, if the competition ceases to be free, then you get an unhealthy organism. The natural condition would be to have such free competition of these various centers that each would yield in turn according to the needs of the whole organism to the others, so that you would get continual redistribution of the tensions, a continued variation in the focusing of energy.

If we say that the first is the principle of individualization and of com-petition for active control, the second aspect is that of interdependence, of mutual subordination, leading to cooperation. Of course the point is that those principles as thus stated, antithetical and opposed to each other, are the two necessary aspects of an organism as already defined. This latter, this subordination, the capacity of each to be stimulated by the other in such a way as to become tributary to the other, is that which gives us the functional unity of the whole. But this principle of specialization and com-petition on the part of each to be for the time the representative of the in-terests of the whole organism, that is, to be the center, is the counterpart principle in the distinction or differentiation which maintains functional unity.

As would be obvious from what was said the other day, the competitive aspect of the various members or subactivities would become most marked at such periods of reconstruction as to demand a good deal of variation. We would get then competition with reference to imitation, with reference to the tentative starting up of various modes of activity, while cooperation would express the outcome, would express the result. They would be related as mechanism and function. The mechanism is competitive; but unless the organism is going to pieces, the outcome of that competitive effort must be to set up the consensus of the various parts. The terms cooperation and competition are taken here in as literal and broad a sense as possible—cooperation being their working together, their functional harmony, and competition the fact that since each organ is the organ of an organism, it strives to embody, to manifest itself in itself the activity of the entire organism. We would have, then, competition as the mechanism of growth, and cooperation as the reestablished harmony of function.

We may stop for a moment here and take stock, to see what [the] concept of individuality would be. So far as it would emerge from the biological distinction we would get two distinct views of the individual. I do not mean by calling them distinct to call them separate, but to mark the fact that the individual will present itself in two different aspects according to the stage at which we take the process we have been discussing. We get a different view of it as we take the reconstruction while it is still going on, while it is still struggling to accomplish itself, while it is still problematic, and [when] we take this process as having succeeded and reestablished unity. In the latter sense the individual will be identical with function. Everything that we have said about functional unity would be said about individuality. In that sense of course individuality is simply this active unity of process of the sort described. It may be said that for that reason it should not be called individuality. It is just as universal, so to speak, as it is individual; it is this harmonized organized unity, it is the whole system of action as it displays itself, and if anybody objected to applying the term individuality to it on that score, I should not insist upon the term. Otherwise I should use it as describing the fact that this process is a unity and that it is a unity of absolute reference. We cannot say that it is unity of conscious self-reference, but that it must put some sort of teleological unity of conscious interest as underlying all special changes which take place.

If we define "individual" with reference to the process of reconstruction while it is still going on and is therefore more or less tentative, the individual is practically identical not with function but with organism. In order to have a convenient term I would call the first functional individual and I would call this the tensional individual, to signify that it marks something which is set off as a factor in a whole process, and that this factor is not in thoroughly adapted relations to the other factors, but that the factors are in relation of temporary opposition to each other, in the relation of tension to each other. If you take a thoroughly established constitutive organism, you do not get any basis for drawing any line between it as organism and its environment at all. You can look at it as the whole universe which is flowering at a given point. You cannot even call it a result or effect of the universe. That would imply a certain dualism between it and the universe, and there is none. It is simply a universe as it is defining itself at that particular point and spot. If you take any healthy organism it is certainly possible to look at it simply as so much of the energy of universe itself, as being simply a specification or differentiation of that whole, and apart from some reconstruction or readjustment which has to be effected, that would be the most natural way in which to take it.

Now our problems as conscious beings are practically on the intellectual side; at least our problems of readjustment and hence our unified point of view is one which we comparatively rarely assume. We take it in the heights of our religious consciousness, and we take it to a certain extent at least in our aesthetic consciousness, and that is the point of view which, so to speak, we are trying to attain in philosophy; but our everyday life is a continuous problem of particular adjustments which have to be effected, and as a result our ordinary point of view is dualistic, that of the tensional individual as distinct from the functional individual, that of the individual which is marked off, set over against something outside of itself—organism and environment, and in conscious terms subject and object. But of course so far as the previous analysis is correct, it would be at least true that on the biological side we have to conceive of this tensional individual as relative to the functional, we have to conceive of the distinction, the opposition of organism and environment as something which grows out of and in turn tends to the unity of function.

One distinction which I might mention here is that between organ and member. That is of course more or less verbal, but it is well to keep the distinction in mind. If we take any particular structure that is a specific structure, as manifestly a whole organism, as centering or focusing the organism, we should call it organ. It is the specified channel of functional activity; it is taken not at large, not in an individualized way. If we take it in its subordinate aspect, then, which instead of being centered is simply a contributing factor to some other structural center, it is a member. The significance of that distinction, I think, will come out when we come to the more distinctly social discussion. We all have those two aspects socially; we are both members and organs of society. As members of society we have duties, responsibilities, we have to respond to the stimuli which come to us as particular individualizations. As organs we are representatives of the whole, we are embodiments of the whole; we have rights; we have claims; we have specific modes of action. Or putting the whole thing into more distinctly political terms, all members were subjects, all organs were participants in sovereignty, were citizens.

One other example—the periods of growth in the human body. All the time there is growth, there is readjustment. But that is not continuous. There are epochs like that of adolescence when these readjustments become so marked that there is a change in the function itself. We have a series of such periods of marked reconstructive readaptations to be found in the development of the human being. In one sense it is simply a quantitative change, but there are these rhythmical epochs when this quantitative change becomes reactive in previous habits and function. Of course that would be a distinction of degree, different values attaching to the two phases.

NOTES

1. For this aspect of Spencer's view, see his *First Principles* (New York: D. Appleton and Co., 1888), Secs. 152–55, 159–62, 166–69.
2. Baldwin, *Social and Ethical Interpretations in Mental Development,* pp. 39–55; 477–78.
3. James Mark Baldwin, *Mental Development in the Child and the Race: Methods and Processes,* 2nd ed. (New York: The Macmillan Co., 1897), pp. 214–20. The first edition was published in 1895.
4. Probably a reference to Spencer, *Psychology,* Vol. II, Part VIII, Chap. III, "Development of Conceptions."
5. For Spencer's view, see *First Principles,* Part II, Chaps. XIII–XVII, esp. Secs. 101–02.
6. John S. MacKenzie, *An Introduction to Social Philosophy,* 2nd ed. (Glasgow: James Maclehose and Sons, 1895), Chap. III, "The Social Organism." The following appears to be a reworking of MacKenzie's discussion in more biological and functional terms.

CHAPTER 3

THE PSYCHOLOGICAL
PROCESS IN RELATION
TO THE BIOLOGICAL

SECTION 1. THE NERVOUS
SYSTEM AND THE ORGANIC
CIRCUIT; THE SPATIAL-
TEMPORAL ORDER; HABITS

May 5, 1898

I will go on with the statement of the general psychologic process in the discussion of the nervous system as the connecting link between the biological and psychological statement.

We have seen that there is necessarily involved in the organism a differentiation of structure to serve as organs through which the activity of the organism as a whole is specified—the various organs representing the function in its maintenance, in its determinate character. We found also that there is involved an interdependence or reciprocal stimulation of these various organs, so that each reinforces the other. Now the nervous system is a structure which is specialized to represent these organic necessities. The nervous system, unlike the other systems of organs in the human body, has no direct, biologically speaking, purpose of its own; it is simply the mechanism through which these organic requirements of specialization and interaction are effectively carried out. The nervous system is a necessity to any high degree of differentiation or specialization, and it is a necessity to any high degree of interaction, especially in a moving organism. In a nonmoving organism like a plant, the circulatory system serves as a medium of intercommunication, of interaction. But on the whole, excepting as there is a nervous system, the action of various parts on each other must be a direct influence; it must be one, on the whole, of simple push and pull, so that the final action is simply the result of the presence of energy in some part of the organism. If you have more action going on on one side of the organism than there is on the other, that physical fact will of itself determine the result.

Now if we are going to get above the level of this physical or mechanical determination of action, there must be some particular mechanism which serves as an adjuster, or as an umpire, with reference to the particular activities of the various structures which are going on. As far as the nervous system is developed, the resulting activity does not depend merely on the relative amounts of excitation which exist in various parts of the organism. The nervous system is an arrangement which equates these various activities. That is, the stimulation proceeding from a given part of the organism may be quantitatively very much greater than that going on anywhere else at the moment, and yet the final direction of action may not be to that particular structure. Not that there is anywhere a violation of the law of conservation of energy, but the nervous system is a mechanism for using up that quantity of force in indirect ways so that the final outcome will be redirected, may be in quite a different direction. That of course is the very meaning of a nerve center. While on one side it is a reservoir of energy which may reinforce the activity of any particular organ, on the other hand it is such a complicated structure that it can store up or it can switch off and redirect the energy which comes to it as stimulus. In other words, in an organism without a nervous system, the activity of the whole organism is the net outcome of the various pushes and pulls which are immediately going on in various parts of it. The organism which has a nervous system has a device for controlling and modifying this immediate interaction with reference to the welfare of the organism as a whole, with reference to its continuous and persistent welfare.

In serving as an interconnecting mechanism of this sort, the nervous system is itself differentiated into end organs and center organs. The end organs, the so-called sense organs, serve on the side of stimulation or differentiation of activity so as to enable the organism as a whole to respond in the particular limited way which is most desirable. The central organ serves, of course, as an adjuster, a means of effecting harmony and cooperation between these various specialized organs. It represents the side of the unity, as the sense organs represent the side of individualization. We are accustomed to discuss the nervous system along the lines of a dualism between the sense organs and the brain—end organs and central organs—from a genetic standpoint. That is impossible; they are contemporaneous growths; they are simply the two poles of one and the same function. We cannot speak of the sense organs as if they were already there and then (by means of various influences) they serve to build up the brain or central organ. Or in psychological terms we cannot speak as if the sensations were the primary thing and that they then modify themselves until they form thoughts and ideas.

That is the point of view both psychologically and physiologically which the sensational school has taken. If we take the apperception school, it assumes a similar dualism but gives the central organs the preeminence as regards importance and conceives the central organ as having a reservoir of energy which it can send out to the sense organs to modify and change them. That is the idea of James Ward in his article in the *Encyclopaedia Britannica,*[1] the power of attention representing the central activity which introduces arbitrary changes on the sensational side; it is the idea which is back of the freedom of the will, as that concept is often presented. In reality there is but one nervous system and the sense organs, and the central organs represent contemporaneous and correlative growths in the development of that nervous system. We have to conceive of something growing so as to modify itself in two directions rather than to try to put all the start either at one end or the other and then make the other end of the line secondary, and subordinate. Just as, for instance, in the growth of the plant, one would conceive of the root structure and stem structure as correlative growths, we would not try to locate the sorts of growth at one point and regard the other the secondary effect. We can regard the brain simply as a co-adaptation or a coordination of the various sense activities; or we can regard the sense activities as so many outgrowths, extensions, so to speak, from the brain. Either of those views would be truer than the one which attempts to account for brain growth as a secondary result from sense growth, or of sense growth as the mere product of the activity located somehow in the brain.

In terms of the relation of organism and environment, of course the end organs stand for the factor of stimulation, of stimulus, in both of the two senses in which that term is used: in the sense of excitation proceeding from the organism to the environment, and in the sense of that excitation as controlled through reaction in such a way as to be an adequate stimulus. The central organ exercises the particular function of control of response in the two forms. First, of reaction to the excitation. And then as stimulation becomes definite, it controls the excitation—that is, responds in the complete sense of that term. The sense activity is to be conceived in the first place, then, as a specialized signal to action, or as a signal to specialized action. The value to an organism of having the sense organs must be that it gets a better means of determining whether or not to react, or if it decides to react, in telling it better how to react—that is, along what paths, what lines of motion its energy should be directed, whether it is to expend a good deal of energy at this point or only a little, and (whether much or little) just what path of discharge should be followed.

We are accustomed to think of the sense organs as somehow passive and receptive. On the contrary they mark differentiations, specializations into a high degree of functional activity. The sense organ is itself an activity of a highly selective sort. It is merely when we start from this false dualism between the sense organs and the brain that we get the view of all of the sense organs as in any sense receptive. In that it has the function of bringing all the changes in the organism to meet a change in the environment, it may be said to be receptive in function. But that would be better expressed by saying that its purpose was to report, rather than to use the term receive, which seems to imply that it is lying there as a mere inert medium or channel of communication instead of representing really the alertness of the mind as a sentinel or outpost to reveal the changes in the environment to which the organism might adapt itself. It is a case of the historical fallacy again when we say it is the business of the sense organs to be on the alert to find out the changes in the environment to which the organism must adapt itself. That as relative to the adaptation which does take place in the organism it might be said [the sense organ] is receptive in function. But that is only because the work is already done, because the report of the change in the environment has already been sent in. We are too apt to think of the changes as if they connected themselves to the brain as mere passive channels or avenues, instead of realizing that what the sense organs are for is precisely to reveal and determine the nature and quantity of these changes that are going on.

As the central organ exercises the function of response, we may say that it serves to read or interpret the signals. We get a signal. Then the question is: What does it mean? What does it call for? What does it demand? Here is such a change in the environment. What does that mean in terms of change in the organism? And it is the central organ which does the translating, which turns this over into intelligent directions for future action. Saying that sensation is blind is like saying that sensation is merely passive or receptive. It is a mere functional term. It is blind. That is to say it must be read, it must be translated. It is a term which expresses what must be done with the sensation rather than anything in the sensation. Taken as sensation merely, there is nothing blind about it. It is the report of such and such a change in the environment, but the important thing for the organism is what it is going to do about the change, and so from the standpoint of the organism it is blind until it has been given that kind of translation. That translation constitutes the thought side, the ideal side, the meaning side. Now this distinction of stimulus and response is, as I said the other day, a distinction within a unity of function, it is a distinction within a circuit. The response does not answer to the stimulus simply in the sense of coming after, it answers it in the sense of reacting into it so as to modify it. Those in the class last quarter will remember that I criticized the reflex-arc concept on that basis, speaking as if it proceeded from one source and that the response was made in the way of pure sequence.[2]

Now when we realize that the response is not merely to the stimulus but that it is into it, we get what I call the organic circuit as distinct from the simple reflex-arc. This is a distinction simply of the office performed in the continued maintenance of the function. Now this control is nothing separate and distinct, nothing which is exercised by the brain as something separate from the sense organs. This response of control is nothing but the adaptation of various particular organs to each other, nothing but their harmonious interaction. We may speak correctly enough of the control of the hand by the brain, but that phrase needs to be interpreted. What do we mean there by the brain? The brain is nothing but the focusing or meeting point of the various particularized activities of the whole organism of which the hand is one. What is really occurring there is the control of the hand by the eye, by the ear, by the legs and so on. The brain is nothing but the particular structure through which that cooperation [and] adaptation of the various specialized organic activities to each other go on. The control, in other words, represents nothing but the particular activity taking its place as a member of the whole system. It is the whole system through the brain which really exercises the control and not the brain, and that control moreover, as exercised by the whole system, is not a particular kind of activity, as if the organism had an inhibitory activity on tap which it could turn on with reference to particular stimuli when it needed to. That control is nothing but the name for the functional organization; it is nothing but the name for the fact that the particular organ is unified with all the others so that the functional unity of the whole is maintained; it is the name for the effectiveness of the interaction. That conception of control as consisting in thoroughness and completeness of interaction is one which we will have to come back to quite continually; so I hope that the point is fairly clear in this biological statement.

In the interaction of the various organs the space order of the environment and the time order in the organism are built up. The constitution of the environment in space terms—that is, in terms of position, direction, and distance—is a process of the definition of the stimuli to action. The time order of occurrence, duration, and sequence is the definition of the control side, the side of the responses which are made to these stimuli, and just as stimulus and response are correlative, in correspondence, so the building up of the space order and time order are strictly correlative. If it were not for the rule of a central adjustment of acts, there never would be any contemporaneous arrangement of objects. If it were not that the organism must project its own acts in a certain order of succession (that is, must do this thing that afterward it may do that), there would be no necessity for making the space distinction in the environment. The distinction of here and there in the environment is simply the reflex of the distinction of now and then in the acts of the organism. The here is the act that is doing or is to be done right away, the then is the fixing of this particular act with reference to some other act which will come in succession after it. From the standpoint of space we treat the organism as if it were part of the environment. That is, the organism, after all, is one of the possible conditions of action and the environment is a possible condition of action too. If we put them all on the same level as possible conditions of action which have to be arranged together in order that function may go on, we get the space view of the world, that of inventorying the means, the conditions of the function. If we regard these not simply as possible means of action, but as actual means of action—that is, we set them going or realize them as set going—then the attitude is reversed. Instead of projecting the organism into the environment, we introject the environment into the organism. We regard it simply from the part which it plays in the sequence of organic activities.

Supposing a man wants to jump across a brook. He is not quite sure whether he can do it, or just how to do it. So he takes stock, inventorying the conditions of the action. For the time being he loses himself in the environment. He is one point in space and the opposite bank is another point in space and he has to put himself on the same level as the other bank over there. If he does not get outside of himself, he cannot get any clear view of the conditions of action. The moment he begins to jump, if the possible conditions of action become actual conditions of action, the opposite bank, instead of being a mere fixed point in space, is nothing to him excepting the spot where he is going to land. Its whole meaning to him is in terms of the act which he is carrying on. Where he is is the point from which he starts. The opposite bank is only the place where he is going to land, it is only an element in one of his own actions as projected in time. Now this is not directly relevant to the discussion of the nervous system, but it is relevant to the discussion of the function of stimulus and control, and of their respective natures. There would be no space world at all, no space distinctions and space ordering of objects if it were not for the necessity of arranging acts in a sequence.

On the other hand we would not know what the sequential arrangement of acts really meant, we could not turn it over into definite terms, excepting as we put it in terms of the system's position and relations of a variety of things. Just think of any sequence of any activity. You will see how you define it by turning it over into terms of the space where that activity is going to occur, and expecting as you can put it in sense terms you cannot locate it, and excepting as you can locate that place in space relations with the other place you cannot tell how the steps of the activity are related to each other. The quantitative relations mean simply an economical adjustment of the various particular acts which have to be adapted to each other in order to maintain the whole function.

I can arrange a sequence of acts in a vague way by saying that that window is a little way to the right of me in front, and that the [sills] of it are about on the same level with my arm. In saying that, I am adjusting a particular act which I am doing now with one that I am going to do pretty soon, or that I may do. If I can get that in quantitative terms and say that it is so many inches and just such and such a degree to the right of me, and just in such a degree up or down from my hand taken as the axis, I can adjust the sequence of acts to each other with thoroughgoing efficiency, and so this whole quantitative statement of space is simply making explicit the sequential order of acts as they follow upon each other as successive stimulus and response in performing a given function.

May 9, 1898

The point made at the last time was that the central organs and the end organs of the nervous system have to be conceived as the correlative poles of the growth of function, and that the sense organs represent the specializations, high differentiations of activity, and that the brain as the chief central organ represents such a coordination of these various differentiated activities as will enable any one of them adequately to function the whole system. The mechanism for effecting that, the special direction that activity shall take, shall not be disintegration, but shall be a channel, outlet, or expression of the whole organism. The differentiation of activity would be disintegration, unless at the same time it was increasing the mechanism for effecting the interdependence, unless interaction was also in process of building up.

Now this adequate coadaptation so that the particular line which an activity does take shall be reinforced by the other modes of possible action, and shall in turn contribute to them, is impossible excepting as the central apparatus has a registering or cumulative function. The only way in which solution of the tension between various modes of activity can be successfully solved, solved in the interest of the whole function, or the organism as representing the whole function and not a particular structure, is that the various modes of immediate activity should be, so to speak, weighted or loaded with reference to the part which they play upon the whole in maintaining the life experience. The eye center, for example, must of necessity be able to bring out what the eye stands for in the life of the organism, and it cannot do that excepting as it has been modified through previous use in such a way to have its present activity represent in this cumulative or registering way the modes of action which have been found serviceable upon the whole in the past. That is, each organ has to be consolidated so to speak of the whole condensation of the whole organism. That is of course familiar as the idea of habit, and it is obvious enough that if all the activities were writ in water, if there were nothing registrative and cumulative of this sort, there could not be organic development of this nature. That is the very meaning that we do give to the central apparatus, that it is not something swayed by immediate stimulus, or by what is going on at the moment, but that it carries with it the function and uses that have been worked out through previous experience.

That suggests then another distinction to go with this one of stimulus and control of which I spoke the other day, the central organ representing the factor of habit and the end organs representing the variations which call for the use and application of habit. Or the sense organs representing the momentary, the immediate in representing the element of change and variation, while the central organs represent the more enduring, the permanent conditions; and the whole function, as stated in terms of this interaction, representing the reconstruction of function, or the growth of the present identical element in and through variation or difference, the same idea that we have had in so many forms before as the very essence of the idea of organism.

That is a familiar enough conception in that general way, but the fallacy which is likely to arise here is one of which I have spoken before: speaking of conceiving of habit and its adaptation to these varying conditions, the so-called process of accommodation, as if they were two different things, two different processes, as if they were one process by itself of habit, and then as if there were another process of variation, and then through that there arose the necessity of adapting the habit to the changing conditions. Now as against that, it should be clearly seen that habit and changing conditions are terms which have meaning only with reference to some necessary readaptation of function; that is, just as we have to define organism and environment in terms of adaptation, so here with habit and changing conditions. The only definition we can give for either of these is teleological. We can only define them, not as existing processes, but with reference to the particular office that they subserve in effecting the reconstruction of function. Anything is habit which can be used for purposes of control in effecting a reconstruction, whatever can be used without itself requiring attention in order to bring about new functioning.

It is not that something persists in a purely mechanical way and something else does not. Everything persists somehow or other. It is a question of how it persists with reference to the end that we want to reach. Now that phase of previous function that persists in such a way that we can employ it at once without giving thought to it we term habit. That factor which needs attention, that which must be looked after, the factor that sets the problem or makes the demand, is what we would term the varying conditions. Now this distinction between that which can be used at once and that which is problematic and has to be cared for, looked out for, is one then which arises in the process of growth, in the process of the readaptation of function. We get into all kinds of difficulty if we conceive of habit as one separate principle or mode of operation, and the changing sensory conditions as another independent mode of operation; but all the time these two have to be brought into some sort of working relations to each other. Habit is simply that which utilizes and administers the changing conditions. The changing conditions are simply the stimuli which evoke the play of habit and to which the habits must apply themselves, but the single fact is the process of growth which can be termed habit varying itself, or our specialized activities coordinating, unifying themselves. The single process of functional identity is difference.

SECTION 2. CONSCIOUSNESS AND ACTION

Now to come to a little closer quarters to the psychological aspects of the question, it would follow from this that consciousness has to be interpreted with reference to the mediation of action, or with reference to the part which it plays in effecting this reconstruction of function; or on the objective side, in terms of the part that it plays in constituting a real environment, in bringing the conditions of life under control and making them adequate stimuli. I wish expressly to disclaim this as being an adequate account of consciousness. All I mean is that if we consider it from the biological standpoint, it is the result we get; but the biological standpoint is itself of course an abstraction, so that we cannot get an adequate conception of consciousness simply from the biological standpoint. But from the point in which we are now interested in the matter, we can say that consciousness represents such an evaluation of the conditions and the method of the life process as continually enriches it in content.

The control of the conditions constitutes the object in consciouness. The control of the method of action, the plan, scheme of action, constitutes the subject in consciousness. Admitting that this is an inadequate account; that is, that it does not cover the whole ground, it is useful in the first place in this way, that it enables us to avoid an undue antithesis between the biological and psychological, which seems to me to have affected recently some sociological discussions. We have now what is termed the psychological school which rather delights in distinguishing itself from the biological school of sociology, laying stress on the seeing of society as a psychological rather than a biological entity and interpreting it from the standpoint of the psychological process rather than the biological. Undoubtedly a merely biological conception of society is inadequate, but a psychological conception which starts out by making itself as antithetical as possible to biological ideas, which simply emphasizes the distinction between the two, and assumes that the biological categories are misleading or else metaphorical, is unfortunate, for it takes the backbone out of the psychological view, leaving it practically without any controlling method, because it does not enable us to place the psychological activities and see what they mean in the evolutionary process as a whole. From this point of view the psychological process simply represents the biological life process, and this coming to consciousness—the coming to consciousness serving for purposes of better control and direction.

If we begin by postulating action in the biological sense, then we would see that psychical processes represent an awareness of the nature of those life activities, and that in doing that it serves to enrich and to direct the life process itself.

Starting it now in terms of consciousness, the processes referred to [as] the end organs represent the specialized activities. It is only in an external sense, the sense which we apply to some spectator, that we can really talk about the specialization of these activities apart from the state of consciousness. The distinction, say, of light and of darkness would have different chemical reactions in different parts of living matter, and in that sense we might say that those activities, as far as they are different from other things, those called forth by heat and pressure, would be specialized. But we might for all real purposes talk as well about the specialization of the activities which go on when wood burns or when a lump of sugar is attacked by an acid. It is because we are attaching different values to these things that this idea of specialization, realization becomes anything more than the term which holds good from the standpoint of an investigator who reads into the facts distinctions which really do not exist in the facts themselves but in himself. All the quality, in other words, of the content is due to consciousness.

The central side in representing the control of the particular activity by the whole system is, psychically, interpretation through anticipation. The great advantage of being able to think biologically means that the stimulus or the environment can be anticipated, and that therefore the necessary reactions or responses can be prepared in advance without having to wait to make the adjustment under the stress of the existing emergency. The whole thinking process represents preparation based on this power of interpretation of an excitation through placing it consciously in the whole system of experience, so as to give it a meaning in terms of other experiences which it may lead up to or indicate or symbolize. The sensation thus represents a variation of action, it represents a novelty. Every sensation is as such new, there is no possibility of the recurrence of the same sensation. Every sensation is qualitatively speaking a creation, it is an original variation of experience. Now the ideal side, that which corresponds to what is going on in the central organs, stands for the old or habitual as serving to utilize and direct the new element, the variable element.

From this point of view the whole process of consciousness represents a tension between the particular, new, or variable factor in action, and the other activities of the organism as a whole; that in that tension the variable element serves to initiate the new activity and to fix the problem of it, while the central response serves to interpret, to give meaning to and to control. Or put in terms of the extreme of consciousness, it is these breaks, the variations, which constitute the different states as different states of consciousness. That is, the different existences we regard as psychical events, psychical entities. Each of those marks a redirection of functional activity, and as long as it persists so that we will give it individuality as a psychical event or existence, it means that the function continues without readaptation. But now we have not only a series of events which make up a so-called chain, but each of those has a content, a significance, a meaning and import. Just as it as an existence is referred to the sensational side, to the change in the direction of the action, so the import or meaning is given by the place which this particular occupies in the whole system of activity, so that existence and meaning are again the two correlative abstractions. The existence is the activity reflected in consciousness on the side of variation or change as located or referred to some particular organ or mode of action; and content is the immanence of the whole system of activity in that varying mode; and biologically all consciousness has to be interpreted as such a tension in the development of experience between the activity of the particular organ and that of the whole system. Now this tensional activity of that sort, between the organism as a whole and some particular organ—the eye, the ear, or the hand—has both its intellectual and volitional aspects.

Take the volitional first. The change in activity is primarily a demand. It is a demand for response, for redirection of the activities of the organism. As an excitant it is demand. Now in that fact we have the basis of the psychology of wants. In the relation of the whole organic system to this particular variation we have, in volitional terms, the putting forth of energy to meet that want. V represents the variable process as end organ; and P, the permanent, as referred to the central. If we speak of it from the demand which this variation makes for modification, for readjustment from the side of P, we have the want, we have appetite or, in more complicated forms, what we know as desire. If we think of this same process in terms of the response, the readjustment of the permanent element in such a way as to control the change that is taking place, we would term it effort. In reality of course, there is one process which we name differently according to the side from which we are interested in it.

Now for the intellectual aspect. Every state of consciousness, according to this, must begin, in however rudimentary a way, as a want, as an appetite. Now in order that we may react to satisfy that want adequately, we have to know what kind of a demand it is. We want to know what sort of a want it is; what it is after. Now as the reaction takes that form of trying to make out the nature, the quality of the want or demand, it becomes what we would term a sensation in the intellectual sense. The sensation in the intellectual sense is this demand becoming objectified, becoming presented to consciousness with some sort of definite value attaching to it. We get in the first place the shock, the jar. Something happens to you. You have no definite sensory qualities, but you do have the shock of change, the necessity for the redirection of attention. That shock is at least a rudimentary want of some sort; a rudimentary appetite, so to speak. However, you cannot satisfy it until you know more about it. Just as soon as your response takes that form of trying to tell something about it, then your shock as mere shock of change ceases, and you get to have certain definite qualities of consciousness on the basis of which you can react adequately. At the same time that this want or demand side, this shock of change side, is changing into sensation, the return wave of action is becoming the idea which is the interpretation or placing of that sensation. It is the meaning of the sensation in the sense that it states that particular occurrence not as a mere event but in terms of what it is good for in the whole system of experience. It makes of it a symbol or sign, a signal of experiences which are outside of itself and hence the necessary correlation of idea and thought in the process of intelligence or attention. What I said the other day about the reaction of stimulus and response of course holds here in the whole process of transformation by which the interpretation of sensation, the placing of it, makes less and less of it as a mere want and gives it more and more an intelligent place of its own—that is, makes of it a sign or clue to all the suggestions and associations of experience that thus come to cluster about it.

On the volitional side then, every want has to be regarded as originating in such a variation of action as calls for readjustment of the whole action, and its satisfaction is found in the meeting of that demand, in securing a new functional unity; and any psychology therefore which would attempt to conceive of wants either in terms of pleasure/pain or in terms of simple appropriation and possession of external objects would be defective. Those are incidents or factors in the process of the satisfaction of the want, but they do not explain the change of function. The variation accounts for the origin of the want, and the restoration of the unity is the satisfaction of the want. Any theory which regards sensation and idea as independent of action and which attempts to state the intellectual process as if these were separate existences is sure to compromise the whole theory.

May 10, 1898

There are two or three points which I want to note in amplification of what I said yesterday, though they would better have been put in at the time.

In this consciousness as the tension of readjustment of experience, involving a particular and variable element on one side, and a general, relatively identical one which stands for the whole as against the particular on the other, there are two stages, as I said yesterday. The first of these we might term relatively the negative one and then as that gets under greater control, the positive. And if we take the volitional side first in the evolution of the want, what presents itself first in consciousness is the break in the previous activity. The state of things is at first referred to the past; it is contrasted with what has been, with the state of functional unity and harmony which has just preceded it; consequently, relatively to that it is appreciated as a state of lack, a state of loss. But that consciousness of lack, of want in the negative sense (that is, of being without something, there being a gap there, a void) arises simply through the contrast with the previous union which is the standard or organization. Now as that want becomes definite, as the reactions which are made take shape in the form of responses so that that want is specified, characterized in its own particular nature, it becomes more and more positive, and partakes of the nature of a demand: that is, of the capacity for feeling the want. And that is the normal evaluation. The term want, the term capacity, and the term potentiality, each has both of those meanings—on one side relative emptiness and lack, the negative side; and the other the meaning of power.

A person says he wants something. You cannot tell whether he means simply that he is without something that he would like to have, or whether he means that he is going to get it. If it means that he is after that thing, and after it vigorously, it is projected toward the future, it is interpreted by what is going to happen, it is the promise, the earnest of the securing of the thing, or of its own fulfillment. The same way on the intellectual side. Sensation at the period when it presents itself simply as a shock of change is intellectually negative, it marks a period of confusion, of passivity. That side has been emphasized so much in epistemological theory that the subject, the mind here, is passive, and there is some energy outside which is bearing in on the self or the subject, and somehow stamping itself, making an impression. That is to be interpreted also with reference to the present stage of action. It means that something has got out of our control and that passivity is really our helplessness, our relative impotency in knowing how to direct our activities. Now as our adjustments are made, it ceases to be felt simply as a confused impression which is forced on us against our will, and it becomes a sign, a signal, an index of certain other possible experiences. This break in the experience, which is felt first as lack and as passive impression, serves to focus the direction of energy. But the point is that it serves that purpose on the negative rather than the positive side; it focuses energy because it sets the problem.

Relative to attention I have spoken of the fallacy of supposing that there is an objective focus of attention at the outset which means the point of greatest stress. It is the place of greatest weakness, it is the point that must be looked after, the point that has fallen to the greatest extent out of harmony, out of equilibrium. Or it is the next means in action; it is the next step that has to be cared for. Instead of defining attention with reference to a focus which is objectively there, we have to define the focus in terms of the readjustment of energy involved in the change of function. The focus simply locates the stress of the readjustment. But in doing that, it gives the next step to be taken, it is the point from which positive reorganization will proceed. If we master that, then we have an instrument in our hands with which to take the other steps of readjustment which are required. Now the sensation, the want, which are precisely parallel to each other, have that double look—one the retrospective, contrasting with the function from which it is the break, and the other prospective, looking ahead. The first is the directive index to securing the new unity of function. Want and sensation are the crucial, the overt, points of the reconstruction of the experience. It is the point where the change, the readjustment is located at a given time.

I think if you will get that image clearly in your mind of the sensation and the want as simply locating the immediate overt strain and stress in the readjustment of function, that it will simplify a good deal the problem of the relation of subject and object by substituting another mental image for that one of a subject here and an object there and of the object as stamping itself on the mind accidentally, having no rationale in its origin and no constructive element in its function. Of course accidentally it may serve to enrich experience but only by injecting perfectly externally a new element into our experience. But there is no explanation there of its having any systematic relation to our experience. How it is that this new element which is injected into our experience is relevant, how it happens to find it and help build up the continuity and the system of our experience—all that is utterly miraculous. The theory of association is the only apology for an explanation of that fact which has ever been offered, and that of course begs the question, because it implies relevancy in the form of similarity already, and how it should have that relevancy is part of the problem to be explained.

Stating consciousness in more objective terms, it represents the tension between an organized situation which is present in idea, present in conception or image, and a local, partial situation which is immediately and overtly present in sensation, which needs to be set over, which needs to be revalued and modified in operating as a means, in order to realize the organized, unified situation which is only ideally present. All thinking, in other words, using thinking here in its widest sense, all the intellectual process as such, involves a relative opposition between a scheme of things which arranges a situation which we want to get hold of, and some obstruction which is felt as immediately present, but which is, although an obstruction, yet the immediate means to be mastered; or that with reference to which the next step may be taken in order that the ideal situation may become active in our experience. That is the tension stated in terms of content, just as before this I have been stating it in terms of process or form.

SECTION 3. THEORY OF IMITATION

As I said yesterday, at the close of the lecture, that in order to illustrate what is meant by this, I would compare it with a certain suggestion of Professor Baldwin's which turns largely on the category of imitation.

At the outset I would like to say that imitation does not seem to me the name of any psychical process at all. It is the name for a result; it is the name for a product; it is a thing to be explained. In other words, rather than a process which we could use in explanation, it names a thing entirely from the outside. A does something, and then B, seeing A, does something like it. You may call that imitation. There is an interesting fact requiring explanation. By what process, by what mechanism, is this product which we call imitation brought about? It seems to me it would throw just as much light on the subject of a child learning a lesson to say that he had a faculty of lesson-learning and [was] using that as a psychological operation. The thing we want to get at is through what mechanism that lesson is learned. And so with this fact of imitation.

Now that does not of course actually dispose of the question as relates to Mr. Baldwin, because he states quite definitely what process he does apply the term to. But I think there is an ambiguity and confusion in his treatment, that he is thinking of two different things, one a strictly psychological process and the other the social product which happens to be brought about through the operation of this psychical process—a confusion which finds expression, I think, in a sentence on page 264 of his first book on mental development. "An imitation is an ordinary sensori-motor reaction which finds its differentia in the single fact that it imitates.[3] The first half of that, since it is a "sensori-motor reaction," states it is a psychical process, "which finds its differentia in the single fact that it imitates." [But] that is nothing in the process at all. It is simply naming it from the outside, from the peculiarity of the result which it effects. Now if it is conceived of as a case of sensori-motor reaction, it falls under the general head which I have been discussing. What I have called the stimulus-response relationship in its growth is precisely the sensori-motor reaction that takes the form of the organic circuit. That is what you have—the motor response is into the sensation so as to modify the sensation and change it from a mere impression into a definite sign or index to something else.

Mr. Baldwin clearly recognizes that it is a process of that kind. He uses the term circular reaction to signify precisely this fact. It is what he calls a circular activity: brain state due to stimulating conditions, muscular reaction which reproduces or retains the stimulating conditions, same brain state again due to same stimulating conditions, and so on. The reaction is back into the stimulus, and if you go back to his earlier discussion of adaptation in general you will find the same thing. Some variations might react in a way to lay hold of it, and some keep on reacting to it again and again. That point is expressed over and over again. It is summed up on page 216: *"Habit expresses the tendency of the organism to secure and to retain its vital stimulations."* He shows very clearly the fact that the reaction should be of a selective character retaining the stimulations which are favorable, and leaving out those which do not help on the life process.

> The process of habit, having as its end the maintenance of a condition of stimulation, is set in train by the initial stimulus. And the discharge of it in the path which again "hits" the stimulus is the function of this stimulus rather than another (pp. 216–17).

He speaks again there of the circular process in a way that would seem to be practically identical with the statement already made. The only question so far would be a subordinate one about the fitness of calling such a process imitation, and while I should not myself think it a happy term for it, a man may use any terminology which he pleases, if he explains what he means and uses it in a consistent way.

But when we learn why he calls it imitation, a point comes out which seems very important, and which up to this point I have slurred over. He has the conception of simply reproducing or repeating the identical stimulus that you had before. Nature, he suggests, does not repeat itself, does not repeat stimuli with enough regularity to guarantee the existence and welfare of the organism. The organism must have, then, a mechanism which shall secure the repetition of the stimuli which nature itself does not give with sufficient regularity, or in a sufficient number of cases. And the reason that he calls this process imitation is because in being a circular process it reproduces the first. The first stimulus we may say is the copy and the reaction is simply directed to reproducing it in order to reinstate the previous stimulus.

> There is in all the instances some kind of constructive idea, a "copy," in more or less conscious clearness, which calls the action out, and which it is the business of the imitator to reinstate or bring about somehow for himself (p. 267).

Now my point is this, that the mere reinstatement of a stimulus, the mere reproduction of a given stimulus, implies that the whole work has already been done. If you have a stimulus of that kind, it is no trick at all to reinstate it. The fundamental problem is to secure an adequate stimulus. Mr. Baldwin assumes that it is already given and that the only problem is to get it over again. That is nothing but the most mechanical kind of habit. When we get a thoroughly adequate stimulus of that kind, the tendency is for it to become automatic; it drops out of consciousness entirely. There could be no question in such cases of any conscious effort. When there is conscious effort to reproduce the copy, it implies tension, it implies that we have no adequate stimulus.

To illustrate, you can suppose the problem for a child to draw a tree. He already sees the tree, and it is just the question of how he is going to make his hand reinstate that visual tree as the copy that he already has. Everyone knows that you will only get the most schematic drawing of that tree. The problem is for the child to see the tree. If you can reconstruct the stimulus, if you can make him see the tree in the reference which it has to his hand, you can get him to draw it in an artistic way. But if you take it for granted that he already sees the tree and it is only for him to reproduce it, you will get only the most mechanical external sort of a tree. The real problem is to secure the stimulus, and if you have the stimulus, the reaction, the response, will take care of itself. Or in other terms, the real question is not a question of reinstating the previous stimulus, but of controlling it. It is simply a question of detail whether control is best expressed by reinstatement or by introducing a particular new element into the previous stimulus.

It is a psychological fallacy to suppose that the stimulus is already there. If we realize that we do not begin with a perfect stimulus, then the problem is how to secure one. The conception that the fundamental process is one of reproducing a previous copy loses its basis. It is simply a question of sensori-motor adjustment; it is a question of this readaption of which I have been speaking.

Now to illustrate that, take the case, which I think Mr. Baldwin mentions somewhere, of a little child who sees his father putting on a ring, and the child imitates that. Is that to be conceived of in terms of a copy and reproduction of a copy, or in terms of a suggestion or excitation to action which through the reaction is to be transformed into stimulus? If you put it in psychical terms, what you have is a visual activity. The child sees something. Is that the copy? Is that the end? If so, why should the child try to reproduce it? He already has the whole thing. But in reality that is not his copy at all; it is a simple excitation to action. Physiologically the visual energy centers there [by] being coordinated with the hand center. There is a discharge of energy from the eye center to the hand center. Now the problem there is a twofold problem. On one hand it is for the hand to react in such a way as to make the eye an adequate stimulus. Why does the eye keep looking at the ring? Why are all our sensations concentrated with reference to the visual process? Simply to get an adequate stimulus for the hand to do something which it is starting to do. There must be that return wave of the image to select and organize the visual perception of seeing the ring. Then in turn that, as it becomes better organized, sets up a certain kind of hand activity so that the child performs that kind of activity.

Now an onlooker who sees both the parent and the child may say it is a copy which the child is reproducing. But if the child has the whole thing already in his consciousness, if he has the copy and the reproduction, he would not do it at all. All he has is the eye stimulus. The problem is to coordinate it with the hand activity. The tendency to imitate in this way will occur therefore only when the hand-eye coordination is already nascent or struggling for expression. But if you take him before the paths of discharge are being set up in his own system, he will not initiate that particular thing, and if you take him after that coordination is thoroughly organized, he will not imitate it. It is just at this particular time that this or the other particular coordination is being formed that he is liable to imitation in a given direction.

These are simply the criticisms which Mr. Mead made the evening the Philosophical Club took up Mr. Baldwin's book.

There are one or two additional suggestions. One is that conscious imitation involves a sense of lack of control, and therefore psychically involves not mere reproduction or reinstatement, but necessarily involves variation. We imitate, not to do the same thing that we have done before, but for the sake of doing something different. It is only when you look at it socially that it is the same. If you suppose two social units already there, you may refer to imitation as establishing identity of action between the two; but if you take the matter psychologically, as occurring in one and the same person's experience, it is change, variation, originality—or in Mr. Baldwin's terminology, it is invention. I think that would be obvious without further argument. In bringing the excitation under control with reference to a new mode of action the stimulus itself is varied, just as the child who sees the tree for the purpose of drawing it would see it differently from what he would in looking at it ordinarily, or when the child who sees the ring with reference to putting it on his own hand sees it differently than when he was seeing it with reference to other things previously.

There is an interesting recognition of this fact in the second book of Mr. Baldwin,[4] pages 99 to 109, where he shows that the process of invention grows out of the process of imitation. He shows it all right; but if you read it carefully, you will see that he does it by showing that the process of imitation is not imitation; that is, the process of imitation when you concretely carry out the case does not agree with the definition. The definition is that you reproduce the same stimulus, and he shows that invention is because you do not reinstate. Of course [this is] an obvious contradiction. The child

> can only learn by imitating; for if he only acts strictly on the revived elements of content which come up in his own consciousness from within, then he is acting strictly as he acted before and that teaches him nothing. On the other hand, he cannot act in ways absolutely new, for they come into his consciousness with no tendency to stir up any appropriate kinds of action. He cannot act suitably upon them at all. Hence it is only new presentations which are assimilable to old ones that can get the benefit of the habits already attached to the old ones, and so lead to actions more or less suited to the new. But this is imitation (p. 101).

As he ends up, however, he shows that the child really invents a whole lot of new things.

> The outcome—that is new, both in the new picture of finger-movements and in the setting together of the strains, organic sensations, and all. He has a new thing to contemplate, and he is withal a new person to contemplate it (p. 105).

I think there is no doubt about that as a matter of fact, but that shows that the process is not imitation as imitation has been defined. It is the content of sensation and ideas instead of the mere revival of them as they were before. Take the logical contradiction here. If the child has set out merely to reproduce, then all these new things would be to him simply signs of failure and so he would go on to eliminate all these new things till he got back to what he had to begin with. There is the confusion that I spoke of.

My point is if we take it as a psychical process, it is not imitation at all; it is simply a particular case of this organic circuit or the formation of a coordination involving new stimuli and new modes of control. It is the fact that the stimulus, instead of coming from an object, comes from something which another person is doing, and that the outcome is of a nature to give the child the same power of control which the other person has already. That is, A gets the power of doing something which B already has the power to do. That is an interesting fact sociologically, but it is nothing which explains or enters into the process psychically considered.

I will have something to say later on about the significance of imitation on the social side.[5] This will perhaps do for the psychological statement.

SECTION 4. CONSCIOUSNESS, VALUE, AND INDIVIDUALITY

May 11, 1898

The conception of tension as being a number of specific activities, each striving to become the central point of focus of the whole activity, but requiring to be adjusted to each other in a unity of function, accounts for the mechanics of consciousness. I mean by that phrase "mechanics" that it serves to explain how the particular state of consciousness arises, and why this particular state of consciousness has the special content which it has. We get in this conception a method then, as derived from the biological conception of organism and environment, for dealing with that problem of the genesis of particular conscious conditions.

But as I said the other day, I do not see that the biological standpoint, although it gives us the method, the standpoint for treatment, is itself abstract. It does not give the whole meaning of the thing. That there should be consciousness at all, that there should be qualities, values, is not explained by any of these considerations at all. In fact it presupposes really the general fact of consciousness, or of self-appreciated value; and taking that for granted deals simply with the question of how it happens to assume this or that particular form, and how these particular forms happen to string themselves along just as they do. In the conception or organism (that is to say, an identity or function maintained through each successive act, reacting through the conditions which it sets up back into itself, back into the conditions which gave birth to itself) we are really implying a conscious individuality. Even if we do not assume that it is really there, as most people do assume, in the case of a plant, we still speak of it after the analogy of a conscious identity. We at least have to read that category into the facts in order to get this conception of an enduring identity of the self at all. And certainly when we come to the animal, we find this identity of function represented in the persistence of feeling.

Now that suggests that beside this aspect of consciousness there is another. I have spoken of consciousness so far as the process of evaluation, the process of setting up and measuring particular qualities or values. Now that presupposes the fact of value. If consciousness were simply an evaluating process, it would be a means that did not have any end and hence self-contradictory. It would be a process that was forever trying to do something which it could not possibly do. It would be an attempt to solve a problem which essentially is insoluble. Or, the aspect of consciousness on which I have been dwelling so far is that of mediation, of valuation in experience. That presupposes immediate value. Even when our attitude of consciousness is distinctly prospective, when we are simply trying to read signs for future action, still every stage of the process is itself conscious experience, and therefore has a certain immediate value of its own. It is not a mere means to future experience. It is itself an experience, which accordingly has a worth and a content of its own.

We have to recognize therefore a rhythm of typical forms or attitudes in the process of consciousness. One of these phases is that of which I spoke, where the distinction of subject and object arises, where the distinction of particular and universal arises, where we are volitionally in the attitude of desire and effort, and intellectually in the inquiring attitude, having a problem on hand as something which has to be interpreted. Now so far as that phase of consciousness is at any particular time most important, we can say that on the active side consciousness is instrumental in character. That is, the various distinctions that arise are selected and elaborated, not for their own sakes, although they do have a value of their own, but for the sake of a future experience, for the sake of some end which we are trying to reach. Their value to us is in what we can get out of them, in the use which we can make of them as factors in inducing another experience, which as functional unity will satisfy all these needs. Or on the intellectual side we may describe this type of consciousness as indicative, prophetic, symbolic in character. It points on to something which in itself is not an end. Its important value for us is precisely in that office which it performs of signifying, being a sign of something which itself does not actually convey.

Now this other point of consciousness we may call that of consummation or of absorption. I do not lay particular emphasis on these terms, but simply to have some phraseology which would express its general nature as distinct from the other type—the other form always having its reference, its important value, beyond itself, while this type of value I call consummation to express the fact that it gathers up, that it sums up, accumulates in itself, all the various forms of value which have been previously indicated, or have been striven for, aimed at. The term absorption would mean the same thing—that is, as gathering up in that saturated way.

It would take the aesthetic attitude as distinct from that of the scientific inquirer. (The latter aims at reducing everything to symbols.) The immediate quality of the objects only has meaning for him when he can reduce them as signs. They are indices simply of a general process. He eliminates the immediate sensuous value. If he let that absorb his consciousness, if he let his consciousness be saturated with the immediate values of the objects, he would at once drop the inquiring attitude, the whole tension between what he has and what he is after. In the aesthetic consciousness, that is just what we find. The consciousness is satisfied with what is immediately present for its own sake; the perception of the qualities of the flower, of the statue, of the picture, of the music, are their own end, are their own excuse for being. They are not reduced to being mere clues or indices or instruments to something over and beyond themselves.

Now a large part of our ordinary consciousness is aesthetic. As we look around at the objects about us in our ordinary frame of mind, the colors, the forms, the shapes, for the most part do not have a particular indicative value to us. They may have, they will have, if we have a certain end to which they may serve as means. But in our ordinary observations, a large part of our consciousness is of this saturated or consummative type. We may imagine a time, I think, from the biological standpoint, when the green of vegetation was indicative in character, when it was a signal or clue to a particular kind of action which the animal might perform, possibly the appropriation of food. It is difficult to see how the differentiation could have occurred and been selected, excepting on the basis of its having some such immediate value as stimulus to future action. But certainly, for us that quality of green is gratuitous; it sums up and confers upon us an additional richness or value in experience, which is the essence of the aesthetic consciousness. The interest in psychology has been the analysis of the mechanics of consciousness, the explanation of the way in which a given state arises and assumes its place in arrangement with other states; and probably for that reason the tendency has been to ignore this particular type of which I have been speaking. And yet that is presupposed by the mechanism of change and of successive arrangement of the states of consciousness, and the latter would not be consciousness at all, would have no worth, were it not for this presupposition of the immediate value which sums up in itself the various elements and qualities which have been worked out before, under the strain of necessity, and through the process of tension.

The theory of association has been the form in which psychological theory has approximated the view of this type of consciousness, particularly the conception of John Stuart Mill of indissoluble association, two qualities getting so close together that you cannot separate them.[6] But this conception of saturation or consummation seems to me a much more adequate formulation of the fact than that of association, for two reasons. Association begins with the discrete separate states which are to be associated together by some future process and thus at once falls into reasoning in a circle, because we find out from analysis that no one of these particular states would have any meaning if it were not associated. There must be the relationship with the other states in order that there should be any quality there at all; and yet the theory of association implies that there are these psychical entities, each having its value as a separate existence, and then the association simply comes in to fuse them together—the idea expressed best by Hume: Every distinct idea is a separate existence, every distinct value or quality in consciousness is an ontological entity and thing by itself. But our psychological analysis shows us that we cannot find any such psychical existences, which as cut out, as independent, do have any such value. To put the objection in another way, as matter of fact these distinct states of consciousness which the theory of association presupposes, instead of being given antecedents to a mental synthesis or association, are themselves analytic products; they are specifications out of the previous unity, and it is the particular kind of variations out of the unity which each one is that determines its particular value.

The other objection is that if we start with these independent existences, then association cannot, without violating its own logic, ever give us any increased value of content. It can only institute internal conjunction between its various atoms. Now as matter of fact, what is continually taking place is that one mode of experience absolutely absorbs into itself the varieties which have been elaborated in other experiences. We have a process of assimilation, of chemical destruction and recomposition into the new form, and not simply a mechanical union of existences, which is all the theory of association could really give us. The association does not simply connect together two separate states, A and B, without any qualitative change in the A and B. It gives us two qualitatively new experiences which we might term A′ and B′.

Take a comparatively external case of association, take a location where some great tragedy has occurred, or some event full of significance for human destiny, any place rich in historical association, Athens or Jerusalem. You cannot say that you had one experience (that of the place) and another (what has happened there), and that you had conjoined the two. What takes place is an actual assimilation and reconstruction. Athens is the place where these things happened, Jerusalem is the place where those things happened. They enter into and make up its significance and value. The thing cannot be formulated without this conception of assimilation or consummation or saturation, and that is what is continually taking place in experience. One form gathers up into itself as its own significance, its own value, a great variety of other experiences, and in such a way as to do away with them. They are destroyed just as the form of food is destroyed when it is digested, made over into qualitatively new structures, and enters into new processes. In fact, if we are going to borrow analogies from other sciences, it is *a priori* certain that the chemical process would give us metaphors which would come much nearer indicating the real nature of psychical change than is metaphor of contiguity, of mere external association or from mechanical considerations—that is, considerations in time and space, which have been the ruling image in the associational psychology.

Now this has just the same bearing on the question of the nature of the individual or of selfhood, as the similar distinction which was made biologically between the functional individual and the tensional individual. This value of consummation, of absorption, is the psychological counterpart of the organized or functional unity on the biological side; and the consciousness, as referring beyond itself, as having an instrumental office, is the counterpart of what I term the organism in tension with the environment on the biological side. From one point of view the individual is the summing up, the consolidation of the elaborated and attained values of experience. Here it is this vital, immediate unified appreciation.

From the other point of view the self is one of the two factors involved in reconstruction. The self is the immediate instrument, the self is the immediate agent; the self is subject, in other words, and therefore is in correlation with the material conditions, the stuff which must be made over, or with the object. According then as we are taking consciousness as one phase or the other of this rhythm of growth, we will emphasize, or we will get different types of definitions of the self. From one point of view it is simply the conscious focusing into an organized unity of as rich values of experience as are possible. But from the other, the selfhood is not immediately an end in itself, it is simply a way or active form for accomplishing something else. From the intellectual side as subject, it is an organ for interpreting it, that which reads, makes out the signs which are presented on the volitional side. It is the center from which proceeds the changes which are necessary to bring about the end which is set up, it is the factors in attention which serve most immediately to overcome the tension by realizing the unity of situation which is presented at first only in idea. While the function is still problematic, while the reconstruction is still going on, it is necessary for this distinction to be made between the material conditions of action, the means which must be put together, utilized, in order to reach the end and the scheme for putting these means together; and in that abstraction this formal means appears as the self, as the I, taken as subject, while the material means represents them set over against them as object.

In order that we may know just what the means are that must be dealt with, in order that we may know what the conditions of the problem are, the self has to be treated as one of these conditions, it has to be made an object. Just as I said we get the space view of the world when we regard the organism as itself a part of the environment. We must abstract [from] our own particular interests and intentions, we must temporarily suppress them, that we may get an adequate view of what the means for action are. We must look at ourselves as if we were simply one of many. That is what occurs in the knowing process where the interests of the self as the self have to be subordinated. The whole interest is concentrated on the object and any insertion of personal aims is of necessity a factor of error, a perversion, a swerving from the truth. But as soon as these possible conditions are inventoried, as soon as we have what we conceive to be a fair view of the situation, then the means are set in operation, they are transforming merely ideal means into actual means, and the moment the change takes place from knowing to doing, the subject, instead of being the subordinate factor, that which must conform to the object, that which must suppress itself so that it simply reproduces the object, becomes the dominant one.

It is that which initiates the change and the object is regarded as subordinate and simply material for manipulation in order to realize the purpose which the agent has set up for itself. As that process completes itself, we get again the organic unity of function or we get the stage of saturated, consummated experience.

NOTES

1. James Ward, "Psychology," *Encyclopaedia Britannica*, 9th ed. (1889).
2. *Supra*, Chap. 2, Sec. 2.
3. Baldwin, *Mental Development in the Child and the Race*.
4. Baldwin, *Social and Ethical Interpretations in Mental Development*.
5. *Infra*, p. 349.
6. John Stuart Mill, *An Examination of Sir William Hamilton's Philosophy* (New York: Henry Holt and Co., 1874), I, 184–85.

CHAPTER 4

THE SOCIAL PROCESS
AS EVOLUTIONARY

SECTION 1. IS SOCIETY AN
ORGANISM? THREE ISSUES

May 12, 1898

Taking up today the third main head, the statement of the process from the social standpoint, I do not intend of course to go into the details of sociological science, but simply to bring out some of the categories so far as they are necessary in developing method.

It will be found convenient to center the discussion about two main heads, one which is connected more directly with the biological discussion, and the other with psychological. The first of these topics is the question whether society is an organism. The second is whether there is anything which may rightly be called social consciousness, and if so what that is, and what is the connecting link between the two topics. We shall find Mr. Spencer's discussion of the social sensorium a convenient one.

In discussing whether society is or is not an organism, I shall start, as indicated the other day, from the analysis of the conception of an organism and not from the description of certain particular activities actually carried on by organisms. You will remember that in Mr. Spencer's discussion in the first volume of his *Sociology* [1] he bases his argument for society as being an organism upon the discovery in society of certain functions of getting food and keeping up the circulation and regulating functions, to show that processes exactly analogous to those of the animal organism may be found in society, and the point where he draws his line, the point where he says society is not identical, is the point where analogy fails between the biological organism and society. He find that in one important respect, the possession of a common sensorium, the two differ; and in that respect society cannot be like it. That type of argument shows that there are certain processes that resemble each other closely that are found in biological organism and society, but unless we know whether those processes are necessary to an organism, and unless we know how they are necessary, how it is that they maintain the organic function as an organic function, we certainly are far still from having any adequate basis for deciding that society is an organism.

I should say in connection with this that the processes which Mr. Spencer picks out are, it seems to me, much more fundamental than those which other writers have used, and consequently [he] is less open to this type of objection than other sociological writers who have attempted to show the analogy. As a matter of fact he has taken processes which are essential to organic activity, but he has not shown that they are, or how they are bound up with the conception of organism as such. I shall follow the outline definition of organism given the other day and discuss the matter under the same three rubrics. First, the factor of differentiation; secondly, interaction or reciprocal dependence between the differentiated parts; and thirdly, the question as to the unity of function maintained through this differentiation and this reaction.

The first thing which it would be necessary to show in order to justify applying the idea of organism to society is that individuals may be regarded as differentiations or specifications of an underlying unity of process; that instead of being so many independent entities which then happen to come into contact and reciprocal relations to each other, an individual as an individual must be treated from the standpoint of a genetic continuity of process.

Now I am not going to say that that position can be proved, but it may be said hypothetically that if we adopt the theory of evolution in its generality, then there is no better way in which to conceive any particular individual on the basis of the theory of evolution, unless we assume a definite break at some particular point, beyond which the evolutionary process is replaced by some other sort of one. We are forced to the conception of a single process of life which has been variously differentiated in order to be able to deal efficiently with the variety of local environments and conditions which have to be met. An individual on this basis represents the adaptation of the process so as to meet some particular problem, so as to be able to deal effectively with the special conditions which are met in some particular place or at some particular time, in the evolutionary development. That is, an individual objectively regarded, physiologically or biologically regarded, would have to be considered from the standpoint of a unit of ancestry, modified through variations and natural selection, and the continuity maintained through heredity. The conception of evolution certainly lends itself much more necessarily to the conception of society as an organism than the idea of special creation did. If we regard each individual as a special creation, then the relations of continuity, of sequence, of course are not found, and while that would not prove that society was [not] organic because these various entities might function together after all in a unified way, it would not provide a natural basis for such an organic unity.

Now on the physiological side, all that we know about the transmission of life, about heredity, and about the formation of particular individuals leads us to conclude that the natural individual, the psycho-physical individal, is simply a particular variation under particular conditions of a general racial stock. Not that that stock has any existence excepting in such forms or variations, but we have to recognize the element of continuity underlying and determining all the variety of individuals which present themselves. Biologically of course, the idea of heredity is the important one in leading to such a conception.

Now of course we do not get the complete individual here, we get only what we might term the objective individual, the natural equipment of the individual, the individual as he comes into existence, as he is given; as he is given to himself as well as to others. I mean by that, we do not take into account the reconstructions, the reactions, which take place in his own conscious development. This natural individual is, after all, simply so much material which is to be shaped through being used as means for the realization of certain ends. The individual's consciousness gone, this natural, psycho-physical individual becomes more or less of an object to him, it becomes something which he can use, which he can direct with reference to certain ends. So this fact of itself would not establish the idea of the individual as a differentiation of a unified process; it would only show that the material conditions which enter into the makeup of the individual are of such a sort.

We still have to face the question of psychical individualization, that which makes the individual an individual to his own consciousness, that which makes him to himself a center of interest and of the direction of attention, that which makes him to himself a focus and initiator of activities. Now it is out of the question to attempt to prove that the process of psychical individualization is simply a process of specialization, or that the individual represents individualization, limitation of growth in a given direction. I can only say that the individual comes to consciousness of himself as individual; that is, becomes a subjective personality through this process which I have just referred to, that of considering himself in his natural gifts and equipment, his psycho-physical outfit, as the means to be used for the realizing of certain ends. Then the question is, just what end, just what function or use am I fitted for, and just how shall I manage myself in order that I may become active in realizing this function?

History seems to present us with precisely such a growth in the consciousness of individuality. While the eighteenth century began by conceiving a full-fledged individual, born as Minerva was fabled to be born from the head of Jove as complete with the consciousness of individuality from the outset, modern anthropological research makes it quite clear that, relatively speaking, the further we go back, the more we get what we might call the social protoplasm in which the conscious individual is lost.

It is only in very modern times that there is any such thing as private rights, that the individual can assert claims for himself because he is an individual. You do not find it until Roman law. You do not find it in the Orient, you do not even find it with any fit procedure for recognition and enforcement of these rights in Greece. It is as a member of a family, or a clan, or tribe, or later on a city-state or some community that one can assert himself, and the study of religions shows also a similar attachment of the individual to the social whole of which he is a part, of an absorption of a merging of the individual as a whole so far as his consciousness is concerned. The process of individualization has been an historical growth of which many of the steps, at least, can accurately be traced. It is a continual movement in the direction of democracy. It is the substitution of relations of personal initiation and direction for the regulations by the use, custom and wont which are universal in early society. It is obvious that as long as custom is absolutely dominant there can be practically no question of developed individual consciousness.

Now if we take two features of historic development in the direction of differentiation or individualization, we find that it has served on one side to make the individual a center of initiation, a center of what we might call spontaneous variation, using that term spontaneous in a practical rather than in a metaphysical sense. It means practically: You may strike out for yourself. You do not have to do a thing simply because others are doing it. If you can accomplish the same result in anything which applies to you as you in a way better than the customary way, why go ahead, you can make your own destiny in life. The idea of course is commonplace in modern politics, in modern religion, and furnishes at least a center of storm in the modern industrial sphere—this idea of the capacity of the individual to shape his career according to his own interpretations of himself, and what he is good for. That means of course a great increase in the modes of social action, it means a great increase in the variety and therefore in the richness of contributors to the total social welfare and the total social outcome. If you can get a thing done a thousand different ways instead of having them all done with perfect monotony in the same way, you are bound to have more complexity and more richness. There has been, then, economic motive back of this development. It is the same thing which forces the division of labor everywhere. You can get better service at less cost, and greater richness and complexity of product, by specializing your agent, your organs as much as possible. The limiting distinction here as distinct from the ordinary idea of labor is that your standard of specialization is to be found in the individual's own equipment and not in the mere external work which is to be done; that it is to be his own powers that are to be liberated so that he can do the thing in his own way. By increase then of freedom, the power to select and arrange means according to one's own judgment as to their suitability and as to their relative values, we mean simply that we are getting an increased number of centers of social variation, of invention.

Now [on the other side] at the same time that we get these additional starting points, these additional initiators, we get increased definiteness in the location of what I may call points of social pressure, points of social attack; practically an increase of power which holds persons responsible. If your clan is your social unity, your individual responsibility is certainly highly vague, it is diffuse and indeterminate. It is the clan as a whole which is supposed to operate. If the individual operates, it is not as an individual, it is simply as a clan partaker. And one clan member is practically as good as another. If anybody in another clan kills somebody in ours, it is not necessary to find that particular person; it is the clan that is guilty; make the clan as a whole suffer for the wrong or pay money compensation. I use that simply as an illustration, but the student of these facts knows that you cannot get your point of social pressure, the point at which you are going to bring to bear all your social forces, excepting where you have the power of choice located.

Opponents of democracy sometimes write and speak as if the question of social responsibility were opposed to individual freedom, that the development of individual freedom has been upon the whole disintegrating, tending to loosen the bonds of responsibility. Of course just the opposite has been the fact. It is where the individual is merged that the responsibility is loose and uncertain. So from this point of view the development of individuals, the process of individualization, means growth in the complexity of modes of agency with increase of definiteness in the direction of control of those various agents. Now the development of the process of individualization is then simply a question of efficiency.

This point of view was brought out very clearly in one of the papers that was read to the class. You start from the clan as an individual and keep on to what we call an individual; or in certain cases that gets split up, and as it was suggested in that paper, there is a tendency to sprout, to bud. There are plenty of pathological instances of that kind where the tendency is to develop more or less independent centers of personality in the individual, to lose one's integrity, to become disintegrated. There is no fixed limit, in other words, to this process of individualization. Refinement of perception, acuteness, increased subtlety of thought, increased aesthetic discrimination are all of them cases of the continuation of this one and the same process of individualization; and the limit is a working limit which has to be worked out experimentally, to find just the point where you can secure the best equilibrium or adjustment of these two phases of freedom of initiation on one side and definiteness of control on the other. Now this need not be taken as an argument that society is an organism, but simply as an explication of the fact that if society is an organism it is from this point of view that we have to conceive and determine individuality.

The second topical idea involved in organism was said to be that of interaction, reciprocal dependence. Socially this is the idea of association. The individual corresponds to the differentiation of the growth of function; association to the maintenance of relation, of interadjustment between these specified organs.

Association first presents itself as an objective fact just as individuality does. It presents itself in the form of classes, or grades, or castes, temporarily fixed distinctions within society; that is, so far as the individual is not differentiated, so far you have just this merging of the individual in a larger community whole, of which I have just been speaking. Now whenever you have that, you have a class. Take the slave in a form of society where the institution of slavery is not questioned. The individual is born in a certain position in the social whole. It is his destiny to occupy it, he fits right into that niche. Neither he nor anybody else has any judgment to pass on the matter. It is an accepted fact. The regime of custom as custom means always the assumption of such a class as that.

The class represents, then, the material out of which the individual is to be differentiated. It represents the as yet unresolved individual. Association of course then does not accurately describe that state any more than the merely physical individual adequately describes the conscious subjective personality, but its totality, its community in the form of immediate, direct fusion or absorption. It involves the positive and binding relations existing between the objective individual, holding them together practically about as rigidly as physical laws, if we hypostasize them, may be said to be held together. The bonds of custom in the customary type of society are about as inevitable in their workings as the law of gravitation is. The individual cannot do what he pleases because it does not occur to him to please; he cannot question at all.

While relatively speaking this represents an outgrown state of society, yet we are of course still in such a stage with reference to what may be supposed to come after. And any stage of society that we can imagine will always have this factor in it; that is, there are certain things which are not questioned at all, which the individual does not bring out into his own consciousness at all, where he simply falls into line with the established, instituted modes of working. Now what those are at present of course it would be a contradiction to try to tell; they are presuppositions which we do not question, but which some individual will sometime question and thereby make it a new conscious center of personality, introducing new conscious distinctions and values into society. But if we go back, we know there was a time when slavery was not questioned, when warfare was not questioned, when polygamy and a multitude of other things which might be mentioned were not questioned. Those were the customs which formed that particular class of race or nation and in which the individual was assimilated without any tension at all.

Now the question is: What becomes of this form of objective association when the individual does develop as a conscious personality? Of
course the general line of my answer must be clear. Association then becomes a conscious fact also—that is, something which is to be reconstructed and readjusted through the medium of distinct consciousness,
through the medium of specialized impulse and specialized reflection or
deliberation. Just as the individual brings himself to consciousness by
considering himself as a center and means from which a certain kind of
action may proceed, so he brings association to consciousness when he
asks: What kind of ends shall I function with reference to? The association becomes a limiting principle in the direction of individuality. If we
say that individuality represents the development of starting points, of
initiations, the question of association tells you how that is going to end up,
where it is coming out. It determines the further ends of the process, as
the development of individualization determines this end. Or in terms of
our biological discussion, the development of individuality, as such, apart
from its determination by the standard of association, represents simply
the competitive, tentative variation. The individual starts to do a certain
thing. Will he go on? Will that become settled, organized in his functions,
his habits, as an individual?

The moment you raise that kind of a question you bring into consciousness the question of association. That was the point of view that was suggested in another of the papers that I read, where it was said that the
social self comes to light when one wants to do something different from
the expectations, ideals of other people. The feeling of difference, of
course, carries with it as standard the feeling of identity with reference
to which the difference has to be discriminated, has to be valued, so that
one brings to light the question of establishing relationships to others as a
criterion of what one shall do, in order to determine the aim which shall
be sought for in the management of one's own particular equipment considered as means. Leaving out the argument that the term social self would
not be a happy term, we might speak of this as the associated self: that is,
the self defined in terms of association, in terms of the relationship which
one has to others. It is necessary to make that interpretation, to make that
estimation of one's self in terms of relationship to others, in order to get a
standard of reference, and a standard of verification, a standard in the
tentative process of evolving variations, new modes of initiation.

May 16, 1898

I said at the end of the last hour that the principle of association is a
limiting principle by reference to which particular variations, or the movement toward individualization, are tested. It is the standard to which the
movement toward individualization has constantly referred itself to be

checked up. By saying that it is a standard, it is not meant that it is an abstract, intellectual standard, but that it is a working standard, it is the limit with reference to which the variations have to be measured and have their value worked out.

Now that brings us of course to the chief problem involved in the conception of society as organism, as to the real relation between the movement toward differentiation and that toward association, interconnection. Is there any such working relation between these two directions of development as to maintain anything like functional unity? May it not be said that the discrepancy, diversity, is so great, and moreover the associations are so multiple and so complex in character, that at most we get only a loosely interwoven fabric of social groups rather than any approach at social organism?—the point of view which Mr. Leslie Stephen has expressed by saying that we may speak of social tissue, not of social organism.[2] Or if we conceive of it as organism at all, should it not be after the analogy of the lower forms where you have colonies of minute organisms all living in more or less close physical relations, and some functional relations to each other, but after all a comparatively little unity of functional development?

I shall postpone the answer to part of that question till I discuss the problem of the social sensorium, with a view at that time to pointing out that while society may be termed organic, the degree in which it is possible and desirable to speak of it as an organism in the idea of single unity of operation and of end depends upon how far social consciousness has been organized. There is a continual movement in the direction of a single functional unity, but it cannot be said to be realized. That, however, is a question of fact rather than principle as to how far the movement toward organization has actually gone.

There is another type of objection which is brought against the principle of organic unity as manifested in society. That is the theory which supposes that there is an irresolvable unity between the individual and the social whole, and it is that aspect of the question that I will now discuss.

There is no such thing as an immediate unity of the individual with the social whole. If the demand for identification or community of substance and of import between the individual and society depends upon finding a purely immediate point of identification, then I think it must be admitted that the antinomy between the individual and society is irresolvable. I shall try to indicate later that the general fallacy of socialism consists in setting up that immediate identification of the individual with the whole as its end and aim. As matter of fact, whatever identity there is is mediated by the relations of the various individuals to each other. In the biological organism we do not find any continual, immediate identification of any particular organ with the organism; what we find are shifting relations of stimulus and tension between the various organs of the organism; and it is through this interplay of the various organs, that interplay involving competition as well as direct reinforcement, that the functional relation between the organic part and the organic whole is kept up. All the organs of the body, the hand and brain and stomach, as types, are in a way continually competing with each other for their food material, competing with each other for nutritive elements. Moreover, they are continually interacting on each other, stimulating each other, so that each may subordinate the activities of the others to itself as an end. In the nervous system the hand is continually trying to control the eye; the ear is continually trying to control the eye; the eye is continually trying to absorb the values of the activities of the other organs into itself. And the actual condition of consciousness at any time is the net result of these various stimuli on each other. That is, there must be of necessity a tension between the various organs.

Now the bearing of this principle upon the general question of the relation between the individual and the social whole is that we are not to take the evidence of conflict between various individuals, or between various groups or classes of individuals, as necessary evidence of an antagonism between the individual as such and the organism as such. It does not follow that because the eye and the ear are in tension with each other, are in competitive conflict with each other, there is no functional relationship between both of those and the body as a whole. The conflict between the parts may be a necessary factor in the process of maintaining the proper functional relations between the part and the whole. The same thing in other words would be that there is no need of assuming any immediate identity between various individuals, any immediate community of end between various individuals, or that there is any need of assuming it as final.

The proper relationship, the proper association between any two individuals, may require to be mediated also; that is, may require to be set up through a larger movement including other social units within its scope. For instance the tension, the conflict between the capitalist and the laborer would not of itself be proof that there is no functional ethical unity, moral unity, in society. It might be that that very tension was necessary to call into play, to stimulate or evoke, other activities which are necessary to the growth of society as a whole; and that that mediated growth of society as a whole is necessary in order to determine the final real position of both the laborer on one side and the capitalist on the other. It is not a question, then, of ignoring or explaining away the tensions which actually do obtain and operate in society.

Some of the attempts to make out society to be an organism rest on a wholly unjustifiable optimism in the way of ignoring these tensions, or blinking them out of sight, so that you get an organism in name simply, and not an organism in fact. The thing that needs to be shown is how these tensions operate. It is a question of interpreting the tension, not of either saying that the bare fact of it makes it impossible for society to be organic, or of trying to explain it away on the other side. If those tensions are necessary, or are factors which participate in the growth of society, then although perfectly real, their reality is subordinate to the maintenance of a progressive society. It is part of the dynamics of social growth. And in that way the tensions between individual and individual and between class and class are stated in terms of the growing, the developing individual, and not simply of the acquisitive and possessing individual, as instrumentalities in the interest of the individual himself.

Now I put that hypothetically, but certainly that is the principle which does hold in all other forms of organic growth. The tension of the parts, of the constitutive and component units in relation to each other, is brought out in and through readjustment, in and through the process of growth, and itself serves to keep up and maintain the growth. Unless, therefore, social growth is something different in kind from growth as we meet it elsewhere, it is Utopian to expect to eliminate the competitive conflict between individuals and classes. The thing that is not Utopian is to organize those tensions so as to make them as active as possible—that is, to make them operate as much as may be to promote the growth of consciousness, to bring about the recognition of the values involved so that the energy which is aroused through the tension shall not be wasted.

It is possible to go to both extremes. Various social schools have done this—one school holding up the purely Utopian idea of the identification of the individual with the social whole, and of the individuals with each other, an ideal which would give us a fixed society. Plato, who originated this form of social conception, saw that clearly. After the ideal was reached, all change was to retrograde, it was falling away from the attained perfection. And it seems to me that the modern writers who have taught this immediate complete absolute identification of growth have not been as consistent as Plato was, they have not considered what the necessary conditions of change were. Change is not necessarily growth, but certainly all growth involves change; and growth, development, is practically regarded as a higher condition of affairs than the simple monotonous maintenance of any given status.

On the other hand we have some theorists who have made a glorification of struggle, of the principle of conflict, and have held that to be, without limitation, the directive principle in all growth. Now when I said that it is a problem to organize the tension so that it can be made effective, I wish to draw a line between the position stated and that of this latter school. The limiting principle to my mind here is that the value of tension is not in itself, or in anything which it immediately accomplishes. It is in the development of consciousness, particularly of the deliberative and reflective, the symbolizing [?] consciousness. Antagonism which finds a direct outlet in action, which discharges itself without the intervention of a conscious process of reflection, I should say in principle always marks loss, waste. There is no accumulation of energy which is expended without intelligent direction and simply follows the path of least resistance as it exists, but without determining what the line of least resistance or maximum of efficiency with reference to the end is.

Psychologically put, all deliberation is the attempt to avoid conflict in overt action by transferring that conflict over into the region of images, ideas, and their relations to each other. I think exactly the same principle holds socially. What society wants, to be really organic, is that mechanism or development which will allow it to utilize threatening difficulties and obstacles and friction so as to reorganize the system of values, to recognize values that have previously been obscured or hidden, and put those that are recognized into more definite relations to each other so that the action finally comes on the basis of unity.

The measure of civilization is precisely the measure to which these tensions are utilized as factors in the reconstruction of the interpreting consciousness as preparatory to action, instead of the overt action following directly and immediately upon the excitation of the tension itself. It is just the difference between a child when he gets mad letting the energy that is aroused discharge at once in reacting blindly, and the adult, who, when he is stirred up, utilizes that excitation in order to deepen and intensify his interest, uses it to focus his attention upon the problem, and uses it to enable him to concentrate his attention long enough to work out the solution of the problem before he acts.

This principle could best be tested by the definite historical definition of the part played by war in the development of social life. I cannot pretend to have made any particular study of the details, but I would suggest the problem as a very interesting one sociologically, the bearing of the hypothesis which I have advanced upon that particular question being this: If what I have said is true, then war has stimulated civilization insofar as it has brought about the immediate recognition of unities, identities, and thus has led to organization. It is not war as a conflict, as the immediate discharge of the energy excited, which accomplishes anything; it is the intellectual travail of facing a possible conflict and getting ready for it. The anticipation of war—that is, preparation for war—seems to me to have played a very considerable part in primitive societies in the centralization and systematization of central powers and in defining the whole system of social control, but I do not think it is true as Spencer says that primitive organization is entirely on the war basis. It is often on industrial pursuits, and partly organized with reference to the successful waging of war or the defense from enemies. This latter element undoubtedly has come in as one factor which has led men to bring to consciousness these positive relations to each other and to control themselves on the basis of those relations. That means that the functional principle, as far as it has gone, has been on the side of association, on the side of community, not on the side of identification, and that is the contradiction involved in the conception of war as a factor in social progress. It assumes relative identifications, associations; it brings to light the organizing, harmonizing relationships within the group at the same time that that particular group is thrown into conflict with another. But it is on this side of the internal, not on the side of the external, that the progress is made. The contradiction is that it is operating on the principle that as fast as it is generalized, [it] destroys itself.

Put on the other side this hypothesis would say that war as war, the final discharge in overt action, was always detrimental to progress instead of helpful, and the chief reason is the psychological, not the economical one. It is not a question of the immense waste of property or energy or life; it is rather that that marks the point where the problem ceases to be considered. The moment that society, like an individual, begins to fight, at that moment it ceases to locate the difficulty; and the energy which, as long as the process of deliberation is kept up, goes to find out what the matter is and tries to meet the difficulty on a physiological basis now gets a negative direction, simply to wipe out somebody or something. No problem is ever got rid of by wiping a certain number of people out of existence. The problem may be temporarily obscured, but the same difficulty is practically there still.

The same objection in principle would be the objection to capital punishment. It is too easy a solution psychologically. You try to get rid of the difficulty by getting rid of the men without considering the underlying social conditions and causes. As long as society thinks it can get rid of crime by hanging a number of people, it will never make a thoroughgoing study of the nature and causes of crime. When it is recognized that getting rid of the criminal does not reduce criminality, then society must direct its protective energies in a scientific and deliberative way to the remedial agencies and education.

It seems to me the same principle holds, without any limitation, regarding war as a social factor. I think you can apply that to the present war.* If it has any benefits, it is in the intellectual reconsiderations and redeliberations which it involves which bring to light presupposed identities and communities of interest. But war, simply as a display of antagonism in the physical direction, serves here, as well as elsewhere, to relieve people from the stress of thinking. People go to war because they get tired of thinking—it is too hard work and it is easier to go to war then to stop and think the thing out.

---

* The battleship "Maine" was destroyed on February 15, 1898. Spain declared war on the United States on April 24, and on April 25, the Congress declared that a state of war had existed since the 21st. The Cuban phase of the Spanish-American War was concluded by mid-July of 1898.

SECTION 2. CRITICISM
OF SPENCER

May 17, 1898

The point of contrast which Mr. Spencer finds between the biological organism and society is that in the animal economy a certain portion is specially differentiated as the bearer of consciousness, while other portions are nonsensitive. The nervous system is conceived of as having consciousness concentrated in it, and it follows from that that the welfare of the other parts of the organism is subordinated to that of the nervous system, since that is capable of suffering pain and pleasure. In society consciousness is diffused through all the individuals, but not indeed with absolute uniformity. Some persons are callous and others possess a high degree of sensitivity, but there are no social units which are feelingless while others monopolize the possession of consciousness.

As the consequence of that we have a reversal of this relation of subordination in society.[3]

> As, then, there is no social sensorium, the welfare of the aggregate, considered apart from that of the units, is not an end to be sought. The society exists for the benefit of its members; not its members for the benefit of society. (pp. 461–62)

It is almost incredible that anyone should thus naively consider consciousness in the organism to be concentrated in a small part of the aggregate for the benefit of which the rest may be said to exist.

> Though a developed nervous system so directs the actions of the whole body as to preserve its integrity, yet the welfare of the nervous system is the ultimate object of all these actions: damage to any other organ being serious in proportion as it immediately or remotely entails that pain or loss of pleasure which the nervous system suffers. (pp. 460–61)

Then he goes on to say:

> But it is otherwise in a social organism. The units of this, out of contact and much less rigidly held in their relative positions, cannot be so much differentiated as to become feelingless units and units which monopolize feeling. (p. 461)
>
> Hence, then, a cardinal difference in the two kinds of organisms. In the one, consciousness is concentrated in a small part of the aggregate. In the other, it is diffused throughout the aggregate: all the units possess the capacities for happiness and misery, if not in equal degrees, still in degrees that approximate. (p. 461)

And then comes the sentence I quoted before: "It has ever to be remembered that . . . the claims of the body politic are nothing in themselves, and become something only in so far as they embody the claims of its component individuals." (p. 462)

There are two or three assumptions there: one, that in the individual organism some of the parts exist for the benefit of others, that the welfare of the nervous system is alone an end, and on the other side, that in society the whole exists simply for the sake of its parts. There is a sentence which seems to me to embody a confusion that is not confined to Mr. Spencer: "As there is no social sensorium, the welfare of the aggregate, considered apart from that of the units, is not an end to be sought." (p. 462) Well, of course it is not. The problem lies simply in the possibility of making such a distinction anyway. The very assumption seems to contradict the whole idea of an organism. If you had simply a mechanical composite, one might speak of the welfare of the whole as somehow swallowing up the welfare of all its composing parts or units. They would have no individuality of their own at all, they would be simply an aggregation; but as Mr. Spencer himself declares, really the only thing which is essentially characteristic of the organism is the mutual dependence of parts. On page 592 for example, he says:

> Let it . . . be distinctly asserted that there exist no analogies between the body politic and a living body, save those necessitated by that mutual dependence of parts which they display in common. Though, in foregoing chapters, sundry comparisons of social structures and functions to structures and functions in the human body have been made, they have been made only because structures and functions in the human body furnish familiar illustrations of structures and functions in general.
>
> All kinds of creatures are alike in so far as each exhibits cooperation among its components for the benefit of the whole; and this trait, common to them, is a trait common also to society. Further, among individual organisms, the degree of cooperation measures the degree of evolution; and this general truth, too, holds among social organisms.

There he virtually states the same point that I made the other day. I said that all these comparisons are simply illustrations. The fundamental question is that which Mr. Spencer states to be that of mutual dependence and cooperation of parts for the welfare of the whole; that there is no whole excepting that of this mutual interdependence. The effectiveness of this mutual dependence or this coopreation measures the only unity; it is the functional unity of cooperation. It is absurd to think there is a whole apart from its unions. There is no whole excepting in and through the interaction of these unions, so-called. Plainly put, it is impossible that society should have an end of its own apart from that of individuals, because every society is the society of individuals. The welfare of society must be referred to the individuals who are the organs of society. On page 592 Mr. Spencer says that all kinds of creatures are alike for the benefit of the whole, that mutual dependence is the criterion of an organism, and that this trait, common to organisms, is a trait common also to societies. That seems to be in contradiction with the statement which I read that the welfare of society is simply a means to the welfare of its constituent units. Here the units cooperate for the benefit of the whole. Now that contradiction would not be of any particular importance—it might just be a slip in writing—were it not that the mutual dependence has been set up as the criterion of the organism, and yet in that earlier chapter Mr. Spencer virtually denies it: that is, the most essential form of mutual interdependence is denied to society. So it is difficult to see how he can continue to call society an organism any more, excepting in a highly remote and metaphysical sense; and yet in the earlier passage, page 462, he says: "From this last consideration, which is a digression rather than a part of the argument, let us now return . . ." etc.—and he gives less than two pages to the whole matter; that is, he treats it as if it were a very incidental thing that society has not a sensorium or a common consciousness as the individual organism has. And yet how mutual dependence then can exist in society excepting in a purely external and objective sense, excepting in the physical sense, if there is not a common consciousness, if there is no participation of consciousness through the various units, it is difficult to see. Of course one might say that there was as matter of fact such economic interdependence, such physical interdependence, that society presents some the traits of the organism, but if it lacks any recognition of the community of interest, if it has no social sensorium, no social consciousness, certainly the important phase—and the only psychological distinguishing characteristic—of an organism is absent.

Now to turn to the other end of it: Is it true that in any sense in the individual organism the nervous system represents the end? Is it that for the benefit of which the other structures exist as mere means of it? Mr. Spencer recognizes that biologically speaking that is not so. From the biological standpoint the nervous system is tributary, instrumental. But he goes on to say:

> Yet the welfare of the nervous system is the ultimate object of the whole body: damage to any other organ being serious in proportion as it immediately or remotely entails that pain or loss of pleasure which the nervous system suffers. (pp. 460–61)

Is it true in any sense that the nervous system monopolizes feeling? Strictly from the physiological standpoint the material of the nervous system is nonsensitive. There is no pain in cutting or slashing or sticking an instrument into the gray matter of the brain, for instance. The naive consciousness, the person who is uninstructed in physiology and anatomy, would never think of saying it was the nervous system which possesses the pleasure and pain. It seems to belong to one's self, and almost never to be referred to the nervous system. We refer consciousness of pain as a rule to some organ, to the hand or the eye or the ear, the particular organ in which the center of tension is at a given time located. Possibly in neuralgia or toothache you would talk of referring pain particularly to the nervous system. That is simply a question of detail. Under some circumstances we would locate it there and under other circumstances we would locate it in the eye or ear. The question involves, however, a real principle. It is a question of how far the individual can be said to possess or monopolize in any way consciousness.

There are two points of view, according to one of which the individual would represent here the point of reference of consciousness, according to the other of which the individual is supposed to be somehow the owner of consciousness. The latter is a conception which has grown up along with and has been formulated more or less in the older metaphysical conception of the soul, where there was assumed to be a metaphysical entity already in existence having the property of consciousness, for all practical purposes just a metal or an acid has particular properties. The substratum of being is supposed there, and then the properties are the possessions which this substratum of being can lay claim to. Now even where the concept of soul is not used at all, that view of things has permeated men's opinions more or less, until, to a great many people at least, it seems a perfectly matter-of-fact thing to talk of individual consciousness, while social consciousness would appear like an absurdity, because there is no single being of society which can be picked out in order to own or possess this consciousness. John Smith or Richard Row may have consciousness, he may be a proper owner of a certain amount and a certain quality of consciousness, but there is no similar ontological entity of society which is capable of thus monopolizing consciousness.

Now if we follow the analogy (admitting that it is only an analogy) of the biological organism, the individual—that is, the organ, in reference to the whole or organism—represents the point to which consciousness is referred. You cannot say that consciousness belongs, or is owned by anything, whether an organism as a whole or any particular structure of the organism, but it is a characteristic of consciousness to be focused, to be centralized, to have definite points of concentration, of reference, in connection with which the scope and particular contents of the experience are placed and interpreted.

One might compare that to a mathematical locus or to a center of ordinates and abscissas. Of course in one case it is a center of conscious values and in the other not, but both agree in being centers of systems in process of construction defined in terms of the part played in the construction. In neither case is the center an independent existence. It is a center simply in being the immediate point with reference to which other values are determined and interpreted. The conscious individual as the focusing is the point of value from which the survey of other values is made, from which they are measured, which gives a limiting principle with reference to which the significant focus shifts as the total system of experience shifts, yet possesses functional continuity and thus identity.

In other words, instead of first assuming the individual and then attaching consciousness to the individual, the concept of the individual itself has to be explained and stated in terms of the movement of consciousness. I am I, a center of consciousness. I am a certain focus of initiation, a point of departure and a point of return in the movement of consciousness. That is what I intrinsically am, instead of there being first an "I" behind and then this "I" coming to do and possess certain things. As I mentioned earlier in the course, while so-called common sense is perfectly ready to fall in with the conception of individual consciousness in the sense of its being something owned by the individual, and while any other conception often seems strained and unreal, common sense is equally repugnant to subjective idealism which would be the only logical consequence of the supposition of the individual as already in existence with consciousness attached. If consciousness were something attached to the ego, then the range of consciousness, the character of its contents, is accordingly limited; the restriction of the individual to what could only be called his own states of consciousness would be an inevitable necessity.

Put from the other end, the fact that consciousness is objective—that is, that it does lay hold of and report the universe of objects and relations which transcend the existence of particular states of consciousness—shows that the nature of the perceiving and conceiving individual, the ego, must be defined in such way as to render explicable this capacity for knowledge, for getting truth.

I think from this point of view the so-called problem of epistemology as to how a particular individual can transcend the limits of his own consciousness when it comes to comprehend the world is a factitious question. It originates with the supposition that there is any such particular being who owns consciousness as his own private possession. If there were such a thing it would indeed be a problem, it would be an insoluble problem. The problem is simplified when we realize that that assumption is a gratuitous piece of metaphysics. The outcome so far will be that the individual, whether we are thinking of the biological organism, or whether we are thinking of what we ordinarily term the individual in social relationships, is to be interpreted with reference to the whole movement of consciousness. That is one necessary pole in the psychical process. That is, the fact of this centralization, the fact of this focusing, the fact of there being points of departure and of reference for value, is a fact which constitutes the element of immediate existence in our experience; but that is never the whole of any conscious experience. That is simply one pole which by abstraction we recognize.

The other factor that we equally have to recognize is that of content, of meaning, of significance; and that meaning, that content of value, is always found in any conscious experience, and is something which transcends mere immediate existence. Now what ordinary common sense does is, after this abstraction has been worked out, to make a separation, to think of the factor of existence as one thing, the given individual or ego, and [to] think of the factor of content or significance or value as another, and then to raise the problem of how these two disparate things can be connected with each other, can be brought into any relation with each other, instead of saying that they are the antithetical factors recognized by analysis in the unity of conscious experience itself.

This point of view may seem metaphysical, unnecessarily so. But some such conception is necessary if for no other purpose than to recognize that there is an alternative to this popular assumption of consciousness as purely and simply individual, and its further assumption, therefore, that the only problem lies in the person who uses the phrase social consciousness: that the burden of proof is wholly on his side, because individual consciousness is *prima facie* unquestionable—it is there anyhow. That consciousness is individualized there is no doubt, but it is equally certain that consciousness is never *merely* individualized or that we have not an adequate statement of it as long as we can confine ourselves to the proposition that consciousness is individualized. We must also recognize that consciousness has a what as well as a that, that it carries value, and that value, while referring to the individual as the center and limiting point, is a value which transcends the individual.

If I have suggested that it is possible to conceive the relation of the individual to the social whole in this matter of consciousness just as we conceive the relation of the eye or hand or ear to the biological whole, if I have simply indicated the possibility of that conception and that there is no intrinsic contradiction in it, I will go on and take up three or four considerations that seem to give positive content to the conception of social consciousness.

SECTION 3. THE SOCIAL STRUCTURE OF CONSCIOUSNESS

May 18, 1898

Having tried yesterday to suggest that the individual should be considered as a certain factor and point of reference in the determination and growth of consciousness rather than as a being behind consciousness which then possesses consciousness as its property or attribute, I will go on today to suggest three or four positive points of view from which the concept of social consciousness may get its meaning.

The first consideration is that consciousness as referring to the individual is socially conditioned on the genetic side. We are of course very far from having as yet any adequate genetic psychology; in fact, we have hardly made a beginning in that direction. But it is clear, if the hypothesis of evolution is accepted and then is applied as a method in reaching psychological conclusions, that not only does the absurdity of considering consciousness as a private possession of a private individual become greater, but in a positive and definite, not merely a metaphysical, way we can see how the quality and tendencies of consciousness have been socially elaborated.

This perhaps involves an extension of the ordinary concept of society, but in that it brings out in a perfectly concrete and specific way the dependence of the individual on the race, upon the efforts and activities of his ancestry, animal and human, it may fairly be termed social. That is, it brings out the actual mediation and modification of the tendencies and the contents of consciousness as they are realized in the individual upon the consecutive development of a highly consolidated content. We might almost say that man's consciousness, the individual's present consciousness of the world of nature, even of the physical world, is the outcome of the cooperating creation. The individual inherits the values which have been worked out by his progenitors. Primarily the sense consciousness, the sense of qualities of color, of sound, of taste, represent such a conferring upon the individual of the conscious wealth which has been produced and conserved by previous generations. Statements that would be metaphysical to the point of being mystical we ought to expect to have some time worked out and verified in concrete biological terms along this line. That is, as we say I see colors and hear sounds, it would be just as true to say that the whole race, the whole continuous life process, was seeing and appreciating those qualities.

If we limit ourselves to the purely individualistic definition of consciousness, this whole region, the region of the actual qualities, specific values which are actually presented in consciousness, becomes absolutely inexplicable. It is a simple, bare, brutal, ultimate fact that we do see certain colors, and that we do hear certain sounds, but there are absolutely no connecting links between those facts and the nature of the individual to whom all these experiences are referred. But if we take the idea of a continuous life process which has been differentiated through its own functional activity in reference to the environment, then we get the basis of a method of explaining and interpreting all these qualities, however far we are from the actual ability to explain them at present. These things have to be interpreted from the evolutionary point of view, just as any other favorable variations which have been selected in the struggle for existence and which then can be conserved. The capacity to recognize distinctions of light and shade, to recognize distinctions of color, sound, and so on—most all of these have been at one time developed as more adequate stimuli to action or as actual means for the control of the environment, subordinating it to the function of the living organism.

But as we said the other day, the biological point of view itself is an abstraction, in that it does not take account of the fact that these distinctions are not mere stimuli to physical action, but they become actual, immediate, appreciated values in experience. Mr. Huxley* is reported to have said on one occasion that man's aesthetic consciousness, his appreciation of beauty and sublimity, was the only argument that he knew of to contravene the theory of the genetic descent of man from the animals, because such distinctions would not have had any worth in the struggle for existence. These are things with reference to which we are, so to speak, so much ahead; they are matters of gifts, not of works. It seems to me, as it was suggested the other day, that those facts, as the facts of the immediate appreciation in consciousness of things which do not serve simply as signals to further action, while they do not contravene the biological theory, do indicate that the simple biological statement is not complete; that is, that it is abstract, that there is another factor involved there, and that in that light this immediate appreciation of worths is a purely gratuitous thing: it is a gift of the universe to the individual. But it is not on that account to be conceived as a mere anomaly; it becomes a fact of importance in interpreting the organic relation which exists between the universe and the individual.

I should say that it was along this line of genetic psychology that we would get the final solution, in anything like approaching scientific terms, of the old problem of epistemology. The epistemological idealists have always realized that the only way of getting out of the purely subjective individualistic theory of the world, of getting rid of the conception that would reduce the whole world to a mere shifting kaleidoscope of particular states of consciousness, was to assume that mind has something universal, something objective in its own makeup and structure. But that has been left simply as a supposition. Such must be the case if there is any such thing as valid knowledge or any such thing as really law-abiding conduct, but just how mind could have this, or just what was meant by its having it, does not appear to have been satisfactorily explained. But from this point of view those phrases are interpretable as manifestations of the social character of mind and mental operations. It is the whole process, the whole activity of life development, using that term life to include the psychical element as well as the strictly biological, which operates in and through the individual so that a merely individualistic state of consciousness, one which is purely and simply individual, is of necessity an impossibility. The criterion, in other words the definition of objectivity and universality, becomes essentially a social one as that has been experimentally worked out—that is, worked out through the actual struggles of adaptation and readjustment.

The second point of view which I would suggest is that it is only for purposes of theory that we can distinguish the physical environment from the psychical environment. We speak continually, and for purposes of

* Thomas Henry Huxley (1825–1895), British biologist and follower of Darwin.

scientific analysis there is no harm in so doing, as if the stimuli which evoked activity and brought out certain states of consciousness were purely physical. In explaining sensations of sound and of color we refer at once to the vibrations of the medium and to the structure of the optical centers and connections. Now while I say there is no harm in that so far as scientific analysis is concerned, it does become erroneous if we suppose that that is the whole of it. As matter of fact certainly the greater part of such stimuli as really modify consciousness is socially transformed, being interpreted through the social medium to the individual. Of course it is perfectly true physiologically that the sensation of red is excited by vibrations of ether traveling at a certain velocity, but it is also true that the significance that is attached to red, what it concretely means to the individual who experiences it, is influenced very much by its contacts with others. We do not have sensations of red in the abstract or as isolated things. The child gets sensations of red gowns, red stockings, and red brick houses, and a multitude of other forms, and all the relationships and associations that give them value. The particular meaning which "red" has depends upon the values which are communicated to him through what others say to him, and through the way in which others deal with those things.

I do not think of any more striking omission in the ordinary psychology than the ignoring of the tremendous interpreting agency with which society has come in between the various physiological stimuli and the conscious reaction to them. Just follow the development of the child from a few months to a few years old and see how a value is put upon all his contacts with the physical world by others. It is almost impossible to find what we might call a pure, naked, immediate contact of the child with the world which gets permanently grafted into his consciousness. What stays is the attitude that he takes toward that physical stimulus and object, the worth that he attributes to it, because of his habitual association with others. The physical environment is always carried, as a matter of concrete experience, embedded in the social environment, and it gets to the individual only through that social environment. The weather is, from one point of view, as purely an objective physical fact as we could easily find; but the value that we attribute to this phenomenon, the meaning that we actually put into it, is one which is socially determined. Take the great epochs of development, of culture, from the hunting stage of man down through the pastoral, the agricultural, the manufacturing, and consider what a different meaning [is] attached at each stage in the development of such a simple fact as rain or sunshine. It is only in the abstract that rain and sunshine have always been the same: only when we by analysis reduce and eliminate certain of the elements and qualities which as matter of concrete fact always are bound up with them. The only thing that is the same is rain and sunshine as it is for the physicist. As it has been for the ordinary man who directly experiences these facts, they have changed with the change of social occupations and ideals. I simply give that as one illustration which could be worked out indefinitely.

As matter of fact the social occupations and the social endeavors of men are the media through which nature comes home to the individual consciousness; plants, stones, animals, as well as these meteorological phenomena are set in social activities. The history of science itself, the history of the contact of science with morals and religion, is utterly inexplicable on another basis. Why should the view regarding certain abstract astronomical observations make a tremendous change amounting almost to revolution? Nothing could be more indifferent than questions as to the relative size of the sun and the earth and whether the sun moves round the earth or vice versa, concretely considered. The change of the views of men upon these subjects partly grew out of and partly induced, partly was a symptom of and partly was the cause of, a tremendous change in men's whole political and religious consciousness, simply because those things were part of the interpretation of society at large, of humanity at large, of itself, and of its place in nature. And so when you have changed the conception of those facts, it of necessity changed man's interpretation of himself and of the direction of his own ideals and aspirations.

That simply as matter of fact would take us again into the theory of the relation of growth in consciousness, to the tension between stimulus and response, or between the organism and the environment. The economic relationship is the fundamental form of the tension; that is, the economic relationship which describes in its simplest and most ultimate terms the relation which exists at a given time between man and nature; that is, in terms of occupation, in terms of the industrial pursuits, the problem of adjustment is made and solved, and hence from the standpoint of theory the continual correspondence that we must have between the occupations of men and the values which they put upon their physical environment. Well now, of course the individual shares in that prevailing atmosphere of interpretation, of evaluations, and that goes along with the prevalent types of social pursuits. As he is initiated into these occupations, as he comes to play his part in them, he partly consciously but more by unconscious absorption interprets plants, animals, stones, sun, moon, stars, rain, and so on, in the same way as those about him. Every new invention, the application of electricity, for example, to industrial pursuits, makes a new organ of interpretation, a new social organ of interpretation of nature.

The two points of view of which I have spoken so far are, so to speak, unconscious methods of effecting the socialization of consciousness. Neither of them came about through anybody's set purpose; they are simply involved in the working machinery of the things themselves.

The third point of view of which I wish to speak, while by no means wholly or perhaps even predominatingly purposive in its social character, still involves a certain amount of conscious aim and direction. It may be called educational in the broadest possible sense of that term, meaning all the influences which are brought to bear on the individual in order to give character in any way to the values which he puts on his own experience. The individual as a particular individual is all the time a target, a center for influences from others which are bearing in on him, with the unconscious purpose, if I may use the term, of making him put certain values on certain things: to ascribe certain worths to the various items of his experience, to use a certain current standard of measuring worth, to have a certain scale of worths which are current in the community in which that particular individual is born, influences which begin the moment the individual comes into the world and which directly and indirectly never let up. Of course we are accustomed to reserve the term education for the more direct methods of effecting this valuation of experience on the part of an individual. I use the term in its widest sense, to include the indirect as well as the direct methods. Now so far as the term social consciousness is used in the more restrictive sense, we come upon the chief justification for that phrase. Society is all the time discovering more and more that control of action from without by any external agency is superficial and ineffective, that it gets its best hold on the individual by setting the way in which he interprets the world about him, interprets his relations to others, and interprets his own experiences. So far as you can fix the way in which any given individual is going to value things, you have a fundamental hold on him, a fundamental control of him. He can be left perfectly free to initiate and work out all the details of his own conduct and experience, but insofar as you have set the general lines and categories of his interpretation, you have a guarantee insofar forth of the social character of the things that will result.

Now it seems to me that this is the chief point of view not merely of social philosophy but of any philosophy: to get hold of the fact that the world of experience is a world of values and, as such, is in continuous change, in continuous evolution, and it is only certain things which we abstract for specialized purposes of analysis that in any sense remain the same. The world of nature, the physical world, is a world of values in experience, and it is a world of developing values. To get hold of that is the key to the comprehension of history—literary and moral history, as well as political. We tend to assume all the time that somehow this consciousness is a fixed fact, that it was just the same in the Elizabethan age or the age of Pericles as now (it of course would vary in its quantities, having great outbursts at certain times). But as matter of fact the whole history is the history of the evaluation of values, and to explain anything is to see what the current, dominant standard and type of value was and how this or that particular fact was located in the general scheme of values.

May 23, 1898

According to the spirit of what has been said, the content of consciousness is due to the adjustment which takes place in the interplay of excitations, restrictions or inhibitions. Consciousness, if it is not regarded as an immediate possession of some individual who lies behind consciousness, cannot be conceived any longer as having its contents arbitrarily determined. If you conceive of it as the direct property of a self behind it, then its constituent factors may be regarded as escaping any particular law. There is a purely metaphysical entity and that breaks out in a variety of thoughts and ideas. If there is any law or any order at all, it is conceived to be found simply on the sensational side. That is, in the popular conception, this being is partly externally determined, receptive. Certain sensations are forced on it and there of course a causal principle of necessity holds; but the manipulation, or their final acceptance, registration, their final valuation is found in the choice, arbitrary selection of the self behind, so that you get an unregulated freedom set over against a receptive determinism.

Now from the standpoint of the other conception we have neither this forced injection of certain qualities of sensations on one side nor the arbitrary indeterminate reaction to them on the other side. We have the organic development of action with reference to which both initiation and reception in the relative sense have to be interpreted. That is, both initiation and the so-called reception of sensations occur in mediation within the readjustment of this organic activity itself, and the content of consciousness at any given time you might say was a sort of net function of the interaction and interplay that are going on, of the various excitations and the various inhibitions.

Put in social terms the content of individual consciousness will depend upon how one is incited or stimulated by others; it will depend upon how one's actions are restricted or inhibited by others; it will depend upon the excitations which one can put worth as regards others—that is, one's ability to direct the activities of others, so that they respond to the stimuli; and it will depend also upon the restrictions which one is able to exercise over the activities of others. In the consciousness then, just as when we are stating it in purely psychological terms (that is, as something which is going on within one and the same individual), we have to interpret the changes of consciousness with relation to the readjustments of action that are going on, so on the social side it is a question of the adjustments which are made between the activities of various agents, which of course will be reduced to these four main heads. That is, the agent A is at once excited to action and restricted in action by the doings of others, and reciprocally he is able both to call out their actions and to modify their activities.

Now if we could get a statement for how these various actions interplay, how they act and react on each other, we would have a formulation for the content of consciousness at a given time. It is in that kind of consideration that we find the justification for the term social consciousness. It does not mean that consciousness is possessed by society any more than the term individual consciousness means that consciousness is owned in fee simple by an individual. It means that the actual contents of one's consciousness, what one thinks, believes, hopes for, and strives for, are dependent on this continuous and complex interaction going on between these various individual activities.

SECTION 4. SOCIAL ORDER
AND SOCIAL PROGRESS

In the development of this socialized consciousness in the individual, there are two principles to be reckoned with: one, that of social order; and the other, that of social progress. That is, every society must aim at effecting a certain amount of conformity in the individual. The individual must arrive at a certain consensus with the community in which he was born. He must come to think and feel, and put forth endeavors to react in lines that are harmonious with the existing community type. That of course constitutes the essence of what we may call social order. All other forms of so-called order—such order as the policeman can keep, for instance—are of course purely external, what Carlyle very happily and vividly termed "anarchy plus a constable." There is no real order insofar as there is no common consciousness; there is mainly repression, and while that is a phase of social order which is most active, it of course implies a tremendous amount of underlying tradition and continuity which are undisturbed, a core of common purposes and common interpretations and habits with reference to which the disturbances are more or less superficial. It is with reference to this common core that one is first a criminal or a lawbreaker or a social-disturber. It is the established level of values at any given time from the basis of which all departures and changes are estimated.

The analogy that I think I have spoken of before with regard to Weber's law comes in here.[4] There is a social pressure of consciousness as well as an individual one, and changes of action have to get a certain ratio of this habitual assumption of society before they are apperceived as new qualities, new values. We may refer to this in general as the principle of custom, corresponding to the principle of habit in the individual, remembering that custom has to be interpreted socially. It does not merely mean that people do certain things, it means that they attach certain values to these things that they do, and that those values at any given time are, relatively speaking, presupposed, taken for granted, in the unquestioned way.

If we compare various societies historically, we find a very great difference in their conscious attitude with respect to this point. The most primitive societies seem to have hardly enough depth of consciousness to set up this continuity of recognized instituted types of value as ideals. We find particularly in Australia societies which are scarcely more than hordes and which are continually shifting, changing, with very little social tradition. It is said of some of the tribes in Africa that the language changes almost entirely every two or three generations. Of course when that takes place there is very little momentum of values which comes into control and takes possession of the individual.

But when societies get more organized than that, we find that the principle of social order takes possession of consciousness, practically to the exclusion of progress. Conformity is the social ideal and all variation is regarded practically, if not theoretically, as criminal. In his *Physics and Politics* Bagehot mentions some savage tribe where the introduction of the European axe was regarded as criminal.[5] The innovator who first ventured to use the axe was put to death or visited with some marked sign of the disapproval of the tribe, although the environment of these people was such that the use of the axe would have been a very great convenience. But it was a simple variation from the approved methods of doing things, but a variation too great for them to tolerate.

This is as good a place as any to say a few words more about imitation on the social side. I have spoken about it before chiefly on the psychical side. Imitation undoubtedly plays an extremely important role in the maintenance of customs, that is, approved social habits. For the most part, however, I think it is unconscious imitation rather than conscious. It is not that the individual sees other people doing certain things and then makes it a conscious end to go and do likewise, but the stimuli which come to him are, relatively speaking, of one type that are consciously repeated. There are certain things which are done over and again and those are the things which that community tells the individual are of supreme importance. So as matter of fact he falls into the same lines of conduct and he too becomes an organ for upholding those particular variations and impressing them upon others. We get something as a result which may fairly enough be called imitation—that is, in the social sense—but psychically it is hardly imitation because it is not intended. It is not done for the sake of imitation. It is done rather for the sake of winning social approval. Negatively it is done for the sake of not being an outcast, an outlaw. But in this very fact we get the limit of the principle of imitation. It is a principle which holds historically, much more in societies which have not become conscious and where progress is not the general idea. In fact it is the limiting principle to social progress.

In what would be termed progressive societies, the insistence upon any individual's thinking and believing just what other people think and believe is diminished—that pressure lets up. There is still a social criterion, but it is not found so much in the identity of intellectual and emotional content and reaction. The standard is transferred rather to the ultimate purport, the ultimate outcome, relatively speaking. If the individual will do things which contribute to the social welfare, he individually may think and believe what he pleases. So far as a given type of thought, idea or belief is found to incapacitate the individual for reaching a certain kind of end in practice, so far as it is found to work against his making a contribution in action to the common good, that idea as an idea is of course put more or less under the ban. All that is termed the growth of toleration, the rights of individual consciousness and all that, means that imitation, in the sense of establishing identical ideas, common intellectual contents, has been discounted.

It might rather be said that the principle of progressive society is that the community wants the benefit of individual coloring in thinking and emotions. Upon the whole, society will get more if the individual does not think of the thing just as other people do. The personal equation, the variation which he introduces, the different way in which he approaches it intellectually, the different way in which he apperceives the thing which purely objectively considered is identical, leads to a fostering and building up of things.

Modern society tells the individual that if he will do his work, he can think and feel as he pleases, but that there is a certain work which he must do in order that he may take his place within the organized community. I do not think it a fair interpretation of the principle of toleration to suppose that it is not of much importance anyway what any individual thinks, that one idea is about as good as another, and nobody knows much about anything and it is better not to make too much fuss about things. It means that you must recognize the principle of individuality in the intellectual and emotional sphere, that you must make the principle of division of labor spiritual and not simply physical; and that if you can free the individual to value things for himself, and to allow his personal equation to have its subjective equivalent, on the whole the social life will be enriched. And until you can allow the individual to judge for himself of the means that he is going to use and make his own selections and adaptations, your principle of freedom is superficial and external.

We have interpreted this principle so far mainly on the negative side. We have put it that society has no right to try to compel the individual to believe such and such things, or that the individual has a right to judge and believe things for himself. Now what I was suggesting was that that is a social principle, a principle of responsibility, duty, and not a mere principle of individualism or of rights as such; that it is a necessary instrument or organ in maintaining a more socialized type of social unity, a more mediated functional type of unity, because it gives society the benefit of a much greater variety of instruments, it puts at the command of society more tools, and tools which are more refined, which have the shadings further carried out.

The attempt to erect a regime of authority in matters of idea, thought, is not simply an encroachment on the rights of the individual, it is an attack on community welfare. It is an attempt to impoverish the spiritual welfare of society as well as to arrest the media through which society varies and is made progressive. Progressive society therefore is based, even if unconsciously, upon the faith that the individual qua individual is a social instrument; it is based upon the faith in an underlying organic identity. The other principle believes that you cannot get the unity or the community until you can inhibit the individual in some particular way unconsciously. The individual as an individual is believed to be nonsocial and it is therefore the problem of instilling into him beliefs, ideas, which will give some guarantee that he will cooperate with others.

The principle of progressive society is that the individual upon the whole is social and may be trusted to act in the social interests, and therefore you can afford to stimulate him, to develop him in his individuality. Modern society would be crazed, would be perfectly at anarchy, with all its opportunities and schemes for developing the individual and bringing out differences between different individuals, unless there were some reason for the faith that upon the whole the individual is organically related to society, that when he is free as an individual he will still continue to function as a social organ.

May 24, 1898

A progressive society is one in which the stimuli between classes and individuals are so arranged as to induce variation, or so as to increase the amount of differentiation as measured by comparing different individuals with each other. The individual marks the point of initiation and, as the initiator, is therefore the medium through which the changes which lead to growth must be effected. In other words, it is not a mere empirical fact that social progress is brought about through the instrumentality of an individual as an individual. It is a matter of necessity. That is what the individual as a particular individual, that is what the specialized individual is, the originator, the initiator.

As was said yesterday, it is a progressive society, then, that presumes a certain faith or belief in the organically social character of individuality. That is, it would be guilty of suicide unless it believed that in stimulating these variations, or in hastening the process of differentiation, it is not also increasing the ultimate amount of social values realized. It implies more, however, than simple faith in the social character of the results of individualization. It presupposes also a system of indirect or highly mediated control capable of utilizing these individual variations and holding them within certain limits, preventing their going to a point which would be excessive or disintegrated.

These two aspects, the increasing complication of social relations which determine the direction of individual variations and the increased encouragement and fostering of these variations, go together. That is, only a society that was already so highly organized that it had a great number of flexible institutions so that it could utilize originalities, new modes of initiation in individuals, could possibly afford to stimulate and encourage those variations. Thus we come here upon the same principle that we found to constitute the definition of an organism: the reciprocity of individualization and of interdependence.

It is because there are a great many more hooks for the individual variations to catch onto, or a great many more cogs and a great many more teeth in the cogs in which the individual's variations may adjust themselves, that it is possible for society to move rapidly in the direction of individualization. Unless the society is complex, unless its arrangements are highly indirect, the variations on the part of the individual would be a threat to social order. There must be some way on the part of society to function these individual variations, it must be capable of setting them to work to operate in some direction, and the general framework for utilizing them must be already there.

It is in progressive society, as it has been said before, that the apparent fixed oppositions between the individual and society present themselves—that is, that its variation in the direction of individualization can be judged from either of two points of view: either with reference to the past or with reference to the future; with reference to what has been accomplished and elaborated, or with reference to adjustments still to be made. Now if we judge with reference to the past, this variation appears, if not antisocial, at least nonsocial. The very fact that it is different makes it insofar disintegrating with reference to what has become fixed in positive institutional types, or anything which has become rigidly organized into custom. The individual there appears as the basis, then, of new social forms. He is a transitional point, a nodal point in the social reconstruction; and unless we look both ways, unless we see how the individual operates there as a factor of reconstruction in society, we will naturally fall into the fallacy of either saying that the individual is antisocial, because we are judging simply with reference to what has gone before, or else as presocial, and as the unit, the basis of social arrangements looking simply toward the future.

As I mentioned before the political philosophy of the sixteenth and seventeenth centuries conceived the individual as essentially presocial, and society as arising out of a mutual compact made between these various nonsocial individuals. Now while the historical school and the philosophical school of the present century have pointed out the errors in that conception, there is a certain truth in it viewed historically. These centuries were the centuries of reconstruction, they were times when the individual had been set from his previous modes of organization in institutional life and when new equally organized modes of socialization had been called into being. Looking then toward the future, the interest being prospective, it was practically inevitable to conceive of the individual as the unit of social organization and to conceive of individuals as being the determinants of government and of all social organization. Of course when that view was read back into the past, was given as an account of the actual historical origin of society, it was radically false; but taken as expressing the problem which was immanent in economic and political matters it had its relative truth. At the periods of great social reconstruction the individual is necessarily thrown into relief, as contrasted with the institutions as they have been, with reference to which he is a distinguishing factor, and also is thrown into relief relative to the outlook upon future social changes with reference to which the individual is regarded as the determining cause, as the center of stress and of strain, as the responsible agent for effecting these changes.

These are not then cases intrinsically of opposition between the individual and society as such; they are cases of oppositions between individuals in society, or between classes or communities in society—that opposition, whether located between individuals or located between classes, being a symptom and a factor in social reconstruction.

There will always be some whose interests will be bound up with the maintenance of the institutions as they have been. There will be those who are the particular beneficiaries of the existing social habits. They will be the preferred creditors of society. They represent the vested interests. In general the conservative class is conservative of course on the whole because their interests are sufficiently maintained and protected in the existing organization.

Now on the other side there will be those whose interests are conceived to be subserved by change, those who can say that they are not getting a fair share of social values, or who do not find themselves capable of exercising the capacities of which they are possessed. That is, they find themselves possessed of powers which they are unable to utilize freely. That is the class then that will favor change; they are social radicals. It is the very nature of any tension accompanying social readjustment to polarize society more or less, to that extent. It is exactly the same thing that occurs in the individual himself at a time of necessary readjustment: the throwing of habit on one side in antagonism over against the ideal, the anticipated future, on the other side.

So here, the conservative class, the institutional interests, the interests which have been worked out and recognized stand out over against the conceptions of social reorganization which will bring into play the impulses or the powers which up to this time have not found adequate expression. Now judged from either end, there will appear all the time, then, to be an opposition between society and the individual. If you judge from the standpoint of the conservative, put yourself at that pole, the radical is an anarchic individual who is simply bound on making inroads into those institutions which have made life what it is, and upon whose continuity all civilization depends. That is, the conservative will identify the element which is bent on introducing change with the individual who has broken loose from the social order and who is attacking it.

You get a quite different interpretation if you put yourself at the pole of the radical. You get the point of view expressed in its most radical and exaggerated form by Rousseau, that man is by nature free and good but has been corrupted and enslaved by institutions. Society from that point of view is that which restricts the individual, is that which hems him in, is that enslaves him, is that which prevents the natural good impulses that well up in his soul from having any outlet. From that standpoint the thing is to loosen all these social bonds and ties and release the individual, let him have something to say for himself and determine his own life. We find as matter of fact that when we judge, not from the standpoint of the growth of social relationships as a whole, but from the one-sided standpoint of either the two factors which are concerned in that social change, there arises naturally the conception of some intrinsic opposition between social welfare and individual freedom and interests.

SECTION 5. IS THE INDIVIDUAL OPPOSED TO SOCIETY? CRIMINAL AND GENIUS AS TEST CASES

There are two forms of the individual which can serve as test cases upon which to try on any theory of individual and social interest. They are the crminal and the genius, respectively. In the criminal we appear to have a case of a conscious and voluntary assertion of the individual against society. In the genius we seem to have a case of the transcendence of society by the individual. In both cases, then, there is a lack of any organic relationship between the two, although expressing itself in different ways.

I do not pretend that the interpretation of the criminal that I am going to give is a proved one, but I give it simply as a hypothesis, as a suggestion to be taken for what it is worth. The valid or the even approximately valid establishment of any theory of criminality is not possible at present, for the data—the physiological, the psychological and the sociological data—have not been sufficiently gathered and reflected upon, but from all those points of view the conception may be advanced independently that crimi-nality is a form of survival.

The Italian school, working from the physiological side, attempted to show that criminality represents atavism, reversion to a more primitive type.* Alexander in his *Moral Order and Progress,* speaking entirely from a psychological and ethical point of view, I think without any awareness of any point of contact with this other view, has advanced the conception that

* The Italian school of criminology was headed by Cesare Lombroso (1836–1909), who claimed to have discovered a special criminal type who stood midway between the lunatic and the savage.

crime represents the persistence of a previous social form of organization which has not become thoroughly assimilated to the current types of social organization.[6] I think it is Carpenter who says that poaching, for example, is a habit of the hunting and fishing stage which persists when society in general is organized on quite a different economic basis (that of agriculture and commerce, and so on), and that in general murder, theft, and all the chief forms of criminality represent something which at one time were by no means considered crimes but which were either innocent or actual virtues.[7] I doubt if there could be found any form of criminality which was not an approved and authorized mode of social action at some period of historic development. It has persisted, however, practically unmodified and therefore does not fit into the moving, the dynamic aspects of existing society. It rather stands athwart the dominant social movements and acts as a continual threat. Now that means unmodified persistence of some one class or some one mode of social action which was appropriate to a simple and more primitive type of social organization. That means that the work of social organization has not been completed. There is a tendency to locate the whole responsibility on the side of the class that has been left behind, upon the side of the class that has not moved on, that has not readjusted itself; but of course you cannot have adjustments made from one side only. It cannot be simply that that one class has got out of balance, out of focus. Things are out of balance somewhere else too, and the relatively unmodified persistence of this class is due to lack of sufficient power of assimilation and interest in assimilation somewhere else.

Generalizing that, society is still, to a very considerable extent, a number of societies which are in juxtaposition with each other, which have physical points of contact with each other, but which psychically are still comparatively discrete, and the interests of those various local social groups are more or less in antagonism with each other. It is just the same thing to my mind being transferred with one and the same geographical area, and within what, physically speaking, is one and the same society. In the early period of distinct geographical societies, the things that you are to do to members of your own tribe are the things that you are not to do to those who belong to other tribes. That is, friendship, mutuality are supposed with[in] the tribe, while hostility is assumed outside. So if it is a virtue to be hospitable and generous inside the clan, it is equally a virtue to be cruel, revengeful to anybody outside. Now [a] lot [of] changes of a physical aspect take place and you, so to speak, dump a lot of those societies down in the same geographical area. While the relations of open hostility may cease, while there is a presumption of unity in a way, yet the mere physical juxtaposition does not prove any psychical unification of interests. That is a matter of slow growth, and while the psychical assimilation and redistribution are going on, there is opportunity for not merely crime but all the forms of class hostility which as matter of fact are characteristic of social life as we now have it.

Simply as a matter of illustration we can conceive of fifty societies which do not come into physical contact at all—between which there are wastes and deserts. We might then have the fabled "golden age" within these societies which are organized more or less on the communal basis. Then you have these various societies reaching out till they come into contact with each other and a period of open and overt hostility setting in. Then you have, as your third type in the illustration, positive relations, relations of travel, commerce, of growing ability to understand each other's language and thoughts, and perhaps a single political regime instituted over all these societies. You get in a physical, external sense one single comprehensive society, but the various constituent groups have not yet become thoroughly reorganized on the basis of their membership in the larger whole. They still retain many of the characteristics that they had as isolated, or as in negative relations to each other, and the process of transformation and growth must keep on until each of those ceases to be independent as a center in any sense and is made over into an organ of the whole.

Suppose that biologically each new form, instead of being specialized and in a way set by the side of other forms, had to take up a lower form into itself. Suppose that the higher forms resulted from the absorption of the coalition of two or three of those lower forms. It is obvious that you would expect a good deal of internal disorder in an organism developed on that basis, for by the principle of momentum they would tend to keep the characteristics previously acquired. They must conform and contribute to the common welfare and participate more or less in the common interest, and the period of mutual conflicts and reactions will have to go on until the whole organism is built up in such a way that each of the previous organisms is now simply an organ. That illustration shows the way in which society as an organ grows. One society is not located simply by the side of another so that each goes on. The newer forms take up and absorb the previous forms and you cannot have complete harmony until the assimilation is complete. It is this conflict of local societies within a growing, single, more comprehensive society which is primarily responsible for the hostilities and conflicts on the negative side which present themselves, criminality being the most marked phase or symptom of this conflict between particular groups.

The criminal is more than a criminal, he is a member of a class. I would not say that that was so in absolutely every case, but it is certainly true as a rule. He comes up to a certain social standard, he needs a certain kind of social approval of his conduct, it is as necessary for him to meet the approval of his class as a certain standard of rectitude is on the part of a businessman. He does function as a member of a certain restricted community. As a representative of that community he is thrown into antagonism with other local groups, and as was suggested before you cannot locate all the responsibility on one side. The criminal class is as much an institution, a social institution, as the nobility of England in a social institution. They are both social products and one is as legitimate an expression of those conditions as they have been as the other is. In other words, any class has to be interpreted in terms of its relation, historic and functional, to society as a whole, and only when thus interpreted do we get the promise and possibility of future harmonious organization.

I will go on to speak of the case of the genius at the next time: the criminal representing, according to this point of view, social survival, the genius representing social anticipation. The main points of the controversy are familar to you as seen in the essays reprinted in James's *Will to Believe* [8] and the essays of Grant Allen and Spencer referred to there.

May 25, 1898

It probably has occurred to you that the problem regarding the relation of the genius to the social group in which he arises is simply a particular case of the separation of the organism and the environment, and then asking the question which is the determining and important relation. On one side there is a school which puts all the determining efficacy in the environment and regards the great man as a simple direct product of his surrounding conditions, thus having for its tendency the reduction of the importance of the great man, his relative elimination so far as having any great part to play in the historical drama. The other side, represented by Mr. James, points out the great part which has been actually played by individuals and dwells on the fact as expressed by Emerson that an institution is simply the shadow of a man, and regards the hero, the leader, as the important factor in all social progress, establishing a certain precedence, so to speak, which is then followed by the mass of men until another great variation arises.

The theory which makes the genius the product of the environment seems inadequate to account for the difference which actually exists between the genius and other men. Everybody is a product of the environment, and why in one and the same environment should there be such great differences? Why should there be anybody to mark off as a genius? Why should variation be so great and so startling? Why should the great man act as he does and make over his environment? It is true that we interpret great men in the light of their surroundings, but it is equally true that it is through the medium of the great man that we appreciate the surroundings. We can say that the Elizabethan age produced Shakespeare, but it is equally true that the Elizabethan age means to us what it does from the fact that Shakespeare lived then and because of what he uttered, that it is through him as an organ that we look at and interpret that mode of civilization.

The theory as stated by James against the Spencerians and Grant Allen in particular seems to make the variation too arbitrary, to throw it outside any amenability to law, as we usually understand law; and in thus making the break, the gap between the genius and his times so very large, it also makes it difficult to account for the influence which he has. If he is such an accidental variation, why should he exert the great influence which he does? We must assume some common element in order to get any purchase for understanding his influence. James's theory of the genius is practically the same as that given in the last chapter of his *Psychology* regarding the origin of *a priori* ideas or the most highly generalized categories. It represents a purely accidental start which somehow transcends the given environment instead of registering it. But why should this variation occur? And if it is a mere variation of such an apparently casual kind, why should it get set? Why should it become an organ for controlling subsequent intellectual operations?

There seems to be a basis for argument on each side. There is something which appeals to the mind on both sides. We feel that the genius must somehow be the product of his environment in the sense of being organically connected with it, and of bringing to light forces that are working there, but we must recognize also that history would be an entirely different thing from what it is if we were to eliminate a dozen great men that might be easily named. If we were to suppose them omitted and wipe out the part which they have actually played in the direction of social forces, certainly as far as we can see a large part of the actual progress that has been made would have to be wiped out too.

Now we are not concerned with all the problems involved in the interpretation of the genius, but taken simply as an extreme case by which to test the apparent independence of the individual from society, it seems to me that what both theories fail to sufficiently notice and emphasize is the importance of the negative element in society and in social growth, and the relation of the genius to that negative element.

The students who had the logical course* will remember the importance that was attached to the negative element in the generation of the universal. That is, the essence of the criticism made on the empirical school, according to which the universal is simply the registration of a number of particulars, was that we have the need for the universal at the time when we have no specific particulars to be registered. Then when we have the particulars already defined and inventoried as particulars, there is no stimulus, no motive to search out any universal. The universal in that case would be nothing but an ideal naming over of what we already have. But we really search for a universal in order to have a method of determining, and controlling, organizing, the particulars. Then the search for the universal always implies some instability in the specific details of

* Presumably a reference to Dewey's course in the fall of 1897 on "The Logic of Ethics."

experience, and implies the need of some instrument by which to catch a firm grip of them, the real function of the universal being to furnish that instrument of location, of interpretation and organization.

Now what I had in mind regarding the genius in relation to society is exactly the same principle psychologically. To say the genius is the product of society, one must recognize the part which is played in stimulating him into being by the deficiencies and excesses, the lack of equilibrium and organization in society, as well as its attained capacities and acquirements. What the empiricist does, the Spencerian school, is to virtually assume the society as there and as smoothly working, as an environment which somehow suddenly consolidates itself or sums itself up into the great man. Of course if society were simply unorganized, if there were merely elements of lack and maladjustment, you could not get the genius. As was suggested about the origin of any variation, there must be a particular tension between the supply and the demand, between the positive and the negative factors, there must be enough which society has worked out, it must have laid hold of sufficient values in experience, to furnish the nutritive material, to furnish the positive suggestions to the future leader. He must have something positive to get hold of as an instrument. But on the other side he brings this positive element to consciousness, he throws it out into such tremendous relief, making a great idea out of it instead of a commonplace idea simply because he shows its illuminating and organizing function with reference to what has, up to that time, been lacking, been defective in the social form.

Some writer (I regret that I cannot make the reference more definite, but I simply saw this in casual reading and did not make a note of it) has claimed that it is a law of history that every great leader has come from an environment which was alien to the environment in which he did great work, that there is a sort of geographical dislocation in the biographies of great men. Jesus, for example, did not have his training and did not reflect the moral and religious ideas of Jerusalem. Socrates was not an Athenian; he came from a lower class than the usual Athenian gentleman. While he was a free citizen he came from a rather despised level. Napoleon did not come from the center of France at all. There was a long list of such references given, which the writer said established this theory of geographical dislocation. It was an empirical way of getting at it, and I do not know how much there is in it, but it seems to me a particular case of this general principle of the generation of the genius through a certain relation of the positive acquisitions of society to its wants, to its lacks. The genius and the influence which the genius has certainly imply a capacity on the part of society to get outside of itself and to turn round upon itself, to look back at itself and to readjust itself from the standpoint of that outside view which it has.

Now Socrates, for instance, certainly was a typical Athenian product. You could not imagine anybody like him anywhere else, and when you have him in Athens you feel that he is where he belongs, that he fits into that social environment. In that sense he is a product; but after all Socrates affords a typical illustration of just this thing. He universalizes, he generalizes a factor that was involved in Athenian life in such a way as to put it in the strongest possible contrast with the attainments of the Athenians. He brings to consciousness the principle of free inquiry, the principle of social discussion, the principle of the direction of life through the discovery of values by inquiry and reflection. And after he has done that we can see that that had been the moving principle in the whole Athenian civilization. But he brings it out and he utilizes it in such a way as to reveal the defects and inadequacy of its use theretofore, and so he becomes at once a reformer, not because he is entirely outside or ahead of his time or brings in any alien principle. He simply generalizes the principle which had been at work before, but the generalization reveals the defects and then it becomes a factor of reform, making the thing over.

Certainly all political, religious and moral leaders have been reformers. We may perhaps doubt whether they made any improvement or not, but in the literal sense of the term they were reformers. The only possible exception would be the literary genius in whose discussion we find this antinomy in its most extreme form. Some regard him as a reflector of his time, and others regard him as a being who descends from heaven and reveals things which are timeless and spaceless and has nothing to do with environment anyway.

It does not seem to me it is stretching the point to say that the artist as well as the other typical forms of social geniuses are reformers. They are reformers at least in the sense that they set not simply new literary styles, not simply that they create new modes of expression and of workmanship, technique—they are reformers on the side of substance as well. That is to say, they create new organs for valuing experience. The social function of the artist seems to me to be precisely that: that he gives new points of view for considering the facts of life. As far as the average man is concerned, his categories for judging the ordinary things of his experience are derived very largely from the artist. Of course the moral and religious teachers furnish him a great deal of material too, but the permeation of the general principles implied by them down into the details of daily life is largely a secondary work of the artists who show the application. The capacity of the common man for seeing life about him in a dramatic and typical way having certain dominant centers of reference, pigeonholes under which he classifies the various items of his experience as they arise, certainly comes to an extent which can hardly be estimated from the artist. The artist in that sense is a creator. He makes the world, he makes experience look different to people; and that element of reconstruction certainly involves [a] more or less negative attitude to the previous current modes of interpretation. He sets free, he liberates new values which by the nature of the case not merely transcend old values but in certain ways contradict them. Certainly the painter has made nature a conscious fact, a fact of conscious experience, to a very considerable degree.

I should have said the artist instead of the painter. It ought to include the workman in the minor crafts, in textile fabrics for instance, as well as in the interpretation of nature in poetry. They have actually brought out the capacity of recognizing colors, of seeing distinctions and relations of light and shade even in the physical and sensuous sense, to say nothing of idealizing these sensuous qualities in new directions. It is rather an intangible matter to get hold of, but I think we underestimate rather than overestimate the results of this liberation or emancipation of these values by artists.

Now if we come to things which are more immediately matters of experience, the social and moral elements which come up in our everyday life, our dependence on previous interpretations is even greater. If we recognize the part played by the negative element, the tension between the acquistions of society and the need of society, we see that it consists in generalizing a principle which has been working, in getting these acquisitions in such a way as to bring the need also to consciousness, and to furnish an instrument for making good that lack [?]. We seem to be able to utilize the factor of truth in both the theories, the one that makes genius a mere product and the other that it is his very nature to transcend the social environment in which he springs up. In other words, to make the connection with the general principle under discussion, it is a question of social growth, of social progress, of the evaluation of function, and the mistake of the empiricist, of the Spencerian school, is to lose from sight the moving aspect, the dynamic aspect, and treat the environment as a static given thing, as simply a thing of attained, of objectified realization.

The school which emphasizes the importance of the individual as such, as representing society, certainly has a strong feeling for that growing element, for the function of change and variation; but in not connecting it with the development of social function as such, it leaves it as an isolated fact, practically an unaccountable fact. All you can say is that these things do occur by some happy accident.

The conclusion then that I would illustrate rather than positively arrive at in the cases of the criminal and the genius is that the relationships have to be interpreted with reference to social progress. That progress, change, does involve antagonisms, involves relative gaps, chasms, but they are not between the individual as such and society, but between one individual and another, or between one class and another, or between one social force and another social force—the differentiation, the lack of harmony between these forces being itself a stimulus to the determination of a new mode of social evaluation and thus indirectly of a new custom or habit of social action.

SECTION 6. THOUGHT
AND ACTION

Before leaving this point of the psychical aspects of the relation of the individual and society and going on to the economic, I want to say something first about the relation of thought and action, and secondly, regarding the conception of the social sensorium in a somewhat more limited and restricted sense than has hitherto been discussed.

With reference to the first point, the relation of thought and action, Mr. Baldwin's recent book [9] makes a convenient point of departure in his insistence upon thought as the material of social organization. Beginning of Part VI, Chapter XII, page 487: "The matter of social organization consists of thoughts, by which is meant all sorts of intellectual states such as imaginations, knowledges, and informations." It goes on to develop and establish that thesis, and that it is thoughts or knowledges which through the process of imitation constitute the warp and woof of social organization. The theory of course parallels the statement which he repeatedly makes on the psychological side that action is a function of thought content, that both desire and belief are functions of ideas, intellectual contents, so that given that idea, intellectual content, the action follows as its normal development or expression.

The psychological statement there seems to be justified in the emphasis prevalent in psychology at present of ideo-motor action as the outcome of the play of ideas. The defect it seems to me is that there is only a halfway recognition of this principle. I should admit without question that given a certain ideas as a completed idea, as thoroughly worked out, as a matter of course its further expression action would follow. But there is still one problem untouched. How did there come to be that idea, and how did that idea get its elaboration? Through what mechanism did it reach this point of completeness and definiteness where it could pass over into action? When we ask those questions we are thrown over upon action as the beginning as well as the end, as the Alpha as well as the Omega of the process. The idea then appears as the intermediary. The action grows out of the complete idea simply because the idea is action in a partial state psychically considered. Now if we accept that psychological statement, we get a different view on the social side. Thought would then appear as methods of social organization rather than as material of social organization; or more strictly speaking, thoughts, ideas, would appear as modes of social reorganization, rather than basic material of organization as such.

At the next time I will call your attention to the footnote on page 97 of Baldwin's *Mental Development* as suggestive on the psychological side. It is only a footnote but it is a very definite and apt discussion of the relation of thought and action from his point of view. I would also invite your attention to the discussion of the distinction between an idea as a piece of information, as a knowledge, and what we ordinarily term beliefs or convictions. A clear analysis of the difference between a conviction and an idea as a knowledge or piece of information I think would clear up the statement that it is ideas which are the material of social organization.

May 26, 1898

In the winter's course I attempted to develop the general view of the relation of thought to action on the basis of ideas as being born out of conflict in action and serving the purpose of solving the opposition out of which they grow so as to become the instruments or materials of reorganization, and I shall not attempt to go over that ground in general again; but the statement of Mr. Baldwin to which I referred yesterday (the footnote on page 97) makes certain propositions which they serve through criticisms to bring out the same points.[10]

Baldwin's position in criticism of the view similar to the one presented—that thought grows out of the obstruction of action—is in the first place that that affords no criterion for the truth of thinking, that we must first assume that certain thought values have been established in action by movement, as he calls it; that thinking or true thoughts are copy systems of these values originally set up in action, their advantage being that since they are ideal copies they are present and utilizable when the objects with reference to which the movements originally took place are not present. Now there is the same conception which runs through all of his book and which of course is extremely current in existing logic: that truth is the correspondence of an idea with the established fact or object, that correspondence consisting in being some kind of a copy, a conception of an agreement of connection between an experience which gives us an object and an idea which simply represents that object. With reference to the question how thoughts can be true, he says it is natural to suppose that the existing adapted or fact-revealing movements have gone before and that thought is in some way a form of inner reestablishing, without consent dependence on real objects, of the system of values first revealed by such movements: "The movement-variations would go ahead of the thought-variations, and the growth of thought would depend upon successful movement, rather than upon its obstruction and damming up." If the thought is a copy of the value revealed in a previous act without the presence of the object itself, then of course that movement must come first—the original must come before the copy as a matter of course. "On the 'obstruction' view, on the contrary, the thought-variations could prove their value, or get to be judged true, only through their issue in movement." That of course is a perfectly correct statement. Truth on that basis is established not be comparison of something that goes before but with reference to something that comes after it by its motor efficacy. But he has some objections to that point of view.

Besides the difficulty of doing this under the conditions of obstruction (whatever that means), there would have to be the same selecting process acting upon movements, which would have been invoked in case the simple movement variations went ahead. It seems to me to involve, when we reflect upon it, a sort of cart-before-the-horse all through the evolution of mind. It is much truer to the facts to say that simple motor adaptations—in *thinking* they are adaptations of *attention*—go before thought, and that the brain variations which perpetuate and stand for these adaptations are *ipso facto* selected in the selection of the movements; *with them come the true thoughts.*

Just what he means by the difficulty of the thought finding issue in movement under the conditions of obstruction is not quite clear. Of course if the obstruction were complete, there would be no issue in movement; but so far as I know, none of these writers have taken the ground that the inhibition is absolute. If it [the obstruction] did [obstruct completely] it would amount to complete paralysis of action.

Another objection certainly has more force; it is that you must have some standard for testing your movement. Which movement is the right movement? Mr. Baldwin to answer that question seems to require that there is some idea already in consciousness on the basis of which you can tell what is right and what is wrong. If I have a clear idea of hitting the bull's eye in the target, I have a standard for telling which movements are successful and which are unsuccessful. His point is, if I have not a clear idea in advance I cannot tell which of my various actions are to be selected, so that in any case the selection of the proper movement depends upon a thought being already in existence. His position is elaborated more extensively in an article in the March number, I think, of the *Philosophical Review* on "Selective Thinking," but I do not think he makes the gist of the position any clearer than it is here in this footnote.[11]

I am going to, without direct reference to Mr. Baldwin again, go on and indicate various points in which his statements seem to me to be open to criticism.

In the first place the statement that a thoroughly adapted movement reports objects seems to me to have no adequate psychological justification. A thoroughly adapted movement or action, one which hits its mark without any difficulty or friction at all, one which therefore raises no doubts, no queries, can hardly be said to be one which reveals or establishes any objects as objects. There is nothing in such a thoroughly harmonious or organized action to make the object, as an object, stand out at all. Undoubtedly such actions may have value; they will have value so far as they take up into themselves the significance of various other actions of which they are not the outcome. But these values are not ideas; they are not thoughts about objects; they are not pieces of information; they are neither percepts nor concepts. That is to say they are in no sense abstract; the value is in no way detached from the action. It is simply the recognized, appreciated value of the action itself. It is not cut loose from the action and located in the object on one side, nor in the subject on the other side.

For further verification of that subject I can refer only to your own experience in cases of thoroughly systematized activity. Do you in such cases stop to detach the significance which your action has and project it with reference to an object distinct from your own operation or connected with yourself as something distinct from what you are doing? Or is it not true in those cases of thoroughly harmonized action that both the object as a conscious object and the subject as a conscious subject are absorbed as integral values into the action itself?

The reference of the value to an object, that is, to make a percept of it, or the reference of it to the subject, to make a thought or concept of it, occurs then, secondly, only when there is sufficient resistance or inhibition in the action to settle it. It would be a great waste of energy, it would be against the whole principles of economy to make these abstractions when there is no necessity for them; and it would be against all the principles of psychical mechanism to cut off, to detach these values when there is nothing to stimulate such an analytic process. But whenever there is resistance, whenever there is opposition, then we have the machinery which will shake the values (which were previously identified), will shake them loose and make them intellectual, make them objects of inquiry, or contemplation or reflection as ideas. Or in terms of Mr. Baldwin's proposition, even if we were to admit, which we cannot do, that a thoroughly adapted movement reveals facts or objects as such, there would still be no basis for an inner reestablishing of these ideas or thought values unless there were some obstruction somewhere, some friction or opposition. As he says, it is "a form of inner reestablishing, without constant dependence on real objects, of the system of values first revealed by such movements." The analysis of that sentence shows the importance of some incompatibility there, some opposition. If the real object is not there, how can you get set up or copy just the same mental state, as when the object was there, and what would be the use of doing it? The conception implies really that you want the object, that you want to use it in some way, and that therefore you feel the lack of it and there is a struggle, or movement of desire in some way for the possession or the control of an object which is now gone.

In mere reverie we have on the surface the reinstatement of ideas, the reinstatement or development of images and thought values when the object is not present and without any direct function or use for such images, but it would require a good deal of stretching to suppose that our mental life is built up out of these reveries as their basis, that thinking and the deliberative processes are simply utilizing the images which come up in this purely chance way in reverie. It is a good deal more natural to interpret this from the other end and say that after the habit of forming ideas with reference to the securing of objects, or the control of objects which have temporarily fallen out of control; that after that habit has been set up, it will at times run of itself, that it will take free play even when there is no direct use for it, for that is a principle that we find everywhere—that habits that were set up for use, after they are developed into powers, do unroll for themselves, for the mere satisfaction to be got out of their own play back and forth.

Now in the third place this difficulty about selecting the right movement can certainly be turned against Mr. Baldwin's own statement. If you have the idea already which simply reestablishes the value previously presented in action, and if your next movement follows directly from that idea, where is there any need for selection? You already have what you want, the thing takes care of itself.

The need for selection is when there are actions taking place which are superfluous, or which are in the wrong direction. It implies sufficient previous conflict or tension to account for two different kinds of movements, some which are in the desirable direction and others which are not. How can you get those two more or less opposed movements going on without having some opposition in the previous sensorial stimuli, it is difficult to see. If the obstruction which gives rise to thinking is absolutely complete, there certainly would be no basis for selecting movements, because there would be no movements. But if we suppose that it is partial (that is, that there is a tension between discharges and obstructions, that activity is dammed up in certain directions, while there is a motor overflow in others), we would be sure to have all the basis that is required for selection. The primary and immediate basis of selection in such a case would be of those movements which relieve the pressure. Any movements which escaping along certain channels reacted so as to open up other channels, or in such a way as to drain out the activity in such a way as to do away with the feeling of obstruction, would certainly be selected.

It is only in highly reflective cases that we stop and judge of success by conscious comparison with an already set up intellectual standard. We go, as we say, by our feelings, our feelings in that case being our various sensations of pressure and relief of pressure. Whenever we get ease in action, we take it for granted that we have relative success, that we are on the right track. We are guided by the "fringe" in James's terminology, by the feeling of direction, rather than by the conscious intellectual comparison between a given result and an antecedent which is supposed to serve as its copy. Of course we make errors in that way. It is not an infallible guide. The feeling of ease may mark simply a temporary relief of the tension, a temporary getting rid of the obstruction, and in the long run or afterwards, the difficulty may turn up in an aggravated form; but, after all, that criterion of success in reaching an end, that feeling of the unified consciousness which gives us the feeling of ease, is the standard by which we go.

Put still in other terms, except by contrast with the previous tension there would be no basis at all for selection. It is because a given action brings relief as compared with the previous pressure, or brings unity as compared with previous discrepancy, that we select it. A man who is shooting anywhere, shooting wildly, would not select any particular movement. A man who could hit the center of a target every time would have no necessity for selecting any particular movement. There must be before that the tension of division in his consciousness, he must have the contrast between the actual and the ideal. He must have a felt incompatibility, an actual consciousness of incompatibility between what he wants to do and what he is doing; otherwise the man shooting at a mark would be engaged in an actually habitual action which would not engage his consciousness at all, any more than taking his leg up and putting it down in walking usually attracts his attention. If there were no absolute obstruction, there would be no selection and no basis on which to select. On the other hand if there were unhindered discharge there would be no selection and no basis for which to select. But given a tension between the obstruction of action and discharge and we have both the necessity for selection and a basis upon which the selection can be made.

Now on that conception of the thinking as arising through obstruction, but as not to be identified with mere obstruction, the mere idea is such a report of existing action as is available for the direction of future action. The conflict reports itself in our sensations; that is, discharges do take place which make themselves felt. Now if the thing simply stopped there, there would be no idea and no utility in ideas, but let one of these reports of the existing state be selected to serve as the organ or instrument of further action and it has become abstracted, it has become an idea, and the peculiarity, the psychical characteristic of an idea as an idea, is that it is precisely that value abstracted out of the past thrown into relief by conflict; it is that utilized, or made serviceable with reference to the future. The process of verification is the projective process rather than a retrospective one. The standard of thought is in the capacity of this idea to unify, to organize the situation. If the idea which is abstracted does serve to reorganize action and unify consciousness on the emotional side, gives a feeling of relief, of the smoothing out of the creases of consciousness, it is taken to be true.

Now the importance of those considerations is their application on the side of social consciousness. Adopting this general point of view what conception do we get as a substitute of the notion that the ideas are the material of social organization? From this point of view ideas have their social significance in being methods or instruments rather than in any sense its raw material. The value of any idea is in its functional efficacy, in its capacity to lay hold of the *disjecta membra* in experience and put them together again in an orderly whole of action and of appreciated value. The idea is a point of view, it is a mode, it is a form, not the matter of organization. The matter, according to this, is found of course in the motor tendencies or in the activities which need to be organized, which have become conflicting and which need systematizing. They are the counterparts on the social side of the impulse, individually speaking. That is, the idea serves to combine together, to direct a variety of impulses which are working more or less at cross purposes. So the thought, the idea, socially considered, is a way of bringing into unity, and so into greater efficiency, various conflicting tendencies in social action.

Take one illustration, the thought, the invention of the sewing machine. Now according to Mr. Baldwin that thought is the material of social organization and imitation is the process by which this thought, arising first simply in an individual and therefore being private, is generalized and made over adequately into social organization. According to the other point of view the thought of the sewing machine is an instrument for relating social tendencies, social activities already in existence but which are not functioning adequately. A negative element comes in there, the element of obstruction somewhere, just as much as it does in the individual. The idea of the sewing machine is the conception of social relief, it is an idea which has the function of alleviation, of systematization. It is that which calls for it, which stimulates it; otherwise a man in the middle of a desert who has never had any social connection would be as apt to invent the sewing machine as anybody else. It is a matter of good philosophy that need is the mother of invention and that need consists of the recognition of conflict which wastes energy, tendencies which are at least not reinforcing each other, and there is felt to be the possibility of coordination, and the idea arises as the instrument or mode of coordination, the material being these various activities which are not organically related to each other.

It is hopeless task to set out to look for the matter of social organization. You can find the matter of social reorganization, but to attempt to find the matter of social organization is to fall into the fallacy of supposing that you have something prior to society which by some future operation on it is going to be socialized. Relatively and historically the various activities which are coordinated through the sewing machine are nonsocial; but that simply means that they are not operating with their full social efficacy, that they have fallen out of position, that there is a disturbance of their relations of positive equilibrium and that they need to be laid hold of and utilized again so that they do become positively contributory to social welfare, and the idea or the invention is the means by which that is brought about.

May 31, 1898

If an idea as a piece of knowledge is to be conceived essentially as a method or an instrument in the development of experience, then the idea, insofar, already is universal. Mr. Baldwin's point is that the idea, as it originates in the individual, is particular, that as such it furnishes the material for social organization, but it becomes universal only through the process of assimilative imitation or absorption on the part of others, and that is one reason that he lays so much stress in the social significance of imitation. It is the process which is necessary to relieve the idea of its isolation and clothe it with a social character by making it generic. Such a conception rests upon the quantitative idea of what the universal is. Its universality, according to that point of view, would seem to be dependent upon the number of people who possess it. It is of course a different way of getting at a very common conception in logic, that universality of an idea depends not upon the number of people by whom it has been used but the number of objects to which it applies, instead of being found in the function which it subserves with reference to the construction of objectivity.

Mr. Baldwin corrects that point of view by another one, without however reconciling the two at all. According to that other point of view the idea is from the first the thought of the situation. It is not any idea, every idea, that is social material, but the ideas that are thoughts of social situations. If we follow out that line of argument, then the universality would be something intrinsic in the idea itself; it would be found in the fact that it is the thought of what is generic in the situation and that it operates with reference to the maintenance of the situation. If the idea is essentially method for action, then that is what constitutes its universality. We get a different criterion of the nature of university than we have upon the view which simply looks at it from the side of its quantitative range. Every idea is at least implicitly or virtually a formulated one. Those mathematical statements to which we do not restrict the term formulation simply represent the highly elaborated ideas. They are the ideas in their purest form, which have been stripped of all irrelevant and incongruous associations. The formulation in the mechanical sense is the idea which serves only for action and all of which serves for action.

While our ideas as we ordinarily hold them are by no means purely intellectual, they are aesthetical and emotional in character, they have a certain surcharge of content from a strictly intellectual point of view, and as a result they are more than mere methods or instruments of action, and also they are not perfectly specific, they are not perfectly defined in their reference to action. The formulation, especially in its mathematical shape, gives the element of the strict, pure idea reduced to its lowest terms and termed in its nakedness an idea. But so far as we make any ordinary idea an intellectual one, make it an information merely, insofar it becomes essentially an attitude toward action. The whole import of information that such and such is the state of affairs means that we have such a statement of the situation insofar as it is regarded as reliable, as determining succeeding action.

All such universals, however, are hypothetical as ideas; they are abstract. There is necessarily then a further process, the process which is the reality, I think, of that which Mr. Baldwin lays a great deal of stress on all through his book. The idea has to be submitted as a proposition to social approval, there is a process of social acceptance and rejection which goes on, a process of social testing and verification. But the misconception, to my mind, comes in in supposing that the idea up to that time, the idea as it presents itself to the individual, is merely particular, and that the social process is wholly the generalizing one. It is rather that the idea, until it has been acted on, is purely tentative, purely hypothetical, and the process of socialization which the idea goes through is then not a process of imitative assimilation primarily; it is primarily the process of attempting to utilize the idea as a method of stimulating and directing action. It is that which transforms it from simply a hypothetical universal into a dynamic, working universal. As a result the quantitative range of the idea may be greatly extended. If the idea is regarded as true, thus holding good for social action, the quantitative extension will be very great; but that is the result or the aspect of the working out of the qualitative universality which it already possesses—it is not the cause of its having a universal nature. The acceptance and rejection which go on are for the purposes of action, not for the mere reception of a certain content in consciousness and the stamping of that with some sort of intellectual approval. It is emphasizing what is purely incidental to conceive of that as essentially an imitative process.

I will refer again to the example used the other day—the invention of the sewing machine. Now that thought when first developed out of social needs was a universal insofar as it was a scheme or formulation for readjusting certain modes of industrial action. It had to go through a process of social acceptance, rejection and modification. But that did not depend primarily upon the number of people who at once began to use sewing machines. It was not that somebody saw somebody else using a sewing machine and then proceeded to imitate him; it was rather that any use of the sewing machine involved a change in doing business, it compelled other people to follow the same line of action. It was not left for them merely to imitate or not to imitate. They had to do something about it or else be left behind in the business competition. Moreover, it is theoretically conceivable that such an invention would become socialized, socially available, and next to nobody [would] ever copy it or imitate it in any way. If somebody could invent a sewing machine that would do the sewing for the whole world, the determination of action would certainly be just as great and just as effective as if one million people copied the invention. The number of people that happen to utilize that particular thing, or happen to be directly related to it, is purely a secondary matter. The activities of people who have never used a sewing machine have been as much affected as those who have used it. It is the effect upon those who do not use it that is more important than that upon those who do use it. It is a social tool to which a variety of other social activities have to be adjusted.

It is the same way with any invention. It is not the number of people who take up and use the invention that determines its socialization. It is the reorganizing influence which it has on a great number of apparently quite different but actually interdependent modes of action. The self-binding reaper gets its social effects when anybody buys a barrel of flour as much as it does when the farmer actually uses it in the harvest. It is the capacity of the idea to compel other adjustments, it is its capacity to function in a directive capacity, in a way which presents stimuli which others must notice and to which they must adapt their activities that furnishes the criterion for its social quality. Ideas then are social, but it is truer to speak of them as social modes or instruments than to call them social material, and their sociology is found not in the degree to which their content is agreed to, accepted in the purely intellectual sense by others, but in the influence which they exert upon the current modes of action and the values which cohere with these modes of action.

We come now to the distinction of the idea in a purely intellectual sense, from what we may call convictions. The unity of a society may be said to be measured by the community of convictions or active beliefs which animate it. Now such assurances, convictions, always have an intellectual aspect which can be segregated by reflection. Thus a conviction can be reduced to a simple idea. But that is always an external operation which some thinker performs upon the conviction. Conviction as a conviction, as it excites and motivates the ordinary consciousness, is a good deal more than an idea, and that "more" is not the simple quantitative moreness, it is not other things added on to the idea. It means that the idea as a formulative statement has no separate existence at all.

Of course all books on psychology and sociology, or any scientific subject, are written by students and these students are a comparatively small portion of society, men who have formed the habit of analyzing the current convictions and beliefs in order to get at and criticize their exact objective influence. That is, the work is done by those who have formed the habit of this analysis and have the power of making over their personal convictions which are just as much emotional and just as much volitional as they are intellectual, making them over into their intellectual equivalents, and for those persons there merely arises an unconscious tendency to identify the purely intellectual equivalents with the assurance or conviction as it vitally excites and animates consciousness.

But from the standpoint of the mass of men, that process is of course fallacious. The comparatively small number of people who can argue about politics or religion without losing their tempers is a concrete example of the point I am trying to make here. People do not get excited about the criticism of ideas as ideas. When one has the attitude toward it that it is an idea, his business is to criticize it in the intellectual examination of it. The difficulty is for the average man to take that attitude toward his vital convictions. They are too real, too much bound up with his life. He has no desire to get outside of them in that way and to dissect them. In fact the whole procedure strikes the common consciousness as too cold-blooded and one who does it lacks an appreciation of the values concerned. If he really valued them, he could not dissect them in that way.

Convictions, assurances, in the sense, are identical with a man's interest, the personal values that are put on things. These common convictions, beliefs, persuasions, common points of view, common principles of value, are not in any sense material for organization; they are rather the outcome, the phases of social organization. They are the social organization as it is worked out; they are not in any sense something which is antecedent to the social organization as the material out of which it is to be composed. Because they are the phases of social organization, of course it would be impossible to exaggerate their social significance. But they have that social significance just because they do lay hold of the whole person, because they express his entire attitude toward life and toward action and are not simply ideas in the sense of pieces of knowledge or of information.* They are the ideas which have ceased to be hypothetical universals and which have become organized into the conduct of life; they constitute the structure of life itself, they are so thoroughly organized into it.

Hence, while it is desirable that somebody should always be in a critical attitude toward some, at least, of these organized values, and while it is desirable that everybody should have the capacity of becoming critical on occasion of some of them, it is not desirable that the emphasis in the life of everybody should be thrown on the side of the strictly intellectual examination. There is not only division of labor as matter of fact, as regards the power of transforming these into abstract statements and criticizing them, but such a division of labor seems to be as important, as serviceable there, as it is in any other direction of life. Of course that is not to be exaggerated into a dualism, that there are to be some persons who are to be in a simply critical attitude and others in a purely receptive and acquiescent attitude, but simply that the class who make it their main business to be engaged in inquiry and criticism and reflection is by the nature of the case a somewhat limited class. Everybody of course ought to have the intelligence and the faculty to use inquiry and criticism when the need for it presents itself, but with the mass of people it is only incidental. It is only with the scholar as a scholar that it becomes a dominant function of life.

* A sentence is obliterated in the original hectograph copy at this point.

SECTION 7. LANGUAGE AS "SOCIAL SENSORIUM" OR "OBJECTIVE MIND"

This makes a convenient point of transition to the discussion of Spencer's social sensorium in the more limited sense. An intelligible sense can be given to that term by conceiving of it as the intelligence which at any given time is available to direct the activities of the individual in social channels. I use the term available in an active, not merely a passive, sense—that is, not simply available in the sense that it [is] stored up somewhere and that the individual can get at it if he tries hard enough, but that it is so actively available that he has to take account of it, that it is so thoroughly organized into him that it does control his conduct for social ends. Plato laid it down as an indispensable condition of community life that it should be small enough so that all its free citizens should be acquainted with each other. That idea was practically realized in Athens; and to Plato living there, it seemed impossible that you could have any human organization of society excepting on that basis. Of course you could have an external organization, you could have a great military empire, but Plato was conscious of the difference between the oriental state and Athens where the various ends were individually participated in by the various citizens and where in turn each citizen was responsible for giving something back to the state. Now that personal acquaintance and the constant communication, converse back and forth, sharing of ideas, commerce of thoughts, constitutes this social sensorium in its simplest form. It is a condition which is met practically in all more primitive social forms. But it involves not only this contemporaneous intercourse, it involves also continuity in time. That is, not merely that all the persons at a given time should be in this action and reaction so that one is influenced by the deeds and thoughts of others, but also that he should be directed in his activities by the previous acquisitions, that there should be an inheritance from past generations. More specifically that social consciousness then is found in language. Not again passive language, or language as a vocabulry which is stored away somewhere, but language as the vital active force of intercommunication, language as the organ of communication.

There is a difference between being objectively stimulated to do social work and being socially stimulated and directed in doing it. The slave is undoubtedly performing a useful social function when he tills the ground and raises crops, and provided his labor is as efficient as free labor, from a purely objective standpoint he would be as social an organ as anybody could be; but in those cases the stimulus is purely direct and because it is direct it is physical. Now language represents the stimuli to action becoming indirect—that is, passing through the medium of consciousness and being reinterpreted before the action finally takes place. In other words, language (using it not in the sense of a repository) does for society what the central nervous system does for the individual. It is the medium for robbing the stimulus of its direct, immediate character and having it influence action finally on the basis of its coordinations and contacts with a great variety of other agencies and influences. A command represents the stimulus in its most direct form which you can get in language, but a verbal command is not so direct as a whiplash or as other forms of purely physical agency. Even in the command there is a certain amount of flexibility, or the possibility of reinterpretation. You may take a suggestion as the middle term. As a suggestion intended to influence action, it of course has a certain amount of directness or stimulation still left in it; but simply as a suggestion, distinct from a command, it is obvious that your final outcome in action depends upon the way he takes to this suggestion, whether it fits into his own individuality or not.

Now if you take intelligence simply as intelligence, it has lost all its direct relationship to action. It becomes simply an objective statement of the situation, and the individual is left to himself to translate that into terms of his own action. The situation is so and so, make up your mind what you will do in such a situation, or do as you think best in such a situation; and in the progressive evolution of society there is a larger and larger amount of the content of truth which is depersonalized, thus being put in such shape that the final outcome in action is dependent upon a much larger number of influences in much more complicated relations to each other.

Instead of saying that intelligence begins with the impersonal form and gradually becomes more and more social, as Mr. Baldwin appears to think, it would be truer to say that intelligence begins in the more personal— that is, the more direct and immediate form. Language takes the form of injunctions and prohibitions. The connection between the thought and the action is of a highly immediate kind, but as society develops, truth loses largely its personal association and becomes depersonalized, its immediate interest is eliminated and is projected out into the thing world, into the objective world, and then the individual indirectly gets the indirect stimulus to his final action through the reaction, through the interaction of the world which is thus presented to him and his own impulses and tastes and inclinations.

Now that implies of course that as society advances, you must have some substitute for what Plato conceived could be done only by personal acquaintance and communication. You must have this social consciousness in some form—that is, you must have society putting itself and its conditions before the individual in the form of ideas, so that the individual can take account of society and social interests, but yet have his own individuality have play also, without hemming in his freedom. And there we come upon, it seems to me, the most peculiar problem of modern society, because as individuality is developed, the need for this indirect social control through a knowledge of the social environment and a knowledge of social values becomes greater and greater, unless the whole thing is to go to pieces in some kind of anarchic disintegration. This is the standpoint from which it is most important and most fruitful for a social philosophy to consider social life in all its forms, from the standpoint of the organization of intelligence which is put at the disposal of the individual in such a way as to secure the equation of these two results: first, his contributing something to the community and, secondly, his getting from the community a sense of the worth, the value and meaning of what he is doing.

Now objectively you can get the solution of that question on an objective basis. You can say that the individual shall contribute so many food units to society and that in return society shall give him so much food and physical comfort. But the essence of the whole thing lies in the sphere of consciousness—that is, the individual getting a sense of what he is doing. Is he coming to consciousness in what he is doing? Is what he is doing with his muscles, his nerves, his physical being, is that saturated with conscious meaning for him? That can be only through the instrumentality of the social consciousness, or through language as the organ of communication. On the other hand, what is he contributing to society—not merely the material of society—but contributing actually to the values of life? Of course these values can be found ultimately only in consciousness.

June 1, 1898

Yesterday I stated that the concept of associated or objective mind might be identified with what we empirically know as language, using language to include all the instrumentalities of communication which enable anyone to interpret his own action, or to value [it] in experience on the basis of the experience of others. As was pointed out before, in general, experience is cumulative in its content; it is socially cumulative through this function of communication. But experience is curiously conditioned. What any individual gets out of his activities and contacts depends upon what the race and nationality to which he belongs has hitherto experienced and subserved and what it is now getting out of it.

As suggested, the import of the term language has to be taken in a very wide sense. It will be possible, however, to draw a line between language as the indirect mode of stimulation and control through interaction in the individual's own consciousness and that direct or physical control of which I spoke yesterday. While the concept of language has to be widened for this purpose (not only to include gesture—but we have to put under the term gesture many activities which we would not ordinarily place there), still there is a criterion by which we can discriminate between those activities which would be considered simply as direct and those which we would put under the head of language. If the activity of another communicates a new idea, a new thought, a new belief or a new interest—that is, influences his action through the intermediary of its translation over into consciousness—then it belongs psychologically to the caption of language. I see a certain person do something. I wonder why he does it, and I finally figure out a reason which is satisfactory to myself and which throws new light upon the proper motives for action, and that in turn modifies my own future conduct. Now psychologically that would come under this head of communication, of language. The only difference between that and gesture or speech, in the ordinary sense, would be that in this particular case the other person did not intend his action to have that particular mediating effect upon my own consciousness, but as matter of fact it did so, just as much as if he had stated that such and such were the proper motives for action in such and such a situation.

On the other hand we may have a form of speech which in reality simply has direct action. If one sees a child running into the fire and one calls to him to keep away, it may be simply the tone of voice and the mere shock which affects the child's action, with no realization of the significance there. There may be no translation over into an interpretation of his own of the situation. What is obvious in that trivial case holds also in many cases that are by no means either so obvious or so trivial. A large part of moral instruction that is objectively moral in that it modifies the conduct of persons in directions that are right is simply an example of that direct authoritative control. There is no intermediary passage through one's own [?] processes of understanding and of valuation. In fact a good many of our ordinary actions are more or less a mixture of this personal reinterpretation and the more direct stimulus or excitation of one act by another.

The reason for identifying associated mind with language or communication may be considered from either end—either from the standpoint of the one who communicates or the one who is communicated to. The latter end is the more apparent. That is, we have only to think how words have become saturated with meaning, with values which have cost in the past a great deal of effort and experimentation, and how certain cores of value have finally precipitated and crystallized, to see what it is that language means to the individual who is at the receptive pole. But the reason holds good equally at the other end. The test for the vitality of an idea, the test for whether significant value is really or merely nominally attached to it— the test, in other words, for whether one conceives the idea as objective or still holds it simply as subjective, as in process of elaboration—is found precisely in the fact whether or not it is used, whether or not it is embodied and thus communicated. Of course all kinds of thoughts are going through one's consciousness all the time, the silent thoughts being much the larger part quantitatively; but they influence action by giving it a certain color and atmosphere which it would not have if it were not for the periods of silent or suppressed thinking.

It may be laid down as a general principle, however, that all those thoughts which are neither uttered nor issue in the form or content of conduct do not do so because they are regarded, they are stamped, as invalid objectively. They may not be condemned to complete uselessness; they may be used as stepping stones; they may be stages in the process by which one finally attains to the idea which he does regard as valid, as holding the really good. But since they have only that instrumental value, they are naturally suppressed. It is only the culmination in the truth, in the conclusion arrived at, which is uttered or which expresses itself in action. Or more strictly speaking that culmination is the communication or the expression in some form or other.

Speech, language, then, cannot possibly be regarded as the mere external clothing which thought puts on itself, as if there were a distinction, a dualism, between the process of thinking as such and the process of expression as such. The expression is, psychologically, simply the adequate culmination of the thinking; it marks the point where it is regarded as ceasing to be simply subjective and becomes objective; it is testimony to the universal character of thinking; it should manifest itself in communication.

The identity of thought and language has been a favorite thesis with a number of writers both from the logical and psychological side, as for example Max Müller,[12] but so far as I know the doctrine of that identity has almost always been formulated simply from the internal logical side. That one cannot think without language is the point which is generally emphasized, that the being who did not have the language would not be capable of reflection. While there is sufficient testimony of the dependence of the individual on social forces in thinking, that needs to be supplemented from the other standpoint. The identity of thought and speech is directly a social fact and not merely a logical and psychological fact. If thought must utter itself, then thought is intrinsically social in its motivation and in its function. The only aspect of thinking that is merely subjective is simply that instrumental manipulation of the symbol, which one goes through with for the sake of reaching the conclusion. The form of the thinking, the machinery of it, may be merely subjective and individual, but the content, the values set up, established, are by their nature objective, and language is simply the appearance in which that objectivity shows itself.

In a more extended discussion it would be useful to consider communication both as regards extent and content, both as regards its range and its depth. Historically we find that the evolution of language has been in both directions—that is, the evolution of associative mind. The range of language is exceedingly limited in primitive societies, and the depth of meaning, the import which is put into any given word, is correspondingly superficial. You have the relatively small number of people who speak the same language or who habitually have commerce with each other through the medium of language, while the amount of experience that is conveyed in the word is correspondingly restricted.

Now if we compare the state of things today with one of these earlier forms, we find the change has been both on the side of range and of depth. The number of persons with whom one directly converses may not be indeed any larger than it would have been two thousand years ago, but through the instrumentalities of printed books, pamphlets and newspapers, through the circulation of intelligence in the form of mail and through the use of the telegraph system as well as in the extension of personal contents [contacts?] in travel, the actual range within which any idea finds utterance for social purposes is indefinitely multiplied. Moreover the continual contact between people speaking externally different languages and the interchange of literature, the use of translations, and so on extend the range, make it even wider in reality than it is in appearance. Now that fact means that the scope of associated or objective mind is becoming indefinitely multiplied, the time range is widening as well as the space range.

It is instructive to know that in primitive societies tribal community is maintained through this function of the associated mind, that is, through the function of tradition. The religious class *par excellence,* the priesthood as such, is precisely the class which keeps the tribal records, the mementos, the memorials, which preserves them physically and which keeps alive their interpretation. The whole matter of social continuity, historical identity, simply focuses about and crystallizes in that element of communication by which the contact with the past is kept up. It is probably that the beginnings of written language were for the sake of securing records which would maintain connection with the past. Written language does not seem to have originated in any direct economic need for literary and aesthetic purposes, but rather as a political instrument through which the associated consciousness on the temporal side can be kept alive. The part played by memorial tablets, pillars and the inscriptions upon them, and so on, is large, but of course all this connection with the past is comparatively limited by the side of what we have today, where the multiplication of printed matter and the historical research that has gone along with that has broken down, in theory at least, all the barriers and has brought the present in a continuous line of descent, not only with the historical human past but with the animal past as well.

On the side of content, perhaps there is no more striking phase of the enrichment of import than the development of science. We are apt to think of science along the same line with the doctrine of the identity of thought and language. It is generally conceived of simply as a highly interesting intellectual development, but its chief significance is of course its social want.* Science as an intellectual growth simply marks the increased definiteness, accuracy and precision, and the increased verifiable content

* Dewey possibly said "won't" at this point.

which is put into the media of communication. It means that one individual is able to mediate—that is, to interpret—his own action and contacts through the experience of others in a definite and reliable way. Science is the social traditions purified, criticized and put in the hands of the individual in a form where he can test it for himself, and I close this point simply by commending to you a further consideration in your own thoughts of science as the content of social communication, instead of simply as the accumulation of a certain body of facts. The very reason that we do ordinarily think of its as classified facts is just because we take for granted the function of communication of applicability from one mind to another. We do abstract it and set it off by itself simply because as matter of fact it is in continuous communication, and it is that fact with the future control of action which gives to science its social meaning.

One more point in conclusion regarding this social sensorium. The problem, as I said yesterday, was to make available to the individual the experience of the race so as to socialize, put that content into his experience without restricting, without infringing upon the initiative, the freedom of the individual—and that language did that through its very indirectness of method. I have just spoken of the tremendous significance of the development of science with reference to the content of communication. The limitation upon the organization, the social sensorium, will be primarily the limitation in the development of science. It is curious, but nonetheless a certain fact, that it is those phases of experience which lie most remote from the experience available and therefore have the least directive, interpretive capacity, which are first put into scientific form.

I say it is curious, but of course it is not, on reflection. The more remote it is, the more readily it lends itself to abstraction and thus to scientific formulation. It is the general features of space construction and of astronomy, things which apparently have the least immediate influence upon the welfare of the individual and society, which first become put into scientific form, and naturally enough, because the fact that they are not of such immediate interest means that it is easier for one to get outside of them, to look at them in an objective way.

To say that a things is of deep personal interest means that it offers a resistance to objective formulation. The meaning of that is that the present limitation of the organization of the objective mind is the lack of development in the sciences of psychology and sociology. As sciences, or as attempts at sciences, they do attempt to deal with the points of immediate and ultimate contact and position in actual experience; that is, they are attempts to apply the abstractions which are found in the other sciences to life itself. They are dependent then upon the development of the other sciences, because on the side of method they require the generalizations and abstractions of the other sciences as points of departure and as instruments of attack and application. They cannot go any faster than the other sciences can go, but they have to meet the resistance of the fact that they are dealing with the concrete, the really concrete interests, customs, habits, as they are actually operative, and not as they may be merely objective by analysis.

Now there is a certain conception of the nature of psychology and sociology as sciences which follows as a corollary from that, which might not at first thought occur to you. It is this. The only thing that can be formulated in these sciences is the method. Just because their material is concrete, is ultimate, it is hopeless as well as useless to attempt any complete or systematic organization of those facts. Life itself is the facts and you cannot possibly salt down that life as you can the facts of the other sciences. What you can do is to state those facts insofar as they grow light on method, or insofar as they give you tools, instruments for further concrete application.

To make the statement concrete, an organized science of sociology would to my mind be practically identical with an organized newspaper, an organized system of the continuous statement and interpretation of the facts of social life which are relevant to the needs of the individual. It is a good deal of an assumption to suppose that a newspaper could be made scientific, but what I have in mind is that you have the two sides. On one side sociology as method—that is, sufficient interest in the structure and workings of society to enable one to interpret the particular social facts as they come up. But they are so numerous and changing that the attempt to get them in a book once for all or even in a series of books of an encyclopedic character is utterly impossible. The facts must be got at and must be made known as they happen, and they happen all the time.

The present newspaper would, from that point of view, represent the disorganization, the limitation, as well as the degree of positive organization attained in the existing objective mind, or social consciousness. Physically the instrumentalities for publicity, that is, for making known to the individual the movements of society, its railroads, mails, telegraphs, and so on, have outrun the spiritual side, that is, the power of systematizing, of coordinating, of interpreting these facts. The result is that we have a greater variety of facts simply in the form of an aggregate with only a rudimentary organization and interpretation of these particular facts in the relation which they bear to the whole. The attempt at interpretation, at systematization is supposed to be given in the editorials. Now the fact that you get your facts in one place and your ideas in another simply shows the lack of scientific method of development.

Of course in anything approaching an ideal social science your ideas would be the working hypotheses by which the facts were systematized, were correlated; that is, they would be worked into the facts as the import of the facts themselves. It would be simply the placing of the particular fact of which it is simply the particular symptom, having only sensational value when it is located. The human mind of course cannot put up with that mere isolation, and the result is that the interpretation is given us in the form of opinions, what some particular man or class of men happen to think about these particular facts. That is to say, the editorial on the part of the individual means the placing of the fact with reference to the class interest, with reference to the particular party or business interest, instead of the strictly objective placing of it; that is, the placing of it as a fact in chemistry or physics is placed with reference to the whole body of facts to which it belongs and indicative of the single movement behind [ahead?].

The two chief modes of organization of the associated mind would be through education and through the function of social publicity. It is something of this latter sort which would have to take the place in modern society of what to Plato was got at by personal acquaintance and conversation. The organization of education is that which, so to speak, gives the individual his bearings, his power to interpret; it puts at his disposal the past with reference to the possible determination of the future. This function of social publicity enables the individual to orientate himself with reference to the actual present, to realize the existing situation and the demands of that situation with reference to the future direction of his own action. In that publicity you have to take account of books, of newspapers, and not merely the daily newspapers but the trade journals, at the number of which one would be much surprised, business catalogues, and all the various ramifications of agencies which put before the individual the whole situation, or the large situation into which his own particular activities must fit if they are to succeed, and thus to enable him to determine freely and intelligently the direction of his own action.

One other aspect of publicity is found in the governmental function. It would be interesting as a political study to work out the variety of ways in which modern societies attempt to regulate social matters through securing and publishing the necessary intelligence. The former attempts on the part of government to regulate affairs directly tend to give way to indirect control through the operation of publicity. The socialist must face the question whether direct control which is always relatively physical in character is not ultimately inferior to this indirect method. Education as carried on by the state may be considered from this point of view since it is an organized method of putting the individual in possession of intelligence with reference to past attainments which is useful in directing his future action. The distinction between the direct ownership of railroads by the government and the attempts at indirect control by the Interstate Commerce Commission would be illustrative of that point.

It seems to me the chief function of a legislative body is not so much to make laws as it is in the discussion which leads up to the passage of those laws, the discussion which ramifies itself all the way through in political campaigns, newspaper and periodical discussions, as well as the discussion which takes place in the legislative body itself. Carlyle's idea of a government by talk has a good deal of truth in it, and a truth which has not merely negative significance; it does involve a period of antecedent communication, of discussion, so that the final legislation is simply an act of registering the conclusion which has been arrived at in the process of discussion. It bears about the same relation to the social process that the expression of an idea does to the individual's own previous elaboration of that idea; it is simply its consummation, its fulfillment, and not an independent volitional act.

It would of course require practically a course to work out in an adequate way the various aspects of the social consciousness, but I shall have to leave the matter here.

SECTION 8. ECONOMICS, POLITICS AND ETHICS SELECT OUT DIFFERENT ASPECTS OF A SINGLE SOCIAL PROCESS

June 2, 1898

I will now apply the general principles reached regarding the psychology of social action to a statement of the relations of the three types of social sciences, economics, politics, and ethics, to one another.

I referred, I believe, earlier in the course, to an account that might stand for popular assumptions on that point, namely, that ethics is an account of altruistic action, benevolent action; economics is an account of self-seeking action; and that politics deals with the regulations that are necessary in order to maintain the proper equilibrium between the egoistic and altruistic, to prevent the egoistic from unduly encroaching on the possibilities and actualities of benevolent action.[13] I do not maintain that anybody has ever specifically announced that view, but it serves to illustrate at least the fact that the various social sciences are frequently classified by describing quite diverse fundamental principles to each one, that they are often supposed to be phases which mark off distinct areas of social action. Each has its own particular set of facts and of principles, and it is possible to draw the boundary lines on the basis of where one set of facts leaves off and another commences.

Now as set over against that conception, we would have the idea of social experience with the various values realized in it and with the two movements of social action in the direction of individualization and association, and then it would be necessary to define each of these and to determine the relations of one to another on the basis of that underlying conception. We would have, in other words, these types of social sciences discriminated, but [not?] by reference to the [various?] separate bodies of fact, but by reference to the various points of view or the various interests with which one and the same body of facts would be approached; we would have aspects or phases of one and the same social experience. The point then would be to ascertain what the fundamental points of view, the fundamental modes of approach are, which give rise to these various phases.

The economic process would be described then as that which effects the evolution of value. It is the machinery of the growth of the values that are realized. It is essentially then an account of means; it presupposes ends, and because it presupposes them it does not inquire into them. It does not even attempt to state what the actual ends or positive values realized are, much less to determine the respective worthiness or validity of these ends. It simply takes it for granted that there are these ends and then asks for the conditions of the evolution of value, the setting up and establishing of these elements which are appreciated and have worth in experience. Economic science might be said to give us the mechanics or dynamics of social experience, because it takes it from this point of view of abstract analyzing simply the means side; it takes, so to speak, a physical view, a mechanical view. That is, both the individual and association are simply factors, simply agencies, instrumentalities. That is to say, it is interested in the individual, or in a given mode of association simply from the part which it plays in this evolution of value; it is interested in them simply as means. The individual as an end, or a form of associated life as an end, does not and need not appeal to it, occupy its attention. It is the very nature of the economic science to make that particular abstraction simply because it approaches the whole thing from the point of view of trying to find out what the methodological or instrumental side of the experience is.

To condemn economics because it makes this abstraction would be the same as condemning physics or chemistry because the account which they give of the universe does not absolutely equate the whole content of the universe. It is not the intention of any one of these sciences to give an account of the thing in its entirety and ultimate meaning, and therefore as long as it knows what it is about and does not claim to be doing something which it is not doing there can be no criticism on that score. The criticism made on economic science that it ignores ethical considerations might equally be brought against mathematics or physics. It is its business to ignore ethical considerations, not in the sense of denying that there are such things, but it is not aims that it is interested in. It is taken for granted that the whole point of attack is on the side of the machinery through which these ends taken for granted are evolved. So, for example, there is the popular objection that it reduces labor to a commodity and does not take account of the individual in labor. Since its interest is simply in means, it follows from necessity that it should reduce the laborer simply to an instrument and the only point then is as regards the efficiency of this particular tool or instrument.

Of course that point of view would become fallacious if the economist should suppose that that was all there was to an individual, that that exhausted his whole sphere of being, or if an individual acted from the assumption that the definition of the individual in terms of efficiency to supply the demand were the final one. We do not, however, attack chemistry, criticize chemistry, because the formulation which it gives for the constitution of sugar is not good to eat. We do not expect the chemist as a chemist to supply us with the actual sugar for consumption. His business is simply in the mechanical side, in an account of the process of construction of the sugar, and the individual as a concrete individual, the person who eats sugar, must make his allowances accordingly. Equally so on the economic side.

That then gives it differentiation from ethics, in that in ethics we recognize the values as values and inquire into the rationale for this and into the justification of the value. We attempt to get a system of valuation and to test any assumed value by reference to the system as a system.

Now in political science we recognize also the ends, or values, which have been actually attained, realized in experience, but we take them simply as attained, as realized. We take them as *de facto,* without attempting a criticism of them with reference to reconstruction. There is an attempt to organize these values, to state the place and limitation of one in relation to the other, to say just what are the rights and responsibilities of this individual with relation to that, or this form of organization with reference to that form of association; but all that is taken simply as the organization of the material of the institutions which are at hand. We might say thus that politics gives us a static view, not meaning by static anything which is dead or inert but simply that it takes a cross section of the activity. It takes it as the moving equilibrium which at any given time has been effected independent of the question of whether that particular equilibrium does really meet all the necessities of the case or whether there are defects in it which call for a further readjustment. It gives us the anatomy, the morphology of society in that way. It deals with the ends which are at the same time means, or with means which are at the same time ends: therefore with concrete means and not simply with purely abstract means as economics does. It takes the given structure of institutions and shows that [how?] that, as matter of fact, controls and incites the individual. It takes the institution as operative. It is not static in the sense of taking the thing as dead; it takes the institution as operating and asks how, as matter of fact, that supplies the individual with a certain capacity or power of action, and how it as a situation exacts of him certain offices, imposes on him certain responsibilities which correspond to the rights or power which it confers on him.

I said that economics takes means as abstract; it takes the conditions under which capacity in general is evolved, but it is the conditions taken from the political side which tell us how that capacity is actually realized and operative at any given time. The difference might be illustrated briefly by reference to property. All economies would show is the conditions under which property was evolved, the conditions which generate the fact of ownership. The political point of view would be interested in showing how property as an institution, as an end which has been realized, functions as the means in maintaining and controlling the activities of various individuals. What is it that property does? What power, what capacity of initiation and direction does that confer on the individual? That is, how does it stimulate him on the other side? How does it control him? What objects does it make necessary for him to realize?

Now if we go on to the ethical science, it may be said to consist in bringing to critical consciousness the values which are assumed as possible by economics, and which are assumed as given by politics. Taking property, for example. Instead of contenting itself, as the political view would, by asking what it actually does for the individual in the way of stimulus and control, it inquires whether these things which it does are justifiable or not; it brings in the question of the reference of these facts to a standard of value taken as a basis for examination and for criticism.

Of course that standard is not an external standard. Any legitimate criticism always consists in the more definite placing of the part with reference to the whole. So the ethical point of view simply consists in bringing to consciousness more adequately the nature of the whole social movement, taking that as the test for any particular phase or part of the social movement. The possibility of social ethics depends upon the possibility of penetrating into the general character of the social movement and of the normal ends, therefore, which as such a movement it is working towards, and then inquiring whether as a given phase of that movement, say, property or the family as it is now, it contributes adequately to the movement, or whether it needs readjustment, reconstruction, in order to play its due function in the whole. The ethical questions, then, arise simply when we have reasons for criticizing some value which hitherto has been taken for granted. We may say that politics deals with an ethical content in the sense that the values of experience as realized through business life, through family life, through school life, are assumed as there. But now some hitch arises of some sort, some friction, and the question then comes up: Is this value what it purports to be, or is this institution giving us, realizing for us, the values which reference to which it was instituted and with reference to which it ought to function?

There is no such thing, then, as an absolute ethical science in the sense that it requires once for all into the values of everything in experience. There are always certain values which are assumed, which are taken for granted, and the point of ethical stress is the point of relative disintegration, the point of relative failure where inquiry must be directed in order to get a reconstruction of values. Ethics looks at these values from the standpoint of their reconstruction, as politics from the standpoint of their attainment. Roughly speaking, we could say that politics looks toward the past or takes the present from the side of the past as the limit reached at any given time. Ethics takes it with reference to the future as the point of departure for a further growth or development. While economics, abstracting from both ends, simply gives us an account of the machinery of the process that lies between. It takes for granted the political conditions as really conditioning, and it takes for granted some end in human life which is being effected by it, but what that end is and just what the actual conditions at a given time are it does not inquire into. As matter of fact the economic process is historically conditioned. You could not possibly have the same concrete economic process in Patagonia that you would have in Greece, or in Greece that you would have in Illinois today; there is always that institutional background. And there is always on the other side the kinds of ends and aims which actual individuals are proposing to themselves; that is, there is the ethical side. But there are certain general relations of man to nature, certain mechanical relations or certain relations of machinery, which are involved at any period, and it appears to me that it is with reference to that phase of the matter that economic science has to be discriminated.

NOTES

1. Herbert Spencer, *The Principles of Sociology,* I, Part II, Chap. II, "A Society Is an Organism."

2. Leslie Stephen, *The Science of Ethics* (London: Smith, Elder, and Co., 1882), p. 126.

3. The following quotations are all from Spencer's, *The Principles of Sociology,* I.

4. *Supra,* p. 19.

5. Apparently a mistaken reference, although Bagehot does express the basic viewpoint to which Dewey refers. See Walter Bagehot, *Physics and Politics* (Boston: Beacon Press, 1956), pp. 75–77.

6. Samuel Alexander, *Moral Order and Progress* (London: Trübner and Co., 1889), pp. 306–08.

7. See the essay "Defence of Criminals: A Criticism of Morality," in Edward Carpenter, *Civilization, Its Cause and Cure* (London: Swan Sonnenschein and Co., 1891).

8. James, *The Will to Believe and Other Essays in Popular Philosophy,* essays on "Great Men and Their Environment" and "The Importance of Individuals."

9. Baldwin, *Social and Ethical Interpretations in Mental Development.*

10. Quotations in the following paraphrase of Baldwin are all from *Social and Ethical Interpretations in Mental Development,* p. 97, note.

11. Summary of James Mark Baldwin's "On Selective Thinking," by Stella E. Sharp, *Philosophical Review* VII (March, 1898), 200–01. The original article is in *Psychological Review* V (January, 1898), 1–24.

12. F. Max Müller, *Chips from a German Workshop* (New York: Charles Scribner's Sons, 1890), IV 484–88.

13. *Supra,* pp. 244–245.

CHAPTER 5

THE ECONOMIC PROCESS

SECTION 1. INTRODUCTION

To go on with the fourth general head, the economic process, I have already defined that as concerned with the means or instrumentalities of social development. The first question that suggests itself, then, is: When and why do we concern ourselves with science? How does this particular point of view come to generalize itself so as to give rise to a science? In answer I will refer to a point which has been dwelt upon before, that it is tension in action, conflict in action, which makes us examine the instrumentalities of action. The only possible motive we could have for investigating and inventing means would be that there is a difficulty which needs to be overcome, and that we cannot get at that difficulty without a more thorough survey of the ground, to see what our resources are. There would be no economic science in the "golden age." If everybody's wants were supplied as soon as he had them, there would be no motive or purchase for this abstraction, or for the setting off of the considerations of means by themselves.

The next point is that we have a contrast between the immediate means and the indirect means. The direct means is the economic individual, the laborer (using that term laborer in the most inclusive sense, to mean anybody who initiates any movement which goes to supply a want). The indirect means, of course, are nature, the forces of the environment. It is the tension between the indirect and the direct means—that is, between the worker on one side and nature on the other side—which is the key to the economic process. The worker represents primarily possible supply: not actual supply but the possibility of the satisfaction of this want. Now it is the friction in action which polarizes the situation in this way, so that we locate the actual lack on one side (the want in the individual) and the possible means (the indirect means of supplying that want in the external world) on the other side.

I simply refer you again to the discussion under the biological head of the organism and environment.[1] The biological relationship is the economic relationship in its essence—conceiving of the organism as primarily that side of action which represents the lack, the break, and [conceiving of] nature, the environment, as that which may, and under certain conditions will, satisfy or make good this want and thus restore the unity of action or, in biological terms, the continuity of function.

June 6, 1898

At the last time I was taking up the relations involved in the economic process which, as I stated at the end of the hour, involves essentially the same factors as the biological process. In fact the biological process, simply as biological from the standpoint of the development of structure which facilitates the control of the environment, is essentially the economic process; and the economic process as we ordinarily regard it, the industrial process of society, is simply an extension of this differentiation of structures and tools adapted to purposes of controlling the environment, save that of course the latter has become conscious and has become more indirect, so that organs, structures, have become tools, become instrumentalities, not simply in the immediate and objective sense but in the directed sense. But the tools of society are extensions of exactly the same principle as specific organs adapted to specific utilization of the environment on the biological side, and the industrial divisions of labor are the precise analogs of the development of new genera or new species biologically.

It is hardly possible to avoid the conclusion that after giving up the old static definition of species the [proper] point of view of conceiving species is from the side of morphology and genetic descent. The only criterion that has been got for a species is the particular way in which those special forms get their living. They represent the industrial aspects; and the morphological side, the structure side, is secondary—that is, the particular instruments which enable it to perform its particular form of life process. The organization of the particular type of industrial work and the organization of the structure of a particular type of fishes has to be conceived essentially on the same basis. They have the same generating conditions and they subserve the same purposes, taking this abstraction of the simple relation of the living form to the environment.

It was also pointed out in the biological discussion that the distinction between organism and environment is the tension which is the readjustment of function, the same as the two factors of the economic process, which as I pointed out at the last time is between the mediate and immediate instrumentalities of action. Now the problem is then again the same—that is, what on the biological side is the organization of the factors of the tension so as to make it effective? The tension first presents itself in the form of resistance, of obstruction, and inhibition. Consciously that reflects itself in a feeling of want, of lack of satisfaction on one side and the obscure apprehension of what it is that causes the lack and what it is that will satisfy the need, on the other side.

The economic development consists essentially in the defining of these two factors; or, put in economic language, consists in the evolution of wants into effective demands on one side and the evolution of nature into serviceable commodities on the other side. The fundamental economic category is the reciprocal one of demand and supply. The want as it becomes translated out of the lack of satisfaction into organized tools or powers for supplying those wants becomes demand. The mere object, the mere material thing which is felt over against us as at once obstructing and inciting us becomes translated into commodities, into serviceable material, or supplies. The unifying point, then, is the development of capacity on one side (using that as a synonym of effective demand) and the evolution of commodity on the other side, meaning by commodity that phrase of the environment which serves to function the capacity and thus to subserve the function. The complete evolution of the want up to the point of effective demand implies of course the other side. That is, it implies the reestablishing of the unity of function and thus the fact of the commodity is present equally. Taking it from the objective side, the evolution of commodity to the point of its actual concrete uses implies the want which is met through the commodity on the other side. That is, while the tension begins with the setting over against each other of the individual agents in the state of lack and at the same time a state of reaction, of incitation to react to nature, and the crude world matter which is set over against the want because it is not directly serviceable or utilizable, but which is capable of becoming so—while it begins in that tension, the very nature of the tension is to reestablish a unity of differentiated, organized activities.

SECTION 2. THE IMPORTANCE OF SCIENCE FOR THE SUPPLY OF COMMODITIES

Taking first the objective development, the development of commodity, in general terms that consists in the continual liberation of the energy of nature in such a way as to make it serviceable for ends—just the point again that we saw on the biological side. The economic process, objectively considered, is one of securing the redistribution of the foci of energy in such a way that the lines of discharge of that energy shall effect more with relation to the maintenance of life activity.

The philosophy of current economics seems to me weak at just this point—the failure to realize that the economic process is intrinsically and from one point of view simply an objective development in simple redistribution of energy which is found in nature. It would hardly be true to say that there has been an overemphasis of the psychological side, because in the current philosophy certain phases of that have been overlooked, but the tendency has been to look on the side of human selfishness, the attempt to satisfy these wants, and to get more pleasure for one's self. Well, people might have wants, might have all of this desire to get the maximum of pleasure and possession for themselves, and might put forth their efforts for their attainment; and the results, if they were not of a particular kind, would not be the relatively consistent and orderly sphere of industrial activities which we have now in the development, on the objective side, of tools, of machinery and invention.

Every machine consists simply in the redistribution of the tensions of energy, of potential energy, so that the manifestations of it, the forms which it takes kinetically, accomplish more than if these changes in space and time had not been effected. While there is no quantitative increase in the amount of energy, it is so rearranged that it effects more. Now that rearrangement is essentially a question of effecting certain coordinations in space and time. Take the steam engine as simply one example. There is no creation of coal or iron, no creation [of] water, no creation of the quantity of energy involved. What we have is a simple rearrangement, a coordination of those various factors.

From an objective point of view, human thought (the thought of the inventer) and human labor (the labor of those who construct the machine) are so much force, so much physical energy of a nervous and muscular kind which is also a part of this coordination. They are one of the factors in the coordination, the more immediate and responsible factor in the coordination, but from a strictly economic standpoint they are actually on a level with the other forms of energy which enter into it. From that point of view it is just as natural a growth as the growth of a tree or the birth and development of an animal, which are simply rearrangements of energy which is already there.

Now of course I cannot develop that thought, but it seems to me that to clearly grasp it is to see that what occurs here is a natural development in the way of a coordination of natural factors; that there is nothing artificial about it; and that in one sense there is nothing in it which is to be regarded as attributable to a will or an intelligence which is outside. From this point of view the will and the intelligence enter in simply as forces and factors in the coordination. That they are the form of the coordination while the physical world is the material of that coordination is the necessary key to any unified economic philosophy. The prevailing economic philosophy is, I should say, distinctly dualistic. It assumes an intelligence and want on one side and it happens to find itself in a material world of forces on the other side. Then it happens that certain reactions take place between these and we have certain results. Instead of that we have a single movement in the direction of this more effective coordination of the factors of activity.

From this standpoint the beginning would consist in a consideration of elements, of climate, soil, etc., which at once obstruct and incite the other factor of want, and of reflective consideration, so as to utilize these in order to effect new combinations of them which will meet the wants which arise; and we would have the development up through the raw material, the history of the evolution of tools, machines, the growing complications through the use of tools, the increasing multiplication of forces in which the materials of nature are utilizable, and then the history of the various ways in which potential commodities thus brought into being become actual commodities, become materials of consumption and become direct stimuli to further functional activity—in other words, become wealth. The concept of wealth from this point of view would be then simply nature, or any natural force so coordinated as to be serviceable as material of, or stimulus to, social functioning, either in the direction of individualization or of association. The consideration of that evolution through its three stages of (first) external nature, (second) raw material, and (third) wealth, or utilized commodity, would involve a consideration on one side of science as the means of effecting this coordination, and would involve on the other side a consideration of space and time relations as involved in the coordination.

There is another point in which the current economic philosophy seems to me defective: the neglect of the part played by the evolution of science in the development of industries. In the emphasis on want, simply as want, desire, and the hedonistic psychology of the mere satisfaction of the want, the tendency has been to overlook the fact that the economic development is conditioned on scientific method and data, that the industrial process is simply a case of applied science. It must be so by the nature of the case. It will always share then in the limitations of the science of the times, and the ultimate means of effecting any further development must be found in the matter of the evolution of science.

Supposing one were attempting really to account for the industries of today, for the use and application, say, of steam and electricity on the basis of the fact that man is a greedy being and that he puts forth his activities simply to satisfy his wants, or get the largest possession with the least effort. How far could one derive the actual facts of industrial life from any of these purely subjective and so-called psychological premises? The mere asking the question suggests that all the connecting links are assumed. The telegraph, telephone, and so on are all cases of the development of a knowledge of the environment, a question of the development of science. They are simply the various arts in which the knowledge of the environment is applied to the control of the environment. If you take the historical view, in the comparison of the various types, modes of industrial life, that point becomes so obvious that while it would be interesting to work it out in detail, the details would hardly succeed in making the principle itself more obvious. If the general principle laid down at the first is true, this must be the case. If the development is an objective development along the line of more complex coordination, then science, which is simply the theory of such coordination, which is simply the facts of nature reduced to coordinated form, must be the necessary antecedent of this economic development. Anything else would be a mere matter of luck and chance, and even if hit upon would have no way to insure itself any permanence in life.

By the way of testing that doctrine I would suggest its consideration with reference to questions of social reform. If the current science or economic philosophy overestimates the material, hedonistic wants and satisfactions with reference to this actual growth of science as the knowledge of the environment and the conditions to its use, is it not equally true on the other side that the average reformer overestimates what can be effected by the mere change in subjective motives, a mere change in people's states of mind and desires, as compared with the actual dependence of reform upon increased knowledge of conditions? Supposing you could change people's states of mind in general, their ideals and desires. Supposing you could make them more altruistic, more interested in serving society simply as such. How would you ever evolve an invention; how would you ever derive the telephone or steam engine from that, any more than from egoistic wants and desires taken by themselves? If I were the greatest reformer of society in the world, I would be helpless in inventing the telephone unless I had acquainted myself with the facts and relationships involved. It is a question principally of science itself.

Take the socialistic progress of reform, for example. Is it not true that its fundamental fallacy is the overemphasis of what can be effected by simple changes in mere states of consciousness (to say nothing of the psychological point of the impossibility of bringing all those changes into consciousness without some purchase in the objective world)? Putting the question from the socialistic side and putting it more specifically, can any such scheme of collective ownership be made without practically complete knowledge of all the conditions that must be met, of the needs and capacities of various individuals, and of the various resources that are available? If you could get that complete publicity, would there be any need of this governmental ownership and control? If you could once secure something like an adequate knowledge of the conditions, would not the thing go on practically automatically? I have only time to put that as a problem. I hope you will think it out as much as you can for yourselves. As I said, the defects from this point of view, the defects as well as the attainments, would have to be measured with reference to the status of science or intelligence at any given time.

Now to apply that thought briefly to the present condition of things, it would mean that there has been a tremendous development of physical and chemical science which has abstractly put at our disposal a much greater variety of materials and which has put at our control a greater variety and complexity of processes with which to handle these materials. The agencies that relate to production and distribution have been greatly increased and refined, so much so that it is beyond the capacity of the imagination to conceive the change that has taken place within the last twenty-five years.

Now that coordination, however, the completion of that coordination, involves the introduction of the organism and of the environment.

In other words, these things must be brought into contact with the human individual even in a merely biological way; they must become materials of personal consumption and use. Now when we come to that factor which is necessary to complete this coordination with reference to which the development of physical and chemical science has given the first set of conditions, we find a different state of the case. We find the sciences which deal with the points of contact, of application of life—that is, which deal with the points where the conditions cease to be abstract and become concrete, where they cease to be partial and have the necessity of junction with the other factors, the factors of consumption and application that are necessary to complete the circuit—we find these sciences relatively in a very backward condition. Of course biology and physiology have made technically very great strides, but that is very recent and very partial as compared with the physical and chemical sciences.

The Supreme Court of Missouri decided the other day that certain city ordinances in St. Louis which were directed toward abating the smoke nuisance by compelling the use of smoke consumers on the chimneys were unconstitutional because they infringed upon the natural rights of the individual. He has a right to burn what he pleases and you cannot infringe on the right of the individual to smoke as he pleases. That would serve as an instance to show how comparatively little headway biological science has made in permeating the social consciousness and action. That seems to us incredibly stupid and prehistoric in character. It cannot be accounted for on the supposition that they were willfully stupid and selfish. It shows a lack of knowledge of the real part played by such functions as that in the life process. People know if you hit a man on the head that it hurts him. That is an established fact that the Supreme Court will recognize, but that smoke in the atmosphere has an important bearing on physical life is not, at least in Missouri, understood.

All the legislation in the last few years opposed to the alleviation of conditions in factories, etc., has to be interpreted with reference to the backwardness of science, and not simply from the standpoint of human greed and selfishness. When the biological sciences have the same hold on the mind as the physical and chemical sciences have now, such legislation will be as little called for as certain other legislation has [is?] now, [and] the relation of those facts to human activity will be understood. While one must sympathize with the keen consciousness which the socialist has of all these ills and of the necessity of paying more attention to human life and not sacrificing life itself in carrying out the physical conditions of wealth, the question still comes up whether the most effective method of producing that result in the long run is not in the element of intelligence and that he is advancing that in the stimulus which he gives to inquiry.

If we go a point further and consider, not the application of materials, of the abstract commodities as conditioned by biological science, but as conditioned by sociological science, of course that science, considered from the standpoint of method, is even more backward. Take the particular problem regarding the possibility which I raised the other day. Consider how much the average manufacturer today is working in the dark as regards the conditions which are necessary really to give success to his endeavors, and consider what an amount of waste, misdirected energy must result from that working in the dark. It is a question in my mind whether a good deal of the excessive competition and of the evils which result from this uncontrolled competition at present are not due more simply to having to put forth a lot of energy to meet a lot of half-understood conditions, rather than to the mere desire of people to get as much wealth as possible, much less to get it at the expense of other people. Working in the dark, not knowing the conditions that their own activity has to meet, to which it has to be adjusted, that activity is almost sure to take to itself a relatively physical form; it must depend upon the mere massive accumulation of power which can down the various obstacles as they arise. Very much of that power and skill now wasted with greater knowledge of the conditions would undoubtedly be directed toward refining the product.

It is of course a commonplace today that production is now quantitative rather than qualitative in character, and that involves the submergence of the individual, the enslavement of the individual to machinery, and the neglecting of the personal and artistic factors. This is attributed to the competitive and capitalistic system. But there is certainly just as much chance for the employment of skill, more chance for the effective control of conditions when the energy can be put forth toward the refinement of the product than there is in the mere turning out of the greatest possible number of units of product. If you could get an adequate stimulus, people's energies would go as naturally to the improvement of quality and the introduction of the artistic element as it now goes to the numerical side. Now that chance, that which makes that opportunity, is simply adequate intelligence.

Physically the world has become practically one through the use of steam and electricity, the railroads, telegraphs, mails, steamboats; and activity that is going on here is affected by other activities all over the world. There is practically now a world market and world conditions of production. That means of course also that consumption and application of these things to life is conditioned upon an area as wide as the world. Now the physical unification, the physical coordination, has outrun the intellectual one. That is, the mutual contact and reaction of materials on each other as a fact have gone before the development of a method of organizing these and relating them to each other: it must, from the necessity of the case. There would be no demand unless there had been a certain congestion and accumulation and friction on the product side that called for it.

June 7, 1898

On the basis of what I said last yesterday regarding the part played by science, socialized intelligence, in the economic process, commodity might be defined as the immediate physical object idealized. That is to say, regarded from the standpoint of an idea, the idea being the method of establishing such a coordination with other natural objects as to make it availble. That point relates to coordination on the side of form, on the side of the method, the way in which the coordinating is done. Science is the formulation of the coordinating.

If we turn to the other aspect, the material coordinated, we shall find that the categories center about the conceptions of space and time and their relations to each other. Space and time considerations give the conditions of this coordination in a most general framework. That generalization or distribution of energy so as to get the tensions, the different foci of energy marked off from each other in such a way that their interaction will accomplish something is this space side. It is the same idea from another point of view that is found designated by the term division of labor. But speaking strictly from the side here of the utilization of natural energy through its proper adjustments, what we have is a continually growing extension of the materials, both of production and of consumption, involving therefore continually greater and more complicated processes of exchange as intermediary between the various steps of the production, respectively, and the consumption, respectively, and between the production and the consumption. One of the most obvious features, superficially, of the economic development is precisely that the area is continually extending. The local centers of production and consumption are absorbed into larger and larger areas all the time, and the purely local features of them are disintegrated; they have to give way to meet the conditions of this absorption into the larger whole.

Now this growth on the side of area is meaningless save as we note the greater differentiation or intensification involved of the various parts which enter into the space-whole. There is that idea of increasing differentiation of energy so as to create a tension, a mutual interaction, therefore, between its various parts. If you have a dozen towns all practically doing the same thing, you will have twelve economic areas, not one. If you get one area which now comprehends all there, it must be because the work in those twelve centers has been specialized, it has been differentiated in such a way that there is a reciprocal relationship of supply and demand set up between them. In order to designate that process on the space side by one word, we might speak of it as the extension of the market, meaning by market not merely the place where the things are sold but the whole influence of that upon the process of production and commercial exchange.

Now with this extension on the space side due to the intensification of centers of energy and specialization goes the corresponding change on the time side. The larger space area means a prolonged temporal period of necessity. Where you have a restricted economic area, you will have a very short time intervening between production and consumption. Production for a nearby market means, relatively speaking, production for immediate use. Now as the factors there on the space side grow more differentiated and complicated in order to manufacture a certain product, you have first to gather together other products and other materials from a number of widely separate areas, and on the other side, in order that the product may get into use, it may have to be distributed or transported to a very considerable distance and the method of handling material has to be changed. You must get facilities for bridging over the time that is necessary to eliminate this distance.

If we say that the space side of the economic process is due to specialization, the time aspect is that of bringing these various separated centers into again-working harmonious relations to each other. Now the important consideration there corresponding to the enlargement of the market on the other side is postponement or deferment, the postponement of utilization and the intervention of a large number of intervening, mediated processes. Now it is the reaction of that which is the essential explanation of the development of capitalism. What we ordinarily call machinery is the physical side of the activities involved in bridging the space gaps and making all these separate things work together harmoniously. Capital is the corresponding instrumentality on the intellectual and the social side; it is the tool by which results can be accomplished at remote points in space, and therefore at comparatively remote intervals in time. In the restricted or local economic areas, you do not find any marked accumulation of capital or any problem of the relation of capital to labor. There are more personal questions, such as slavery, etc., but to carry on a long series of operations where fruition, consumption, or actual application to life is postponed, you must have something to fall back on, something to make and keep the connection during that long period of time, and capital is that instrument. It is a necessary correlate then of the extension of the space area, or the market.

What was said in classic economics about the origin of capital in abstinence and sacrifice seems to me simply the reflection of this principle on the subjective side, and in terms of a rather individualistic psychology. It is that personal inhibition, that saving up something instead of using it right away, or going without something in order that you may do something with it in the future. They are mere incidental and personal accompaniments of this larger process of objective mediation. I cannot imagine anything more futile than the savage proceeding to sacrifice himself in that way, abstaining from immediate consumption that he might pile up something else—I mean, to do that *systematically*. The dog saves bones, but he saves them for a future time, they are in no sense capital, tools, to do something with. Now in a restricted local area, abstinence leading to saving would be futile. A man can only use up about so much stuff anyway, and simply to save it till tomorrow that you may have twice as much as today would be an irrational thing.

The defect of the origin of capital for mere saving is that it does not afford any motivation for the process of saving, nor any explanation of the function to which the savings are put, if it is a mere question of saving it, a mere question of concentrating consumption, of alternating periods of going without things with periods of satiety. The real motive for saving is the necessity of covering a more complex period of production with reference to the needs and the use of the thing by somebody else distant in space and involving mutual exchange and transportation. On that basis the saving not only gets subjective motive into the individual, but it gets its function.

Capital is the medium of carrying out production and getting control of the market in a more effective way. The use development of money, not as a mere counter in exchange, but as itself an economic tool, and the consequent demand for the use of that tool would find its explanation here. On one side its accumulation marks the gathering together of resources to cover a certain span of time. On the other side, the demand for, the borrowing of it, means that it can enter in as the means of bridging the individual over to a comparatively remote point of time.

While it is a trivial enough thing of itself, the relation of the rate of interest—that is, the size of the rate—to space remoteness may have some significance as an illustration of the point involved there—the fact that the rate of interest is always lowest at the relatively dense centers of population where things are highly concentrated and highly assured, while when you get to a more remote [area] physically, where the strain of mediation is greater, where the connection must be made at more remote points in order that there may be effective work done and the range of uncertainty is greater, the amount that has to be paid becomes greatly increased. The economic antagonism that we find between agricultural districts at present and city districts, with reference to banking and the nature and use of money, would be, I think, another phase of precisely this same relationship taken at a period when the coordinations were not well established.

SECTION 3. THE DEVELOPMENT OF VALUES AS RESPONSE TO DEMAND

If we say that on the objective side the evolution of commodities represents the development of natural energy in such a way as to make it available for the life process, we would say that the evolution of wants into effective powers represents the converse movement of the realization of the ideal or subjective side. The important idea, the important concept which would have to be traced out here is that of value in its various ramifications: concepts of value in use, value in exchange, so-called objective or market value, and subjective value, marginal value, price, cost—all these familiar terms.

Without attempting at all to place these various conceptions in any systematized way in relation to each other, it is obvious that an antinomy has come into economic theory with relation to this category of value. On the one hand there has been the attempt to identify value with exchange value, marking it off carefully from value in use or consumption, treating the latter as noneconomic, lying outside of the ethical sphere so that all economic theory would have to do with it would be the relation of the market in supply and demand which affects cost and price. Now there has been the other more recent movement represented by Austrian economists* who have insisted on the recognition of the subjective and personal elements of pleasures to be gained and in connection with that have worked out a complex theory of marginal utilities and final utilities and their relation to each other.

If we compare these, the idea suggests itself that in the concept of exchange values we have really a consideration of the processes of measuring value. The things that are abstracted there and set up for analysis are the various ways in which it is decided what value is put upon things; it represents the process of objectifying the values, of stating the worth of one activity in relation to another. It marks the process of the coordination of activities, just as we were considering on the commodity side the coordination of materials. That a thing is worth so much in the market, that it costs such and such a price marks the analysis, the particular equilibrium which has been established between one side and another side of activities; it forms the means of effecting an equation between one side and another, money of course being the abstract statement or medium of that objectification.

To say that a pair of shoes is worth so much means that a certain kind of satisfaction has been measured over against certain other kinds of satisfaction. The various inhibitions, restrictions involved in the securing or the going without of each have been set over against those involved in the going without or the getting the others; and the stimuli to activity, the inciting and controlling power in activity of the one has been actually measured and equated over against the others. That at least is the point of view which I would suggest.

Concerning the considerations which center around cost and price and money, the part which is played in reference to these is that they do give us the machinery by which individuals and society have estimated the worth

* A school of economists who held essentially that value springs from utility and that successive portions of goods have a diminishing marginal utility.

of wants and of the satisfaction of those wants. As was brought out in the psychological statement, where there is purely direct, immediate satisfaction, there is no motive for objectifying the want, reflecting on it, seeing how much importance is attached to the satisfying of it. But the moment remoteness of time or distance comes in, then the question arises: Shall I do this or shall I do that? Shall I attempt to satisfy this want or that, to manifest this power or that? And then there comes the need of a standard of reference, a common denominator, a process of mutual comparison and interaction, looking at one in the light of another, and with that the evolution of a scale of values—that is, the transformation of a general abstract standard of value into a series of graduated forms of measurement which can be applied to particular activities as they arise.

It is clearly an extremely complicated process of which the mechanism is intricate. If one attempted to work out by reflection all the considerations that enter into the simple statement that the price of a pair of shoes is $2.50, it would certainly tax the most gigantic intellect and the most thoroughgoing and accurate access to information. All the activities of life, all the wants of life enter into some relation to that statement. It represents a solution for the time being, an adjustment for the time being, of all these activities in relation to the others so that the individual may now utilize it in order to direct his own activities by. It puts at the disposal of a particular individual this whole social mechanism in enabling him to measure the importance of the various wants, and enabling him to arrive at those preferences and choices which are the necessary antecedents of overt action.

The classic economists cannot have been wrong in spending so much time in the analysis of the ideas of price and cost and all that goes with them in relation to labor, raw material, market, and all the rest of it. But the defect from the standpoint of philosophy consists simply in isolating them. It is a mechanism, it is a mediating process, and stated by itself in an isolated way it leaves out of account the terms between which the interaction is taking place. It fails to recognize this process of measuring values in the growing specialization and interdependence of the various wants which maintain society, and it fails to see how that process operates in enabling the individual to adjust the kind and range of his own activities to those of others. He may have a very accurate descriptive account of a piece of machinery without any statement of why it was invented or what the outcome is of its running. The question which has occupied attention has been: What is the real measure or standard of value there?

One answer has been that the real measure is that of labor, that the real worth is dependent upon the amount of labor that is put into it. Karl Marx endeavored to give a sort of quasi-mathematical statement of so many units of labor operating for so much time, establishing such and such value. The difficulty with that point of view is to get a criterion for the value of labor. What is the difference between useful labor and that which is useless? What is the difference between the labor that is expended in a well-conducted factor and that which would be expended in sifting sand through a sieve? You could get the same number of physical units, but is the resulting value the same? Can the laborer justly claim the same pay in both cases? Of course no one would say so. It is interesting to note that Karl Marx gets over that difficulty by shoving in two or three words. After saying that the value depends upon the labor, he uses this qualifying adjective "socially available" labor,* which of course begs the whole question. Instead of making labor the standard, it makes something else the standard for the value of the labor.

Now the theory which has been worked out gives a clue, I think, to the right conception there. It is not the amount of labor that it took to produce anything which measures its value; but the quickest way of estimating its value in terms of cost is to ascertain what it would take to replace it under given conditions. And that implies a demand for its replacement, it implies an active need for the thing somewhere. You cannot measure that value in terms of the past, you can really only measure it in terms of the future; that is, the considerations which determine value are not the considerations which precede, which are antecedent. There are conditions which are operating from the other side, as regards the part which that particular thing can play in effecting future coordinations. For that reason an immense amount of labor can be expended on something which has practically no value, and a very little labor may be expended on something of the very highest value. In the first case the thing does not fit in anywhere; in the other it may be the key to the whole situation and its value is estimated by what can be done with it, not from the standpoint of what has been done to it before, its efficacy in effecting direction, in effecting excitation, in effecting control which we attempt to express in terms of the market value.

The bearings of that point on further points of economic theory I cannot indicate, but it seems to suggest a weakness in all socialistic plans for getting a set scheme of values and of rewards. Any such set, formulated scheme would be dependent upon past conditions. Of course some capacity to anticipate might come in and modify the correctness of my statement, but upon the whole the whole scale of values in their return back to the individual would have to be adjusted upon past conditions of labor and of satisfaction. Now in progressive society it is certainly important that the side of use, function, should dominate over the side of attainment and past realization. You must have the possibility of putting a premium on the thing in terms of the readjustments which it can now effect as distinct from the particular part which it may have played in the past.

---

* Perhaps a misreading of Marx or a misquote. Marx does say, "The character that his own labor possesses of being *socially useful* takes the form of the condition, that the product must be not only useful, but *useful for others*" (Karl Marx, *Capital* [New York: The Modern Library, n.d.], p. 85, italics added).

June [?], 1898

With reference to the school that has attempted to state value from the subjective and personal side as consisting in the actual satisfaction afforded, and that attempted to take account of the part played in the estimate of values in the actual determination of economic relations, it may be said that while it has clearly recognized the element which the older school has rather ruled out, it has interpreted the nature of this individual satisfaction and of the part which it plays in too individualized and rigid a sense. That is, it has adopted the hedonistic psychology, identifying satisfaction simply with the enjoyment of certain things and thus has regarded the mental processes which lead up to the final choice as simply a comparison of these given units of pleasure and pain.

Without attempting to go over once more these criticisms of the hedonistic psychology, the point where this conception has led the economic considerations astray may be put about as follows: the weakness is in taking these values as something already fixed and given. If the value is simply a matter of experience in feeling, then of course your deliberative process, your process of the estimation of possible competing values leading up to choice, will consist in nothing but the mechanical comparison of these values which are already there present in consciousness. Now as a matter of fact, the nature of preference is not deciding between values which are already specifically present to the mind as completed; it is essentially a process of bringing value to consciousness. There is not first a value and then an estimate of it in comparison with another. The whole process is the process of valuation. It is a process of objectifying, or bringing out clearly the nature of the want, its quality, and the importance attaching to it. One would get the impression, I think, from reading these accounts, that it was already perfectly clear to the person concerned just how much value attached to a loaf of bread, to a horse, and going to a concert, and that the mind simply derived these quantitative chunks of value and, by putting them in the scale, said, I want this more than the others. The real meaning of having to make an economic preference in any one of these lines is that at the outset one does not know how much these wants amount to, and the very process of concluding which values one prefers is the bringing to light through the antagonisms of the place which each occupies in the whole system of life. It is a process of measuring the value through the organic position which is attributed to it in life as a whole.

I attempted to bring out before, on the psychological side strictly, that preference was always a process of evaluation, and the choice simply marks the point where the value was subjectified. It seems to me it is even clearer if you take it on the objective economic side than on the psychological side. It is a dynamic process in the adjustment of the various factors of activity to each other, and the element of satisfaction is determined as the consequence of that consideration of the adjustment of activities to each other, instead of being somethnig which goes before as antecedent and preconditions the active part. I will conclude this point by saying simply that all such economic categories as profit, wages, etc., as well as the nature of capital, exchange and use, would seem to have a necessary explanation along this line of consideration.

The ultimate point, of course, which has to be kept in view is satisfaction. That is to say, not merely the feeling of satisfaction, not the mere pleasure or pain, but the application of the commodity in question to human life, to enriching its scope, making more out of it: wealth in the broadest sense of the term. All these intermediate processes have finally then to be interpreted with reference to the part which they play in constituting this ultimate valuable application to life. Consumption is too narrow a term as it is used, because it implies too much of the mere using up of the thing. It would be helpful if we had a term which included not only that passive or receptive side which is found in the work [word?] consumption, but also the positive utilization of the thing in the direction of energy, and the satisfaction which is got from that positive output of energy. Consumption of course is not finally for its own sake. The consumption is to reinforce the life process; it is to make good the waste and to increase the amount of energy available to the individual to be put forth in making his life worth living.

SECTION 4. THE LABOR QUESTION; SOCIALISM

Now as we noticed on the objective side there was a growing complexity in the space and time factors which enter in, so of course on the psychical side there is a growing mediation—that is, a growth in the amount of indirectness and dependence involved in the securing of this final value of life itself. The return to the individual, in other words, is more and more dependent upon intermediate social processes. In the hunting condition of life the activity put forth by the individual and the return are of course closely connected together. A man takes [a] weapon and goes out and kills the game and he eats it. He does that as a rule as a member of a family or clan. Now under modern conditions where the individual does his work and gets his return, not in any products which he himself calls into being but simply in money compensation which he then is left to expend for himself in getting his own satisfaction, these intermediate factors are obviously very numerous and very complex.

That constitutes the essence, it seems to me, of the so-called labor question. The difficulty of it is establishing the proper equation between the effort expended in social service and the return in individual satisfaction which society makes. The problem of doing that is so difficult because the factors which enter in are so numerous, and because many of them are so remote from immediate control and many of them are obscure, so uncertain, that it is impossible adequately to take them into account; that is (going back to the point I mentioned the other day), that the physical interdependence has got ahead of the psychical interdependence. Socially, that is, what is being done in different parts is as a matter of fact influencing what is being done in other places, without a sufficient consciousness of how it does that to enable us to control it, and introduces an element of uncertainty and risk which becomes a very dominating factor in the present state of the case. It bears equally on the remuneration of the laborer. Where the risk of uncertainty is so great, the chance for profit to those who undertake the risk must be correspondingly greater. It seems to me that this factor of profit as distinct from the return for social services has to be interpreted along that line of the amount of uncertainty, the experimental character of the coordination which is effected. That would imply that every new undertaking was what some people would call disproportionately rewarded because it involved the effecting of a coordination with a new method and on a larger scale. There are elements entering in which naturally produce what often is considered an excessive profit. But in those cases even where it is not so much a question of doing a thing in a new way or on a much larger scale, the fact of risk enters so largely into existing production that the person who takes the risk, intellectually and emotionally as well as financially, would get a share in the profit which would be disproportionate to that received by the individuals who assist in carrying out the details of the scheme, providing the whole situation were more organized on the intellectual side.

I made incidentally a number of criticisms on socialistic schemes and I will make one more at this point. Their ideal seems to me to conceive of too immediate a relationship between the matter of social service and the return which society makes to the individual. That is, it seems to involve an attempt to fix too specifically and definitely the exact amount and nature of the work which the individual would do and the exact sort of the return which society through the government would make to that individual. It fails to notice, in my judgment, the amount of automatic interplay which goes on and the complexity of that interplay in effecting the proper equation between the outgrowth and the return which comes back to the individual. It fails to notice the number and the kind of factors which influence the values which the individual can really get out of what is physically given back to him; how much it depends upon his education, upon the consciousness of power, of initiation, and of self-direction. It fails to notice how organically freedom and indirectness of relationship are bound up together.

The progress of society, it seems to me, necessarily consists in putting in a process of some sort between the relationship which one individual has to another, or to another body of individuals; it consists in making individual relationships to each other determined by these mutual relationships to something else, instead of there being a direct connection between the persons concerned. The elements of choice of profession, of vocation, of labor, of the place where the labor will be done; the power of choosing the way in which the remuneration for that shall be utilized or applied to life—it is along these directions that actual social progress goes, instead of simply in a more definite, fixed-once-for-all-by-an-outside-authority decision of just the amount and kind of labor an individual would do and just the amount and kind of remuneration he would get for doing it. It is whether the most effective justice would be worked out in the long run and upon the whole by setting up a particular centralized authority which would make this adjustment, or whether the social process is itself so organic in principle that the adjustments must be effected in the organic working out of the process itself. The ordinary economic conceptions certainly stand in very peculiar relations to the notion that society is in any sense organic. Insofar as society is organic, it would seem to follow as a necessary corollary that the adjustments between the labor and the individual, between the effort which he puts forth, the energy which he puts into society, and the values which he gets back, should be adjusted, not by some particular agency, but by the whole complex system of mutual stimuli and control. It is no particular part of the body which controls the demand for food and the process of nutrition and the distribution of food products. That whole thing is effected in the organic interplay. So far as society is in any sense an organism, we would expect the final solution, the final selection and distribution, to be made similarly there by the interplay of all the various parts of the organism.

Government undoubtedly comes in as one of the organs, just as the brain comes in as one of the organs of the whole system; it comes in to set certain limits, to hasten, to accelerate movement in certain directions, to remove certain obstructions which have grown up in the past and deprive the moving forces from having full efficiency, and so on. There is plenty of room for government as one organ among the others to exercise a certain supervision over the adjustments which are going on, and for attempting in the main to keep these adjustments moving in the right direction, but that is quite a different thing from puting the actual control of the whole process into the hands of any particular agency.

It seems to me that there is a failure on the part of the socialist to recognize the factors in historic development. There is a tendency to make a cross section of the existing state of society at a given time with all the evils that are found in it and to take that as finality, apart from any anticipations of a more favorable condition of things which may be worked out through the normal movement of the forces themselves. The philosophical dualism between the ethical and the natural has gone further than appears at first sight, and it shows itself in unexpected places, but it seems to me that the notion of processes which do not intrinsically work for social ends but must be put under government before their outcomes will be distinctly social and ethical is a survival of just this dualism between the material and the spiritual sides of life, between the natural and the ethical sides.

Among the writers and thinkers who have not the slightest notion that there are any metaphysical theories involved, and who would pride themselves in sticking to the facts, there is the assumption that the economic process is a merely natural thing, or if it is psychical at all it is psychical simply on the more physical side of wants, appetites, feelings of pleasure and pain, and that therefore if you get in the ethical factor at all, it must be got in from the outside and you have your choice between two ways of getting it in, either through government or through the conversion of a sufficient number of individuals to altruistic motives. If you leave individuals simply to themselves in the way of doing business, the result will be self-aggrandizement, and a crowding down of others, but if you can get the state to come in and direct it to a common interest, or if you can work on the individual's own motives so that he will accept the golden rule, you can get a better condition of things. The point is, insofar as society is organic, the ethical element, the factor of social justice, must be found in the workings of the economic process itself. The problem is not subjective to outside influences and agencies, but deliberative, to give it [the economic process?] free working. And the condition of doing that is the growth of the knowledge available of conditions of production, conditions of consumption, of distribution, and finally the conditions of real application to life, involving in that the education of the individual along scientific and aesthetic lines.

SECTION 5. THE CONNECTION BETWEEN THE ECONOMIC AND THE POLITICAL

The connecting link between the consideration of the economic process and the political is found in noting the fact that just as function is the working unity of what we distinguished as organism and environment, so occupation or pursuit, calling, industrial interest, is the unification of what we have considered separately on the side of commodity or product and want or capacity; that is, the consideration so far has been of the categories involved in the economic process. The economic process itself as a concrete thing is found in the development of occupation. Just as the concrete biological fact is the exercise of function, it is in the occupation that a concrete adjustment of the physical side and the psychical side is made. Concrete economic history would consist in the history of the evolution of occupations, not merely on the formal side, but the conditions under which it is developed and the part which it plays, the values which it realizes in the social life.

There are two larger factors of this development on the side of location of which I will speak. One is the organic segregation of social groups loosely knit in primitive hordes and then more consolidated in clans, tribes, villages, communities, and so on. The point is that individuals are primarily held together on the basis of their relations to nature. Of course that is never the whole bond of unity, and in later and more complex societies it is very difficult to find even that primitive bond of union. But the immediate conjunction, the immediate connections, I think, are always found, even in the more developed societies, in the common relation of attack, so to speak, upon nature—the control and utilization of nature. And certainly in the primitive forms that bond constitutes a very large part of the whole social bond. The individuals are virtually forced together in virtue of certain immediate economic needs, and the kind of society will depend upon the kind of occupation which is adapted to the particular local development. We have there the key to the development of the family life in all the earlier forms, ramifications, every species of which has been traced out with care by a variety of observers. The fundamental clue to look for in this development is always, I think, the kind of economic life which was suited to the particular physical environment and to the particular traditions and resources in that environment which the people had inherited.

Take one example in modern conditions. There is a great deal of talk about the disintegration of the family through the prevalence of divorce, etc., and a great deal of reflection as to how that supposed disintegration of the family can be checked. Now why should such a phenomenon come up at this particular time? The reason could be stated from many points of view, but the dominating one is precisely the industrial changes. When the household is the center of industry as it was on the whole one hundred and fifty years ago, the family has a very different motivation, a very different immediate necessity from that which is had when the products of society have passed over into factories, and where only the more trivial and, so to speak, belated forms are left to household life. On one hand the almost physical necessity for a compact household life is relaxed, and at the same time the opportunities for activity beyond the range of the household, the stimuli to activity in outlying regions, are indefinitely increased. The net result of the relaxing of pressure on one side, combined with the opportunity for activity beyond, would hardly have any other effect than the readjustment of forces and relationships in which for the time being the family would appear to be going backward. The unit of organization is transferring itself from the family to the particular capacity of the individual, woman as well as man, within the family, and the family life of the future will have to be one in which the basis of unification will be of a distinctly different sort. I use that simply as an illustration of the interdependence between the particular type of economic function involved and the corresponding forms of organization on the associated side.

A great many recent students of religious phenomena have shown how largely the religious associations of primitive society are reflections of fundamental economic relationships. I refer to Robertson Smith's *Religion of the Semites,*[2] as he seems to me to have a firmer grasp on that conception than anyone else that I know of. The pressure of getting a living is so great, and the interests of the men are so immediately and consciously concerned with the conditions of food supply, with all the factors which facilitate living, that it seems to me that it is psychologically almost impossible that the fundamental directions of attention should not come to center about such processes. Thus the great gods are objectifications of the interests bound up in such occupations. The great myths and rites are all of them related directly or indirectly with these same forms of social occupation. Nor is this a simply utilitarian and materialistic conception. The ethical side, the spiritual side, is found in the fact that these occupations have a social significance; they have to do not merely with the physical satisfactions which an individual secures, but with the corporate relations to the environment which are necessary to community existence and growth. Individuals are bound together by these common necessary activities and satisfactions. The gods and the cults manifest these relationships and serve to bring to consciousness the social or ethical factors which lie back of the economic occupations. The religious sanction and consecration are the mark of tremendous social import involved.

The second type is found where these locally segregated groups begin to interact with each other. Here we have simply the principle of the division of labor. Up to this time in a crude way, any given clan, any given tribe or city is itself a whole within itself but is specialized more or less according to the environment. That is, the prevailing industry in one place is either fishing, agriculture, or pasturage, because these occupations represent the adjustment of the organism and environment under particular conditions. But with exchange of course this distribution becomes more internal. Specialization is carried to a much greater point of refinement, and we get within one and the same society the agricultural class, the mining class, the manufacturing class, the artistic class, and the professional classes. It is those differentiations of occupation in classes considered as social organs which become the chief thing, at least become an extremely important thing, a dominant principle in the organization of social institution.

I will leave the economic process at this point and go on to take up the political question a little more specifically.

NOTES

1. *Supra,* Chap. 2, Sec. 1.
2. William Robertson Smith, *Lectures on the Religion of the Semites* (Edinburgh: A. and C. Black, 1889).

CHAPTER 6

ETHICAL ASPECTS OF
POLITICAL INSTITUTIONS

SECTION 1. THE PROBLEM OF
SOVEREIGNTY AND THE
FUNCTIONS OF GOVERNMENT

June 10, 1898

The point suggested yesterday was that the associations of persons are fundamentally determined by the relation of the community to nature; that is, [it is] with reference to a common work and with reference to the particular part played by any organ in accomplishing that common work that the relations of individuals to each other are adjusted.

This brings us to the fifth general head which I gave at the outset, the political aspects of society. As already explained, by political aspect is meant the attained organization of the various modes, organs of social action, with reference to the social function. The economic process is treated as the abstraction of the process by which these organs are evolved, differentiated. If we view these organs as existing and operating in relation to each other from the standpoint of how their interaction maintains society as an organism, we get the political view.

I can only go over briefly some of the main heads involved on the side of politics. The obvious fact that occurs to us when we speak of politics is the conception of authority which is defined in law. Where there is anything which deserves the term political, there are definite instrumentalities for controlling the activities of the minor social units so as to make them subservient within certain limits to the ends and aims of the whole social group; or technically, that idea of authority and subordination is known as sovereignty. Laws are the various particular formulated expressions in which the authority finds its objectification.

On the working side the purpose of law is to define rights and obligations as respects the various social organs, that is, whether units or minor groups or associations. The function of law is to define, in other words, the sphere and place of any given social organ with reference to other organs, and that definition has two sides: the side of rights is the side of differentiation, the side by which the organ is constituted an individual organ. The side of obligation or responsibility is the side of its reaction. As thus defined with other organs it is the side of association.

Going back to the first point, the nature of authority or sovereignty, we find that discussions in the main have centered around the topics of the relative part played by the conception of force, and by the conception of end in its definition. Is authority to be identified with supreme force, or with coercing force? Or is relationship to an end necessarily involved in the idea? Shall we define sovereignty in physical terms? Or shall we define it in psychological terms, in terms of volition? If it is to be defined simply as supreme or coercive force, then our category is a physical one. If we define it primarily in terms of an end, then we are virtually in the sphere of volition and our category is a psychical one. As a corollary to that distinction we have the question as to whether sovereignty is limited or unlimited in its nature. If we can get a criterion for answering the former question, there will be no difficulty in answering the latter.

The other type of problem historically has been as to the residence or location of sovereignty. We have had historically such theories as held that sovereignty was located always in the particular group or particular class who exercise the authority over others, the views most clearly expressed in modern times, or at least first, by Hobbes and then restated as a basis of actual jurisprudence in the present century by Austin, the English representative of the so-called school of jurisprudence, in his lectures on jurisprudence.[1] Over against that we have a conception of popular sovereignty, which finds its suggestion in Locke and its most definite working out in Rousseau, and in all the modern democratic schools, especially on the radical and revolutionary side. Then in popular terms, in this country at least, we have had the conception of the sovereignty of the individual—the individual as such is sovereign—a doctrine which cannot be connected with the name of any political philosopher, but [which] has played a great part as a phrase in American politics.

The question on the philosophic side underlying that question of the residence of sovereignty is, as I shall try to bring out, the question of the relation of the individual and the social whole, the question of the relation of a particular social organ to the entire social organization. And I discuss that question in terms of the residence or location of sovereignty simply because it is a convenient way of leading up to the larger question. So much for the general problems on the political side.

The identification of sovereignty or authority, political authority, with force, dominant force, is a common assumption. You will find it attributed by Green to Austin as well as to Hobbes. The facts regarding the various theories held on sovereignty in modern times are as well stated by Green in his lectures on political obligation[2] as anywhere else. He states the views from Hobbes's times on with criticisms; but while the view is rightly ascribed to Hobbes, Austin is quite clear in his statements that while sovereignty does upon the whole exercise superior force, it is always more or less on sufferance. It is because the mass of people are willing to obey rather than make a fuss; and as a matter of fact the subjects, as distinct from the sovereign, always do have a superior power—only they do not care about exercising it. So it is not fair to identify the conception of supreme force, or even of a superior force of sovereignty, with Austin's view.

There is a little book by Dr. Salter entitled *Anarchy or Government*[3] which is an examination on a philosophical basis of the reasons for government and for yielding obedience to government. It is the examination on philosophical grounds of anarchy versus government, no government versus government. The statements are very clear and the development of the idea is extremely moderate, and I would refer to that as a basis. His whole conception is that government does equal coercive force, it does mean that the individual, against his own desires, may be compelled to act in certain ways. It logically follows, then, that anarchy is ideally the best form of social arrangement. Or as it is more commonly put, government is simply a necessary evil. If everyone were sufficiently well intentioned, there would be no need of political authority; individuals could be left to their own interests and moral judgments in order to do the right thing.

But according to Mr. Salter, we are not sufficiently unselfish to be capable of taking such an ideal view of things. The limitations of persons' knowledge and the defects in their motives are so great that in order that we may approximate nearer to this idea of individual self-control, coercion is a necessity within certain limits. The individual may, and does at the present, threaten the rights and interests of others; and it is in the interests not simply of the whole as a whole, but of all individuals as individuals, that any particular individual who makes these threats should be restrained from these violations of the claims of others.

There [in Salter] is the antithesis between political authority as meaning coercive power and natural associations, voluntary associations, which are the normal outworkings of the individual as such, as volitional in character, resting on persuasion rather than coercion, the personal convictions and the capacity of persuading others through appeals to interest to take such and such a course of action. It follows that the political organization is marked off quite definitely from social organization. When people come together, say, as in family life, simply on the basis of personal volition and individual recognition of mutual interest, and agree of their own accord to cooperate in life for certain ends, you have a strictly voluntary association. But in the government as representing the consolidation, so to speak, of power, in order to coerce refractory individuals and to present motives of possible coercion to those who would otherwise be refractory but would be restrained by knowing that they will be whipped into line if they try to get out too far, we have the essence of the political as such.

You will notice that there are three sets of ideas naturally going together: the concept of government as coercive, in antithesis to matters of personal interest and insight, and in antithesis to voluntary normal social organization. From this point of view political authority represents simply the limitation, the negative side in social organization. So far as community ideas are really realized, so far the foundations of government are relegated to the background. I refer to Mr. Salter's book not because it seems erroneous above others, but because it is clearer in its statement of what is often assumed in a more or less confused manner.

Now that brings us at once to the question which may be stated in this way on the psychological side: Is the distinction between force and will valid? If there any form of will or voluntary association which does not imply the exercise of force? In the conception that the use of force is antithetical to will, [that is,] represents an external restriction brought to bear on will, you get a survival of that idea that will is simply a matter of motive in the purely internal sense of motive. There is the doctrine of a free intermediate factor implied there which operates simply within the inside of consciousness so to speak, without showing itself anywhere in the actual world. Will is identified with choice, and choice is conceived, if not actually defined, as something which is quite preliminary to overt action. A man may have a motive and make up his mind without effecting any actual change in the world. The muscular change acting on the motive is regarded as the mere physical consequence; the psychical side has all come before, but now, as the physical succeedent, we have the putting forth of force and the making of changes in the world. Metaphysically the same dualism between the internal and external, subject and object, is implied here.

Now as against that conception the theory so far advanced requires of course a conception which makes will itself essentially forceful. It is the very nature of will to find expression, to seek execution or realization. Whether that execution will be found just exactly as it is intended or not will depend upon considerations that are more or less within the range of foresight, and in that sense are external; but some effort, some rearrangement, some action, in the overt sense, is absolutely necessary to a concept of will simply as will. Unless overt action does take place, it is proof positive that we are still within the intellectual and emotional aspect. Of course even that involves more separation than there really is, even the deliberative and emotive process involves a certain amount of putting forth of energy, involves rearrangements in the molecules and tensions of the brain and discharges to the muscles. From one point of view any emotional stress is overt action. It simply does not reach the point of integration so that it becomes visible, but it is there. Without going into that phase of the matter, the moment we give up the conception of will as a separate factor which can exercise choice in the purely transcendental region, then of necessity volition must mean an effective determination of that individual himself. And since the individual does not live in a vacuum, since the individual lives in a world of forces, that effective determination of the individual, that recoordination of himself which we find in volition, must have its effect, its expression, outwardly.

When a man says that he did not accomplish anything, really he did accomplish something. Perhaps it was not satisfactory to him, but of course he does make some change in the world, he does put forth force. It is simply that the force which he puts forth is deflected by other forces so that it does not bring about the precise result that he desired. But the conception of an absolutely ineffective will, a will entirely lacking in the elements of execution or of force, is simply a psychological nonentity. Will cannot be defined, that is to say, in terms merely of ends, or merely of ideals, abstract ends and ideals. Will implies that the end becomes to some extent a means and thus points toward operation or effectiveness.

On the logical side we must include as elements in our conception of will both means and end: that is to say, both force (that is the means side operating to realize an end) and an ideal which is sufficiently concrete, embodied in working powers and impulses, habits, to find some overt manifestation of itself. On the biological side this separation between means and end, or between force and idea, between the physical and the psychical, is like conceiving organs which are not the organs of any organism, or of an organism which has no organs. The end side, the idea side, is simply the conception of a coordination, of a unification of the various means or habits, and so the organs as particularized realities, actual structures, or the particular exercising of force are the specifications, the realizations of the idea which is involved in the organism, the totality side.

Now applying that general psychological conception to society, the exercise of force, instead of being something external to and restrictive to aims, is the measure of the reality of the aim. Just as you would measure the sincerity of the individual, the extent to which he really believes in his professed ideal by the efforts he is willing to put forth to realize it, so our test for the reality of the social conception is the amount of stir it can make in the world, the amount of positive effective application to life which it can find in the sphere of space and time. Any other conception leaves us in this thoroughgoing dualism between the moral and physical, or the moral and the social. The moral becomes a mere ideal something—desirable to have realized, very nice if it could be realized—but it has no intrinsic force of its own. There are no guarantees that it may have or should have any realization. It is simply left to the arbitrary choice of a lot of particular individuals to decide whether or not they will choose to accept this ideal and try to carry it into effect. According to the other point of view, every ideal, so far as it is genuine, is operative; and the force side, the execution side, is nothing but the objective uttering and the objective measuring of the worth or significance of the ideal.

June 13, 1898

From what we said at the last hour it would follow that the exercise of force is not a matter which can be restricted to a particular social agency.

Wherever we have social ends that are in process of realization, there we would find the exercise of force. The end would always enact itself just in the way that it was really an end and that self-enactment is forceful. Taken from the side of concrete fact, it is almost grotesque to limit the use of force to a particular organ particularly denominated political. The organization of every form of association involves the use of force, and involves it not merely in positive or liberating directions, but also in restrictive and inhibitory directions. The family as an institution involves the use of force, so does the school—and force of as immediate and physical a type as we ever find exercised by government.

Now those who would identify sovereignty with the exercise of power account for that by the general principle that whatever the government does not forbid it permits, and what it permits it virtually performs, in which case the position of corporal punishment in family discipline would be regarded as really due to governmental action; it would be simply a form in which sovereignty was exercised, say, in a delegated manner. Now I do not question the principle of truth involved in such a statement; but if we generalize that principle of truth, it carries us a good ways. The moment we say that every such exercise of power is virtually an exercise of sovereignty in some delegated or mediated form, we have to apply that statement all the way through, and the very conception of sovereignty as a specialized institution like the government, which exercises force all through the voluntary associations, breaks down; this element of force becomes projected into what had previously been set over against sovereignty and conceived as voluntary association.

So accepting the element of truth in the proposition that all such exercise of force is virtually as the instrument or organ of sovereignty, it would follow that the whole rigid dualism between sovereignty as coercive force and voluntary association as resting on the play of insight and interest would break loose. In all other forms of association where we really see force used in direct forms (that is, physical coercion), force nevertheless plays a large part. It becomes more clothed with psychical associations, it becomes more indirect; but when we simply recognize what a tremendous part is played in all society by the pressure which individuals, separately and in association, exercise on each other, and how largely the running machinery of society consists simply in these mutual pressures and resistances, and how much the efficiency of those pressures does depend upon the presence of a force which may display itself in some more overt manner, it seems to me there is very little left of this attempt to put voluntary association as a psychical thing, a volitional thing over against the exercise of force as of a physical and coercive nature.

Social boycotts, industrial boycotts, strikes, lockouts are only the more obvious instances of this exercise of pressure. If you think how far the principle of boycotts goes in society, how much men are influenced in their action by the fear of certain unfavorable reactions by other people, or by threats, we begin to see the principle through more disguised modes of expression. The difference is simply one of direction: between giving a man to understand that he will not get work to do and therefore will not get enough to eat unless he prescribes to certain conditions, and saying we will lock you up. Only government operates in the latter form, but all kinds of voluntary associations operate in the former way. It is a mere distinction of details in the mode of applying the force, and not a distinction of principle.

Every positive relation, to extend the principle further, into which any individual enters with another individual has its compelling side to it. The very fact that he is in that relationship, that another voluntarily, or by birth or stress of circumstances, has come into a certain institution puts a positive influence on him, which, while it is interpreted and clothed more or less in psychical forms, has its physical structure.

Now we must remember that on the other side the operation of the state is not merely physical, it has a certain amount of psychical investiture. The threat of punishment is not the same, or the threat of arrest is not the same as the mere direct physical restraints. The force is not operating absolutely directly, it is acting through the medium of a stimulus which appeals to consciousness and which is interpreted in consciousness. The only difference between the more explicit threat of the state to punish and the pressure which a religious organization puts upon one of its members either to act or to believe in a certain way is simply one of detail, of degree; it concerns the amount of mediation is consciousness that takes place between the merely physical aspect of the stimulus and its final effect upon the conduct.

We would still have to deal, however, with the question of this difference in detail. How does it happen that the government does for the most part (if we except, say, family life and the school) reserve the right of the most immediate or physical form of the exercise of force? How is that to be accounted for? I should say in a general way on the theory of units.* If all voluntary organization involves the exercise of force, that means a certain power which is really holding the individual in certain lines of activity by positive stimulus and by negative inhibition. Then the question of the exercise of those modes of force becomes an important thing, it marks the difference between order and anarchy, in the sense that anarchy means complete disorder and chaos. We must, in other words, interpret and control units by the use of force, by the utilization of end[s?], and since the variety of institutions and associations and relationships involves a great variety of ends, that involves some positive organization of ends in relation to each other. If family life were carried on simply by one set of people in one spot of the earth, and business partnerships were equally segregated, and so on, we would have to organize each within itself, make an adaptation of the means of execution within it. But since they are equally pulling on each other, since they are all bound up together in the larger movements

* Possibly Dewey really said "limits." See *infra*, p. 415.

of society, there must be equally a reciprocal adjustment of each to the other.

The sphere of the exercise of force, the control of the means necessary to execute these ends, must be similarly definite. That is, certain powers of the individual will be ascribed to the family as the family, or as an individual of the family, others as a member of the joint stock association. He will have other powers as the member of a club, others as a member of the church. He will have other powers as a citizen and political subject, as a civic political integer. That involves some rule of distribution. This assignment, so to speak, of powers must be conducted on the general principle that negatively they shall not clash and positively shall assist each other. There would be disintegration, not only to society as such, but to the individual as an individual, if the force which he could exercise as a member of industrial associations clashed to the point of much friction with the capacities which he exercises as a member of a family. On the principle of the division of labor we should naturally expect the evolution of some social order which should have for its special benefit the adjustment of the distribution and relationship of these powers with special reference to the probable points of strain.

That is what I meant by reference to the principle of limits. The government involves a social organ just as the family or the business partnership does; and instead of having a monopoly of the exercise of force, it as a division of labor, as a particular organ, simply marks the instrumentality through which the adjustment of the lines of force that are operative in the other modes of association are adjusted to each other. It is a matter of convenience, it is a teleological matter, or an economical matter, to have a particular instrumentality which shall be charged with the supervision and oversight for making these adjustments in a general way instead of leaving them to be settled according to the mere circumstances of the moment. Thus the business of government comes to be to formulate the lines along which these adjustments are naturally made, with a view to application to doubtful cases.

There once more is what I meant by reference to the principle of limits. It would be just as absurd for the government to attempt to formulate in law, in legislative enactment, all possible modes or forms [?] of social activity as it would be for the individual similarly to bring to formulated intellectual consciousness all his various impulses and habits. There is a final motive for reflection in the individuals. That is, either the actual clashing of various habits and impulses or the anticipation of a possible clash. It is with reference to those actual or possible strains that the individual reflects. Carrying the principle of deliberation beyond that point is to weaken his available executive ability. Now similarly, in the state, there are a great many adjustments which are at any given particular time fairly able to take care of themselves; they are the habitual thing, the points that are not questioned either theoretically or practically. There are other matters lying, so to speak, nearer the surface where the adjustments and readjustments are in process of making, and with reference to which, therefore, the formulations are particularly in demand.

The clerical function of government, the so-called legislative function is found in an attempt to locate these points of tension and lay down a general formulation for dealing with them. That is only rather an elaborate way of expressing what might be termed the relativity of legislation. The explicit lawmaking activity of the Romans in the third century before Christ was not that of the fifth, and that in turn was not that of today. It is not the business of the government to make an inventory of all modes of activity and tell how they ought to be carried on, but to adapt its formulation to the needs of the situation, those needs being interpreted along the line of the adjustment of forces which is most problematic at that particular period. Beyond certain limits, in other words, which are determined for the most part experimentally, it is found desirable to leave the working out of these distributions of force to the natural interplay of social life itself, to be determined by the occasions, and the need of the occasion.

That might be illustrated by the principle of strikes. The very nature of the strike is to come as near the exercise of overt force, without overstepping the bounds, as it can. People may deplore that, but its effectiveness depends upon the fact that it does do that. Now that a given community allows a strike to be carried on means that under its particular conditions it finds it more advisable to let the thing be worked out in that experimental manner than it would be to attempt to prescribe for it in advance. According to its interpretations of the situation, it is the most feasible way of accomplishing the final distribution.

Now another community of different historical antecedents and traditions may put the limit somewhere else. There is a very obvious difference, for example, between the place where the Latin races in Europe, the Teutonic races, and the English and American people draw those lines. The English and American tradition is evidently to have a good deal more as regards distribution of power left to the external out-working of the elements themselves, and to tolerate more disorder in bringing that about than some of the European peoples. In continental Europe we find quite different modes of getting at it between the French and the Germans. They agree, as against our method of doing business, in attempting to formulate the various contingencies that arise and provide for them by general rule in advance; which means that the government is given more power—but their principle of getting at it is quite different within themselves. They appeal to the expert formulation of the situation, among the Teutonic; and more to centralization on the executive side, among Latin people.

As for the recent time where a rigid line is so often drawn between voluntary association and sovereignty, it is a well-known fact that the purely habitual factors do not attract attention. It is simply the points of readjustment that we are conscious of, and so we overlook the tremendous exercise of power which is involved within the voluntary organizations themselves. It goes on naturally all the time and we do not stop to think of it, and our attention is more attracted to the obvious and overt actions of government, although if we could get a statement in qualitative terms the ratio might be not more than as one to one thousand. But it is the one which attracts the attention, and so we tend to ignore the remaining nine hundred and ninety-nine thousandths, and to deify that particular element.

If we come now to the phases of this operation of force by government, we find it convenient to specify three general heads—those which we know as the constitutional, the civil, and the criminal.

The constitutional law aspect of governmental declaration and operation represents clearly the more fundamental and organic ways in which the community interprets its own activity. The lateness of the written constitution simply shows how great the tendency is for the people to take itself [themselves?] for granted. Just because these lines of action are so fundamental, they are hardly brought to consciousness at all, they are simply assumed. As in the case of England the thing comes to consciousness only as a particular occasion arises, it is only when some special adjustment has to be made, and in the case of England, in this particular adjustment the tendency is to think of it simply as a particular case, and then it has weight as a precedent.

Well, there is a difference in our way of doing things. Such a constitution as ours only attempts to state the fundamental distribution of powers in a very general way and with reference to certain clashes, the adjustment of which at the time could be most easily attempted. Experience taught them that it was a problem as to how the various states were going to operate in relation to each other and to the federation. Also how judicial and legislative powers could most readily function with reference to each other. There were a number of particular difficulties that had actually to be adjusted, and when we say that the American constitution was a practical document and not merely an academic or professorial constitution, it means that it confined itself to indicating forms, methods, for dealing with the more particular points of tension as they have been revealed by experience up to date.

But distinguishing constitutional law from the two other forms, it would indicate reference to interest in those habits which are considered as necessary to the integrity of the individual in question. In this case the individual means the nation; it represents its self-consciousness along the lines of what is considered indispensable to its own continued functioning.

Now to take the second type, civil law, using that not in a technical sense but in a general way to include everything that lies between the determination of the character of government and the violations of law which we term criminal. We find that we have here simply the machinery for effecting the solution of social tensions as they arise. The point that differentiates it from the criminal side is that virtually, unconsciously, these tensions are regarded as normal, and as not threatening social welfare. They are regarded as incidental to social movement, to social progress; they are practically regarded indeed as actual instruments or organs in social development. We leave the individual to institute a civil suit. The government takes upon itself the responsibility of a criminal suit. In case it is decided that the individual has been injured from a civil point of view, the act is not considered criminal and therefore as demanding punishment. It is regarded technically as an injury which the individual has received and with reference to which redress does not take the form of punishment, but of restitution, or of injunction, prohibition in some form or another, of similar activities in the future.

It is clear that no objective line can be drawn between these two forms of conduct, but [one of them] would be regarded as within the civil sphere at one time and in the criminal at another, or even vice versa. Going on another man's land under certain circumstances or social conditions will be regarded as a crime against the state and the state will take action. At another time it will be considered simply as a mode of trespass and unless some individual considers himself injured and takes proceedings, no notice of it will be taken at all. On the movement in the other direction certain forms of carelessness at one time will be considered as simply things of which the injured individual will take notice, while later the same objective act may be treated as indicating a disposition which is threatening to society as such and which therefore falls within the criminal scope. Taking these two differentia (that is, the way in which legal distinctions are set up and the kind of redress which is decided), it seems to me to come out quite clearly that in one case society thinks upon the whole that more can be gained through the onus of action upon some individual. If the individual does not care enough about his rights to be interested in personally asserting them, why then it is better to let them be trampled on.

But in other cases, and this I think forms the great mass of important litigation, the simple fact is that the distribution of rights has not yet been determined. Society is changing. Just what claims under those changed conditions a given individual has as against another is not certain, and the tendency among the English-speaking people, at least in those cases, is to say: You would better wait until the problem arises and then make your conclusions with reference to the concrete circumstances which enter into this particular case, comparing this so far as possible with others of the same general sort, making some sort of a classification as you go along. It relies then mainly upon custom.

Historically statutory law is a very late development, just as a written constitution is a very late development. They are the counterparts of each other in these two forms. Statutory law means simply that a given line of experience has been worked out to the point where it is found useful to abstract the methods involved, to generalize them and to set them up. Here again you find difference in type—but the difference is psychological—between the continental people and our own. In Roman law the tendency has been to carry the general modification side very much further, while the Anglo-Saxon tradition has been to make the adjustment consciously on the basis of the relation of particulars to each other, bringing the universal involved to consciousness only so far as it is necessary to deal with the particular case. We find historically that great legislative movements have taken place at periods of reconstruction; then a given social form has fairly worked itself out and a new one is coming in. That the adjustment between past and present be made without too great a break, it is necessary to have some more legislation. You find that first in Greece in a tendency toward more definite legislation, later in Rome, and in this present century among all peoples a great increase of legislative activity coincidental with the change in industrial conditions and commercial relationships.

One word on the criminal side here. A given act or given line of conduct which has previously been considered as coming within the civil scope is transferred to the criminal when it is believed, whether rightly or wrongly, that the doing of this particular deed involves a habit, a disposition, or interest, which is hostile to society. The line is drawn carefully between those acts which an individual does in pursuit of his own interests which may threaten the interest of others, and those which are regarded as being signs of a lack of proper socialization. If I do a certain thing, the government virtually says: Maybe that was done fraudulently at bottom but it is better for the social welfare to throw the responsibility to act on the aggrieved individual. The right of the particular case is not clear yet, there is only half truth on both sides, some more comprehensive act will come between and it is referred to the civil sphere. Again the state will say: I take what that person does to be indicative of a habit which by its very existence threatens society; therefore society in its more collective aspect, through this particular organ set up for the purpose, must take notice of that particular act. The aggrieved individual might be willing to overlook it, but the disposition is still there. The habit is a threat to others; it is general, in other words. So the same overt act would be referred either to the civil sphere or the criminal, according as it was regarded, or not regarded, as resulting from the generalized attitude of social opposition.

SECTION 2. FORCE CAN EITHER BE LIBERATING OR RESTRICTIVE

June 14, 1898

An illustration of law in its criminal aspects brings us clearly the question of the use of force in a direction which to a particular individual is coercive, restrictive, in character. At the outset we have to notice that that is only one, and only an incidental and comparatively limited aspect of the operation of sovereignty. As is implied by what has been said in the previous discussion, it is the organization of force which liberates the individual. That is, even if we are emphasizing the element of force in our differentia of sovereignty, we have to recognize that this force is exercised normally not to coerce the individual but to stimulate him, to define for him the sphere of action within which he can have practically free play; that through the adjustments which are made by law, through the limits and definitions that are set up, each individual has definite lines for the direction of his energy presented to him. He becomes a centralization of force himself, he becomes a concentration of power which he could not otherwise be, and he has provided for him and suggested to him certain channels along which, if he exercises his force, it will be effective, it will accomplish something.

It is certainly then a very one-sided view which overlooks that aspect of the use of force which serves to, as I said, liberate the individual—that is, to help him to define his own powers, and direct and utilize his own powers, so that they amount to something. That is the normal side, the positive side; and the coercive or restrictive is related to that as the pathological is always related to the normal, or as the negative is always related to the positive.

The objection is sometimes made on the moral side that the law, since it claims to possess authority and therefore compelling power in relation to the individual, restricts the sphere of moral action. The objection is made by the school of ethical individualists (as distinct from the economic), for example, that the public school system is a bad thing, and of course much more so the compulsory phase in that system. The moral ideal would be that each individual voluntarily saw and chose the good, that he should possess sufficient interest in proper human development and proper affection for his own children to see that they are properly cared for. The point of view may seem somewhat strained, but it is one which has actually been taken. To bring all such matter as that under legal enactment is to tend to make the individual have external motives for his action, to act from fear or hope of reward, or some kind of psychical, if not physical, compulsion, instead of freely; and [acting] freely of course is the very essence of moral action—that is, that the act proceed from the individual's insight and his own choice and interest.

Now in relation to what has been said before the psychological fallacy is in supposing that any individual under any circumstances has within his own isolated consciousness any insight or any working motives, any actual power of choice. It makes of the individual a sort of deity, and a deity which can work in a vacuum, which can present to itself without any relationships a scheme of life, a project of values, and then some way select among these various values. The relation in the way of stimulus and the contact with that stimulus involves certainly the use of force; it is necessary to bring the individual to the point of having any insight, to give him anything to think about and any motives for reflection; and equally so on the side of choice. The objection is an extreme case of the psychological fallacy. It puts in at the outset and takes for granted what can be there only after the whole intermediate machinery has done its work. After the individual has been brought, through contact with others and through the necessity of organizing his own activities and powers, into relation with the powers of others then we may say: "Why, leave the matter entirely to the insight, interest and choice of the individual." But that represents the last term, the outcome of the decision. It presupposes virtually that all the operating agencies of society in which the organization of force is involved have been at work all the time to stimulate this individual into consciousness and to arouse him to a sense of what the actual values in the matter are.

If we take also the side of the carrying of decisions into effect, we find the same sort of dualism that we have run across before, the identification of will with the merely internal, the identification of consciousness or the psychical with something which can be complete in itself without relation to the environment.

As I pointed out at the outset[4] a certain class of writers, represented by Kant and Green, hold that the government must not use force to affect the motives of the individual because that is getting over into the spiritual region where the individual's own deliberation and motives must be supreme; but that the use of force is justifiable in order that things may be so arranged that the individual will have a chance to carry his right decisions, his good motives, into effect. In the way of removing obstructions to the execution of the motive, or in the way of promoting conditions to facilitate the realization of the moral motives, the use of force is justifiable.

Now the fallacy there is in supposing that the consideration of the so-called external conditions, those which have to do with the execution of motive, will not react in the formation of the motive itself. You would think from this view that it was entirely one set of considerations that related to the formation of the motive and another set which determined the matter of its being carried into effect, and that these two sets of data have only the most superficial and external connections with each other. But any concrete observation or reflection will convince us that as a matter of fact the individual always forms his motives with reference to execution. The conditions which one conceives as entering into the possibility of action, into the possibility of realization, are at once reflected in the quality and makeup of the motive itself. It is always true indeed that there are certain considerations, objectively, which enter into the matter of carrying out the intention, which one has not foreseen. But that does not alter the fact that the motive, as it is actually formed in one's consciousness, is conditioned in every way upon what one believes and thinks concerning the conditions in which he is going to act.

I am simply saying that people never form motives at large or in the air; they form motives with regard to particular things which must be done and in that way enter into the actual present conditions of the environment.

The most that one could get on that basis would be a motive to be good in general, or something like the Kantian motive of doing the right because it is right. I do not admit logically that one could get even that much, that is, simply the abstraction of a most highly generalized and schematic relation to the government. There would be nothing there by which to outline the conception of the good or the right, even in this most vague way, unless one had the conception of some kind of a world, some kind of a vague environment in which he was going to operate.

When it comes to the more specific question: What shall I do in order to be good? What is right? What is the particular thing which is my duty? then it seems to me argument is hardly necessary to point out that everything that this set [Kant and Green] have waived one side [sic] and related simply to conditions of application comes in. The really practicable thing must be the right thing, and the only criterion for the right, unless we fall back on a purely abstract, unrelated mental faculty which isuues its *dicta* as so many absolute *ipse dixets* [*dixits*], is whatever is really practicable— that is, whatever is consistent with the conditions of action in such a way as to organize them so that the deed shall be the summing up of the real conditions.

Now the bearing of this question on the so-called restrictive or coercive aspect of force is just here. If an individual has a wrong basis for considering the situation, if he has a false standard for measuring values, some stimulus or other must be used to bring him to himself, to change the direction of his attention, to bring to light factors which he has been ignoring, and to help him to put in a better perspective those which he has been overestimating or exaggerating. Now under certain conditions that stimulus will present itself simply as check, or mainly as check, mainly as running up against a force, up against a sharp obstruction. Now that is not because it is simply force, or because it is simply obstruction. It is because the state of the individual's consciousness is such that he interprets it as simple force, or simple coercion.

If a child attempts to do something which is physically impossible he tumbles down and gets hurt, and we might as well object that the law of gravitation [w]as being restrictive of freedom, of individuality. [Similarly,] because he cannot do this impossible thing without getting hurt, was to consider certain modes of social action as merely restrictive or coercive of the individual. There lies back of both [these conclusions] an absolutely abstract idea of freedom. We set up an individual at large, having no concrete powers or relationships, and then freedom is supposed to be found in the activity of that empty thing. The necessity of the conditions, and the relation of the activity to the conditions, is perfectly obvious on the physical side. Everyone would admit that the agent has to act physically in an environment and that he can accomplish something only as he uses the forces of that physical environment. One would not object to the law of gravitation because it restricted the individuality by making it impossible for one to jump into the air a thousand feet, or leap into a precipice without being injured. Such a conception would not have much sense. One's physical freedom would be found in his active use of physical powers.

The view I am trying to present is simple: that we must look at moral and social relationships in precisely the same way, and that if the individual has set up abstract conceptions, if he has set up one-sided ends or aims which are impossible under the conditions, there is bound to be a reaction as much in one case as in the other. It is not because the reaction there is intrinsically an expression of simply coercive force, but because the individual, on account of his previous habits and interests, makes it such. A man who is interested in the education of his children does not find anything coercive in the public school system. He simply finds that his powers of carrying certain ideas into effect that would otherwise be abstract are greatly facilitated. He finds increase in his power of vision to see what he really wants, and also increase in the instruments that he can use in carrying out his ideas. To him it is simply organization on the positive side. If the person runs up against the machinery of organization he naturally gets a different result than when he runs with that machinery.

Now of course that notion cuts both ways. It not only gives a justification for what may be termed the coercive use of social forces, but it also gives a standard for determining their proper use. Their real function, as has been said, is to bring the individual to consciousness. Insofar as specifically social administration in relation to the criminal is not calculated up to the limits of possibility to effect this, insofar it may be condemned, not because it is coercive, but because it does not perform the function which coercion should perform. The use of it as a stimulus on the negative side, to show the individual why he is out of proper relationship, to show him where he is not making his connections right, to bring home to him the abstractness and real impossibility of his animating ideas, of his controlling interests: that gives the standard for the amount of force which can be used and for the way in which it should be used. In other words, the standard for the kind of mode of the administration of punishment.

If we take the three conceptions regarding the nature of punishment: first, that it should be retributive, second, that it should be preventive, and third, that it should be reformatory, the formulation that we would get on this basis is that punishment is retributive but never for the sake of retribution. The actual form of it is retributive—that is to say, the action and reaction are equal. The individual that is out of line with society finds society out of line with him, and the bringing home of that may be termed compensation; but that is not the end or aim, it is simply the nature of the thing as it goes on. It is through prevention, restriction—that is, the individual is put under circumstances where he cannot do that thing again, or is less likely to do it again. The prevention side gives punishment on the side of means, but the end must always be reformatory—that is, the modification of the individual's consciousness, such a change in his attitude as will make him look at himself in a new way, in a new scale of values, and of course not merely theoretically so, but in a new practical judgment of himself and of his place in the social situation.

SECTION 3. SOVEREIGNTY AS UNIFICATION OF MEANS AND END, FORCE AND IDEA

I have put under this discussion of sovereignty what might equally well have been discussed somewhere else, and what I should have discussed somewhere else if I had more time. But they are all connected with the general conception of sovereignty as equivalent to social will, and will as involving an organized unification of means and end, or of force and ideas, and the subsequent impossibility of arriving at correct conclusions from the standpoint of a theory which makes an unreal separation between these two phases of will. More technically speaking, the conclusion we would arrive at concerning the nature of sovereignty is that sovereignty represents the working organization, at a given time, of the social consciousness; it represents the effective, operative ideals; it represents those social aims and purposes which have become so thoroughly embodied in habits and in acts that they make themselves felt, that they carry themselves out. In psychological language sovereignty is the motor force of the social idea. Now because it is that, we cannot identify sovereignty with any particular social order. That has been implied already. We cannot identify government and sovereignty.

Government is simply one organ of sovereignty, simply one mode of effecting social action. You cannot even say it is *the* organ of sovereignty. It is not the chief preeminent representative of social aims. Industrial life, family life, the school, are all of them *the* organs just as much as it is. It does not have a particular function on the formal side—that is, it is an organ which deals with the conscious adjustment of other organs in cases of probable or possible collision. From one point of view that is less an end in itself than any other social organ. Its importance is practically as instrumental. The family has a certain final end, it represents the embodiment of an aim concretely, and so does business life, and so does artistic and intellectual life. The government is simply a scheme or piece of machinery for facilitating the proper interaction of these other organs. On the side of form as distinct from that of content, it does have a certain preeminence. It represents the direction of social consciousness, or the direction of attention with respect to the more important forms of the tensions which arise. It is by no means the whole social consciousness, or the whole social attention, but it is that social attention as concerned with matters which, if allowed to go too far, would make serious breaks. Or on the positive side it is concerned with anticipating and thus preventing more serious forms of social collision.

In reaching this conclusion, we have come to the second point with regard to sovereignty: its residence or location. We have a point of view from which to consider, then, the so-called residence or location of sovereignty. It is seen to be equal to the means which carry into effect social aims. Every institution has its claim from that point of view. Each is a mode or organ for realizing social value. Each then is an instrument of sovereignty. Not in the external sense, as if this power was delegated to it from without, as if it really belonged to government and government had chosen to allow the individual, or the institution in question, to utilize a certain amount of the force which practically belonged to it, but in an intrinsic organic sense the individual or the particular institution does represent sovereignty. And that is the element of truth in that conception of the state as permitting whatever it does not forbid, and enacting whatever it permits. But that is to be interpreted in the most direct and intrinsic sense, not in the derivative sense, as if the expression of this power came from somewhere outside of itself. The institution is simply a working phase of sovereignty.

If we take the three different views which have been held in modern times historically, we find the view of Hobbes is that sovereignty resides in the few, but that its power is unlimited and that it therefore can operate as it pleases; that is the source of all law and order. There we have in the most extreme form the conception of the relations of individuals as a whole being utterly lawless. The particular power, the crystallizing center, is the source from which any other radiates.

Then we have the view of Locke which also identifies sovereignty with the government, that is, with the few, but which says it is essentially limited. Government has this force for the sake of realizing social ends, and consequently when it begins to utilize this force for itself, or in any way against the general interest, it virtually abdicates. You do not have to have a revolution, government itself has made the revolution. There we have the conception of sovereignty as condensed in the few but operative for the good of all.

Then, at the other end from Hobbes we have Rousseau with the doctrine of popular sovereignty, according to which people as a whole, what he termed the common will, is the sovereign and acts also for the good of the whole. Rousseau went so far as to deny the possibility of representative government in legislative matters. In adminstrative matters it would be possible, but from that point of view it is servile. Society hires certain administrative agents just as you hire a laborer. But on the legislative side, society as a whole being sovereign, society as a whole must make the laws, all legislation must be directly the issue of a pure democracy.

Now that conception of sovereignty as equivalent to common will has clearly certain points of identity with the view that has already been expressed, but the weakness of Rousseau's conception is that he insists that the general which he gets, the universal, is an abstract and formal one. There is not, on his basis, any organized scheme by which sovereignty operates. You have this general will at large, but there is no provision in the general will for defining in a systematic way its own modes of exercise. The general will has been erected in a force or faculty or entity which lies back of and outside of particular acts and individuals. The point where Rousseau is weak practically is also where he is weak theoretically His general [will] is not an organizing principle. His general will is not the will that is manifest in a concrete organization of society at a given time; it is a sort of abstract identity of purpose whcih lies behind it all. For instance, Rousseau distinguishes between the common will and the will of all. The will of all is the sum of the individual will[s]. The common will is that which is actually common. It is the abstract universal of the formal logic. According to that, social action, legislation, must be unanimous. The law is the expression of the common will. Rousseau gets around that by saying that people vote simply to find out as to whether there is a general will. If thcrc is a majority of one, the vote is still unanimous. It is not the majority that makes the law. The majority is the common will and the voting is the device to bring out what the general will is. The grotesqueness of that comes from his notion of the nature of a common will.

What Hobbes got hold of was the necessity of specification, of having some particular way in which the general will is made known and through which it operates. It comes out better in Austin than it does in Hobbes or Locke. He says it is the very nature of sovereignty to be a determinate body. An indeterminate body may have public sentiment and that may act in a more or less vague way to accomplish something that is not sovereignty. What characterizes sovereignty is that there should be some particular individual responsible for its execution. That emphasis on determinateness brings out the necessary element in the conception of sovereignty.

The trouble with those who have insisted on the location of sovereignty in a particular body is that they only want one particular body. This view would correspond biologically to one which would insist that the organism could not be an organism without a brain, and that it was the brain and only the brain which made it an organism. Rousseau's view would be that which insisted that there must be an entity back, an organism, but which left it to the matter of chance whether that organism had any particular organs for doing anything.

I will leave this matter of sovereignty. I am going on to take up the matter of right and duty, their basis, and the principles of classification.

SECTION 4. THE RELATION BETWEEN THE IDEAL AND THE ACTUAL IN SOCIAL CHANGE

June 15, 1898

The working action of sovereignty is found in institutions, the self-conscious action of sovereignty is found in law. I use "law" here in the most comprehensive sense, equivalent to the term *jus* in Latin and the term *Recht* in German, these terms meaning both obligations which are imposed and rights which are conferred. They have a double meaning for which there is no actual equivalent in English, and I use the term law to express the formulation by means of which powers or rights are defined on one side and obligations on the other.

The point that I have just made as to the distinction between the working operation of sovereignty and its reflective or self-conscious operation is necessary in order to get a clear conception of the position and limitation of the legal concepts. According to one view the legal and political are coextensive. Such a course would be the necessary result from the standpoint of Hobbes, or the standpoint of Austin. The sovereign is the determinate body who promulgates law, from which commands and privileges proceed. The sphere of necessity would be exercised then, in the region of these laws.

The analytic school had some difficulty in meeting the objections brought by the historical school, which pointed out that in all earlier forms of society you do not find any express law-promulgating body, but the appeal is always to custom. In these primitive societies, as you know, the only question which arises, which the judges have to decide, nominally at least, is: What is the custom? As soon as custom is detected, then everything else follows at once.

The way in which the analytical school met that objection was on the basis mentioned yesterday, that whatever the sovereign permits it virtually commands. That is, customs by it are regarded as being given the form of law through the judicial decision. Prior to that time they were not really law. The objection to that is that the thought of the people, whatever was custom, had been law all the time and the judicial decision did not make it so. There is another objection which is indicated in the distinction between institutions and law. There are a great many influences which really determine the course of events, which really control action, besides these formulated in any way.

Austin recognizes that in the distinction which he makes between the legal and the moral. The legal is the formulated or objectified side of the political, while the moral represents the influences which proceed from indefinite, unspecified sources. Public opinion is a typical example of what he means by the moral in distinction from the political. There is not a certain body which imposes on the people. It is floating around, it is in the air, and yet it does have a great deal of power ultimately. Austin recognizes that, but Hobbes did not recognize that the intangible influence controlled the determinate activity of the sovereign. That is, what the sovereign really commands will be dependent upon this incoherent body of convictions and beliefs which lie behind, and people on the whole must believe that the action of the sovereign is in line with that vaguer, wider sphere of influence, or else they will not put up with it.

Now the difficulty in marking off that sphere of influence and control as moral and setting it up so definitely over against the political is that it does not give any coherent working theory for the interaction of the two spheres. The point comes out most concretely in dealing with the question of change of government. You see at once, according to Austin's theory, that any change in the governing body itself must be extrapolitical, must be revolutionary. As long as the political sphere proceeds from the sovereign, if there is any change in the sovereign that must come from the outside.

For instance, you could not treat the formation of the thirteen American colonies into an independent state as itself a political change on this basis at all. You could not treat it as a thing which could be stated at all in legal terms. You have there a change in the sovereign and all you can see is that you have a break. First you had one sovereignty and that somehow disappeared and another came, you do not know where from—that is, politically you do not. If you get into the sphere of the moral, you can find various influences. Was not such a revolution the formation of the North German Confederation into the modern German Empire? That could be treated as a political evolution on this basis of Austin's, insofar as the government was modified. As it moved on along new directions, so far you have a change which is revolutionary, extrapolitical. That is the specific, concrete point where the weakness of his theory comes out.

Now the meaning of that is that such a view would identify the political simply with that which had been formulated in an objective sense. It takes society practically as a dead thing, it takes it as if all the machinery were suddenly stopped. It gives you a sort of fossilized or frozen view of society, as if you could get the whole political action in a snapshot and that photographic static outlook were the whole thing. We all know that behind that cross section, behind that which can thus be put in concluded terms, there is the movement, the life to which all that is relative, and for the sake of which the more static side exists, of which it is simply the instruments for the future direction.

In any working conception of sovereignty, therefore, we have to include these directions in which institutions are developed, have to include the tendency as well as the formulative attainment. And if we identify the legal with that which can be formulated, this stands over against the legal [moral?], but not over against the political. It is just as real politically, it is just as much a matter of sovereignty, as the legal side is, but it simply gives us the two aspects, the practical and the ideal, the dynamic and static, of sovereignty itself. The ratio between the working institutional side and the formulated legal side is a varying one.

It is like the matter of self-consciousness in the individual. Sometimes the individual will get along very well with only a little, and again he must have a good deal; it depends upon the amount of [readjustment that is required in?] the development of the American nation and American constitution from the formation of the constitution up to the end of the Civil War. Now the legalist view, as we know, was that the thing was unchanged all the time. It assumes that either the secession view was there and right from the outset, or else the other conception was absolutely there and was right from the outset, and you get into all these interminable arguments which as matter of fact made up so much of the discussion before the Civil War as to what the constitution said on such a point. I do not pretend to speak with authority as a historian in this matter, but it seems to me fairly obvious that there were certain relations that were not definite all the time, for two reasons. It was partly that they were withheld voluntarily because if they were formulated it would make trouble and it was easier to withhold them; and partly because the problem itself had not come into existence enough so that any authoritative declaration of the exact rights of particular states and of the central government as such was called for, and that [our?] political history had been a continual evolution or bringing out into more definite explicit shape the forces which were at work there from the start, but which it was not possible or at the time seemed desirable to put into explicit shape. The growth, in other words, of constitutions, the growth of governments, the whole matter of evolution, becomes practically inexplicable on the conception which would identify sovereignty with that which is specifically formulated.

One more example illustrating the practical bearings of the thing, the question of international law and international relations. From one view, that of the formulated legal view, sovereignty is restricted to independent nationalities. On that point of view, international law is termed law only by courtesy. Austin would take that position. We call it law but it is not law in any sense at all, because it does not proceed from any definite superior, but means simply that nations agree on a moral basis to do things in a certain way. There is no wrong then, in the legal sense, in violating any one of these principles. As matter of fact the international relationships do have a very binding force on so-called independent isolated sovereignties. Of course there are various degrees of obligation. There are certain things that no nation would ever dream of violating; it subjects its action just as definitely as any individual subjects his action to the authority of the state.

Now if we take this working institutional conception of sovereignty, we

can only say that the larger evolution of sovereignty is going on and is finding its expression in these international relations. They are just as much expressions of the real sovereignty as the independent nationalities themselves
are. The nation becomes in turn an organ of sovereignty. The exact relation
of these various organs of sovereignty to each other still remains indefinite,
but that there is a movement toward a more specific and definite adjustment with reference to which the independent nations become cooperative
instruments of execution seems to me unquestionable. In any case it is
only on some such conception as that, of a larger sovereignty which is in
process of evolution, that we can put any political meaning into international law or international rights. Without that conception it would become simply a matter of courtesy.

This signifiies a further distinction with reference to the distinction between the positive and what is variously called the ideal and the natural,
or between the *de facto* and the *de jure,* not simply as relates to sovereignty,
but to law and rights. You will find in the various writers on the more
speculative aspects of jurisprudence discussions as to what the distinction
between positive law and natural or normal law is. I would apply the
distinction just made to the interpretation of these terms.

The positive or *de facto* is that which has been found useful, valuable
to formulate. That formulation is never anything final, it is always to
get a basis for further action, it is an inventory. We have to take a survey
of the existing situation and formulate it in order to get an idea of the
direction in which action is moving and consequently in the line in which
we shall direct our efforts profitably. So the *de facto* is not opposed to the
de jure.

On the other side, the so-called natural or ideal side of law would
consist in abstracting and making stand out the movement of social forces,
and putting that movement, for the sake of greater clearness, into contrast
with the attained conditions. That is, we view it as arrested, as if it were
fixed, as if there were an ultimate on one side. That is not the whole fact.
Society is really moving, the very fixing of it makes the line of movement
stand out more explicitly on the other side, and that becomes our ideal,
becomes the standard, the norm, with reference to which we judge the
availability of what we consider ourselves to have already reached.

In other words the political always involves a synthesis of what we
abstract, separate, in the legal and the moral. As I said before, the legal
is the formulated or objectified side of the political; and the moral, as
contrasted with the legal, represents a consciousness of what it is good
for, of the uses to which it may be put. In biological terms it is the relation
of structure to function. Function always gives the standard from which we
consider, criticize and test, structure. Structure is only for the sake of
function. Does it do what it purports to do? Does it really free movement
and facilitate it, or does it tend to obstruct, congest, or impoverish?

There is another sense in which the term natural has been used as distinct from the political, especially in connection with the term rights. Natural law and the law of nature are generally to be interpreted on the basis of the principle just suggested. For example, the formulation of a law of nature among the Romans as over against positive enactment was clearly the recognition of the social principles which would hold in the larger more comprehensive society that was coming into existence as contrasted with the previous local communities. The Romans had one set of laws, the Germans another, the Greeks another, the Egyptians another, and so on. As travel and intercourse increased, these people became acquainted with one another and had to have some principle of adjustment. The law of nature formed by the Romans was projected backward as if the principle had been uniform and recognized by all these people all the time. They said that was the law which was stamped by nature itself in men's minds, or from the teleological point of view by God Himself in men's mind; but that was simply reading backward what they needed for the future. This natural law was not really something which all these people had always recognized. It was simply the principle which they must now recognize in order that they might work harmoniously together, that this movement toward integration might continue. The real significance was in the stimulus that it gave to accelerate the breaking down of the barrier between the separated communities and the organization of a larger world state.

But if we turn to the term natural rights, we find that it has a different meaning, a new sense of the term nature comes into view. By the term natural rights has practically always been meant the rights which the individual had as an individual prior to any political organization and limiting conditions. It is a doctrine which has played a very large part in history since the sixteenth century. We find it in our own Declaration of Independence, in the so-called Bills of Right which precede a great number of the state constitutions; we find it expressly stated at the time of the French Revolution: the individual has a right to life, liberty, and the pursuit of happiness. These rights inhere in him before political society is organized, before there are any relations of superiority or inferiority, before the exercise of authority at all. And these inalienable rights which belong to the individual furnish the limits within which political activity must be confined. It must not do anything which will infringe on these natural rights of the individual. You find that doctrine of course in the war cry of the liberal democratic school in politics from the sixteenth century on. That was the war cry which met and conquered the doctrine of the divine right of kings on the other side.

Now we might argue that there are no such things as natural rights in that sense. The outcome of the whole previous discussion was that there was an could not be any individual prior to social organization. So "natural" as something which is prior to and which measures the conditions of the political must be rejected. Of course the conclusions of the historical school are just the same sort as are reached on the philosophical basis. We do not find historically any individuals preceding society; and the further we go back, the more the statement is true, the more we find a social aggregate, a collective state of things in which individuality is, relatively speaking, merged.

But the fact that this conception of natural rights has had so much practical power, that it has been an instrument, a most determining influence in modern movements, shows that there are practical realities latent there which are simply misinterpreted in this particular definition of the natural rights. And if we try to get hold of these realities, I think we get the same interpretation of "natural" here as applied to right that we had before as applied to law. It represents a consciousness, not of something which preceded political organization, but of the working tendency of political organization. It really represents the future. It was, as so frequently happens, simply turned around and applied to primitive historical conditions. It means virtually that the psycho-physical individual is the ultimate organ of sovereignty. The whole problem is the question of organization, of finding the various organs, and this war cry of inalienable natural rights of the free and independent individual means simply that the individual was coming to consciousness of himself as possessing new capacities and therefore demanding new spheres of exercise.

It is not surprising that the doctrine was first formulated in England, because we know it was on that basis the whole English development was carried on. The people did not say, these things are wrong and must be changed, but they threw them back into the past: We used to have such rights; the kings are trying to take them away from us, and we are simply preserving what has always belonged to us. Of course, there was a certain amount of truth in that, but literally speaking it was the truth of the spirit and not of the letter. They had always had certain principles of free action which implied the capacity of self-direction, self-control, and they felt that these things would be an infringement on the right of self-control. As matter of fact it was the new occasion which demanded new differentia of the powers of initiation. The natural right meant really the consciousness of progress, the consciousness of further development which seemed to be logically and legitimately away from the activities which had been exercised in the past. It recognized that the doctrine did stand for a great truth and therefore did accomplish a great deal.

It ought to be recognized also that it resulted in a great deal of harm. It taught that the presumption is always on the side of the individual, that the approach to association is secondary an relatively artificial, that the burden of proof is always on the individual side. The right of the individual to do as he pleases is the primary thing and anything else is restriction, limitation, or coercion for which some very ample justification must be found. Putting the same thing morally it resulted in an exaggerated sense of right against the sense of duty and threw the conception of right more or less out of focus. The real justification of the demand for right is that it is a necessary instrument for doing something else. It is necessary to further functioning. Justification is simply a means to [a] further end, and this isolation, this setting up of natural rights as an entity by itself, is responsible for transforming these rights from means into ends. Thus the democratic movement lost much of the ethical imputation which really belongs to it. It got an overindividualistic interpretation, and also an economic interpretation as against an ethical one. That is, it came to be a demand for comforts, for possessions, instead of for powers which were requisite for social development and progress.

SECTION 5. RIGHTS AND OBLIGATIONS

June 16, 1898

It has been assumed several times in what has been said that rights and obligations are the correlative phases of the manifestation of sovereignty, or they are the two forms in which political organization finds its expression. At this point that statement will have to be left for the most part as a simple empirical fact, but recourse to the theory of organization previously advanced will suffice to suggest its rational basis. Right represents the phases of organization which correspond to differentiation, or the movement toward individualization. Politically speaking it is the body of rights, the system of rights, which constitute the individual.

We might almost say the rights are the individual and the individual is the rights which he possesses. The responsibilities, the obligations, are the organization on the side of association, on the side of interaction. I tried to show before that the organization necessarily, as well as matter of historical fact, did involve those two sides of the evolution of the particular organ; the aspect of individualization, the reciprocal relations of stimulus and response in which a given organ stands to others, summed up under the term association or interaction.[5] The rights taken collectively give the political category, then, of freedom. The obligations taken together give the political category of responsibility.

More specifically, a right is the power of initiative and control in a sphere of action which is secured to the individual by the community, because of that individual's membership in the community. The definition, then, includes three points: first that it is the capacity of self-determination; secondly that that is guaranteed to the individual. It is not a mere desirable claim on the part of the individual, it is not, insofar as it is right, something that he can have if he can get it, but there is a certain security, definiteness, attaching to it. The community assumes responsibility when the individual has rights, to see that he has them really and not merely in name. Thirdly, the ground, the basis for the right being given to the individual—it is a fact of his social membership; that is, as it was said yesterday, the right is the definition of his function.

Perhaps no more need be said on that last point than was said yesterday in the criticism of the identification of natural rights with purely individualistic claims. It may be enough to recall that such an isolated individual is an historical nonentity; that even if he existed historically, he would be psychologically incapacitated, that he could not present ends to himself with reference to which he would conceive these claims in his rights, and that, politically speaking, such a conception would end only in fatality or in anarchy—that is, if rights were purely individualistic in their basis. The element of social guarantee, of assertion, becomes virtually inexplicable. If the right is individual, it would seem that it ought to be left to the right of the individual to enforce that right. Why should society interfere even to enforce the individual's claims? That has been the rock on which the individualistic school has split. If it has not led to anarchy, it at least has been at the expense of its consistency

The individualistic school has attempted to justify the action of government in enforcing the individual's rights. The justification has been sought in the negative statement that the individual has these rights subject only to his not using them so as to interfere with the equivalent exercise of the same rights on the part of others, and that therefore when one individual does use his powers so as to prevent someone else from using his, the government is called on to interfere. But the action of government is to be restricted to that minimum, and to that negative matter.

That, however, is simply stating the positive fact of association of community on its obverse side. Why should not the individual, if his rights are individual purely, interfere with the corresponding exercise on the part of others? Or putting the question in a better way: What does such a statement mean? What is the equivalent exercise of rights on the part of others? What is the basis on which you determine that the individual is infringing on this equivalency of those powers on the part of others? What is the basis on which you can get any other meaning into the terms powers, exercise, equivalent, excepting as you have in mind some sort of an organization in which these individuals are trying to play their part? If these were really so isolated as the theory sets out by supposing them to be, how would you get any basis for comparing these different powers and establishing anything like the legitimate use, or equivalency respecting one or the other? You would seem to be turned back to the position of Hobbes: everybody has a right to get everything he can get, if he can get it. The only test for power is power; the only test for the right is whether it can be exercised or not, and that is a purely physical question. If I can do a thing, that is proof that I can, and that I have a right to do it. If I appropriate one thousand acres of land to myself, upon what basis can it be said that I am interfering with equivalent rights on the part of somebody else? He had the same chance I did and he did not do it. If he did not, it is because he could not, and he can do something else. That is the only logical conclusion that I can see, unless you put in there some common end, some binding relationship from which you criticize the real operations of the different individuals, and the individuals have presupposed some such end and community of interest.

More technically, the difficulty which the individualistic school could not get over is the origin of government at all. It has used the contract theory in one form or another to account for calling the government into existence. But aside from the historical objection to the compact or contract theory, there is the point that the contract implies *already* social relationships. This very act of agreeing, this act of consent could not have any binding force unless it were simply the enactment of a real consensus of the underlying purpose and interest which found expression. Contract is a significant thing if you assume a working organization somewhat incoherent, which is seeking through the medium of mutual discussion of interest and a final reciprocal conclusion to formulate itself in more specific and definite ways.

There is a sense in which modern governments may be said, with some show of historical truth, to rest on the consent of the governed, to be in that sense the outgrowth of contract. But that simply means that in the determination of the form of government existing social organization has found it more and more expedient and possible to make provision for utilizing the interests and intentions of the individual. It is simply a way of saying that the individual, as such, is operating more and more as the organ of sovereignty, with reference to which the activities of other organs have to be interpreted.

But of course that conception of the individual operating as the active instrument of social organization is just the reverse of the conception of the individual acting as an individual prior to the social organization, and then the different nonsocial individuals proceed to evolve somehow the social conditions. The contradiction comes out in Hobbes in relation to this fact. Why should the individual yield unrestricted obedience to the sovereign after it has come into existence? Before that he had a natural claim to everything. After the state comes into existence he has no naural claims to anything, he simply has the duty of obedience. The enactments of the state are morality. Why should not the individual, when he feels like it, have recourse to the state of nature? Why should he not resolve himself into his previous conditions? Why should he not secede, in other words? As long as he stays in the state, he is bound to obey it; but let him go back to the state of nature where there are no obligations. Hobbes says there are, after all, natural obligations—obligations to keep your promises, to seek your own happiness and security—and since the state is the necessary instrument of securing your own happiness and security, you are bound to stick to it.

Rousseau states the problem from the other end in this way: The problem is to find a condition of affairs where the powers of each shall be reinforced by the powers of all without any abridgment of his natural powers. But after [that] the state is called into existence, after [that] you get this general will which is operative and with reference to which the individual has no more power virtually than he had in Hobbes's scheme. The absolute form under the French Revolution (the Committee of Safety) was not only logical but was the conscious outgrowth of Rousseau's conception of the general will and of the subordination of the individual to it.

The liberal school, says Locke, represents an attempt at compromise. Various individuals do find that they have certain interests in common and that they are very important, and they voluntarily agree to restrict certain privileges for the sake of being more secure with reference to these common interests. A says, for example, I will give up the right to N, and B says that he will give up the right to M, in order that we may all enjoy the rights A, B, C, D, F. The individual voluntarily agrees to restrict his own freedom and that is the origin of government. But that involves again putting in the conception of a common interest as being already there and as being really the criterion with reference to which the value of individual interests is determined.

The second point mentioned, the securing to the individual of the exercise of his rights by society, is simply the realization of this fact that we have already considered, that the right is grounded in social membership. It is simply making overt, making objective, that relationship. Society, in other words, is looking after itself, its own interests in guaranteeing rights, because the political individual as such, who finds embodiment in rights, is a social organ. It is simply the care of the organism for its own organs. It cannot be an organization excepting in and through its members and that particular expression of itself is the right. It is implying more separation than there is to say it is the basis of the right, it is the right itself. The first point simply characterizes the nature of any right more explicitly. In the psychical statement it always reduces itself to capacity to initiate and to direct a given line of action.

There are certain general classifications of rights which you find in books of jurisprudence, which may be referred to here. Their interpretation will, perhaps, bring out the general point.

One of the oldest classifications, coming down from Roman law, is expressed clumsily by the terms rights of persons and rights of things. It is clumsy because there is no such thing as rights of things at all; rights are of necessity rights of persons. What is meant by rights of persons is rights which depend upon status. If you take the feudal times it is obvious that before you could tell what an individual's rights were you had first to characterize very specifically his station, and you had a number of gradations of station, and the rights would vary all along. In modern times with the democratic movement these distinctions have been swept away. There are still distinctions between man and woman, between the unmarried and the married woman, and so far as rights are determined by such considerations as these they are rights of persons. Rights of things, rights over things, are virtually rights of control of inanimate objects. Now the philosophical value of that distinction may be stated in this way: in a certain state of political progress, power of nature is dependent upon a given fixed status. As society advances, the relationship is reversed and status is determined virtually by function. That is, each individual status does not cease; in one sense it becomes generalized. Everybody of age has his own status, he has his own particular social locus; and that is virtually dependent upon the way in which he can control his environment, or it is dependent upon the way in which he can utilize his environment.

At least the only point that I would call to your attention there is the changed significance of the meaning of social status from something fixed as predetermined action to something movable and dynamic, which is really simply the summing up of the powers of action.

The second great distinction which has been made in jurisprudence is that of rights *in rem* and rights *in personam*. The terminology again is awkward because the rights *in rem* would seem to be the same rights over things. In reality it means the right which holds as against everybody. A right *in personam* is a right which holds only against some certain person. Property right is a case of a right *in rem*. I do not exercise it with reference to one person more than with reference to anybody else. It holds absolutely and indifferently. Rights that arise out of contract or out of the marriage relationship are rights *in personam*. If you make a contract with a person, you have certain rights, but you can enforce them only with reference to that particular person. You cannot compel somebody else to do this particular thing.

Now the philosophic significance of that would come out by observing that the rights which are held against everybody can be stated only in a negative form. Rights *in personam* may be stated in a positive form. A general property right can only be stated in this way: that nobody else can interfere with you. You can say just what you are going to do with your property. The right *in personam* is a right to a specific matter which can be stated positively. Somebody must deliver a certain amount of goods, pay me a certain amount of money at a certain date, or render some sort of effective service to me. The rights *in rem,* then, are simply highly generalized statements in the abstract, while the right *in personam* is the right in its concrete expression. Rights *in rem* are the conditions, really, of concrete exercise of rights. When anything is actually done, it must be done by some particular person in a particular way and at some particular time. The abstract right to property is a pro condition of any effective use of property, but after all it does not insure that I have any property. I may be utterly poverty stricken and still I have that right. But if some right *in personam* came in question, it would simply mean that that possible right, that abstract right, was being realized and was operative.

Again then, the right *in personam* arises through the operation of an abstract right *in rem*. The moment a person begins to use his property, he assumes virtual obligations to others which can be enforced. If you offer a given thing for sale that carries with it legally certain obligations, you have virtually entered into a contract with the person to whom to sell that thing. If you start out in business as a doctor you make virtual contracts with any persons who engage your services. They get a definite right which they can enforce against you. But if we connect this with the previous statements, we find that those considerations during the Middle Ages which were largely determined by status are now determined by contract, that there is a tendency for social relationships to take on themselves the form either of virtual or implied contract.

Take the old dispute as to whether marriage is or is not a contract. Thus the argument for marriage as being a contract means that it arises through the voluntary assent of two persons with reference to an end which they have in common. Those who object to calling marriage a contract mean that the substance of the marriage relationship cannot be reduced to a mere exchange of personal services, that there are deeper relationships involved than could be found in the statement that A would give B certain things and that B would give A certain things. It seems to me that what holds there quite clearly is also true of all social arrangement. The right *in personam* is the growing individualized form which abstract rights take to themselves in becoming operative.

Another distinction is that between antecedent or remedial rights. It is a commonplace of law that no right is really a right unless it carries with it some means of enforcement. Theoretically, by the common law a wife has had a right for a good while to certain support from her husband. As a matter of fact that right has been inoperative because no procedure was set up by which it could be carried into effect. The remedial right simply means, then, the definite social procedure to which recourse can be had in order to carry out the antecedent right. It is the difference between a nominal and an effective right.

The laissez-faire school has objected to making many things matter of statutory enactment on the grounds that they would better be made matters of contract. That school objected in England to the compulsory provision in factories of certain safeguards of life. They said: The individual is a free being and he can refuse to work there unless he chooses. Let that be a matter of free contract between him and his employer.

After the object of such legislation has been gained, that type of objection has much force, but it does not have until that time. The individual who could easily, naturally, make contracts on that basis would not of course be in need of legislation. But the fact that all the time there are many rights which are nominal but of which the social conditions do not at the time provide active means for realization; and the significance of bringing these matters under express legislation is that it does prevent just that recourse to a specific mode of procedure by which the individual can make his professed right an actuality.

It is not really a question of the enlargement of the function of government. That is merely an incidental aspect of it. The real problem in these cases is the one of expediency as regards the securing of means for making a nominal right effective. The individual already has a nominal right to life and to an unhampered use of his own body. How shall that right be made effective? If it cannot be made effective by contract, then the presumption is there; but that it can be nominally made effective by contract is no guarantee that it can be actually made so effective. It is obvious that there are such contradictions all the time in society. Every individual has a nominal right to life, to liberty. But if that were realized, he would have all possible rights. There is no right you could not put under that head of the right of life and liberty. But as time goes on it is found that the individual's possession of such a right is only partial, and hence the necessity of the evolution of further rights involving recourse to definite modes of procedure which shall make the previously assumed rights valid.

For example, referring to international relationships, until international rights are secured, the person has no right to his own life. As long as nations are likely to go to war over the individual's disposal of his body is limited by that fact. He is likely to have to go to war and be maimed or killed. The development of international relations is only making explicit what is implied in the most positive and simplest form of right, the right to control body and limb.

The fourth great classification of rights has been into *private* and *public*. The right to make contracts and insist on enforcement would be private. The right to vote, to hold office, and so on would be public rights. Now that distinction, while its practical worth is obvious without any argument, cannot be interpreted theoretically to mean there is a fixed limit between private and public rights; that takes us back again into the old individualistic philosophy of society as a late arrangement growing out of purely individual considerations. What it means, I think, is definitely indicated by the brief discussion that I gave the other day of the place and nature of government. Taken in connection with what has just been said about the distinction between the nominal or professed and actual or operative rights, all rights are public in the sense that they have a social genesis, social conditions and a social function. The right to property is in that sense just as much a public right as is the right to vote. The ultimate object of both is exactly alike, in order to make the individual operative on one side and social values available to the individual on the other side. As matter of fact the individual has been found not to be able to make effective his assumed right to property unless he has his hand to a certain extent on the machinery of government. As I said the other day, the government is a particular organ through which the adjustment of the other organs is made, and the public right means that the individual can direct his powers with reference to the particular center from which the other adjustments proceed.

You have only to think of English history to see to what a tremendous extent that principle has operated there. The individual has increased his political power all the time as a better means of protection and of utilization for his previously assumed rights to life and to the accumulation and use of property. The development of representative government in England would not be applicable at all if it were not for the assertion of these personal rights by the individual. In other words, we have here simply a working illustration of the impossibility of separating the two: the so-called private and the so-called public. The public is necessary as the guarantee and assurance of the private; and on the other side as the individual has the capacity to make these initiations with reference to his own body and with reference to property, he of necessity demands, insists upon having more to say about the immediate control of the governmental power itself. The democratic movement politically can be treated from this point of view as the absolutely necessary expression of the organic character of all rights. That is the way in which they all depend on each other and act in each other.

It has been a dream, of course, of thinkers of the aristocratic type in politics (Plato, for example) of rights which would be guaranteed to the individual from above by those wisest and most competent. Here is the situation. A should have rights of controlling his own body, of property, pursuit of happiness, guaranteed to him by the governing class outside of himself. That theoretical dualism has proved practically untenable, and the democratic movement is the objective demonstration of the impossibility of any such arrangement. As matter of simple historical fact the individual cannot get these more simple and rudimentary rights secured to him from any source which is extrinsic to himself. He must have his own finger in the pie to be sure that it is parcelled out rightly; and that fact is not a mere economic fact, it is an ethical fact. It is simply evidence that society is a community, it is organic, and its interests are all bound up together. You cannot set one set here and another somewhere else and then get the working relation between the two.

June 20, 1898

As I said the other day rights and obligations are to be considered as the counterpart of structure and function, biologically. The rights are the conditions which are requisite for complete action, and the obligations, the duties, are simply the abstraction of the various modes of operation involved in this complete function. One has rights in order that he may fulfill his duties, and the motive which has prompted the continual expansion of rights has been at bottom the sense of the growing opportunities of life, the growing demands of life, the enlargement of the range and content of action, and consequently the necessity of securing to the agents of action more secure hold of their possession of the instrumentalities of action and a wider and more adequate accessibility to the materials and the methods which were necessary for the effective fulfillment of life. The rights from that basis are simply the specification or the unfolding of the nature of the individual. Rights are the various specified directions in which the individual finds himself, in which he finds realization, in which he comes to be truly an individual, and not merely a physical individual.

SECTION 6. LIBERTY, EQUALITY, AND FRATERNITY AS EXPRESSIONS OF THE MODERN DEMOCRATIC IDEAL

If we take the motto of the French Revolution—liberty, equality, and fraternity—as expressing in a general way the modern democratic ideal, the conception of liberty is of course simply the conception of individuality brought to definite consciousness. It is the assertion of rights, and that generalized assertion of rights is simply self-consciousness on the part of the individual, of himself. It is not that there is first an individual and then after that he is to be free and have liberty, but the conscious individual is simply in liberty; that is, the individual is to be defined in terms of power of initiative and power of controlling action through the medium of deliberation: initiative as opposed to taking things on authority under somebody else's control, and deliberation as opposed to custom, which of course simply as custom always takes the form of authority in relation to the individual.

Fraternity represents the side of association, the side of the function of active relationships. It is the statement of the unity of interaction which is a correlate of the differentiating principle which is registered under the title of liberty.

Equality represents naturally the mean term. It is, so to speak, society, stated in terms of the individual, or the individual stated in terms of association, relationships. Given liberty then, and you would not necessarily have equality, because if the conception of freedom is isolated, or the conception of individuals is isolated, you get no criterion to determine the direction of it, you get no limit. If you have fraternity as an ideal which is generalized, that becomes the interpreting principle which really defines the liberty. If then you have liberty operating, or individuality operating in and for the end of the common interest, the common values, then of necessity you have this further conception, this intermediate conception of equality.

And that gives, it seems to me, the content to that conception: not as is asserted to be by its followers and its opponents, a declaration that all men have just the same intellectual and moral powers, that they are all on exactly the same footing as to their structure and as to their attainments. That idea of course is an impossible idea. It is negated by the very conception of individuality, of liberty, which makes impossible any such quantitative interpretation of the idea of equality by nature. The phrase "all equal before the law" is part of the idea that all individuals shall have the same sort of treatment, equitable consideration, from the legal authority, and all should have equal claims to redress of wrongs; but if the other conception of equality is altogether to undefined and vague in scope, then equality before the law is too restricted.

The equality is simply equality with reference to the opportunity of each to be himself, not that he should have the same amount of property, or the same privileges, or the same recognition in a quantitative state from society, as everybody else has, any more than he should have exactly the same amount of physical strength, or be so many inches high the same as everybody else; but that liberty is a fraternity. That is, it is an association based on the common good. Each individual would of necessity be provided with whatever is necessary for his realization, for his development, whatever is necessary to develop him to enable him to function adequately.

The principle there, instead of being a quantitative one, is essentially a qualitative one. Instead of being a leveling idea, reducing things to a monotony in which all distinction is swallowed up, it is a differentiating principle ultimately. It is no object for one to be like somebody else. What everybody wants to be, at bottom, is himself, that particular differentiation of energy and of consciousness; but he does require, in order that he may actually function his whole intrinsic capacity, to show himself actively as he is. He must have certain opportunities provided for him. He must have just the same provision made, the same equipment for enabling him to get all that is in him, that anybody else has.

Of course then the limit of what it supplies to the individual can only be stated in general terms, but the principle is there: whatever is necessary to enable him to put his powers thoroughly at the service of society. There would still be a distinction between rich and poor, just as between those who are more intellectually gifted and those less so; but the poorest would not be poor in one sense, quantitatively that is, as compared with somebody else on the basis of an adequate unit, but qualitatively in the sense that he should be deprived of whatever was necessary for him to get for himself and to give to society the full benefit of what is in him. The same way about political offices. It would not follow that all these things must be passed around, but that each individual should have the same opportunity, the same accessibility to them, the determining principle simply being whether that is necessary for him in his own movement toward self-realization and toward functioning in the interests of the whole.

SECTION 7. ANARCHISM
AND SOCIALISM

I think perhaps this would be as good a place as any to say a few words on the imposed ideals of socialism and anarchism, using anarchism, not in its popular scarecrow sense, but as the philosophical equivalent of thorough-going individualism, the theory which holds that state activity is essentially restrictive and negative, and that the problem is to make all social arrange-ments imply the free and voluntary determination of the individuals con-cerned. The essence of the individualists's position on the philosophical side is that there are certain intrinsic laws which control society, just as there are physical laws; that legislative enactments on the contrary are al-most certain to be arbitrary and therefore confusing; that the less there is of that element, the more likely the internal regulating principles are to show themselves and to compel the individuals to live in conformity with them: so hands are to be kept off in order that these intrinsic qualities in the natures of individuals may come out and show themselves, so that social arrangements shall be simply the natural and spontaneous adjustment of those forces. You might let society go the way it will and not legislate for this, that, and the other thing in society any more than you would attempt to lay down from the outside how a tree shall grow.

Now the contradiction in the extreme individualistic position comes out in the fact that all excepting the absolutely most extreme ones hold that the state is to have the power to secure life and rights; in other words, the in-dividual must be negatively secure against violation of his individuality on the part of others.

I suggested the other day that all rights, because on one hand they grow out of a unified personality and on the other hand refer to a unified society, are so interdependent that no fixed separation can be made between them. Now here is an attempt to set off certain rights within certain limits just because of their interorganic dependence. The limits of these things are purely working limits, they vary from age to age and from country to coun-try.

As a matter of practical politics I doubt if there are any proposals of the extreme socialists which might not be debated from this point of view: Are they, or are they not, necessary to the adequate securing to the individ-ual of his rights to life and his rights to property, that is, to sufficient con-trol over the environment? The socialist must argue for complete collectiv-ism, that that is the only sure way for the individual as an individual to really get a free life, and to get a property right which is anything more than in the merely legal sense. Rights to life and rights to property are so related that they practically cover the whole sphere of action. The right to life might be said, stated psychologically, to be the organism or the subject; the right to property is the statement of the function on the side of the rela-tion to the environment. When you have activity stated on the two sides, you have practically made provision for everything.

The confusion which underlies the anarchistic conception is that be-tween the real and the nominal, between the positive and the negative. An individual does not have the right to life simply because it is laid down in the statutes that he has such a right; it is a matter of conditions, relationships. There is no such thing as a purely abstract capacity of power, it is a question of what anybody can really do. It is a question of where he is, what his position is and what the conditions are in which he is placed. And to secure the active enforcement, operation, of that positive power or capacity may involve, theoretically, almost any amount of governmental action. The socialist always claims that his collectivism is simply a means, that it is not an end in itself, that all he is concerned in is the fullest and freest living on the part of all individuals; and that existing arrangements are so practically inequitable, and so restrictive, so inhibitory upon the average individual that our present individualism is not real.

Now the socialist on the other hand (using this term in a very broad sense as antithetical to the unrestricted [anarchist's] individualism) finds its [sic] contradiction in precisely this assertion of collectivism as the means by which to secure individualism as the end. The popular objection against socialism is that it involves a certain element of slavery, a certain suppression of individual initiative and capacity; and that in shutting out competition the motives which stimulate and appeal to the play of individuals and the development of their particular powers has its basis in the recognition of precisely this contradiction. So far as the individualist is to be the end, he must be the means also. You cannot supply an individual with his development; the very nature of his individuality is that he must work the thing out for himself, and that shall involve experimentation, shall involve that certain limits are not well defined. He is to have an opportunity to try for himself and see what he can do; and the responsibility for the control is to be found, not in any outside organized agency, but in his own rational processes, in his own powers of deliberation.

These two schools, in other words, represent the abstractions of the two factors which are necessarily involved in social activity. Each recognizes these two factors but does not put them in organic relationship to each other. Individualism says that government is a mere external scheme. Society is a mere arrangement for developing the welfare of the individual. Now socialism at bottom would be the same logic. It insists much more on the importance of association, on the importance of community, but at the same time the very fact that it is compelled to set up a particular agency which is the special representative of society, the fact that it has to make a distinct entity out of what it calls the state, shows that it has the same dualism at bottom between society and the individual.

As I said the other day, if society is really an organism it must carry its operating and controlling principles in its own functioning. The progress of social life itself must be the chief instrument for the realization of desirable ends and for reform; and to single out some special agency, to suppose that property relations, that business, for instance, commerce, has simply an evil and individualistic tendency and that evil tendency must be held in check by another power, the state, which alone makes for justice, is to say that there is a fundamental split between the nature of individuals and the requirements of association. There is a split between liberty and fraternity and you must bring in this outside power to bridge the gap or minimize its evil results.

Putting the proposition in more concrete terms, it is that the question of the range of governmental action is always of details, and the error of both [socialists and anarchists] is that they attempt to defend it on some purely general principle. There is nothing which it is intrinsically desirable for government to do and there is nothing intrinsically which it is not desirable for it to do under certain circumstances; it is simply a question of what the facts of the case are. As a matter of fact will it be more expedient to do it in this way or in that way? Such questions cannot be argued at large. It is simply noting the actual circumstances that enter in and what the forces at work are. That has been the historical solution found by the practical man. However much as a theorist one has inclined to the side of individualism or socialism, certainly upon the whole up to the present time all these questions have been decided on an opportunist basis. Under certain conditions a great deal of governmental action would be called for without being interference, and at other times very little of it would be called for. The presumption and burden of proof would simply shift from time to time according to the conditions involved. The only things that remain permanent are the general ends: the movement toward individualization on one hand and toward association on the other.

SECTION 8. A CLASSIFICATION OF RIGHTS AND DUTIES

I will now give very briefly a suggestion of a scheme for classification of rights and duties.

1. Right to life
2. Right to property
3. Right to expression

The basis underlying the whole scheme is that all rights are to be treated as phases of the development of social consciousness, or phases of the social will. What we are studying is the development of will, and that will can be defined only as the combination of force or means, and end or ideal. It is like the organic relations of mind and body. The two must go together. There is not a split between the individual's brain and muscles. So in the social region there is a social relationship between the idea and the control of nature, the possession of the force which is requisite to realize that end.

The right to life represents the end in its broadest and most indefinite forms. You cannot give any particular content to life. On the side of means, however, you can state the content very specifically. It is the control of the body as an organism and the protection of that body from all the influences which tend to destroy it, or in any way to weaken it. So of course, as a matter of fact, the rights of life are stated on the side of means. You must not kill a person, must not maim or wound him, must not maintain nuisances that are obviously detrimental to his health; and in the modern expression of that idea, society is responsible for the hygienic well being of individuals, that work shall be done under certain conditions of healthfulness. The peculiarity of the rights that are actually put legally under the head of rights to life is that they are so very indefinite on the side of the end involved, while they are narrow on the side of means. Life is treated as if it were merely a physical thing. The more we know of psychology and physiology, the more these two things shade into each other.

I referred the other day to the fact that so much of our important knowledge has not affected the popular consciousness at all. So here the brain is a part of the physical body, and in the long run it must be seen that a healthy free brain is necessary to life, as necessary as the more obvious control of the body, the hands, legs, and arms is. When that fact is once realized, that the brain is really a part of the body and is the organic instrument of thinking, the most immediate tool of the spiritual life, necessarily the content of what is put under what an individual has a right to claim as part of human life must be broadened. For instance, education now is referred to some other right, the right to participate in political life. But if we knew more of psychology and physiology we should know that the right of education is the right of his own body. The individual in the long run cannot really control his muscles and movements excepting as he develops and educates his brain.

The right to property represents the right to life through the environment; it is the will expressing itself. We cannot talk about the body isolated from other natural conditions and forces. It is always in an environment, and right to property is the explicit recognition of this relationship. It simply makes overt the interdependence of organism and environment in the life process. The right of property in essence is the capacity to embody an idea in material form. The essence of property is that it is such a projection, such a realization of a purpose in concrete form, in terms of energy and motion. That general idea would be more specific by referring to what was said about the whole economic process as a process of the liberation of the forces of nature.

Under the third head, rights to expression (which is not a technical legal term), I mean what is ordinarily termed the rights of conscience, rights of communication, the right of the individual to choose his own form of religion, the right to free speech, free thought. You see that is simply a continuation of the same general principle. We may have an idea embodied in material form and it may be so thoroughly embodied that it is lost, it is swamped, the psychical meaning in which it is wrapped up, the thought, does not come out. If you idealize that thought element, make it more flexible, less tied up to the material form, if you give it range, if you consider it as embodied in movement, instead of simply matter, you get this conception of the right of the individual to himself on the side of the determination, expression, communication of his own ideals and purposes.

The history of the fight for these rights has never been written, so far as I know, but anyone with a passing acquaintance with modern, especially English and French history, knows what a tremendous struggle it was to get the right to conscience and the right of free speech. It is a thing which now we practically take for granted. Occasionally thumbscrews are put on individuals, but in a general way it is a right which is generally recognized in the abstract as the right to life. And yet that conscious recognition of it is only a few hundred years old. It was recognized in Athens, but there only for free citizens and in a limited area. Now, in theory, it is a right which the individual as an individual can claim. It involves a complete reconstruction of governmental methods. The right to life or the right to property are, relatively speaking, physical rights. They become spiritualized, ethical, when they pass over into the right of the individual to make himself valid on the side of his power to objectify and communicate to the consciousness of others his own particular interpretation of life.

Just as the first class defined rights to the individual, the second class would define them more distinctly with reference to association. Under the first we would have the rights which an individual has as a natural member of any institution. I do not know any word that expresses it very well and will say "rights of status." The moment an infant is born into the world it has rights as a member of the family. There are certain claims which can be made on behalf of it, if not consciously for itself. But it is because it is already a member of the social institution. Parents have certain definite obligations by the very fact that the child is born. The fact that he is a member of the community gives him certain claims. It is the counterpart of rights to life, it is taking it on the social side. What discriminates it from the other two is that it is essentially a natural relationship, not dependent upon what the individual has previously done, but upon the mere fact that he is there.

As volition enters in, we have contract, which represents an idea becoming consciously adopted by two different individuals and each specializing the performance of a certain part with reference to that common end. It involves the principle of exchange. A will do something for B on condition that B does something for A—a recognition that there is a common element on which they can serve each other. It is the recognition of mutuality of interest in its mechanical form, rather than in the organic form. It would be the counterpart of property on the more individualistic side. It is an immediate and somewhat mechanical relationship.

Then we have the rights of voluntary association, the difference here being, of course, that the relations into which the individual enters are larger than those entered into by contract. The nature of contract is that it should be specific. These voluntary associations have so much more range and content that they cannot be brought down to any such limits. A free family life, a family life which individuals determine for themselves instead of being determined by society or by the parents, trades unions, churches, etc., would be examples of these voluntary associations. We forget what a very large part these voluntary associations have played in social evolution. I may underestimate the part played relatively by government, but it seems to me, as between the two, these voluntary associations have been much greater determining elements than anything which the government has done. The part played by trades unions, for example, where there was a great struggle for the right of association on the basis of interest in labor and to get the right of free expression—but after that right is once recognized, you have a new social instrumentality, a new organ for arriving at decisions and for putting these decisions in execution.

The third class are what are ordinarily put under the head of strictly political or public rights: the right of the individual to determine the sovereign, to actively participate in the direction of the social movement, and to do it in overt ways. According to the principle already laid down, this third class cannot be marked off rigidly from the others. When the individual exercises any of his so-called personal rights or any rights of association, he is virtually becoming an element of sovereignty, he is deciding what the future society will be, but not at the most overt point. And the political rights are the rights to exercise direction at points where the strain is obvious and where the application of force is also obvious. The right to vote, the right to hold office, of course would be examples of these public or political rights. I hope the point is clear why I mark them as the third class: not that they are different in principle but they make the principle which is implicit in the others, the active relationship of the individual to the social movement, explicit. They provide a definite external mode of expression for it. They supply the particular outlet or channel instead of having to make itself felt in more indirect ways. I call attention again to the fact that they must all be treated as interdependent.

The great legal vice, or the vice of the legal mind, is to attempt to make such a classification into a hierarchical order, to make it into a static arrangement where each set of rights is isolated, pigeonholed and labeled by itself. The element of definition is very valuable, it is important, but that is only one side of it. There is the interaction side as well as the side of definition. The social movement is going on and hence the exact definition of any one of these is simply a working device; and when this tendency to fix the classification and make it rigid becomes uppermost, then we get sheer abstraction. The rights are found only as there is movement, and there is continual change involved there. Because of this interaction, when one right, say, that of voluntary association, changes, the right to life gets a new import also. That is most clear in the case of political life. Why do various classes demand suffrage? Why do women want the suffrage? It is practically because of the reaction that it has on the other classes of rights.

They are moving, and to get hold of these rights means a modification all along the line.

SECTION 9. THE DEVELOPMENT OF RIGHTS THROUGH TENSION

Following out the same idea, we have the principle for the development of rights. The development is through conflict, through tensions. The right to life and the right to property come into conflict with each other in these present formulated modes of exercise. Harmonization must be effected, and that involves a modification of both.

Take one example, the laws relating to factories, compelling certain guards to be put around machinery in motion to protect the life of employees, laws enforcing proper conditions of ventilation, those which give the employee the right to compensation in case of injury. Historically these have been urged by certain schools, all socialistic at bottom. They are simply questions of conflict between two sets of existing rights. Here is the right of life on one side in the case of the employee and on the other the right of property in the case of the employer. If you take either of the two points of view as ultimate, you will get a very different interpretation. One school virtually has taken the ground that the individual should have the right of his own life. Another opposed to it asserts the right of property, that a man has the right to arrange his property as he pleases and if the person does not want to work for him he need not. There is a form of right worked out under certain social conditions and certain political conditions. Those conditions have changed and these rights are now at cross-purposes with each other. So some new legislation comes in which practically has put new content into both the right to life and the right to property, and has given them a new significance.

Personally I believe that most of the practical political questions that come up of any large nature can be most effectively considered from the standpoint of conflict of rights involved there. It is not that one side is right and another wrong, but that in the given historical environment certain modes of operation were set in motion which met the need of that environment and that the two things get into balance. But in a change of environment they are likely to get at cross-purposes to each other, and a system must be effected which involves a change in both, and it is in that way that the active, living development of rights is kept up.

Take one example with reference to the right of life, the movement for the abolition of slavery. Where did the consciousness on the part of the individual come from? How does it happen that at some times people will put up with slavery and sometimes will not? It is a matter of consciousness. When it is recognized as slavery then people begin to object. People are slaves only so long as they don't know that they are slaves. What is it that causes that change in the consciousness so that they begin to conceive themselves as slaves and to think of themselves and of their rights in a different way? It is simply because there is always a certain amount of function which the individual has and exercises, and as society develops, as the function of the government becomes increased, the significance of what he is doing comes home to him. The individual sees what is involved in what he is doing and he makes a demand that the thing which is involved shall become explicit, recognized and appreciated by all.

You can transfer that from the slave to the labor question at present. What is it that makes the labor question on the conscious side? Why is it putting forth claims and agitating in certain directions? Simply because in the industrial function previously exercised, certain relations were involved which are now being evolved in consciousness. The significance of the function of work is coming to consciousness. Because of the changed conditions under which it is operating, it ceases to be a customary, physical thing, and appears as a psychical thing which shows itself in certain demands. You cannot treat it as simply a revolt against wrong which superior force has imposed on the laboring class. Neither can you dispose of it as an outbreak of unregulated feeling and impulse and ambition, a sort of disease which a certain social section has become possessed of at a certain time. It has to be treated from the standpoint of the evolution of social consciousness as a whole, bringing out in a psychical way the powers and the relations which previously had been latent, that coming to consciousness involving a readjustment in action. That is the principle which has been insisted on all the time, that that coming to consciousness and readjustment in action are two statements of the same thing.

NOTES

1. John Austin, *Lectures on Jurisprudence; or, The Philosophy of Positive Law* (2 vols.; London: J. Murray, 1869).
2. Green, *Lectures on the Principles of Political Obligation*, Secs. 32–79.
3. William MacKintire Salter, *Anarchy or Government, An Inquiry in Fundamental Politics* (New York: T. Y. Crowell and Co., 1895).
4. *Supra*, pp. 229–35.
5. *Supra*, Chap. 4, Sec. 1.

SELECTED BIBLIOGRAPHY

ADDAMS, JANE. *Democracy and Social Ethics*. New York: The Macmillan Co., 1902.

Virtually a companion volume to Dewey's 1898 *Lectures on Political Ethics*. More practical in orientation.

ALEXANDER, SAMUEL. *Moral Order and Progress, an Analysis of Ethical Conceptions*. London: Trübner and Co., 1889.

A sophisticated formulation of the naturalist standpoint, and a strong influence on Dewey.

AUSTIN, JOHN. *Lectures on Jurisprudence, or The Philosophy of Positive Law*, 3rd. ed. London: John Murray, 1869.

A key element in Austin's theory of sovereignty that was retained by Dewey is the requirement that sovereignty always be specific, actual.

BAGEHOT, WALTER. *Physics and Politics*. Boston: Beacon Press, 1956.

One of the earliest (1867) applications of Darwin to political theory. The emphasis on government by discussion may have influenced Dewey.

BOYDSTON, JO ANN (ed.). *Guide to the Works of John Dewey*. Carbondale and Edwardsville, Ill.: Southern Illinois University Press, 1970.

The most complete Dewey bibliography, with helpful introductory essays on various aspects of his thought.

DARWIN, CHARLES. *The Descent of Man,* new ed. New York: D. Appleton and Co., 1890.

More important for its influence on Dewey's methodology than for its substantive conclusions.

DEWEY, JOHN. *The Early Works*. 5 vols. Carbondale and Edwardsville, Ill.: Southern Illinois University Press, 1967–1972.

The standard edition of Dewey's published writings during the period 1882–1898.

———. *Freedom and Culture*. New York: G. P. Putnam's Sons, 1939.

Dewey's final and one of his most interesting works in social philosophy.

———. *The Public and Its Problems*. New York: Henry Holt and Co., 1927.

Stresses the location of a "public" or group suffering from the indirect consequences of social activity as the essential factor in furthering political change.

451

GREEN, THOMAS HILL. *Lectures on the Principles of Political Obligation,* reprinted from Green's *Philosophical Works,* Vol. II. London and New York: Longmans, Green, 1941, 1950.

The model for Dewey's early, idealist-oriented, political theory.

———. *Prolegomena to Ethics,* 2nd. ed. Oxford, Eng.: The Clarendon Press, 1884.

Posits a strict dichotomy between the natural and the moral. Dewey's ethical naturalism grew out of his criticism of Green on this point.

HEGEL, G. W. F. *The Philosophy of Right,* trans. and ed. T. M. KNOX. Oxford, Eng.: Oxford University Press, 1942.

Grandfather of the Deweyan approach to moral and social philosophy.

HOFSTADER, RICHARD. *Social Darwinism in American Thought,* rev. ed. Boston: Beacon Press, 1955.

The classic study of the impact of Darwinism in America and the reaction of American social thinkers to it.

JAMES, WILLIAM. *The Principles of Psychology.* 2 vols. New York: Henry Holt and Co., 1890.

The major influence in Dewey's development of his functionally oriented, naturalistic psychology.

MEAD, GEORGE HERBERT. *Mind, Self, and Society, from the Standpoint of a Social Behaviorist.* Chicago: The University of Chicago Press, 1934.

A major work by Dewey's colleague at Chicago, well worth comparing with the 1898 lectures.

RUCKER, DARNELL. *The Chicago Pragmatists.* Minneapolis: University of Minnesota Press, 1969.

The intellectual and social background during Dewey's Chicago years.

SPENCER, HERBERT. *First Principles.* New York: D. Appleton and Co., 1888.

The preface contains the complete program of Spencer's "Synthetic Philosophy." Dewey said of Spencer that his system *"seems* to fix the limits of all further effort, to define its aims and to assign its methods. But this is an illusion of the moment. In reality this wholesale disposal of material clears the ground for new, untried initiatives" ("Herbert Spencer," in Dewey's *Characters and Events* [New York: Henry Holt and Co., 1929], I, 60).

INDEX

INDEX

the biological process, 253–54, 387–88; expresses fundamental relationship between man and nature, 345; concerns evolution of value, 383, 387; supply-demand defined biologically, 388–89; price as a measure of value, 397–99; labor theory of value, 399–400; and profit, 403; and the labor question, 402–403; importance of social groups in its history, 405–407. *See also* Biological Process

Economics: as one of the social sciences, 221; as expressing a natural relationship of man to material goods, 244–45; dualism between it, the political, and the ethical, 245–46, 250–51, 256–59, 382; and dualistic theory of self, 251–53; not to be condemned because abstract, 383–84; its inadequate theory of commodities, 389–91; its neglect of science, 391–94; spatial-temporal basis of its categories, 395–97

Educational Theory: mistaken emphasis upon discipline, 146–48; and upon sugar coating everything, 148–49

Effort: always implies desire, 29, 142–44; physical versus intellectual, 150–52

Egoism: Dewey and the problem of, xxv–xxvii; and self-realization, 208–209; element of truth in, 212; reflective, 213; in Hobbes, 224–25. *See also* Altruism

Eliot, George: on duty and self-interest, 208

Emotion: as immediate sense of value, 28; as projective and retractive, 29; distinguished from feeling, 111–13; distinguished from interest, 112; definition of, 114; Darwin's theory of, 114–15; Dewey's theory of, 114–22; James's theory of, 117–18; classification of, 119–23; as tension reflected in consciousness, 134–35; moral significance of, 137–42; not to be suppressed, 140–42. *See also* Desire

Environment: in the evaluative process, 175–78; ordinarily a part of function, 276; as resistance and stimulus, 278; represents a demand for variation, 279; can't directly influence organism, 284–85; physical and psychical distinguished, 343–45. *See also* Organism

Ethics: psychologic and social distinguished, 9–10; three theories of the role of social force in individual moralization, 221–23; as one of social sciences, 221; distinguished from the economic sphere, 245; dualism between it, the political, and the economic, 245–46, 250–51, 382; concerns the rationale of values, 384–85; social, 385; cannot be absolute, 385–86

Evolution: not contrary to morality, xxxii, xliv, 95–96; and the economic process, 253; various theories of, 280–84; process of, 271–99; absence of transitional forms in, 291; in relation to cosmological process, 291–93

Feeling: as immediate consciousness of worth, 110; distinguished from emotion, 111–13; as checking the intellectual process, 111; distinguished from interest, 112; and object of desire, 161

Force: doesn't resolve problems, xlii, 249–50; problem of its relation to will, 243; and sovereignty, 409, 411–19; not limited to the political organ, 413; three phases in government, 417–19; a limited aspect of sovereignty, 419–20; as liberating or restrictive, 419–24. *See also* Will

Freedom: indeterminists concerned with initiation, 170; James on, 170; as coming to self-consciousness, 173–74. *See also* Determinism

Genius: not simply a product of environment, 357; or a function of the individual, 358; utilizes society to bring out its defects, 359–60

Goethe: on desire, 163

Good: related to prospective function of conscientiousness, 187; defined, 192–93

Government: only one organ of sovereignty, xli, 424; functions to make adjustments, 404, 415; its legislative function, 416; constitutional, civil, and criminal phases, 417–19. *See also* Social Sensorium

Green, Thomas Hill: characterization of progress, xxix; theory of the common good, xxxix, 232, 234; critique of hedonism, 158–59; on social element in self-realization, 207; on indirect

17.95